Punjab Reconsidered

Punjab Reconsidered

History, Culture, and Practice

edited by
Anshu Malhotra
and
Farina Mir

OXFORD
UNIVERSITY PRESS

OXFORD
UNIVERSITY PRESS

Oxford University Press is a department of the University of Oxford. It furthers
the University's objective of excellence in research, scholarship, and education by
publishing worldwide. Oxford is a registered trademark of
Oxford University Press in the UK and in certain other countries

Published in India by
Oxford University Press
YMCA Library Building, 1 Jai Singh Road, New Delhi 110 001, India

ISBN 13: 978-0-19-807801-2
ISBN 10: 0-19-807801-3

Typeset in Adobe Garamond Pro 11/13.6
by BeSpoke Integrated Solutions, Puducherry, India 605 008
Printed in India at Rakmo Press, New Delhi 110 020

Contents

Figures

Acknowledgements

The volume editors and the publisher gratefully acknowledge the publishers and copyright holders of the journals cited below for permission to publish the following articles:

Cambridge University Press for

Alyssa Ayres, 'Language, the Nation, and Symbolic Capital: The Case of Punjab', *Journal of Asian Studies*, 67 (3), 2008, pp. 917–46. © The Association for Asian Studies, Inc., published by Cambridge University Press, reproduced with permission.

Harjot Oberoi, 'Brotherhood of the Pure: The Poetics and Politics of Cultural Transgression', *Modern Asian Studies*, 26 (1), 1992, pp. 157–97. © Cambridge University Press, reproduced with permission.

Farina Mir, 'Genre and Devotion in Punjabi Popular Narratives: Rethinking Cultural and Religious Syncretism', *Comparative Studies in Society and History*, 48 (3), 2006, pp. 727–58. © Society for the Comparative Study of Society and History, published by Cambridge University Press.

Center for Sikh and Punjab Studies, University of California for

Gurinder Singh Mann, 'Guru Nanak's Life and Legacy', *Journal of Punjab Studies*, 17 (1–2), 2010, pp. 3–44.

William J. Glover, 'Construing Urban Space as "Public" in Colonial India: Some Notes from the Punjab', *Journal of Punjab Studies*, 14 (2), 2007, pp. 211–24.

Acknowledgements

The volume editors and the publisher gratefully acknowledge the publishers and copyright holders of the terms deriving below for permission to publish the following articles:

Cambridge University Press for...

Abbreviations

BJP	Bharatiya Janata Party
BNP	British National Party
CRCI	Cultural Resource Conservation Initiative
EDL	English Defence League
IWAs	Indian Workers' Associations
MLA	Member of Legislative Assembly
NWFP	North-West Frontier Province
RSS	Rashtriya Swayamsevak Sangh
UNCHR	United Nations Commission on Human Rights
UP	United Provinces
USCIRF	United States Commission on International Religious Freedom

Note on Translation, Transliteration, and Diacritics

The essays in this volume use many Hindi, Persian, Punjabi, and Urdu words. Except in the case of proper nouns or terms that are familiar in English, such words are defined the first time they are used either through context, a parenthetical or bracketed remark, or in a note. All translations from these languages are by the essay's author(s), unless otherwise noted. In transliterating from Indian languages, authors were asked to use the system they preferred. Some essays thus have a simple form of transliteration rather than using diacritical marks, where terms are transliterated in a way that renders them phonetically correct for an English reader. In other essays, authors have employed diacritics, following standard academic usage. In each case, the prevailing principle has been to render the text as accessible as possible to readers.

Anshu Malhotra and Farina Mir[†]

Punjab in History and Historiography

AN INTRODUCTION

This volume seeks to consider the notion of *Punjabiyat*, a loosely defined term often used to describe a sentiment of belonging or attachment to Punjab and/or the foundations of a shared, cross-religious, cross-caste, cross-class culture. Is there an 'idea of Punjab' or 'ideas of Punjab' that help ground—as Punjabi—people from the region, now scattered across the globe? Or that connect those in Indian and Pakistani Punjab, divided by what is for most of them an impermeable border? In other words, despite political, social, religious—indeed, historical—differences, are there notions of Punjabiyat/*Punjabiness* that constitute Punjab as a region conceptually in history, culture, and practice? The essays in this volume, through their careful analyses of aspects of Punjabi social, cultural, political, and religious history, taken collectively suggest that there are, indeed.

Part of the impetus for this collection is that volumes on Punjabi culture/s or histories—especially of its modern period—have not been commonplace in academic circles. One is more likely to come across

† This Introduction has benefitted from careful readings by David Gilmartin and Gurinder Singh Mann. We would like to thank them for their helpful comments.

titles that delve into specific aspects of its culture or people, for instance works on 'Sikh religion' or the 'Sikh people', 'Islamic identity' or 'Hindu reform' in their Punjabi regional context. Such endeavours are entirely valid and reasonable, and perhaps even necessary, but it is difficult to comprehend the elision if not erasure of Punjabi identity from academic writing. Given that it has been easier for diasporic Punjabis to evoke a much wider and an inclusive Punjabi identity than it has been for Punjabis residing in India or Pakistan, one wonders if this elision is yet another result of the political divisions that have marked Punjab's twentieth-century history? Have these divisions, whether of 1947 or the postcolonial period, made other identity markers more apt or emotionally more satisfying than the idea of belonging/originating/associating with a region? Or could it be that Punjabi identity is particularly open to appropriation, and even incorporation within other identities—for instance Sikh identity in Indian Punjab?

We think this is the right moment to re-imagine and re-configure Punjab and notions of Punjabiyat, not only in light of a complex past, but also on the threshold of a globalizing future that is reconstituting both subjects and subjectivity. Each essay in this volume attempts to do this to some extent, while engaging with a specific aspect of Punjabi history and culture. Taken as a whole, the volume both presents critical and varied analyses of Punjab's complex cultures and helps reflect on Punjabiyat in its many manifestations.

It is of course difficult to measure, calibrate, or concretize the multiple ways in which Punjabiyat was—and is—lived, experienced, and vitalized. However we wish to make an effort to capture a somewhat elusive, often unstable and shifting 'idea of Punjab'. If we can propose a *raison d'être* for this volume, it is surely the need to explore this 'idea' in its myriad forms. The temptation is to define it as a primordial, patriotic feeling localized around a region and its culture. But that would be misleading, historically speaking, as Punjab neither had a stable region nor a single culture. In this volume, the perspectives presented on Punjabiyat include in their reach people physically present in politically split but geographically contiguous Punjab and those who left its environs long ago yet continue to call themselves Punjabi and/or engage in and identify with aspects of its culture/s. The emotions associated with Punjabiyat might be ethereal, but that does not make them unreal. The idea of Punjab, or Punjabiness might live in the imagination, but such is the nature of identity. The attempt in this volume is not to lend s(t)olidity to the concept, but to capture its variability in different forms, and over a period of time, including its contemporary manifestations.

METHODOLOGICAL FOUNDATIONS

This volume marks a point of departure in the study of Punjab by emphasizing a cultural history of the region and its peoples. The turn towards cultural history is now established and is particularly apposite in contending with questions of what constitutes communities, peoples, selves, or how these are represented. As a volume that brings together diverse perspectives on Punjabi cultures, the term 'culture' is understood in the widest possible sense—mentalities and social texts, symbols and cultural representations, elite and popular cultures, social codes and their performance and reception[1] —and a variety of methodological and disciplinary techniques have been employed for its analysis. For example, as we use the term, it also refers to the material cultures of a period, or even a culture specific to class/es. Thus the Annales school's foundational emphasis on studying mentalities—mental habits and the barely perceptible changes therein, especially in the *longue duree*—continues to be of vital significance. The anthropological perspective on studying cultural codes of societies, whether through 'thick description' or by analysing the symbols and rituals of a culture is equally important, as is the desire to study cultural texts for their meanings; so too is Foucault's notion of discursive practices as sites both for constituting power and for its subversion. Each of these methods has been crucial to contemporary scholarship on Punjab, as they have to studies of identities. Beyond these foundations, the power of discourses, signs of change, and modes of subversion are a significant constituent of this volume as well, as are insights from literary criticism. The latter have facilitated the deconstruction of social and discursive practices and the de-centring of cultural texts, loosened societies and cultures from stable moorings, and encouraged an examination of diverse voices.

Cultural texts are surely an important site of analysis in the essays that follow, and texts have been interrogated not only for their meanings, but also for how they work, their manifold reception, and their appropriation to new and different ends. The linguistic turn with its emphasis on cultural self-expression through language, and the feminist perspective, which has helped unravel the gendered aspects of language, have been influential theories whose impact will also be visible in the following pages. Indeed, the essays in this volume use these and other methods to provide compelling and sophisticated analyses of the cultural foundations of historical change.

Most of the contributors in this volume, though not all, are historians, and though the interdisciplinarity that the linguistic and cultural turns in history have encouraged is undoubtedly evidenced here, so is the historian's preoccupation with context. Readers will thus find the specificity of social or political milieus carefully laid out for them, rather than an adherence to post-modernist trends that pursue the study of cultural texts and artefacts as free-floating signs, capable of generating endless interpretive possibilities. We use the term practice to capture this emphasis on context, particularly to draw attention to the importance of historical time, and to ground cultural praxis in temporal frames and social networks.

Our underscoring of practice is also grounded in the work it allows us to do in analysing the relationship between ideality, ideology and lived histories. How are the ideals of a society transmitted among its various constituents, and how are they appropriated, accepted, inverted or abandoned? How do some ideals become commonplace, so much a part of life that their fabrication or artifice is naturalized? On the other hand, how do societies move to newer ideals, insert change in the midst of the mundane and the ordinary? While a discussion of the nature of historical sources falls outside the scope of this introduction, we would nonetheless like to note that a number of our sources, especially the textual ones, speak of ideal societies in order to construct them. Some are also concerned with ideologies, narratives structured in distinct ways to propagate specific agendas. The intertwining of myth, legend and history in our sources is a particular challenge. Their untangling requires us to tease out the various strands in the narratives of the past, and pushes us to decipher how our contemporary notions of myth, legend, and history as distinct categories of analysis are not shared by our historical subjects. Coaxing sources to yield more than the obvious is a challenge to most historians, and by emphasizing practise we hope to point to our sensitivity towards the issue of sources and their interpretation in given social locales. This volume thus foregrounds both (Punjabi) cultures in practice and the practice or method of the scholar of Punjab. We turn now to contextualizing the latter—scholarship on the Punjab—by providing a historical and historiographical framework in which to locate the essays in this volume. But first, we think it critical to define our subject of study: what, after all, constitutes Punjab? Do its land, people, language (s), cultural practices, religious beliefs, and/or material cultures constitute the region? Or are these rather categories of representation, while the region is constituted by our imagination? Let us turn, then, to the fundamental question of territoriality.

TERRITORIALITY

The idea of Punjab—as is that of any region—is grounded in complex concepts of territoriality. While these concepts are perhaps as varied as those who hold them dear, we focus attention on three concepts of territoriality in particular. We identify these as the historical, the spatial, and the imaginary. While we disaggregate these concepts from one another in order to facilitate our discussion, it must be underscored at the outset that in practice, in the way that people identify with a region as a geographic/territorial entity and incorporate this into their notions of self—into their identity—these three aspects of territoriality easily meld into one another producing precisely the complexity of experience that the essays in this volume all point to.

Any understanding of Punjab's territoriality in historical terms is a complicated matter, not least because of a glaring anachronism common to both popular and scholarly treatments of the region. Namely, that the term Punjab emerged only in the late sixteenth century—in references to a *sarkar-i-Punjab* (the Government of Punjab) and a *suba-i-Punjab* (Punjab province) in Mughal documents[2]—yet it is used to refer to a geographic entity in the northwestern part of the Indian subcontinent (presumably a 'land of five rivers', from the literal translation of the Persian term) irrespective of the era under discussion. Even as careful a scholar as J.S. Grewal, whose research has been central to establishing the historicity of the term, has published such works as, *Social and Cultural History of the Punjab: Prehistoric, Ancient, and Early Medieval*.[3] Undoubtedly, this anachronistic use of the term serves to reify the notion of a coherent region stretching back to time immemorial—a notion that must surely be interrogated rather than assumed. This is not to suggest, however, that historians have taken a static view of Punjab's territoriality. Rather, what is perhaps more evident in the existing scholarship is the recognition that embedded in the term from its earliest use is a relationship between a geographic entity—one that is taken to be relatively stable—and administrative entities—whose contours have shifted over time. The latter sometimes map quite comfortably onto the former, and sometimes less so.

To engage with Punjab's territoriality in historical terms, thus, is to anchor the nebulous geographic entity Punjab in time and place: to give it concrete boundaries; to historicize it. Scholars do this most typically by identifying the contours of the various administrative and/or political entities that have constituted Punjab. In the process, they have shown that these administrative borders rarely map onto the geographical conception of Punjab as the land of the five rivers (or six rivers and five doabs, or interriverine tracts). To put this somewhat differently, what is most evident in this scholarly approach is that there is a clear 'idea of Punjab' in geographical terms against which historians (and other scholars) measure the administrative units. Thus, for example, although Mughal sources appear to use suba-i-Lahore and sarkar-i-Punjab synonymously, modern historians generally agree that the Mughal suba of Lahore *and* the northern parts of suba Multan *and* the western parts of suba Delhi, taken together, is likely a better representation of 'Punjab'.[4] By the same token, despite the strong association of Sikh political power with Punjab, it is well recognized that Ranjit Singh's kingdom of Lahore does not map comfortably onto the geographic entity Punjab because after 1809 it did not include areas south of the Sutlej river and subsequently included parts of Jammu, Kashmir, and territories across the Hindu Kush mountains (Kabul), all of which scholars take to be distinct from Punjab (Figure 1).[5] What the disjuncture between actual administrative units and the latent notion of Punjab prevalent in scholarship reveals is, of course, that the latter—the idea of Punjab as a geographical entity—borrows heavily from modern, colonial territorial divisions (Figure 2). The influence of modern conceptions of Punjab in the assessment of all periods of Punjab history notwithstanding, British colonial Punjab itself is not coterminous with modern conceptions of Punjab in geographical terms, as outlined above. After all, the colonial entity included Peshawar, Leia, and Hazara at annexation in 1849, and Delhi and its environs were added to the province in 1858. Indeed, the history of colonial Punjab in territorial terms is one of constant remappings, the most dramatic of which is undoubtedly the vivisection of the province in 1947 into Indian and Pakistani halves. The postcolonial history of Indian Punjab has been no less unstable, with first the separation of the PEPSU states, then the creation of a new capital in the city of Chandigarh, and the subsequent trifurcation of the state in 1966 into Punjab, Haryana, and Himachal Pradesh.

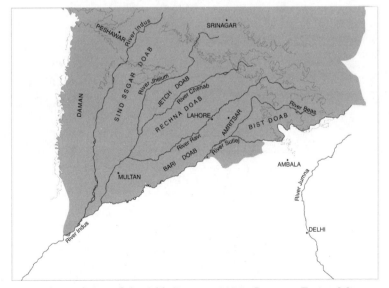

Figure 1 Map of the Sikh Empire, 1839. Courtesy Farina Mir

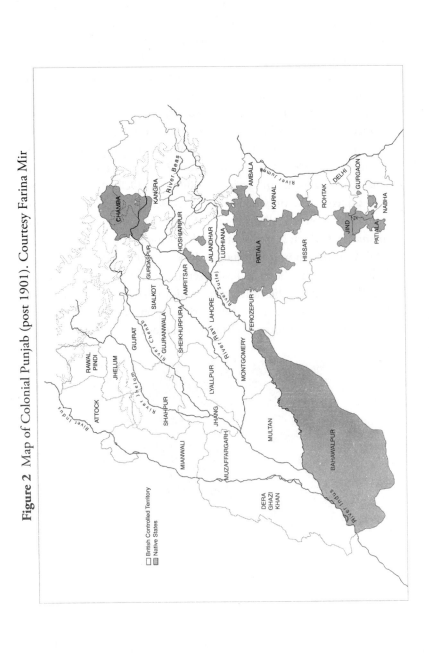

Figure 2 Map of Colonial Punjab (post 1901). Courtesy Farina Mir

Despite these shifting contours of Punjab as an administrative entity, the essays in this volume do not focus so much on this territorial instability of the region as on the geographical stability of the 'idea of Punjab' as it has emerged in the modern period. Put another way, and as Farina Mir has argued elsewhere, despite the waxing and waning of Punjab's administrative borders, 'the Punjab has a geographical–cultural core...whether conceived as an axis connecting the major cities of Amritsar, Lahore, and Multan, or more broadly as the five *doab*s and the cis-Sutlej territory [the area to the south of the Sutlej river, up to Delhi]'.[6] Indeed, this geographical–cultural core corresponds to the rather stable—even if nebulous—notion of Punjab that is a subtext in discussions of the region's territoriality. And it is this notion of Punjab's territoriality that the essays in this volume engage more directly, rather than those of administrative borders. Having said that, the essays also show that this rather stable entity was not in any way insular or unconnected from the regions around it. In particular, the essays by Anshu Malhotra and Christopher Shackle point to the importance of cultural continuities with Sindh, to Punjab's south-west. Both essays hint that these continuities may point to a cultural inheritance from Sindh, or at minimum Sindhi influence on Punjab's literary culture—an influence that has to date been muted in scholarly understandings, at best.

If engaging with Punjab's territoriality requires moving through history to see what this meant at different junctures, then it also requires moving through space. That is, the notion of Punjab explored in this volume extends study of the region to include not only the Punjab of the Indian subcontinent, whether early modern, colonial, Indian, or Pakistani Punjab, but also the places where the 'idea of Punjab' has travelled, and along with it ideas of Punjabiness. We conceptualize this expansion of scope as thinking about Punjab spatially, rather than simply in geographical terms. Thus, we include in this volume an essay by Tony Ballantyne on a particular Punjabi migrant experience—that of Sikhs who migrated from Punjab to Britain in the mid-twentieth century. Ballantyne's essay examines the construction of a Sikh identity in Britain in the latter half of the twentieth century, focusing on Sikh representations of themselves as a distinct community to the British state. This was a deliberate process, and as Ballantyne shows, it had certain outcomes that might be read as 'costs'. One, for example, was that it privileged a particular vision of Sikhism, marginalizing other voices, experiences, and representations of the faithful. Another was that it privileged a religious over a regional identity, thus providing little ground for inter-racial or inter-faith alliances that might have more effectively furthered Sikh political and socio-economic aims. While Ballantyne limits his analysis to the consequences of Sikh political action in the British context, we might add that to think of Punjab in these spatial terms—to ignore, as it were, boundaries or limits as identified on a map—is also to emphasize a recursivity between the Punjab and its diaspora, both historically and to this day. That is, the experience of Punjabi migrants has transported Punjab—as a set of ideas and practices—to other parts of the globe, and the diaspora has similarly played an important role in Punjab's (and India's) history. One need only think of the revolutionary nationalism of the Ghadar Party, started on the west coast of North America in the early twentieth century, or the significance of the diaspora in supporting the Khalistan movement, or the economic impact of migrant labor remittances on Punjab (both Indian and Pakistani) to recognize this recursivity.[7]

If Ballantyne's essay on the Sikh diaspora in Britain reminds us that we should not think of Punjab as isolated from other parts of the world, then Simona Sawhney's essay is crucial to understanding how changing conceptions of other parts of the world influence thinking in Punjab, both historically and today. Sawhney's essay seeks to juxtapose contemporary acts of public violence in Lahore with those of the nationalist figure Bhagat Singh and his comrades. It is a jarring contrast, no doubt, given the iconic status of Bhagat Singh as nationalist hero and the revulsion caused—certainly in liberal circles, but surely beyond, as well—by the depraved violence unleashed on Lahore's citizens in the past few years, particularly its religious minorities such as the Ahmadiyya and the Shi'i. But Sawhney uses the juxtaposition to great effect. Her essay not only elucidates facets of Bhagat Singh's politics, but posits the significance of changing conceptions of the West between Bhagat Singh's time and our own. Among this essay's strengths is how it helps shape an understanding of local politics in the light of these conceptions, showing how the local and nationalist politics of the early twentieth century were

never insular, but rather interwoven with conceptions of the West
that helped sustain them. The sad irony is that the earlier politics of
death and hope that she elucidates has largely become a politics of
death alone.

To turn the discussion to the imaginary aspects of territoriality is
only to make explicit what has thus far been implicit in this discussion. That is, as significant as administrative borders or lines drawn
on maps—perhaps even more significant—is how Punjab figures in
people's imaginaries. Indeed, connections with the landscape seem
critically important to Punjab's inhabitants and to Punjab's history, whether gauged through relationships to land within Punjab,[8]
or in the way that landscape is evoked when people move beyond
its borders. David Gilmartin takes up the issue of the landscape in
his discussion of the making of Pakistan and in particular Pakistani
Punjab. As Gilmartin points out in the opening of his essay, 'the
creation of Pakistan has often been portrayed as a process peculiarly divorced from the history of the land that is today Pakistan'.
Given the significance of land, literally and figuratively, to this
event, this historiographical oversight is indeed astounding. In his
essay, Gilmartin brings a history of the land into the historical narrative of colonial Punjab in new ways—in environmental terms, that
is—and shows how changing relationships with the land, in conjunction with the new colonial dispensation, had resounding effects
on Punjabi notions of self and community by transforming notions
of *biradari* (brotherhood, kinship system, or descent group), a key
facet of Punjab's social organization.

If life on the land, and thus a relationship to it, was transformed
for many during the colonial period, then colonialism's end severed
that relationship altogether for scores of people. The numbers are
staggering and despite being well known are worth repeating: an
estimated 12 million people were on the move in Punjab in the
summer of 1947; that is 12 million people whose lives were severed
from familiar places and landscapes. Yet, for many of Partition's
refugees, while the physical relationship with land/place was irrevo-
cably lost, their 'Punjab' would live on in their imaginaries, and in
the new worlds they constructed for themselves. One example of
this is the names given to some of the refugee colonies of Delhi:

'Gujranwala', 'Bhera' or 'Punjabi Bagh'. Another example is the persistent conversation opener posed to Punjabi settlers in Delhi, even 60-odd years on from Partition: *'tussi pichhon kithon de ho?'* (Where are you from [with clear reference to a 'before': *picchon*]?). Such imaginings extend beyond refugee communities, and are to be found in migrant communities the world over, whether marked in their restaurants (London's plethora of 'Lahore Kebab House (s)', or New York's 'Lahore Deli', for example), their sweet shops (London's famous Ambala *mithai*-makers, for example), or their neighbourhoods (for instance, Vancouver's 'Punjabi Market' area). In each case, an imaginary is at work that maps Punjab without giving credence to international borders either within the subcontinent or beyond it. While no single essay in this volume addresses itself to this imaginary, it is without doubt at play in all of the essays included herein. Indeed, it would not be pushing our point too far to suggest that the region is constituted as much by people's limitless imaginaries as by the borders that define it on any map or the land that such representations signify.

LANGUAGE AND LITERARY CULTURES

We argued above that Punjab has a geographical–cultural core, one that has been relatively stable compared to the shifting contours of the region in administrative terms. Undoubtedly, one of the key conceptual foundations of this cultural core is language. The relationship between region and language, however, is not entirely straightforward. To be sure, we are positing a relationship between Punjab (land) and Punjabi (language), and Punjabis (people). But we are keenly aware that it is a complicated one, and we attempt here to draw out some of that complexity as it relates to language.

We speak of Punjabi in the singular, but it is of course constituted as a language by a number of dialects. Linguists have mapped this out in technical detail, so we need not do so here.[9] What is perhaps more helpful for the purposes of this volume is to think of Punjabi as a language constituted by a range of mutually intelligible dialects spoken in the area from the environs of Delhi to those of Peshawar, including (although not exclusively): Majhi, Siraiki, Malvai, Puadhi,

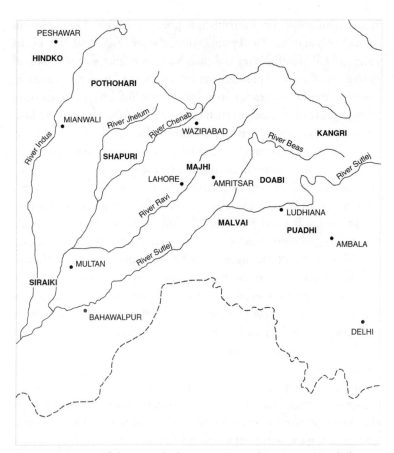

Figure 3 Map of the Punjabi language area, showing major dialects.
Courtesy Farina Mir

Kangri, Doabi, Hindko, Pothohari, Dogri, and Lahnda (Figure 3).[10]
This definition allows us to see the cultural continuities that mark this
area without imposing too singular a view of the language (s) spoken
there. One sees this approach taken, in some ways, by Christopher
Shackle in his essay, 'Punjabi Sufi Poetry from Farid to Farid', where
while recognizing dialectical differences between the compositions of
various authors—most notably the Farids of the title, Baba Farid (d.
1265) and Khwaja Ghulam Farid (1845–1901)—Shackle draws them
into a single tradition, that of Punjabi Sufi poetry. Shackle's essay is
self-consciously revisionist, seeking to question a dominant paradigm

in the scholarship on Punjabi Sufi poetry established by Lajwanti Rama Krishna in her 1938 publication, *Punjabi Sufi Poets*, that posits a rise and fall of Sufi poetry and casts Sufis 'as religiously universalized exponents of a shared pre-modern Indian spiritual understanding'. In contrast, Shackle argues for an era of vibrant Sufi literary production that ranges from the late-twelfth century Sufi Baba Farid to the late-nineteenth century Sufi Khwaja Ghulam Farid. More importantly, perhaps, he recontextualizes their literature away from Krishna's emphasis on its 'universalism inspired by the monism of Vedanta' by arguing that it is critical to see this literature in its Islamic context. This is not, of course, to deny that Punjabi Sufi poetry had a profound impact beyond Sufi and Muslim circles, or that there could be 'theological equivalences' between Vedantic monism and certain Sufi ideas, as Malhotra discusses in her essay in this volume. Rather, it is to suggest that we be more attentive to the context in which Punjabi Sufi poetry was produced. Shackle's essay not only does this, but also posits an argument for why the Islamic context of Punjabi Sufi poetry's production became opaque, suggesting that it was the result of Punjabi Sufi poets and their poetry being appropriated in the modern period to contemporary political exigencies.

Shackle's essay is an important reminder that in examining a regional literature, we do not want to collapse important distinctions that were germane to the context of its production. Thus, without undermining the notion of a regional literature, we can recognize distinct strands within that tradition. We can suggest, thus, that between the sixteenth and eighteenth centuries two distinct literary traditions emerged in Punjab. One was of the Sufis, who expressed their mystical experience in poetry that deployed the dominant Punjabi dialects Majhi and Multani. By using symbols and metaphors in their poetry that were steeped in the practices of everyday life—such as the spinning wheel, a prospective bride collecting her dowry, or popular characters from Punjab's ubiquitous *qisse* (epic stories/romances), such as Hir and Ranjha—Sufis produced an emotional connection with their listeners. The other was the Sikh tradition, which from the time of Guru Nanak had turned to the *nirguni* bhakti that was spreading across north India for spiritual inspiration and sustenance. The languages of this universalist bhakti, Sant Bhasha and later Braj, were the preferred modes of transmission of Sikh literature.[11] There were, nevertheless, many points of intersection between the two, whether the mode of 'masquerading' in feminine voice adopted by male poets when addressing the beloved (God),[12] the use of bridal mysticism, or the presence of Baba Farid's poetry in the Adi Granth. Indeed, Shackle, who in his essay briefly explores the historical and literary problems of the Farid verses in the Adi Granth is more aware than most of the complex relationship between the two traditions, being one of the few scholars to have worked on both.

As the discussion above suggests, Punjabi linguistic and literary cultures are marked by pluralities. They are also marked by ironies, not least of which is their relationship to the state. Members of all of Punjab's religious communities—Hindu, Muslim, Sikh, Christian—speak Punjabi, and have done so historically. Although it has been a vibrant vernacular tradition since the time of Baba Farid, Punjabi has never enjoyed state support. Mughal rulers reinforced the policy of their Sultanate predecessors to use Persian as the administrative language in the areas where Punjabi was spoken, a practice continued by Mughal successor states, including Ranjit Singh's early nineteenth-century kingdom. While the colonial period should have seen the adoption of Punjabi as the language of administration in colonial Punjab because of colonial language policy, the colonial state chose to use Urdu as the official language in its stead.[13] Part of the colonial rationale for not using Punjabi was the plurality of its scripts (Indo-Persian, Gurmukhi, and Devnagari), none of which dominated. While the use of Devnagari for Punjabi was relatively rare in the nineteenth century (or before or since), Indo-Persian and Gurmukhi were both so common that neither could easily be adopted over the other. Each of these scripts was also implicated in language–community claims by the latter half of the nineteenth century, which further complicated the issue (Indo-Persian–Muslim; Gurmukhi–Sikh; Devnagari–Hindu). If the absence of state patronage meant little in the way of the standardization of modern Punjabi (it might be noted that most modern Indian vernaculars were standardized through their relationship with the colonial state), then the late-nineteenth century context of communal claims on language(s) sealed its fate in this regard.

Vernacular languages were politicized in new ways in the late nineteenth century that had implications for Punjabi as a ground for cross-communal ethno-linguistic claims. Sikh reformers, particularly those associated with the Singh Sabha (a Sikh socio-religious organization established in 1873), promoted Punjabi in the Gurmukhi script as the language of Sikh aspirations. Similarly, at about the same time—the 1880s—Hindus, particularly those associated with the Arya Samaj (a Hindu reform movement established in 1875), sought to bring the Hindu–Hindu–Hindustan triumvirate that animated United Province politics to bear on Punjab politics. Muslims too played their part in these partisan politics. Thus, we see petitions in the late nineteenth century from Muslim organizations to the colonial state advocating for Urdu as 'their' language. One such example is provided by the Anjuman-i-Hamdardi Islamiya, which petitioned the Hunter Commission in 1882 to maintain Urdu as the official language of Punjab.[14] This political terrain produced a number of ironies, some of which surface in the essays in this volume. Simona Sawhney's essay, for example, points to the tension between Bhagat Singh's advocacy for Hindi and his simultaneous conviction in the emotive power of Punjabi for its speakers. Although exploring this latter point is beyond the scope of Sawhney's essay, it nonetheless reminds us that despite the divisive terrain of late nineteenth- and early twentieth-century language politics, the affinity of Punjabi speakers for their language remained vital.

Alyssa Ayres's essay follows a different set of ironies around language, these in postcolonial Pakistan, where despite Punjabi dominance of the Pakistani state, Punjabi is the only major regional language in Pakistan with no official status. Ayres focuses her attention on what she terms a '*Punjabiyat* movement', which she defines as 'seeking to "restore" a role for Punjabi, justified entirely in terms of aesthetics and pursued through the development of a respected Punjabi-language written public sphere'. Ayres helps us understand what is at stake in this movement, which defies the logics of the usual explanation for language movements: nationalism. As Ayres rightly points out, the arbiters of this movement enjoy political power and influence, suggesting that this is not their motivation. She provides a sophisticated analysis that relies on notions of symbolic capital. Ayres focuses specifically on Pakistani Punjab, but her argument has relevance for a broader cross-border perspective, in at least two specific ways. First, it underscores the affective ties that undergird for many a relationship to Punjabi despite the minimal state space accorded to it in much of its postcolonial history. Put somewhat differently, despite the absence of any official status for Punjabi in Pakistan and the divisive language politics that wracked Indian Punjab in the aftermath of independence until the state was further partitioned in 1966, Punjabi continues to have immense emotive power for its speakers in both countries, and for migrants from Punjab—and often their descendants—the world over. Second is a countervailing trend. Namely, that in the contemporary period there has been an impact of the absence of state support and the instrumental advantages of other languages—whether Urdu in Pakistan, Hindi in India, or English in both countries; for some the ties of language are indeed eroding. Thus, the Punjabi movement that Ayres documents in Pakistan is one that has never enjoyed widespread popular support. Similarly, one can note that in places like Delhi, young urbane professionals today are less likely to be proficient in Punjabi than their parents' and grandparents' generations. This, however, seems not to undermine their identity as Punjabi. Thus, we might posit that while the link between language and territory was surely critical to establishing Punjabi subjectivity historically, it is not necessarily constitutive of all contemporary Punjabi experience.

COLONIALISM IN PUNJAB

Interrogating the idea of Punjab becomes particularly salient if we consider how historians have engaged with Punjabi history, particularly its modern period. It is perhaps not surprising that the workings of the colonial state—its administrative and technological innovations, for example—and the sheer power of its imperial interventions in Punjab have been a mainstay of postcolonial history writing on the region. As a people still coming to terms with the short but transformative hundred years of colonial history and its consequences, it was imperative to examine how the colonial state had instituted its power. The peculiarities of the paternalistic 'Punjab School' of administration were understood and explained in terms of the colonial state seeing Punjab as the last bastion of conquest, and the colonial rulers' paranoia of being hemmed in by a turbulent frontier and the designs of powers beyond it.[15]

An important element of the colonial state's Punjab project, if we can call it that, was to recognize/shape the 'tribal' character of the province's 'agricultural classes' and to nurture them as the 'natural' leaders of Punjabi society, both of which were to the disadvantage of *kirars*, moneylenders, and traders, most of whom were Hindu.[16] The colonial state did this through legal and administrative structures that had a profound impact on Punjabi society. Two interventions that stand out in particular are the division of Punjabis into 'agricultural' and 'non-agricultural' tribes and the application of 'customary law' for all Punjabis.[17] Generally viewing Punjabi land-owning Jats (and Rajputs) as a flat, seamless category of middle-ranking peasants encouraged such policies.[18] Indeed, the colonial understanding of caste in Punjab viewed it as a system of ranking social hierarchy, one that pertained to social customs and purity/pollution taboos in particular. These customs and taboos were thought to have less traction among Punjab's Jats—something belied by contemporary scholarship, including Oberoi's essay in this volume—than among its urban mercantile classes; it was these urban mercantilists who were seen to preserve the ideals of caste.[19] In other words, notions of agricultural/non-agricultural, tribe/caste became foundational to colonial policies in Punjab. Among the consequence of such categorization was the enactment at the *fin de siècle* of the Punjab Land Alienation Act which proscribed 'urban castes/classes' from owning agricultural land. In sum, the consequences of these policies were that they favoured the land-owning castes and classes over urban professional and trading ones.

The workings of the British Raj then—its apparently limitless power to intervene and change things—whether in taming nature by creating the famous irrigation canals or in compartmentalizing people through their census and other ethnological/ethnographical logics have received due attention.[20] This research continues to be significant, even as newer research further unravels the workings of colonial institutions such as the police and the army or dismantles the apparently monolithic structure of the colonial state.[21] While disaggregating the colonial state and, increasingly, looking beyond it through histories grounded in social and cultural perspectives, there are significant ways in which these two impact areas of Punjab historiography—that is, the state's attempt at socio-legal restructuring and its will to refashion the landscape—have come together as well.

In this context, David Gilmartin's essay in this volume is important for linking the power of the colonial state and its transformative capacities to cultural changes that came to define the new rural elites. He draws on earlier research to show how the colonial state produced an immense ecological transformation of Punjab through technological innovation specifically, in creating the irrigation canals.[22] The drive for increasing agricultural productivity and thus revenues was linked to marginalizing and criminalizing the pastoral/semi-pastoral communities of western Punjab. Gilmartin notes the tensions between the settled agriculturists and the pastoralists of Punjab and underlines the role of Sufi *pirs* (saints/mystics) as intermediaries between the two. The pious pirs, as Richard Eaton's articles on Baba Farid's establishment at Pakpattan have shown, played a crucial role in the gradual Islamization and settling of these areas.[23] Subsequently, the sacred genealogies emanating from them became the foundation for and affirmed the power of local families of substance.

Under colonialism the new rural elite, guided by the state's moral universalism that emphasized private property and individual responsibility, came to rework genealogy as the fluid notion of biradari. While contractual law structured dealings in property, customary law came to organize patterns of inheritance and other matters that fell in the domain of personal law in large parts of colonial India. Besides nurturing a loyal rural elite, these changes also created a more patriarchal society. With the state's insistence on the division between agricultural and non-agricultural classes with the implementation of the Land Alienation Act in 1900, sharp cleavages between the favoured rural elite and the urban non-agricultural elite came into play, as demonstrated above. Rural low class/caste tenants, labourers and artisans, and women were also losers in this peculiar social engineering. Gilmartin traces the impact of this policy in the cultural adoption and adaptation of biradari, and the manner in which it came to define social and political relations in colonial and contemporary Pakistani Punjab. The tensions between Punjabi cultural identity and the developmental policies of the Pakistani state, or between the Islamist *shari'at* laws and skepticism about their need, in Gilmartin's view, can be partially traced to the rural elite's social investment in the idea of biradari. Through the subtle shifts in the social institution of this idea in the pre-colonial, colonial, and postcolonial periods, Gilmartin demonstrates how we might understand society through cultural transitions.

The collusion between the colonial state and indigenous elites that Gilmartin illustrates through his analysis of the working of the concept of biradari has been taken up by feminist historians, who have shown its particularly detrimental effects on women. Though Gilmartin's essay only hints at the hardships women had to face due to the patriarchal institutions that were constructed under colonialism, others have demonstrated the very real losses that women suffered. The process of codification of customary laws, for instance, in which the state and patriarchal elites collaborated, actively worked against women's usufructuary and other rights on land. Prem Chowdhry has shown the effects that usurping women's rights had on the widows of landed Jats,[24] while Veena Oldenburg has elucidated long-term changes in the institution of dowry against the background of new revenue demands and the freezing of patriarchally-informed customary laws.[25] The changes in rural Punjabi society in the colonial period thus remain a significant area of interest. Although the essays in this volume do not directly address how historical change impacted women per se, much of the work presented here obviously owes a debt of gratitude to this feminist scholarship, and many of the essays are sensitive to the changing contexts and expressions of patriarchy and gender relations.

The historiography of modern Punjab thus has given a fair degree of attention to the structures and institutions of the colonial state, particularly for their role in making a rural elite. It has also focused attention on this rural elite, showing for example how it participated and dominated the politics of the province in the early twentieth century through webs of patronage and the workings of the Unionist Party.[26] The process of urbanization, however, or the characteristics of urban classes have received much less attention. The impact of the British Raj on urban areas was in fact enormous, in Punjab as across British India, as a growing body of scholarship has shown.[27] But this scholarship has mostly focused on capital cities—both of presidencies and provinces. Urban history, particularly in the Punjab context, is still in a nascent phase, and despite the strides made, much is still to be done.[28] We know little about the travails of the urban poor, for example, and not much about the middle classes either. Though some historians working on changing gender relations have drawn attention to the new demands of domesticity among the emerging upper caste, middle classes—speaking of the newly envisaged appropriate roles for women, and the disciplining required in the ostensibly emancipatory programmes of education that centrally shaped the middle classes or exposed its anxieties—other aspects that defined middle class-ness have received far less attention.[29] One exception is perhaps the over-explored area of the communalizing of the middle classes, to which we will turn our attention shortly. Markus Daechsel's work therefore marks something of a departure, and his essay here carries forward his earlier writing on the self-expression of the Urdu middle class of late colonial Punjab.[30]

Daechsel examines the remarkable division between the agricultural/non-agricultural classes mentioned above to show how in Punjab this pushed some classes away from investing in land. However, the relationship of the middle class to commercial or industrial ventures remained tenuous, with high-risk financial institutions flopping more often than succeeding, as Daechsel's brief sketches of some of the representatives of this class illustrate. Daechsel notes the dependence of the middle classes on patronage from both rural elites and the state. Middle-class education programmes, even its reformism as seen in the various *anjumans* (associations) that constituted a defining aspect of urban life or the printing presses that shaped debates in the public sphere, remained captured by key elitist patrons who imposed cultural norms in the 'micro-fabric' of middle class life. It is in the changing relationship of the middle class to material objects—its consumerism—that Daechsel discerns a class coming into its own. He argues that as the middle class changed its relationship from use-value of material objects to a more confident consumption of sign-objects between the two World Wars, a more self-assured class took birth.

If Daechsel looks at middle-class culture, then William Glover shifts attention to another dimension of urban life. His essay examines the meanings congealed in the term 'public space' and the relationship between Punjabi publics and the spatial use of the corporeal city once municipal committees were established in 1862. Tracing the specific understanding of the term 'public space' from its western European usage in the medieval period, Glover shows the particular ways in which municipalities employed the term in Punjab (as elsewhere in colonial India). Though in the pre-colonial period there were spaces in the city that were accessible to almost all of its residents, spaces that were in many ways physically similar to what the colonial government would call 'public' urban space, the change in the situation, according to Glover, was in the instituting and strict implementation of new laws and rules that defined how public space could be used. Glover traces for us in Punjab a more general colonial phenomenon: how colonial authorities interpreted the density and filth of indigenous Indian cities as symptomatic of social malaise. His intervention, however, is to draw our attention to the concomitant emphasis on transforming public spaces to engineer a socio-cultural change among the denizens of the city. Once again, the ambitions of Punjab's colonial administration are laid bare. The most exciting aspect of Glover's essay is his reading of legal cases from nineteenth- and twentieth-century Punjab where he analyses how the term 'public' was applied to the spatial use of the city. Glover speaks of the 'translation' of the language of 'public', and therefore the contestation over the use of 'public space' among Punjabis. He points to the increasingly sophisticated manner in which Punjabis imbibed, transmuted and re-deployed the term 'public', with its baggage of rules, delineating the complex processes that shaped the cityscape in the colonial period. By showcasing Daechsel's and Glover's essays, we point to the exciting new research on Punjab's cities, their physical appearance and material cultures, and the classes who inhabited, transformed and consumed the city.

RELIGIOUS IDENTITIES IN PUNJAB

As Daechsel notes, and as other writings on the reformist middle classes have underscored, existing studies depict these classes as deeply divided along religious lines. This historiographical representation is to an extent a discourse of Partition, an event that has encouraged writing about Hindus, Muslims and Sikhs as if they were self-contained communities with little interaction and intermingling, even though they lived in the same region and grappled with the same forces of economic, social, and political change. The emphasis on religious community and identity is surely grounded in scholars' desire to reflect the long term or deep-rooted 'communal' antipathies that created purportedly rigid and separate communities of Punjab. Without a sense of such a history, after all, partition and its accompanying violence and the brutal uprooting of peoples would seem a mystery condemned to be in the shadow of either atavistic animalism or elided by pinning the blame on a few hate-inciting figures.

An examination of the historiography of Punjab reveals that scholarly energy has been devoted not so much to cultural history, but much more to the cultural fault lines in Punjabi society, concentrating on moments of rupture. We know why/how religious antagonisms became entrenched in society, but less about mental states, for example, that encouraged the shared veneration of saintly lives.[31] We know how different religious communities came to see themselves as distinct from each other, and how soured relations between them sowed the seeds of an irrevocable political parting of ways. Indeed, these processes have garnered so much attention that one might wonder, is there more to Punjabi culture/s than antagonistic religious identities? Is there more to religious identities than acrimony and debate?

While we hope to demonstrate the relevance of these latter questions in the pages of this volume, there is no getting away from the divisive consequences of sectarian politics. And, despite over a half century of interrogation into communalism—often, however, with a telos to Partition—much work is yet to be done. The enlarged discursive fields in which religious communities were constructed and the insidious ways in which refashioned religious rituals and symbols became hegemonic, for example, must be better understood. We do not wish to deny the ramifications of conflict, nor leave it unaccounted for. However, we wish to underscore two points. First, that religious conflict/communalism was always coterminous with a thriving cultural world where religious difference—however contentious in some spheres—did not inhibit common, shared praxis in others. Punjab historiography, buttressed by the broader work of many of the contributors to this volume, is illustrating this with increasing efficacy. The challenge that our historiography has yet to take up effectively, however, is to push beyond understanding communalism and Punjabiyat as parallel phenomena, and to interrogate the ways in which they may be imbricated in one another, and how they together produce modern Punjab.[32] Second, that there was no teleological one-way street built into identity politics leading inevitably to the partition of the subcontinent; the politics of the late colonial period were always contingent. Thus, we argue for examining the 'processual' and 'in-the-making' aspects of identity politics, which in effect give any society the possibilities of multitudinous trajectories. Put another way, to understand the reach of religion in shaping lives and cultures without obsessively relating this to the deployment of communal identities in arenas of politics is critical to how religious identities and cultures are studied in this volume.

The colonial period in Punjab was a turbulent one, and seminal studies have focused on this era as a time when the language and form of religious discourse were forever changed. After all, this was the time when various organizations and movements including the Arya Samaj, the Singh Sabhas, the Ahmadiyya, and numerous Muslim anjumans emerged, all composed of elites eager to gain space and recognition in the new public sphere.[33] The logic of their social and cultural politics depended on mustering and maintaining the support of their 'cadres', engaging in bellicose rhetoric, the discursive domains of which have been well documented and analysed. The impetus of this research is far from over, and as we continue to grapple with religious and ethnic conflicts in South Asia—whether of our own making or those received as a legacy of the colonial state—its momentum is not likely to abate.

C.S. Adcock's essay in this regard disturbs and unsettles some of the given assumptions about the nature of public discourse and the ostensibly entrenched positions that various reform and political organizations were committed to. She questions the assumed linkages often made by historians between the Arya Samaj of the late nineteenth and the first decade of the twentieth centuries to Hindu nationalism as it grew after the 1920s.[34] The framing of the debate on communalism by the Indian National Congress in terms of 'Hindu Tolerance', that is, Hinduism as a 'tolerant' religion that did not condone proselytization, as against the attack on Muslims by Hindu nationalists in this matter, had significant consequences in polarizing public debate. The representation of the early twentieth century by historians in similar terms—the continuum between the Arya Samaj and Hindu nationalism—has obscured important moments in the Arya Samaj's history. One of these, for example, is that of the Arya Samaj struggling to live up to its ideals of reform on caste.[35]

Adcock brings a new perspective to scholarship on the Arya Samaj's *shuddhi* programme—the proselytizing that earned the Samaj the dubious tag of indulging in 'semiticism'—by foregrounding the point of view of those who chose to be 'purified' and 'converted'. Shifting attention away from shuddhi as a Hindu–Muslim question, Adcock highlights issues of dalit identity instead. This is a particularly compelling approach given that the 'dalit question', as it were, was at this time agitating reformers, nationalists and the 'low' castes themselves.[36] She shows how 'untouchability' and Dayananda Sarasvati's idea of caste based on merit—the Vedic universalism of the Samaj— was often raised by converts. The continuum between Muslims, untouchables and women as the other(s) of the upper-caste Hindu male that her essay hints at opens up important questions about those who claimed the nation. The careers of some of the polemicists and controversialists she discusses ironically also point to the fluidity of identities in so far as many of them changed the religions and reform organizations they supported frequently enough to render meaningless the idea of loyalty to any given identity; or, to think of this a little differently, it demonstrates the accumulation of multiple identities.

The 'performance' of controversy—given that conversion theatricals were geared towards attracting public attention—and by implication the 'performance' of identity in the public sphere of colonial north India opened the question of identity to public moods, scrutiny and participation. Conversion as a form of dissent and as creating novel situations and rituals of belonging emerged as an arena for commenting on society itself.[37] In the context of Punjab, then, uncomfortable questions are raised: were genuine moments that could have re-defined Punjabi attitudes towards the dalit question not capitalized upon by their ostensible supporters? Was the 'communal' issue more complex than the assumption of straightforward loyalties of defined communities/religiosities that we assume? To what extent did it become imperative for dalits to define their identity in their own terms—whether through their 'traditional' religion or by instituting or appropriating newer identities such as Ad Dharmi, Valmiki Sabha, Buddhist, and Christian?[38]

A salient contribution of this volume are essays that examine the eighteenth and the nineteenth centuries, opening up key concepts like 'religion' or 'community' or 'piety' for careful interrogation in the pre-colonial and early colonial periods. Can the European Enlightenment's universalizing of religion, and the importation of that idea in the colonies be held responsible for obscuring indigenous traditions that grasped and performed religiosity in different ways?[39] Did the stance of the 'Orientalists', with their focus on textual traditions create a warped understanding of Indian religious phenomena? Was 'Hinduism' never studied on its own terms, marking as different the colonized and their religious expression from their imperial rulers?[40] The essays highlighted below show the local lineages of holy men and regional traditions that so significantly defined people's relationship to the sacred. They also illuminate the interlocution, appropriation and intermeshing with the greater Indic traditions that created the templates on which the local was inscribed. The idea of a community was also undoubtedly present, but what made the community distinct was a much more complex process than the categories Hindu, Muslim or Sikh allow for. In other words, it might be more useful to look at society in relational terms, marking out distinctions not in sharp cleavages but in chains of connectedness.

One example of such a palimpsest would be the new state structure of the Sikhs, built on the political and statist imaginary fed by the culturally hegemonic Mughal state. Another would be the reach and play of the Pauranic mythologies to understand and experience the world. Alternatively we can speak of the sheer power of the holy personage in Punjab disbursing sacred charisma on the temporal or spiritual efforts of humans. This could be a *sant* or a pir, a living guru or a human conduit carrying forward saintly *baraka* (grace), performing salutary and obligatory miracles, affirming life and its course for most Punjabis.

The study of the Kukas by Harjot Oberoi, and the Gulabdasi sect by Anshu Malhotra, point to ways in which the guru lineages (a parallel tradition being the veneration of the pirs) played an important part in expressing piety in this region. Though these essays also affirm the notion of Hindu, Sikh and Musalman/Turak in Punjabi society, they are circumspect about using them as self-evident categories. Oberoi depicts the centrality of the purity/pollution binary for the millenarian Kukas (though they rejected the caste system) who literally invested everything to maintain the symbolic purity of the cow. The attack on the butchers of first Amritsar, then Raikot, and finally an apocalyptic moment at Malerkotla in 1872 was not a case of 'religious riot' that we have become familiar with in the colonial chronicles from the end of the nineteenth century, but symptomatic of a state of anomie for the Kuka protectors of the cow. It was the *mlechha* (impure; barbarian) British with their increasing tolerance for cow-slaughter that forced the hand of the Kukas, who rose against the destruction of what they held to be inviolable. The Kukas drew inspiration from the miracle-making guru Ram Singh, proximity to his physical presence and the power of his teachings. The guru himself freely borrowed, adapted and internalized from the Sikh tradition, whose imagined pristine past he wished to recreate.

While the Kukas were keen on drawing boundaries in their own way and distinguishing between the sacred and the profane, the Gulabdasis seemingly welcomed all to their *dera* (establishment). These included men and women, persons of all religions, the high castes and the low. Malhotra shows how the charisma of the guru was important in this rather literary sect whose last decades, as those of the Kukas, intersected with the colonial period. It was guru Gulabdas's particular interpretation of Vedantic monism that encouraged the openness of the sect that apparently embraced all. Malhotra re-explores the concept of 'syncretism' to demonstrate the manner in which specific appropriations from bhakti, Sufi and Sikh traditions created the multiple inheritances that the sect revelled in.

Taking a slightly different approach, Mir looks at another instantiation of the overlaps between bhakti, Sufi, and Sikh traditions in her essay on Punjabi popular narratives. Mir's main focus is on the representation of saint veneration within Punjabi qisse, and *Hir–Ranjha* in particular. Through an analysis of a number of late-nineteenth century Hir-Ranjha texts, she argues that saint veneration is consistently represented as both a legitimate and a preferred form of religious devotion. By historicizing these texts and their popularity, Mir argues for their significance as historical sources, and as representations of contemporary popular attitudes. In contemplating how best to analyse this discourse and the historical practices it signifies, she argues for thinking of it as a regional form of piety. Indeed, she argues that this is more helpful in thinking about questions of religious identity in late nineteenth- and early twentieth-century Punjab than the concept of syncretism, a concept that Malhotra finds helpful for the same historical context.

Despite Malhotra's invocation of syncretism and its value for analytical purposes, that is not to suggest that her reading of the Gulabdasi sect shies away from interrogating what might be described metaphorically as discordant notes in the sect's history. She attempts to decipher these discordant notes as they emerge from the Gulabdasi Piro's writings, which underline Hindu-Turak (as Muslims are referred to in the contemporary literature) differentiation, on the face of it a strange juxtaposition in a sect known for subversions of orthodoxies. Piro's putative 'conversion' from a Muslim to a Gulabdasi (Sikh/Hindu) neophyte is a reminder that 'conversions', whether in the pre-colonial or the colonial periods, demonstrated both the fluidity of identities as they also became occasions for plugging the porosity of community borders. Inclusiveness and distancing were intrinsically part of the enterprise of crossing religio-cultural borders.

Oberoi's and Malhotra's essays also link up with Adcock's essay on the important issue of the low castes and untouchables of Punjab. While Oberoi shows that the Kukas had a number of Jat followers,[41] Guru Ram Singh was from the artisanal Tarkhan caste and there were other 'low' caste disciples. On the other hand, though Gulabdas was himself a Jat, sources show that his sect had many low caste and untouchable followers.[42] This fluidity tells us something about the intellectual, social, and religious subject positions available to some low castes in nineteenth-century Punjab. Despite the polemical dimensions the 'untouchability' question acquired in the late nineteenth and the twentieth centuries, as Adcock shows, we know that these social spaces continued to exist. The continuous histories of the Namdharis (Kukas) and the Gulabdasis to our present times indicate that, even though the sects may have changed in varied ways over time. The present flaring up of Sikh/Ravidasi/dalit identity issues, clustered around various popular deras in Indian Punjab and in the diaspora, point to the need to examine the history of these older deras, which could scupper and subvert given ritual and social hierarchies of Punjabi society.

Two more essays in this volume further complicate our understanding of how community and religious identity came to be experienced and addressed in the eighteenth century. Discussing the specific genre of history writing within the Sikh tradition, the *Gurbilas* literature, they attempt to unravel how the notion of a Sikh community was constructed and built. Before we take these up for discussion, a few preliminary words about the flourishing discipline of 'Sikh Studies' will help in apprehending them.

SIKH STUDIES AND QUESTIONS OF IDENTITY

Demographic, political and cultural factors have considerably influenced the growth of Sikh Studies. The second Partition of Punjab, in 1966, created an Indian state in which Sikhs constituted upwards of sixty per cent of the population, a demographic shift that changed forever the status of Sikhs from a small minority in colonial Punjab (a mere 7 per cent according to the 1891 census)[43] to a conspicuous majority. The success of the Green Revolution in Punjab in the 1960s and the 1970s made it one of the most prosperous states of India. Academic life in Indian Punjab developed apace with at least three large universities, in Chandigarh, Patiala, and Amritsar. While much of the research produced at these sites assumed—as it contributed to—the idea of a Sikh nation, equally important was scholarship that examined or projected the history of a region.[44] The tension between these two projects—Sikh history and Punjabi history—was particularly acute during the Khalistan movement in the early 1980s, which demanded for itself a history of Sikh nationhood.[45]

Other tensions and opportunities have also influenced the field of Sikh Studies. One of these, for example, is the massive emigration from Punjab from the late nineteenth century which created a need for host communities to incorporate this diaspora in what have often been evolving discourses on multiculturalism. The large migrations from the Sikh community, and its success in terms of both economic well-being and integration in host societies—the latter demonstrated by Ballantyne in this volume—has meant a significant presence and growth of Sikh Studies in Western academia. In recent years the discipline has engaged in debates about Sikh identity and opened questions about the perennial ambivalence of identities and the state of flux in which they are constantly negotiated.[46] The discipline has encouraged a range of research into the pre-modern period, spurred on in the first instance by locating and studying texts and manuscripts associated with the gurus.[47]

Gurinder Singh Mann makes a critical intervention in precisely such scholarship, as well as in the broader analysis of Sikh Studies in his essay, 'Guru Nanak's Life and Legacy: A Reappraisal'. Here, Mann focuses attention of scholarship on the first Guru, in particular, assessing the state of scholarship on this seminal figure in Sikh and Punjabi (and Indian) history, and uses this as an opportunity to explore the future possibilities of research in the broader field of Sikh Studies. His essay provides a reconsideration of the foundational work of W.H. McLeod and suggests the ways it has perhaps unduly influenced Sikh scholarship decisively. While cognizant of McLeod's significant achievements both within and for the field of Sikh Studies, Mann is nonetheless willing to underscore the interpretive strategies or paths that McLeod's scholarship foreclosed; he, in turn, presents us with a glimpse of those that he sees as most vital to an understanding of the Sikh religion and Sikh social history. Two of Mann's revisionist stances are of particular note. First, based upon his reading of the earliest Sikh scriptures, Mann overturns the traditional quietist image of Nanak to present him as an energetic and self-conscious religious and social institution builder. Second, he asserts that the Jats, and some artisanal castes, were an important component of the earliest Sikh community under Nanak, in contrast to the scholarly consensus that Jats entered the Sikh fold in large numbers only in the seventeenth century.[48] Mann's analyses, thus, nudges historians to re-examine the given contours of Sikh history. At minimum, he opens up the question of re-assessing important phases in Sikh history: the role of various gurus in building the Sikh community; and the complex interplay between Punjab's political, social and cultural histories and Sikh history. Different genres of Sikh literature—the *janam-sakhis, rahit-namas*, the gurbilas eulogies, as well as the various recensions of the Adi Granth—allow for a careful analysis of the evolving dynamics of the Sikh community. Some will surely find Mann's analysis provocative, as they may his prescriptions for future research. We see his essay as marking our contemporary moment as both a crucial and transformative juncture—one in which we can both take stock of the past and look forward to the future—in the field of Sikh Studies, rife with possibilities as a new generation of scholars enter the field and new institutional spaces are garnered for the study of Sikh and Punjabi history.

Among the many accomplishments of Sikh Studies as a field is the way it has complicated our understanding of the seventeenth, eighteenth, and the first half of the nineteenth centuries, particularly through scholarship that has highlighted the power of the Khalsa—as an idea, an incipient organization, and as an imperial *darbar* (court).[49] Sometimes the intimate relationship between the history of the Sikhs and its historians, contemporary as well as those of earlier generations, has also led to more polemical efforts to exhibit a continuous history of Sikh 'nationhood', its locus apparently embedded in old manuscripts, but also dressed in newer nationalist sensibilities.

However, as research has become more sophisticated, particularly in its examination of what went into the making of Sikh senses of the self, the Sikh community's relationship to its past has also become more nuanced.

Louis Fenech in this volume studies the complex and fascinating history of the *Zafar-namah* (Epistle of Victory) attributed to the tenth guru Gobind Singh. Dismissing the banality of questions that try to establish whether the tenth guru did/did not, could/could not have written the *Zafar-namah*, or whether he would have entered into a dialogue with the Mughal emperor Aurangzeb, Fenech is more interested in the history of the *Zafar-namah* itself. Fenech simultaneously unpacks the manner in which Gobind Singh's court and his literary composition can be placed within what he calls a 'larger South Asian Islamicate' culture, and how over time the text came to stand for the guru in the Sikh imagination. From what was purportedly the guru's letter to the emperor, this text's transition and transformation into sacred writing, and its emplacement within the *Dasam Granth* is the unfolding story of Sikh subjectivity and selfhood. Fenech's adept handling of diverse sources, drawing out the contours of the Perso-Islamic heritage of north India even as he shows how a sense of Sikh community was born, enriches our understanding of this period as it does of Sikh identity.

In a similar vein, Anne Murphy examines Kuir Singh's *Gurbilas Patshahi Das* and delves into the larger Pauranic mythological world that animated this genre of literature, showing at the same time the interpretive load a term like 'community' carried in the eighteenth and the early nineteenth centuries. Focusing on Kuir Singh's portrayal of the martyrdom of the ninth guru Tegh Bahadur, Murphy too weaves her discussion around the persistent and troubling question of conversion. Noting that the idea of religion in this period and region must be seen to be relational (rather than as dualistic, as it developed in the west), Murphy investigates what Turak, Hindu or Sikh meant at this time. She delineates the concept of 'commensurability' to give a perspective on how Turaks were constructed as the others of Sikhs in this literature, but also how the commensurable institution of conversion mirrored aspects common to both.

CONVERSION AND THE POLITICS OF DIFFERENCE

The heuristic load that the term 'conversion' carries in Punjab is then explored in three different essays in this volume, pertaining to different but linked periods (Murphy's, Malhotra's, and Adcock's). In recent years in the historiography of South Asia, the term 'conversion' has been complicated to show many gradual, novel, and complex ways in which communities or individuals change their religious affiliations.[50] The term is no longer deployed primarily to open up the domain of the evangelizing ambitions of the Christian missionaries, though this continues to be an area of investigation,[51] or to discuss the apparently intractable problem of the spread of Islam in India, though path-breaking contributions have been made in this area.[52] In the context of Punjab these essays show that there were ways in which the idea of conversion simultaneously hardened community boundaries even as it allowed the breaching of those divisions. Murphy's essay, by elaborating the theme of 'martyrdom' explored in Fenech's earlier work,[53] dwells on how martyrdom developed as a central thematic in Sikh representations of the self through the trope of 'conversion'. Yet the moment of conversion, even if presented as a choice between martyrdom and ignominy, inexorably drew the self close to its supposed other. The gradual reifying of the idea of conversion within the Sikh tradition (along with that of martyrdom) pushes us to investigate its meanings in the changing political contexts of Punjab. Significantly, the representation of 'conversion' against the background of conflict over political power, as was the context of Gurbilas literature, directs attention to the insight provided by Talal Asad; he argues for the importance of power and its configurations in any analysis of religion in a socio-historical situation, rather than perceiving religion as a universalist phenomena standing on its own.[54] Thus the changing understandings of Hindu, Sikh, and Musalman/Turaks in Punjab must also be seen to be contingent upon the political situation at a given time, even as accretions of cultural markers contributed to identity.

The saga of Haqiqat Rai as represented in the nineteenth century that Malhotra discusses briefly in her essay highlights how Hindu and Sikh groups came to associate conversion with the abuse of political power by the Turaks in Punjab. Malhotra elaborates this idea in her discussion of Piro, showing how by the mid-nineteenth century the conversion trope could plausibly be displaced to any supposed abuse of power by the 'Musalmans'—even when the Sikhs ruled. However, the putative conversion of the Muslim Piro to the Gulabdasi sect points to how this conversion also allowed for the reifying of religious identities, if only to exhibit in the larger context the speciousness of divisions in the first place. This latter attitude—that religious divisions were specious—had a long history within bhakti literature, and was used to mock the ritual-oriented religiosity of authority figures. Finally, Adcock examines the shrill polemics of the early twentieth century and shows that those who thrived on controversies that demarcated community boundaries, themselves moved between different identities. Taken together, these essays complicate both the term conversion and its articulation in Punjabi society. Indeed, conversion, it seems, was implicated in the complex and multi-dimensional ways in which modern communities came to be constructed.

Anna Bigelow, who delineates the symbolic power of three shared sacred sites in contemporary Indian Punjab draws out another aspect of inter-community relations, namely what she calls 'pro-social encounters'. All the sites she discusses are associated with different expressions of Islamic piety—the *dargah* (tomb) of Hyder Shaikh in Malerkotla, shrines commemorating events from the life of the famous Chisti Sufi Shaikh Farid in Faridkot, and a *maseet* (mosque) in Gobindpura. Rather than reading tolerance at these places as the outcome of passive non-interference, Bigelow suggests in her analysis of shared sacred sites that it is the positive effort on the part of various interested parties to work towards promoting peace that makes space for varied—and not contestatory—interpretations of the power of the sacred. Importantly, this desire for harmony does not mean the erasure of difference. In fact, different ritual specialists and those with a stake in a site's continuing religious life often understood the power of the sacred in separate ways. What is critical, and Bigelow's essay lays this out clearly, is people's ability to make space for alternate and pluralistic understanding of a site's religious meaning.

What Bigelow has observed in the course of her fieldwork and discussed with theoretical clarity, has been a kind of movement in contemporary Indian Punjab. It seems the dominant Punjabi Jat-Sikhs and their Hindu neighbours have over the last decade restored and rebuilt over two hundred mosques destroyed in partition riots. This has been accomplished either with their resources and initiative, sometimes at the behest of the *Jamaat-e-Islami*, and at times with the help of funds remitted from relatives in the Sikh diaspora. It is with this background that the latest case of the Ghumman family's similar effort in Sarwarpur has received celebratory acknowledgement.[55] Is this the case of post colonial Indian Punjab's remorse over the extremities of violence during the Partition? Undoubtedly this gesture of symbolic amity has enormous power, not least because Punjab saw the worst of partition violence. However, this magnanimity for a mere 1.5 per cent Muslim population of the state, many of whom are migrant labour, must be put in perspective. On the one hand it shows how the trend of hardening of religious lines and political posturing on the issue since the demolition of the Babri Masjid is bucked in Punjab, exemplified by the pro-social encounters that Bigelow highlights. On the other hand, it must be kept in mind that the miniscule Muslim population of Indian Punjab is not a threat in terms of numbers, economic presence, nor does it spawn a fear of cultural conquest, both of which are anti-Muslim bogies favoured by the Hindu Right. The saga of conflict in Indian Punjab is being played out with a sharper edge in relation to the dalits, who have larger numbers and represent greater prosperity. Nevertheless there is no doubt that pro-sociality encourages people to look at themselves as tolerant and multi-dimensional.

In contrast to the edifices of amity being constructed in Indian Punjab, Pakistani Punjab is perhaps going through the worst period of intra-community conflict in its history. In a country that is more than 95 per cent Muslim, it is astounding that the tag of '*kafir*' or infidel is being bandied about to brand people.[56] It is not just Hindu, Sikh and Christian minorities who are victimized, but also the Shi'i and Ahmadiyya 'minorities'.[57] Increasingly the divisions between the Wahabi and the Barelvi factions of the majority Sunni sect are coming to the fore, seen for instance in the targeting of the shrines of revered

Sufi saints; suicide bombers targeted Data Ganj Baksh's shrine in the heart of Lahore on 1 July 2010 and Sakhi Sarwar's shrine in Dera Ghazi Khan on 3 April 2011. As Ayesha Jalal has shown, the idea of jihad has undergone unimaginable metamorphosis in recent years. From a concept that was historically deployed in the South Asian context as much to promote peace as war, it is now understood primarily as an individual's right to fight not just the 'West', but others perceived to be enemies and infidels. The ethical aspect of the >t, the greater jihad, has given way, as has the right of the state iate it.[58] The attack on the Sufi shrine represents a desire to a quintessentially shared feature of Punjabis' piety, the faith shrines with their spiritual sweep and miraculous powers.[59]

ona Sawhney picks just this ominous moment of violence—of men willingly sacrificing life for a cause perceived as greater emselves by exploding bombs at an Ahmadiyya mosque—to inquire into an earlier phenomenon of 'revolutionary terrorism'. While the romance of sacrifice and death are linked with the idea of patriotic exhortation directed at the youth, Sawhney turns to the writings of the young man gifted with clear thinking—Bhagat Singh. Using the canvas of a range of writings emanating from the radical, socialist and democratic traditions of the West in the nineteenth and early twentieth centuries, Bhagat Singh displayed an astonishing cosmopolitanism in order to forge a democratic nationalism. What makes a hero and what gives the hero the right to inflict violence, including on the self, were issues that troubled Bhagat Singh. The similarities with Gandhi were only too visible, but so were the enormous differences. Similarly the case for drawing parallels with the present manifestations of terrorist violence is there, but so are very significant distinctions. One of the distinguishing points that Sawhney highlights with subtlety is the manner in which the perception of the 'West' has undergone a change. From a beacon of hope and cosmopolitanism, the West is viewed by many youth growing up in the third world today as the seedbed for spawning prejudiced neo-imperialists. Hope and cosmopolitanism have had a conjoint death. And the line dividing the romance of death with its sheer brutality erased. The projected essentialism of cultures then seems the unfortunate fallout of a globalizing world.

Punjabiyat and the 'Idea(s) of Punjab'

In this volume, then, we bring together essays with disparate and related themes, from historical and contemporary times, collectively investigating or alluding to different facets of a lived Punjabiyat. By encouraging our contributors to think about aspects of Punjabi culture and history, we hope we have added to the strength of a growing discipline of cultural history from an important region in South Asia, the complexity of whose cultural and historical inheritance has not received adequate attention. We have not only emphasized the amorphous and shadowy nature of our nodal idea of Punjabiyat, but also underlined that for all its ambiguity, the notion is real in so far as it exercises people's imaginations, emotions, experiences, and a sense of self. For far too long, we contend, the idea has been ignored because it does not fit into given neat boundaries, whether political or religious. The messiness inherent in the plethora of new questions, or in rethinking older engagements with newer insights, is a welcome disorder that we hope this volume ushers.

While we have spoken of the nebulousness of Punjabiyat, we would also, perhaps paradoxically, argue that it is pervasive; indeed, its pervasiveness may play some role in its vitality as an identity going largely unexplored. Punjabiness slips into so many aspects of popular culture that there seems to be no need to explicate it separately. Punjabiyat's wholehearted embrace by the Bombay film industry is a case in point. Bollywood's hybrid Hindi-Punjabi-Urdu lyrics, the musical genius of some Punjabi emigrants recognized and nurtured by the film industry, or the use of lilting Punjabi folk melodies and tunes that carried the flavour of Punjab, as for example in the unforgettable beats of O.P. Nayyar, indicate this ubiquitous presence. Something similar is happening with Punjabi poetry. The perennial popularity of Bulleh Shah in Punjab has now become a larger phenomenon with broad celebration of his compositions in both India and Pakistan thanks to the reach of cinema and music. From the film *Bobby*'s (1971) adaptation of Bulleh Shah's poetry—*beshak mandir masjid todo Bulleh Shah yeh kahta* (made by Raj Kapoor, the Peshawar-born thespian of the foremost family of migrant Punjabis in Bollywood)—to Rabbi Shergill's 2005 chart buster *Bulla ki Jaana*, to the recent *Ranjha Ranjha kardi main ape Ranjha hoi* from the film *Raavan* (2010; directed by the Tamil Mani Ratnam), Bulleh Shah has become synonymous with Punjabi *sufiana kalaam*. The celebration of the Hindu upper caste Khatri identity, often lovingly (if garishly) depicted in extravagant marriages and rituals, is the most recent expression of second and third generation Punjabis in the Bombay film industry whose parents/grandparents came from Punjab.[60] In recent decades Punjabi identity in diaspora communities too has been partly coalesced by musical experimentation, creating hybridized sounds nevertheless sutured to ethnic identities.[61] This has helped shape South Asian identity for numerous youth growing up in western and other countries. However, the very ubiquity of this apparently familiar and loved (or denigrated) Punjabi culture should not mean that it does not require rigorous study.

By delving into variegated aspects of Punjab's culture and history, we hope to elucidate the idea of Punjabiyat, as well as to complicate it. We do not imagine the volume as a source for a definitive list of criteria that might tell us what it means to be Punjabi. Nor is this volume an attempt to posit a simple, hydraulic relationship— historically or today—between Punjabiyat, on the one hand, and communalism, religious conflict and violence, on the other. Lived realities are, of course, much more complex than such a dichotomy allows for. And certainly, we are acutely aware that Punjabiyat and the articulation of oppositional or conflictual religious identities are implicated in the same historical processes. At the same time, however—and undoubtedly underscoring the complexity of the issue at hand—we want to gesture towards the potential of Punjabiyat to act as an antidote to the politics of antagonism.

Our endeavour is to foreground the complexities of such issues, and to put forward different perspectives on and approaches to engage with them. In doing so, we hope this volume will both historicize and complicate the idea of Punjab and Punjabiyat, and provide an important comparative perspective for the study of Indian regions.

Notes

1   The following discussion has benefited from theoretical insights on cultural history in Lynn Hunt, 'Introduction: History, Culture and Text',

in Lynn Hunt (ed.), *The New Cultural History*, Berkeley: University of California Press, 1989, pp. 1–22; Victoria Bonnell and Lynn Hunt (eds), *Beyond the Cultural Turn: Directions in the Study of Society and Culture*, Berkeley: University of California Press, 1999.

2 J.S. Grewal, 'The Historian's Panjab', in his *Miscellaneous Articles*, Amritsar: Guru Nanak Dev University, 1974, pp. 1–10.

3 J.S. Grewal, *Social and Cultural History of the Punjab: Prehistoric, Ancient, and Early Medieval*, New Delhi: Manohar, 2004.

4 This is evident in Muzaffar Alam's *The Crisis of Empire in Mughal North India*, New Delhi: Oxford University Press, 1993, for example. One also sees this reflected in Chetan Singh's *Region and Empire: Panjab in the Seventeenth Century*, New Delhi: Oxford University Press, 1991.

5 J.S. Grewal, *The Sikhs of the Punjab*, Cambridge: Cambridge University Press, 1990, pp. 99–127.

6 Farina Mir, *The Social Space of Language: Vernacular Culture in British Colonial Punjab*, Berkeley: University of California Press, 2010; Ranikhet: Permanent Black, 2010, p. 27.

7 On the Ghadar movement, see the seminal study by Harish K. Puri, *Ghadar Movement: Ideology, Organization & Strategy*, Amritsar: Guru Nanak Dev University, 1983. On the Khalistan movement, see Giorgio Shani, *Sikh Nationalism and Identity in a Global Age*, New York: Routledge, 2008, esp. pp. 40–99. On remittances from the Gulf to Pakistan, see Jonathan Addleton, *Undermining the Centre: The Gulf Migration and Pakistan*, Karachi: Oxford University Press, 1992.

8 This could include anything on a spectrum between deeply-sedimented emotive ties to native place/locality, on the one hand, to itinerancy, on the other hand. On ties to native place/locality, see Mir, *The Social Space of Language*, chap. 4. On itinerancy in Punjab, see Neeladri Bhattacharya, 'Predicaments of Mobility: Peddlers and Itinerants in Nineteenth-century Northwestern India', in Claude Makovits, Jacques Pouchepadass, and Sanjay Subrahmanyam (eds), *Society and Circulation: Mobile People and Itinerant Cultures in South Asia 1750–1950*, Ranikhet: Permanent Black, 2003, pp. 163–214.

9 The clearest linguistic exposition of the language is Christopher Shackle, 'Panjabi', in Dhanesh Jain and George Cardona (eds), *The Indo-Aryan Languages*, New York: Routledge, 2003, pp. 581–621. We should note that Shackle considers Siraiki a separate language, but for the purposes of this volume we choose to subsume it in Punjabi not for political, but rather for historical reasons. The Siraiki movement is a modern phenomenon, dating from the 1970s, and is situated in a very particular context of Pakistani politics. To treat it as a separate language for the period under study in this volume, which ranges from the medieval to the contemporary periods strikes us as

anachronistic. On the movement, see Christopher Shackle, 'Siraiki: A Language Movement in Pakistan', *Modern Asian Studies*, 11 (3), 1977, pp. 379–403; and Tariq Rahman, 'The Siraiki Movement in Pakistan', *Language Problems and Language Planning*, 19 (1), 1995, pp. 1–25.

10 We should note that of these dialects, Lahnda alone is no longer common in linguistic discussions of Punjabi dialects. Shackle, for example, does not include it in his exposition of the language in his essay, 'Panjabi'. Today, linguists generally use the term to refer to a distinct Indo-Aryan language. One finds a number of such references in Dhanesh Jain and George Cardona (eds), *The Indo-Aryan Languages*, New York: Routledge, 2003. See, for example, pp. 240, 545, 652, and 898. This dovetails with colonial linguist George Grierson's analysis in his famous linguistic survey of Indian languages, where he identified Lahnda as the language spoken in Western Punjab. See George Grierson, *Grierson on Punjabi* [reprint of Punjabi sections of *Linguistic Survey of India*, vol. 9], Patiala: Languages Department, 1961 [1919]. For our purposes, however, we follow the tradition of Punjabi literary criticism that views Lahnda as a dialect of Punjabi, one particularly significant to medieval and early modern literary production. See, for example, Mohan Singh Uberoi's foundational text, *A History of Panjabi Literature (1100–1932)*, Jalandhar: Bharat Prakashan, 1971 [1933].

11 Denis Matringe, 'Hir Varis Shah, A Story Retold', in Vasudha Dalmia and Theo Damsteegt (eds), *Narrative Strategies: Essays on South Asian Literature and Film*, New Delhi: Oxford University Press. 1998, p. 19.

12 Carla Petievich, *When Men Speak as Women: Vocal Masquerade in Indo-Muslim Poetry*, New Delhi: Oxford University Press, 2007.

13 The reasons for this are explored in Farina Mir, 'Imperial Policy, Provincial Practices: Colonial Language Policy in Nineteenth Century India', *Indian Economic and Social History Review*, 43 (4), 2006, pp. 395–427.

14 See Mir, *The Social Space of Language*, pp. 84–5.

15 P.H.M. van den Dungen, *The Punjab Tradition: Influence and Authority in Nineteenth Century India*, London: George Allen and Unwin Ltd, 1972.

16 N.G. Barrier, *The Punjab Alienation of Land Bill of 1900*, Durham, NC: Duke University Press, 1966.

17 On designating 'agricultural' and 'non-agricultural' tribes, see Barrier, *The Punjab Alienation of Land Bill*. On the creation of customary law, see Neeladri Bhattacharya, 'Remaking Custom: The Discourse and Practice of Colonial Codification', in R. Champakalakshmi and S. Gopal (eds),

Tradition, Dissent, and Ideology, New Delhi: Oxford University Press, 1996, pp. 20–51; and David Gilmartin, 'Customary Law and *Shari'at* in British Punjab', in Katherine P. Ewing (ed.), *Shari'at and Ambiguity in South Asian Islam*, Berkeley: University of California Press, 1988, pp. 43–62.

18 It should be noted that some colonial officials had more nuanced understandings of Jat identity. Denzil Ibbetson, for example, noted important distinctions within this group.

19 Anshu Malhotra, *Gender, Caste and Religious Identities: Restructuring Class in Colonial Punjab*, New Delhi: Oxford University Press, 2002, pp. 24–34.

20 On the canal colonies, see Imran Ali, *The Punjab Under Imperialism 1885–1947*, Princeton: Princeton University Press, 1988. On colonial ethnographic logics, see Richard Fox, *The Lions of the Punjab*, Berkeley: University of California Press, 1985.

21 See, for example: Arnaud Sauli, 'Circulation and Authority: Police, Public Space and Territorial Control in Punjab, 1861–1920', in Markovits *et al.* (eds), *Society and Circulation*, pp. 215–39; Rajit Mazumder, *The Indian Army and the Making of Punjab*, Ranikhet: Permanent Black, 2003; and Tan Tai Yong, *The Garrison State: the Military, Government and Society in Colonial Punjab, 1849–1947*, Thousand Oaks, CA: Sage Publications, 2005.

22 Ali, *The Punjab Under Imperialism*.

23 Richard Eaton, 'The Political and Religious Authority of the Shrine of Baba Farid', and 'Court of Man, Court of God: Local Perceptions of the Shrine of Baba Farid, Pakpattan, Punjab', in his *Essays on Islam and Indian History*, New Delhi: Oxford University Press, 2001, pp. 203–46.

24 Prem Chowdhry, *The Veiled Women: Shifting Gender Equations in Rural Haryana 1880–1990*, New Delhi: Oxford University Press, 1994. For how the laws affected 'high caste' widows, see Anshu Malhotra, 'Ascetic Widowhood or Widow Remarriage? Dilemma for the New Punjabi Elite', in her *Gender, Caste and Religious Identities*, pp. 82–115.

25 Veena Talwar Oldenburg, *Dowry Murder: The Imperial Origins of a Cultural Crime*, New York: Oxford University Press, 2002.

26 Ian Talbot, *Punjab and the Raj 1849–1947*, New Delhi: Manohar, 1988.

27 See, for example, on Calcutta, Lahore, and Bombay, respectively: Swati Chattopadhyay, *Representing Calcutta: Modernity, Nationalism, and the Colonial Uncanny*, London: Routledge, 2005; William J. Glover, *Making Lahore Modern: Constructing and Imagining a Colonial City*, Minneapolis: University of Minnesota Press, 2008; and Preeti Chopra, *A Joint Enterprise: The Indian Making of British Bombay, 1854–1918*, Minneapolis: University of Minnesota Press, 2011.

28 In addition to Glover 2008, see Ian Talbot, 'A Tale of Two Cities: The Aftermath of Partition for Lahore and Amritsar 1947–1957', *Modern Asian Studies*, 41 (1), 2007, pp. 151–85.

29 Malhotra, *Gender, Caste and Religious Identities*.

30 Markus Daechsel, *The Politics of Self-Expression: The Urdu Middleclass Milieu in Mid-Twentieth Century India and Pakistan*, London: Routledge, 2006.

31 There are, however, increasingly scholarly correctives to this. See Anna Bigelow's essay in this volume as well as her, *Sharing the Sacred: Practicing Pluralism in Muslim North India*, New York: Oxford University Press, 2010.

32 Our thanks to David Gilmartin for this point, whose own work is at the vanguard in this respect.

33 K.W. Jones, *Arya Dharm: Hindu Consciousness in Nineteenth Century Punjab*, New Delhi: Manohar, 1975; David Gilmartin, *Empire and Islam: Punjab and the Making of Pakistan*, Berkeley: University of California Press, 1988; Harjot Oberoi, *The Construction of Religious Boundaries: Culture, Identity and Diversity in the Sikh Tradition*, New Delhi: Oxford University Press, 1994; Bob van der Linden, *Moral Languages from Colonial Punjab: The Singh Sabha, Arya Samaj and Ahmadiyahs*, New Delhi: Manohar, 2008; Spencer Lavan, *The Ahmadiyah Movement: A History and Perspectives*, New Delhi: Manohar, 1974; and Yohanan Friedmann, *Prophecy Continuous: Aspects of Ahmadi Religious Thought and its Medieval Background*, Berkeley: University of California Press, 1989.

34 For such a stance, see Christophe Jaffrelot, *The Hindu Nationalist Movement and Indian Politics 1925 to the 1990s: Strategies of Identity-Building, Implantation and Mobilisation*, Delhi: Viking, 1996.

35 Jones contended that in his *Satyarth Prakash* Dayananda Sarasvati, the founder of the Arya Samaj, argued for caste based on the merit of a person rather than birth, advocating an 'open social system'. See Jones, *Arya Dharm*, p. 33. For a different view that argues for Dayananda's ambivalence on caste reforms, see Anshu Malhotra, 'The Body as a Metaphor for the Nation: Caste, Masculinity and Femininity in the Satyarth Prakash of Dayananda Sarasvati', in A.A. Powell and S. Lambert-Hurley (eds), *Rhetoric and Reality: Gender and Colonial Experience in South Asia*, New Delhi: Oxford University Press, 2006, pp. 121–53.

36 On the dalit Ad Dharm movement of Punjab, see Mark Juergensmeyer, *Religious Rebels in the Punjab: The Social Vision of Untouchables*, Delhi: Ajanta Publications, 1988.

37 On the diverse aspects of 'conversion' and the different modes and motivations for such an occurrence, see Rowena Robinson and Sathianathan

Clarke, 'Introduction', in Rowena Robinson and Sathianathan Clarke (eds), *Religious Conversion in India: Modes, Motivations, and Meanings*, New Delhi: Oxford University Press, 2003, pp. 1–21.

38 John C.B. Webster, *Religion and Dalit Liberation: An Examination of Perspectives*, New Delhi: Manohar, 2002.

39 On the manner in which religion developed as a transhistorical and transcultural category see Talal Asad, *Genealogies of Religion: Discipline and Reasons of Power in Christianity and Islam*, Baltimore: The Johns Hopkins University Press, 1993; and Tomoko Masuzawa, *The Invention of World Religions*, Chicago: University of Chicago Press, 2005. On the usage of the term 'Hinduism', see Heinrich von Stietencron, 'Hinduism: On the Proper Use of a Deceptive Term', in his *Hindu Myth, Hindu History: Religion, Art and Politics*, Ranikhet: Permanent Black, 2005, pp. 227–48. On different components constituting Hinduism, see Gunther-Dietz Sontheimer, 'Hinduism: The Five Components and Their Interaction', in Heidrun Bruckner, Anne Feldhaus and Aditya Malik (eds), *Gunther-Dietz Sontheimer: Essays on Religion, Literature and Law*, New Delhi: Manohar, 2004, pp. 401–19.

40 Gauri Vishwanathan, 'Colonialism and the Construction of Hinduism', in Gavin Flood (ed.), *Blackwell Companion to Hinduism*, Oxford: Blackwell Publishing, 2003, pp. 23–44.

41 Though Jats are placed as *shudra*s in the Hindu caste hierarchy, they were the powerful land-owning dominant caste of Punjab.

42 These included the later fiery Singh Sabha supporter Ditt Singh, the harijan Tara Singh and the prostitute Piro.

43 *Census of India 1891 – Vol. XIX – The Punjab and Its Feudatories*, Calcutta: Government Printing, 1892, p. 88.

44 This is seen, for example, in the bi-annual journal *The Panjab Past and Present* started by Ganda Singh of Punjabi University, Patiala in 1967; and the *The Journal of Regional History*, established in 1980 and published by Guru Nanak Dev University, Amritsar.

45 J.S. Grewal, *The Sikhs of the Punjab*, Cambridge: Cambridge University Press, 1990; and Harnik Deol, *Religion and Nationalism in India: The Case of the Punjab*, London: Routledge, 2000.

46 Some aspects of these debates have been captured well in J.S. Grewal, *Contesting Interpretations of the Sikh Tradition*, New Delhi: Manohar, 1998.

47 The literature here is too vast to be referenced fully except mentioning a few outstanding examples. W.H. McLeod, *Guru Nanak and the Sikh Tradition*, New Delhi: Oxford University Press, 1986; Gurinder Singh Mann, *The Making of Sikh Scripture*, New York: Oxford University Press, 2001; and Pashaura Singh, *Life and Work of Guru Arjan: History,*

Memory, and Biography in the Sikh Tradition, New Delhi: Oxford University Press, 2006.

48 W.H. McLeod, 'The Development of the Sikh Panth', in his *Exploring Sikhism: Aspects of Sikh Identity, Culture, and Thought*, New Delhi: Oxford University Press, 2004, pp. 49–69.

49 Louis E. Fenech, *The Darbar of the Sikh Gurus: The Court of God in the World of Men*, New Delhi: Oxford University Press, 2008.

50 Robinson and Clarke, *Religious Conversion in India*.

51 Robert E. Frykenberg (ed.) *Christians and Missionaries in India: Cross-Cultural Communication Since 1500*, London: Routledge, Curzon, 2003.

52 Richard M. Eaton, *The Rise of Islam and the Bengal Frontier 1204–1760*, Berkeley: University of California Press, 1993.

53 Louis E. Fenech, *Martyrdom in the Sikh Tradition: Playing the 'Game of Love'*, New Delhi: Oxford University Press, 2000.

54 Talal Asad, 'Anthropological Conceptions of Religion: Reflections on Geertz', *Man*, 18 (2), 1983, pp. 237–59.

55 Khushwant Singh, 'Rebuilding Secularism, Gandhi Style', *Hindustan Times* (New Delhi), 13 June 2010, p. 15; Chander S. Dogra, 'Shades of the Old Punjab', *Outlook* (New Delhi), 5 July 2010, pp. 58–61. More recently, a Muslim industrial house based in Malerkotla—the Sohrab Group of Industries—running the Hars Charitable Trust has restored a church targeted in the wake of the threat to burn Qurans (in the USA). 'Muslim Trust Restores Church', *The Times of India* (New Delhi), 20 September 2010, p. 13.

56 Amir Mir, 'Just Who is not a Kafir?' *Outlook* (New Delhi), 19 July 2010, pp. 54–6.

57 A controversy erupted over the branding 'kafir' on the coffin of the young Hindu Prem Chand of Pakistan who died in a plane crash near Islamabad. Mohammad Wajihuddin, 'Don't Use the K Word', *The Times of India* (New Delhi), 20 September 2010, p. 13.

58 Ayesha Jalal, *Partisans of Allah: Jihad in South Asia*, Cambridge: Harvard University Press, 2008; Ranikhet: Permanent Black, 2008.

59 See Farina Mir's essay in this volume.

60 Srijana Mitra Das, 'Partition and Punjabiyat in Bombay Cinema: The Cinematic Perspective of Yash Chopra and Others', *Contemporary South Asia*, 15 (4), 2006, pp. 453–71.

61 Ananya Jahanara Kabir, 'Musical Recall: Postmemory and the Punjabi Diaspora', *Alif: Journal of Comparative Poetics*, vol. 24, 2004, pp. 172–89.

Part I

Literary Cultures and Language Politics

Christopher Shackle

Punjabi Sufi Poetry from Farid to Farid

Originally completed as a moderately-sized PhD over three-quarters of a century ago, Lajwanti Rama Krishna's *Pañjābī Ṣūfī Poets*[1] rather remarkably remains the nearest thing to a standard work in English on its subject. It is the purpose of this chapter to suggest that a proper understanding of the full evolution of tradition of Sufi poetry in Punjabi requires a rather radically revised approach.

Her account is one of rise and fall. Beginning with a chapter on the poetry of Farid included in the Ādi Granth, which she attributes to Baba Farid's early sixteenth century successor 'Farid II', she goes on to outline the lives and poetry of Shah Husain (d. 1593) and Sultan Bahu (d. 1691) before providing a more elaborate treatment of Bullhe Shah (d. 1758), whom she rightly describes as the greatest of all Punjabi Sufi poets. Much more questionably, however, she sees that greatness as being the product of a progressive move away from his circumscribed Islamic origins, eventually culminating in a fully fledged universalism inspired by the monism of Vedanta. The five remaining chapters then pay decreasing attention to Bullhe Shah's more significant successors, such as Ali Haidar (d. 1785) and Hashim Shah (d. 1823) and their lesser contemporaries, before finally petering out with a desultory mention of a few very minor nineteenth-century poets. The influence of Rama Krishna's approach remains significantly evident in later studies, notably including quite a number of those similarly written in English by Indian authors.[2]

In reaching for a better understanding of Punjabi Sufi poetry, the present chapter tries to open up new ways of understanding this wonderfully rich tradition by coming at it rather differently. We begin with some general reflections on the special problematics of Punjabi literary history, with particular reference to the Sufi poetic tradition. It is suggested that the writing of the history of Punjabi literature of the pre-colonial period is an exceptionally difficult undertaking. Not only is the surviving material frequently rather sparse in quantity, and often very imperfectly preserved textually,[3] but it is also quite heterogeneous in inspiration, comprising a whole variety of traditions far from being confined to the familiar Sufi and Sikh types.

We then approach the Sufi poetic tradition not as usual from its fragmentary beginnings, but from its end in the later nineteenth century. Not only are the lives and circumstances of the last great exponents of the tradition far better attested than those of the earlier poets, but the fact that they were active in the period when the introduction of printing had established an active vernacular publishing industry in the Punjab means that the texts of their poetry are far more reliably preserved. This relative abundance of reliable evidence can, it is argued, afford a much better basis for understanding the Sufi poetry of earlier periods than *a priori* generalizations about the ecumenical character of medieval Indian spirituality, allowing the construction of a fuller picture of the tradition by giving as much weight to its late classics as to its fragmentary earliest records.

We then move back in time to a summary consideration of the contrasting special characteristics of the earliest Punjabi Sufi poetry, the verses of Farid preserved in the Sikh Ādi Granth (1604), and the vexed question of their precise relationship to the famous figure of Baba Farid (d. 1265). Here it is suggested that in the absence of direct attestation of links between the poetry and the life in the case of Farid, not to speak of other Punjabi Sufi poets, much may usefully be suggested by comparative study of evidence from Sindhi, the nearest regional tradition of vernacular Sufi poetry. This is illustrated with particular reference to the early Sindhi Sufi poet Shah Karim (d. 1623).

The final sections of the essay then deal with the three best known poets of the Mughal period, whose three centuries are sparsely represented respectively by Shah Husain, Sultan Bahu, and Bullhe Shah. Attention is drawn both to characteristic features of stylistic evolution, which it is possible to begin to discern only from this period, to typical differences between these poets, and to the serious flaws in Lajwanti Rama Krishna's re-casting of these Sufis as religiously universalized exponents of a shared pre-modern Indian spiritual understanding. It is also emphasized how the textual evidence for this period is much more poorly established than it is for the later Sufi poets of the nineteenth century with whom we began.

PUNJABI LITERARY HISTORY

Literary history might be minimally defined as the diachronic arrangement of texts and their authors. As such, it is an untidy exercise at best, since it must awkwardly straddle the divides between history and criticism as it tries to organize all sorts of different literary materials produced across time into intelligible schemes of classification.[4] In the case of pre-modern South Asia, the writing of literary history is made even less tidy by overlapping boundaries of language, religion and poetic genre, not to speak of the massive gaps and the many well known historical difficulties which are presented by uncertain biographical data, unreliably dated texts, and poorly established textual transmission. This pervasive absence of objectively verifiable data can often make it difficult to establish agreed standards of authenticity.[5]

Given the cultural and political divides which characterize the region, it is no surprise that the history of Punjabi literature has always been a particularly problematic one to write. It is, for instance, notable that there is no coverage of Punjabi literature in the two major recent English-language histories of Indian literatures published in the West: the multi-volume *History of Indian Literatures* published by Brill in the 1970s under the general editorship of J.S. Gonda and the large multi-authored single volume more recently edited by Sheldon Pollock.[6] A similar gap existed for a long time in the Sahitya Akademi's major English-language series of histories of Indian literatures. In the end this was partially filled by the dual-authored history by Sekhon and Duggal, which in its turn was then supplemented by two separately published volumes authored by Sekhon alone.[7]

Like some of the Punjabi-language histories published in India since 1947, the failure of the Sekhon–Duggal volumes to construct a persuasive single narrative illustrates the intrinsic difficulties of finding a satisfactory arrangement for a comprehensive Punjabi literary history. Historians of Hindi literature can achieve this through depicting the parallel traditions of *sagun bhakti* and *nirgun bhakti* and of Muslim and courtly literature, variously written during the premodern period in Braj Bhasha, Avadhi or Khari Boli, as all leading to the unitary modern literature written in the modern standard Hindi which was developed to express an Indian national consciousness.[8]

In a way, this was also the approach attempted early in the last century for Punjabi by Bava Budh Singh, the amateur enthusiast who created Punjabi literary history, and whose work was extensively cited by Lajwanti Rama Krishna. Loosely designed as a kind of encyclopaedic anthology, Budh Singh's three pioneering volumes[9] began with a celebration of the primacy of Guru Nanak and the contributions of the later Sikh Gurus, then detailed the poetry of the Sufis and other mostly Muslim authors which dominated the following period, before describing the modern Punjabi literature then being created by the authors of the Sikh renaissance led by Bhai Vir Singh.

In reality, however, the attempted harmonization of the Muslim with the Sikh tradition, with its more or less explicit idealization of a single Punjabi cultural identity, conspicuously failed to achieve political embodiment when Punjab was divided along religious lines in the Partition of 1947. For the few historians of Punjabi literature in Pakistan,[10] this has allowed medieval or modern writings in Gurmukhi script to be almost completely ignored. Indian scholars writing in either English or Punjabi, on the other hand, in their attempts to embrace the hugely significant pre-modern Muslim Punjabi poetry, especially that of the Sufis, have often been led into maintaining the over-readiness to smooth over the differences of Sufi from Sikh and other bhakti literature which was so characteristic of the nationalist period during which Lajwanti Rama Krishna's thesis was written. These dangers seem best avoided now by adopting the alternative encyclopaedic approach[11] exemplified to good effect in R.S. Jaggi's five-volume literary history,[12] which prefers to offer separate parallel descriptions in order to do justice to the parallel traditions of pre-modern Punjabi literature, even at the risk of sacrificing the attractive simplicity of the nationalist agenda's unitary narrative.

Against these general considerations, we may now move on to a characterization of some of the salient features of Punjabi Sufi poetry in relation to other pre-modern literary traditions. Here we shall reverse the usual order of leading from a sketch of the beginnings of Sufism in India through to its first local poetic manifestations, and we shall begin instead with the culmination of the tradition in nineteenth-century Punjab. It is in fact a significant weakness of Lajwanti Rama Krishna's book, in which she is followed by many later Indian critics and literary historians, that quite inadequate coverage is given to the nineteenth century, when she asserts that 'the real Sufi ceased to exist'[13] due to the new outlook produced by political change and to the degeneracy of Sufi institutions. However convenient it may be to a nationalist reading of Indian history, this judgement seriously spoils the whole story of Punjabi Sufi poetry by altogether leaving out any serious engagement with its last and best attested period, which saw the production of poetic masterpieces little known in India, but continuing to possess great living significance in Pakistan.

SUFI POETRY IN NINETEENTH-CENTURY PUNJAB

One of these great nineteenth-century Sufi saint-poets is Khwaja Ghulam Farid (1845–1901), who succeeded his father and elder brother to the leadership of a prominent Sufi lineage which commanded the allegiance of the nawabs of the princely state of Bahawalpur, then a remote and largely desert region situated in the extreme south-western corner of Punjab. Khwaja Ghulam Farid's lineage dated from the eighteenth century revival of the same Chishti order (*tariqa*) first founded in Punjab by the great medieval saint Baba Farid Shakarganj, with whom he is not to be confused, although he too used the poetic signature 'Farid'. As a poet, Khwaja Farid is mainly known for his *dīvān*, a wonderful collection of 272 mystical *kāfīs* and the hymns which are the main genre of lyrical Sufi poetry. Designed for singing by professional musicians in *qavvālī* at the tombs of the saints which are the centres of Sufi cultic activity, Khwaja Farid's kāfīs are especially notable for the sophisticated variety of their language, style and content.

Exceptionally carefully organized, first by the final letter of the main rhyme (*radīf*) and then by the initial letter of the first verse, Khwaja Farid's dīvān was first published one year after his death in the Lahore-printed 1902 edition authorized by his son and successor. This was followed in 1944 by a magnificent edition with Urdu commentary and introduction produced under the auspices of the Nawab of Bahawalpur.[14] The kāfīs are predominantly written in a rather pure form of the local speech traditionally labelled 'Multani', which is nowadays generally known in Pakistan as 'Siraiki',[15] but they also include numerous verses in other languages such as Braj Bhasha, Urdu, Persian, even Sindhi.

Khwaja Farid's Sufi message of celebration of both the pains and the joys of mystical love for the Divine Beloved is expressed in a rich multiplicity of styles and images, which famously includes both very frequent special reference to the romantic legend of Sassi and Punnun and remarkably original evocations of the natural beauties of the deserts of Bahawalpur which were of special significance to Khwaja Farid as manifestations of divine beauty. They also include many striking uses of the love-imagery of the Persian ghazal and a whole range of Islamic and Indian references in celebration of mystical experience of oneness:

> *Ḏīhāṅ rātīṅ sanjh subāhīṅ*
> *Kanṛīṅ Kāṇ bajāvim bīn*
> *Qudsī bansī anhad azlūṅ*
> *Rānjhan phūk suṇāvim fazlūṅ*
> *Rakh rakh vahdat dī ā'īn*

> Day and night, morn and eve
> My ears hear Krishna's lute.
> From the first day Ranjha graciously
> Plays his holy flute and lets me hear
> Celestial music in the mode of unity.[16]

Other unpublished works attributed to Khwaja Farid include some Siraiki *dohṛās* in the couplet form used by the Sufis for their shorter verses, besides a collection of rather run-of-the-mill Urdu ghazals,[17] and a short Sufi treatise written in Persian prose. Persian prose was also the medium used for the hagiographic literature devoutly composed by his disciples, notably the *Maqābīs ul Majālis* [*The Sparks of the Assemblies*] relating to the last decade of Khwaja Farid's life which was composed in five volumes by his follower Rukn ud Din in the *malfūzāt* genre used to record a Sufi saint's sayings and actions.[18] There is also quite a considerable secondary literature in Urdu which casts light on matters passed over by the early hagiographers, such as Khwaja Farid's romantic attachment to a girl of the desert tribe which is celebrated in some of his kāfīs.[19]

The other great Sufi poet of the period is also a Pir from a remote frontier region, this time the Mirpur District which was then a part of the Dogra state of Jammu and Kashmir. This was Khwaja Farid's close contemporary Mian Muhammad Bakhsh (1830–1907), who succeeded his elder brother to the headship of one of the very numerous local lineages of the Qadiri tarīqa which had become by far the most widespread of the Sufi orders after its introduction into Punjab in the later fifteenth century. Writing in the standard pre-modern Muslim poetic language, with some use of distinctive local vocabulary, Mian Muhammad worked primarily in the genre of the *qissa*, the verse romance which is the main narrative genre of pre-modern Punjabi literature, and which in his hands becomes a vehicle for the direct expression of Sufi ideas.

Besides an encyclopaedic oeuvre which includes several treatments of local romances like those of Sohni-Mahinval and Mirza Sahiban, reworkings of Persian romantic narratives, and hagiographic poems on the miracles of the Prophet and of Shaikh Abdul Qadir Jilani (d. 1166), the founding saint of the Qadiri order, he is best known for his great poem *Saif ul Mulūk* (1863), a lengthy retelling in some 9000 verses from a profoundly Sufi perspective of a story familiar from the *Arabian Nights*.[20] Published in at least fifty different editions since its first printing in 1880, and frequently recited to a distinctive melody (*lai*), Mian Muhammad's *Saif ul Mulūk*, properly called *Safar ul 'Ishq* (The Journey of Love), continues to enjoy a massive local popularity which is entirely comparable to the reputation of Varis Shah's *Hīr* (1766) in central Punjab.

Along with the oral composition of a great quantity of occasional verse, which is only imperfectly preserved, Mian Muhammad later wrote a spirited defence in Punjabi verse of the practice of devotion to Sufi tombs, then coming under attack by Muslim reformists, while in Persian prose he updated a lengthy memoir of his spiritual lineage, which was later published in an Urdu translation by his leading disciple Malik Muhammad, a contractor from Jhelum.[21] Malik Muhammad also wrote a valuable Urdu life of his master, which emphasizes the intensity of his devotion to the Prophet, to Shaikh Abdul Qadir and to the Pirs of his own lineage, and his personal combination of intense mystical devotion with strict Islamic observance, as well as his miraculous powers and his poetic creativity.[22]

Exceptionally full records thus exist for these two great Sufi poets, whose maturity coincided with the establishment of the new print culture promoted by the Lahore publishing industry. All their most significant works are available in authentic contemporary editions, often also in corrected versions by later editors, making it possible to offer confident comment both on such detailed matters as their language and style, and on the general emphasis and content of their oeuvre, with its characteristic creative combination of elements from their shared triple heritage of the Islamic learning which underpinned their Sufi understanding, the Persian poetry which suffused their literary culture, and the local stories, conventions and images which give their poetry so much of its distinctive appeal.[23] Complementing each other in genre and coverage, the extensive poetic output of these two very different poets collectively constitutes a uniquely comprehensive statement of the pre-modern Sufi literary tradition in the final decades of its vital period, and offers a uniquely rich textual resource against which to understand the work of the earlier Punjabi Sufi poets.

We are also quite well provided with a wider context for the activities of these two poets. The nineteenth century, thanks to its comparative closeness to our own time and to the relative abundance of available contemporary materials, is in general a period easier to grasp than the pre-modern centuries of the Mughal era. Although the written biographical records are of course heavily slanted towards hagiography, they were composed very near the lifetimes of their subjects, and their relative fullness makes it possible both to feel some confidence in establishing links between the poets' lives and their poetry. Both were defined in life by their hereditary connection with Sufi shrines sited out in the far west of the region and by their formal role as Pirs, but Khwaja Farid's status as personal spiritual guide to a major ruling prince and the twin poetic celebrations in his lyrics of his beloved desert and of his desert beloved were very different from Mian Muhammad's reluctant assumption of responsibility in middle life for a relatively minor local shrine and his combination of a strict personal celibacy with repeated poetic expression in his extended narratives of a passionate devotion to the miraculously all-powerful master-saint Shaikh Abdul Qadir. We can therefore see how the collective label of 'Punjabi Sufi poet' can embrace rather different kinds of Sufi and different kinds of poet.

In other words, it is with this period around these two major poets that a literary history of Punjabi Sufi poetry becomes a truly realistic undertaking rather than a speculative and uncertain enterprise of reconstruction. As may already have become apparent through what has not been said, the Islamic context in which they defined themselves is sufficient for understanding both these poets. Both of them were based in Muslim majority areas out to the west situated so far from the central Punjab heartlands that Sikhs hardly figure in their imagination, and Hindus are background figures only, albeit politically significant if spiritually subordinate ones in Mian Muhammad's Jammu. Their frequent celebration of the central mystical conception of the unity of Being (*vahdat ul vujūd*) or 'all is He' (*hama ūst*) is certainly reflected in the poetic expression of the meaninglessness of outward religious distinctions. But, outside their Sufi poetry, this did not stop them from revealing indifference, at best, to non-Muslims or from expressing strongly negative views of the position of other Muslims, whether in Khwaja Farid's strongly anti-Shia sentiments or Mian Muhammad's opposition to the anti-Sufi stance of the Wahhabi reformists.[24] Nor did it mean that their literary inspiration is not entirely explicable in terms of an exclusively Muslim spiritual universe, requiring no invocation of a supposedly more significant Indic framework.

FARID AND EARLY SINDHI SUFI POETRY

The lengthy conclusion to Mian Muhammad's *Saif ul Mulūk* includes an extended evocation of his poetic predecessors. This pioneering poetic history of Punjabi Muslim literature begins with a catalogue of the main genres before listing the great Sufis of the past:

The land of Punjab has had many poets full of wisdom, who have composed brilliant kāfis, *bārān-māh*s, dohṛās and *bait*s. Some have composed and written books, qissas and *risāla*s. Where now has that company gone, Muhammad? Look and take careful stock.

First is Shaikh Farid Shakarganj, true knower and possessor of sainthood. Every utterance of his tongue is a guide on the true path.

Then there was a Sultan Bahu, a special hero in the cause of truth. The dohṛās which he uttered shine out in both worlds.

On listening to the kāfis of Bullhe Shah, inner unbelief is broken. He swims about in the ocean of Oneness.[25]

In this passage we are taken straight back to the head of the list of Punjabi poets, with the praise of Shaikh Farid Shakarganj (1173-1265) whose life as the great Chishti Pir of Ajodhan in Punjab during the period of the Delhi Sultanate is notably recorded in the wonderful *malfūzāt* of Farid's most famous disciple, Khwaja Nizam ud Din Auliya, completed in 1322 by Amir Hasan as *Favā'id al-Fu'ād* (The Morals for the Heart).[26] But while the records of Shaikh Farid's life are quite comparable in approach and authenticity to those available for our nineteenth-century Sufi saint-poets, they have nothing to say about him as a Punjabi poet. It has therefore been something of a problem for Punjabi literary historians to link the historically well established Shaikh Farid with the so-called *Farīd-bāṇī*, the small corpus of poetry attributed to Farid in the Sikh Ādi Granth compiled some 350 years after the saint's death by Guru Arjan.

This disjuncture between text and context has made the authorship and authenticity of the *Farīd-bāṇī* one of the most vexed questions of Punjabi literary history. The controversy need not be gone into here, since ample accounts of the latest scholarly consensus are available.[27] This overturns the now quite outdated attribution of the *Farīd-bāṇī* by Lajwanti Rama Krishna,[28] following Macauliffe and others, not to Farid himself but to his sixteenth-century successor Shaikh Ibrahim known as 'Farid Sani' or Farid II, a contemporary of Guru

Nanak's who figures in the later Sikh *janamsākhī* literature. Instead, the modern position reasserts the traditional identification of Shaikh Farid himself as the putative author of the *Farīd-bāṇī*, with the necessary scholarly caveats taking account of the strong probability of accretion and textual corruption through presumed oral transmission in the period preceding the compilation of the Ādi Granth.

As the only part of the Ādi Granth of discernibly Sufi inspiration, the *Farīd-bāṇī* is certainly of exceptional intrinsic interest as well as symbolic importance. It is however quite difficult to reach a full understanding, partly because there is so little of it, only 112 short shaloks of very miscellaneous content plus four short hymns, amounting only to some seven printed pages of the massive scripture. Interspersed verses by the Sikh Gurus suggest that Farid, like Kabir and other nirguṇ Sants, was taken as a figure of parallel spiritual prestige whose message was in partial if imperfect harmony with their own, an understanding heavily underscored in the later *janamsākhī* literature, where verses of Farid are cited in reconstructed disputations designed to show the superiority of Guru Nanak.

Like the couplets of the Gurus and the Bhagats, the Farid *shalok*s are in the familiar mediaeval style particularly favoured in the nirguṇ tradition but also adopted by some early Indian Sufis. Most are in the metrical form of the dohā,[29] whose four short half-verses are cast in the highly compressed style still made possible by the richly inflected language of the period. Their most typical theme is that of the urgent need for loving devotion to the eternal Beloved as the only antidote to the inexorable passage of a human life towards old age and death:

> *Farīdā: kālīṅ jinī na rāviā, dhaulī rāvai koi*
> *Kari sāṅī siu piraharī, raṅgu navelā hoi*

> Farid: who delights with white who did not delight with black?
> Practise tender love for the Lord, the colour will be renewed.[30]

In many of the shaloks the poet's signature is superfluous to the metre, as here, so in itself provides no guarantee of authenticity. But a recognizable poetic persona underlies most of the shaloks, and clearly apparent connections of content across the corpus are reinforced by a notably distinct preference for dialectal words and forms from south-western Punjab:

Farīdā: nandhī kantu na rāvio, vaḍḍī thī muīāsu
Dhana kūkendī gora men, tai saha na milīāsu
Farid: when young she did not delight her spouse, when old she died
In the grave the woman cries, 'I did not find you, Lord!'[31]

On the basis of this typical feature of the Farid shaloks, it may be suggested that there was a particular association between south-western Punjabi and the early Sufi literary tradition.[32] This would be consistent with the importance of such sites as Multan and Uch as centres of Sufi activity, and would be a further illustration of the characteristic association of languages of particular regions with the verse literatures of the various religious traditions of the mediaeval period. Thus in the east of the 'Hindi' area, the tradition of devotional writing in Avadhi was first established by the Sufis, then taken over for Ram bhakti by Tulsi Das, and Braj Bhasha was of course naturally always closely associated with Krishna bhakti, while Khari Boli had particular associations with the nirgun Sants, and is also prominent in the mixed language of the Sikh Gurus, along with central-western forms of Punjabi.

The evidence from the Farid verses in support of this suggestion is further underlined by the imitative use by the fifth Sikh Guru Arjan of a distinctive language in some of his shaloks, which are separately labelled as *Ḍakhaṇe* or 'southern verses', as in the set which precede the stanzas of his *Vār* in Rag Maru:

[*Ḍakhaṇe M5*]
Jā mū passī haṭṭha main, pirī mahinjai nāli
Habbhe ḍukkha ulāhiamu, Nānaka nadari nihāli

When I look into my heart, the Beloved is there with me
And through His grace is Nanak from all griefs set free.[33]

Here the Guru catches the distinctive Faridian tone while even exaggerating the linguistic peculiarities of the Faridian style by adding to south-western Punjabi forms such distinctively Sindhi items as *mū[n] passī[n]* 'I see' or *mahinjai* 'mine'.

Since such items are not characteristic of the Farid shaloks them-selves, the claim sometimes advanced by Sindhi scholars that Farid may be seen as a pioneer of Sindhi literature[34] might be dismissed as an untenable expression of modern linguistic chauvinism. But it would be unwise similarly to dismiss the comparative value of early Sindhi literary evidence in amplifying our understanding of the context and character of the Farid shaloks as the isolated sole record of the early Sufi tradition of Punjabi literature. The much more conservative linguistic character of Sindhi, as compared to all main varieties of Punjabi, encouraged the cultivation of the compressed dohā form long after its obsolescence in Punjabi, well into the era of more abundant contemporary Persian hagiographic records.

Here the prime relevant text is the Persian *malfūzāt* of Guru Arjan's older contemporary, the Sindhi Sufi poet Shah Abdul Karim of Bulri (1536-1623). Written around 1630 by one of his disciples with the title *Bayān ul 'Ārifīn* (Account of the Gnostics), this book contains ninety-three verses in Sindhi by Shah Karim, along with seven others by his predecessor Qazi Qadan (1463-1551), who became a devotee of the Mahdi of Jaunpur and who was appointed qazi of Bakhar in Upper Sindh. Verses by these two poets, of exactly the same formal type as those of Farid, that is the dohā or its reverse the *soraṭhā*, are here each preceded by anecdotes which authentically reflect early Sufi understandings of their genesis.

Sometimes these stories are of a familiar type, like the one which tells how Qazi Qadan was one day alerted to the entry into his mosque of a naked ascetic who had laid down and gone to sleep with his feet pointing towards Mecca. Outraged by this disrespect the Qazi rushed in to beat him, but when he went to his feet found his head there instead and vice versa. When he was reduced to despair, the holy man looked at him and said, 'Set the feet whither you will, but keep the heart towards the Lord.' So the Qazi put down his stick and became a seeker of God, uttering this verse:

Jogiya jāgā'iyosi, sutto hu'asu niṇda meṅ
Tihāṇ po'i tha'osi, sandī piryāṅ pechare

The yogi woke me up when I lay asleep
Afterwards I recognized the path to the Beloved.[35]

Elsewhere, however, the connection between anecdote and verse is more surprising. One feature of the early Sindhi verses notably lacking in Farid is the incorporation of references to the famous local romantic legends, whose tragic heroines are used to symbolize the yearning of the Sufi for his divine Beloved. In the following episode from the seventh chapter of the *Bayān ul 'Ārifīn,* devoted to the description of ecstasy and passion, Shah Karim is first overcome by his meditation on the memory of the martyrdom of Imam Husain:

One day the holy Pir remembered the story of the fair Imams in his heart and was moved to shed floods of tears. Then he sat in focused meditation. Raising his head again and again, he uttered the name of Imam Husain, with the tears pouring from his eyes for a long time. He remained seated in meditation, uttering the name of the holy Imam, and lamenting all the while, unable to speak because of his weeping:

He is then moved to utter a verse which expresses the same sort of passionate lament by invoking the romantic legend of Sohni, the heroine about to drown while seeking her beloved Mehar (the Punjabi Mahinval):

> *Ghoriya bī na tāti, mihāro'ī mana men*
> *Jo puṇa pe'ī rāti, ta hū sā'iru hū'a sohaṇī*
>
> Aware of nothing else, the poor girl has only Mehar in her heart.
> When the night falls, there is the same river, the same Sohni.[36]

Shah Karim is thus in more ways than one the true ancestor of the rich later tradition of Sufi poetry in Sindhi, with its characteristically interwoven simultaneous reference to local and to Islamic materials. The treatment of all these materials has its apogee in the greatest Sindhi literary classic, the *Risālo* of Shah Karim's great-great-grandson, Shah Abdul Latif of Bhit (1689-1752). Arranged by the ragas to which they are performed, also according to their subject matter in the case of the sets of verses celebrating the fate of individual legendary heroines, the verses in this very large collection are still in the classic medieval form of the dohā, corresponding to the genre labelled shalok of the Ādi Granth, but called by the Arabic word *bait* in Sindhi. The long retention down to the nineteenth century of this succinct metrical form in Sindhi may partly be accounted for by the way that the relative conservatism of Sindhi grammatical morphology makes for brevity. It may however be noted that many modern accounts of Sindhi Sufi poetry by Hindu authors writing in English tend to minimize its clearly Islamic character in favour of the wishful argument that its Sufi emphasis on the oneness of being must clearly derive from the unique inspiration of Vedantic monism.[37]

Punjabi Sufi Poets of the Mughal Period

In the light of the comparative perspective provided by this detour into Sindhi, we may now resume our account of the earlier Punjabi Sufi poets by first observing that, in contrast to the unbroken Sindhi poetic tradition, there is in Punjabi a marked disjuncture between the earlier poetry uniquely represented by the Farid verses on the one hand and the later Sufi poetry of the Mughal period on the other. The textual evidence for this period is again patchy, making it necessary to approach it with a good deal of caution. For a start, while the overall linguistic style of the poetry may be characterized as being marked by a continuing preference for western Punjabi forms along with a naturally considerable use of Perso-Arabic vocabulary, there is for two or three centuries no textual evidence for any of the Punjabi works attributed to the three main figures of the period, until the appearance of the first printed editions of the 1880s and 1890s which were compiled from the oral tradition of the *qavvāl*s who sang their lyrics. The very unevenly available biographical and other textual sources are also seldom well matched to the extant poetry in terms of directly yielding clear contemporary contexts for it in the way which has been seen to be possible for the Sindhi verses of Shah Karim.

One of the misleading features of Lajwanti Rama Krishna's pioneering study is the way in which it blurs the differences between the Farid verses and the classic Sufi poetry of the Mughal period through her attribution of the Farid corpus to the early sixteenth-century Shaikh Ibrahim called Farid Sani ('Farid II'). The date of the corpus is thus advanced by some three centuries, bringing it close to the time of the next significant Punjabi Sufi poet, Shah Husain of Lahore (1539-93). Shah Husain was a close contemporary of Guru Arjan, and was indeed portrayed in the later Sikh tradition conveyed by the encyclopaedic memorialist Santokh Singh as having tried unsuccessfully to get his poetry included in the Ādi Granth.[38] He was also a contemporary of the Sindhi Shah Karim, and like the latter he was affiliated to the Qadiriyya which after its introduction into the region in the preceding century rapidly became the leading Sufi order in Punjab.

Shah Husain was a figure whose far-out life style as a *malāmatī* Sufi who rejected many social norms attracted considerable contemporary attention. Known in his day to members of the imperial family, he later received mention in the *Hasanāt ul 'Ārifīn* (Beauties of the Gnostics), a brief account of the outspoken utterances of the Sufis compiled in 1652 by the Mughal prince Dara Shikoh.[39] A fuller account of Shah Husain's life was also recorded in Persian verse by his devotee Shaikh Mahmud in the remarkable lengthy memoir called *Haqīqat ul Fuqarā* (The Reality of the Sufis) which dates from 1662. Besides the usual descriptions of his vast following and numerous miracles, this gives often very explicit details of his antinomian life style, including his drinking and his homoerotic infatuation with the beautiful young Brahmin boy Madho Lal, which has caused particular problems for many twentieth-century critics like Lajwanti Rama Krishna.[40]

In Shah Husain's case, the hagiographic record is certainly more reliably attested than the Punjabi poetry. While these early sources also speak of Shah Husain's fondness for dancing and singing, none of them quote any Punjabi or Persian verses by him. The only composition which seems to be reliably attributed to him is a Persian treatise on Sufism,[41] which suggests a rather different profile from the Punjabi poetry on which his fame rests today. Moreover, since the first printed edition of the Punjabi poems dates only from 1897,[42] that is 300 years after his death, it has to be uncertain how many of the existing kāfīs attributed to Husain are authentic, or indeed if others may have been lost. It is also perhaps significant that he is not prominently listed in the rather comprehensive catalogue of some forty Punjabi poets compiled by Mian Muhammad in the 1860s.

Whatever the authenticity of the extant Punjabi poetry may be, it certainly does not offer any clear reflection of Husain's way of life, which seems to have been more attuned to the urban world of the Persian ghazal than to the more sedate rural setting of most Punjabi poetry. It is certainly notably different in style, language and content from the Farid corpus. Instead of the shalok, the dominant form is the kāfī, with its characteristically more relaxed and lyrical expression. Most of the 150 or so kāfīs attributed to Shah Husain are quite brief compositions consisting of a limited number of simple verses.

Their typical themes, which were to be much more fully exploited in the kāfīs of Bullhe Shah, partly overlap with those found in Farid. Examples include the description of the demands of the mystical path in the well-known short kāfī with the refrain *Mushkil ghāṭ faqīrī dā* 'The faqir's path is hard!',[43] or the continual need for vigilance with death always lurking just round the corner, as in the refrain of another poem *Vela simran dā nī uṭh Rām dhiāe* 'Now is the time to remember, girl, arise and meditate on God!'[44] Besides this occasional use of the name 'Ram' for the Divine, there is however little of the kind of Hindu reference which might be expected from the connection with Madho. Instead, Shah Husain's verse is distinguished by a notable use of themes clearly related to folk-poetry, such as the songs associated with the spinning-parties which were an important part of a young girl's life.

The most notable innovation evident in Shah Husain's poetry as compared with the Farid verses is one which was to become a central feature of the Punjabi Sufi poetic tradition. This is the frequent reference for the first time to the great Punjabi romantic legend of Hir-Ranjha. In many of his most affecting lyrics the poet adopts the female persona of the heroine in her desperate love for Ranjha, who symbolizes the Divine, as in the following kāfī:

My heart begs for Ranjha
I roam the forests searching
For Ranjha to be with me.
Here come the buffaloes, but not my love:
Hir cries out in Jhang.
I wander madly night and day
The sharp thorns scratch my feet.
Husain the humble faqir says:
How can I find Ranjha.[45]

The next Punjabi Sufi poet placed after Shah Husain by Lajwanti Rama Krishna and most later literary historians is Sultan Bahu of

Jhang (1631–91), who directly follows Farid in Mian Muhammad's catalogue. He too was affiliated with the Qadiriyya, although through quite different connections, and he later established his own branch of the tarīqa, which he called Sarvari Qadiri. All modern accounts of Sultan Bahu's life[46] depend on a much later source, the hagiographic memoir *Manāqib-e Sultānī* (Glories of the Sultan), compiled some six generations later by a descendant called Sultan Hamid. This depicts him as a powerful Pir with a devoted local following in western Punjab, a profile not unlike that which was drawn earlier in this chapter for our nineteenth-century Sufi poets, albeit one which Lajwanti Rama Krishna[47] found awkward to fit with her idealized model of the Punjabi Sufi poet as a free spirit transcending communal ties.

Confirmation of Sultan Bahu's self-definition as an authoritative teacher of Sufi doctrine and practice comes from his own writings, of which far more have been preserved than is the case for any of the other Punjabi Sufi poets. By far the greatest part of his comprehensively recorded output is not in Punjabi at all, however, taking instead the form of Persian prose treatises.[48] Said originally to number over 140, over two dozen of these survive with many available in modern Urdu translations. Their typically didactic tone may be illustrated in this brief extract from his Persian treatise called *Mihakk ul Fuqarā* (The Sufis' Touchstone), which demonstrates the characteristic use of acrostic formulae as mnemonic devices and of scriptural quotation and commentary to give authority to the argument:

O true seeker, know that the path of the journey is the way of divine knowledge. So any seeker of the Lord who has no knowledge of Sufism is utterly lost. The word for Sufism, thai is *TaSaVvuF*, consists of four letters:[49]

The first letter is T, which stands for *Tasarruf*, or applying the self to the path to God;

The second letter is S, which stands for *Sirāt*, the straight path, i.e. proceeding on the way to God;

The third letter is V, which stands for *Va'da*, the false promise which is to be avoided;

The fourth letter is F, which stands for *Fath ul Ghaib*, or conquest of the unseen, and for *Fanā fi'n Nafs*, or annihilation in the self.

Anyone who does not possess the knowledge of these letters and who does not act upon them can never know about Sufism.

The other meaning of Sufism is that it comes from the name of Allah, that is, the knowledge of A, and the meaning of A is written in the holy verse 'He taught Adam the names [of them all]' [*Qur'ān* 2:31], i.e. 'We taught Adam (upon whom be peace!) all the names'. The Sufis say that here 'all the names' mean all types of knowledge, of intellects and of degrees, which lead from theory to reality and whose outer and inner degrees are with the Lord.[50]

Like so many other Sufi teachers from Rumi onwards, Sultan Bahu also had an ecstatic side which he expressed in poetry. This is notably revealed in some of his Persian ghazals which are of the ecstatic mystical kind which so memorably fill in Rumi's great *Dīvān-e Shams-e Tabrīzī*:

Az man hazār man man v'az man hazār hai hai
Hai hai hazār az man az man hazār hai hai

From me there came a thousand 'I's, from 'I' a thousand 'ah, ah's
A thousand 'ah, ah's from me, from 'I' a thousand 'ah, ah's![51]

Nowadays, though, the Persian poetry of Sultan Bahu has become largely unknown, just like the equally forgotten if more polished courtly verse produced over the centuries in such quantities by local poets writing in Lahore and other centres. What he is instead remembered for are the 190-odd verses he wrote in Punjabi, which in Pakistan at least seem to have gained considerable popularity since Lajwanti Rama Krishna's day.[52] Once again the textual record goes back only to the first printed edition, published about 200 years after the poet's death.[53] Here Sultan Bahu's verses are mechanically arranged by their first letter to form a sort of *sī-harfī* sequence, that is, a poem consisting of thirty stanzas each commencing with the successive letters of the Arabic alphabet with which their initial words begin. In the case of Sultan Bahu's collection, however, there is no thematic connection between the verses. They are collectively known as *abyāt*, the Arabic plural of *bait* 'verse', the same term confusingly used to mean a dohā in Sindhi, whereas Sultan Bahu uses the longer *davayye* metre also commonly employed in narrative *qissa* poems such as Mian Muhammad's *Saif ul Mulūk*. Since he usually writes four-line verses, there is characteristically much less compression in their expression than in the shaloks of Farid. A further characteristic of Bahu's abyāt is that *hū,* the syllable used by the Sufis to evoke the Divine 'He', is added to the end of each line.[54]

In some ways, the abyāt are closer to the teaching style of the Farid shaloks than to the lyric kāfis of Shah Husain or Bullhe Shah. The poet normally speaks as male teacher rather than as female lover, and there is virtually no reference to local stories although there is plentiful mention of Sufi and other Islamic doctrine. Perhaps the most notable new topos found in Bahu's abyāt is the frequent proclamation of the superior validity of true devotees over superficial differences between Hindu and Muslim, as illustrated along with the formal characteristics of the language and the metre in the following example:

> *Nūn: na oh hindū na momin, na sijda den masītī, hū*
> *Dam dam de vich vekhan maulā, jinhāṅ qazā na kītī, hū*
> *Āhe dāne bane divāne, zāt sahī vanj kītī, hū*
> *Maiṅ qurbān tinhāṅ toṅ, Bāhū, 'ishq bāzī jin lītī, hū*

(N) Not Hindus or believers, not bowing down in mosques, Hu
With every breath they see the Lord, and never skip a prayer, Hu
They once were wise and then went mad, by truly knowing God, Hu
I am devoted, Bahu, to those who have chosen the game of love, Hu[55]

As should be apparent from what has been said about Sultan Bahu's Persian writings, this poetic rejection of Hindu–Muslim distinctions certainly does not entail rejection of a Muslim spiritual identity.

BULLHE SHAH

The same issue arises with even more force in considering the work of the third poet on Mian Muhammad's list, the great Bullhe Shah of Kasur (1680–1758). Here for once we need not differ from Lajwanti Rama Krishna's opening assessment:

Bullhe Shah is universally admitted to have been the greatest of the Panjabi mystics. No Panjabi mystic poet enjoys a wider celebrity and a great reputation. His kāfis have gained unique popularity.[56]

Bullhe Shah is indeed by far the most famous and popular of all the Punjabi Sufi poets, and his poetry continues to exert a wide and powerful appeal across religious boundaries. For long pre-served orally, it first began to appear in printed editions in the late nineteenth century. Fittingly enough, of the two significant early editions one was published by a Muslim devotee, the other by a local Sikh enthusiast.[57] Consisting of about 160 kāfīs, which are generally more substantial in size as well as being consistently finer in poetic and spiritual quality than Shah Husain's, along with miscellaneous Punjabi verses in other genres, Bullhe Shah's oeuvre is bulkier than the preserved Punjabi poetry of either Shah Husain or Sultan Bahu. Given the history of its transmission, some questions of textual authenticity must apply here too, but the power and coherence of Bullhe Shah's poetic personality is certainly a sufficient guarantee of the genuineness of the core corpus.

Considering the enduring subsequent fame of his lyrics, it is on the other hand remarkable that there seems to be no early written record at all of Bullhe Shah's life, although the area in which he lived in central Punjab is evident from his tomb at Kasur and the expressions in his poetry of his utter devotion to his Pir, Shah Inayat of Lahore, who is regarded as a manifestation of the Divine Beloved:

You hastened to me of Your own accord
How long can You remain in hiding?
You have come as Shah Inayat
Peeping out at me![58]

Shah Inayat is known to have been affiliated both to the Qadiriyya and to the Shattari order, which was notable for its particular interest in Hindu esoteric religious practice, as evidenced in the writings of two of its earlier Shaikhs, Abdul Quddus Gangohi (d. 1537) and Muhammad Ghaus (d. 1563). The Shattari connection may help account for the notable proclamations of the meaninglessness of outer religious distinctions—far more explicitly expressed than those found in Sultan Bahu's Punjabi verses—which are so marked a feature of Bullhe Shah's poetry.

Bullhe Shah's cross-communal appeal of course importantly derives in part from this very feature. The classic status of his poetry is, however, equally due to his extraordinary gift for the seemingly simple use of natural Punjabi language to express profound spiritual truths. The refrains of quite a number of his kāfīs show this gift of combining familiarity with suggestiveness so strikingly as to have become virtually proverbial sayings. Examples include *Uṭh jāg ghurāṛe mār nahīṅ* (6) 'Get up, awake and do not snore'; *Sab ikko rang kapāhīṅ dā* (70) 'All cotton bolls are coloured white'; *'Ishq dī naviyoṅ navīṅ bahar* (76) 'The spring of love is ever new'; *Katt kuṛe nā vatt kuṛe* (81) 'Stay put and spin, my girl'; *Merī bukkal de vich chor* (118) 'There's a thief in the folds of my veil'; *Munh āī bāt na raihndī e* (113) 'I can't help myself saying'; or the famous *Hindū nāṅ nahīṅ mussalman* (153) 'Neither Hindu nor Muslim'.

The verses of Bullhe Shah's lyrics are equally remarkable for the comprehensiveness and variety of their content, making them so successful a medium for imparting that sense of universality which is necessary for openness to the Sufi understanding of the 'Unity of Being'. As in all Sufi poetry, there is a frequent expression of contempt for mere learning: *'Ilmoṅ bas karīṅ o yār* (79) 'That's enough of learning, friend'. So too is there a regular dismissal of outward ritual: *Roze hajj namāz nī māe, mainūṅ piyā ne ān bhulāe* (64) 'Fasting, pilgrimage and prayers, mother, all these the Beloved has made me forget'. Equally characteristic of Sufi poetry, though, is the regular citation of key scriptural texts in Arabic: 'Thumma wajhu'llāh' *dasnāeṅ aj o yār* (80) 'Today, Beloved, you tell us that "[Wherever you look,] there is the face of God".'

The sheer range of reference in Bullhe Shah's poetry is in fact one of its most remarkable features. Thus the universal operation of the divine power of love is celebrated in catalogues which embrace the prophets of Islam, the Sufi martyrs, the lovers of Punjabi legend, and the figures of Hindu mythology, as in the long kāfī with the refrain *Rahu rahu oe 'ishqā māryā ī*:

> Stop, stop, love, you have slain me
> Did you ever deliver anyone safe?
> You made Moses climb up Sinai
> You had Isma'il sacrificed
> You had Jonah swallowed by the whale

Oh, how you exalted them…
You had the throat of Sarmad split
You made Shams utter the words:
'Arise by my command' and then
You had him flayed from head to foot…
Sir love then rushed on Hir
Then made Ranjha pierce his ears
When he came to marry Sahiban
Mirza's head was sacrificed…
And what did you do to the Gopis
You had Krishna steal their butter
You had king Kans dragged before him
To be tugged by his topknot and thrown down…[59]

Of all these sets of figures, it is of course the Hir-Ranjha pair who carry the greatest emotional affect in Bullhe Shah's poetry. As in most other respects, here too the poet's adoption of the persona of Hir is more powerfully expressive than is generally the case in Shah Husain's kāfīs. Contrast with the example of the latter cited above the famous verses of Bullhe Shah:

Rānjhā Rānjhā kardī nī main āpe Rānjhā hoī
Saddo nī mainūn Dhīdo Rānjhā Hīr na ākho koī

Repeating Ranjha's name I've myself become Ranjha
Call me Dhido Ranjha, let no one call me Hir![60]

An important reason for the poetic exploitation of the Hir-Ranjha story above all the other Punjabi romantic legends is the double suggestiveness of Ranjha's initial similarity as flute-playing herdsman to Krishna, then later in the story of his emergence in the guise of a yogi coming to win back Hir after her enforced marriage: *Rānjhā jogīṛā ban āyā, vāh sāngī sāng rachāyā* (61) 'Ranjha has come as a yogi, oh what a show he's put on'. It is in Bullhe Shah that we first find this twin takeover into the Sufi poetic tradition of central themes from both Nath yoga and Krishnaite saguṇ bhakti.[61] So the kāfī by Khwaja Farid which we quoted earlier in this paper derives directly from Bullhe Shah's *Bansī Kāhn acharaj bajāī*:

Krishna has played wonderful music on his flute
O flute playing herdsman Ranjha
Your music is in tune with all things…[62]

This range of cross-religious reference, along with the frequently expressed repudiation of narrow credal definitions and their associated rituals has encouraged twentieth-century critics to construct a whole variety of 'Bullhe Shahs' to suit their own preconceptions. Thus the pioneering Punjabi literary scholar Mohan Singh in his 1930 Gurmukhi edition of selected kāfis [63] emphasizes Bullhe Shah's essential harmony with the Sikh Gurus, while some Pakistani critics are conversely anxious to emphasize his credentials as an orthodox Muslim.[64] Given the virtual absence of reliable biographical data to which to anchor the interpretation of this subtle poetry, it is perhaps unsurprising that, more than any other Punjabi Sufi poet, Bullhe Shah has provoked such confusions of understanding. These have been very usefully mapped in two articles by Robin Rinehart on the reception history of Bullhe Shah's poetry, although she is perhaps insufficiently dismissive of some of the extremer readings.[65]

While fully recognizing that the apparent simplicity of Bullhe Shah's poetry can make it difficult to pin down, we would once again argue that it is best appreciated in its own Sufi context. Take for example the refrain and opening verse of one of his most familiar lyrics:

> *Bullhā kih jānāṅ maiṅ kaun*
> Bullha, how can I know who I am?
> I'm not a believer in the mosque
> Nor taken up with the ways of unbelief
> Nor am pure amongst the defiled
> Nor am I Moses, nor am I Pharaoh [66]

For Lajwanti Rama Krishna, who places this as a work of his maturest period according to her quite unsubstantiated chronological division of Bullhe Shah's poetry, which sees him as moving from being a mainstream Sufi to becoming an out-and-out Vedantic monist, this celebration of having broken 'all shackles of country, religion, convention and sect' is taken as evidence that his pantheism 'was Hindu in his entirety and therefore differed a good deal from the pantheism of the Sufis'.[67] It is true that the contrary position, that Indian Sufi poets reiterate the message of Rumi and the other Persian masters, which was notably espoused by, for instance, the great scholar of Sufi literature Annemarie Schimmel,[68] can be open to accusations of excessive vagueness, and of not doing sufficient justice to local difference. But in this particular instance as elsewhere, Bullhe Shah's *Bullhā kīh jānāṅ maiṅ kaun* surely effects a direct transcreation from an Anatolian to an Indian context a famous Persian ghazal written some five centuries earlier by the great Jalal ud Din Rumi (d. 1273):

Chi tadbīr ai musalmāṇān ki man khud-rā namīdānam
Na tarsā nai yahūdam man na gabram nai musalmānam

What can I do, o Muslims, for I do not know myself
I'm not a Christian nor a Jew, not a Zoroastrian nor a Muslim.[69]

Enough, though, has perhaps now been said to indicate how a history of Punjabi Sufi poetry more satisfying than the partisan and incomplete narrative set out by Lajwanti Rama Krishna might be conceived. While having to cope as best it can with the inadequacies and silences in the historical record, such a literary history might hope to do justice to the different individual characteristics as much as to the generic similarities observable between those few collections which have come down to us from earlier centuries. Our argument has been that the gaps can be partly filled in by using comparative evidence from neighbouring literatures, but also by looking at the tradition across the whole period of its quite lengthy if hardly continuous evolution.

In this way, it might at last be possible properly to understand Punjabi Sufi poetry as a literary tradition in its own right, distinguished in both its inspiration and expression from the various parallel literary traditions of Punjab, most notably of course the Sikh literature but also the products of other nirguṇ bhakti and saguṇ bhakti traditions. Although the argument is still perhaps too easily attractive to Indian nationalist sentiment, it can hardly be maintained that just because it too strives towards the ideal realization of the Unity of Being, the best Indian Sufi poetry must be essentially Indian in its inspiration, having nothing much to do with Islam.

As human beings, we may all assent to the essential identity of the spiritual message of the great teachers and poets of the past.

As literary historians, though, we need to do proper justice to the differences in expression of that message observable from one tradition to another and from one period to another. In this way might hope to tell the whole story of the Punjabi Sufi poetic tradition from Baba Farid to Khwaja Ghulam Farid, or what in Pakistan is sometimes more succinctly denoted as *Farīd se Farīd tak* 'from Farid to Farid'.

NOTES

1 Lajwanti Rama Krishna, *Pañjābī Ṣūfī Poets A.D 1460–1900*, London [Calcutta printed]: Oxford University Press, 1938, abbreviated as *PSP* in subsequent references below. Originally submitted as a University of London PhD in 1934, the book has been subsequently reprinted in India, Delhi: Ashajanak, 1973 and translated into Urdu in Pakistan as *Panjābī ke Sūfī Shā'ir*, trans. Amjad Ali Bhatti, Lahore: Book Home, 2004. Described as coming from a Hindu family with Sikh connections, Lajwanti Rama Krishna was clearly a person of considerable determination, being the first Indian woman to obtain a doctorate in France, her thesis being, published as *Les Sikhs: Origine et développement de la communauté jusqu'à nos jours (1469–1930)* [*The Sikhs: origin and development of the community down to the present day (1469–1930)*], Paris: Maisonneuve, 1933. Anyway marginalized by its language and adding little to English-language studies of the time, this was a rather conventional survey compiled from an uncritically nationalist perspective. Unlike *PSP*, it has thus long been forgotten, partly also no doubt because of the much more active cultivation of Sikh studies since the 1930s, as compared to research in Punjabi Muslim studies.

2 For example, S.R. Sharda, *Sufi Thought: Its Development in Panjab and its Impact on Panjabi Literature from Baba Farid to 1850 A.D*, New Delhi: Munshiram Manoharlal, 1974, Surindar Singh Kohli, *Bulhe Shah*, New Delhi: Sahitya Akademi, 1987, published in the Makers of Indian Literature series, or Lochan Singh Buxi, *Prominent Mystic Poets of Punjab*, New Delhi: Ministry of Information and Broadcasting, 1994.

3 That is, outside the abundant Sikh scriptural tradition (whose language is itself, however, only partly to be properly identified as Punjabi).

4 For a stimulating general discussion of the problematics of the genre, see David Perkins, *Is Literary History Possible?*, Baltimore and London: John Hopkins University Press, 1982.

5   This is not of course to deny the validity of other approaches. While the lack of evidence for earlier periods must probably confine, for example reception histories to recent decades, the possibilities of a synchronic approach to the published Punjabi literature of the earlier colonial period have been very interestingly explored in Farina Mir, *The Social Space of Language: Vernacular Culture in British Colonial Punjab*, Berkeley and Los Angeles: University of California Press, 2010.

6   Sheldon Pollock (ed.), *Literary Cultures in History: Reconstructions from South Asia*, Berkeley: University of California Press, 2002.

7   Sant Singh Sekhon and Kartar Singh Duggal, *A History of Punjabi Literature*, New Delhi: Sahitya Akademi, 1992, with two chapters on the Sufi poets on pp. 16–25 and pp. 64–73, was followed by Sant Singh Sekhon, *A History of Panjabi* [sic] *Literature*, 2 vols, Patiala: Punjabi University, 1993, 1996, which deals with the Sufi poetry in vol. 1, pp. 15–33, and vol. 2, pp. 1–49.

8. Cf. the classic accounts by Hazariprasad Dvivedi, *Hindī Sāhitya: Uskā Udbhav aur Vikās*, Delhi: Attarchand Kapur, 1955, and Ramchandra Shukla, *Hindi Sāhitya ka Itihās*, Kashi: Nagari Pracharini Sabha, 2008, a seventh edition which confirms its enduring status since its first publication in 1951. As has often been observed, however, the apparent coherence of such versions of Hindi literary history is achieved only by the negation of Urdu. While that is another story which can hardly be gone into here, the great difficulty of achieving an integrated Hindi-Urdu literary history was recently brought home to me by the perceived necessity for two separate introductions (by Vasudha Dalmia and myself) to the anthology of translations from both languages published as Shobna Nijhawan (ed.), *Nationalism in the Vernacular: Hindi, Urdu, and the Literature of Indian Freedom*, New Delhi: Permanent Black, 2009.

9   Budh Singh, *Hans Chog* (1915), *Koil Kū* (1916), *Baṅbīhā Bol* (1925), all published Amritsar: Phulvari Agency. See further my chapter 'Making Punjabi Literary History', in Christopher Shackle, Gurharpal Singh, and Arvind-Pal Mandair (eds), *Sikh Religion, Culture and Ethnicity*, Richmond: Curzon, 2001, pp. 97–117.

10 Cf. Abdul Ghafur Quraishi, *Panjābī Adab dī Kahānī*, Lahore: Aziz Book Depot, 1972, Hamidullah Shah Hashimi, *Panjābī Adab dī Mukhtasar Tārīkh*, Lahore: Taj Book Depot, c.1973, Faqir Muhammad Faqir, *Panjābī Zabān va Adab kī Tārīkh*, Lahore: Sang-e Mil, 2002. But see Shackle, 'Making Punjabi Literary History', for the more catholic approach of the older Muslim pioneer of Punjabi literary history Maula Bakhsh Kushta in his *Panjāb de Hīre*, Amritsar: Dhani Ram Chatrik,

1939 and *Panjābī Shā'irāṅ dā Tazkira*, Lahore: Maula Bakhsh Kushta and Sons, 1960.

11 Cf. Perkins 1992, pp. 29–60 for the perennial tension between encyclopaedic and narrative approaches to literary history.

12 Ratan Singh Jaggi, *Pañjābī Sāhitt da Sarot-Mūlak Itihās*, 5 vols, Patiala: Punjabi University, 1998–2002. Jaggi's approach entails the disconnected treatment of the Sufi poets across several volumes, so vol.1, pp. 239–79 deal with Farid, vol. 3, pp. 158–216 with Shah Husain and Sultan Bahu, and vol. 5, pp. 135–74 with poets from Bullhe Shah down to Khwaja Farid.

13 *PSP*, p.125.

14 *Dīvān-e Farīd* (ed.) Aziz ur Rahman, Bahawalpur: Aziz ul Matabi', 1944. A partial translation is available in *Fifty Poems of Khawaja* [sic] *Farid*, trans. Christopher Shackle, Multan: Bazm-e-Saqafat, 1983

15 As a result of his combination of purity of local idiom with regional spiritual prestige, Khwaja Farid has since the 1960s become a prime symbol for the movement for the separate recognition of Siraiki cultural and political identity in Pakistan, cf. Christopher Shackle, 'Siraiki: A Language Movement in Pakistan', *Modern Asian Studies*, 11(3), 1977, pp. 379–403. For the purposes of the present argument, however, the exclusivist rival claims laid by modern protagonists of Punjabi and Siraiki to the largely overlapping Muslim poetic heritage of the past are set aside, in the same way that a comprehensive Punjabi language area may be constructed as embracing divergent regional standards like Siraiki as well as the more narrowly defined standard Punjabi based on the Majhi dialect of Lahore and Amritsar, cf. Christopher Shackle, 'Panjabi', in George Cardona and Dhanesh Jain (eds), *The Indo-Aryan Languages*, London and New York: Routledge, 2003, pp. 581–621.

16 *Dīvān* (ed.) Aziz ur Rahman, kāfī 110, p. 367.

17 See further my summary treatment in 'Urdu as a Sideline', in Christopher Shackle (ed.), *Urdu and Muslim South Asia: Studies in Honour of Ralph Russell*, London: SOAS, 1989, pp. 77–91.

18 Cf. the Urdu translation published as *Maqābīs ul Majālis* (ed. and trans. Vahid Bakhsh Sial), Lahore: Islamic Book Foundation, 1979 and my English translation of the first volume published as *The Teachings of Khwaja Farid*, Multan, Bazm-e Saqafat, 1978.

19 See further Masud Hasan Shihab, *Khwāja Ghulām Farīd (Hayāt va Shā'irī)*, Bahawalpur: Urdu Academy, 1963, and Christopher Shackle, 'The Shifting Sands of Love', in Francesca Orsini (ed.), *Love in Many Languages: A Cultural History of Love in South Asia*, Cambridge: Cambridge University Press, 2006, pp. 87–108.

20 The best edition, with complete verse-numbering, is *Saif ul Mulūk* (ed.) Muhammad Sharif Sabir, Lahore: Sayyid Ajmal Husain Memorial Society, 2002, while a complete Urdu prose translation is available as *Saif ul Mulūk*, trans. Mian Zafar Maqbul, Lahore: Shaikh Muhammad Bashir and Sons, n.d.. The South Asian context of the story is described in C. Shackle, 'The Story of Saif ul Mulūk in South Asia', *Journal of the Royal Asiatic Society*, Series 3, 17 (2), 2007, pp. 1–15. One of Mian Muhammad's shorter early poems, his *Qissa Shaikh Sun'ān* in which Shaikh Abdul Qadir becomes a prominent figure in the well-known story by 'Attār', is described in my chapter 'Representations of 'Attār in the West and in the East: Translations of the *Mantiq al-Tayr*', in Leonard Lewisohn and Christopher Shackle (eds), *'Attār and the Persian Sufi Tradition: The Art of Spiritual Flight*, London: I.B. Tauris, 2006, pp. 165–93.

21 Published as *Bostān-e Qalandarī* (The Orchard of Dervishry), Jhelum: Munshi Muhammad Hasan ud Din, 1930.

22 Commissioned by a Jhelum bookseller to accompany an edition of *Saif ul Mulūk* and completed less than two decades after Mian Muhammad's death, Malik Muhammad's memoir is also appended as 'Savānih-'umrī' to one edition of *Saif ul Mulūk*, Muzaffarabad: Nizamat-e Auqaf, 1994, pp. 570–638.

23 This threefold profile is developed further in Christopher Shackle, 'Styles and Themes in the Siraiki Mystical Poetry of Sind', in Hamida Khuhro (ed.), *Sind through the Centuries,* Karachi: Oxford University Press, 1981, pp. 252–69.

24 For the former's anti-Shia views cf. my translation of *The Teachings of Khwaja Farid*, pp. 41–2. Mian Muhammad's strong anti-Wahhabi stance is set out in his 1877 poem *Hidāyat ul Muslimīn* (Guidance to Muslims) (ed.) Mahbub Ali, Muzaffarabad: Nizamat-e Auqaf, 1980.

25 *Saif ul Mulūk* (ed.) Sabir, verses 9018–22, p. 487.

26 Available in English as Amir Hasan Sijzi, *Nizam ad-Din Awliya: Morals for the Heart* (ed.) and trans. Bruce B. Lawrence, New York and Mahwah: Paulist Press, 1992.

27 See particularly the careful discussion in Ratan Singh Jaggi, *Panjābī Sāhitt,* vol. 1, pp. 240–80 and the late Pritam Singh's substantial monograph *Sri Gurū Granth Sahib vāle 'Sekh Farīd' di Bhāl* (The Search for the 'Shaikh Farid' of the Guru Granth Sahib), Amritsar: Singh Brothers, 2008. In broad harmony with these authorities, my own understanding is set out in the as yet unpublished paper 'Sikh and Muslim Understandings of Baba Farid', delivered as the Amrit Kaur Ahluwalia Memorial Lecture at UC Berkeley in April 2008.

28 *PSP,* p. 6.
29 Cf. Karine Schomer, 'The *Dohā* as a Vehicle of Sant Teachings', in K. Schomer and W.H. McLeod (eds), *The Sants: Studies in a Devotional Tradition of India,* Delhi: Motilal Banarsidass, 1987, pp. 61–90.
30 *Shalok Farīd* 12, *Ādi Granth* [hereafter *AG*], p. 1378.
31 *Shalok Farīd* 54, *AG,* p.1380.
32 Cf. my earlier study, 'Early Vernacular Poetry in the Indus Valley: Its Contexts and its Character', in A.L. Dallapiccola and S. Z.-A. Lallemant (eds), *Islam and Indian Regions,* Stuttgart: Steiner, 1993, vol. 1, pp. 259–89.
33 *Mārū kī Vār* M5 4.1, AG, p. 1095.
34 As, for instance, in the introduction to an edition of the *Farīd-bāṇī* in Sindhi script, *Bābā Farīd Ganj-e Shakar jā Dohā* (ed. and trans. Agha Salim), Jamshoro: Institute of Sindhology, University of Sindh, 1990, pp. 26–30.
35 *Shāh Karīm Bulṛī'a vāre jo Kalām* (ed.) Umar b. Muhammad Daudpoto, Bhitshah: Shah Abd ul Latif Cultural Centre Committee, 1977, p. 129.
36 Ibid., pp. 102–3.
37 Notable examples of this reading of Sindhi Sufi poetry, which is exactly comparable to the approach of *PSP,* include such standard studies as L.H. Ajwani, *History of Sindhi Literature,* New Delhi: Sahitya Akademi, 1970 or Motilal Jotwani, *Sufis of Sindh,* New Delhi: Ministry of Information and Broadcasting, 1996. Cf. Ajwani 1970, p. 75: 'The great defect of Sorley's study of Shah Abdul Latif of Bhit is that he wants to crib and confine him into the narrow mould of a dogma that he calls Islam, instead of viewing him as a typical, true Indian *rishi,* the man who had a *darshan* or vision of God, and who passed on that vision in ecstatic words to his rapt hearers.'
38 Santokh Singh's account is reproduced in M.A. Macauliffe, *The Sikh Religion,* Oxford: Clarendon Press, 1909, vol. 3, pp. 62–3.
39 Dara Shikoh, *Hasanāt ul 'Ārifīn* (ed.) Makhdum Rahin, Tehran: Visman, AH 1352sh. = 1973, pp. 57–8.
40 *PSP,* pp. 16–19. The short monograph in the Makers of Indian Literature series by Harjinder Singh Dhillon, *Shah Husain,* New Delhi: Sahitya Akademi, 2000 focuses on the Punjabi poetry and avoids too many awkward details of Husain's life in favour of a generalized characterization of Shah Husain as a *malāmatī* Sufi. For a more insightful creative interpretation of the significance of the extraordinary depiction of the saint in the *Haqīqat ul Fuqarā,* see now Scott Kugle, *Sufis and Saint's Bodies: Mysticism, Corporeality, and Sacred Power in Islam,* Chapel Hill: University of North Carolina Press, 2007, pp. 181–220. But his chapter pays only passing attention to Shah Husain's Punjabi poetry.

41   I have been unable to obtain a copy of the modern edition of this work, reported as 'Risāla-e Tahniyat' (ed.) M. Iqbal Mujaddidi, published in *Ma'ārif* (Azamgarh), August 1970, also in *Sahīfa*, Lahore, July 1972.

42   This was *Kāfiyāṅ Shāh Husain*, Lahore: Dayal Singh, 1897, according to Shahbaz Malik, *Panjābī Kitābiyāt*, Islamabad: Pakistan Academy of Letters, 1991, no. 3300/1, p. 185.

43   *Kāfiyāṅ Shāh Husain* (ed. and trans.) Abdul Majid Bhatti, Islamabad: Lok Virsa, 1977, kāfī 107, p. 120.

44   Bhatti (ed.), kāfī 138, p. 152.

45   Bhatti (ed.), kāfī 9, p.10, where the refrain appears as *Maiṇḍā dil Rānjhan rāval mange* In other editions the opening words 'my heart' are regularized to the standard modern Punjabi *merā dil,* while in the slightly more critical edition *Hālāt va Kāfiyāṅ Mādholāl Husain* (ed.) Mohan Singh Divan, rev. M. Habibullah, Lahore, Malik Nazir Ahmad, n.d., *kāfī* 18, p. 28, they are written as *maiṇḍī dil,* that is, with *dil* as feminine, as in modern Siraiki *meḏī dil.* This is a small but typical illustration of the impossibility of fitting the pre-modern literary heritage into neat modern linguistic categories on the basis of very imperfectly established texts, cf. note 15 above.

46   Cf. Ahmad Saeed Hamadani, *Hazrat Sultān Bāhū: Hayāt va Ta'līmāt,* Lahore: Sultan Bahu Academy, 1987.

47   *PSP,* p. 29.

48   Cf. Zuhur ud Din Ahmad, *Pākistān meṅ Fārsī Adab kī Tārīkh,* vol. 3, Lahore: Majlis-e Taraqqi-e Adab, 1974, pp. 165–74, also Hamadani 1987, pp. 70–2.

49   That is, as written in the Persian script.

50   *Sirr ul 'Urafā Kalāṅ* (Urdu version of *Mihakk ul Fuqarā Kalāṅ*), trans. Muhammad Sharif, Faruqabad: Maktaba-e Naqshbandiyya Qadiriyya, c.1993, pp. 75–6.

51   *Dīvān-e Bāhū* (ed.) Ahmad Saeed Hamadani, Jhang: Hadrat Ghulam Dastgir Academy, 1998, *ghazal* 31, p. 35.

52   *PSP,* p. 32.

53   Early editions are helpfully discussed in *Kalām-e Sultān Bāhū* (ed.) Nazir Ahmad, Lahore: Packages, 1981, pp. x–xix, beginning with an edition of 1891. But an edition of 1878 is listed in Malik 1991, no. 3052/, p. 176.

54   Doubts have been plausibly voiced as to whether this characteristic *hū* is any more original to the *abyāt* than the acrostic *sī-harfī* arrangement of all modern editions of Sultan Bahu. Cf. *Kalām* (ed.) Nazir Ahmad, pp. xix–20, also *Abyāt-e Sultān Bāhū*(ed. and trans.) Sultan Altaf Ali, Lahore: Haji Muhammad Ashfaq Qadiri, 1975, pp. 18–21

55 *Kalām,* (ed.) Nazir Ahmad, no.181, p. 87. The best of the several available translations of the *abyāt* is *Death before Dying: The Sufi Poems of Sultan Bahu* (trans. Jamal J. Elias), Berkeley: University of California Press, 1998.

56 *PSP*, p. 40.

57 *Qānūn-e 'Ishq,* ed. Anvar Ali Rohtaki, Lahore: Allah-vale ki Qaumi Dukan, 1889, and *Kāfihā-e Hazrat Bullhe Shāh Sahib Qasūrī* by Bhai Prem Singh Qasuri, Kasur: The editor, 1896).

58 *Kulliyāt-e Bullhe Shāh,* (ed.) Faqir Muhammad Faqir, Lahore: Panjabi Adabi Academy, 1960), kāfī 95, p. 206. The following numerical references in the text are to the kāfī numbers of this edition.

59 Faqir (ed.), kāfī 65, pp. 126–34. For an English version of the whole poem, cf. J.R. Puri and T. Shangari , Dera Baba Jaimal Singh: Radha Soami Satsang Beas, 1986, pp. 335–9. A full edition of the poetry in Gurmukhi script with facing English translation is to appear in the new Murty Classical Library of India series as Bullhe Shah, *Sufi Lyrics,* trans. Christopher Shackle, Cambridge Mass.: Harvard University Press, forthcoming.

60 Faqir (ed.), kāfī 62, p.123.

61 Cf. Denis Matringe, 'Krṣnaite and Nāth Elements in the Poetry of the Eighteenth-Century Panjabi Sūfī Poet Bullhe Śāh', in R.S. McGregor (ed.), *Devotional Literature in South Asia,* Cambridge: Cambridge University Press, 1991, pp.190–206.

62 Faqir (ed.), kāfī 28, p.46.

63 Bullhe Shah, *50 Kāfiāṅ* (ed.), Mohan Singh Ubirai, Lahore: University of the Punjab, 1930.

64 For example, Nazir Ahmad in his fine edition published as *Kalām-e Bullhe Shāh,* Lahore: Packages, 1976.

65 Robin Rinehart, 'Interpretations of the Poetry of Bullhe Shah', *International Journal of Punjab Studies,* 3 (1), 1996, pp. 45–63; and 'The Portable Bullhe Shah: Biography Categorization, and Authorship in the Study of Punjabi Sufi Poetry', *Numen,* vol. 46, 1999, pp. 53–87.

66 Faqir (ed.), kāfī 27, p. 44.

67 *PSP*, pp. 58–9.

68 Cf. for example, her classic study *As Through a Veil: Mystical Poetry in Islam,* New York: Columbia University Press, 1982, especially the chapter on 'Mystical Poetry in the Vernaculars', pp. 135–69.

69 Jalal al-Din Rumi, *Barguzīda-e Dīvān e Shams-e Tabrīzī,* Tehran: Amir Kabir, n.d., p.115. Cf. *Kalām* (ed.), Nazir Ahmad, p.106, and the numerous parallels with Persian Sufi poetry adduced in *Qānūn-e 'Ishq* (ed.), Anvar Ali Rohtaki.

2

Alyssa Ayres[†]

Language, the Nation, and Symbolic Capital

THE CASE OF PUNJAB[*]

Since gaining independence in 1947, the attainment of a unified national identity has been, as with many ethnically diverse postcolonial states, an important pursuit of the Pakistani state. As a result, the overt assertion of regional identities has been construed, for decades, as a problem of 'centrifugal forces' perennially in danger of spinning out of control. The state-instantiated official nationalism gives primacy to an imagined nation, present in some nascent form from Muhammad bin Qasim's invasion of Sindh in 712 CE and culminating in the political creation of Pakistan in 1947,[1] with a literary–historical culture that authorizes the Urdu language as a cor-

[*] This is an abridged version of Alyssa Ayres, 'Language, the Nation, and Symbolic Capital: The Case of Punjab', *Journal of Asian Studies,* 67 (3), 2008, pp. 917–46. © The Association for Asian Studies, Inc., published by Cambridge University Press, reproduced with permission.
[†] This essay was researched and composed prior to the author's appointment to the US Department of State. The views expressed here are those of the author and do not necessarily reflect those of the US Department of State or the US government.

nerstone of its national expression.[2] Within this national framework, a widespread belief that Punjabi is a language of 'low' culture and one without official recognition, has pushed Punjabi to the shadows of official life.

From the days of the Pakistan Movement even prior to partition, and explicitly so after the creation of the country in 1947, a relational cultural hierarchy symbolically linked the notion of Pakistan's legitimacy with a national cultural heritage emblematized by Urdu and its literary–cultural history.[3] That Punjabi lacks official status, even in Punjab, provides the necessity for its revival. But the more recent visibility of a *Punjabiyat* movement suggests deep implications for our most powerful theories charting the relationship of language to the nation and its political imagination. Although this movement bears the surface features of a classical nationalist formation—insistence upon recovering an unfairly oppressed history and literature, one unique on earth and uniquely imbued with the spirit of the local people and the local land—the structural features of this process differ markedly from those we have come to understand as classical nationalisms.

The Punjabiyat movement in Pakistan has not been propelled by newly literate but disenfranchised individuals recognizing inequality or social difference as they gain education in the transition to industrial society, leading to a search to overturn an urban cultural elite in favour of a vernacular populism.[4] Given Punjab's well-noted dominance in Pakistan, it is hard to explain as an effort by political entrepreneurs seeking advantage through incorporation with, or resistance to, the 'centre', as is the case with classic models of language revivalism and language nationalism.[5] Moreover, with the positions of power—social, political, economic—enjoyed by the Punjabiyat movement's actors, the explanation of symbol manipulation or theory of instrumental, even opportunistic, choice in search of electoral or other competitive gain appears an insufficient logic.[6]

As confounding, the Punjabiyat movement raises questions about the role of language, reading, and the textual transmission of powerful ideas of belonging. It is hard to situate the Punjabiyat case within Benedict Anderson's sophisticated models, and it seems a particularly poor fit for causal explanations involving print capitalism. It appears to be a reaction to rather than an instance of official nationalism, creating a confusing paradox.[7] Rather, it has been slowly growing out of the work of an urban cultural and political elite—fluent in Urdu and English as well—some of whom have maintained comfortable positions of power for some time. Yet they seek to 'restore' a role for Punjabi, justified entirely in terms of aesthetics and pursued through the development of a respected Punjabi-language written public sphere. The Punjabiyat movement seems to be concerned with *creating* the key tools that theories of nationalism posit as necessary for its emergence.[8]

Given the intriguing questions this case poses about the mechanisms of nationalism, the Punjabiyat movement marks an opportunity to explore the importance of symbolic capital in efforts to maintain cultural forms against a national identity that would supplant them.[9] Pierre Bourdieu's elaboration of the forces of symbolic domination and the working of the linguistic market—a market in which social exchange produces distinction in social value—allows us to better isolate and explain the phenomena at stake in the case of Punjab. By virtue of the dynamics of the movement's emergence from within the dominant 'core' of the country, this case allows an abstraction away from the functionalist and instrumentalist explanations that have been powerfully convincing elsewhere. For we see in the case examined here precisely what Bourdieu understood as a struggle for recognition—a struggle for a particular language tradition to gain acceptance as a legitimate language—in a context entirely without the analytic interference of economic, political, or even demographic distractions.[10]

Panjāb kā Muqaddama, 'The Case of Punjab'

The broad contours of Pakistan's creation as a homeland for South Asian Muslims are well known. Pakistan's difficulties forging a cohesive sense of nationality, one able to include its diverse citizenry, has been the subject of scholarly work in particular on the 1971 breakup of the country.[11] During the 1990s, ethnic conflict in Sindh was the focus of scholarship on Pakistan's nation–region problems.[12] The current resurgence of Baloch nationalism reprises the armed conflict in the province in the 1970s. Zones of national contestation are so numerous that a recent edited volume on Pakistan bears the subtitle 'Nationalism without a Nation?'.[13] In all of the scholarship on Pakistan's nation–region dilemmas, Punjab's dominance has been a central feature. And rightly so: with a population somewhere between 77 million and 83 million, Punjab is the most populous province of Pakistan. Its residents make up 55.6 per cent of the population of the country, according to the 1998 census.[14] Punjabis dominate Pakistan's major institutions: Though clear current statistics are not available, Punjabis have composed as much as 80 per cent of the Pakistani Army and 55 per cent of the federal bureaucracy, according to figures as of 1987.[15] Virtually since the country's birth, other ethnic groups in Pakistan have accused Punjab of seizing national spoils for its own benefit at the expense of others. Punjab is perceived to have 'captured' Pakistan's national institutions through nepotism and other patronage networks.[16] Ideas about Punjab's dominance—it is often called a hegemon—are so commonplace that the word '*Punjabistan*' serves as a shorthand for the national conundrum.[17]

The 'Punjabistan' idea has to do with a widespread resentment of Punjab's numerical dominance and, as important, its prosperity and perceived greed. Pakistan's Punjab enjoys natural advantages: it is the most fertile province in a country in which some 44 per cent of the population makes its living off the land.[18] But many of its man-made advantages indeed suggest a preference for the province: Updating Ian Talbot's earlier observations,[19] Punjab's farms have 84 per cent of all the owned tractors in the entire country, as well as 94.6 per cent of the tube wells, two important development indicators.[20] The literacy rate in Punjab is about the same as that in Sindh (47.4 per cent and 46.7 per cent, respectively), though higher than that in the North-West Frontier Province (NWFP) and in Balochistan (37.3 per cent and 26.6 per cent, respectively). Punjab's women are the most literate in the country, with 57.2 per cent of the urban and 25.1 per cent of the rural female populations able to read.[21] The urban female literacy rate is comparable to that of Sindh, but Punjab's rural female literacy rate is nearly twice that of Sindh and the NWFP and more than triple Balochistan's.[22] All these indicators tell us, in short, that there are more Punjabis than anyone else in Pakistan, and they are better off than everyone else, with more productive land, cleaner water, better technology, and better educated families.

The education–literacy dimension is important, not least because it is one of the core components of the two most widely cited theories about the mechanisms of nationalism, those of Benedict Anderson and Ernest Gellner. [23] Anderson's elegant theory relies upon print capitalism (in particular, newspapers and novels) as the primary vector for creating a cohesive sense of shared belonging—a shared sense of space-time—across large populations. Gellner's exploration of modernization and the gradual transformation of agricultural societies to industrial modes require the expansion of bureaucracies and the '*Mamlukization*' of society. This functional explanation relies on a state-directed ability to institute literacy in an official language, which regional elites become aware of as a point of difference from their 'own' regional language-culture complex. An obvious problem here lies in the issue of much less than universal literacy, despite Punjab's relative performance compared with other parts of Pakistan. Given that slightly more than half of Punjab is adjudged illiterate (and here we should recall that such surveys skew toward reporting higher rather than lower literacy), the situation poses clear limitations for the explanatory or catalytic value of print textual forms to engage this large population in a common sense of national belonging.[24]

But in addition, what we find in Pakistan's Punjab is an extremely curious situation: formal literacy in Punjab means literacy in Urdu, for literary, official, and daily 'documentary' public life in Punjab has taken place in Urdu since the British Raj. After annexing the province from the Sikhs in 1849, the British decided to substitute Urdu for Persian as the state language in the later part of the nineteenth century.[25] The colonial policy privileging Urdu as the official language of Punjab continued with the creation of Pakistan in 1947, although a broader institutionalization of Urdu across the territories that became part of this new country—territories with longer histories of regional language use, such as Sindhi, Pashto, Bengali, Balochi, and Siraiki—would require a significant capital and epistemological project on the part of the central government. Census figures illustrate that Urdu was and still is the first language of a very small percentage of the population of Pakistan—7.3 per cent in 1951, rising to 7.6 per cent by 1981, and 7.53 per cent in the 1998 census (but as high as 20 per cent for urban areas). The choice of Urdu as the national language for Pakistan (rather than any of the other languages that could have been selected and had wider presences as first languages) was intimately related to a language ideology that posited Urdu as the bearer of high Muslim culture in the region—indeed, as the preferred bearer of *religious identity*, although Urdu has never been a language of religious text in the way that Arabic (for Islam) or Sanskrit (for Hinduism) could claim.[26]

In addition to the privileging of Urdu for administrative and official life, English—at varying levels of competence—has been regarded since at least the late nineteenth century as a necessary tool for elite economic and social advancement. In modern Pakistan, state education planning documents from 1947 forward identify the necessity to 'change over' the elite schools from an English medium to Urdu as a means of levelling the educational playing field for all and of building a country of citizens equally fluent in Urdu. However, these proposed changeovers never took place, and elite educational institutions remain English medium. In recognition of this severe stratification, as early as the 1980s, private English-medium schools emerged to service upper-middle and middle-class families unable to gain admission to the most elite schools.[27] The confluence of two prestige languages with official patronage has created an unusual situation for Punjabi, rendering it peripheral to the longer history of an Urdu-language official sphere and the unceasing dominance of the English language at the upper levels of bureaucratic life. Thus, Punjabi is truly doubly marginal.

Examined in terms of direct economic or social benefit, the Punjabiyat movement does not easily fit into any of our theoretical categories of explanation. From an instrumentalist perspective, the movement does not make any sense, as noted sociolinguist Tariq Rahman has observed in frustration.[28] It is not about seeking power: the movement's key protagonists are all successful public intellectuals whose advocacy of the language *followed* their success in electoral or bureaucratic politics or in the private sector. It does not appear to be about financial gain, given the limited arena of Punjabi publishing. Although Punjabiyat activists have been called antinational,[29] the Punjabiyat movement itself does not claim a separatist agenda. The Punjabiyat activists instead want Punjabi to claim its rightful inheritance as one of the great world languages. Its rhetoric is entirely framed in terms of affect and the urgency of recovering a 'lost' identity. That Punjab, widely perceived as the most 'vested' of Pakistan's 'vested interests', should nurture a growing ethnic nationalism eager to rehabilitate itself from a perceived cultural alienation perpetrated by some *other* vested interests suggests the need for more inquiry into the reasons for the emergence of this 'case of Punjab'.

Recovering the Cultural Self

As is typical in cases of cultural revival worldwide, the Punjabiyat project's roots can be traced to lone intellectuals—cultural entrepreneurs—working in the 1960s.[30] Among them, Najm Hosain Syed (1936–) was central. He actively began creating new literary works in Punjabi—criticism, poetry, and plays—in the late 1960s, with several of his key texts emerging in the next decades. Syed was a core participant in the *Majlis Shah Hussain*, a literary association celebrating the Sufi poet Shah Hussain (1539–1599) through literary readings and an annual festival, the *cirāghān dā melā*.[31] Syed's writings clearly inaugurated the discourse of recovery that marks all the Punjabiyat efforts. His narrative forms drew from old Punjabi poetry and folktales, using them as alternative historical sources. Importantly, Syed established his notion of Punjabi heroism in opposition to what he viewed as the received wisdom of Punjab as a land and a people of submission. This belief that Punjab has been characterized as submissive and stripped of its historical valor resounds throughout the Punjabiyat texts.

In essays written in Punjabi and English,[32] Syed wrote of the *vār*, a Punjabi epic–martial verse form, composed by Qādiryār, a nineteenth-century poet (ca. 1800–50) whose verses recovered the story of the pre-Islamic hero Puran of Sialkot (ca. 100–200 CE).[33] Syed then composed his own *vār*, *Takht-e-Lāhor*,[34] which used Shah Hussain's poetry as historical source material for a drama based on the character Dulla Bhatti.[35] Dulla Bhatti, leader of a revolt against Mughal emperor Akbar, was hanged in 1599. In the annals of received history, he was a criminal, but in the verses of his contemporary Shah Hussain, Dulla Bhatti was a resistant hero of the land. His dying words as recorded by Shah Hussain were, 'No honorable son of Punjab will ever sell the soil of Punjab.'[36] Syed published a series of poetry collections in the 1970s, as well as another drama exemplifying this new Punjabi heroism in 1983. His *Ik Rāt Rāvī Dī* featured Rai Ahmed Khan Kharal (1803–1857), a participant in the 1857 revolt against the British, as a hero for Punjabis to call their own. As with *Takht-e-Lāhor*, *Ik Rāt Rāvī Dī* drew upon alternative historical sources, in this case folk songs of the Ravi riverbank area—Kharal's birthplace—to fashion a hero whom the British state had seen a criminal.[37] By employing these indigenous forms, with sons of the soil reinterpreted heroically through the textual source of Punjabi poetry rather than the annals of the Mughal victors, Syed presented a new kind of Punjabi person—strong, valiant, unfazed by confronting authority. Most important, this new Punjabi person could lay claim to his own language as the form most appropriate for cultural expression.

During the early to mid-1970s, under the country's first democratically elected government, headed by Zulfiqar Ali Bhutto (1972–77), a sense of intellectual openness coincided with the search for national redefinition in the aftermath of the 1971 breakup. During this short half-decade, a greater emphasis on the legitimacy of local ethnic identities—in no small part attributed to Bhutto's own recognition of Sindh's unique cultural heritage—resulted in the state creation of institutions such as *Lok Virsa* (1974) and regional literary boards such as the Pakistan Panjabi Adabi Board. Writers such as Fakhar Zaman, Munnoo Bhai, and Shafqat Tanveer Mirza began to establish themselves in Punjabi. Mohammad Hanif Ramey, whose work will be engaged later, served as the chief minister of Punjab during the Bhutto years. Yet following General Zia ul-Haq's military coup in 1977, opportunities to openly write about a 'Punjabi identity' (or any other) were curtailed, particularly during the first half of his decade of dictatorship. Poet and fiction writer Fakhar Zaman saw his works banned.

By the mid-1980s, this ethnoliterary project began to take on a more openly declared agenda through treatises that expanded upon the themes of the literary forms. Mohammad Hanif Ramey returned from self-imposed exile and penned *Panjāb kā Muqaddama* (The Case of Punjab), published in 1985. Manifesto-length responses from other regions followed within two years.[38] The year 1985 also witnessed the publication of Fateh Muhammad Malik's *Punjabi Identity*.[39] In 1986 the World Punjabi Congress, spearheaded by Fakhar Zaman, convened for the first time.[40] The year 1988 brought *Panjābī Zabān Nahīn Maregī* (The Punjabi Language Will Never Die)[41]; 1989, *Panjāb kā Maslā: Dīpoliṭsizeshan aur Awāmī Tahrīk kā na Calnā* (The Problem of Punjab: Depoliticization and the Non-Movement of the People's Movement)[42]; and 1992, *Āo, Panjābī ko Qatl Kareṇ!* (Come, Let's Kill Punjabi!) and Shafqat Tanveer Mirza's *Resistance Themes in Punjabi Literature*.[43]

In a parallel development in the 1980s, Punjabi cinema rose to a position of market dominance, primarily through the iconic revenge-seeking peasant-warrior 'Maulā Jaṭ', played by Sultan Rahi (1938–1996), who by the mid-1990s came to embody the genre. Though this literature and film have not been examined in any detail in the academic analyses of centre–province relations in Pakistan, it is a rich source, in some cases, explicitly describing the relationship between the Punjabi people and their language in filial terms; in other cases, making use of powerful, violent allegory to convey such affect; and most of all, establishing a set of iconic figures to embody a new notion of Punjab and the Punjabi language as strong and resistant. These texts offer important examples of the way Punjabi language, history, and ethnicity were undergoing revision in Pakistan.

The Hegemon's Lost Self

The most surprising aspect of the Punjabiyat literature is the extent to which the Punjabi language is characterized as 'lost', lost through the oppression of Urdu. This stance turns upside-down the idea of 'Punjabistan' as an oppressor. In this view, the Punjab of Punjabiyat is itself a kindred spirit to the other ethnic victims of the Pakistani state, making common cause with Bengal and Bengali in particular.

One critical dimension of the relationship in the region between the Punjabi and Urdu languages lies in the fact that the Punjabi language has had a more limited role in print life, particularly in its Arabic script form. The Punjabiyat literature points to these separate spheres of language life in Punjab as evidence of an internal loss of self. At the same time, however, these writers frequently address the paradox of a lost self alongside the politically dominant idea of Punjabistan, acknowledging the acquiescence of many Punjabis in the oppression of other language-ethnic groups in Pakistan through a sort of false consciousness, illustrated by three examples:

> For the past forty-one years... Punjabis have mixed the sweet poison of alien languages with the blood of the generations, and to kill off their own Punjabiyat became a participant in profiteering and opportunism, swinging their axe on their own two feet... For the sake of murderous Urdu, first they slit the throat of our Punjab and murdered hundreds of thousands of Punjabis. Then, for this man-eating language, [they] wanted to make the Bengalis slaves. They tried to rob them of their freedom. And having become the spokesmen of the other brothers, they spilled the blood of Bengalis. And not just Bengalis, but for this murderous language they also fired bullets upon Sindhis, the next-door neighbors for thousands of years.[44]
>
> Having given up their identity, and through Punjab built a tradition of living as a Pakistani, in this way, they became intellectually developed but their emotional development remained halfway, and they became the prey of several such dreams, on account of which not just they but Pakistan as well was harmed... Punjab's new generations are not proud of Punjabi, but are excluded from it; in a bid to walk like a swan, the crow forgot its own gait.[45]
>
> I am also a migrant. I am from Faisalabad. My home is a true United Nations: the cook is Bengali. The servant is Sri Lankan. The driver is a Pathan and the gardener is a Sindhi. My children speak Urdu, not Punjabi. When I started to put a tape of Punjabi songs on in the car, my four-year-old son said 'Please turn it off'. I asked 'Why?' He said 'Only dogs speak this language'....We don't live in Pakistan, our place is air-conditioned. Air-conditioned cars and videos. We have a satellite antenna; we have lost our link and connection with our own country.[46]

These passages, all from texts that appeared in the mid-1980s to the early 1990s, are linked by the notion that a process of identification with the nation-state—Pakistan and its national language—has brought disaster upon themselves as well as the nation. Speaking Urdu rather than Punjabi is like a 'sweet poison', an aping of an incommensurate other genus or a lost link to an inner essence. These expressions of disaffection within Punjab are difficult to understand through the 'Punjabistan' model. How does an ethnic group said to be politically, economically, and culturally dominant in a polity suffer from a 'lost' self?

These narratives illustrate how Punjabi speakers fare poorly in status consciousness, a finding that coincides with the surveys carried out by sociolinguist Sabiha Mansoor. Her survey asked various groups of students (Punjabis in both Urdu- and English-medium schools) to rate their 'native language groups' on aspects such as 'social grace', 'modern', and 'cultured'. Contrary to her guiding hypothesis, she found that the Punjabi students consistently rated themselves lower in these aspects than they rated their Urdu-speaking peers.[47] This sense of dual consciousness is portrayed here as a burden on Punjabis, whose perceived linguistic and cultural limitations in Urdu are marks of inferiority, and who are simultaneously denied knowledge of literatures in their own language.

The late Mohammad Hanif Ramey's *Panjāb kā Muqaddama* gives extended attention to the problems of a dual consciousness and loss of self, making the argument that this loss forms Pakistan's core problem. His treatise, a 159-page manifesto and revisionist history, attributes the breakup of Pakistan in 1971 to Punjabis' false identification with an idea of Pakistan narrowly defined to exclude the cultural richness of Punjab. In one chapter, he lays the blame for the secession of East Pakistan squarely on the shoulders of Punjab—as do most Bangladeshi accounts of that history—but for an entirely different set of reasons:

> The mistake here was not that Bengali along with Urdu was not made the national language.... With respect to Urdu, because of Punjabis' erroneous and emotional attitudes, Bengalis had the feeling that Urdu is the language of Punjabis. They rightly thought that if the language of Punjabis, Urdu, can be the national language, then why can't their language, Bengali, be so— especially when in terms of national population they had the majority. If the people of Punjab had demonstrated such love for the Punjabi language, to which it was entitled by status of being our mother tongue, then the situation would not have deteriorated, it would have become apparent to all that Urdu,

if it wasn't the language of the Baluch, nor of the Pathans, nor of the Sindhis, wasn't the Punjabis' either. And if the peoples of the four provinces would have kept their respective mother tongues, then they would have been ready to accept Urdu as their national language, so then it may have been possible for the Bengalis also to accept Urdu as their national language while also having their own mother tongue. I blame myself above all, and then all the Punjabis, for having betrayed our mother tongue Punjabi. We not only erected the language problem in Pakistan, but also caused terrible damage to Urdu.[48]

This 'lost self' interpretation depends on the perception of Punjab as having sacrificed itself—its tongue, its way of being—in service to the unmet promise of Pakistan. Yet instead of conceptualizing the strong presence of Urdu in Punjab as advantageous in an 'Urdu-speaking' nation-state, these writers instead locate their national, provincial, and personal struggles in the psychological discourse of language loss as a loss of self.

The 'lost self' model leads to a corollary conundrum having to do with opportunity and participation in the national cultural economy. In terms of agrarian development, Punjab is far more prosperous than any other province of Pakistan. But in the 'lost self' understanding, Punjabis face hardship purely by virtue of the language they were born to speak first. The idea of Punjabi economic desperation is possible not by juxtaposing Punjabi wealth with Balochi deprivation but instead through comparison with English- and Urdu-speaking elites, an interpretive sleight of hand seen in two cartoons from another Punjabi proponent, 'Kammi', in his polemic *Panjābī Zabān Nahīn Maregī* (The Punjabi Language Will Never Die).

The cartoon in Figure 2.1 depicts the Punjabi language embodied as a villager shivering without cover on a cold desert night while Urdu and English—indicated by the caption and by the cap and necktie on the camel, symbolizing the Urdu-speaking and English-speaking elite—lie protected in a tent. The image invokes the 'Camel and the Tent' story, allegorizing Urdu and English as the uninvited guests who gradually displace Punjabi.[49] The second cartoon (Fig. 2.2) grotesquely depicts the Urdu- and English-speaking 'everymen' drinking milk directly from a cow's udder while hapless Punjabis stand watching, unable to wrest a drop for themselves. Perhaps fortunately, it is captioned 'Untitled'.[50]

Figure 2.1 'Punjabi? Urdu, English Inside?'. Sa'id Farani Kammi, *Panjābī Zabān Nahīṇ Maregī: Panjābī kā Muqaddamah Panjāb Meṇ* [The Punjabi language will never die: The case of Punjabi in Punjab] (Jhelum: Punjabi Esperanto Academy, 1988), p. 53. Cartoon reproduced with permission of the author

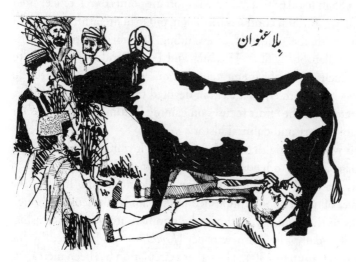

Figure 2.2 'Untitled'. Kammi, *Panjābī Zabān Nahīṇ Maregī*, p.127. Cartoons reproduced with permission of the author

The sentiments expressed in these political cartoons, as with the 'lost self' narrative, invert the standard understanding of Punjab as a rapacious 'Punjabistan' and instead present a self-portrayal of a subaltern victim. Reading these political cartoons against social statistics and human development indicators that clearly establish Punjab as the wealthiest and most privileged provides insight into the degree to which ideas about prosperity are linked to those of prestige and are as much imagined as real.

Historical Recovery: Local Literature and Stories from the Soil

The new Punjabiyat literature asserts that the project of 'recovering' Punjabi for the psychological well-being of the Punjabi people must go hand in hand with a recovery of Punjab's history, including its literary traditions and its martial past. One strand of this thinking focuses on the literary merits of Punjabi, primarily the devotional poetry of Sufis and the romance tales—the famed *Hīr-Rānjha, Sāhibāṇ-Mirza, Sohnī-Mahiwāl,* and *Sassī-Punnūṇ* in particular.[51] The *Hīr-Rānjhā* romance of Waris Shah (ca. 1722–1798) and the mystical poetry of Bulleh Shah (ca. 1680–1758) are important points of reference, cited routinely.[52] Kammi contrasts the 'reign' of Urdu literature in Punjabi schools with the 'injustice' of excluding Punjabi literature—Waris Shah, Bulleh Shah, Shah Hussain, and Baba Farīd.[53] The effort to create such a Punjabi literary culture, one on a par with the Urdu language and with equal attention devoted to it in state institutions, illustrates how the effort focuses on gaining legitimacy and status for Punjabi literary and cultural history.

It is worth noting that in this context of low literacy, the Punjabi language appears to have a print life only at the lowest levels and in arenas marginal to formal education and 'official' life. Indeed, the number of quality books published in Punjabi is miniscule, although thanks to the Punjabiyat efforts, the numbers are slowly increasing. As well, a daily Punjabi newspaper (*Khabrān*) was launched by the Khabrain Group in 2004. The paper's circulation has been increasing rapidly, likely accounting for the 67 per cent rise over the previous year in Punjabi-language newspaper circulation enumerated by the Audit Bureau of Circulations in 2004, with another 62 per cent increase in 2005, and 53 per cent for 2006. Even with the circulation boost of recent years, however, Punjabi-language newspaper circulation measured a mere 0.68 per cent of Urdu and 4.87 per cent of English-language circulations in 2006.[54] But in the world of 'chapbooks', or small stapled books, the best available survey—albeit more than a decade old now—reveals that approximately 39 per cent of such printed artifacts are written in Punjabi, compared with 36 per cent in Pashto and 23 per cent in Urdu. Their content ranges from poetry (religious and secular) to romance stories, film songs, magical spells, humor, and the lives of religious figures.[55] Again, the prevalence of written Punjabi circulating primarily within this quasi-literate sphere serves to illustrate the doubly marginal dimension of Punjabi in Pakistan. The Punjabiyat proponents advocate a qualitative change in Punjabi's relationship to official state institutions, for a simple quantitative change would not achieve the goal of gaining respect, recognition, and symbolic capital that the Punjabiyat proponents see as its due.

This core challenge of creating greater symbolic capital for Punjabi was taken up with revolutionary gusto by Fakhar Zaman. His allegorical Punjabi novel *Bandīwān* developed an extraordinary argument about language and literature in the nation-state, the latter depicted as the perpetrator of bondage and oppressor of subjectivity. *Bandīwān* is a political manifesto in the form of a novel, and it invokes Franz Kafka's *The Trial* stylistically and directly. It opens with the central character, 'Z', in solitary confinement, awaiting trial and punishment for charges of conspiracy to commit murder. Z claims he has committed no crime, only that he has written in 'the people's language', having rejected the national 'double standard', and with his writing seeks to battle the 'inverted subjectivity' that is the great enemy of Pakistan. In the novel's climactic fourteenth chapter, we find Z strapped on a rack, enduring repeated floggings. After each lash, Z expounds upon his philosophy of Punjabi language and its centrality to restoring proper psychic health to political life in Pakistan. Z's long speeches about Punjabi, while undergoing lash after lash of a leather whip, form the novel's centre-piece, culminating in a manifesto for a new birth of Punjabi literature to assuage the problem of 'inverted subjectivity':

...Unfortunately, for several generations the history of Punjabi was written according to the whims of the white rulers, and Punjabis were called obedient and 'devoted servants'. These 'devoted servants', quickly submitted to the domination of the newly arrived outsiders. The current batch of Punjabi poets, writers, and intellectuals have completely re-analysed Punjabi character and its history. A new movement has emerged in this other kind of poetry, novels, drama, and literature, which is giving shape to the consciousness of Punjab. The young poets and writers are giving new meaning to Punjab's classic writings. Having given the discourses of Sufi poetry new shape, instead of the poetry of resignation, they have shown it the poetry of opposition, against oppression and domination. This literary movement is the first step in a historical sequence of importance that will bring Punjabi language on a par with other languages.[56]

By the end of the novel, Z has been condemned to death, convicted of trumped-up charges designed to rid society of his revolutionary interpretations that emphasize Pakistan's regional languages—notably, Punjabi—and the novel closes, bleakly, from death row.

While this effort to rehabilitate Punjabi language, literature, and history and to elevate it to a prestige position in Pakistani literary and official life has been taking place through theatre, poetry, literary magazines, and essays, at the other end of the textual spectrum, a different sort of process has been under way, yet with similar implications for the political economy of language. Let us recall that even among the most literate population in Pakistan, Punjab's literacy rate hovers at only slightly under half the population. These 'masses' appear to have declared their allegiance to a contemporary heroic character who, though he does not explicitly reference any single historical figure, could have been drawn from any of the resistant heroes featured in the Punjabiyat literature. This hero, 'Maulā Jaṭ', has transformed Pakistani popular cinema.

THE RISE OF THE POPULAR VIOLENT PUNJABI HERO

In 1979 *Maulā Jaṭ*, a rough-and-tumble extravaganza of violence, hit the theatres in Punjab and revolutionized Pakistani cinema.[57] The film's unequalled success—spawning numerous sequels and knock-offs—resulted in Punjabi eclipsing Urdu as the most prolific and highest grossing cinema in the country, and the star, Sultan Rahi, earned him an entry in the *Encyclopedia Britannica* as the one who 'established Punjabi as the major language of Pakistani cinema'

Figure 2.3 Maulā Jaṭ

(see Figs 2.3 and 2.4). This was an unusual turning point, for the Pakistani film industry had long indulged in a more genteel aesthetic, epitomized by actors like Nadeem: handsome, speaking chaste Urdu, educated, often dressed in Western suits, and clean shaven. Sultan Rahi's iconic Maulā Jaṭ character could not have been more different: rough, dressed in the *lungi-kurta* of a Punjabi peasant, a skilled horse rider as well as master of the *gaṇḍāsā* (a long-handled axe), possessing an enormous and hypermasculine moustache, and given to demonstrations of brute physical strength. He quickly came to symbolize a new privileging of Punjab and Punjabi in the nonofficial, low-prestige arenas of Pakistani public life. This shift did not take place to universal acclaim, however, as can be seen in the writings of prominent critic Gillani Kamran, who castigated Punjabi film for 'defin[ing] the Punjabi culture as something primitive, noisy, vociferous, and highly pugnacious…crude, vulgar, morally degrading and without any decorum'.[58] While Kamran may not have been alone in his sentiments, the question arises whether some different aesthetic was at work here.

Against Kamran, those who loved the Maulā Jaṭ genre found the choice of language the very source of cheer, especially an aspect of

Figure 2.4 Maulā Jaṭ in London

the performance that drew upon a type of Punjabi-language verbal duel called *barrak*. According to Pakistani film director and historian Mushtaq Gazdar, barrak epitomized Punjabi bellicosity:

The verbal brawl called barrak, in Punjabi slang, is the hallmark of the movie. It can be taken as comic or serious, real or grotesque, depending on the nature of the audience. But such scenes stir audiences immensely. Barrak is a high-pitched, full-throated, threatening yell, a sort of warming up, a prelude to a brawl...[it is] a part of Punjabi life and culture. It is a bold challenge to the opponent.[59]

The Maulā Jaṭ character engages in this particularly Punjabi behaviour, and, in addition, every aspect of his character showcases a strong, brave, Punjabi masculinity. He rescues a Punjabi girl about to be raped when other 'sons of Punjab' refuse out of fear. He combats evil, personified by a fictionalized version of a real Punjabi village don, Nuri Nath. He displays physical strength, pulling a heavily loaded oxcart out of a bog, thus demonstrating that he is *stronger* than an ox. He fights enemies in hand-to-hand combat, using the traditional tool for cutting sugarcane (the gaṇḍāsā). The Zia ul-Haq regime tried to ban *Maulā Jaṭ*, yet somehow the film's producer managed to get a two-year stay order against its prohibition, and it went on to a record run.[60]

The proliferation of Jaṭ films displaced Urdu as the primary language of Pakistani cinema and Punjab, rather than Pakistan, seem to structure the landscape. Characters refer to Punjab, not Pakistan, as being very big, or that 'all of Punjab' will come to a festival. The central hero invokes, by name alone, pre-Islamic caste identities native to Punjab, Jats and Gujjars. These traditional agricultural castes exist in both Pakistani and Indian Punjab. Thus, ethnic as well as geographic horizons valourize a view of Punjab that pays little heed to the necessity of defining Pakistan in national terms, terms that have come to ignore the non-Islamic dimensions of social life.

Maulā Jaṭ and the many spin-offs (*Maulā Jaṭ in Landan*, *Maulā Jaṭ te Nūri Nath*, *Jaṭṭī dā Vīr*, *Jaṭ Gujjar*, *Jaṭ Gujjar te Nath*, *Makhā Jaṭ*, *Bāli Jaṭṭī*, *Ik Dhī Panjāb Dī*, *Desān dā Rājā*, *Wehshī Jaṭ*, and *Wehshī Gujjar*, to name just a few) represent a rethinking of the language of popular culture and the representation of heroism in Pakistan. Just as Ramey, Mirza, and Syed sought to reclaim strong Punjabi heroes for the current generation, Maulā Jaṭ became the cinematic embodiment of Punjabi strength, nobility, and honour, mediated by the pugnacious pleasures of the Punjabi language. If the proponents of Punjabiyat worried about reclaiming a Punjabi *imaginaire* in which Punjab would no longer be viewed as submissive, Maulā Jaṭ fulfilled this wish from the 1980s forward. From 1979 until his death in 1996, Sultan Rahi's Punjabi hero destroyed in a bloody frenzy anyone who crossed his path. Punjab had indeed found itself a hero who could not be called submissive.

The emergence of Maulā Jaṭ as a hero and the Punjabi film aesthetic's eclipse of Urdu offer a proxy point of comparison to the literature being produced by the elite actors of the Punjabiyat movement. Yet despite their social disconnect, and while occupying other ends of the literacy spectrum, both forms of Punjabi text from the 1980s forward mirror the incomplete quality of attachment to the national authorized culture, suggesting very interesting implications for Pakistan's national project, as well as our understanding of language and nationalism, and the functions thereof.

THEORETICAL LESSONS FROM THE CASE OF PUNJAB

More than sixty years have passed since Pakistan's creation, decades of challenges to the official national vision from virtually all corners—East Bengal, Balochistan, Sindh, and the NWFP's recurrent Pashtun nationalism. Each of these challenges has fit the region-versus-centre model, and in each one, the centre has been ethnically labelled 'Punjabi'. But the 'case of Punjab', as it were, bears the markers of a classic nationalist movement, albeit with a different underlying structure. Indeed, this elite is not one whom we would expect to find engaging in such a process of cultural revival, for the idea that Punjab and Punjabis have a politically, culturally, and economically dominant existence in Pakistan has become a virtual truism. It is as if the protagonists are in opposition to themselves, adopting the stance of a minority or regional elite against some *other* majority or centre oppressor. In fact, one of the more self-conscious arguments of the Punjabiyat literature is precisely this, that they must battle 'inverted subjectivity' or the 'loss of self'. The long-assumed 'centre' of political power finds the national legitimate language *insufficient*, illustrating the limits of symbolic domination, even over decades, and even over the consciousness of those exercising dominance. In this way, the case of Punjab offers the unusual situation of a living counterfactual: Without clear instrumental motivations or other functionalist explanations that rely on the use of language politics to achieve other kinds of power, it becomes easier to perceive that the Punjabiyat ethnoreclamation project is a movement to elevate the Punjabi linguistic and literary sphere from a position of marginality in the national aesthetic order—again, a strategy entirely focused on increasing symbolic capital as *an end in itself.*

As we have seen, Pakistan's early leaders chose to pursue a national language project that relied upon a language ideology that portrayed Urdu as the appropriate language of South Asian Islam. Other language traditions in Pakistan were subordinated, and in the cases of Bengali and Punjabi, were perceived as having non-Islamic linkages (Hinduism, Sikhism) that made it difficult for them to achieve recognition as equal participants in the nation. This underscores the force of language ideologies in making language policy choices in a modern polity and how those choices impact ideas about cultural spaces and their relative value. Perhaps as important, this relational language hierarchy has been reproduced in the economic sphere, in which, against all social statistics to the contrary, Punjabiyat proponents conceptualize themselves as victims, oppressed, lost, and deprived. These ideas about Punjabi being an inferior language to Urdu have led to a movement that seeks specifically to refute these same contentions through forging new literature that draw upon the contributions of Islamic Sufi thinkers. This move works to undo the boundaries between 'high' Urdu culture and 'low' Punjabi by highlighting the philosophical contributions of the latter, and the effort has performative analogues, such as the annual celebration at Shah Hussain's tomb, which invokes the Punjabi past while simultaneously flagging Punjabi's role in furthering Islamic traditions as the language of creative Sufi thought.

The second intriguing lesson from the case of Punjab relates to perduring historical memory and the unsatisfying primordial versus constructivist dichotomy for explaining cultural formations. Punjab's much longer (nearly seventy years longer) experience with Urdu as an official language would perhaps have pointed to a more extensive displacement—or even atrophy—of Punjabi, particularly given the language ideological hierarchy that has relegated Punjabi to the low end of this prestige scale. That Punjabi has not experienced a more extensive erosion suggests some limits on a wholly constructivist position, for if that were the case, the national language/national culture project in Pakistan should have been a far easier task with far greater impact. But again, even during colonial rule, the historical record shows that Punjabi never 'disappeared' without state patronage; it simply moved to, and was maintained in, spheres beyond those constrained by state practices.[61] One does not need to posit a sort of romantic primordialism or Herderian rapture over the autarkic existence of national cultures in order to make sense of this, but we certainly need to recognize that the production and reproduction of a particular cultural space, via oral poetic forms, historical tales that 'pass down' exemplary heroes, and texts (written or oral) invested with spiritual authority, illustrate the conceptual importance of symbolic value of a language–culture complex, particularly when placed in a relational hierarchical matrix that assesses that value negatively in relation to others.

The close, indeed legitimizing, relationship of history to the modern nation-state[62] requires that the national past tell a story that results in the creation of the national present. But this teleological lens, with its narrow field of vision, always excludes other kinds of stories, especially if those other stories exist in a linguistic medium without state patronage. Thus, the historiographical effort of the Punjabiyat movement to 'reclaim' important figures from a Punjabi-language regional past has led to a new canon of heroes: Raja Poras, Dulla Bhatti, Rai Ahmed K̲h̲an Kharal, Puran of Sialkot, and his half-brother Raja Rasalu, to name a few. These resistant fighters, featured precisely to 'rescue' Punjab from a self-perception of submissive victim, have been drawn from all periods of Punjab's history and from other kinds of literatures not present in official life. Notably, this movement's idea of claiming 'Punjabiyat' does not limit itself to a post-Islamic world, something rather unexpected in light of official Pakistani state narratives. In fact, this is precisely where the Punjabiyat debate cross-cuts that of the nation-state: Whereas the state locates heroism in the great men of the Pakistan movement, the coming of Islam to the subcontinent, and the Muslim rulers of prepartition India—all chronicled in an overtly supraregional Urdu or English textual corpus—the Punjabiyat hero reclamation project explicitly seeks to reincorporate heroes marginal to national memory by drawing from folk songs and poetic forms, forms that can perdure through oral transmission even if excluded from formal historiography. The growth of this movement illustrates how processes of national legitimation through literary-historical exclusions that clearly sideline the contributions of constituent peoples create the perceived need to carve space for their inclusion.

NOTES

1 On the problem of Pakistani history's point of origin, see Ayesha Jalal, 'Conjuring Pakistan: History as Official Imagining', *International Journal of Middle East Studies*, 27 (1), 1995, pp. 73–89, esp. pp. 78–81.

2 Pierre Bourdieu, (trans. from French by Gino Raymond and Matthew Adamson), *Language and Symbolic Power,* Cambridge, Mass.: Harvard University Press, 1991.

3 Tariq Rahman, *Language, Ideology and Power: Language-Learning among the Muslims of Pakistan and North India,* Karachi: Oxford University Press, 2002, pp. 262–87.

4 Ernest Gellner, *Nations and Nationalism,* Ithaca, NY: Cornell University Press, 1983.

5 David D. Laitin, 'Language Games', *Comparative Politics,* 20 (3), 1988, pp. 289–302; David D. Laitin, *Identity in Formation: The Russian-Speaking Populations in the Near Abroad,* Ithaca, NY: Cornell University Press, 1998.

6 Paul R. Brass, *Language, Religion and Politics in North India,* Cambridge: Cambridge University Press, 1974; and Laitin, 'Language Games'.

7 Benedict Anderson, *Imagined Communities: Reflections on the Origin and Spread of Nationalism,* 2nd edn, London: Verso, 1991.

8 See E.J. Hobsbawm, *Nations and Nationalism since 1780: Programme, Myth, Reality,* 2nd edn, Cambridge: Cambridge University Press, 1992, pp. 54–63, esp. p. 54.

9 Bourdieu, *Language and Symbolic Power.*

10 On symbolic capital and the production of legitimate language, see especially Bourdieu, *Language and Symbolic Power,* pp. 43–65, 72–76.

11 Rounaq Jahan, *Pakistan: Failure in National Integration,* Dhaka: Oxford University Press, 1973. Philip Oldenburg, '"A Place Insufficiently Imagined": Language, Belief, and the Pakistan Crisis of 1971', *Journal of Asian Studies,* 44 (4), 1985, pp. 711–33.

12 Adeel Khan, 'Ethnicity, Islam and National Identity in Pakistan', Special issue, *South Asia,* vol. 22, 1999, pp.167–82; Stanley J. Tambiah, *Leveling Crowds: Ethnonationalist Conflicts and Collective Violence in South Asia,* Berkeley and Los Angeles: University of California Press, 1996.

13   Christophe Jaffrelot, *Pakistan: Nationalism without a Nation?*, New Delhi: Manohar/Zed Books, 2002.

14   Government of Pakistan, *Population and Housing Census of Pakistan 1998*, vols 1–5, Islamabad: Population Census Organisation, 1998.

15   Yunus Samad, 'Pakistan or Punjabistan: Crisis of National Identity', in Gurharpal Singh and Ian Talbot (eds), *Punjabi Identity: Continuity and Change*, New Delhi: Manohar, 1996, p. 67.

16   Oskar Verkaaik, 'The Captive State: Corruption, Intelligence Agencies, and Ethnicity in Pakistan', in Thomas Blom Hansen and Finn Stepputat (eds), *States of Imagination: Ethnographic Explorations of the Postcolonial State*, Durham, NC: Duke University Press, 2001, pp. 345–64.

17   Samad, 'Pakistan or Punjabistan'; Ian Talbot, 'From Pakistan to Punjabistan? Region, State and Nation Building', *International Journal of Punjabi Studies*, 5 (2), 1998, pp. 179–91. Ian Talbot, 'The Punjabization of Pakistan: Myth or Reality?', in Jaffrelot, *Pakistan: Nationalism without a Nation?*, pp.51–62.

18   Government of Pakistan, *Pakistan 2000 Agricultural Census,* Islamabad: Federal Bureau of Statistics, 2000.

19   Talbot, 'The Punjabization of Pakistan', p. 56.

20   Government of Pakistan, *Pakistan 2000 Agricultural Census,* Table 10.6.

21   Aamir Latif, 'Alarming Situation of Education in Pakistan', http://www.unesco.org/education/wef/en-news/pakistan.shtm, 2001, accessed 10 April 2008.

22   Government of Pakistan, *Population and Housing census of Pakistan: Advance Tabulation on sex, Age Group, Marital Status, Literacy and Educational Attainment (Figures Provisional)*, vol. 6, Islamabad: Population Census Organisation, Statistics Division, 1998, p. iv.

23   Anderson, *Imagined Communities*; Gellner, *Nations and Nationalism*.

24   Satish Deshpande, 'Imagined Economies: Styles of Nation Building in Twentieth-Century India', *Journal of Arts and Ideas,* nos 25–6, 1993, pp. 5–36; see especially p.10. E.J. Hobsbawm, *Nations and Nationalism,* pp. 56, 62. See also Lisa N.Trivedi, 'Visually Mapping the 'Nation': Swadeshi Politics in Nationalist India, 1920–30', *Journal of Asian Studies,* 62 (1), 2003, pp. 11–41; esp. p.12.

25   Nazir Ahmad Chaudhry, *Development of Urdu as Official Language in the Punjab (1849–1974),* Lahore: Government of Punjab, Directorate of Archives, 1977, p. 169. Ayesha Jalal, *Self and Sovereignty: Individual and Community in South Asian Islam since 1850,* New York: Routledge, 2000, pp. 102–38. Farina Mir, 'Imperial Policy, Provincial Practices:

Colonial Language Policy in Nineteenth-century India', *Indian Economic and Social History Review*, 43 (4), 2006, pp. 392–47.

26 Here I am relying upon linguistic anthropology's important concept of language ideology.

27 Mukhtar Zaman, (trans. from Urdu by S. Faizi), *Thoughts on National Language Policy* [*Qaumī Zabān kī Pālisī ke bare men̥ Cand K̲h̲yālāt*], Islamabad: National Language Authority/Muqtādira-e-Qaumī Zabān, 1985, p. 13.

28 Tariq Rahman, *Language and Politics in Pakistan,* Karachi: Oxford University Press, 1996, pp. 191, 208–9.

29 Punjabi proponents Fakhar Zaman, Aitzaz Ahsan, and Mohammad Hanif Ramey have all spent time in jail; Najm Hosein Syed was removed from his position as head of the Punjabi Department at Punjab University during the Zia regime, under the same accusation. See also Tariq Rahman, 'The Punjabi Movement in Pakistan', *International Journal of the Sociology of Language*, vol. 122, 1996, pp. 73–88.

30 Ronald Grigor Suny, and Michael D. Kennedy (eds), *Intellectuals and the Articulation of the Nation,* Ann Arbor: University of Michigan Press, 1999.

31 Christopher Shackle, 'Punjabi in Lahore', *Modern Asian Studies,* 4 (3), 1970, pp. 239–67.

32 Najm Hosain Syed, *Sīdhān,* 2nd edn, Lahore: Majlis Shah Hussein, 1973, pp. 77–121.

33 See also 'Puran of Sialkot', in Najm Hosain Syed, *Recurrent Patterns in Punjabi Poetry,* Lahore: Majlis Shah Hussein, 1968, pp. 73–112. For the Punjabi text, see Taufiq Rafat (trans. by Taufiq Rafat), *Qādir Yār: Puran Bhagat,* Lahore: Vanguard.

34 Najm Hosain Syed, *Tak̲h̲t-e-Lāhor: Dulla dī Vār,* Lahore: Majlis Shah Hussein, 1972.

35 Ibid.

36 See Mohammad Hanif Ramey, *Panjāb kā Muqaddama* [The case of Punjab]. Lahore: Jang, 1985, pp. 111–30.

37 Najm Hosain Syed, *Ik Rāt Rāvī Dī,* 2nd edn, Lahore: Rut Lekha, 2000. [Original edition, Idarah-e-Punjabi Adab, 1983]

38 Syed Massod Zahidi, *Pākistān kā Muqaddama* [The case of Pakistan]. Lahore: Classic, 1988; Zia, Shakil Ahmed, *Sindh kā Muqaddama: Hanīf Rāme ke Muqaddama-e-Panjāb Par Ahl-e-Sindh kā Jawāb-e Da'va* [The Case of Sindh: The People of Sindh's response to Hanif Ramey's 'Case of Punjab], Karachi: Shabil, 1987.

39 Fateh Mohammad Malik, *Punjabi Identity,* Lahore: Sang-e-Meel, 1989.

40 The World Punjabi Congress inaugurated its global activities with the 1986 conference, followed by another in 1989, and then intermittent gatherings throughout the 1990s. By the late 1990s, the frequency of these collective gatherings picked up, with meetings around the world as well as in Pakistan and India.

41 Sa'id Farani Kammi, *Panjābī Zabān Nahīṇ Maregī: Panjābī kā Muqaddama Panjāb Meṇ* (The Punjabi Language will Never Die: The Case of Punjabi in Punjab), Jhelum: Punjabi Esperanto Academy, 1988.

42 Farrukh Suhail Goindi, *Panjāb ka Maslā: Dīpoliṭsizeshan aur Awāmī Tahrık kā na Calnā* (The Problem of Punjab: Depoliticization and the Non-Movement of the People's Movement), Lahore: Jamhūrī Pablikeshanz, 1988.

43 Chaudhry Nazir Kahut, *Āo, Panjābī Ko Qatl Kareṇ* (Come, Let's Kill Punjabi!), Karachi: Wāris Shah, 1992. Shafqat Tanveer Mirza, *Resistance Themes in Punjabi Literature*, Lahore: Sang-e-Meel, 1992.

44 Sa'id Farani Kammi, *Panjābī Zabān Nahīṇ Maregī*, p. 7.

45 Ramey, *Panjāb kā Muqaddama*, pp. 76, 97.

46 Kahut, *Āo, Panjābī Ko Qatl Kareṇ*, p. 253.

47 Mansoor, *Punjabi, Urdu, English*, pp. 46–57.

48 Mohammad Ramey, *Panjāb kā Muqaddama*, pp. 93–4.

49 Kammi, *Panjābī Zabān Nahīṇ Maregī*, p. 53.

50 Ibid., p. 127.

51 Sikh literature, for the most part, does not find a place in this canon-in-formation. However, in 2000, an Arabic-script transliteration of the writings of Guru Nanak (the founder of the Sikh religion) was produced in Lahore. The volume is enormous, some thousand pages, and nearly three times the cost of an average book in Pakistan.

52 According to Farina Mir, *Hīr Rānjhā*, a Punjabi-language romance dating from at least the sixteenth century, was widely hailed—despite the British promulgation of Urdu as the state language—as a seminal text for Punjabis during the colonial period. In an apocryphal story, illustrative of the value placed on this literature, one Punjabi revolutionary, on trial for the murder of the former British governor of Punjab, was said to refuse taking oath on any book but Waris Shah's *Hīr*. See Farina Mir, *The Social Space of Language: Vernacular Culture in British Colonial Punjab*, Berkeley: University of California Press, 2010. Also Mirza, *Resistance Themes*, p. 210.

53 Kammi, *Panjābī Zabān Nahīṇ Maregī*, p. 27.

54 Government of Pakistan, 'Average Circulation of Newspapers and Periodicals by Langauge/Type, 1996–2006', http://www.statpak.gov.pk/depts/fbs/statistics/social_statistics/periodicals_by_language.pdf, 2007 accessed 10 April 2008.

55 William L. Hanaway, and Mumtaz Nasir, 'Chapbook Publishing in Pakistan', in William L. Hanaway and Wilma Heston (eds), *Studies in Pakistani Popular Culture*, Lahore: Lok Virsa/Sang-e-Meel, 1996.

56 Fakhar Zaman, *Bandīwān,* pp. 148–9; Fakhar Zaman, *Qaidī,* p. 119.

57 Images of Maulā Jaṭ are from the private collection of Lollywood Billboard Art, owned by Omar and Mariyam Khan, and were part of a larger exhibition at the Commonwealth Institute in London, 15 September–5 November 2001. Reproduced with permission of the owner.

58 Gillani Kamran, *Pakistan: A Cultural Metaphor,* Lahore: Ravian English Masters Association/Nadeem Book House, 1993, p. 247.

59 Mushtaq Gazdar, *Pakistan Cinema, 1947–1997,* Karachi: Oxford University Press, 1997, p. 134.

60 See 'Maula Jat—The Director's Cut', from the Hot Spot Online (www.thehotspotonline.com). The Hot Spot Web site is the most comprehensive source of film reviews, billboard art, and information on Pakistani cinema. The company holds video compact disc rights to *Maulā Jaṭ* and many other films.

61 Mir, *Social Space of Language.*

62 Prasenjit Duara, *Rescuing History from the Nation: Questioning Narratives of Modern China,* Chicago: University of Chicago Press, 1995; Ronald Grigor Suny, 'History', in Alexander J. Motyl (ed.), *Encyclopedia of Nationalism,* vol. 1, San Diego, CA: Academic Press, 2001, pp. 335–58.

Part II

Texts, Contexts, and Religious Identities

3

Louis E. Fenech

The History of the *Ẓafar-nāmah* of Guru Gobind Singh

I will carry a message to him and its words will be as a blade drawn from its scabbard. [Indeed,] a letter must be written whose edge is as sharp as a sword's and whose message booms like the thunder cloud.[1]

Shāh-nāmah Ferdausī

The *Ẓafar-nāmah* (Epistle of Victory) attributed to the tenth Sikh Guru, Guru Gobind Singh (d. 1708) has not been given its just due.[2] This assessment includes the fact that it is often appropriated as the historical source narrating the events surrounding the Khalsa Sikh evacuation of the fort of Anandpur in 1705 and the subsequent Battle of Chamkaur in which the Guru escaped with his life. Today, apart from its ostensible historical narrative, both the focus on and the focus of the text lies principally upon what scholars refer to as its moral emphasis; of holding true to one's vows and of galvanizing one's faith in protective embrace of Akal Purakh or God, values in good accord with those of the Guru Granth Sahib, the Sikh scripture, and well in keeping with the mandate of the late nineteenth-century Sikh reform movement, the Singh Sabha.[3] In this way the *Ẓafar-nāmah* serves to complement the *Khalsa Rahit* which gradually evolved during the eighteenth and nineteenth centuries and, as well, to support one of the central teachings found within the principal Sikh scripture, the Adi Granth, that is the supreme power of remembrance of and reliance upon the *nām*, the divine self-expression of the Eternal Guru.[4]

The letter has over the last fifty years, furthermore, become a controversial one with academics keenly arguing on the question as to whether it was written by Guru Gobind Singh or not. The majority of these scholars, however, work within the exact same framework despite their differences of opinion and as a result fail to apprehend the true worth of the document. Both interpretations situate the *Zafarnāmah* within the type of positivistic and structured historiography of the present, but its true value is as an eighteenth-century testament to the Sikh understanding not just of one episode in the later years of Guru Gobind Singh's life, but a demonstration of its way of constructing Sikh personhood, of 'Sikhness' or being Sikh, and of its way of simultaneously relaying information about the past, the present, and of course of the future, namely the Khalsa's eighteenth and nineteenth-century place in the South Asian Islamicate in the context of their loss of Guru Gobind Singh and his continuing presence in them and in the scripture.[5] In many ways the question as to its authorship is as doomed to failure as any search for origins.[6]

ZAFAR-NĀMAH, ḤIKĀYATS, AND THE DASAM GRANTH

Not only does the *Zafar-nāmah* narrate the evacuation of Anandpur but this forced departure is the act which precipitated its writing. With the death of the ninth Sikh Guru, Guru Tegh Bahadar at the hands of the Mughal executioner in 1675, his young son, Gobind, inherited the town of Anandpur, the site upon which was earlier situated the village of Makhowal on land purchased by the ninth Sikh Master from the raja of that area. It was perhaps the young Guru's expanding popular support in Anandpur specifically and the *pahaṛī* (hilly) region generally, coupled with his diplomatic fluency and efficiency and the power these developments suggested which caused the emperor Aurangzeb (d. 1707) to issue orders to local officials to prevent Sikhs and others from gathering at Anandpur in large numbers as early as 1693.[7] Sikh traditions tell us clearly of these increasing numbers by the early 1700s.[8] Such expansion led to Sikhs from Anandpur raiding neighbouring villages for supplies and this, in turn, dramatically enhanced the frustrations of the local pahaṛī rajas who were finally led to bury their differences, mount attacks against the Guru's patrimony, and lay collective siege to Anandpur in May 1704.

By December, frustrated by the Khalsa's tenacity, the representatives of the emperor and perhaps Aurangzeb himself had guaranteed the Guru's and his Khalsa's safe passage from the city were they to abandon the town's fort of Anandgarh, a promise which we are told was written on a copy of the Quran itself (as was standard practice in such matters since such a vessel sanctified one's oath).[9] The Guru was, tradition continues, well aware of the duplicitious nature of both the pahaṛī rulers and the Mughal authorities but he was nevertheless persuaded to accept this condition against his better judgement through the force brought to bear upon him by both his mother and his Sikhs according to later Sikh tradition. As Ratan Singh Bhangu, whose poetic *Srī Gur-panth Prakāś* (1841 CE) may be deemed illustrative of such tradition, states:

What could the Guru do when they refused to accept his advice? [What could the Guru do when] the people [of Anandpur] ran to all four directions [seeking safety]?[10]

The Guru along with his family and his Sikhs thus left the town behind and were almost immediately set upon by Mughal and Pahaṛī forces, as the Guru had inevitably foreseen. As the Guru and his Sikhs prepared to fend off their enemies, the Mughals captured his family and trapped the Guru in a small fort in the town of Chamkaur with a small number of his Khalsa. Fortunately the Guru survived this battle and made his way further westwards towards the villages of Dina-Kangar. It was here that the *Zafar-nāmah* was written.

According to tradition, this epistle was sent to the Emperor Aurangzeb as a rebuke for the emperor's failure to ensure the honourable conduct of both himself and his representatives in the Punjab during the siege of Anandpur and immediately afterwards.[11] Although the original letter is not extant, there are several early copies which have survived which only slightly differ from one another.[12] Many of these are likely to have been consulted in producing the numerous hand-written Gurmukhi manuscript copies of the *Zafar-nāmah* scattered throughout archives in northern India, almost all in Gurmukhi script and in the Persian language although occasionally in Punjabi translation.[13] Relatively rare are those manuscripts in Perso-Arabic script.[14]

The standard version of the letter is today found within the Dasam Granth and as such forms a revered part of the sacred Sikh inheritance, at least to most Sikhs.[15] For many Sikhs of course it is beyond doubt that the *Zafar-nāmah* was composed by the Guru himself as it begins with the phrase *Srī mukh vāk pātśāhī 10* 'Uttered from the blessed mouth of the tenth lord'.[16] Although many contemporary scholars see the *Zafar-nāmah* as a unique text within the Dasam Granth, it does appear as the first of twelve 'stories' or *Hikāyat*s written also in Persian and transcribed into Gurmukhi script.[17] The *Hikāyat*s may seem unrelated to the letter as these are generally composed of stories much like those in the *Pakhyān Charitr* sans the latter's more scatological and erotic dimensions;[18] but these nevertheless share with the Guru's epistle the narrative format; at least a fourth of the *Zafar-nāmah* attempts to narrate the Sikh past.[19] In the vast majority of eighteenth and nineteenth-century *Zafar-nāmah* manuscripts the *Hikāyat*s are an inextricable part of the *Zafar-nāmah*.[20] The bundling within the Dasam Granth therefore follows precedents we find in these, a model which has been in place since at least the early to mid eighteenth century.[21]

As to when the *Zafar-nāmah–Hikāyat*s became securely set within the canon, that is the Dasam Granth, we cannot say with certainty at this time. On the one hand one may conjecture that it was only relatively recently, that is in the past hundred years, as there are a number of eighteenth and nineteenth-century manuscripts of this massive compendium of texts which do not include it.[22] On the other hand, however, one can also assume that these were included (or better yet revered as the Dasam Granth was not compiled until well after the tenth Guru's demise) relatively early, perhaps within just a few years of Guru Gobind Singh's death in 1708. Here we turn to the question of why these compositions were included in a text the majority of whose compositions were in Brajbhasha and whose materials derived exclusively from Puranic and *itihāsic* Indic sources. Certainly there are themes within the *Ẓafar-nāmah* that are consonant with those in the Puranic sources, particularly notions of *razm* (battle) and *bazm* (delight) in Persian *masnavīs* which are not altogether dissimilar from the *vīr-ras* (heroic sentiment) and *śrǹgar-ras* (erotic sentiment) of Sanskrit, Hindi, and Brajbhasha poetics,[23] but inclusion in the Dasam Granth was not based solely upon corresponding values and subjects (if at all). Indeed, not only were these Persian compositions attributed to the tenth Guru and thus sacred— both because of the Guru's apparent allocation of Guruship to the words uttered by, with all due respect, the dead Gurus (that is, the Guru Granth) before his own death and the belief that this letter contained his 'essence' (that is, Guru substance) in the sense that this substance passed through his hand which came into contact with the instrument which wrote out these texts—but also such an inclusion would have rounded out his court culturally and politically. After all, the standard of courtly comportment and ceremony which was generally followed and simultaneously contested by the tenth Guru and his courtly entourage was that of the Mughal *darbar* (recall that this was the only style of government and court with which the tenth Guru and his Sikhs were intimately familiar) and thus the inclusion of Persian compositions in his court's oeuvre would have most likely been deemed essential and have served the aims of later Sikh hagi-ographers who looked back nostalgically to the Guru's beloved (and now mythic) darbar assigning to that period a heightened morality and grandeur in a current time of despair, crisis, and, frankly put for later poets, lack of patronage.

THE TEXT OF THE *ẒAFAR-NĀMAH*

As a text in itself the *Ẓafar-nāmah* follows the standards of all good Persian poetry, particularly the *masnavī* of which it is an example. The text today contains 111 *bait*s or couplets[24] all of which follow a strict rhyme scheme and a specific metre, in the latter case that of Ferdausi's famous *S̲h̲āh-nāmah* written in the *mutaqārib* metre.[25] Its first twelve baits form an invocation to the divine, an exordium one discovers in many classical Persian texts, such as for example Sadi's *Būstān*,[26] while its next ninety-nine baits are composed of the *dāstān* or 'story'. The *dāstān* begins by castigating Aurangzeb's apparent perfidy (baits 13–15; followed with further remonstrations in baits 45–50).[27] Although the author then explains his reason for doing so by perhaps alluding to the events of the siege of Anandpur and its abandonment by the Sikhs after assurances and oaths from the Mughal commanders (baits 18, 21, 57), we can only imagine how the author felt towards the man who was directly responsible for the murder of the tenth Master's father and indirectly for the murder of his sons.[28] After some moralizing which is clearly Islamicate in tenor (baits 16–17, 22), we then hear of what may be occurrences during the Battle of Chamkaur in which two of the Guru's sons were killed (baits 19–21, 26–41, 44) after which we become privy to the Guru's movements (bait 59). Finally the Guru actually makes his petition by requesting Aurangzeb to visit him in Kangra to set matters straight if the emperor is in fact 'a man who believes in the one God' (baits 58–60, 63–4). This is not so much a petition in the traditional sense as it is an order, a breach of which will result in the most severe consequences for Aurangzeb.[29]

Interspaced within these and often overlapping are maxims and morals regarding the importance of upholding one's oaths (baits 43, 44, 50–3, 55, 56, 57, 76–7, 84, 87, 109); further condemnations of the emperor who killed his own brothers and imprisoned his father (48, 49, 50, 66, 67–8, 69, 70, 79, 81, 85, 86, 87, and the second mesra of 94) along with his praises (89–93 and the first mesra of 94); descriptions of the Guru himself, especially his trust in God (43–4, 60, 63–4, 88, 95, 98, 105–6); and a healthy dose of soteriological dictums (65, 66, 82, 83, 84, 96, 107–8). This is therefore far more than a mere linear story, far more than a dāstān.

The Guru's *Zafar-nāmah* also includes allusions to the Persian canon, namely the works of Ferdausi and Sadi in this case, which writers used over many centuries to construct a literary culture with which all educated men and women throughout the Islamicate would have been familiar.[30] We have already witnessed this in regard to the *Zafar-nāmah's* references to the *Shāh-nāmah* but perhaps the most famous couplet of the tenth Guru's poem, bait 22, is in fact a direct borrowing from a couplet which appears in both Shaikh Sadi's *Gulistān* and *Būstān* texts with which Aurangzeb was undoubtedly familiar:

Zafar-nāmah	*Gulistān/Būstān*
When all strategies brought to bear are exhausted it is then lawful to draw the sword. [31]	When the hand is foiled at every turn it is then permitted to take the sword in hand.[32]

The exposition of this specific couplet is warranted as for Sikhs today the entire text of the *Zafar-nāmah* has been effectively collapsed into this single bait which provides sanction for earlier Sikh ideas of *mīrī-pīrī* (secular and spiritual sovereignty) and righteous battle (*dharam yuddh*). This hegemonic understanding may be credited in large part to the Sikh intellectuals of the aforementioned late nineteenth-century Singh Sabha reform movement who appropriated the couplet and attuned it to resonate with their modernist and colonial orientation.[33] By modernist and colonial what I mean to emphasize is an epistemological and political environment, largely (though by no means completely) Orientalist and essentialist in nature, in which identifiable groups (or better, groups made to be rigidly identifiable) within the British Punjab competed amongst one another for resources and privilege.[34] The Singh Sabha reading of bait 22 as premise for future action rather than justification for past activities, is in this light a facet of what Doris Jakobsh calls the 'politics of similarity' and Tony Ballantyne refers to as 'points of recognition', namely those mores, ideals, and values which both Sikhs and Britons believed they held in common. In this case the vigour and 'manliness' tempered by caution, rationality, and the rule of law in deciding to finally resort to armed struggle (more as an ideal of course in both cases as both British and Sikh history makes abundantly clear).[35] It is most likely that the Singh Sabha also read bait 22 in this manner as it tended to distance the Sikhs from both their Muslim (who were constructed as venal and violent, often drawing the sword out of its scabbard with impunity) and Hindu (who were portrayed as weak and effeminate, far too timid to ever draw weapons) Others. As Ballantyne tells us these 'points of recognition' rested on the 'identification and marginalization of other groups that lacked those qualities that the Sikhs and Britons suppos-edly shared'.[36] As a result bait 22 often becomes the pitch to which the entire *Zafar-nāmah* is adjusted at least in regard to modern Sikh identity politics.[37]

It is likely that pre-colonial Sikh traditions would not have rejected such an interpretation of Muslim and Hindu others out of hand nor would the assessment of Sikhness itself, as neither Hindu nor Muslim, have been fundamentally different. Certainly western Orientalism served the Singh Sabha project well as in the words of Christopher Bayly, it provided 'conditions, practical and ideologi-cal, which allowed people to reproduce...forms of social power and division',[38] but it would be an exaggeration to claim that Hindu and Muslim identities in pre-Singh Sabha literature were not caricatured in just this way (although pre-colonial Sikh tradition would most likely have targetted its ire towards the brahman imaginary rather than to local expressions of Hinduness). A quick read through either the *rahit-nama*s or Ratan Singh Bhangu's pre-eminent *gur-bilās* text makes this claim abundantly clear.[39]

AUTHORSHIP

Because of such references to classical Persian poetry the *Zafar-nāmah* is often surrounded by controversy: there are, as a consequence, Sikh scholars and scholars of Sikh history who find it quite unlikely that the *Zafar-nāmah* before us today was written by the Guru and sent to the emperor. This is not an unreasonable assumption since on the one hand, Guru Gobind Singh was the Guru and was thus beholden to no human being but to the One Lord alone in whom apparently the Guru has complete trust (a point the *Zafar-nāmah* often repeats) while on the other, tradition implies, one may ask how the tenth Master could bring himself to petition the emperor who had not only evicted the tenth Guru from his patrimony but had also visited much tragedy upon the Guru's family.[40] Scholars such as Gurbachan Singh Talib, however, say that the Guru could not have written the text because he was too well versed with Mughal literary and diplomatic conventions. How could he be otherwise when his literary court was staffed by poet-courtiers such as Bhai Nand Lal Goya and Kavi

Alam both of whose many years in the service of the Indo-Timurids, as the *mīr-munshī* or principal scribe of Prince Mu'azzam/Bahadar Shah himself in Nand Lal's case, made them thoroughly cognisant of Mughal etiquette and literary standards?[41] Sikh tradition also adamantly claims that as a child the Guru himself was as rigorously trained in the courtly arts as the princes of the royal Timurid line.[42] Would either Guru Gobind Singh or an erudite courtier like Nand Lal allow such an extraordinary, versed (rather than prose) petition to make its way to the emperor's court and perhaps be rejected out of hand?[43] Traditional *'arż dāsht,* Talib argues were straightforward documents in 'extremely courteous' and 'decorous' prose often petitioning the Mughal court to correct a local situation gone askew.[44] These were certainly not admonishing letters, however much deserved, which accused the Mughal ruler and his representatives in the harshest of terms, of breaking oaths upon the Quran, being ungodly, and straying from the principles of Islam (*dūr ast dīn*— 'he is far from faith').[45]

The counter to this claim, of course, is that educated Sikh courtiers and poets would indeed have encouraged the Guru to petition the Mughal in a style unlike what we find in the standard *'arż dāsht* to thus ensure that the tenth Master's requests caught the eye of some official and ultimately came under the emperor's gaze. After all if his court did indeed include ex-Mughal courtiers and poets it is likely that the Guru was aware that Aurangzeb's literary tastes tended towards poetry (despite the tenacious claims of the emperor's later biographers), especially poetry which included a strong moral emphasis, as the *Ẓafar-nāmah* most certainly does.[46] Furthermore, the receipt of uncommon form letters it appears did have precedents during the Indo-Timurid period of Indian history. Epistolographers and clerks, and writers and poets, both within and outside of the Mughal court were often guaranteed an audience with the emperor or his courtiers through the latter's receipt of the former's innovative prose or verse: 'Everyone writing a letter', claims Muhammad Ghani, '...endeavoured to produce as beautiful letters as he could [*sic*] so as to attract the notice of the addressee...'.[47] These included poets and litterateurs as revered as Akbar's *malikushshuarā* or poet laureate (made so in 1588) Abul Faiz ibn Mubaraq Allami known by the *takhallus* Faizi

(954–1004 H./1547–95 CE) the brother of Abul Fazl, many of whose *'arż dāsht* 'break away from the bondage of conventional phraseology and the rigid beginnings of the *murāfaāt* (citations employing expressions of humility)...'.[48] There is moreover the possibility that the *arż dāsht* in reference was not the *Zafar-nāmah* but a different text.[49]

One may be tempted to argue that the very title of the text would have reminded its intended royal Mughal audience of their own grand lineage as the term *Zafar-nāmah* is exactly the title of Amir Timur's famous biography completed well after his death in 1424–5 CE by Sharafuddin Ali of Yazd and reproduced within the darbars of various Timurid rulers throughout the eastern Islamicate, including both the Uzbeks and the Mughals.[50] 'Mullá Yazdí', we are told, 'was held in high estimation for his *inshá'* in his own country and in India'.[51] Surprisingly, the title of the work is, as we shall see, not noted within the Guru's letter itself (although the earliest *nastalīq* copy I have seen does begin with this title),[52] a fact which forces us to defer such speculation in this direction. We shall take up this theme of naming later on.

INTERNAL EVIDENCE

These conjectures are clearly justified as, once again, there appears to be no original text. Ultimately, therefore, one must suspend judgement on both the question of the *Zafar-nāmah*'s authorship and whether this was in fact the letter sent to Aurangzeb. There is little doubt that eighteenth-century Sikhs knew that the Guru had sent some letter to the emperor as word of such had spread throughout the oral narrative-scape of eighteenth-century Punjab and beyond very soon after the Guru's death in 1708 CE and perhaps earlier. Under the loving hand of tradition, moreover, the letter's very journey becomes a story unto itself, an arduous *sevā* undertaken by Bhai Daya Singh. Although Sainapati has the tenth Guru encourage Daya Singh to take a number of Khalsa Sikhs along with him as travelling companions[53] later accounts go so far as to include the four other members of the Panj Piare as Daya Singh's escorts despite the strong tradition which claims that at least three of these five were killed in the Battle of Chamkaur.[54] In the end, however, only Bhai Dharam Singh remains mentioned alongside Daya Singh.[55]

With these limitations in mind therefore let us take the internal evidence of the *Zafar-nāmah* on its own merit. As an account of the Sikh past the *Zafar-nāmah* continues the narrative which abruptly ends in the thirteenth chapter of the *Bachitar Nāṭak*. Although the *Zafar-nāmah* is not in the typical Brajbhasha of eighteenth-century Sikh texts its format is not dissimilar from most gurbilas literature, particularly the *Bachitar Nāṭak* as both works are in the first person: it interweaves divine praises and Sikh teachings with narratives of the Guru's battles and wanderings and affectionately crafted images of the tenth Guru, the latter of whom is portrayed as the righteous foil to the (mostly) wicked Aurangzeb (see particularly baits 106–10), an opposition which orients much of the action and helps structure its narrative. Indeed, the image of the Guru which we discover here is quite Islamicate in nature. Most telling perhaps is bait 16:

Anyone who comes under the shadow of the *humā* cannot be grasped by even the craftiest of crows.[56]

The next baits make clear the implicit idea here, that Guru Gobind Singh himself has been 'touched' by the humā's shade, the mythic Islamicate bird which grants sovereignty to all those who come into contact with its shadow. For this reason, the tenth Guru and many of his Sikhs escaped Anandpur and Chamkaur and for this reason as well, the text implies, the first course of action the Guru undertakes afterwards is to confront Aurangzeb in this versed letter as an equal. This is therefore a testament to the sovereignty of Guru Gobind Singh and, by extension, the independence of his Sikhs. The humā couplet above thus foreshadows bait 61 which relates Guru Gobind Singh's implicit rejection of an offer which Aurangzeb presented the Guru, induction and incorporation into the Mughal system of *mansabdārī*. Here the tenth Guru is reminding the emperor of his earlier proposal:

Your title will be one thousand horse if you come to this area and meet me.[57]

This dismissal once again makes the implicit claim of collective sovereignty for the Sikhs as the Guru refuses to take on a sub imperial title.

The *Zafar-nāmah* also devotes baits to the praise of the Guru's Sikhs. Although the many references to Guru Gobind Singh's devotion to the Lord may also be taken by extension to apply to his warriors, it is in the act of battle that the Sikhs merit particular attention. The account of the Battle of Chamkaur begins with a rhetorical question:

What could a small number of starved men do when an army ten lakhs strong attacked without warning?[58]

The answer is a great deal as the next twenty or so baits make clear. At the end we see a battlefield which runs red with blood. Here then we find another opposition, Aurangzeb's near infinite resources against those few of the Guru which also helps situate the narrative, an opposition we hear at length in the *Zafar-nāmah*'s closing baits (105–11). Let us be clear that the tenth Guru in no way desires to fight, but fight he and his Sikhs must when such action is forced upon them (baits 18, 20–2).[59] This will become the typical way in which Sikhs will understand themselves and their reactions to armed struggle and violence, playing into and enhancing ideas already present in such notions as *mīrī-pīrī*.[60] The final bait narrating the battle (bait 41) likewise ends with the same rhetorical question in bait 19 bringing to a close that particular segment of the *Zafar-nāmah* (although bait 44 briefly reintroduces the battle in the context of the theme of divine protection) adding a particular texture and depth to this document to which eighteenth- and nineteenth-century Sikh audiences. This is a glorious testament to Sikh mettle in both battle and prayer, and was crafted as a Sikh *Shāh-nāmah,* the text which supplies the mythic template for the *Zafar-nāmah*'s author and which accounts for the choice of metre. This is therefore a text which portrays an indigenous Sikh understanding of the past in much the same way as the *charitr*s I spoke about in an earlier study.[61]

This awareness allows us to couple the text with another which likewise narrates Sikh interpretations of the past. It seems clear that the *Bachitar Nāṭak* and the *Zafar-nāmah* are closely related. The *Bachitar Nāṭak* as it stands today ends at its fourteenth chapter which forms a closing invocation to the divine thus paralleling those we find at the beginning of the Wonderful Drama. The thirteenth is contextually far more crucial in my opinion as it forms the end of the *apnī kathā* which begins in chapter six. What makes the strongest claim for the Guru's authorship of this text is the fact that the narrative ends just here, in 1696 right after Prince Mu'azzam makes his way into the Punjab. Chapter thirteen does provide a valid end to this narrative as we here see the Indo-Timurid recognition of the Guru's authority. While the *Bachitar Nāṭak* ends with the Guru's recognition by the state, the *Ẓafar-nāmah* portrays the Guru's attempt to engage the state diplomatically as an equal. Certainly the number of diplomatic treatises which had been written by his kavi darbars suggests that Guru Gobind Singh was more than familiar with the arts of diplomacy.[62] The *Ẓafar-nāmah* may thus be understood as extending this apnī kathā narrative into the early eighteenth century.

THE HISTORIOGRAPHY OF THE *ẒAFAR-NĀMAH*

I wish to turn now to how Sikhs understood the *Ẓafar-nāmah* in the eighteenth and nineteenth centuries. The earliest written Sikh source to mention the letter was *Gur Sobhā* (Radiance of the Guru). Its narrative is one which will continue with little change over the next century.[63] Sainapati begins by telling us that the Guru decided to write an epistle to Aurangzeb after having been deceived by him at Anandpur (1–13). The Guru summoned Daya Singh and explained the situation to him, asking him to collect a number of Sikhs and march down to southern India to hand the emperor this letter (14). Disguising themselves as Mughal soldiers (*ahadī*) the Singhs set off southwards (15–16), travelling first to Delhi and then through a number of towns, all the while meeting up with local *sangats* (17–20) and visiting *dharamsalas* every dawn. Eventually they made it to the house of the Sikh merchant Bhai Jetha in Ahmedabad (21) where they set up camp for a few days.

Over time, Bhai Daya Singh, unable to see Aurangzeb, becomes despondent and sends off a letter to the Guru in the hands of two couriers requesting help in securing a meeting with the emperor (25–30). The tenth Guru then asks the couriers to make all haste back to Daya Singh (29–30) after which he relates the contents of the letter (31–7) noting that he had himself desired to visit the emperor but was unable to because of the deceit in which all of the emperor's people engaged (33). Eventually Bhai Daya Singh meets Aurangzeb who reads the letter and sends a macebearer off with the loyal Sikh, with his response to the Guru's petition for the long and demanding return trip to the Guru (38–40). The arduous nature of the letter's journey makes its presentation very significant, enhancing the letter's prestige and importance. Bhai Daya Singh only meets again with the Guru at the beginning of the fifteenth chapter after a difficult trek back home, and gives him the news that Aurangzeb had died in Ahmadnagar.[64]

It is perhaps because the letter's journey is so fraught with danger and so underscores the rare bravery of the Sikhs involved that it retains this basic outline. Some minor changes do, however, appear in later texts. Although both *Mahimā Prakaś* texts all but ignore the narrative journey, it is taken up with much enthusiasm in Kesar Singh Chhibbar's account. In the *Baṅsāvalī-nāmā* Daya Singh makes his way to Aurangzeb disguised as a Hajji with a new copy of the Quran which he claims was brought directly from Mecca (10:589–92). Here we once again become privy to an exchange between Bhai Daya Singh and Aurangzeb in which Aurangzeb asks if the Khalsa has been created:

whilst reading the *pothī* [that is the Guru's letter] Aurangzeb's face went black. Having finally finished reading it the emperor asked, 'Has this [new] panth [the Khalsa] come into existence?' Daya Singh answered, 'Yes, majesty, it has'. [65]

In reply to which [Aurangzeb] commanded [in Persian]: *īnrā qatl mīkonam*, 'I will kill it.' [66]

This exchange in later works will become both more dramatic and more heated, and will ultimately demonstrate once again the independent sovereignty of the tenth Guru and his Sikhs. Such may be witnessed symbolically in the *Mahimā Prakaś Kavitā* (1776 CE). Terribly remorseful after becoming aware of how much suffering he has caused the tenth Sikh Guru Aurangzeb voices a desire to meet him. To this end,

[The emperor] then spoke to [Daya Singh] in this manner: '[Take] this attire [*bhes*] to your Guru. On the right side [of it] there is a single white hair from the hair of my beard'.[67]

This gifting is reminiscent of the ritual of robing ceremonies in which the emperor shares his person/substance with the grantee, symbolically incorporating him into his own person, a ritual that lay at the very heart of Mughal diplomacy. Indeed as far as such rituals are concerned the most precious and desirable garments are those actually worn by the emperor himself where contact with the emperor's substance is the most intimate, which seems to be the situation here. As such the suggestion of the sovereignty of the tenth Guru is unmistakable and for Sarup Das Bhalla inevitable.[68]

This suggestion becomes far more explicit in both the *Sau Sākhīān* and *Sūraj Prakāś* the latest of the gurbilas texts (1843 CE), as Daya Singh and his now frequent companion Dharam Singh have entered into the august presence of the emperor and presented him with the Guru's letter:

They presented the Guru's letter and having so placed it in front of the emperor they uttered [the Sikh battle cry], '*Vahiguru!* Victory belongs to the Guru!' As they said this they looked towards and contemplated the written instructions [of the Guru thus averting their eyes from the emperor's person]. They came forward with the Guru's order (*parvānā*) thus demonstrating their commitment to Sikhi.[69]

By failing to comport themselves in the prescribed manner while in the emperor's presence and purposefully averting their gaze to focus upon the letter of the Guru as his symbolic representation, Bhais Daya and Dharam Singh are clearly asserting the Guru's independence, their independence, and as well that of the collective Sikh panth.[70] This is the very prognostication which Santokh Singh elaborates in a number of lines after these.[71] Indeed, in Santokh Singh's early to mid nineteenth-century environment this was a very commonplace way of appreciating Guru Gobind Singh's continued dynamic presence amongst the Sikhs. It is just a small step from the ideas implicit in this narrative to the eventual understanding of the *Zafar-nāmah* as *bāṇī*, sacred writ. Here the text itself stands in for the Guru.

But let us now return to Sainapati. It is difficult to know beyond doubt if the letter about which Sainapati is speaking is today's *Zafar-nāmah*.[72] We come close when we compare *Gur Sobhā* with certain baits.

A man should keep his word. He should not have something on his lips and something else in his heart. [73]

Know that a man must keep his promise (*sukhan*) to someone. A promise given should be kept. Know that the task [explicit in the oath] must be undertaken by heart or by life: It must certainly be done with no delay.[74]

But whether Sainapati read the letter or not is not the point I wish to make here. In the light of the evidence available there is simply no way we can know the answer to this question. What seems quite significant and compounds our ignorance is the fact that Sainapati only refers to the text throughout his account as nothing more than a 'letter', *likhā*.[75]

The failure to name the text seems to indicate that for Sainapati and other court poets what would eventually become the *Zafar-nāmah* was not particularly revered at the start; certainly worth mentioning as it was written by the Guru but nothing more than a document that one ruler would send to another. It is perhaps for this reason that the *Zafar-nāmah* was not entered into what became the Dasam Granth until the later nineteenth century. I must add that such an understanding of this letter was not true for all Sikhs who, it appears, did very much prize and revere even the succinctly written *hukam-nama*s of their day.

Sainapati's view of the document was not to last as within a year of the tenth Guru's death a series of anecdotes conveyed not by a Khalsa Sikh as one would expect but rather by an Udasi Sikh named Sewa Das appears. The *Parchīān Pātśāhī Dasvīn kī* apparently found a ready audience well into nineteenth century as evinced by its influence on later works.[76] The episode which merits our consideration is the thirteenth which modifies Sainapati's quite dramatically and forms the principal way of understanding the *Zafar-nāmah* until the early twentieth century. Guru Gobind Singh condemned the 'Turks' and commanded the Khalsa:

'Go, battle the Turks and slay them.' The Khalsa replied, 'O true king, the emperor of the Turks has ten lakhs of cavalry. We will nevertheless obey your command'. [The Guru then said,] 'A letter will be written to the [emperor of the] Turks [which when read] will kill him'. The Khalsa then said, 'O true king, if the emperor will die in this way tremendous praise will ensue'.

The Guru Baba then wrote the letter and titled it *Zafar-nāmā*, the Epistle of Victory.[77]

Here for the first time we are presented with the name of the text, The Epistle of Victory,[78] an interesting title given the Guru's circumstances. What type of victory does our author here suggest? The explicit victory here it appears is not a singularly moral one.[79] The victory rather is complete, a triumph which ultimately leaves Aurangzeb dead.

When Aurangzeb recited [the *Zafar-nāmah*] aloud he looked at and addressed Bhai Daya Singh. He asked, 'Has the Khalsa been created?' Bhai Daya Singh replied, 'Indeed, sir, it has'. Aurangzeb spoke again, 'It should not have been created now. Catastrophe lies ahead'. As soon as Aurangzeb spoke these words his face turned [ghostly] white and he died.[80]

The *Zafar-nāmah* thus appears to accrue supernatural power over time. Indeed, the mere reading of the text is an act which destroys the wicked whilst fulfilling the requests of the righteous, a claim often enunciated clearly in the closing lines of many *Zafar-nāmah* manuscripts:

Any Sikh of the Guru who reads, hears, and/or contemplates [the *Zafar-nāmah*] will have his wishes (*bhāvnā*) all fulfilled. He will obtain release as well as destroy the [endless] cycle of birth and death. This is the greatest fruit. No other fruit exists like it. [That Sikh] who goes to battle and hears and/or reads the *Zafarnāmā* will be victorious. As Aurangzeb was killed and victory obtained so will the person who listens to and/or reads the *Zafar-nāmā* procure victory. [Reflect on this] and say '*Vāhigurū Vāhigurū Vāhigurū jī!*' [81]

Of course such claims as to the power of the Guru's words whether written or heard should elicit little surprise in the light of doctrines such as Guru Granth. Since the time of the Gurus themselves their words have held a tremendously powerful place in the collective Sikh imagination, playing a very important role in the construction of Sikh personhood.

Sikh texts which appear after the *Parchīān* continue to suffuse their *Zafar-nāmah* narratives with such ultimate power. This is the case in Sarup Das Bhalla's text[81] as too in Sukkha Singh's gurbilas:

The place [at which] the divine Guru who is the Ocean of Mercy stopped was the village of Kaṅgaṛ [about 1.5 kilometres south of Dina]. At that time, he spoke the following words to the Khalsa: 'Who is there to kill the emperor? Either kill him with a written letter (*kāgad likh*) or smite him [while] facing the battlefield'. [82]

It is of course the former course of action which the Guru takes and the end result although not immediate is easily as miraculous:

After having read the Epistle of Victory (*Bij-nāmā*) the emperor suffered afflictions [of various types] as if the 'Servant of God' (*jan*) himself had held [Aurangzeb's] breath and heart with power. The red colour of his body turned into a disagreeable (jaundiced) appearance. The emperor then became distressed and died. The empire of the Turk (*grih turk*) was thrown into lamentation. The many days of grief cannot be reckoned. No one came outside for even a small amount of time. In this way the respectable Daya Singh had obtained victory on the field and returned [to the Guru]. [83]

Whilst in the *Bansāvalī-nāmā*:

[Aurangzeb] continued reading [the *Zafar-nāmah*] inside [his palace] for forty days. He only came outside when he died.' [84]

There is a nice symmetry observed in these accounts. While Guru Nanak brings a descendant of Timur to the throne through his blessings,[85] Guru Gobind Singh destroys another through his reproach. It is only fitting in this light therefore that in these same and other accounts dealing with the life of Guru Gobind Singh, the tenth Guru embraces Guru Nanak's legacy by both ensuring and blessing the succession of Aurangzeb's eldest son, Prince Muazzam/Bahadar Shah.[86]

Let us finally conclude with Santokh Singh, the preeminent conveyer of gurbilas tradition. It is likely that by Santokh Singh's time as new networks of communication were being established by both the kingdom of Ranjit Singh and the British presence in India, literate Sikhs had become somewhat more familiar with the historiography surrounding Aurangzeb, in that he had died many months if not a year after the letter of the tenth Guru had been delivered. Nevertheless *Sūraj Prakaś* still manages to modify the miraculous in the *Zafar-nāmah* narratives to accommodate this annoying truth. To this end Aurangzeb finishes hearing the *Zafar-nāmah* after which he is asked by Daya Singh to give back the quiver which the Guru had given him as a keepsake (*amānat; dhrohar*) after the two had transported themselves to Mecca through supernatural means. Earlier upon receiving the said quiver the Guru explained that it was to be returned upon his meeting with the Guru's Sikhs (1:31:23–4):

He gave both the quiver and written orders [of safe conduct] to Daya Singh. Having dismissed them (Daya and Dharam Singh) [the emperor] became very anxious. Afterwards [as a result] a sickness sprouted within him. He knew completely that this would lead to his own death. [87]

Aurangzeb's death would wait until the thirty-seventh section of the first *ain* of *Sūraj Prakāś* in time for Daya Singh's long and arduous journey back to the Guru with Aurangzeb's two macebearers to come to an end. Their reunion is a joyous one during which Daya Singh quickly relays all of the information of his encounter with the emperor to the Guru and his gathered Sikhs, finally handing over to the tenth Master the quiver-deposit. It is then that Daya Singh tells the Guru of Aurangzeb's condition after the emperor had read the *Zafar-nāmah*. Once again, the main cause of illness is familiarity with the contents of the Guru's missive. Daya Singh explains:

[after I gave the emperor] the *Zafar-nāmā* which you wrote, we withdrew and were sent outside. Immediately, the emperor became distressed and going inside once again we could not see him. He became aware of his sins and these set upon every direction of his heart. It was said that he lay seriously ill but there was no outcry [as he was hidden from view].[88]

To this the Guru replies:

Hearing [Daya Singh's report] the True Guru said, 'Well done. Aurangzeb's death will be deprived of delay'. [89]

Here Santokh Singh like the gurbilas authors before him is expressing a theme of destruction which is also tantalizingly hidden within the intertextual resonances of the *Zafar-nāmah*. But this is a story for another day and another paper.

Today the *Zafar-nāmah* has been almost completely shorn of its miraculous content thanks, in part, to the tireless campaigns of the Singh Sabha and those erudite and passionate Sikhs who have inherited its renown.[90] Its words still possess a supernatural power of course as its inclusion within the Dasam Granth testifies, although it is rarely sung during *kirtan* or in kirtan darbars. It is certainly used in *katha* however to help buttress popular Sikh traditions regarding the evacuation of Anandpur, the Battles of Chamkaur and Muktsar, and as well the deaths of the Four Sahibzade. All this notwithstanding, controversy over its authorship remains, and will most likely do so until the text is finally appreciated for what it does contribute to Sikh understandings of Sikh personhood for within its poetry we find expressions of a Sikh identity distinguished from other specific identities within the Punjab and as well a declaration of Sikh sovereignty well in keeping with the claim of both the rahit-nama and the gurbilas literature.

NOTES

1 *Shāh-nāmah Ferdausī* (6th edn, Tehran: Ansharat Khushah, 1382/2003), p. 98. Rostam the hero of Iran is here speaking to Shah of Iran, Kai Kavus after the latter has read a letter sent by the antagonistic Shah of Mazendaran. This article is part of a much larger study on the *Zafar-nāmah* of Guru Gobind Singh. Fenech (forthcoming).

2 The copy of the *Zafar-nāmah* which I will reference throughout this essay appears in Ganda Singh (ed.), *Maākhiz-i Tavārīkh-i Sikhān jild avval: Ahd-i Gurū Sahibān* (Sources of Sikh History volume 1: the Age of the Sikh Gurus), Amritsar: Sikh History Society, 1949, pp. 64–71.

3 Kahn Singh Nabha, *Gurmat Sudhākar*, 4th edn, Patiala: Bhasha Vibhag, Punjab, 1970, pp. 84–5.

4 The Khalsa Rahit is the Khalsa Sikh code of conduct which was, according to Sikh tradition, dictated by Guru Gobind Singh before his death in 1708. Although there are many different Rahit traditions in the precolonial Sikh period, today the Rahit has been standardized as the Sikh Rahit Maryada. It is in this document for example that we hear of the five symbols of corporate Khalsa Sikh identity, the Five Ks (uncut hair, comb, breeches, bangle, dagger). The Adi Granth (Primal Text), also known as the Guru Granth Sahib, is the Sikh scripture and understood as *gurbāṇī* (uttererances of the Guru), and as such is believed to contain the mystical presence of the divine.

5 This accounts for the eighteenth-century understanding of what Sikhs call Guru Granth-Guru Panth. Under this rubric the eternal Guru is mystically present in both the scripture and the gathered Sikh community.

6 My understanding of Islamicate draws upon the work of Marshall Hodgson, *The Venture of Islam: Conscience and Change in a World*

Civilization I: The Classical Age of Islam, Chicago: University of Chicago Press, 1974, pp. 57–60. Extending this geo-cultural paradigm eastwards towards South Asia we discover a dynamic, South Asian Islamicate culture whose strands include Central Asian nomadic war bands, Persian, Rajput, and other local groups in the service of the imperial and subimperial darbars of the Mughal empire.

7 Chetan Singh refers to this order from a collection of *Akhbarāt* issued in the 36th regnal year. These are not included in Ganda Singh's collection. Chetan Singh, *Region and Empire: Panjab in the Seventeenth Century*, New Delhi: Oxford University Press, 1991, p. 300, n. 120. Ratan Singh Bhangu tells us of growing Sikh numbers and the consequences of these: Jit Singh Sital (ed.), *Srī Gur-panth Prakāś krit Bhāī Ratan Singh Bhangū Śahīd* 16:31, Amritsar: Shiromani Gurdwara Parbandhak Committee, 1994, p. 82; also 18:6, p. 87.

8 Ganda Singh (ed.), *Kavī Saināpati Rachit Srī Gur Sobhā* 11:2–4, Patiala: Punjabi University Publication Bureau, 1988, p. 116:Daily the Khalsa took the Guru's darshan and was pleased. Regularly such divine vision was obtained. The Sikhs of the Khalsa served the True Guru selflessly and love blossomed within their hearts. They came from towns [throughout the Punjab] and settled at that place [Anandpur]. They took the darshan of the Lord (*prabh purakh*) and no doubt remained [within them]. The Khalsa overcame as many villages as resided nearby. Two years and a number of days were passed in this way.

9 Online edition of Santokh Singh, *Gur-pratāp Sūraj Granth*, 6:27:25–6, p. 212 at http://www.ik13. com/sri_gur_ partap_ suraj_garanth.htm. (popularly known as *Sūraj Prakāś*). Here Aurangzeb says the following:From the beginning I had sworn an oath on the Quran that no harm whatsoever would ever come your way.Also see 6:30:1–2, p. 230.

10 Sital (ed.), *Srī Gur-panth Prakāś* 18:31, p. 90.

11 See Ganda Singh's comments in his *Kavī Saināpati Rachit Srī Gur Sobhā*, Patiala: Punjabi University Publication Bureau, 1988, pp. 39–41; 134, footnote 2. [Hereafter *Gur Sobhā*]. Within the *Zafar-nāmah* itself bait 14 informs the reader of the dishonesty of Aurangzeb's representatives, the *bakhshī* and *dīvān*. *Zafar-nāmah* 14, Ganda Singh (ed.), *Maākhiz-i Tavārīkh-i Sikhān*, p. 66.

12 Slight differences in Persian masnavis and ghazals are also not altogether uncommon. There are versions of the *Zafar-nāmah* which have fewer than 111 baits whilst others claim more. See Shahryar (trans.), *Śrī Gurū Gobind Singh jī Rachit Zafarnāmā [Panjābī vich kāvi-anuvād]*, Amritsar: Singh Brothers, 5th edn, 2003.

13 For example, Guru Nanak Dev University mss. 59*a*; 199*kh* and 1116, fols. 1a–26a; 292; 464*a*; as well as mss. SHR 1540 and SHR 2218 at

the Khalsa College Sikh History Research Department in Amritsar; and Punjabi University, Patiala ms. 115665, fols 1a–6b.

14 Guru Nanak Dev University ms. 5043, fols 1a–4a.

15 The Dasam Granth includes compositions attributed to the tenth Guru in both Brajbhasha and Persian. As the Brajbhasha compositions draw heavily from Hindu mythology, many Sikhs refuse to accept the text as the work of the Guru although traditions of it having been the work of the Guru are found as early as the mid eighteenth century. The *Zafar-nāmah* is however generally agreed to be the work of Guru Gobind Singh. The Dasam Granth stands apart from the central Sikh scripture, the Adi Granth. This latter text is believed to contain the mystical presence of God (Akal Purakh or the True Guru) and is such particularly revered.

16 Guru Nanak Dev University ms. 1000, f. 1a.

17 See Kahn Singh Nabha, *Gurmat Sudhākar*, 4th edn, Patiala: Bhasha Vibhag, Punjab, 1970, p. 84, fn. 1.

18 The *Pakhyān Charitr* (Stories upon stories) is the longest segment of the Dasam Granth and is generally known in English as the 'Wiles of Women'. This text is composed of 403 stories the majority of which deal with the moral complexity of women although a number of these also point to the moral lapses of men. These stories are akin to the erotic banter and small talk often heard in the women's quarters and so it is likely that the appellation stuck, based not so much on the fact that these stories were about women but rather that these were recited by women in the privacy of the women's quarters or *zenana*.

19 For history and literary genre see V.N. Rao, David Shulman, and Sanjay Subrahmanyam, *Textures of Time: Writing History in South India 1600–1800*, New York: Other Press, 2003, pp. 3–5.

20 See for example mss. SHR 1456, 2244c, 1540, 2218, 2243b, and 2300b at Khalsa College all of which combine the two. Many printed editions of the *Zafar-nāmah* in Gurmukhi also include the *Hikāyats* such as Gurbachan Singh 'Makin' (trans.), *Zafarnamah* (Epistle of Victory), Ludhiana: Lahore Book Shop, 2005.

21 See Piara Singh Padam (ed.), *Bhāī Kesar Singh Chhibbar Krit Bansāvalī-nāmā Dasān Pātsāhīān kā* 10:587, Amritsar: Singh Brothers, 1997, p. 180. *The Parchīān Pātisāhī Dasvīn kī* attributed to Sewa Das Udasi is a much earlier source apparently, perhaps dating back to 1709 CE. Kharak Singh and Gurtej Singh (ed.), *Parchian Sewadas*, Punjabi text on p. 133 [hereafter *Parchīān*]. An almost identical sākhī is related in Kirpal Das Bhalla's *Mahimā Prakāś Vārtak* completed sometime in the later 1740s. See Kulvinder Singh Bajwa (ed.), *Mahimā Prakāś Vārtak*, Amritsar: Singh Brothers, 2004, sakhi 126, pp. 177–81.

22 W.H McLeod, *Sikhism*, New York: Penguin, 1997, p. 178 and the famous 1897 report by Munna Singh *et al.*, *Rapoṭ*, pp. 4, 6. Some Dasam Granth manuscripts which include neither the *Ẓafar-nāmah* nor the *Ḥikāyats* are Punjabi University ms. 115648 and 115407 although these seem incomplete for the most part. See also Ratan Singh Jaggi, *Dasam Granth dā Krtritav* [The Authorship of the Dasam Granth], New Delhi: Punjabi Sahit Sabha, 1966, pp. 101–2, 108. Later nineteenth and early twentieth-century versions do, however, include the text. See for example Punjabi University mss. 115595 and 115596. In these it is clear that the *Ḥikāyats* are a part of the *Ẓafar-nāmah*.

23 Recently, Shackle has suggested that the *Ẓafar-nāmah–Ḥikāyats* form a binary of *razm* and *bazm* symmetrical to the *Bachitar Nāṭak* and the *Pakhyān Charitr as vīr-ras* and *śriṅgar-ras*. Christopher Shackle, 'Zafar-nama', *Journal of Punjab Studies*, 15 (2), 2008, p. 165.

24 There are many printed and online editions of the 111-bait text, some of which package it with the *Ḥikāyats*. In the latter there are four additional Brajbhasha couplets inserted at the end of bait 111 (sometimes claimed to be the invocation beginning the second of the *Ḥikāyats*). *Ẓafar-nāmā* 112–15, Dasam Granth, p. 1394.

25 Traditionally the *mutaqārib* metre consists of a short-long-long syllable scheme repeated eight times within a bait with slight variations.

26 See G.M. Wickens (trans.), *Morals Pointed and Tales Adorned: The Būstān of Sadī*, Toronto: University of Toronto Press, reprint, 1978.

27 *Ẓafar-nāmah* 13, Ganda Singh (ed.), *Maākhiz-i Tavārīkh-i Sikhān*, p. 66.

28 See for example Piara Singh Padam, '*Zafarnāmā*', in Mohinder Kaur Gill, *Dasam Gurū Rachnā Saṅsar*, Delhi: Sanpreet Prakashan, 1999, pp. 119–23, esp. p. 119.

29 *Ẓafar-nāmah* 82 in Ganda Singh (ed.), *Maākhiz-i Tavārīkh-i Sikhān*, p. 70:To do something other than fulfill your oath [and meet me] will ensure that the Lord himself forgets you [on the Day of Judgment].

30 Muzaffar Alam, 'The Pursuit of Persian: Language in Mughal Politics', *Modern Asian Studies*, 32 (2), 1998, and his 'The Culture and Politics of Persian in Precolonial Hindustan', in Sheldon Pollock (ed.), *Literary Cultures in History: Reconstructions from South Asia*, Berkeley: University of California Press, 2003. Both Babur and Jahangir in their respective personal chronicles mention such.

31 *Ẓafar-nāmah* 22, Ganda Singh (ed.), *Maākhiz-i Tavārīkh-i Sikhān*, p. 66.

32 M.H. Tasbihi (ed.), *The Persian–English Gulistan or Rose Garden of Sadi* [trans. Edward Rehatsek], Tehran: Shargh's Press, 1967, p.

575. Nurallah Iranparast (ed.), *Būstān-i Sadī*, Tehran: Danesh, CE 1352/1973, p. 90, line 12 in this text.

33 During the eighteenth and early to mid nineteenth-century this focus was altogether absent as Sikhs of this period by contrast did not seem to give any preference to this bait at all nor to any extracanonical interpretations of it let alone casting it as the epistle's guiding principal. Indeed, *Zafar-nāmā Saṭīk* (Commentary upon the *Zafar-nāmah*) manuscripts of this period provide quite straightforward Punjabi translations of this passage without any further elaboration nor without mentioning its earlier incarnations within either the *Gulistān* or the *Būstān*, essential in more comprehensively working through the robust texture of the couplet itself and its relation to the *Zafar-nāmah* as a whole, something I do in Fenech (forthcoming).

34 The most recent commentary and description of the environment I have in mind appears in Giorgio Shani, *Sikh Nationalism and Identity in a Global Age*, London and New York: Routledge, 2008, pp. 11–14. Further background appears in Harjot Oberoi, *The Construction of Religious Boundaries: Culture, Identity and Diversity in the Sikh Tradition*, New Delhi: Oxford University Press, 1994; Kenneth W. Jones, *Arya Dharam: Hindu Consciousness in 19th-Century Punjab*, Berkeley: University of California Press, 1976; and N.G. Barrier, *The Sikhs and Their Literature (A Guide to Tracts, Books and Periodicals, 1849–1919)*, Delhi: Manohar Book Service, 1970.

35 Doris Jakobsh, *Relocating Gender in Sikh History: Transformation, Meaning and Identity*, New Delhi: Oxford Unviersity Press, 2003, pp. 58–69; Tony Ballantyne, *Sikh Cultural Formations in an Imperial World*, Durham and London: Duke University Press, 2006, p. 26.

36 Ballantyne, *Between Colonialism and Diaspora*, p. 26. The original context of bait 22 within both the *Gulistān* and *Būstān* is not a justification for action previously taken but rather as a maxim to follow. In a sense therefore the Singh Sabha helped recapture the couplet's original intent. For a thorough elaboration of the dense intertextuality at play in the Guru's use of this couplet, see Fenech forthcoming.

37 See for example 'Zafarnāmah', in Harbans Singh (ed.), *The Encyclopaedia of Sikhism* IV, pp. 451–2. In this brief article bait 22 caps off the following essentialist description of the epistle: The central theme of the composition is the presentation of the ethical principle as the supreme law in matters of public policy as well as in private behaviour. Of course the late twentieth-century *Encyclopaedia of Sikhism* is itself a testament to the strength and longevity of the Singh Sabha interpretation of Sikhism as it near perfectly accords with this reading of Sikh history and religion.

38 Christopher Bayly, *Empire and Information: Intelligence Gathering and Social Communication in India, 1780–1870,* Cambridge: Cambridge University Press, 1996, p. 168.

39 The gur-bilas genre (splendour of the Guru) deals specifically with the history and mighty deeds of the sixth and tenth Gurus. In these, most Muslims are construed as violent and untrustworthy while brahmans are often said to engage in deceit.

40 It seems to me that the only power to which the Guru could address any complaints was that of the emperor, as the most powerful rulers in the pahari region and too many Mughal commanders themselves were opposed to him.

41 Bhai Nand Lal has been the subject of many of my articles. For one, see Louis E. Fenech, 'Bhai Nand Lal Goya and the Sikh Religion', in Tony Ballantyne (ed.), *Textures of the Sikh Past,* New Delhi: Oxford University Press, 2007. For Kavi Alam see Piara Singh Padam, *Srī Gurū Gobind Siṅgh jī de Darbārī Ratan,* Patiala: New Patiala Printers, 1976, p. 173.

42 Fenech, *Darbar of the Sikh Gurus,* pp. 143–5.

43 Gurbachan Singh Talib, 'The Zafar-Namah', in Parkash Singh (ed.), *The Saint-Warrior Guru Gobind Singh,* Amritsar: Khalsa College, 1967, pp. 33–8. The question of courtly etiquette and literary conventions is often voiced in the *Ḥikāyat*s. For one example see *Ḥikāyat* 2:2, Dasam Granth, pp. 1394–5. Mughal sources make clear that the Guru sent a petition or *'arż dāsht* to the emperor's darbar. Ganda Singh (ed.), *Maākhiz-i Tavārīkh-i Sikhān,* p. 74.

44 For the accepted forms and language of the typical Indo-Timurid *'arż dāsht* see Momin Mohiuddin, *The Chancellery and Persian Epistolography under the Mughals,* p. 155. It appears that G.S. Talib's understanding of the *'arż dāsht* is much more restrictive than the texts labelled so by the Mughals themselves.

45 This phrase occurs in bait 94. Amongst other baits see *Ẕafar-nāmah* 45, Ganda Singh (ed.), *Maākhiz-i Tavārīkh-i Sikhān,* p. 67, for example: I did not know that this man was an oath-breaker; that he worships [worldly] wealth and has destroyed [his] faith.

46 See my reassessment of the emperor's literary tastes in Fenech, *The Darbar of the Sikh Gurus,* chapter 4. Let us recall that a guide to writing official letters is also attributed to Bhai Nand Lal Goya. Many of these Indo-Timurid guides included in their lists *sanads* and *'arż dāshts.* See for example the *Munshalātalnamakīn* of Mir Abulqasim Namakin as noted in Momin Mohiuddin, *The Chancellery and Persian Epistolography under the Mughals,* pp. 173–8. A few brief portions of Nand Lal's Persian

Dastūrulinsha appear in Ganda Singh (ed.), *Kulliyāt-i Bhāī Nand Lal Goyā*, pp. 185–205 whose abridged Punjabi translation one may find in Ganda Singh (ed.), *Bhāī Nand Lāl Granthāvalī*, Patiala: Punjabi University Press, 1989, pp. 230–41.

47 Ghani, *A History of Persian Literature at the Mughal Court III: Akbar the Great*, pp. 254–5.

48 Momin Mohiuddin, *The Chancellery and Persian Epistolography under the Mughals From Bábur to Sháh Jahán: The Study of Inshá/, Dár ul-Inshá/ and Munshis based on Original Documents (1526–1658)*, Calcutta: Iran Society, 1971, p. 191.

49 This is what Dalip Singh claims in his *Life of Sri Guru Gobind Singh ji*, pp. 240–50.

50 The first Mughal emperor, Zahiruddin Babur was descended on his father's side from the conqueror Amir Timur. Because of this and because of Timur's extraordinary reputation throughout the eastern Islamicate the Mughal emperors were quite keen on ensuring that their lineage was well known. Indeed, Aurangzeb's father himself took the title *Sāḥib-i Qiran-i Thānī*, an allusion to Timur's own title 'Master of the Auspicious Conjunction', *Sāḥib-i Qiran*. The text itself is reproduced in Maulawi Muhammad Ilahdád (ed.), *The Zafarnámah by Mauláná Sharfuddìn 'Alì of Yazd*, volume 1, Calcutta: Baptist Mission Press, 1887. An image of the Mughal copy of the Timurid *Zafar-nāmah* complete with Shah Jahan's hand-written praises of the text appears in Michael Brand and Glenn Lowry, *Akbar's India: Art from the Mughal City of Victory*, New York: Asia Society Galleries, 1985, pp. 150–1. Muhammad Ghani claims that Abul Fazl prepared his *Akbar-nāmah* with Yazdi's *Zafar-nāmah* in mind. M. Ghani, *A History of Persian Language and Literature at the Mughal Court* III, p. 245.

51 Momin, *The Chancellery and Persian Epistolography under the Mughals*, p. 20. Indeed, Babur himself mentions Yazdi's *Zafar-nāmah*. Thackston (ed.), *The Baburnama*, pp. 354–5. Also Richard C. Foltz, *Mughal India and Central Asia*, Karachi: Oxford University Press, 1998, pp. 23–4.

52 *New Delhi Bīrh* folio 1095a (Gurmukhi pagination).

53 Ganda Singh (ed.), *Gur Sobhā* 13:14, p. 133.

54 Guru Nanak Dev University ms. 59*b Zafarnāme bāre*, fols 222a–b.

55 Dharam Singh alone is first mentioned in the *Sau Sākkhīān*. G.S. Naiar (ed.), *Gur-ratan Māl: Sau Sākhī*, pp. 42–3.

56 *Zafar-nāmah* 16, Ganda Singh (ed.), *Maākhiz-i Tavārīkh-i Sikhān*, p. 66.

57 *Zafar-nāmah* 61, Ganda Singh (ed.), *Maākhiz-i Tavārīkh-i Sikhān*, p. 68.

58 Zafar-nāmah 19, Ganda Singh (ed.), Maākhiz-i Tavārīkh-i Sikhān, p. 66. Also see bait 104, p. 70 for a similar sentiment.

59 Kirpal Das Bhalla's Zafar-nāmah narrative (sakhi 126) elaborates further. MPV 126, pp. 177–8 and Parchīān p. 133.

60 See Vir Singh (ed.), Srī Gurū Granth Sāhib jī dī Kuñjī: Vārān Bhāī Gurdās Saṭīk Bhāv Prakāśanī Ṭīkā Samet Mukammal, New Delhi: Bhai Vir Singh Sahit Sadan, 1997, vār 26, pauṛī 4, p. 417.

61 Fenech, Darbar of the Sikh Gurus, chapter four.

62 See Piara Singh Padam, Srī Gurū Gobind Singh jī de Darbārī Ratan, Patiala: New Patiala Printers, 1976, p. 98.

63 Surprisingly the journey narratives in the Parchīān, MPV, and in Sarup Das Bhalla's Mahimā Prakāś Kavitā (1769 CE) is reduced to a single line. See Parchīān, p. 135; MPV 26, pp. 180-81; and Sarup Das Bhalla, Mahimā Prakāś 2 volumes [ed. Gobind Singh Lamba and Khazan Singh], Patiala: Bhasha Vibhag, Punjab, 1971, vol. 2, 26:9, p. 886 [Hereafter MP II].

64 Ganda Singh (ed.), Gur Sobhā 15:2, p. 150.

65 Padam (ed.), Bhāī Kesar Singh Chhibbar Krit Bansāvalī-nāmā 10:601–02, p. 182. This exchange appears earlier in MPV 126, p. 181. Also Jaggi (ed.), Gurbilās Pātiśāhī Dasvīn 22:193, p. 350; and Santokh Singh's SP 1:31:48–9.

66 Padam (ed.), Bansāvalī-nāmā 10:604, p. 182.

67 MP II 26:30, p. 890.

68 The issue of robing and symbolic incorporation within the darbar of the Sikh Gurus is examined in my Darbar of the Sikh Gurus, chapter three.

69 SP 1:31:32–3 and MP II 26:2–5, p. 886.

70 This may also be understood as a challenge to the emperor, reflecting in this gurbilas text what Santokh Singh may well have understood the Zafar-nāmah to manifest.

71 SP 1:31:58–60.

72 A profoundly negative assessment appears in Dalip Singh's Life of Sri Guru Gobind Singh ji, pp. 240–50.

73 Zafar-nāmah 55, Ganda Singh (ed.), Maākhiz-i Tavārīkh-i Sikhān, p. 67.

74 Ganda Singh (ed.), Gur Sobhā 13:35, p. 137.

75 Ibid.,13:14, 13:22, pp. 133, 135. In 13:31, p. 136 it is also called a letter, varkī.

76 Although there is one pseudonymous manuscript of the Parchīān dated 1709 later recensions supply the author's name as Sewa Das Udasi.

77 Parchīān, p. 133. Also MPV 126, p. 177.

78 There are a small number of Punjabi texts written after Bhalla's account which also specifically name the Guru's letter, but with different titles. Sarup Das Bhalla for example calls it the *Shauq-nāmā* which may be translated as 'petition' whilst Sukkha Singh uses the Sanskritic equivalent of the Persian *Zafar, bij* and so *bij-nāmā*. See *MP* II 26:1, 17 p. 886, 887 and Jaggi (ed.), *Gurbilās Pātiśāhī Dasvīn* 22:198, p. 350.

79 See J.S. Grewal's interpretation of the *Zafar-nāmah* in his 'The Zafarnama: The Epistle of Moral Victory', in J.S. Grewal, *From Guru Nanak to Maharaja Ranjit Singh*, Amritsar: Guru Nanak Dev University Press, 1983.

80 Ms. 199*kh* Guru Nanak Dev University, fol. 50b.

81 In the *Mahimā Prakāś Kavitā* Aurangzeb reads the *Zafar-nāmah* and *tab uṭhe śāh mahal mo gae / udāsīn hoi baiṭhe rahe*, 'The emperor then rose and went to the palace. He became detached and indifferent and continued sitting' 26:18. *MP* II 26:32–3, p. 890.

82 Jaggi (ed.), *Gurbilās Pātiśāhī Dasvīn* 22:113–14, p. 343.

83 Ibid., 22:198–200, p. 350.

84 Piara Singh Padam (ed.), *Baṅsāvalī-nāmā* 10:604, p. 182.

85 Padam (ed.), *Baṅsāvalī-nāmā* 6:124-6, p. 98.

86 For example see Guru Nanak Dev University ms. 19*c Bahādar Shāh nāl Mulākat kā Prasaṅg* fols 101b-114a. Also Gian Singh, *Tavārīkh Gurū Khālsā* I, Patiala: Bhasha Vibhag Punjab, 1980, p. 863. Also *Gur Sobhā* 15:9, p. 151 and *Baṅsāvalī-nāmā* 10:611, p. 182.

87 *SP* 1:31:61.

88 *SP* 1:37:43–4.

89 *SP* 1:37:45.

90 Harjot Oberoi, *The Construction of Religious Boundaries: Culture, Identity and Diversity in the Sikh Tradition*, New Delhi: Oxford University Press, 1994.

4

Anne Murphy[†]

An Idea of Religion

IDENTITY, DIFFERENCE, AND COMPARISON IN THE
GURBILĀS

The *gurbilās* literature describes the lives of the Gurus, and in particular
that of the tenth human living Guru of the Sikh tradition, Guru Gobind
Singh, (b. 1666, Guru 1675–1708), and the history of the community
after this time. One incident that is portrayed for the first time in this
genre of literature is the martyrdom of the Ninth Guru, and father of
Guru Gobind Singh, Guru Tegh Bahadur (b. 1621, Guru 1664–75).
This essay will explore one exemplary portrayal of this incident, in the
mid- to late-eighteenth century account of the life of the Tenth Guru,
Guru Gobind Singh, by Kuir Singh, entitled *Gurbilās Patshāhī Das*, as
published by Punjabi University in 1999.[1] The portrayal of the Ninth
Guru's martyrdom in Kuir Singh is in many ways typical of contemporary and later accounts of the martyrdom, based as it was (like most

[†]I thank Anshu Malhotra and Farina Mir for their insightful comments. A
shortened and modified version was presented at the European Conference
on Modern South Asian Studies, 26–29 July 2010 in Bonn, Germany. I
thank the participants of the conference for their excellent comments and
criticism. Special thanks to Ananya Bedi of the University of Delhi, for her
comments and assistance.

accounts) on the portrayal within the *Bachittar Nāṭak,* a text attributed to the Tenth Guru that is generally seen to inaugurate the genre of the gurbilās. As will be seen, however, the Kuir Singh narrative elaborates significantly on that version, providing a compelling articulation of one author's understanding of religious difference and identity, and the category of the 'religious' that informs this understanding.

The goal of this essay is not to assess the historicity of this incident—sources outside Sikh tradition do corroborate it—nor to analyse its complex theological dimensions.[2] The concern here is with how the idea of religion has been imagined and expressed through its portrayal. The martyrdom of the Ninth Guru is an important event for a number of reasons that relate directly to the broader issues I address here. The martyrdom of Guru Tegh Bahadur is often invoked today in discussion of the relationship between Hindus and Sikhs, since Guru Tegh Bahadur is said to have given his life in defence of the rights of Hindus—specifically, the Kashmiri *pandit*s who are said to have sought his help.[3] In its elaborated version, such as is found in Kuir Singh's text, the incident also revolves around the issue of conversion, as these Hindus and the Guru himself are said to have been brought under pressure to convert to Islam. In this, the narrative invokes a much larger trope in the description of Islam in South Asia: the issue of 'forced conversion', which is discounted by most historians as a significant aspect of conversion to Islam in the region but has had an enduring political significance in the representation of Islam in South Asia up to the present day.[4] I cannot at this time account for why the theme of conversion assumes importance at the time of this text's composition; such an accounting would require analysis and broader historical grounding that would bring us too far from the scope of this essay.[5] The representation and meaning of the incident in this particular expression are of concern here for what they tell us about the idea of religion that undergirds them.

THE IDEA OF RELIGION IN THE COLONIAL AND PRE-COLONIAL PERIODS

This essay takes as its starting point the debate regarding the formation of South Asian religious communitarian definitions and individual subjectivities before, in contrast to within, the British colonial idiom, a subject that has occupied a prominent place in the historiography of South Asia, and of Punjab. Brilliant early work by Kenneth Jones on the census, for example, showed how religious identities were formed in relation to the practices and as well as ideologies of British governance not only in Punjab, but in the subcontinent as a whole.[6] In *Religion and the Specter of the West*, Arvind Mandair describes how Sikhism was produced as a religion within the colonial field through a process predetermined in meaning and effect by Western knowledge formations.[7] The category of religion and its attendant assumptions, he argues, act within a regime of translation that denies the complexity and relationality of pre-modern South Asian cultures, fundamentally changing how a religious community could be conceived.[8]

Critique of the category of 'religion' is not new: W.C. Smith, early on, and Talal Asad, and others such as Mandair more recently, have made persuasive arguments regarding the inapplicability of the category of 'religion' as a universal category.[9] Asad's discomfort with 'universal definitions of religion is that by insisting on an essential singularity, they divert us from asking questions about what the definition includes and what it excludes—how, by whom, for what purpose, and so on. And in what historical context a particular definition of religion makes good sense'. Instead, the 'identifying work' needed to define religion must be done with 'doctrine, behaviors, texts, songs, pictures...and so on...[the definitions of which] are embedded in passionate social disputes on which the law of the state pronounces'.[10] Religion and the religious are therefore configured within embedded social practices and operations of power (state and non-state driven) that defy singular and universal characterization. Will Sweetman has shown how the rejection of the category of religion itself relies upon western European and Christian notions of the same, such that it is 'precisely the claim that Hinduism is not a religion which reveals lingering Christian and theological influence even in the works of those who explicitly disclaim such influence'.[11] Mandair argues that this is inevitable; the concept of religion in the western secular humanities relies upon an ontotheological premise that presupposes a particular nature of the transcendent and the existence of God; this is not shorn from it easily. Mandair has thus endorsed Derrida's suggestion that *religio* remain untranslatable, to hold the category of religion at critical distance.[12] Along similar lines, in recent work Ronald Inden and co-authors have attempted to rework the conventional vocabulary used for religious communities and sects in South Asia to avoid the category of 'religion' and related ideas, and in so doing to avoid the problem of designating the religious as a universally translatable aspect of human experience.[13]

The questioning of the nature of religion as a category has as its necessary corollary the task of critical evaluation of the religious categories and community formations we might assume operated in the pre-colonial period, as the work of Inden and colleagues suggests. Significant work has already been done on this topic, particularly with reference to the construction of the category 'Hindu'. The use of quotation marks around the term 'Hindu' will be unfamiliar to few reading this volume, as it reflects a long debate within both academic and popular circles about the production in the nineteenth century of 'Hindu' as a term and an identity as a product of colonial codification of the non-Muslim and non-Christian religious practices of the subcontinent.[14] Mandair has argued that the pre-colonial period in general—with reference to the category 'Sikh' as well as 'Hindu'—was characterized by 'a complex or relational logic, according to which it would be perfectly valid to suggest that A=B, the implication of which would be the existence of relatively fluid social and individual boundaries'.[15] This formulation follows an earlier argument articulated most famously by Harjot Oberoi, who sketched an 'older, pluralist paradigm of Sikh faith [that] was displaced forever by a highly uniform Sikh identity, to one we know today as modern Sikhism'.[16] Tony Ballantyne has demonstrated that such uniformity was never actually achieved in the modern period: just as Sikh identity was undergoing definition and restriction, Sikh identities were also becoming increasingly diverse in diasporic and other contexts, so we would be wrong to assume uniformity in Sikh enunciations in the late nineteenth and twentieth centuries, in contrast to a fundamentally different past.[17] Nonetheless, religious communitarian identities were defined in the colonial period in new ways, both as a direct result of specific instruments of British governance, such as the apportionment of representation within government representational structures based on religious identity and corresponding census figures, and the effects of the institutions and practices of modernity more generally.

Wherever one stands within these debates it is also clear that critique of the applicability of religious terms in the pre-modern period—except in its most extreme form—does *not* necessarily mean that such terms and attendant meanings did not exist in *some* sense in the pre-colonial period. There are clear enunciations of identity and community in the pre-colonial period that therefore must be accounted for, enunciations that inspired David Lorenzen's forceful argument for the applicability of the term 'Hindu' before 1800.[18] Brian Pennington has thus described how 'the historical role of the colonizer was not to invent Hinduism either by blunder or by design, but to introduce an economy of concepts and power relations that dramatically enhanced the value of such identity markers'.[19] Mandair argues along similar lines that 'the enunciation of a Sikh identity does not begin in the colonial period… [and] a Sikh identity had already emerged in the sixteenth and seventeenth centuries'.[20] Indeed, much work has been done on Sikh enunciations before the onset of British colonial formations of knowledge; the oeuvre of J.S. Grewal is exemplary of the body of literature that explores these Sikh modes of being and their articulation in that period. 'What changes in the colonial period', Mandair rightfully argues, 'is the way in which identity was conceived'.[21]

The same may indeed be true of the idea of 'religion': that there are ways we must consider the operation of such a category in multiple modes, and in non-Western universalist terms, in the pre-colonial period, regardless of the particular changes wrought by a Western notion of 'religion' introduced in the context of colonial rule.[22] This essay represents an inquiry along such lines in historical terms, with both a recognition of how religious community definitions changed in the colonial period and appreciation of their pre-colonial resonances, to consider an exemplary articulation of the enunciation of being Sikh in the eighteenth to early nineteenth century, and in particular its relationship to the idea of religion in more general terms. By carefully examining one instance of the pre-colonial enunciation of Sikh subjectivity, the aim here is to assess the understanding of the category of the 'religious' within it, and what such an enunciation can tell us about the idea of such an arena of human experience and expression in this period. To repeat, this is not to argue that 'religion' existed in the *same sense* in the pre-colonial past that it did in the colonial period, nor that British interventions in the field of the religious did not create novel forms of enunciating and living religious identity. The argument is that the operation of the category of the 'religious' as a complex and dynamic marker of a universal aspect of human experience may be relevant to our reading of the pre-colonial period—in its own terms.

TEXT AND CONTEXT

First, some notes on the text and the genre it represents. The dating of Kuir Singh's *Gurbilās Patshāhī Das* has caused significant debate. While a date of 1751 is mentioned in the text itself, there are metrical problems with the relevant line that leads to doubts about its authenticity.[23] Surjit Hans argues for a late eighteenth or early nineteenth century date for the text, drawing in part on what he argues is Kuir Singh's awareness of the British presence in the country, while Madanjit Kaur argues strenuously for taking the text as the product of the mid-eighteenth century.[24] The genre the text represents, as has been mentioned, is the gurbilās literature: literally, the 'sport' or 'play' of the Guru.[25] The genre begins with writings attributed to the Tenth Guru, particularly his *Bachittar Nāṭak*. Texts in the genre are strongly intertextually related, as is visible in Kuir Singh's text: it is clear that in addition to relying upon the teachings and narratives related by the close disciple of the Guru, Bhai Mani Singh—as asserted by the author—he also relied upon other texts in the gurbilās genre, such as the earliest examples of the form, *Gur Sobhā* and the *Bachittar Nāṭak*, among others.[26] Sukha Singh's *Gurbilās Patshāhī Das* is another important text to account for in relation to Kuir Singh's, although scholars debate their chronological arrangement.[27] Sukha Singh's text, however, features a much shorter description of the martyrdom and associated events.[28] Another contemporary text, Kesar Singh Chibber's *Baṃsāvalīnāmā Dasāṃ Pātshāhīāṃ kā* (mid-eighteenth century), features a more extensive description of the event that emphasizes the role of the author's relations, Satidās and Matidās; that version quotes the *Bachittar Nāṭak* directly.[29] As will be discussed, the *Bachittar Nāṭak* provides a particularly powerful model for the portrayal under consideration, since it is the first description of the events in question, and occupies a central place in the tradition of representing the event.

I have written elsewhere about the idea of the community as a continuing presence of the past, of the gurbilās literature and the question of the historical.[30] In that discussion, I noted that the notion of the *panth* or 'community' takes shape as a Sikh form of collective organization that is not reducible to statist forms of sovereignty in the work of Sainapati, *Gur Sobhā,* generally attributed to the beginning of the eighteenth century and the earliest example of this genre of text not attributed to the Tenth Guru.[31] That text, which is generally dated to 1711, was produced as the Sikh community transitioned from the period of living Guruship to the articulation of ultimate authority within the sacred canon (the Adi Granth or Guru Granth Sahib) and the community—the paired principles of *granth* (text) and panth (community) articulated by the tenth and final living Guru, Guru Gobind Singh.[32] *Gur Sobhā*, like Kuir Singh's *Gurbilās Patshāhī Das*, provides a narrative description in poetry of the life of the final living Guru and the formation of the Sikh community in this period. The transformations evident within these and other texts in the genre reflect the transition from the period of living Guruship in the beginning of the eighteenth century, to the post-living-Guru period, and the political instability in Punjab as successor groups began to vie for power as Mughal power began to fracture. This process was only beginning at the time of the writing of *Gur Sobhā*, but by the end of the eighteenth century, the political landscape across the subcontinent was transformed into a range of post-Mughal polities (many of which still paid nominal allegiance to the Mughal state) and the eventual establishment of a sovereign state in Punjab under a Sikh ruler. Conflicts in the period reflect the growing stature of the Sikh community in this unstable political field.

Kuir Singh's *Gurbilās Patshāhī Das* is similar in organization to *Gur Sobhā* but features strong mythological content and a clearer political sensibility, appropriate to its later time of composition, as political sovereignty in relation to the Mughal state and other smaller Hindu kings from the Punjab Hills was being won with greater and greater confidence and stability among Sikh chiefs, culminating in the establishment of the kingdom of Lahore under Maharaja Ranjit Singh at the close of the eighteenth century. In general terms, a central concern for all gurbilās from the late eighteenth and early nineteenth centuries is the articulation of connections between the Guru and the panth. In this way the narration of the Guru's life constitutes the means for the formation of the Sikh community. Sikh expression of the past through the eighteenth century is also fundamentally shaped by the redefinition of sovereign relations within a post-Mughal Punjab, building upon the broader non-statist, theologically-driven orientation that can be seen in the early example of the genre, *Gur Sobhā*. Thus Kuir Singh's text, which hails from later in the eighteenth century, complicates the theologically inflected historical sensibility associated with the Tenth Guru in *Gur Sobhā*. In later examples of the gurbilās genre, in general, mythological associations of the Guru are further developed, and the Guru is seen to be connected to other religious authorities, particularly but not exclusively Ram; as Kuir Singh writes, some see the Guru and call him Ram, and others see Shankar or Shiva.[33] Such broad references are mobilized to position the Guru in relation to a larger cosmology, within a vision of the pre-eminence of the Guru.[34] In this, Kuir Singh's text strongly resonates with aspects of the Dasam Granth, which features extensive mythological references; indeed, a bulk of the Dasam Granth is dedicated to the description of the incarnations of Vishnu and the Goddess figures prominently.[35]

In Kuir Singh's text, there are also clearly state-oriented articulations of the meanings of sovereignty: the Guru is explicitly called upon to counter repressive state powers, and the Guru is meant to 'destroy the Mlechas' or foreigners, just as he destroys desire and anger in the mind.[36] This vilification of the foreigners or 'Turks' is directly related to state power and its 'religious' meanings are ambiguous, as will be explored here. Such a distinction has been observed in other texts that articulate the distinction between *mlechha* or 'barbarian' and not; in times of greater peace, accommodation and appreciation are viewed, and at other times a portrayal of difference.[37] The trappings of the Guru's authority are explicitly royal in form, and the vocabulary of state sovereignty runs through the text.[38] As has been noted, this development reflects the ascendancy of sovereignty among the successors to Mughal authority, including Sikh chiefs, as the eighteenth century progressed. The sovereignty of the Guru with reference to the community at this point is imagined in terms of state sovereignty, within a complex and changing political field.

IMAGINING THE RELIGIOUS SELF

Kuir Singh's quite lengthy work on the life of the Tenth Guru features not only mention of the martyrdom of the Ninth Guru, which is also a feature of other similar texts, such as Sukha Singh's probably earlier text by the same name and Chibber's text from the mid-eighteenth century. It also includes a particularly elaborate description of a debate between the Ninth Guru and father of Guru Gobind Singh, Guru Tegh Bahadur, with the Mughal emperor Aurangzeb, and the subsequent martyrdom of the Guru after his refusal to convert to Islam. As noted by Fauja Singh, there is no historical possibility of such a debate taking place, as Aurangzeb at the time of the death of Guru Tegh Bahadur was not in Delhi; similar debates with a *qāzī* and other religious figures—common in the text—are equally unattested in the historical record.[39] But, as Fauja Singh also suggests, the exchange does have value for giving readers/hearers (when the text was recited) a sense of Kuir Singh's vision of the meaning of the martyrdom, and how it articulates larger issues around the formulation of religious difference and identity. More specifically, the incident and its portrayal reveal how religious subjectivities are and are not perceived as commensurable in the formulation of conversion, within a larger comparative framework that relies upon an underlying categorical similarity between two entities from which and to which conversion occurs. Understanding religious identity through conversion is revealing; Heinrich von Stietencron for example argued for deconstruction of the category 'Hindu' based on the use of conversion to 'change' a person from a Vaishnava to a Shaiva.[40] Conversion in the case at hand, in eighteenth-century Punjab, demonstrates how the idea of the religious as a meaningful category operated in pre-colonial terms, in a Sikh discursive context, and what it can tell us about religious difference and its resolution.

As has been noted, the incident regarding the Ninth Guru is well known. Outside of its obvious significance within Sikh history, it has constituted a central motif in the portrayal of the Sikhs as protectors of the Hindu community. It is also an early example of the valourization of martyrdom in the Sikh tradition. Louis Fenech argues that the portrayal of the Ninth Guru's execution represents 'the first in Sikh literature to aver that the "great deed" (*mahi sākā*) of stoically sacrificing one's life for the "purpose of righteousness" (*dharam het*) ensures one a spot in paradise'[41] and, as such is 'something entirely new in the Sikh tradition'.[42] As he further notes, the popularity of the relevant passage of the *Bachittar Nāṭak* 'seems to indicate that a fascination with heroic sacrifice animated some members of the eighteenth century Panth'.[43] The relevant sections of the *Bachittar Nāṭak* are as follows:

> *tilak jaṃñū rākhā prabh tā kā| kīno baḍo kalū mahi sākā |*
>
> For the sacred threads and forehead marks of those he protected, In time he did this great sacrifice/historic act.

> *sādhani heti itī jinī karī | sīsu dīā par sī na ucarī | (13)*
>
> For the good ones[44] he did this much, He gave his head but did not speak.[45]

> *dharma het sākā jinni kīā | sīsu dīā par siraru na dīā |*
>
> For the sake of *Dharm*, he did this great act. He gave his head but did not give *siraru*[46]

nāṭāk ceṭak kīe kukājā | prabh logan kah āvat lājā | **(14)**

This show of relish and bad work [such as the showing of miracles]—
shame would come to the men of God [who would perform them]

doharā | ṭhīkari ḍhori dilasi siri prabh pur kīyā pyān |
teg bahādar sī krīā karī na kinahūṃ ān | **(15)**

Breaking the pot shard (*ṭhīkar*) [of the body], on the leader of Delhi,
he left.
That which Teg Bahadur did, no one else could have done.

teg bahādur ke calat bhayo jagat ko sok |
hai hai hai sabh jag bhayo jai jai jai sur lok | **(16)**

At the departure of Teg Bahadur, all the world was filled with grief
The world cried out in despair, and his victory was hailed in the
world of the Gods.[47]

The *Bachittar Nāṭak* account foregrounds Tegh Bahadur's sacrifice for the sake of dharm, and for the 'good ones'. For Fenech, the
notion of Gugu Tegh Bahadur sacrificing his life for a religion other
than his own is anachronistic, and assumes a level of differentiation inappropriate to the configuration of religious identities of the
period: 'The earliest evidence is clear on that fact that he did [die the
death of a martyr], and that he was understood to be a martyr by the
Sikhs of the eighteenth century... [but it is necessary] to dispel the
Tat Khalsa notion that the community for which the Guru died was
a different one from his own'.[48] This assumption, he argues, is one of
a later period, and that divisions between Hindu and Sikh were not
clearly drawn enough in the period of the martyrdom to consider the
Guru's sacrifice as being one for another religion. We'll address this
issue in Kuir Singh's text, below.

First however I will focus on another aspect of the *Bachittar
Nāṭak* account. In this version, there is no specific accounting of
the relationship between Sikhism and Islam. Conversion is referred
to obliquely, with reference to those protected, 'with sacred threads
and forehead marks'. The demonstration of a miracle receives
greater attention. We see the theme of miracles in the Kuir Singh
account as well: the Guru's refusal to perform them, to show his
strength and mastery, emphasizes the role of God in such events:
'*karāmāt sahī prabh ke ḍhig hai ham to in dāsan dās pakārī* [Miracles

are in the hands of the lord, we are the servants].[49] Indeed, at one point the endurance of the tortures given to the Guru is seen as proof of a miracle, but not fully.[50] Religious power can be expressed in multiple terms, but a true miracle exhibits intent. This aspect of the incident is in itself of interest. While it is the case that the demonstration of miracles as an expression of religious power was not unknown within Sikh literature—they are quite common in the Janam-Sakhis, accounts of the life of the first of the Sikh Gurus, Guru Nanak Dev—the performance of miracles is also downplayed.[51] The stories of Baba Atal Rai and Baby Gurditta, the sons of the Sixth Guru, Guru Hargobind, who performed miracles too readily in their father's eyes, provide well-known popular examples of this. The *intentional* demonstration of power, particularly on demand, is what is at issue. This is articulated in the response of the Guru noted above: miracles are the workings of the Lord, and are thus in his control. It is not right for humans to conjure them at will.

In Kuir Singh's text discussion of conversion is expanded.[52] Islam and the practices and commitments of the Guru are portrayed in agonistic terms that are resolved through conversion—the choice between one or another faith or tradition reveals difference that is only resolved through identity, through becoming the same. Yet, at the same time, since this difference can be overcome through conversion, the traditions/faiths/religions so named (and what name we use here is important) are staked out in the encounter as commensurable, two things that are made equivalent through this act of moving *in-between* and *across*. Islam and Sikhism, then, are two of a kind. This rhetoric of conversion in Kuir Singh's more elaborate rendition of this encounter thus tells us how religion as a broader category might be understood. ˙

Kuir Singh's attitude towards Islam and Muslims is ambiguous and multi-dimensional. This indeed has resulted in two very different accountings of the text in the scholarly literature. Among the few in-depth analyses of the text is one by Surjit Hans—an account that has provided the premier scholarly reference on the gurbilās literature for some time—and a recent article by Gurtej

Singh.[53] Hans positions the Kuir Singh text as relatively late, as has been noted. One reason for this is the 'conciliatory tone' of the author towards Muslims.[54] For Hans, this provides evidence of the late provenance of the text, and likely reveals 'a strong imprint of Sikh rule under Ranjit Singh for whom it was absolutely necessary to hold the three communities in some kind of balance'.[55] Hans acknowledges what Gurtej Singh notes—'a deep hatred of Muslims'[56] in Kuir Singh's text—but senses a conciliatory approach in Kuir Singh because 'an impression is given that the term covered the tyrannical rulers only'.[57] He then notes a conversation between qāzīs and the Guru wherein Sikhism and Islam are 'only marginally different'.[58] Surjit Hans thus expresses consternation at the statement of Guru Gobind Singh, in the writing of Kuir Singh, that 'your religion is good for you and ours is good for us'.[59] On the other hand, Gurtej Singh notes that 'the key to the author's character, and consequently to that of his work, lies in his intense hatred of Muslims. Hopes of prayers for their ruination are the most numerous to come across', although, as he also avers, this is certainly directly related to political domination by Muslims.[60]

These two readers of this text, therefore, have provided different estimations of its attitude towards Islam and Muslims. This is because the text engages with religious difference, and conversion, in multiple ways. One of the direct references to conversion in the text associates it directly with state/political power, as Gurtej Singh and Surjit Hans both note. Conversion in what we might call 'religious' terms is actually political in nature:

puni āp auraṃg ayo tin pai, tin hain kahai, tin bain kahai bhal bhāt bicārī |

Then Aurangzeb came again, then he said these words, thinking well

karāmāt dijai kat dūkh saho, natu lehu sutā ham dīn sudhārī |

Give us a miracle, why endure misery? Otherwise, take our daughter and accept our faith

kāṃgaṛ aṭak pisor lahor ko, deu sūbā tum ho nrip dhāro |

We will appoint you leader and give you the provinces of Kangra Atak, Peshawar and Lahore.[61]

At other times, however, conversion is characterized as a matter of the mind or heart.[62] Conversion is also enacted through practices: a Hindu compromises Hindu identity with the eating of the cow, and thus the status of being 'Hindu' is determined through rules around commensality and the consumption of beef.[63] A counterargument is presented by the Guru, in debate with a qāzī, comparing the distinction between *harām* and *halāl* in Islam with eating prohibitions in Hindu contexts. Such practices are seen as commensurable, and here the Guru is victorious in debate with the qāzī over the nature of the importance of the cow and the taboo against eating beef.[64] Alongside the issue of conversion in Kuir Singh, we thus also see extended comparisons between religions and religious practices. Through the text at different points we see multiple visions of Islam: a debate with a pīr, for example, as well as debate with a qāzī. Descriptions of Sikh practice are also quite detailed throughout, and not surprisingly significant details are given in association with the narration of the founding of the Khalsa, where elements of the code of conduct known as *rahit* are given.[65]

David Lorenzen has shown that religious difference was described in pre-colonial literature, and this forms part of his argument for the applicability of the term 'Hindu' before the colonial period.[66] But difference can also lead to commonality. The resolution of a sense of conflict or difference between religions overall is found by Guru Tegh Bahadur in conventional devotional terms, by resorting to a particular set of practices and ways of being that foreground the relationship to the divine and realization of it within:

> *guro vāc, sun kājī | pyāre | jo sāhib ko simran dhāre |*
> *binā yād sāhib ke aise | murad simgār lakho bidh taise |* (35)

All must engage in remembrance of the name, without it there is nothing.
Without memory of the lord it is as if one looks upon a corpse, in lavish adornment.

Along such lines, the writer tells us that the Guru equates Turk and Hindu.[67] This text, then, features an incident of 'forced conversion', but does so in a way that forces consideration of complex relations between Islam and the community and teachings of the Guru and the Sikhs. The two are shown as a kind: comparable, and in some senses equivalent. The differences between the two can be elided in different ways: through conversion, or through an underlying shared experience, or through a phenomenological comparison of practices and beliefs, as seen in the discussion of eating restrictions within Islam and among the Hindus.

This brings us back to the question of the relationship between the terms 'Sikh' and 'Hindu' in the text. 'Sikh' clearly refers in the text to a follower of the Guru, and 'Hindu' as a general category that is opposed to the category of Turk. The Guru is addressed by the qāzī as 'Hindu'.[68] But it is clearly not *equivalent* to Sikh in religious terms: in terms of practices or beliefs portrayed, or allegiance to the Guru. For these, that which is 'Sikh' is defined and not called 'Hindu'. The category of 'Hindu' is set up in opposition to the category of Turk (and in this conversation, Turk clearly means Muslim). Fenech's contention that there is *not* a sense of distinction between that which is done for and by the Sikhs, and that which is done for and by the 'Hindus' as a general category, therefore, is misplaced. In Kuir Singh, Hindu is a term that is oppositional in meaning, defining a relationship more than a set of attributes, and clearly—along the lines Mandair, Talbot, and others have outlined—not a single identity.[69] Being 'Hindu' therefore is akin in this text to not being Turk, not to being of a particular religious stance. The eating of cows does define one as either Hindu or non-Hindu/Turk. But this does not define the contents of 'Hindu'. In one of many examples, it is noted that, in describing the mission of the Guru, '*himdūate mai uh paṃth calai hai | turakan nās karai sukh pai hai |* He was born among the Hindus and would find happiness in the destruction of the Turks'.[70] Elsewhere it is noted that this panth overall was formed for the purpose of the destruction of the mlechas.[71] Clearly, then, this panth was created for a given purpose—implying a separate identity. The definition of Sikh practices is clear in the text, and is not equivalent to being Hindu, but instead to being a follower of the Guru and a practitioner of specific practices.[72] The panth, then, is not equated with being Hindu, and 'Hindu' operates in the text in relatively vague terms. One cannot clearly define it, nor subsume that which is clearly defined in relation to the Guru—that is, in relation to being Sikh—within it.

On Comparability and the Idea of Religion

Farina Mir has noted in her recent exploration of nineteenth century *qissa* literature that 'Punjabis shared notions of pious behavior irrespective of their affiliations to different religions'.[73] This argument for the qissa world can be recast in interesting ways in the earlier, more explicitly sectarian literature under examination here. The text under consideration here clearly addresses itself to Sikh concerns. Thus while 'what *qisse* underscore is the multiplicity of religious practices in which Punjabis participated',[74] the text under consideration here seems to underscore the sense of exclusions that accompanied such multiplicity, and the articulation of a particular religious subjectivity within a larger field. This is that which the qissa seems to counter, and is in keeping with our conventional understanding of how a 'Sikh text' would operate. Yet, religiously directed texts—that is, texts that are directed towards the articulation of religious boundaries and the communities thereby defined—can also express dynamics of shared religious ideologies and practices. Mir notes that the idea of syncretism is *not* the key to understanding the kind of shared religious–cultural sphere exemplified by the qissa, since such an understanding implies a necessarily agonistic relationship between those entities being syncretized.[75] Instead, 'the devotional practices described and privileged in Punjabi qisse are better understood as reflecting shared notions of piety, and that participating in the forms of devotion that accompanied this piety was not predicated on one's pre-existing religious identity'.[76] This shared religious space is saint veneration which is better understood as 'constituting a parallel, alternative spiritual practice that was accessible to all of Punjab's inhabitants'.[77]

A shared notion of piety may have significance outside the qissa world as well. Clearly there are real elements of difference articulated in Kuir Singh's text, and the issue of coerced conversion that predominates in the portrayal of the lead-up to the martyrdom of Guru Tegh Bahadur cannot be dismissed lightly. The examples given briefly here, however, show how commensurability is articulated even in conflict. Through this process, the 'religious' as a category is created, and equivalences are articulated within it. The 'religious' is a way of being that is shared; at times it is politically inflected, at others is an aspect of the mind/heart. It also reflects power through the miraculous act available in all religions. Religious difference is asserted, but commensurability accompanies this assertion, through discussion of differences and similarities. Indeed, the Guru is asked to *'kahai sāc bānī, tumai nāhi māro'* [Say the true words, and you will not be beaten].[78] Practices are compared; the Guru asserts that God is the source of all of these; if the words are true, they are true for all. Equivalences, and comparable differences, are demonstrated. Such tensions are not always resolved. Conversion, in political terms, is the only way to resolve political difference. To assert commonality, the Guru resorts to a common devotional, trans-community source that underlies all. This 'core' is close here to a definition of religion, shared among the practices and embodiments that we might call the religious in this text. Thus Mir's observations on shared religious experience in the qissa can be discerned, in certain senses, as a sense of shared religiosity even when religious *difference* is not only accepted, but asserted.

Taking a lead from Muzaffar Alam's work on the languages of political Islam, where at times difference is maintained while commensurability is argued for, we can see in Kuir Singh how moments of comparability are articulated, where difference is asserted, but also a sense of equivalence that does not argue for equation or sharing but for something that is different and related in kind.[79] Such a moment is important, if we are to understand more fully the dynamics of difference and coexistence, or commensurability, in our understanding of the past. In the contradictions in Kuir Singh's text—its generosity and its sense of conflict—we see the negotiation of the social fact of difference, through the establishment of a comparative framework within which both a Sikh position, and an Islamic one, reside. This reveals an underlying universal aspect of human experience that can be understood as 'religion', and senses of difference within that category. This difference can create movement between, the creation of sameness. Or it can be resolved in the moment of devotion, and the movement beyond.

NOTES

1 Kuir Singh, *Gurbilās Patshāhī Das*, (ed.) Shamsher Singh Alok, introduction by Fauja Singh, Patiala, Punjab: Publications Bureau, Punjabi University, 1999.

2 For an example of such theological dimensions, see: Gurbachan Singh Talib (ed.), *Guru Tegh Bahadur: Background and the Supreme Sacrifice, A Collection of Research Articles*, Patiala: Punjabi University, 1976. On evidence regarding martyrdom, see J.S. Grewal and Irfan Habib, *Sikh History from Persian Sources*, New Delhi: Tulika, 2001, pp. 12–14, 105, 113.

3 See for example http://www.hinduwisdom.info/articles_hinduism/99. htm, accessed 28 July 2010; http://www.sarbloh.info/htmls/guru_ bahadur.html, accessed 14 June 2010; and http://www.hindutva.org/ sikhism.html, accessed 14 June 2010. See counterargument: http:// www.info-sikh.com/PageRSS2.html, accessed 14 June 2010.

4 See discussion in Richard Eaton, 'Introduction' in his *India's Islamic Traditions, 711–1750*, New Delhi: Oxford University Press, 2003, pp. 1–34.

5 I thank Anshu Malhotra for bringing up this issue in discussion at the ECMSAS conference, July 2010. I hope to pursue this theme in further work.

6 Kenneth Jones, 'Religious Identity and the Indian Census', in N. Gerald Barrier (ed.), *The Census in British India: New Perspectives*, New Delhi: Manohar, 1981, pp. 75–101.

7 Arvind-pal Singh Mandair, *Religion and the Specter of the West: Sikhism, India, Postcoloniality, and the Politics of Translation*, New York: Columbia University Press, 2009.

8 Mandair, *Religion and the Specter of the West*, pp. 418, 420 on South Asian heteronomy and 414 on pre-modern complexity. As he says elsewhere, in the colonial period 'the logic of identity changes from complex or relational to dualistic', Mandair *Religion and the Specter of the West*, p. 236.

9 See Talal Asad, *Genealogies of Religion: Discipline and Reasons of Power in Christianity and Islam*, Baltimore: Johns Hopkins University Press, 1993; W.C. Smith, *The Meaning and End of Religion*, New York: Harper & Row, 1978. More importantly, see Asad's recent article on Smith: Talal Asad, 'Reading a Modern Classic: W.C. Smith's *The Meaning and End of Religion*', *History of Religions*, 40 (3), 2001, pp. 204–22.

10 Asad, 'Reading', p. 220.

11 Will Sweetman, '"Hinduism" and the History of "Religion": Protestant Presuppositions in the Critique of the Concept of Hinduism', *Method & Theory in the Study of Religion*, 15 (4), 2003, p. 330.

12 Mandair, *Religion and the Specter of the West*, p. 423.

13 Ronald Inden, Jonathan Walters, and Daud Ali, *Querying the Medieval: Texts and the History of Practices in South Asia*, Oxford and New York: Oxford University Press, 2000, 20 ff.

14 Brian Pennington's book *Was Hinduism Invented? Britons, Indians, and the Colonial Construction of Religion*, New York: Oxford University Press, 2005 provides a comprehensive and balanced account of the debate. See Asad, 'Smith' for a fruitful intervention in the terms of debate on reification.

15 Mandair, *Religion and the Specter of the West*, p. 236.

16 Harjot Oberoi, *The Construction of Religious Boundaries: Culture, Identity and Diversity in the Sikh Tradition*, New Delhi: Oxford University Press, 1997, p. 25.

17 Tony Ballantyne, *Between Colonialism and Diaspora: Sikh Cultural Formations in an Imperial World*, Durham, London: Duke University Press, 2006, p. 66 ff.

18 David Lorenzen, 'Who Invented Hinduism?', *Comparative Studies in Society and History*, vol. 41, 1999, pp. 630–59

19 Brian Pennington, *Was Hinduism Invented? Britons, Indians, and the Colonial Construction of Religion*, New York: Oxford University Press, 2005, p. 172.

20 Mandair, *Religion and the Specter of the West*, p. 236.

21 Ibid.

22 Indeed, Mandair explores such a theme in his exposition of the *bani* or sacred writings of the Gurus.

23 Kuir Singh, *Gurbilās Patshāhī Das*, p. 277.

24 Surjit Hans, *A Reconstruction of Sikh History from Sikh Literature*, Jalandhar: ABS Publishers, 1988, pp. 266, 269; see Kuir Singh, *Gurbilās Patshāhī Das,* p. 259 and mention of *firang*. Madanjit Kaur 'Koer Singh's Gurbilas Patshahi 10:An Eighteenth Century Sikh Literature'. http://sikhinstitute.org/recent_res/ch13.html accessed 13 June 2010.

25 On the genre and the major texts associated with it, see Purnima Dhavan 'The Warrior's Way: The Making of the Eighteenth-Century Khalsa Panth', PhD dissertation, University of Virginia, (2003), 13, 15, 90ff., 141, chapter 4, *passim*; Louis Fenech, *Martyrdom in the Sikh Tradition: Playing the 'Game of Love'*, New Delhi: Oxford University Press, 2000, p. 123ff; W.H. McLeod, 'The Hagiography of the Sikhs', in Winand M. Callewaert and Rupert Snell (eds), *According to Tradition: Hagiographical Writing in India*, Wiesbaden: Harrassowitz Verlag, 1994, p. 33ff.; W.H. McLeod (ed.), *Textual Sources for the Study of Sikhism*, Chicago: University of Chicago Press, 1984, p. 11ff., and McLeod, *Who is a Sikh?*,

p. 51. For discussion of the term '*Bilas*', see Anne Murphy, 'History in the Sikh Past', *History and Theory,* 46 (2), October 2007, pp. 345–65.

26 See introduction to Kuir Singh, ix and Gurtej Singh, 'Compromising the Khalsa Tradition: Koer Singh's *Gurbilās*', in J.S. Grewal (ed.), *The Khalsa: Sikh and Non-Sikh Perspectives*, pp. 47–58, New Delhi: Manohar, 2004, pp. 48–9.

27 See Hans, *Reconstruction,* pp. 250–3.

28 Sukha Singh, *Gurbilas Patshahi Das* (ed.) Gursharan Kaur Jaggi, 2nd edn, Patiala: Bhasha Vibhag, 1989. See the fifth section, p. 64 ff., for this description.

29 Kesar Singh Chibber *Baṃsāvalīnāmā Dasāṃ Pātshāhīāṃ kā* (ed.) Piara Singh Padam, Amritsar: Singh Brothers, 1997, pp. 115–22 for Satidās and Matidās and the incident, pp. 120 and 122 for reference to the *Bachittar Nāṭak*. J.S. Grewal argues the text is neither an example of *gurbilās*, nor a genealogy, as the title would suggest: J.S. Grewal 'Brahmanizing the Tradition: Chibber's *Baṃsāvalīnāmā*' in J.S. Grewal (ed.), *The Khalsa: Sikh and Non-Sikh Perspectives*, pp. 59–87, New Delhi: Manohar, 2004, p. 61.

30 Murphy, 'History in the Sikh Past', 2007.

31 Ganda Singh (ed.) [1967], *Kavī Saināpati Racit Srī Gur Sobhā*, Patiala: Publications Bureau, Punjabi University, 1988 (hereafter *Gur Sobhā*). See general discussion on dating in Murphy 2007, and, for an argument for an earlier date, Gurinder S. Mann 'Sources for the Study of Guru Gobind Singh's Life and Times', *The International Journal of Punjab Studies*, 15 (1 and 2), pp. 229–84.

32 For discussion of the authority invested in *granth* and *panth*, see Harjot Oberoi, 'From Punjab to "Khalistan": Territoriality and Metacommentary', *Pacific Affairs*, 60 (1), 1987, pp. 26–41, 33ff.

33 For examples of references to Ram, see Kuir Singh, *Gurbilās Patshāhī Das,* pp. 15, 18–20, 50; the reference to both Ram and Shiva is on p. 21.

34 See discussion of Vaishnava references in Jeevan Deol, 'Eighteenth Century Khalsa Identity: Discourse, Praxis, and Narrative', in Christopher Shackle, Gurharpal Singh, and Arvind-pal Singh Mandair (eds), *Sikh Religion, Culture, and Ethnicity*, Surrey, England: Curzon Press, 2001, pp. 25–46.

35 *Sri Dasam Granth Sahib*, trans. Dr Surindar Singh Kohli, vols 1–3, Birmingham, UK: The Sikh National Heritage Trust, 2003.

36 See Kuir Singh, *Gurbilās Patshāhī Das,* pp. 12 and 50.

37 See, for instance, Cynthia Talbot, 'Inscribing the Other, Inscribing the Self: Hindu–Muslim Identities in Pre-Colonial India', *Comparative*

Studies in Society and History, 37 (4), 1995, pp. 692–722. Indeed, distinctions between Muslim and non-Muslim shift in the text overall. There is not room to explore this further here; see Hans, *A Reconstruction of Sikh History*, for some discussion.

38 See, for example, Kuir Singh, *Gurbilās Patshāhī Das*, chapter five. In this it carries forward themes central to Sikh tradition particularly as expressed in the Dasam Granth. See Louis Fenech, *The Darbar of the Sikh Gurus: The Court of God in the World of Men*, New Delhi: Oxford University Press, 2008 and Robin Rinehart, *Debating the Dasam Granth*, New York: Oxford University Press and AAR, 2011.

39 Fauja Singh, 'Introduction', in Kuir Singh, *Gurbilās Patshāhī Das* (ed.) Shamsher Singh Alok, Patiala, Punjab: Publications Bureau, Punjabi University, 1999, p. xix. For another discussion of the relative historicity of the events and alternative versions, see Sher Singh 'Guru Tegh Bahadur courted Shahidi for Milat-e-Nau' http://www.sikhreview. org/pdf/january2008/pdf-files/history3.pdf, accessed 14 June 2010. Encounters with religious figures abound in the text. See, for example, also pp. 25–6, for an interchange with a *pir.*

40 Heinrich von Stietencron, 'Religious Configurations in Pre-Muslim India and the Modern Concept of Hinduism', in Vasudha Dalmia and Heinrich von Stietencron (eds), *Representing Hinduism: The Construction of Religious Traditions and National Identity*, Thousand Oaks, California and New Delhi: Sage Publications, 1995, pp. 51–81; Gauri Viswanathan's exploration of conversion in the articulation of modern social subjectivities is also exemplary: *Outside the Fold: Conversion, Modernity and Belief*, Princeton: Princeton University Press, 1998.

41 Fenech, *Martyrdom in the Sikh Tradition*, pp. 124–5.

42 Ibid., p. 125.

43 Ibid., p. 124.

44 Given the reference to forehead marks and sacred threads above, this term could specifically refer to those bearing these marks, or could refer to a more general category of person.

45 There is no negation in the line in the Punjabi published print version (with commentary) by the Shiromani Gurdwara Parbandhak Committee (SGPC), but other published versions of the text feature the negation and it is standard to include it. See for example, *Sri Dasam Granth Sahib*, vol. 1, Surindar Singh Kohli (trans.), Birmingham: The Sikh National Heritage Trust, 2003, p. 128.

46 This is translated as miracle in the SGPC published version of the text, with commentary; It is translated as faith at http://www.sikhiwiki.org/

index.php/Bachitar_Natak, accessed 14 June 2010 and his creed in Kohli, *Sri Dasam Granth*, 128. I leave it untranslated in the light of the disagreement over its meaning.

47 In section 5 of the text, the final lines of the section.

48 Fenech, *Martyrdom in the Sikh Tsradition*, pp. 153–4.

49 Kuir Singh, *Gurbilās Patshāhī Das*, p. 35; line 23.

50 Ibid., p. 40.

51 I thank Francessca Orsini for this observation, which in the confines of this short paper I cannot do justice to.

52 This is present in Chibber's text as well, for example, Kesar Singh Chibber, *Baṃsāvalīnāmā*, pp. 225–6.

53 Gurtej Singh 'Compromising the Khalsa Tradition'.

54 Hans, *Reconstruction*, p. 269.

55 Ibid.

56 Gurtej Singh, 'Compromising the Khalsa Tradition', p. 49.

57 Hans, *Reconstruction*, p. 269.

58 Ibid.

59 Ibid., p. 267.

60 Gurtej Singh, 'Compromising the Khalsa Tradition', p. 52.

61 Kuir Singh, *Gurbilās Patshāhī Das,* p. 37; see also similar reference on p. 35.

62 Ibid., p. 35; line 20.

63 Ibid., p. 34; line 36.

64 Ibid.; line 40. Sohan Singh Sheetal summarizes this exchange as being one about which is better, Islam or Sikhism. Sohan Singh Sheetal, *Sikh Itihas de some*, Ludhiana: Lahore Book Shop, 1981, p. 142.

65 Kuir Singh, *Gurbilās Patshāhī Das*, pp. 110–13.

66 Lorenzen, 'Who Invented Hinduism?', pp. 648–52.

67 Kuir Singh, *Gurbilās Patshāhī Das*, p. 38.

68 Ibid., p. 43.

69 See Talbot, 'Inscribing the Other', p. 91ff.

70 Kuir Singh, *Gurbilās Patshāhī Das,* p. 11, line 15. A prophecy of the downfall of the Turks is given at numerous places; see p. 42.

71 Ibid., p. 14.

72 Ibid., see for example p. 42.

73 Farina Mir, 'Genre and Devotion in Punjabi Popular Narratives: Rethinking Cultural and Religious Syncretism', *Comparative Studies in Society and History*, 2006, 48 (3), p. 729.

74 Ibid., p. 730.

75 Ibid., pp. 732–3.

76 Ibid., p. 734.

77 Ibid., p. 755.
78 Kuir Singh, *Gurbilās Patshāhī Das*, p. 36, line 49.
79 Muzaffar Alam, *The Languages of Political Islam: India 1200–1800*, Chicago: University of Chicago Press, 2004.

5

Gurinder Singh Mann[†]

Guru Nanak's Life and Legacy

AN APPRAISAL[*]

Guru Nanak (1469–1539), the founder of the Sikh community, is a subject of perennial interest for the Sikhs and their scholars, and a quick look at any bibliography on the subject would reflect the range and the depth of writings available on various aspects of his life and teachings. Given his relatively recent dates, there is a wide variety of sources available about his life and mission (*Jagat nistaran*).[1] These comprise texts, including his poetic compositions and the writings of his immediate successors and early followers; sites such as Talwandi, the place of his birth, and Kartarpur (The Town of the Creator), the centre he established; and two known artefacts associated with his life.[2] These sources provide primary information for a scholarly reconstruction of the Guru's life.

[*] This is a revised version of Gurinder Singh Mann, 'Guru Nanak's Life and Legacy', *Journal of Punjab Studies*, 17 (1–2), 2010, pp. 3–44.
[†] J.S. Ahluwalia, Rahuldeep S. Gill, J.S. Grewal, John S. Hawley, Kristina Myrvold, Christopher Shackle, Ami P. Shah, Harpreet Singh, and Shinder S. Thandi commented on its contents at various stages of its development, I am indebted to them all.

Among the studies that have shaped the discussion on this issue in recent scholarship, *Guru Nanak and the Sikh Religion* (Oxford: Clarendon Press, 1968) by W.H. McLeod (1932–2009) would be the first to come to mind. Since its publication, this book has served as a key source of information on the Guru and the founding of the Sikh tradition in the English language.[3] Its conclusions pertaining to the details of the Guru's life, the import of his teachings, and the nature of his legacy in the rise of the Sikh community have remained dominant in scholarship on Guru Nanak and early Sikh history created during the last quarter of the twentieth century.[4]

With the post-Partition generation's work in Sikh studies reaching a close, it seems reasonable to begin reflecting on the field's future expansion.[5] Beginning this process with a discussion on Guru Nanak and the origins of the Sikh community is logical, and making *Guru Nanak and the Sikh Religion* the point of departure seems pragmatic. This creates the opportunity to review a scholarly icon of the past generation, assess the state of scholarship around one of the most significant themes in Sikh history, and simultaneously explore the possibilities for future research in the field. Working on this assumption, this essay deals with the issues pertaining to Guru Nanak's life, teachings, and activity at Kartarpur, which are addressed in three stages: how McLeod treats them in *Guru Nanak and the Sikh Religion*, my assessment of his positions, and the possible ways to expand this discussion.

My work in recent years with the early Sikh sources has convinced me that the interpretation of Guru Nanak's life and legacy, which resulted in the beginnings of the Sikh community, needs close scrutiny. This project involves a fresh look at the issues related to the life of the founder, interpretation of his beliefs, and a clearer sense of the sociocultural background of the early Sikh community. A greater understanding of this phase of the Sikh community's history would serve both as a foundation to interpret developments in subsequent Sikh history and a window into the medieval north Indian religious landscape.

Constructing Guru Nanak's Life

The opening part of *Guru Nanak and the Sikh Religion* presents a discussion of the Guru's life (pp. 7–147). It begins with an introduction to the sources: the Guru Granth (a largely pre-1604 text), the opening section of the *Vars* (ballads) of Bhai Gurdas (d. 1629), and a set of the Janam Sakhis (life stories [of Guru Nanak]) written over a period of two centuries (1600–1800), and goes on to present summaries of the Guru's life in these texts.[6] From this extensive literary corpus, McLeod selects 124 stories, subjects each one of them to a close scrutiny, and places them under the categories of 'possible' (30), 'probable' (37), 'improbable' (18), and 'impossible' (39) (pp. 92–4). This discussion is followed by an examination of the details regarding the Guru's dates of birth and death (pp. 94–9), and closes with a page and a half summary of his life that is believed to be historically verifiable (pp. 146–7).

Reactions to McLeod's work on the Janam Sakhis as a source of early Sikh history range from denunciation to a sense of awe, but there cannot be any disagreement that he is correct in starting his discussion with early sources on the life and mission of the Guru.[7] In addition to his historical approach, McLeod's attempt to introduce Sikh sources in translation was also a major contribution to the field.[8] Despite these methodological strengths, however, the assumptions that McLeod brought to bear on these sources are problematic. For instance, right at the outset McLeod argues that the Janam Sakhis as a source for the Guru's life are 'highly unsatisfactory', and the challenge is 'to determine how much of their material can be accepted as historical' (p. 8). Instead of replacing these low-value texts with some more useful sources for the purpose of writing a biography of the Guru, McLeod subjects them to an elaborate analysis that ultimately confirms his basic point regarding their limited historical value (pp. 71–147).

Without making a distinction between an analysis of the literary form of the Janam Sakhis and making use of them as a source for reconstructing Guru Nanak's life, McLeod introduces selected episodes from these texts, offers critical assessment of their historical value, and adjudicates the nature of their contents. While following this method, McLeod does not pay the requisite attention to the chronology of the texts under discussion, with the result that his analysis turns out to be synthetic in nature. Selecting, swapping, and blending episodes created by individuals belonging to diverse groups with sectarian agendas, writing over two and half centuries after the death of Guru Nanak, has its own problems.[9] The resulting discussion remains centred on a formalist literary study of the Janam Sakhis and makes little advance toward delineating the Nanak of history.

McLeod's tendency to label the episodes of the Guru's life as possible, probable, improbable, or impossible, or to interpret them as hagiography has not been very productive. Let me illustrate the limitation of his approach with reference to a story involving Guru Nanak's journey to Mount Sumeru that McLeod refers to several times in his *Guru Nanak and the Sikh Religion*.[10] He writes, 'This [Sakhi] indicates a very strong tradition and one which cannot be lightly set aside. When Bhai Gurdas and all of the janam-sakhis unite in testifying to a particular claim we shall need compelling arguments in order to dismiss it' (p. 119). As far as I understand, historians are expected to make sense of the information available to them, not find 'compelling arguments' to dismiss it, and McLeod's rejection of the story on the grounds that Mount Sumeru 'exists only in legend, not in fact' deserves further scrutiny.

In the Puratan Janam Sakhi manuscripts, the description of the Guru's journey to Sumeru is part of his return from Kashmir and is restricted to a short opening sentence of Sakhi 50. This reads: 'Having crossed the Savalakhu hills, [the Guru] climbed Sumeru and arrived at a place (*asthan*) associated with Mahadev'. The remaining story is built around the debate between the Guru and Mahadev and other Shaivite ascetics living at this location regarding the relevance of their spiritual practices and the need for social responsibility and productivity. The episode concludes on a seeming note of congeniality and an agreement between them that they all should meet again to continue this conversation at the annual fair of Shivratari to be held at Achal, which we are told was 'a three-day walk from there'. The location of Achal, a Shaivite site, is well known and is around 20 miles from Kartarpur.

How did the Sumeru apparently located in the Punjab hills become the 'legendary' Mount Sumeru? There are several interesting details that converge here. First, Vir Singh (1872–1957), the editor of the printed edition of the Puratan Janam Sakhi that McLeod uses, interprets *Savalakhu parbat* as 125,000 hills (*sava* is ¼ of 100,000 = 25,000 and *lakhu* is 100,000) instead of Shivalik hills, and on the basis of this reading claims that Guru Nanak crossed these many hills to reach Sumeru.[11] Second, instead of looking toward the south from the Kashmir valley with Srinagar at its centre, Vir Singh takes the reverse direction and envisions Guru Nanak travelling north. Finally, building against the backdrop of Hindu–Puranic mythology and the accounts that appear in the later Janam Sakhis, he concludes that Sumeru is in the vicinity of Lake Mansarovar.[12]

Not interested in making the distinction between the details of the Puratan account of Guru Nanak's visit to Sumeru and its elaboration in the later Janam Sakhis, including the speculative commentary of Vir Singh, and as a result unable to imagine that Sumeru could be a modest seat of the Shaivite ascetics that was 'a three-day walk from Achal', McLeod is quick to reject the possibility of 'Sumeru' being an actual mountain and the Guru having made this journey.[13] Rather than focus on this original episode for the information embedded within it—the prominence of Shaivite ascetics in both the Punjab and the bordering hills; Guru Nanak's debates with these figures; his unequivocal rejection of their way of life and the need for its replacement with a life based on personal, family, and social commitment; and a degree of amiability of the dialogue—McLeod's primary concern is on the physical location of Sumeru. His inability to grasp the details of this episode results in seeking its dismissal. Interestingly, McLeod's effort does not remain restricted to scholarly analysis of the Janam Sakhis but goes beyond to advise the Sikhs to discard them from their literary reservoir for the benefit of the coming generations, as 'seemingly harmless stories can be lethal to one's faith'.[14]

In my view, McLeod's analysis of the Janam Sakhis is less informed by the nature and use of these sources within Sikh literature than by an interpretive lens that views the Janam Sakhi literature as Sikh counterparts of the gospels.[15] As a result, he invested a great deal of time and energy to the study of this literary corpus, but was deeply saddened by the Sikh response to his 'best scholarly work'.[16] Unlike the gospels, however, the Janam Sakhis are not considered authoritative sources of belief, nor are their authors committed to the divine status of their subject. In their own unique ways, these texts attempt to narrate what the Guru did and said, generate feelings of devotion among their listeners/readers as the followers of the path paved by him, and in the process preserve his remembrance.[17]

Rather than trying to overturn these accounts along the lines McLeod established, I believe that scholars need to study early Sikh sources such as the Janam Sakhis by developing a clearer understanding of their dates of origin and the context of their production.[18] The field is fortunate to have sufficient manuscript data and related historical evidence to address these issues, and the critical editions of these texts are slowly becoming available.[19] This seems to be the only way to flesh out significant information available there.

Let me explain what I mean with some details. On the basis of my work with the Janam Sakhi manuscripts, the evidence seems to point to the rise of the Janam Sakhis in the following sequence: Puratan (pre-1600), Miharban (pre-1620), and Bala (1648–58).[20] The dates of the Puratan are suggestive of an early period in the history of the community, when the people who had met the Guru and had the opportunity to hear his message from him may still have been around (*Guru Nanaku jin sunia pekhia se phiri garbhasi na parai re*, M5, GG, 612). The evidence indicates that this text was created by someone who was part of the group that later emerged as the mainstream Sikh community. The possibility that the author of this text and some of his listeners knew Guru Nanak as a real person—who bathed, ate food, worked in the fields, rested at night, and had to deal with sons who were not always obedient—makes this text an invaluable source of information on the Guru's life.

Unlike the Puratan, the importance of the Miharban and Bala Janam Sakhis falls in a different arena. Elaborating on the Puratan narrative, these two Janam Sakhis expand the scope of the Guru's travels and introduce a circle of people who would have made up the third and fourth generation of his followers.[21] Whereas the farthest limit of travels to the east in Puratan is Banaras, Miharban extends the travels to Assam and Puri. Also as sectarian documents, they both reflect the points of view of the groups that created them and mirror the divisions within the community and the polemics involved in presenting the founder in the middle decades of the seventeenth century.[22] Given the variations in time of their origin and context of production, it is essential to study each of these texts separately to see what they have to offer on the Guru's life and the early Sikh community.

Let me present some details available in the Puratan Janam Sakhi to support its relevance for understanding the Guru's life, his primary concerns, and the contours of the early Sikh community. With regard to the founding of Kartarpur, the Puratan narrates that it was established after the first long journey (*udasi*) of the Guru, and not after the completion of his travels, as it is commonly presented in current scholarship.[23] As for the daily routine at Kartarpur, we are told that the Sikhs gathered at the Guru's place (*dargah*), recited his compositions as part of their daily prayers (*kirtan*), listened to his exposition of the ideas therein (*katha*), and shared a community meal (*parsad/rasoi/langar*).

Given this description, his residence would have been a sizeable establishment large enough to accommodate congregational prayers the year round, rain or shine, provide facilities for the making and serving of the food, and put up visitors.[24] The Puratan refers to the recitation of Guru Nanak's *Alahania* (songs of death) and *Sohila* (praise) at the time of his death (Sakhi 57).[25] There is also the firm belief that the Sikhs in their religious life did not follow what others around them practiced (Sakhi 41). In no uncertain terms, the Puratan reports that Kartarpur with the Guru's dargah at its centre represented the sacred site for the Sikhs.[26] The presence of the Guru sanctified it, his abode served as the meeting place, and there is an expectation that the Sikhs living in distant places should make a pilgrimage, have an audience with the Guru, and meet their fellow Sikhs living there.

These details align well with the ideas of Guru Nanak. His compositions represent wisdom (*Sabhi nad bed gurbani*, M1, GG, 879); he is available to provide exegesis to help the Sikhs understand them (*Suni sikhvante Nanaku binavai*, M1, GG, 503); and the text refers to the role of holy places, festivals, and the chanting of sacred verses as an integral part of religious life (*Athsathi tirath devi thape purabi lagai bani*, M1, GG, 150). The Guru is the central figure in this vision, and there is nothing that could compare with his presence (*Guru saru sagaru bohithho guru tirathu dariau*, M1, GG, 17; *Nanak gur samani tirathi nahi koi sache gur gopala*, M1, GG, 437; *Guru sagaru amritsaru jo ichhe so phalu pave*, M1, GG, 1011, and *Guru dariau sada jalu nirmalu*, M1, GG, 1328).

After the establishment of Kartarpur, the Puratan reports four long missionary journeys—to the region of Sindh in the south, the Himalayan foothills in the north, Mecca in the west, and the present-day Peshawar area in the northwest.[27] During these travels, the Guru is reported to have initiated people into the Sikh fold through the use of the ceremony called the 'nectar of the feet' (*charanamrit*), organized Sikh congregations in distant places, and assigned *manjis* ('cots', positions of authority) to local Sikhs, who were given authority to oversee the daily routine of their congregations. Whereas the narrator of the Puratan leaves no doubt that a full-fledged effort at the founding and maintenance of a community occurred at Kartarpur, and that the Guru continued his travels after its establishment, scholars are convinced that Kartarpur came at the end of the Guru's travels, and that he had no interest in building institutions.

Rather than attribute the institutional founding of a community to Guru Nanak, scholars of the past generation have highlighted the activities of later Gurus, especially Guru Amardas (b. 1509?, Guru 1552–74) and Guru Arjan (b. 1563, Guru 1581–1606).[28] Working on the basis of his belief that Guru Nanak rejected the institution of scripture and that it started with Guru Arjan, McLeod and his generation missed the importance of the facts that Guru Nanak evolved a new script, Gurmukhi (the script of the Gurmukhs/Sikhs); committed to writing his compositions in the form of a *pothi* (book) bound in leather; and passed it on ceremonially to his successor, Guru Angad.[29]

The Puratan also informs us that the succession ceremony of Guru Nanak was performed in two stages. In the first stage, the Guru offered some coins to Angad, which in all likelihood indicated transference of the control of the daily affairs (*dunia*) of the Sikh community to him (Sakhi 56). In the second part, the Guru presented the pothi containing his compositions to Angad, which implies that from that point on Angad was in charge of the spiritual affairs (*din*), with the result that he was his formal successor and the leader of the Sikhs (Sakhi 57). The Guru is presented as having conducted an open search for a successor, declaring the succession in a public ceremony, and making sure that all concerned accept the transmission of authority before his death.

EXAMINING GURU NANAK'S BELIEFS

In the second half of *Guru Nanak and the Sikh Religion*, McLeod presents his interpretation of Guru Nanak's teachings (pp. 148–226). He begins by underlining the need to base this discussion on the Guru's compositions and interpret them by situating them in their historical context. He argues that Guru Nanak's writings can be understood within the paradigm of the 'Sant tradition', which he defines as a synthesis of elements from 'Vaishnava Bhakti', 'hatha-yoga', and 'a marginal contribution from Sufism'. He assumes Guru Nanak to be 'a mystic' seeking an 'ineffable union with God' (pp. 149–50). Working on this understanding, he then lays out the Guru's teachings under the headings of 'The Nature of God', 'The Nature of Unregenerate Man', 'The Divine Self-Expression', and 'The Discipline'.[30]

While supporting McLeod's use of Guru Nanak's compositions as the source materials and the need to situate the Guru within the context of his times, one cannot help but raise issues with how he accomplished this task.[31] Explaining his formulation of the 'Sant synthesis' as a reservoir from which the religious poets of the time, including Guru Nanak, drew their ideas, McLeod writes: 'Many of these concepts Guru Nanak shared with the earlier and contemporary religious figures, including Kabir. It is at once evident that his thought is closely related to that of the Sant tradition of Northern India and there can be no doubt that much of it was derived directly from this source' (p. 151).[32] There is no denying that Guru Nanak shared ideas, categories, and terminology with fellow poet saints, but McLeod pushes this position to a point that leaves little provision for any significant originality for any of these individuals' respective ideas.

It is interesting to examine how McLeod arrived at this conclusion to assess the legitimacy of this conceptualization.[33] Writing in 2004, McLeod reports that he started the research that resulted in *Guru Nanak and the Sikh Religion* with the compositions of non-Sikh saints recorded in the Guru Granth, but found that 'their thought was rather difficult to work into a coherent system'. He then 'turned to the works of Guru Nanak', and seemingly reached his formulation that all of them drew their ideas 'Sant synthesis'.

Within the context of the Guru Granth, it is fair to claim that there is a relative homogeneity of overall beliefs between the writings of the non-Sikh saints and those of Guru Nanak, and this is the reason why these people's compositions appear there in the first place. It is thus true that the compositions of these saints in the Guru Granth carry themes that align with those of Guru Nanak, and since these people came prior to the time of the Guru, it is reasonable to infer that he must have borrowed these ideas from them. But the initial difficulty that McLeod faced in reducing the writing of the non-Sikh saints into 'a coherent system' points to the complexity of their thinking and needs to be taken into consideration when arguing for their mutual influence upon one another.

We know that the compositions of the non-Sikh saints that appear in the Guru Granth represent an edited version of their literary production and thus reflect what largely suited the Sikh religious and social thinking. McLeod's discussion here, however, does not provide evidence that he had made any effort to study the writings of these figures that appear outside the Sikh canon.[34] Barring Kabir (292 *chaupada*s and 249 *shalok*s), Namdev (60 chaupadas), and Ravidas (41 chaupadas), the remaining ten 'Sants' have a total of nineteen chaupadas. As far as I can see, McLeod's building the argument of the 'Sant synthesis' involved reading Kabir and then extending his ideas to Namdev and Ravidas, on the one hand, and Guru Nanak, on the other. I believe that each of these figures has to be studied in depth before one could make a firm claim of the type McLeod made, and there was no way to do that, given the state of knowledge in the mid-1960s.[35]

In addition, McLeod assumed that since the Guru's ideas were available in the writings of Kabir, he must have borrowed them from his predecessor. This position served as a launching pad for his twofold analysis. It made the Guru a firm part of 'Sant synthesis', and little basis was left for a belief in the originality found in his writings. There is, however, no evidence to support the assumption that

Guru Nanak knew or had access to the writings of Kabir or those of the other non-Sikh saints, and the manuscript evidence points toward the compositions of these poets entering the Sikh scriptural text during the period of Guru Amardas.[36]

Built on inadequate data, this problematic concept of the 'Sant synthesis' went on to provide the framework for McLeod's 'historical analysis' of the Guru's writings. It resulted in his overemphasizing the similarities between the ideas of the Guru and Kabir, and his dismissal of the links between the Guru's ideas and those of the Sufis such as Farid and Bhikhaṇ.[37] McLeod does not take any note of the presence of Farid's compositions in the Guru Granth, which constitutes the largest single unit (4 chaupadas and 130 shaloks) after Kabir, and thus takes no interest in explaining their significance. Rather than address the role of Islam in Guru Nanak's thinking, McLeod dismisses that role as 'marginal' at best.[38]

In addition to the difficulties inherent in McLeod's formulation of the 'Sant synthesis', one cannot help but question McLeod's selection of what he thinks constitute the primary themes in Guru Nanak's compositions. For instance, while it is true that the nature of God is an important theme in Guru Nanak's poetry, it is important not to miss the specific aspects of the divine nature that fired the Guru's imagination. While singing about God, the Guru is focused on the creative aspect that brought the universe into being (*Ja tisu bhaṇa ta jagatu upia*, M1, GG, 1036), and is immanent in it (*Sabh teri qudrati tun qadiru karta paki nai paqu*, M1, GG, 464). Simultaneously, the Creator turned Sovereign (*Sahibul Patshahi*), is understood to be deeply involved in the day-to-day making and dismantling of the world (*Bhani bhani ghaṛiai ghaṛi ghaṛhi bhanai bhaji usarai usare dhahai*, M1, GG, 935; *Vaikhe vigsai kari vicharu*, M1, GG 8), and initiating radical changes in the natural state of things when necessary (*Nadia vichi tibe dikhale thali kare asgah*, M1, GG, 144). Guru Nanak's interest in divine nature is thus geared toward describing how the Sovereign runs the universe and the implications of this belief for orienting human life.

Let me illustrate this with reference to the Guru's composition entitled *So Daru* ('That Abode'), which enjoys the distinction of appearing three times in the Guru Granth (M1, GG, 6, 8–9, and

347–8) and is part of Sikh prayers recited at both sunrise and sunset. It begins with a question: What is the nature of the abode where the Divine sits and takes care of the universe (*sarab samale*)? The answer to this appears in twenty-one verses, of which seventeen evoke various levels of creation and four underscore divine sovereignty.[39] This interest in the creation as divine manifestation is representative of the Guru's thinking in general and appears in many of his other compositions.[40]

It may be helpful for scholars to consider that Guru Nanak's reflection on the Divine is actually focused on the theocentric nature of the universe. As for more philosophical aspects of divine nature, the Guru seems perfectly at peace with the position that they cannot be expressed in human language and conceptual categories (*Tini samavai chauthai vasa*, M1, GG, 839). For him, the divine mystery has not been fathomed in human history (*Ast dasi chahu bhedu na paia*, M1, GG, 355; *Bed katabi bhedu na jata*, M1, GG, 1021), and what human beings are left with is to accept this limitation and make the best of the situation (*Tu dariao dana bina mai machhuli kaise antu laha, Jah jah dekha taha taha tu hai tujh te nikasi phuti mara*, M1, GG, 25).

Given this context of understanding, the primary responsibility of human beings is to grasp the values that underline the divine creation of (*rachna*) and caring for (*samal*) the world, apply them to use in their daily routine, and in the process become an active part of the universal harmony as well as contribute toward it (*Gagan mahi thal ravi chand dipak bane*, M1, GG, 13).[41] For Guru Nanak, there are two stages of spiritual development: acquiring the knowledge of truth, which seems to be easily accessible from Guru Nanak himself (*Bade bhag guru savahi apuna bhed nahi gurdev murar*, M1, GG, 504), and translating this acquisition into one's life (*Guri kahia so kar kamavahu*, M1, GG, 933; *Sachahu urai sabhu ko upar sachu achar*, M1, GG, 62) through labor and perseverance (*Jah karni tah puri mat, karni bajhahu ghate ghat*, M1, GG, 25). The goal of life is not to be reached in the possession of truth but in its application in one's day-to-day activities (*Jehe karam kamie teha hoisi*, M1, GG, 730; *Jete jia likhi siri kar, karani upari hovagi sar*, M1, GG, 1169; *Sa jati sa pati hai jehe karam kamai*, M1, GG, 1330).

McLeod's elaborate exposition of Guru Nanak's teachings remained centred on his 'theology' and allows no room for ethics. There is no reference to the Guru's crucial stress   a life centred on core values such as personal purity (*ishnan*), social involvement with charity (*dan*), forgiveness (*khima*), honor (*pati*), humility (*halimi*), rightful share (*haq halal*), and service (*Vichi dunia sev kamiai ta dargahi basa,ni paiai*, M1, GG, 26; *Ghari rahu re man mughadh iane*, M1, GG, 1030; *Ghali khai kichhu hathahu de*, M1, GG, 1245). Nor is McLeod able to take note of the Guru's overarching belief that liberation is to be attained collectively (*Api tarai sangati kul tarahi*, M1, GG, 353, 662, 877, 944, and 1039), emphasizing the need for communal living and social productivity. Unlike other medieval poet saints, the Guru also spoke emphatically of collective liberation (*Api tarahi sangati kul tarahi tin safal janamu jagi aia*, M1, GG, 1039), and went beyond singing about human equality to actually challenging the Hindu caste hierarchy (*Sabhana jia ika chhau*, M1, GG, 83) by starting the langar (communal meal), which represented rejection of any social, age, or gender-related distinctions.

McLeod's categorization of Guru Nanak's teachings brings to the forefront issues pertaining to the most effective way to interpret Guru Nanak's beliefs. As for traditional Sikh scholarship, there have been two distinct ways to expound on his compositions.[42] The primary method has been to focus on Guru Nanak's compositions. The author would introduce the context in which the Guru is believed to have written the composition under discussion, would then quote its text, and explain its message in the medium of prose. These commentaries, as well as anthologies of the compositions used for the purpose of exegesis in devotional sessions, are extant beginning with the late sixteenth century.[43] This method of analysis of the Guru's compositions continues till the present day and can be seen working in the writings of scholars trained in the *taksals* ('mints', Sikh seminaries).[44]

The second type of analysis of Guru Nanak's and his successors' teachings begins with Bhai Gurdas, who selected a set of themes that he wanted to share with his audience, and then elaborated upon them by paraphrasing the Guru's writings in his own poetry. Beginning with the last quarter of the nineteenth century, the writers working along these lines began to use prose as their medium of expression, and from this point on these writings emerged as an important genre.[45] This approach achieved a high degree of expansion in the works of Jodh Singh (1930s), Sher Singh (1940s), and McLeod (1960s).[46]

Whereas the commentators of the former version aimed to contextualize the composition under discussion within Guru Nanak's life and deal with its total contents, the latter option involved an exercise in formal analysis, with the presentation of a particular theme without having to clarify its precise position in the larger context of Guru Nanak's beliefs, let alone situating it in the activity of his life. While the first had some sense of episodic completeness in its devotion to Guru Nanak's thinking, the second in all likelihood began as answers to questions from the audience by those who had an overall understanding of the message of the Gurus. As it developed, however, it involved the author's mechanical selection of themes, and the resulting imposition of a system on the Guru's ideas may have its strengths but also has the potential to become a problem, as in the case of McLeod.

In my view, the aforementioned approaches that analyse Guru Nanak's teaching by focusing on his compositions need to be refined as well as expanded to include the details of his life, the nature of his activity particularly at Kartarpur, and the information about the context in which these unfolded. The effort in the past years to take up a theme, catalogue its appearances in the writings of the Gurus, and essentially summarize these quotations remains limited. In other words, a computer search of, say, the term *seva* (service) in the verses of Guru Nanak can only provide the basic data, which needs to be situated within the larger context of his writings and those of his successors to arrive at its significance in the Sikh thinking.

THE FOUNDING OF KARTARPUR

When constructing Guru Nanak's life, McLeod focused on the early sources such as the Janam Sakhis, and for the exposition of his teaching he was content with a formal analysis of the Guru's compositions. The sections devoted to the Guru's life and his teachings in *Guru Nanak and the Sikh Religion* remain mechanically juxtaposed, and the two decades of the Guru's life at Kartarpur are covered in the concluding page and half.[47] There is no move toward linking the Guru's beliefs with what he did during the course of his life, especially the founding of Kartarpur, and the legacy that he left for posterity.

McLeod has little to say on the Kartarpur phase of the Guru's life, which resulted in the gathering of a community, the self-imposed responsibility of overseeing its welfare, and the creation of a blueprint to ensure its future stability. For him, 'the pattern evolved by Guru Nanak is a reworking of the Sant synthesis, one which does not depart far from Sant sources as its fundamental components are concerned. The categories employed by Guru Nanak are the categories of the Sants, the terminology he uses is their terminology, and the doctrine he affirms is their doctrine' (p. 161). McLeod believes that the term 'founder' implies that someone 'originated not merely a group of followers but also a school of thought, or set of teachings', and it applies to Guru Nanak in 'a highly qualified sense'.[48] Having argued this with considerable vigor, McLeod shows no interest in addressing the issue of why he was the only one among his peers to think of founding a community.

Fully convinced of Guru Nanak's rejection of 'external authority', 'ceremonies', 'religious texts', 'pilgrimage', 'ritual bathing', and so on, McLeod is reluctant to explain why the Guru got into the enterprise of gathering a community with numerous institutional structures (p. 153). By emphasizing the 'religious' nature of Guru Nanak's life and legacy, he undercuts the importance of such institutional structures, on the one hand, and seems to point toward its being some sort of 'Hindu' group centred on meditation, on the other.[49] For him, the lives of the people at Kartarpur were oriented around three primary rhythms: meditation, search for liberation, and work in the fields. He misses the interwoven vision of liberation and landscape as reflected in Guru Nanak's poetry saturated with the images of the soil, plants, animals, migratory birds, rain, the Persian wheel, sacred centres, shops, bazaars, and so on. He misses Guru Nanak's recognition of the beauty of creation and his keenness to see the world before replicating it in Kartarpur (*Sabh dunia subhannu sachi samaiai*, M1, GG, 142; *Tat tirath ham nav khand dekhe hat patan bazara*, M1, GG, 156).[50]

Guru Nanak's emphasis on radical monotheism, a life that follows a balance of religious and sociopolitical commitment, and a proactive belief in human equality and so on, which distinguish him from his fellow Shaivite or Vaishnava saints of the period, are not taken into consideration at all. The Guru's vision of social commitment was also deeply informed by his interest in and commentary on contemporary political developments. For example, the Guru's father, Kalu Bedi, and his father-in-law, Mula Chona, were both revenue collectors and were thus part of the political hierarchy of the time.[51] As a teenager, the Guru had to present himself in front of the village elders (*panch, chaudhari, muqadam, mahajan*) and offer defense against the accusations that his buffaloes had damaged the neighbour's wheat crop (Puratan, Sakhi 4).[52] He also worked for a decade or so in Sultanpur, a district headquarter for Daulat Khan, who later emerged as the most powerful political leader in Lahore and was instrumental in inviting the ruler of Kabul, Babur (d. 1529), to invade the region in the 1520s. The Guru's travels further exposed him to political realities, and it is significant to register that those who took up the Guru's path at Kartarpur comprised a revenue-paying farming community with close contact to the powers of the time who determined the terms of revenue and then ensured its collection.

Guru Nanak's compositions reflect his extensive interest in and knowledge of politics and his discomfort with the prevailing corruption around the key political institutions (*Raje sih muqadam kute, jai jagain baitthe sute*, M1, GG, 1288).[53] He took notice of the Mughal invasions, and was the only spiritual figure of his time to have written on the subject (which he did in the form of a set of four compositions: M1, GG, 360, 417–18, 722). He himself was no pacifist and accepted confrontation between opposing political powers and the ensuing bloodshed as a way of life, but he could not accept violence in which the innocent and the hapless bore the brunt of political conflict (*Je sakata sakate ko mare ta man rosu na hoi, Sakata sihu mare pai vagai khasmai sa pursai*, M1, GG, 360). In light of his belief in divine justice as the organizing principle in the world, Guru Nanak rejected any justification for a system based on bribes and false witnesses (*Vaddhi lai ke haqu gavai*, M1, GG, 951; *Lai ki vaddhi den ugahi*, M1, GG, 1032).

In other words, the Guru's early upbringing provided him the opportunity to know how the political authority functioned in the village (Sakhi 3, Puratan), the nature of its relationship with that of the local headquarters (*shiq*), and then through it to the centre at

Lahore (*suba*). His compositions underscore the need to be involved in life at all levels (*Jab lagu dunia reahie Nanaku kichhu sunie kichhu kahie*, M1, GG, 661; *Ghali khai kichhu hathahu dehi Nanaku rahu pachhanahi sei*, M1, GG, 1245), and condemn any tendency that may lead toward an ascetic path (*Makhatu hoi ke kan parae phakar kare horu jat gavai*, M1, GG, 1245). It is reasonable to argue that these ideas played an important role in his decision first to gather a community at Kartarpur and then to prepare a blueprint for its future. Remaining fixated on the 'religious' nature of the community, scholars have totally missed the possibility that Guru Nanak's effort at Kartarpur may have been patterned on the model of Lahore, but at the same time, was creating a better version of it.

This position comes into focus in the light of the early Sikh community's understanding of Guru Nanak's life and activity. The first account of the founding of Kartarpur, which appears a decade or so after the Guru's death, explains it in terms of the establishment of a kingdom with a castle at its base (*Nanaki raju chalia sachu kotu satani niv dai*, Rai Balwand and Satta Dum, GG, 966), and his nomination of a successor is described in metaphors of the transference of his royal throne to Guru Angad (b. 1504, Guru 1539–52, *Lehene dhareou chhatu siri kari sifati amritu pivade*, Rai Balwand and Satta Dum, GG, 966). The Goindval Pothis compiled in the early 1570s refer to Guru Nanak as the 'Bedi King', who supports both the religious and the temporal dimensions of the world (*Baba Nanak Vedi Patisahu din dunia ki tek*, Pinjore, folio 215), and call him and his successors as the 'True Kings' (*Baba Nanaku, Angad, Amardas, Sache Patisah*, Jalandhar, folio 8).[54] The bards at the Sikh court of the subsequent decades categorized the activity of Guru Nanak in the areas of politics (*raj*) and spirituality (*jog*), and presented his line of successors as a divinely sanctioned royal dynasty (*Sri guru raj abichalu atalu ad purakhi furmaio*, the Bhatts, GG, 1390).[55] In his vars, Bhai Gurdas presented the establishment of the Kartarpur community in terms of the minting of a new coin (*Maria sika jagati vich, Nanak nirmal panthu chalia*, 1: 45).

As mentioned earlier, the Guru enjoyed the supreme authority at Kartarpur; the *manjis* represented this in distant congregations, and the pothi containing his compositions marked a symbolic version of it. In addition, the Guru's *dargah* served as the Sikh *tirath* (sacred spot)

and the destination of pilgrimage, and the charanamrit (initiation ceremony) brought new people into the community. The daily prayers
based on the recitation of the compositions of the Guru, followed
by the langar, which involved communal cooking and sharing food,
served as agencies of internal solidarity as well as distinction from
others such as Shaivites, Vaishanavites, Shaktas, Sufis, and Sunnis.

   In addition to the institutional markers present at Kartarpur, scholars
have not paid adequate attention to the geographical and demographic
considerations that governed Guru Nanak's decision to settle there.
Though the archeological remains of Kartarpur are not available, references to its establishment in the early texts and its geographical location
offer interesting data. The Puratan reports that Guru Nanak started
some sort of communal activity at Talwandi (Sakhi 38), his native
village, but soon decided to move on and establish Kartarpur (Sakhi
40). We know that Talwandi was founded by Rai Bhoa, a high-caste
Hindu convert to Islam, and given this situation, the layout of the village would have a mosque at its center. The Puratan also mentions the
presence of a temple there, which would be in proximity to the Hindu
quarters, as we can guess from the layout of villages of the time.

   It seems reasonable to assume that once Guru Nanak saw his
communal experiment to be taking off in Talwandi, he thought of a
more congenial location for its development, rather than having to
function in an environment of competition with Hindu and Muslim
neighbours on a daily basis (Sakhi 41). A host of reasons seem to
be in place for his choice of the Kartarpur area. His father-in-law,
Mulah Chona, worked for Ajita Randhawa, a Jat village chief in the
area, and would have been of help in making this move possible.
This situation would also imply that the Guru knew the area well,
and was aware of the fertility of the soil with plenty of rain and sub-
soil water ensuring the economic viability of the new community.
His compositions manifest a high degree of sensitivity to the beauty
of the natural world, and the area around Kartarpur, with the river
Ravi entering the Punjab plains and the Shivalik foothills in view,
would have been attractive for the Guru. Its location on the pilgrimage routes marked a potential for access to a stream of spiritual
seekers open to taking up a new way of life. Kartarpur was thus an
ideal location for the founding of a community.[56]

With regards to the demographic composition of the community at Kartarpur, McLeod and scholars of his generation took for granted that the early Sikhs came from the Hindu fold, but new information sheds a different light on their socio-religious background.[57] The received wisdom states that the Khatris, an upper-caste (Vaishiya) group within the Hindu social hierarchy to which Guru Nanak's family belonged, constituted the original Sikh community. This understanding is, it is argued, based on the evidence that appears in the early sources. We are then told that the Khatris were 'the teachers of the Jats', and that this relationship resulted in the large-scale entry of Jats into the Sikh community in the closing decades of the sixteenth century, during a period of growing hostility with the Mughals.[58]

However, a closer examination of evidence from the Puratan and the Vars of Bhai Gurdas regarding the prominent Sikhs of Guru Nanak's day does not seem to support this demographic portrait.

The Puratan	(8 Names)
2 Khatris	Bhagirath and Lehiṇa
3 Jats	*Buddha Randhawa, Saido, and Gheho
1 calico printer (*chhimba*)	Siho
1 blacksmith (*lohar*)	Hassu
1 Muslim (*mirasi*)	*Mardana
The *Vars*	(15 names)
9 Khatris	Taru Popat, Mula Kir, Pirtha Soiri, Kheda Soiri, Pirthi Mal Saihgal, Rama Didi, Bhagta Ohri, Shihan, and Gajaṇ Upal
3 Jats	Ajita, *Buddha Randhawa, and Firaṇa Khaihra
1 blacksmith	Gujar
1 barber (*nai*)	Dhinga
1 Muslim	*Mardana

(*Buddha Randhawa and Mardana appear twice, which leaves us with 21 names)[59]

These statistics are clearly not substantial enough to provide a firm basis to judge the precise social composition of the early Sikh community. In my view, the simple fact that these texts produced by the Sikhs of Khatri background recorded half of the early Sikh leadership (ten out of twenty-one names mentioned above) to have come from the lower caste/outcaste/nomadic backgrounds does not point to the type of the Khatri hegemony argued for in current scholarship. It may also be useful to reiterate there is no reference to any large Khatri movement to Kartarpur from Talwandi, the Guru's village, or any other place, and that all five people who accompanied the Guru during his travels are presented to have come from an outcaste background.[60]

Given this context, I believe that an alternative scenario of the composition of the original Sikh community is worth considering. As for the history of the central Punjab during this period, the local traditions mention the region's devastation by the Mongols (1390s), its development under the Sultans (fifteenth century), and further consolidation under the Mughals (1526–1706).[61] The arrival of the Persian wheel (*harahat*) was the key instrument in the region's development. A survey of the names of the villages in the vicinity of Kartarpur also shows that the Jats and those who worked for them (*Kalals, Lohar, Nais, Tarkhaṇs*, etc.) were its primary inhabitants, and that by the 1520s these people were sufficiently powerful to enter the memoirs of the ruler of Kabul, who was on his way to become Emperor Babur, the founder of the great Mughal dynasty.[62] He remembers them as troublesome and problematic, and their resistance to external interference also surfaces in the sources such as the *Chachnama* (eighth century with a Farsi version prepared in the thirteenth century), and Gardizi's *Zainul Akhbar* (eleventh century).[63]

As for the social history of the Jats, the textual sources record an interesting evolution of this group in the first half of the second millennium. The *Al Hind* (early eleventh century) labels these nomads as the 'low Shudras'; Abul Fazal's *Ain-i-Akbari* (late sixteenth century) records some of them in the list of the large landholders (zamindars) on both sides of the river Ravi; and the *Dabistan-i-Mazahib* (mid-seventeenth century) elevates them a notch up to the lowest rung of the Vaishiyas.[64] It is not hard to explain the Jat elevation in the hierarchy from a low caste to the bottom of an upper-caste level. These centuries had seen the Jats take up settled agriculture and become primary producers of the food that the urban society consumed. No city-dwelling Hindu would have relished the idea of eating the stuff produced by supposedly low or outcaste people.

It is also important to register that we cannot take it for granted that the Jats perceived themselves as Shudras, Vaishiyas, or even part of this caste-based society at all. Once settled, however, they would be in search of ways to construct ties with the society around them. As part of this agenda, we can understand their large-scale entry into Islam in west Punjab, the Sikh path in the central areas, and the beginning of a tedious process of working out a relationship with the caste hierarchy within Hindu society in the areas now known as Haryana and western Uttar Pradesh.[65]

Guru Nanak's move to Kartarpur raises the possibility that he was aware of this sociodemographic situation, and that this might even be a factor in his decision to go there. The place offered fertile soil as well as a large constituency of rural people who were in search of a socio-religious identity. Given his own landowning, farming family setting—the only Sikh Guru to have come from this background—Guru Nanak would have had no problems in building ties with the Jat neighbours and invite them to join his path. His calling the Creator the Great Farmer, seeing the beginning of the universe in terms of sowing seed (*Api sujanu na bhulai sacha vad kirsanu, pahila dharti sadhi kai sachu namu de danu*, M1, GG, 19), and interpreting the key values in terms related to farming would have been of considerable fascination for these people (*Amalu kari dharati biju sabdo kari sachu ki ab nit dehi pani, Hoi kirsanu imanu jamai lai bhistu dozaku murai ev jani*, M1, GG, 24; *Man hali kisrani karani saramu pani tanu khetu, namu biju santokhu sauhaga rakhu gharibi vesu*, M1, GG, 595; M1, GG, 1171).[66] Guru Nanak's concerns with corruption associated with political institutions and discomfort with injustice referred to earlier would have worked well with these people, given their own traditions of tribal justice and resistance to any outside infringement in their activity.

Kartarpur's location thus points toward the possibility of an interesting meeting between a substantive figure, who believed that he had been assigned a mission of creating a new dispensation (*Dhadhi sachai mahali khasami bulia sachi sifiti salah kapaṛa paia*, M1, GG, 150; *Hari kirati rahiras hamari Gurmukhi Panth atitang*, M1, GG, 360; *Api tarahi sangati kul tarahi tin safal janamu jagi aia*, M1, GG, 1039), and people who lived in its vicinity and were searching for a community that could help their transition from a nomadic to sedentary lifestyle. Joining a leader who affirmed human equality (*Sabhana jia ika chhau*, M1, GG, 83) and dreamed of building a society without corruption and oppression would have offered a more attractive alternative than becoming part of the Hindu social hierarchy or locate themselves within the class differentiations prevalent within Muslim society.[67]

The evidence at our disposal points to an impressive presence of the Jats at the time of Guru Nanak's death in 1539. For instance, the village of Guru Angad, Khadur, which served as the primary Sikh seat after the death of Guru Nanak, belonged to the tribe of the Khaira Jats; and the land for Dehra Baba Nanak, the village that Guru Nanak's son, Sri Chand, established after the flooding of Kartarpur came as a gift from Ajita, a Randhawa Jat. In other words, the two Sikh sites that rose to prominence after the disappearance of Kartarpur were directly associated with the Jats. Furthermore, following the authority of Guru Nanak's successor, Guru Angad, the two most prominent figures of the time, Buddha Randhawa, who was also a potential candidate for the guruship, and Ajita Randhawa, who helped rehabilitate the Guru's family at Dehra Baba Nanak, came from a Jat background.[68]

The location of Kartarpur seems to support the view that the Jats and their rural ancillaries constituted the core of the original Sikh community, and scholars in the field need to examine this issue in the days ahead. If found viable, this shift of stance in the social composition of the early Sikh community would call for a new set of parameters to understand the origin as well as later developments in Sikh history. What was there in Guru Nanak's message that attracted these people? How did these erstwhile nomads adopt the contents of his message to their needs and aspirations? Was the early Jat experience of joining the Sikh community so successful that this prepared the ground for the other Jat tribes living around to follow suit in the subsequent decades? These questions would need to be addressed as scholarship develops.

Furthermore, little is known about the life and ethos of the Jats and their outcaste rural ancillaries but, as mentioned earlier, it seems reasonable to argue that being nomads they had no organic relationship with the Hindu caste hierarchy. Making this distinction would have huge implications for our understanding of the concerns and motivations of the early Sikh community. Emerging from McLeod's *Guru Nanak and the Sikh Religion*, the overarching perceptions that Sikh beliefs as well as social constituency essentially emerged from the larger Hindu context, and that their history is one of carving out of a distinct identity from that of the parent community, need to be reassessed.[69]

This discussion would also have a direct bearing on issues related to caste and gender within Sikh society. If the overwhelming majority of the original community was not part of the caste hierarchy, how appropriate is it to use caste-related categories to explain early Sikh society? If the Sikhs themselves now use these terms, then it would be helpful to locate the reasons and precise point of their entry into the Sikh discourse. In the same vein, the treatment of women in the nomadic society and customs such as widow marriage and the absence of sati (burning alive on the pyre of the dead husband), and so on, need to be brought into focus to help understand the happenings within the early Sikh community.[70]

In my view, a narrative of the origin of the Sikh community needs to incorporate an understanding of the life of the master (*khasam*) of Kartarpur (Nanak), the nature of the seed he sowed there (his beliefs), and the sociocultural background of the early caretakers (Sikhs). Having accomplished this task, scholars can attempt to assess how the original seedlings thrived in their subsequent transplantations in different locations, changed circumstances, and the variations among different caretakers. Building on the evidence whose bulk, range, and depth expand with the passage of time, scholars can think through these issues and create a narrative that can provide a higher degree of historical accuracy than the one in current circulation. After all, the Sikhs may be the only major tradition where the origin of the community can be constructed strictly from contemporaneous sources.

Where do scholars in Sikh studies go from here? Three options seem to be available. First, there is a large constituency of scholars in the field who believe that *Guru Nanak and the Sikh Religion* marked a 'paradigm-shift' in 'a historiographical revolution' in Sikh studies, and they would expect future research to build and expand on its conclusions.[71] This understanding implies that *Guru Nanak and the Sikh Religion* is secure as the master narrative of the founding of the Sikh tradition, and as a corollary of this, McLeod's later writings and those of others that were crafted around its arguments deserve the currency they have enjoyed in the past decades.

The second option has appeared in J.S. Grewal's recent writings, where he points out the limitations of McLeod's research findings pertainingto different periods and themes of Sikh history.[72] While arguing that McLeod did not really grasp the details of Guru Nanak's life and his teachings, Grewal points out that McLeod's 'attitude, his approach and his method have often resulted in premature hypotheses', and 'his position as a historian ... aligns him with the "orientalists", with a certain degree of inbuilt Eurocentricism'.[73]

On the basis of my reading of *Guru Nanak and the Sikh Religion* presented here and my past years' immersion in the early documents, I believe that efforts to build on the received wisdom or keep ourselves restricted to critiquing McLeod would be counterproductive for the field.[74] While fully agreeing with Grewal about the limitations of McLeod's work, my primary interest lies in how to move forward and develop a fresh narrative of Guru Nanak's life, beliefs, and legacy. Given the critical mass of scholars presently working in the field and the availability of the large corpus of published materials, this goal does not seem beyond reach.[75]

I suggest a three-stage process to execute this agenda. First, scholars need to return to the early textual sources, date them with some degree of precision, situate them in their socioliterary contexts, and flesh out historical details from them. Second, they need to expand the pool of information by including art, artefacts, iconography, numismatics, sites, and so on, and then seek out information that these sources can provide. Finally, the information gathered around the landmarks in Sikh history should be presented in emic Sikh terminology.[76] As I have attempted to show that the terms such as the 'Sant synthesis', 'unregenerate man', and 'the discipline' popularized by *Guru Nanak and the Sikh Religion* would not do, but more work needs to be done before we can cull out a set of terms that may present the frame of reference adequately.

Let me close this essay by underlining the need for precision in scholarly understanding of Guru Nanak and early Sikh history. Two events associated with Guru Nanak's fifth birth centennial that unfolded on the campuses of the universities in the Punjab serve as interesting pointers in this direction. The first relates to the name of Guru Nanak. The Akali Dal, a Sikh political party, which ruled the Punjab in the late 1960s, sponsored a set of public celebrations in 1969 to commemorate the Guru's birth, and the establishment of a new university in Amritsar was the jewel in this crown. The institution was named 'Guru Nanak University' and was inaugurated with great fanfare. After the graduation of the first batch of students, a public controversy erupted that resulted in the rise of a political campaign to expand its name. The people spearheading this move were emphatic that the institution named in honour of the Guru must carry his 'full name', which they argued was 'Guru Nanak Dev'. The state government, after protracted resistance, buckled under and granted their wish by expanding the name of the university by a legislative act in 1975. As far as I know, there is no reference to 'Dev' in the writings of Guru Nanak or those of his successors or early Sikhs. Is it part of the name or does it mark an honorific that was added later? No one seemed to be clear about these issues while changing the name in the 1970s, and the present generation does not even seem to remember that this controversy erupted in the early history of their university.[77]

The next instance concerns the date of birth of Guru Nanak and the debate that unfolded around it on the campus of Punjabi

University, Patiala. In the fall of 1969, this university organized an array of activities to celebrate the event, of which an international conference held in September was the prize item. On this occasion, a special issue of *The Panjab Past and Present*, a university-based journal of history, was released, entitled *Sources on the Life and Teachings of Guru Nanak*; it was edited by Ganda Singh (1900–87), a highly respected historian of the time, and was distributed to the participants. While the conference at the university campus was synchronized with the celebrations of the Guru's birth, believed to have been in late November (*Katak di Puranmashi*), the editorial appearing in the journal issue argued for 15 April 1469 (*Visakh*) as his date of birth. A generation of scholars has come and gone since the event, but no clarity seems to have emerged on this basic issue.

A final detail revolves around the reference to the early Sikh community as the 'Nanak Panth'.[78] Although scholars such as McLeod and many others of his generation use this label freely and without question, it must be underscored that this term does not appear in the writings of Guru Nanak, or those of his successors and their followers.[79] It first shows up in the Janam Sakhi attributed to Miharban (d. 1640), a first cousin of the sixth Sikh Guru, Guru Hargobind (b. 1595?, Guru 1606–44), and even more important for us, the leader of a major Sikh sectarian group of the time (Miṇas/Chhota Mel).[80] The *Dabistan-i-Mazahib*, a mid-seventeenth-century Farsi text, is the first non-Sikh document to use the name the Nanak Panthi along with the Gursikh to refer to the community.[81] Furthermore, it is important to point out that a name such as the Nanak Panth, which evokes the idea of 'personal' following of a leader, is criticized in the writings of Bhai Gurdas and is categorically denounced in the poetry created during the period of Guru Gobind Singh (1675–1708).[82] In other words, the name assigned to the early Sikh community in current scholarship is not a self-designation, but a sectarian/external label the nature of which is criticized in the mainstream Sikh literature.

Focusing on details such as these would help scholars work toward developing a more accurate and nuanced narrative of the happenings during this early phase of Sikh history. Once the details of the founding of the Sikh community and the terms required to name and explain them are in place, people in the field can then move on to interpret the developments in subsequent history. I believe a clean start is necessary to delineate the origin of the Sikh Panth (the path of the Sikhs), and then one can map how it turned into the *gaddi rah* (big path) of Bhai Gurdas and the *param marag* (great path) of the late seventeenth-century anonymous author at the court of Guru Gobind Singh.[83]

NOTES

1 A recent bibliography of writings in English records over 600 entries on Guru Nanak; see Rajwant Singh Chilana, *International Bibliography of Sikh Studies*, Dordrecht: Springer, 2005, pp. 30–60. The writings in Punjabi on the Guru are far more extensive and spread over a much longer period of time. The opening statement of the Puratan Janam Sakhi reads: 'The life story of Baba Nanak from the beginning to the end [who] came to liberate the world'. For its published edition, see Rattan Singh Jaggi (ed.), *Puratan Janam Sakhi*, Patiala: Pepsu Book Depot, 1977.

2 Scholars count Guru Nanak's compositions recorded in the Guru Granth (GG) in different ways. Charan Singh provides the figure of 974 poetic stanzas; see his *Bani Biaura* [1902], Amritsar: Khalsa Tract Society, 1945, pp. 124–5; Kahn Singh Nabha presents the number as 947 in his *Mahan Kosh* [1930], Patiala: Bhasha Vibhag, 1981, p. 437; Sahib Singh counts them as 357 compositions and 3 Vars in his *Sri Guru Granth Darpan*, Jalandhr: Raj Publishers, 1961, 1: 17; and Piara Singh Padam supports the figure of 974; see his *Sri Guru Granth Prakash*[1977], Patiala: Kalam Mandir, 1990, p. 58.

As for the artefacts, a pothi and a chola associated with the Guru are extant. For details, see 'The Guru Harsahai Pothi', in my *Making of Sikh Scripture*, New York: Oxford University Press, 2001, pp. 33–40; and entries on the chola in Tara Singh Narotam, *Sri Guru Tirath Sangraih*, Kankhal: Sri Nirmal Panchayati Akhara, 1884, 288–9; Giani Gyan Singh, *Tvarikh Gurdarian*, Amritsar: Buta Singh Pratap Singh, undated [1919?]), 36; Kahn Singh Nabha, *Mahan Kosh*, p. 477.

For references to the Guru in the writings of his successors and early followers, see Ganda Singh (ed.), *Sources on the Life and Teachings of Guru Nanak*, Patiala: Punjabi University, 1969, pp. 26–44. For the details of his life, see Kirpal Singh and Parkash Singh (eds), *Puratan Janam Sakhi*; *Janam Sakhi Miharban*, 2 volumes, Amritsar: Khalsa College, 1962, 1969; Gurbachan Kaur (ed.), *Janam Sakhi Bhai Bala*, Patiala: Bhasha Vibahg, 1987; and Gursharan Kaur Jaggi (ed.), *Varan*

Bhai Gurdas, New Delhi, Arsi Publishers, 2010. For the latest research on Bhai Gurdas, see Rahuldeep Singh Gill, 'Growing the Banyan Tree: Early Sikh Tradition in the Works of Bhai Gurdas Bhalla', PhD dissertation, University of California, Santa Barbara, 2009.

3 When discussing the impact of McLeod's book, one must be clear that the traditional Sikh scholars worked in Punjabi, and as a result had no direct access to the book. They receive eight to ten years of training in the *taksals*, which involves learning the recitation and interpretation of the Guru Granth, the study of Sikh historical writings, practice in *kirtan*, and extensive travels to Sikh pilgrimage centres. Their work prepares them to become *granthi*s. Unfortunately, there is very little scholarly literature available on the *taksals*, and many scholars writing in English are not even aware of the presence of these institutions. From among the products of these *taksals*, Randhir Singh (1898–1972), Shamsher Singh Ashok (1903–86), Piara Singh Padam (1923–2001), and Joginder Singh Vedanti (1940–). could be counted as the major figures of the past century. For information on the early history of the taksals, see G.W. Leitner, *History of Indigenous Education in the Punjab* [1883], Patiala: Bhasha Vibhag, 1971, pp. 28–37.

Among scholars who work in English, there were efforts to register differences with *Guru Nanak and the Sikh Religion*. Fauja Singh Bajwa (1918–83), a historian based in Punjabi University, engaged with McLeod's argument with a high degree of seriousness; see his 'Guru Nanak and the Social Problem', in Harbans Singh, (ed.), *Perspectives on Guru Nanak*, Patiala: Punjabi University, 1975, pp.141–50. In this essay originally presented at a conference in 1969, he made a two-pronged argument: Guru Nanak was deeply concerned about the social issues of his times, and given this area of his interest, his message differed in fundamental ways from those of his contemporaries. Unfortunately, Fauja Singh got embroiled in a controversy of his own in 1975, when he was attacked by university-based scholars as well as those outside academia, pushing him out of any public role. For details, see his 'Execution of Guru Tegh Bahadur: A New Look' [1966], *Journal of Sikh Studies*, February 1974, pp. 79–89, and responses to it by Trilochan Singh's 'Letter to the Editor', August 1974, pp. 122–6; and J.S. Grewal's 'Freedom and Responsibility in Historical Scholarship', *Journal of Sikh Studies*, February 1975, pp. 124–33.

Simon Digby (1932–2010), an expert on Islamic literature of South Asia, was the only Western scholar to present a substantive review of McLeod's work, which he described as 'the latest and one of the most valuable additions to the corpus of Christian missionary writings on the religious sociology of India, whose type and pattern were established early in the century'. Having situated McLeod's work in this tradition, Digby registers his discomfort with his 'ruthless approach' to unearth the 'Nanak of history', his use of 'Protestant theological terms' to explain Guru Nanak's ideas, and his 'weak grasp of Sufi literature'. For this review, see the *Indian Economic and Social History Review*, 7 (2), 1970, pp. 301–13. Published in a Bombay-based journal, Digby's ideas seemingly did not reach the Punjab and as a result could not become part of the discussion of McLeod's work in any important way.

Some scholars attempted to engage with McLeod's approach and argued that there are different ways to understand the Guru's life, but none of these succeeded in challenging McLeod's argument in any significant way or emerge as a viable alternative to his presentation. For early efforts in this direction, see Harbans Singh (1923–95), *Guru Nanak and the Origin of the Sikh Faith*, Patiala: Punjabi University, 1969, and J.S. Grewal (1927–), *Guru Nanak in History*, Chandigarh: Panjab University, 1969.

It might also be useful to mention that McLeod's writings evoked a hostile response within some circles. He reports that he was not invited to the international conference arranged by Punjabi University in September 1969, and Kapur Singh denounced the book there; see his *Discovering the Sikh: Autobiography of a Historian*, New Delhi: Permanent Black, 2004, pp. 63–4. Early responses to the book included Kirpal Singh's critique published in *The Sikh Review*, February–March 1970. Daljeet Singh (1911–94), whose interest in Sikh studies followed his retirement from Indian Administrative Services in 1969, spearheaded the second round of this attack. As McLeod's status rose on the North American academic scene in the 1980s, Daljeet Singh's opposition to his works became increasingly strident. With some degree of effort, he was able to bring together some supporters who were ready to help him save 'Sikh scholarship from the missionary onslaught'. This denunciation of McLeod's writings and, by extension, those of others who were thought to have been working with him largely unfolded in North America. This criticism barred the Sikh studies programs at Toronto University (1986–92) and Columbia University (1988–99) from attaining permanence, and stunted the growth of the programs at the University of British Columbia (1987–97) and the University of Michigan (1992–2004) during the nascent stages of its development. For details of these debates, see Gurdev Singh (ed.), *Perspectives on the Sikh Tradition*, Patiala: Siddharth, 1986; J.S. Grewal, *Contesting Interpretations of the Sikh Tradition*, New Delhi: Manohar, 1998, pp. 215–37; and McLeod, *Discovering the Sikh*, pp. 154–91.

In my view, Daljeet Singh and his associates could not distinguish between McLeod's training in biblical studies and what they perceived as his 'missionary designs' to erode the foundation of the Sikh tradition; see Grewal, *Contesting Interpretations of the Sikh Tradition*, 128. As a result, they could not identify the precise nature of what irked them in McLeod's writings. McLeod's response to their criticism was no less enigmatic. He argued that he was an atheist and attack on his research was part of an effort to protect the Sikh traditions from historical scrutiny; see his 'Cries of Outrage: History versus Tradition in the Study of Sikh Community', *South Asia Research*, vol. 14, 1994, pp. 121–35. Given the fact that the people McLeod refer to in his discussion were products of Western modes of education and wrote in English, I am not convinced that McLeod's characterization of them as 'traditional scholars' and their motivation as being centred on protecting 'traditions' had much justification.

4 The authority of *Guru Nanak and the Sikh Religion* was established soon after its publication. McLeod himself and some other scholars built their interpretation of the events in later Sikh history on the research results of this book, thereby further strengthening its influence and authority in the field. See his *Evolution of the Sikh Community*, Oxford: Clarendon Press, 1976; *Who Is a Sikh? The Problem of Sikh Identity*, Oxford: Clarendon Press, 1989; and *Sikhism*, New York: Penguin, 1997. For those who built on McLeod's interpretation of early Sikh history, see Harjot Oberoi, *The Construction of Religious Boundaries*, New Delhi: Oxford University Press, 1994, pp. 47–91; for its critique, see J.S. Grewal, *Historical Perspectives on Sikh Identity*, Patiala: Punjabi University, 1997, pp. 33–47.

As for general acceptance of the conclusions of the book in the 1980s, see John S. Hawley and Mark Juergensmeyer, *Songs of the Saints of India*, New York: Oxford University Press, 1988; and A.T. Embree (ed.), *The Sources of Indian Tradition*, New York: Columbia University Press, 1988 [1958], and many others that deal with the Sikh tradition in a limited way. The impression that McLeod had acquired a mastery of Punjabi provided a high degree of authenticity and authority to his writings in the eyes of many Western scholars who were happy to use them for basic information they needed about the Sikhs.

5 It may be useful to reiterate the landmarks of this period, which included the establishment of Punjabi University, Patiala (1962), and Guru Nanak Dev University, Amritsar (1969), as well as the celebrations of the centennials of the birth of Guru Gobind Singh (1966) and Guru Nanak (1969), the martyrdom of Guru Tegh Bahadur (1975) and Guru Arjan (2004), the inauguration of the Khalsa (1999), and the elevation of the Granth to the position of the Guru Granth (2008). This period has seen the production of more scholarly literature on the Sikhs than in their entire earlier history.

6 In addition to the texts mentioned in note 2, see Vir Singh (ed.), *Puratan Janam Sakhi*, [1926], Amritsar: Khalsa Samachar, 1986; Jasbir Singh Sabar (ed.), *The Gian Ratanavli*, Amritsar: Guru Nanak Dev University, 1993; and Sarupdas Bhalla, *Mahima Parkash*, ed. Utam Singh Bhatia [1776] Patiala: Bhasha Vibhag, 1971.

7 For criticism of McLeod's use of the Janam Sakhis, see Ganda Singh, 'Editorial', *Panjab Past and Present* (October 1970), pp. i–x. In my view, Ganda Singh's evaluation raises important questions regarding the issue of academic responsibility of a senior scholar toward new research. It seems clear that Ganda Singh had fundamental differences with McLeod's research results, but he did not want to bring them to the forefront lest they provide fuel to the fire already gathering around the book; see note 3. His argument that McLeod's work needs 'sympathy', not 'carping criticism', hurt the rise of a healthy debate so essential for a field at an early stage of growth. For positive assessment of his work on the Janam Sakhis, see Surjit Hans, *A Reconstruction of Sikh History from Sikh Literature*, Jalandhar: ABS Publications, 1988, pp. 198–9; and Nripinder Singh, *The Sikh Moral Tradition*, New Delhi: Manohar, 1990, p.79.

8 For McLeod's translations, see *The B–40 Janam Sakhi*, Amritsar: Guru Nanak Dev University, 1980; *The Textual Sources for the Study of Sikhism*, Totowa: Barnes and Nobel, 1984; *The Chaupa Singh Rahit-Nama*, New Zealand: University of Otago Press, 1987; *Sikhs of the Khalsa Rahit*, New Delhi Oxford University Press, 2003; and *The Prem Sumarag*, New Delhi: Oxford University Press, 2006.

The legitimacy of McLeod's use of an historical approach has also come under attack from diverse quarters; see Noel Q. King's essay in Gurdev Singh (ed.), *Perspectives on the Sikh Tradition*; and Jasbir Singh Mann *et al.* (eds), *Advanced Studies in Sikhism*, Irvine: Sikh Community of North America, 1989. For a recent critique, see the relevant sections in Arvind-Pal Singh Mandair, *Religion and the Specter of the West*, New York: Columbia University Press, 2010.

It seems to me that the historical approach synchronizes well with Sikh understanding of the past. For instance, the Sikh view of time is linear, and Sikhs believe their history to be an integral part of the divine design for human kind. For Guru Nanak, the universe rose as a result of the divine command (*hukam, bhana*) and follows a course set in historical time (see his cosmology hymn GG, 1035–6). The Sikhs began to record their own history soon after the community's founding, and the Puratan Janam Sakhi registers a reasonably good consciousness of issues such as that of historical chronology. The daily *ardas* (Sikh supplication) is essentially a thanksgiving prayer for the divine support through various phases of the community's socio-political and ideological development from the beginnings to the present day. References to historical events begin to appear in the writings that are included in the Guru Granth; see Balwand and Satta, GG, 966, for the developments during the sixteenth century; for a discussion of this issue in Guru Arjan's time, see Surjit Hans, *A Reconstruction of Sikh History*, pp. 137–77. The earliest manuscript of *Sakhi Babe Nanak ki Adi to Ant tak*, dated 1640, was extant until the 1970s; see Rattan Singh Jaggi (ed.), *The Puratan Janam Sakhi*, 1, pp. 36–137. For the text of the ardas, see the English version of *Sikh Rahit Maryada*, Amritsar: Shiromani Gurdwara Parbandhak Committee, 1997, pp. 9–11; for discussion of its history and contents, see Lal Singh Gyani, *Puratan Ardasa te Bhaugati Parbodh*, Amritsar: Panch Khalsa Press, 1920; and *Puratan Sikh Ardasa*, Amritsar: Gurmat Press, 1952, pp. 1–17; and Piara Singh Padam, '*Ardas*', in his *Guru Ghar*, Amritsar: Singh Brothers, 1997, pp. 279–86.

9 For instance, unless the history of the sources employed in an account created in 1776, the year of completion of the *Mahima Parkash*, can be traced back to the times of Guru Nanak (d. 1539), I am not convinced that it could serve as a significant source of information for an 'historian'.

10 *Guru Nanak and the Sikh Religion*, pp. 11, 49, 59–60, 75, 119–22.

11 Given his emphasis on the need for skepticism, it is strange that McLeod seems satisfied to use an edition of the Puratan Janam prepared in 1926 by Vir Singh, the limitations of whose editorial capabilities were a subject of a doctoral research; see Harinder Singh, 'Bhai Vir Singh's Editing of *Panth Parkash* by Rattan Singh Bhangu', PhD thesis, Guru Nanak Dev University, Amritsar, 1990.

12 Vir Singh (ed.), *The Puratan Janam Sakhi*, pp. 175–6.

13 Instead of associating this with the Puranic mythology, it may be useful to think of other possibilities such as the name of the leading Jogi based at this place was named Sumer (There is an interesting portrait of 'Bava Sumerpuri' in the collection of Maharaja Nabha); the Jogis based there called it Sumeru; as part of the belief in their powers the people around began to call this place Sumeru; as part of the vernacularization process, the Punjabi *meru* simply means a 'hill' and *sumeru* thus becomes a 'holy hill'. I became aware of the last meaning while reading Giani Naurang Singh's commentary on the *Sarab Loh Granth*, see MS 766, Guru Nanak Dev University, folio 1930.

14 McLeod writes, 'Sikh children who receive a Western-style education will assuredly imbibe attitudes which encourage skepticism, and

having done so they are most unlikely to view traditional janam-sakhi perceptions with approval. Given the emphasis which is typically laid on stories concerning Guru Nanak there is a risk about Sikhism as a whole may come to be associated with the kind of marvels and miracles which are the janam-sakhi stock-in-trade. For some the price may be worth paying, but at least they should be aware of the risks involved in adopting the traditional approach'. See his *Sikhs: History, Religion, and Society*, New York: Columbia University Press, 1989, pp. 21–2.

15 For commentaries on the Janam Sakhis, see *The Gian Ratanavli*, Sakhi 1; Ratan Singh Bhangu (d. 1847), *Sri Guru Panth Parkash*, Balwant Singh Dhillon (ed.), Amritsar: Singh Brothers, 2004, pp. 16, 178–83; Ernest Trumpp (1828–85), *The Adi Granth* [1877], New Delhi: Munshiram Manoharlal, 1978, pp. i–vii; Gurmukh Singh (1849–98), M. Macauliffe (ed.), *The Janam Sakhi Babe Nanak Ji ki*, Rawalpindi: Gulshan Punjab Press, 1885, pp. 1–10; and Karam Singh (1884–1930), *Katak ke Visakh* [1912], Ludhiana: Lahore Book Shop, 1932. Two doctoral theses, Jagjit Singh's 'A Critical and Comparative Study of the Janam Sakhis of Guru Nanak upto the Middle of the Eighteenth Century' (1967); and Piar Singh's 'A Critical Survey of Punjabi Prose in the Seventeenth Century' (1968), were submitted at Panjab University, Chandigarh.

16 For McLeod's writings on the Janam Sakhis, see his *Early Sikh Tradition: A Study of the Janam Sakhis*, Oxford: Clarendon Press, 1980; *The B–40 Janam-sakhi*, Amritsar: Guru Nanak Dev University, 1980; and 'The Janam-sakhis', in his *Evolution of the Sikh Community*, pp. 20–36; 'The Hagiography of the Sikhs', in *Essays in Sikh History, Tradition, and Society* [1994], New Delhi: Oxford University Press, 2007, pp. 35–53; and 'The Life of Guru Nanak', in Donald S. Lopez, Jr. (ed.), *Religions of India in Practice*, Princeton: Princeton University of Press, 1995, pp. 449–61. For the reception of these writings, see his *Discovering the Sikhs*, pp. 150–1.

17 Within his own writings, Guru Nanak describes himself as an ordinary human being who has been assigned the path of singing the praises of the Creator (*Manas murati Nanaku namu*, M1, GG, 350; *Nanaku bugoyad janu tura tere chakran pakhaq*, M1, GG, 721; *Koi akhe adami Nanaku vechara*, M1, GG, 991; *Kare karae sabh kichhu jane Nanaki sair ev kahie*, M1, GG, 434, and 660; *Hau dhadhi hari prabhu khasam ka hari kai dari aia*, M1, GG, 91, and 150, 468, and 1057).

18 For a creative way to address this issue, see John. S. Hawley, 'Mirabai in Manuscript', in *Three Bhakti Voices: Mirabai, Surdas, and Kabir in Their Times and Ours*, New Delhi: Oxford University Press, 2005, pp. 89–98.

19 The two editions, Rattan Singh Jaggi (ed.), *The Puratan Janam Sakhi*; and Gurbachan Kaur (ed.), *Janam Sakhi Bhai Bala* represent excellent critical scholarship.

20 The earliest known manuscripts include the Puratan Janam Sakhi (1640); the Bala Janam Sakhi (1658); and the Miharban Janam Sakhi (1754). The text of the writing of the Gurus that appear in the early Puratan manuscripts is pre-Kartarpur Pothi (1604). We have on record the claim of Hariji (d. 1696) that his father, Miharban, had completed his Janam Sakhi by 1619; see Krishna Kumari Bansal (ed.), *Sodhi Hariji Krit Goshatan Miharban kian*, Sangrur: the editor, 1977, 234; for reference to a copy of Miharban Janam Sakhi prepared in 1651, see MS 427B, Khalsa College, *Samat 1708 Vaisakh Vadi ekam nu* [Miharban, Hariji, and], *Chatrbhuj pothi puran hoi*, folio 676. There is firm evidence that Bala Janam Sakhi was compiled after the death of Baba Handal (1648), and an elaborately illustrated manuscript dated 1658 was extant until recently, see *Janam Sakhi Bhai Bala*, pp. 149–50.

21 The echoing of the Puratan images in the literature of the Miharban family leaves little doubt that this text was available to them, see the opening and sections of *Sodhi Hariji Krit Goshatan Miharban kian*.

22 The Miharban and the Bala Janam Sakhis were productions of the sectarian groups led by Miharban and Baba Handal, respectively. For *Janam Sakhi of Miharban*, see MS 2306, Khalsa College, dated 1650 (*Sakhi Guru Hariji ke mukh ki likhi Samat 1707*, folio 164b); and *Sodhi Hariji Krit Goshatan Miharban kian*. For additional writings of this family, see Pritam Singh and Joginder Singh Ahluwalia, *Sikhan da Chhota Mel: Itihas te Sarvekhan,* San Leandro, California: Punjab Educational and Cultural Foundation, 2009, pp. 84–97. An undated manuscript entitled, *Janam Sakhi Baba Handal* (folios 1–602), is available with his descendents at Jandiala Guru, near Amritsar. For more on this text and family, see Varinder Kaur, 'Parchi Baba Handal: Sampadan te Itihasik Visleshaṇ', MPhil Thesis, Guru Nanak Dev University, Amritsar, 1989; and Rajinder Pal, *Sankhep Jivan Charitar Sri Guru Baba Handal Ji,* Jandiala: Gurudwara Sri Guru Baba Handal Ji, undated [1990s].

23 It may be useful to point out that this itinerary is not accepted in current scholarship; see Harbans Singh, *Guru Nanak and the Origin of the Sikh Faith,* p. 154.

24 A discussion of the relationship of the position of the Guru and the layout of his house with the model of a Sufi master and his hospices (*khanqah*), on the one hand, and the hillock (*tillas*) of the Shaivite ascetics, on the other, would shed light on the nature of relationship of the early Sikhs to these groups. For general information about the

period, see J.S. Grewal (ed.), *Religious Movements and Institutions in Medieval India*, New Delhi: Oxford University Press, 2006.

25 For the singing of the *Alahania*, see the Puratan Janam Sakhi manuscript dated 1690, folio 273b.

26 For an essay on this important theme, see J.S. Grewal, 'Sacred Space in Sikhism', in Joseph T. O'Connell (ed.), *Organizational and Institutional Aspects of Indian Religious Movements*, Shimla: Indian Institute of Advanced Study, 1999.

27 It is important to reiterate that the Puratan's account of Guru Nanak's travels is much less elaborate than the ones available in the Miharban and the Bala Janam Sakhis.

28 For this interpretation of the rise of institutions such as the *langar*, the *manjis*, and the *Granth*, see W.H. McLeod, *Sikhism*, pp. 23–4, and pp. 30–1. Working within this larger context, Pashaura Singh argues that the compositions of the early Gurus were preserved in both oral and written form (aides-memoire), and the institution of scripture formally started with Guru Arjan, see his *Life and Works of Guru Arjan*, New Delhi: Oxford University, Press, 2006, pp. 134–71; Christopher Shackle's recent statement also attributes the first 'canonical' version of Sikh scripture to Guru Arajn, see his 'Repackaging the Ineffable' Changing Styles of Sikh Scriptural Commentary', *Bulletin of School of Oriental and African Studies,* 71(2) 2008, p. 257.

Another example of McLeod's anachronistic discussion of Guru Nanak's theology based on evidence from the writings of other Gurus can be found in his discussion of the *mangal/mulmantar* ('invocation'/'the root formula')—a string of epithets that refer to different aspects of the Divine. He begins his exposition of Guru Nanak's ideas with an analysis of the mangal but fails to mention that it appears for the first time in the Kartarpur Pothi (1604), completed during the period of Guru Arjan. While explicating the 'Sikh conception' of the Divine, it is fine for Jodh Singh to start his discussion with the mangal—see his *Gurmat Nirṇay* [1932], Patiala: Bhasha Vibhag, 1979, 1—but not for McLeod, who is claiming to deal only with the ideas of Guru Nanak. For a discussion of the mangal, see my *Making of Sikh Scripture*, pp. 53–4. The terms *Satinamu, Akal Murati*, and *Ajuni* that appear in the mangal are not used in Guru Nanak's verses, and his favorite epithets for the Divine such as *Kartaru, Nirankaru*, and *Sahibu* are not available in this text.

For a discussion of Guru Amardas' year of birth, see Raijasbir Singh (ed.), *Guru Amardas: Srot Pustak*, Amritsar: Guru Nanak Dev University, 1986, pp. 227–9.

29 For a discussion of this pothi, see my *Making of Sikh Scripture*, pp. 33–40.

30 There was a general welcome accorded to this section of the book after its publication. Ganda Singh complemented McLeod for 'understanding, appreciating and presenting [the Guru's] teachings in a very lucid and convincing manner'; see *Panjab Past and Present* (October 1970), pp. i–x. Needless to say, McLeod's use of Protestant terms such as 'theology', 'divine self-expression', 'unregenerate man', and 'discipline' to label the Guru's ideas may not have sounded unreasonable to people in the late 1960s, but writing in 2010 we are better equipped to understand this problem.

Although I was vaguely aware of this issue of terminology earlier, it was crystallized for me with John S. Hawley's presentation entitled 'What is Sikh Theology?' at Columbia University on 31 March 1990. In this unpublished paper, he laid out the issues involving the use of terms from one tradition to explain the ideas of the other and the problems inherent in this effort.

31 McLeod's discussion is built around the dichotomy between the supposed Sikh belief in 'divine revelation' and his need to analyse the Guru's beliefs by situating them in their historical context. For me, a historian is obligated to take into account Guru Nanak's belief that his compositions represent the divine voice (*Tabalbaz bichar sabadi sunia*, M1, GG, 142; *Jaisi mai avai khasam ki bani, taisra kari gian ve Lalo*, M1, GG, 722). This comes further into focus when we note that none of the Guru's illustrious contemporaries on the Indian side made claims for divine sanction, and these are an integral part of the prophetic tradition on the Judeo–Christian–Islamic side.

32 There is no evidence to support McLeod's category of a Sant; see Nirvikar Singh, 'Guru Nanak and the "Sants": A Reappraisal', *International Journal of Punjab Studies*, 8 (1), 2001, pp. 1–34; for McLeod's response to this article and Singh's rebuttal to that, see *International Journal of Punjab Studies*, 9 (1), 2002, pp. 137–42.

33 For more on this theme, see Karine Schomer and W.H. McLeod (eds), *The Sants: Studies in Devotional Traditions of India*, Delhi: Motilal Banarsidass, 1987, pp. 1–6; Hawley and Juergensmeyer, *Songs of the Saints of India*, pp. 3–7; Nirvikar Singh, 'Guru Nanak and the "Sants": A Reappraisal', pp. 1–34; and J.S. Grewal, *The Sikhs: Ideology, Institutions, and Identity*, New Delhi: Oxford University Press, 2009, pp. 3–21.

34 The bibliography in the book does not indicate that McLeod paid much attention to the writings of these saints that appear outside the Sikh canon. Nor does he take any note of the effort that went into the selection of these compositions for the Sikh scriptural text. From our knowledge of the early Sikh manuscripts, the writings of the non-Sikh

saints were vetted in two stages. In the first, those who believed in iconic worship were labelled as unbaked stuff (*kachi bani*) and discarded. In the second, the available compositions of those who believed in the formless God were subjected to close scrutiny and the ones that conformed to the Sikh beliefs in family and social life were selected. For these details, see my *Making of Sikh Scripture*, pp. 111–17; Pashaura Singh, *The Bhagats of the Guru Granth Sahib*, New Delhi: Oxford University Press, 2003; Vinay Dharwardkar, *Kabir: The Weaver's Song*, New Delhi: Penguin, 2003, pp. 25–58; and John S. Hawley, 'The Received Kabir: Beginnings to Bly', in *Three Bhakti Voices: Mirabai, Surdas, and Kabir in Their Times and Ours*, pp. 267–78.

35 The secondary literature referred to in this discussion include Ahmad Shah, *The Bijak of Kabir*, Hamirpur, 1917, pp. 1–28; Charlotte Vaudeville, *Kabir Granthavali*, Pondicherry, 1957, pp. iv–v; Vaudeville, *Au Cabaret de l'Amour: Paroles de Kabir*, Paris, 1959, pp. 7–11, Vaudeville, 'Kabir and Interior Religion', *History of Religions*, 3, 1964, pp. 221–2; Bhagirath Misra and Rajnarayn Mauraya, *Sant Namdev ki Padavali*, Poona, 1964, pp. 9–31; and Parasuram Chaturvedi, *Uttari Bharat ki Sant-paramapara*, Prayag, 1951, pp. 709–33. The names of the publishers are not mentioned in the bibliography provided in the book.

36 In my view, the supposed similarities between the two compositions of Kabir and Guru Nanak quoted to make the point that Guru Nanak had access to the writings of his predecessor are too vague to support this argument; see Piara Singh Padam, *Sri Guru Granth Prakash*, pp. 47–8. For the entry of the *bhagat bani* into the Sikh scriptural corpus during the times of Guru Amardas, see my *Goindval Pothis: The Earliest Extant Source of the Sikh Canon*, Cambridge: Harvard Oriental Series, 1996.

37 There is not a single reference to Baba Farid in the second section of the book; see entries under his name in the index, *Guru Nanak and the Sikh Religion*, p. 254.

38 See his 'Influence of Islam upon the Thought of Guru Nanak', in his *Sikhism and Indian Society*, Shimla: Indian Institute of Advanced Studies, 1967, pp. 292–308. Let me present one instance to challenge this situation. McLeod and many others of his generation use *Akal Purakh* (Being beyond time) as the core epithet for God in Guru Nanak's writings. It comes from Indic roots and brings in a set of philosophical connotation to explain the Guru's conception of the divine. The problem with this usage becomes apparent when one presents the simple fact that this epithet appears only once in the Guru's compositions (*Tu akal purakhu nahi siri kala*, M1, GG, 1038). Simultaneously, it might also be intriguing to note that the Guru uses *Sahib*, which

comes from Arabic and means 'Sovereign', more than one hundred times in his compositions.

39 The categories that represent the creation include the musical modes (*rags*), elements (air, water, fire), the deities (Brahma, Shiv, and so on), holy people (Siddh, Jati, Sati, and so on), learned people (such as writers), beautiful women, warriors, rich people, sacred spots, and others. The same type of structure unfolds in his cosmology hymn (M1, GG, 1036), the opening thirteen verses catalogue the absence of what Guru Nanak associates with the world—natural objects (sun, moon, light, sky, rivers, and so on), gods (such as Brahama, Bishanu, Mahesu), humans (men and women), religious personas (jogis, gopis, khans, shaikhs, hajis, mullahs, qazis), sacred texts (Veds, Shashatars, Katebs), sacred spots (*tirath*, Mecca/haj), social hierarchy (Varan)—and the final three declare that the Creator brought all these into being and one can only make sense of this with the help of the Guru.

40 See his fifty-four-stanzas composition entitled *Onkar* (M1, GG, 929–38), which though entitled 'The God', is about the universe and how human beings should function in it.

41 This idea runs though the writings of all the Sikh Gurus, *Sabh srisati seve dini rati jiu, de kanu sunahu ardas jiu*, M5, GG, 74.

42 For traditional Sikh scholarship, see Taran Singh, *Gurbani dian Viakhia Parnalian*, Patiala: Punjabi University, 1980; a summary of his argument appears in Pashaura Singh, *The Guru Granth: Canon, Meaning and Authority*, New Delhi: Oxford University Press, 2000, pp. 241–57. For another statement on this theme, see my '500 years of Sikh Educational Heritage', in Reeta Grewal and Sheena Pall (eds), *Five Centuries of Sikh Tradition*, New Delhi: Manohar, 2005, pp. 335–68.

43 For the commentaries on Guru Nanak's compositions, see the relevant sections in the early Janam Sakhis. The earliest manuscript of this type that has come to my notice contains a collection of the vars in the Guru Granth. Although undated, its orthography belongs to the late sixteenth century, and the texts such as these came to be known as the *Panj Granthi*s and *Das Granthi*s, which contained the core compositions used for daily recitations.

44 Piara Singh Padam, *Guru Nanak Sagar*, Patiala: Kalam Mandir, 1993, pp. 73–178.

45 See Tara Singh Narotam, *Sri Gurmat Nirnay Sagar* [1876], Kankhal: Sri Nirmala Panchaiti Akhara, 1898; Kahn Singh Nabha, *Gurmat Prabhakar* [1898], Amritsar: Chatar Singh Jiivan Singh, 2005, and *Gurmat Sudhakar* [1899], Patiala: Bhasha Vibhag, 1979; Jodh Singh, *Gurmat Nirnay*; and Sher Singh, *Philosophy of Sikhism* [1944], Amritsar:

Shiromani Gurdwara Parbandhak Committee, 1986. Bhagwan Singh's *Rahit Darpaṇ* (pre-1877), which still is in manuscript form with very few scholars aware of its existence, also falls in this category.

46 See previous note. McLeod's discussion does not create the impression that he had the opportunity to immerse himself in the writings of the Guru, think through the nature of the issues related to his life and teachings, and propose a narrative of this crucial period of Sikh history that can be supported with firm evidence. Instead, I see here a young scholar coming to the Guru's compositions with preconceived notions about the medieval religious landscape of north India, and a set of Protestant categories and terms that he thought was adequate to unlock the ideas of any thinker irrespective of his or her linguistic or cultural context.

47 The portrait of the Guru that emerged in *Guru Nanak and the Sikh Religion* coordinates closely with his image of half-closed eyes looking toward the heavens available in the calendar art of the 1960s; see McLeod's *Popular Sikh Art*, New Delhi: Oxford University Press, 1991, Preface. A serious discussion of the iconography of the Guru has yet to appear, but the data at our disposal indicate a shift between the portraits that predated the mid-nineteenth century and the iconography that became popular afterward. For discussion of these issues, see Susan Stronge (ed.), *The Arts of the Sikh Kingdoms*, London: Victoria and Albert Museum, 1999; and B.N. Goswamy, *Piety and Splendour*, New Delhi: National Museum, 2000.

48 W.H. McLeod, *The Evolution of the Sikh Community*, p. 5.

49 See his 'On the Word Panth: A Problem of Terminology and Definition', *Contributions in Sociology*, 12 (2), 1979.

50 For an interesting discussion, see Manmohan Singh, 'Bird Images in Guru Nanak's Hymns', *Panjab Past and Present* (April 1979), pp. 227–31.

51 Kabir refers to the authority and attitudes of the revenue collectors in his verse *Hari ke loga mo kou niti dasai patwari*, GG, 793.

52 Reference to the village elders appears in the Puratan Janam Sakhi manuscript dated 1758, folio 15.

53 The Puratan presents Guru Nanak's critique of the politics of the time in some detail. The Guru is presented as being deeply upset with the prevailing corruption around the political institutions, and its author expresses this forthrightly. It is, however, interesting to reflect on why the Guru's discomfort with the politics of the time is absent in the Miharban Janam Sakhi and the *Gian Ratnavali* (post-1760s). Could it be that by elaborating on this, Miharban did not want to risk annoying the Mughal authorities with whom his family worked closely, and

the author of the *Gian Ratnavali* did not need to bring it into the discussion, as the Sikhs themselves were the rulers by the time of his writing?

54 The sounds 'b' and 'v' are interchangeable in Punjabi, and the *Vedi Patisahu* here refers to Guru Nanak's family caste, Bedi. For an interesting comment on the concept of the king being responsible for the concerns of both *din* and *dunia*, see Abul Fazal, *Ain-i-Akbari*, tr. H. Blochmann [1927] (Delhi: Low Price Publications, 2001), pp.170–2.

55 For more on the Bhatts, see Rattan Singh Jaggi, *Sikh Panth Vishavkosh*, Patiala: Gur Ratan Publishers, 2005, 2, pp. 1334–7.

56 As for the location of Kartarpur, Sialkot was in its north (20 miles), Kalanaur, the town where the Mughal emperor Akbar was coronated in the 1550s, in the southeast, (5 miles), Batala in the south (15 miles), and Lahore in the west (20 miles).

57 For a discussion of the Kartarpur period, see my *Sikhism*, Englewood, NJ: Prentice Hall, 2004, pp. 22–8.

58 McLeod, *Sikhism*, pp. 14–15, and pp. 36–7.

59 In addition, we have six names that do not carry any reference to the social station of these people (Malo, Manga, Kalu, Japuvansi, Bhagirath, Jodh, Jivai); see Bhai Gurdas' *Varan*, 11, pp. 13–14.

60 The Bala Janam Sakhi opens with the claim that Bala, who was supposedly a childhood friend of Guru Nanak, lived in Talwandi, and so did the descendants of Lalu, Guru Nanak's father's elder brother.

61 Sujan Rai Bhandari, *Khulasat-ut-Tavarikh* [1696], tr. Ranjit Singh Gill, Patiala: Punjabi University, 1972, pp.78–9.

62 *The Baburnama*, tr. Annete Susannah Beveridge [1921], Delhi: Low Price Publications, 2003, p. 454; Wheeler M. Thackston (ed.), *The Baburnama*, New York: Oxford University Press, 1996, p. 315. The villages around Kartarpur were inhabited by the tribes of Bajwas, Chahals, Gills, Kahlons, Khairas, Manns, and Randhawas. It might also be useful to mention that the Jats and their rural ancillaries constituted over 90 per cent of the Sikh community when the numbers begin to become available; see Surinderjit Kaur, 'Changes in the Distributional Pattern of the Sikhs in India, 1881–1971: A Geographical Appraisal', PhD thesis, Panjab University, Chandigarh, 1979, p. 34.

63 Cited in Irfan Habib, 'The Jats of Punjab and Sind', in Harbans Singh and N.G. Barrier (eds), *Essays in Honor of Ganda Singh*, Patiala: Punjabi University, 1976, pp. 94–5. Vladimir Minorsky, 'Gardizi in India', *Iranica*, 137, 1948, pp. 200–15, does not seem to include this reference.

64 Ainslie T. Embree (ed.), *Alberuni's India*, New York: Norton Library, 1971, p. 401. It is interesting that this position is tangentially evoked

in Bhai Gurdas's Var 8, devoted to the society around him. Its ninth stanza deals with the Brahmins, tenth with the Kshatriyas, whom he equates with the Khatris, eleventh with the Vaishayas, and twelfth with the Jains, Jats, Lohars, Chhimbas, Oil makers, Barbers, and so on. The placement of the Jats and the Jains with all other outcastes is interesting. For the reference to the Jats in *Dabistan-i-Mazahib*, see Ganda Singh, 'Nanak Panthis', *Panjab Past and Present*, 1, 1967, pp. 54, 57; and for their appearance in the *Ain-i-Akbari*, see Table 1 in Irfan Habib, 'The Jats of Punjab and Sind'.

65 For references to the Jats in later writings, see Joseph Davey Cunnigham, *A History of the Sikhs* [1848], New Delhi: S. Chand, 1985, pp. 299–300; K.R. Qanungo, *History of the Jats* [1925], Delhi: Delhi Originals, 2003; M.C. Pradhan, *The Political System of the the Jats of Northern India*, New Delhi: Oxford University Press, 1966; and Nonika Datta, *Forming an Identity: A Social History of the Jats*, New Delhi: Oxford University Press, 1999. From the press on this issue in 2010:

> 'Amritsar: The All-India Jat Reservation Sangharsh Committee launched its rath yatra from the Golden Temple here today. They are protesting against the government's failure to grant OBC (Other Backward Class) status to the Jat community of Punjab, Haryana and Jammu and Kashmir. The yatra will pass through various districts of three states before culminating on September 13, [2010] at Sonepat (Haryana), which will be observed as "Jat Chetavani Divas". On the day, the district units of various states would hold rallies across the country, said Yashpal Malik, national president of the committee, which had already declared to disrupt the Commonwealth Games. He said the community had been fighting for getting the OBC status for the past 19 years. He alleged that the community was feeling dejected over the continuous indifferent attitude of the governments at the Centre and three states which had adopted double standards by granting the status to other similar caste and communities like Yadav, Ahir, Saini, Kamboj, Gurjar etc.' *The Tribune* (Chandigarh, 29 August 2010).

66 It may also be interesting to point out that the author of the *Dabistan-i-Mazahib* considers Guru Nanak compositions to be in Jataki, 'the language of the Jats', who have 'no regard for Sanskrit language'. See Ganda Singh, 'Nanak Panthis', *Panjab Past and Present*, vol. 1, 1967, p. 54.

67 I have seen this type of process unfolding in my lifetime. Beginning with the early 1960s, I remember the Gujjar pastoralists coming down from the hills and attempting to spend winters or settle down temporarily in the Punjab. While the farmers were happy to offer their fallow

fields for free cattle manure in return, and urban society was happy to buy cheaper milk, the Gujjars were invariably seen as petty criminals who carried arms and were always ready to steal. With the agriculture having become more intensive in the Punjab in the past decades, their plight has worsened, and one often sees them squeezed with their cattle onto the open areas along the roads.

68 This was the only point of transition of leadership in Sikh history when a Jat candidate was in the running for the office of Guruship, see *Janam Sakhi Bhai Bala*, p. 460; and Kulwinder Singh Bajwa (ed.), *Mahima Prakash Vartak*, Amritsar: Singh Brothers, 2004 [1770?]), pp. 51–2. For general references to his life and activity in the eighteenth century writings, see relevant sections in *Gurbilas Patshahi Chhevin*, Amritsar; Shiromani Gurdwara Parbandhak Committee, 1998[1718?]); and Dharm Singh (ed.), *Kavi Saundha*, Amritsar: Guru Nanak Dev University, 1981[1790?]. For recent writings on him, see Jasbir Singh Bhalla, *Baba Buddha Jivani*, Amritsar: Navin Prakashan, 1981; Amarjit Kaur, 'Punjabi Sahit Vich Babe Buddhe da Sarup', PhD thesis, Guru Nanak Dev University, 2002; Sabinderjit Singh Sagar, *Baba Buddha Ji*, Amritsar: Guru Nanak Dev University, 2005; and Harnek Singh, *Sri Guru Granth Sahib: Viakhia te Sandesh*, Patiala: Gurmat Prakashan, 2008, pp. 42–62. Little is written about Ajita Randhawa, but his name appears prominently in the writings of Bhai Gurdas, and an important late seventeenth-century text entitled *Goshati Ajite Randhawe nal hoi* is also available.

69 For the details of McLeod's argument, see his *Evolution of the Sikh Community* (1975), pp. 1–19 and pp. 83–104; *Sikhism* (1997), pp. 3–61 and pp. 228–50; *Essays in Sikh History, Tradition, and Society* (2007), pp. 171–96. For those who built on McLeod's work, see Harjot Oberoi, 'Ritual and Counter Ritual', in J.T. O'Connell, Milton Israel, Willard G. Oxtoby (eds), *Sikh History and Religion in the Twentieth Century*, visiting editors W. H. McLeod, J.S. Grewal, Toronto: University of Toronto Press, 1988.

70 This would also provide the appropriate context to interpret the code of conduct and belief (*rahit*) statements pertaining to the ritual details of the remarriage ceremony of widows, produced around 1700. See *Prem Sumarag*, ed. Randhir Singh [1953], Jalandhar: New Book Company, 2000, pp. 30–5.

71 Tony Ballantyne (ed.), *Textures of the Sikh Past*, New Delhi: Oxford University Press, 2007, p. 3.

72 Grewal's early position was that 'with mild disagreement here' and 'a minor difference there', one could work with McLeod's overall interpretation of Sikh history, see his 'Legacies of the Sikh Past for the Twentieth Century', in J.T. O'Connell *et al.* (eds), *Sikh History and*

Religion in the Twentieth Century, p. 18. More recently, he has registered McLeod's limitations as to how he was not able to achieve the
goals he had set up for himself in his study of the Janam Sakhis; he also
contends that McLeod's argument that Guru Nanak's life story has to
remain brief carries little significance in the light of the fact that we
have far more detailed information about him than any other figure of
his period. See J.S. Grewal, *Lectures on History, Society and Culture of
the Punjab*, Patiala: Punjabi University, 2007, pp. 160–4. Writing in
2009, he expanded on Karine Schomer's argument regarding the nature
of medieval Indian poetry to question McLeod's joining of Guru Nanak
and Kabir as parts of the 'Sant synthesis', as well as his resulting interpretation of the circumstances of the rise of the early Sikh community; see
his *Sikhs: Ideology, Institutions, and Identity*, pp. 3–4.

73 J.S. Grewal, 'W.H. McLeod and Sikh Studies', *Journal of Punjab Studies*,
17 (1–2), 2010, p. 142.

74 I divide McLeod's scholarship into two broad areas: interpretations of
various phases of Sikh history and translations of the early Sikh texts
(see note 8). I have already registered my differences with his research
results regarding the founding of the Sikh community. As for the latter
category, my differences with his work are centred on the dating of the
translated documents. In my view, McLeod did not have the opportunity or the time to study the early manuscripts of these texts, and in the
absence of any empirical evidence he dated these texts where he thought
they fitted best in the trajectory of Sikh history he himself had created. In
the light of the data available to us, there is no basis to support McLeod's
dating of, say, the Vars of Bhai Gurdas before 1604; the Puratan Janam
Sakhi after 1604; The *Chaupa Singh Rahit-Nama* in the mid-eighteenth
century; *The Prem Sumarag* in the early nineteenth/late eighteenth century; and *Sri Guru Panth Prakash* in 1841; for references to these dates,
see his *Textual Sources for the Study of Sikhism*, pp. 17–18.

It has been a deeply agonizing experience to critique McLeod's
scholarship, with which I started my own journey into the wonderland
of Sikh studies in the early 1980s, but I feel obliged to present these
thoughts for the consideration of younger scholars. For the beginning
of my differences with McLeod's interpretations, see my 'Teaching the
Sikh Tradition', in John Stratton Hawley et al. (eds), *Studying the Sikhs:
Issues for North America*, Albany: State University of New York Press,
1993, pp. 142–3.

75 This is an important facet of the previous generation's legacy, which began
with the pioneering efforts of Ganda Singh in the 1930s and manifested
in the selfless service of many others like Randhir Singh, Shamsher Singh
Ashok, and Piara Singh Padam. These scholars were involved in preserving

manuscripts, developing their repositories, preparing their catalogues, and making them available in print. For Ganda Singh's biography, see Rattan Singh Jaggi, *Sikh Panth Vishavkosh*, vol. 1, pp. 714–16. For Randhir Singh, see notes 3, 68, and 81. For Shamsher Singh Ashok's monumental works, see his *Punjabi Hath Likhatan di Suchi*, 2 vols, Patiala: Bhasha Vibhag, 1961 and 1963; and *Sikh Reference Library Amritsar dian Hath Likhat Pustakan di Suchi*, Amritsar: Shiromani Gurdwara Prabandhak Committee, 1968. For Padam's contribution, see his *Rahitname*, Amritsar: Singh Brothers, 1995, and notes 2, 3, 8, 36, 44, and 82.

76 It may be useful to mention another position on this issue. In *Sikh Formations*, 1 (1), June 2005, Arvind-Pal Singh Mandair writes: 'The study of Sikhs and Sikhism today is at a major turning point. The conventional frameworks that have dominated the efforts to carve out a distinct subject area of Sikh Studies over the last four decades appears increasingly unhelpful, if not irrelevant, against the backdrop of globalization and the emergence of new theoretical interventions in the human and social sciences. At the same time as we all, in some measure, come to terms with a 'New Age' in the twenty-first century, when the old certainties are being reassessed or giving way to new modes of thought, there is a serious intellectual challenge for those of us engaged with the study of Sikhs and Sikhism. This challenge is all the more pressing for it has also come at a juncture when there is generational change talking place in the academic leadership of the subject, with the towering 'greats' of the 1960s and 1970s gradually giving way to a new generation who now neither share their mindset nor are any longer comfortable with methodologies that have so long dominated the field'.

Mandair's claim that 'Sikh Studies' need to outgrow the supposedly 'conventional framework' seems perfectly reasonable, but how this goal is to be achieved is the key question. Replacing the model of biblical studies that McLeod brought to Sikh studies in the 1960s with a new one based on the thinking of the towering 'greats' like Hegel and Derrida, as Mandair seems to do in his recently released *Religion and the Specter of the West* (2010), may not be much of an answer to this problem.

77 No reference regarding the change of the name appears in *Guru Nanak Dev University: A Profile* (1994), a publication produced at the time of the university's silver jubilee celebration. It would be interesting to examine this episode and find out the basis on which the present name was argued for by its supporters, the nature of their religious affiliation, and the contribution of the large history and other related departments on the campus in this discussion. The fact stands, however, that there were differences on what name should be used to build an institution honouring the founder of the tradition.

78 See McLeod's 'The Nanak Panth', in *Who Is a Sikh?*, pp. 7–22; 'The Early Nanak Panth', *Sikhism*, pp. 9–15; and Harjot Oberoi, *The Construction of Religious Boundaries*, p. 477 (entries under Nanak-panth and panthis).

79 Guru Nanak calls the people at Kartarpur as the Sikhs (*Suni Sikhvante Nanaku binavai*, M1, GG, 503), and considers them to constitute the Gurmukh Panth (the community of the Gurmukhs, *Hari kirati rahirasi hamari Gurmukhi Panth atitang*, M1, GG, 360); Guru Arjan assigns them the name of Sach da Panth (the path of truth, *Kal jal jam johi na sakai Sach ka Pantha thatio*, M5, GG, 714); the Bhatts describe them as the Utam Panth (the best path/the community of the best, *Ik Utam Panth sunio gur sangat*, GG, 1406) and Dharm Panth (the path of morality, *Lahnai Panth Dharam ka kia*, GG, 1401; *Dharam Panth dhariou*, GG 1406); and Bhai Gurdas uses the epithets of the Nirmal Panth (the pure path/the community of the pure, *Maria sika jagat vichi Nanak Nirmal Panth chalia*, Var, 1: 45), and the Nirala Panth (the unique path, *Sabadi jiti sidhi mandali kitosu apana Panth Nirala*, Var, 1:37). It is interesting to note that the term Nanak Panthi does not appear even in Sujan Rai Bhandari, *Khulasat-ut-Tavarikh* [1696], pp. 80–1.

80 The Miharban Janam Sakhi, 1:8; and *Guru Amardas: Srot Pustak*, 52 and 56. For a discussion on Guru Hargobind's year of birth, see Piara Singh Padam, *Khashtam Guru de Khat Darshan*, Patiala: Kalam Mandir, 1994.

81 For this section in the *Dabistan-i-Mazahib*, see Ganda Singh, 'Nanak Panthis', *Panjab Past and Present* 1, 1967, pp. 47–71.

82 *Bishnai das avatar nav gania* (*Var* 14:4); and *Das avatar akar kari purkharath kari nav ganae* (*Var* 16:10). For a denunciation of personal following, see 'Apani Katha', in Bhai Randhir Singh (ed.), *Shabadarth Dasam Granth*, Patiala: Punjabi University, 1972, 1, pp. 71–2; Sainapati, *Sri Gur Sobha*, ed. Ganda Singh, Patiala: Punjabi University, 1967, p. 65.

83 *Satigur sacha patisahu gurmukhi gaddi rah chalia* (*Var* 5:13); *Satigur sacha patisahu gurmukhi gaddi rah chalande* (*Var* 5:20); *Barah panth sadhie ke gurmukhi gaddi rah chalia* (*Var* 7:12); *Liha andar chaliai jiau gaddi rah, Hukami razai chalana sadh sanghi nibahu* (*Var* 9:14); *Hukami razai chalana gurmukhi gaddi rahu chalia* (*Var* 12:17); *Barah panth ikatar kar gurmukhi gaddi rahu chalia* (*Var* 18:14); *Gurmukhi gaddi rahu sachu nibihiai* (19:19); *Sachu saman sach vich gaddi rah sadh dang vahina* (*Var* 24:6); *Babanai ghari chal hai gurmukhi gaddi rahu nibhai* (*Var* 26:31); and *Sachui vanaji khep lai chale gurmukhi gaddi rahu nisani* (29:12). The name *Param Marag* is an alternative title in the early manuscripts of the text that is known as the *Prem Sumarag* in current scholarship, see notes 8, 7, and 76.

Part III

Religious Cultures: Marginal, Popular, Controversial

6

Harjot Oberoi

Brotherhood of the Pure

THE POETICS AND POLITICS OF CULTURAL TRANSGRESSION*

The spring month of *Magh* heralds festivals, pilgrimages and popular rituals in the north Indian countryside. In 1872, the small village Bhaini, in Ludhiana district, was the scene of feverish activity. Participants in a millenarian community popularly known as Kukas had collected there in connection with the spring festivities on 11 and 12 January. They had, however, very little to celebrate. In the past four months nine of their numbers had been hanged by the colonial authorities on charges of attacking slaughter houses and killing butchers, others had been imprisoned, and many more were subjected to increasing surveillance and restrictions. British officials nervously shifted their views of the Kukas. Earlier seen as religious reformers within the Sikh tradition, they were now deemed to be political rebels.[1] As those present felt heavily suspect in the eyes of the administration, the atmosphere at Bhaini must have been tense and unnerving.

*This is an abridged version of Harjot Oberoi, 'Brotherhood of the Pure: The Poetics and Politics of Cultural Transgression', *Modern Asian Studies*, 26 (1), 1992, pp. 157–97. © Cambridge University Press, reproduced with permission.

On 13 January, the day of the traditional festival of Lohri, a party of Kuka zealots left their leader's village to mount an attack on Malerkotla, the capital of a small Muslim principality of the same name, approximately thirty miles south of Ludhiana. The next day, en route to their destination, the Kuka crowd raided the fort of Malodh, the residence of a Sikh aristocrat related to the Maharaja of Patiala, possibly to avenge through his affine the anti-Kuka policies of the Maharaja and equip themselves with arms and horses. The insurgents met with little material success. Next morning, on 15 January, when a band of approximately 120 Kuka Sikhs attempted against all odds to invade the town of Malerkotla, they were repulsed by trained and well armed state troops. The same afternoon an armed contingent from the Sikh principality of Patiala succeeded in capturing sixty-eight Kukas from the raiding party. They were brought to Malerkotla where L. Cowan, the Officiating Deputy-Commissioner of Ludhiana district, following the hardened traditions of the Punjab school of administration, had forty-nine of them blown away from guns without the niceties of a legal trial. The next day T.D. Forsyth, Commissioner of the Ambala Division, on joining his subordinate, had sixteen more Kukas blown from guns, but this time after the formalities of a brief trial. These drastic measures earned the Kukas a hallowed place in the textbooks of modern Indian history and also made them a part of the 'heroic' Sikh tradition.

Why did a small party of Kuka Sikhs attack the state of Malerkotla? What was the source of their confidence which made them feel invincible against a superior political-military power? Answers to these questions have not been lacking since the Kuka movement reached its climax on the parade ground of Malerkotla. The first to respond were British officials who proposed a simple and straightforward theory to vindicate their actions and the fair name of English justice. In British eyes, the kingdom of Maharaja Ranjit Singh was a Sikh state. Its annexation meant that the Sikhs had lost their superior status in the Punjab and a proud community was humiliated. To avenge their disgraceful defeat and regain past glories Sikhs were constantly on the look out for the first available opportunity to overthrow the British rule. The Kuka movement under the leadership of Ram Singh was a direct manifestation of this basic urge. By suppressing it in time the authorities prevented evil designs from materializing and protected the interests of the civil society.[2]

A second interpretation of the Kuka actions is advanced by nationalist historians. For them the Kukas provided a ready-made illustration of how the Indian people waged war against British imperialism almost immediately after their territories had been unjustly annexed. 'The Kuka struggle was thus part of the gigantic all India struggle for freedom from British colonial oppression. As such, it deserved to be highlighted and commended'.[3]

In retrospect, it is not hard to see through the ideological justifications of British apologists and the persistent efforts of nationalist historians to incorporate all sorts of social movements under the nationalist banner. But no alternative perspective was available until quite recently, when W.H. McLeod re-examined the available materials. With refreshing vigour he broke clear of existing orthodoxies and offered an alternative theory, showing how the Kuka movement constituted a millenarian response emerging from specific socio-economic circumstances, particularly a tremendous rise in population, the failure of the harvest leading to a famine, and the presence of a discontented peasantry, features present in most millenarian uprisings. Significantly, McLeod also noted the striking similarities of the Kuka movement with millenarian stirrings in other parts of the world.[4]

Existing studies of the Kukas, while demonstrating the various facets of the movement, its political dynamics and its close connection with social conditions, much in line with the dominant historiography of Indian nationalism, have shown greater interest in exploring pragmatic themes rather than the semantic aspects. They help us firmly to grasp the underlying causes of the movement and define its character, an essential task for any study, but tell us little of what the movement meant for the participants themselves. To interpret the actors' objectives, their own structures of consciousness and experience, is as crucial as locating the major causes and features of a social movement. Such an exercise requires a study of imagery, symbols, metaphors and codes of behaviour, elements which have not been considered, in earlier studies, as the socio-political circumstances. But if we neglect the former it is hard to understand fully the discourses of Ram Singh and the statements of his followers. In a letter to his disciples, Ram Singh prophesied: 'on a Sunday midnight locks will open and two suns shall appear on the horizon, one on the left and the other on the right. A white elephant will descend on earth...'[5] The message loaded with symbolic language is meaningless without a semiotic analysis. Kaisra Singh, a Kuka Sikh, recorded before he was blown away from a gun at Malerkotla parade grounds

I went to Bhainee for the Maghee Mela [fair]. I sat near where Heera Singh and Lehna Singh were. They did not advise me to join in any enterprise. *God put it into my heart to go with them* ....I left Bhainee with them. We went together to Ruboo, and from Ruboo to Malodh. God ordered me to go there. No one else told me...I had not even a stick. I then came with the party to Kotlah. I came inside the town to the palace gate. I was in fight before the treasury, but had no arms...We came to Kotlah *by God's order* to kill the slayers of kine....[6] (emphasis added)

Kaisra Singh was hardly an exception among the Kuka insurgents. Their ranks were crowded with men who shared similar beliefs—who staunchly believed that their cause was just and that they possessed the power to challenge the alien Raj and its collaborators. For God was on their side, he spoke to them, and they were following his directives. This essay examines the phenomenology of such deeply held beliefs in order to answer such questions as: What convictions made people die for their religion? How does religion play a role in resistance? Why are apocalyptic visions believed in? What evokes the moral indignation of communities?

IN PURSUIT OF HOLINESS

Holiness, a fundamental concern of religions, is a difficult concept to define but, as a preliminary definition, it stands here for a complex of ideas which endows individuals, texts, time, places, institutions and communities with a distinct power and quality of sanctity that distinguishes them from the rest of civil society. The term holiness also includes the meanings evoked by the word sacred and in common practice the two words are often used as synonymous. But as distinct from the sacred, holiness has a moral code inscribed into it, a code that informs of those values, beliefs, concepts and symbols through which a community conceives what is just, legitimate and virtuous. The power of this moral order largely arose from its nexus with the sacred. Holiness, with a moral order encapsulated within it, helped people distinguish the pure from the impure, the right from the wrong, and the sacred from the profane, thereby establishing moral codes of individual and collective conduct.[7]

Those who violated its standards were subjected to the intense rage and indignation of the community, expressed through words, gestures, rumour, signs and, occasionally, weapons. These traditional sanctions against the transgressors of the holy order were easily communicated and comprehended by the constituents of the local society but were not that easily decoded by external observers. For instance, the British officials saw in many of the Kuka actions a primitive mind at work, while for the community their punitive acts were derived from the store house of expressive tradition. The argument which follows places the holy order and its defence at the centre of the analysis of the Kuka movement.

The Kukas did not create the holy order they so zealously chose to pursue; they only extended and interpreted it. The evolution of the Kukas into a 'sect' within the Sikh tradition and their singling out in British files has heavily coloured the readings of the early history of the Kukas. Consequently, it occasionally appears as if their ideology suddenly materialized out of nowhere and was without deep roots in their society. Such a view is erroneous. It is useful for the orthodox Sikh tradition which seeks to view Kukas as a marginal sect that went astray but not permissible historically if one particularly studies them in relation to the larger Sikh society. The Kuka cosmology concerning a holy person, purity, right conduct, dress and food taboos, and sacredness had a long history, both within the Sikh tradition and in the larger framework of the Indic culture.[8] In order to understand the complex history of the Kuka movement and how it relates to the Sikh past let us begin by briefly examining the biography of Bhai Ram Singh, the man who became central to its nineteenth century trajectory.

Very little is known about the early life of Ram Singh. He was born in 1816, in a humble rural family—his father was a carpenter in the village of Bhaini in Ludhiana district. Assisting his father in daily chores, the child Ram Singh grew up memorizing several compositions from the Adi Granth, reciting from the scriptures and acquiring a working knowledge of Panjabi. He may have received some formal education at the hands of a local learned man. By the time he was twenty, like many other young men of his age, he left his village to join an army regiment, named after Prince Nau Nihal Singh, the grandson of Ranjit Singh. During his service years he met Bhai Balak Singh whose personality, convictions, teachings, and vision so impressed him that he became an ardent disciple. Just before the Anglo-Sikh war of 1845, Ram Singh left the army and returned to his native place to work as a sharecropper. In his thirty-fourth year he once again left Bhaini, this time for Ferozepore to work for an uncle who had undertaken to repair a fort and various other buildings. During his stay there legends record his powers to work miracles.[9] According to one account, one Sunday Ram Singh was employed to put a roof on a poor man's house in Ferozepore city. One of the beams proved a foot too short, and the owner begged Ram Singh to remedy the defect without obliging him to buy a new beam, which was more than he could afford. Ram Singh thereupon by his miraculous powers expanded the beam to the required length without adding to it—the beam had grown a foot. According to F.A. Steel, who recorded the above legend, 'hundreds of persons in Ferozepore will attest the above tale, many being eye-witnesses and the house can be shown to the curious'.[10] It is significant that the legend concludes by stating that on the day of this miracle Ram Singh obtained 500 followers. Clearly, in popular sentiment there was a connection between miracles and the sanctity accorded to Ram Singh. Recognizing the elements of holiness in Ram Singh was for many a means of earning religious merit, a claim he never explicitly makes but is granted by others. This process of recognition by the Sikh masses is acknowledged by Ram Singh in a letter: 'first Sikhs generally recognized Bir Singh, then Maharaj Singh and now me'.[11]

Two years before the Uprising of 1857, Ram Singh returned to his native Bhaini and opened a shop dealing in food grains and iron implements. At the same time he collected around him a core group of associates and disciples, most of whom were demobilized soldiers from the former regiments of the Lahore state. From this nucleus were to emerge many of the prominent Kukas of the future. For the benefit of a growing number of adherents who visited Bhaini, Ram Singh, in line with Sikh tradition, set up a langar. In 1862, when Bhai Balak Singh died at Hazro, Ram Singh emerged as one of his three successors. By now he manifested the major characteristics of a Sikh holy man: the ability to expound on scriptures, piety and a demonstrated capacity to work miracles. These features confirmed for his followers that Ram Singh was a holy man whose rise had in fact been predicted in the current prophecies. Let us now turn to what Ram Singh preached to his growing following. What was his message?

If there is one theme that pervades his teachings it is the opposition between pure and impure.[12] Such a recurrent concern on the part of the Kukas may appear to be novel, particularly because interpretations of the Sikh movement always emphasize how Sikhism freed itself of ritual concerns, discounting ideas of purity and impurity. While it is correct that the polarity between purity and impurity as an organizing principle of society exemplified in the Hindu caste system was questioned by the Sikh movement, it must not be overlooked that the Sikhs have always paid great attention to notions of ritual purity both individual and corporate.[13] The third Sikh Guru, Amar Das (1479–1574), constructed a *baoli* or water tank at Goindwal where the Sikhs would go for pilgrimage and bathe in the waters of the tank, thereby ridding themselves of impurities. All major Sikh shrines, including the famous Golden Temple, were to continue with this tradition. On being built, a large water tank was added to their structures where the pilgrims would dutifully undertake ritual purification by immersing themselves in the holy waters of the tank. The purificatory powers of water are universally recognized and in the Indian cultural tradition have always been particularly significant; thus the great tradition of acquiring merit by bathing in the river Ganges. M. Eliade, one of the most creative phenomenologists of this century, notes several features associated with water in religious thinking: it breaks and dissolves all forms, does away with the past, and purifies and regenerates; in short, it is a symbol of renewal.[14]

All visitors to a Sikh shrine, from very early in the history of the *panth* but certainly by the nineteenth century, were required to take off their shoes, if they wore any, and subsequently wash their feet and hands before entering the shrine. Once again this practice illustrates very well Sikh concerns for purity and the efforts to eliminate dirt. The space outside the temple is considered dirty and unclean. To get into the shrine one must undergo cleansing by leaving behind soiled footwear and particularly wash those parts of the body that are constantly exposed to the outside world. The dirt encountered outside is not merely that of soil, excrement and germs, but is a cultural notion embedded in spatial classification. To venture outside means being exposed to pollution, particularly from other people; to gain access to a place where purity is believed to be concentrated it is mandatory to get rid of acquired dirt. Today, all major Sikh shrines, reflecting the old custom, have attendants at the entrance who collect visitors' shoes before they are allowed in.

With this background on ideas and notions of purity in Sikhism, the insistent emphasis in Ram Singh's teachings on avoiding impurities of life should hardly appear surprising. They were in accord with his own religious heritage and meshed in well with the beliefs of the larger society.[15] A state of purity may be a desirable ideal but the organic processes of the human body and social surroundings make its attainment difficult. Impurities arise out of bodily emissions, menstruation among women, *riles de passage* such as birth and death, certain kinds of foods and materials, and anomalous social situations. To negate these polluting forces Ram Singh elaborated a cluster of rituals which would generate purity of body, speech, food, dress and actions. An account of these follows.

According to the hagiographic literature, one of the first ritual acts Ram Singh performed was the initiation of five Sikhs at Bhaini in 1857.[16] In itself this was a minor happening but it marked an important departure in the practice of the initiation ritual. Candidates for initiation mostly visited four or five large Sikh shrines such as the Golden Temple at Amritsar. Ram Singh changed this and literally brought the possibility of the ritual to the doorsteps of those who wanted to participate in it. Literature records how in his extensive tours of central Punjab Ram Singh conducted the initiation ritual in innumerable villages. In his teachings he persistently insisted on the need and importance of the initiation. How is this insistence on the initiation ritual connected to ideas of purity and impurity? The uninitiated were perceived to be in a state of religious marginality, for while they might nominally be Sikhs they had not confirmed this and were therefore liable to the dangers of impurities. In the nineteenth century these impurities, besides those flowing out of bodily processes, had to do with food, dress, speech, social associations and the violation of the Sikh code of conduct. While there is rarely a direct reference to dangers we can infer from contemporary sources at least three forms of danger: being cut off from God, a major source of protection and boons; languishing in the misery of the transmigratory cycle and, sometimes, the possibility of turning into a non-human or *bhut*. These dangers could be eliminated through initiation. An initiated individual stopped occupying a liminal position for he was now a part of a chosen collectivity and in his state of ritual purity was protected from what his society deemed to be impure and dangerous.

But the ritual purity attained through initiation was clearly not permanent. Even if there was no direct transgression of the rules contained in the code to maintain the state of purity, an individual was daily besieged by impurities. To negate their influences Ram Singh untiringly demanded of his followers an early morning bath. It is easy to read into this stricture a call for hygiene. But it is hard to imagine a people in an agrarian society, with blazing temperatures avoiding bathing. Ram Singh is pressing towards a morally clean state and not simply for rules of hygiene. Given the overall context of his teachings, the insistence on a bath before dawn can only be explained within the framework of the purity: impurity opposition. Balak Singh, considered by the Kukas as the founder of their faith, had demanded that his disciples bathe three times a day. Ram Singh is known to have followed this precept of his mentor very seriously. In a *rahit-nama* or code of conduct, issued by him sometime in 1866, to which the Kukas subscribe even today, he demanded: 'Rise during the last watch of the night and taking a pot of water [for cleansing] go out into the fields to relieve nature. When you return scour the pot twice, remove the clothes which you were wearing while in the fields, clean your teeth, bathe, and recite [the prescribed portions] of sacred scripture'.[17]

Defecation not only pollutes the body but also personal clothing and the water pot—objects which were in close proximity during the process. To overcome its negative influence Ram Singh recommends a thorough cleansing of the water pot, disuse of clothing before washing, and a bath. This is to be followed by the recitation of sacred scriptures. The same schedule is followed even today at the Kuka headquarters in Bhaini. According to S.S. Sanehi, 'a namdahri, or Kuka, living at Sri Bhaini Sahib bids good-bye to his bed at about three in the morning...Having been to the toilet, he *purifies his hands seven times* with either sand or ash or earth...He cleans his teeth with a branch of a tree used in India for this purpose instead of a tooth brush. Then he takes a bath either with well water or in the holy tank named Ram Sarovar...Having taken his bath, the Kuka puts on different clothes, not those he had worn going to the toilet...'.[18] The passage of a century has hardly altered the tradition begun by Ram Singh.

In order to construct a comprehensive ideology, the purity principle was further extended to encompass diet restrictions, a code for dress and several commandments for social behaviour. Bhai Ram Singh's spiritual mentor, Balak Singh, had already enjoined his followers not to eat food cooked by those outside the community of disciples and never to drink water from a leather pouch. The latter reflects the reverence for the cow and abomination for anything made out of cow hide. Kuka Sikhs were further prohibited from consuming meat or liquor and smoking tobacco. In one of his writings Ram Singh stated 'meat and liquor are the diet of *mleccha*. Consuming them pollutes consciousness'.[19] Food taboos appear to be the most widely respected rules among the Kuka Sikhs in the nineteenth century.

This discussion poses a central question: what was the reason for the considerable emphasis on ritual purity in the Kuka ideology? I have already pointed out that the Kukas shared their concern for purity with the rest of the Sikh Panth. While the Kuka notions of purity were correlated with the concept of purity and pollution as found in the caste system, the similarity did not extend much further. Caste for the Kukas was unimportant. They did not employ the purity: pollution opposition to assign a group of people the task of being permanent hereditary specialists in impurity so that the other members of society belonging to the 'twice-born' groups could retain their purity. In their consanguinity, marriages, commensality, and most importantly their world view, they overturned the commonly accepted determinants of the caste system. This should not be taken to imply that they did not have any rules governing social relationships, only that their rules at the level of abstraction were not those of the caste hierarchy. To a certain extent the Kuka expression of pure: impure marks a historical continuity with the Sikh conceptual structure briefly delineated earlier which also gave a privileged position to the same dyad and its system of meaning.

The Inspector-General of Police for Punjab seems to have got to the heart of the matter. In a report he commented on how the Kukas 'appear anxious merely to revive the Sikh religion in its original state of purity and to eradicate the errors which have from time to time, defiled it'.[20] Purity, as Louis Dumont and D.F. Pocock argue in an essay cited earlier is an essential prerequisite to approaching the gods. They observe: 'this does not mean their [the gods] nature is purity, but that purity is a condition for the contact with them to be beneficial...'.[21] It is simply a crucial requirement for relating to the gods. By upholding ritual purity, following the dictates of a strong moral code in everyday life and the cleansing of the body, in part represented the efforts of the faithful to establish a firm nexus with the sacred, build up magico–religious defences, create order out of chaos and acquire powers that ordinary people lacked. To recapitulate thus far, Kuka symbolic structure may be represented by the binary opposition purity: pollution. Underlying it was the belief that through purity one was powerful, almost invincible; in a state of impurity one was weak and susceptible. Those who were pure in the mode of the Kukas were part of the brotherhood, those who endangered purity were certainly adversaries. By the late 1860s, for the Kuka Sikhs those who transgressed the boundaries between pure: impure were violating the moral order contained within the framework of holiness and had to be punished for their behavioural improprieties. In other words, upholding holiness called for stern action on the part of the faithful. But who were the adversaries inviting the wrath of the Kukas?

In Defence of Holiness

From 1866 onwards the Kukas, deeply committed to their world-view and with an unshakeable belief that the forces of the cosmos were on their side, spent their energies assailing those they saw as responsible for violating the conceptual principles of holiness. While the colonial authorities in the 1860s were still busy debating what kind of threat the Kuka Sikhs represented to the Raj, four butchers in Amritsar were killed on the night of 15 June 1871. By the time the police had caught up with the suspects and the investigating detective, Christie, had proudly claimed that he had solved the crime, butcher families in the town of Raikot were attacked on 1 July and three people were killed. To the further embarrassment of the authorities, it turned out that the persons apprehended for the Amritsar attack were innocent and had been forced to confess the crime due to third degree methods employed by the police. Now events moved quickly. Exactly a month after the Raikot killings, three Kuka Sikhs held guilty for the murders there were hanged in August outside the slaughter house of Raikot. A month later four of the accused in the Amritsar case were hanged and two of them were transported for life. On 27 November 1871, two more Kuka Sikhs were hanged on charges of abetting the Raikot murders. Barely two months later in January 1872, an irregular mass of Kuka Sikhs started on their famous march to Malerkotla, which ended in the tragic disaster, detailed at the beginning of this essay.

These seemingly bizarre episodes have caused much confusion among historians. Contemporary scholarship finds it hard to untangle the mystery of why the Sikhs should have taken on themselves to protect the cow, particularly in a period when many of their brethren would soon be proclaiming Hindu–Sikh distinctions. Picking up what was visibly a Hindu sacred symbol would hardly have helped any enterprise wanting to establish the independent identity of the Sikhs. Deciphering targets of civil violence and symbolic protest originating from religious communities is never simple, particularly because the unlettered activists do not leave behind textual records containing an account of their *motives* and actions. For contemporary police and military officials tutored in a colonial epistemology which highlighted crime and insurrection as the major motivations of indigenous population, comprehending Kuka actions was not too difficult. Using their evocative vocabulary, they categorized Kuka actions as foolish, dangerous, evil, criminal, and premature. Nationalist historians, as pointed out earlier, read in them the imprint of an anti-imperialist consciousness. A more recent historiographical approach questions this interpretation, claiming that the 'victims of the Kuka's verbal and physical attacks were nearly all fellow Punjabis, not Englishmen'.[22]

The obsessive concern among historians whether the targets chosen were anti-British or not is misplaced. This debate diverts attention away from the more fundamental problems such as why did the Kukas choose to attack and kill butchers rather than local officials, members of police or moneylenders—the frequent victims of peasant jacqueries in nineteenth-century north India? What were the Kuka Sikhs trying to communicate to their fellow comrades in civil society when they decided to act as the defenders of the cow? These issues cannot be answered if the locations of Kuka sacrilege and violence are analysed in isolation. This is perhaps one reason why Kuka responses appear to many historians to be incoherent, spontaneous and ill-conceived. But to be meaningful they have to be treated as a part of a cultural system for even madness, to paraphrase Edmund Leach, has an order.[23] It is the task of a historian to discern that order. In the present case that order was embedded, to use semiotic terminology, in a cultural code that was made up of the antinomy between purity: pollution. Once we place the indices of the Kuka actions within the parameters of this code it becomes easier to recover at least some of their shadowy meanings.

For the Kukas colonial rule switched the existing cultural codes, producing an ambiguity in the given classificatory system governing purity: pollution/ sacred: profane/ morality: immorality/ holy: unholy. The new Christian rulers of Punjab found it hard to apprehend many of the old customary categories regulating social behaviour. As representatives of the most advanced nation on earth, extremely confident in their utilitarian ideology, possessed of an unbounded evangelical zeal, they had little patience with other people's world-views and were keen on imposing their own norms and standards. Having annexed the Lahore state after two stiff wars they had little to fear and were in a mood to innovate despite political risks. The 'Punjab school of administration', charged with messianic fervour, was determined to present Punjab as a model state for the rest of the Empire, almost as if it had been ordained by God. Reform, Progress and Civilization were the three key terms in the vocabulary of the British men asked to administer the newly conquered frontier province. Christian missionaries, English educators and British officials were given a free rein to experiment with their subjects, spread the new civilizing doctrines, and reshape the rustic Punjabis. This imperial trinity spared no efforts to purge old customs and impose Victorian ethics, all in the name of God or enlightenment. In the process of changing the face of the land they quite unwittingly ruptured the symbolic order underpinning local society, generating cultural conflicts British authority would find hard to comprehend or contain.

Unlike the case of earlier empires, political legitimacy was no longer sought in the normative categories of an indigenous culture but in an imperial ideology mixed with racism, superior moral purpose and an arrogant repudiation of local cultural mores.[24] The new rulers did not seek approval or justification for their actions against gods they considered pagan, holy men they thought were crazy, and Oriental beliefs they dismissed as irrational. Men of great piety, who had once been at the top of the social apex under the Sikh Raj, were now easily dispensed with. Those at the bottom, without any ritual standing but useful as political collaborators, were given ample privileges and command posts. Departures from accepted political conventions deeply ingrained in a system of local cultural references and a symbolic sacred order may best be exemplified by the contrasting attitudes between sectors of the local population and the English administration on the issue of cow slaughter in the Punjab.

Although the belief in the sacredness of the cow is widespread today among Hindus and Sikhs, the history of how it came to be considered sacred and why killing a cow became taboo is less easily understood. [25] The cow was frequently alluded to in Vedic texts. By the early Vedic period the cow became a measure of payment, in literary imagery goddesses were compared to cows, the products of the cow were an integral element in Vedic sacrifices and significantly the cow and the bull came to symbolize maternity, fertility, and virility.[26] In the same period, however, beef was regularly consumed and there was no taboo attached to cow slaughter. In the Brahmanical text, the *Shatapatha Brahmana,* a Brahman priest says in answer to a question why the flesh of the cow and the cart-ox should not be eaten, 'that very well may be, but as long as it puts flesh on my body I will continue to eat it'.[27] It is only in the Gupta age, and that, too, within the orbit of the elitist Brahmanic religion, that the cow began to be perceived as inviolable, and according to one source its killing was capital offence.[28] A Chola king ordered executions for cow slaughter. By the early medieval period there is sufficient evidence to show increasing veneration for the cow among the Hindus and also the practice of cow slaughter among Indian Muslims. To placate Hindu feelings, Emperor Akbar prohibited cow slaughter and those who disobeyed the royal edict were faced with capital punishment.

Cow killing or its prevention became an obvious barometer to gauge state policies on religious matters. Once the Mughal empire disintegrated, its successor states across northern India continued respecting the old tradition of banning the killing of cows. Under the Sikh rulers of the Punjab cow slaughter was punishable with death. Even the British authorities, early in their expansionist drive, were not averse to adhering to conventions concerning the killing of cows. In signing treaties with princely states like Kutch the British agreed to uphold the tradition.[29] According to a Muslim Maulvi in 1882, 800 Muslims were in Kashmir prisons on charges of cow slaughter.[30] In the Punjab soon after the First Anglo–Sikh War, when Henry Lawrence was appointed as the British resident at Lahore, he posted orders outside the Golden Temple prohibiting cattle slaughter in the holy city of the Sikhs. This effort to placate Sikh–Hindu sentiments, however, did not last for long.

While this background to India's cattle complex helps us to understand in general terms attitudes towards the cow and cow killing, to comprehend the nature of the Kuka actions against the butchers it is imperative to specify the position of the sacred animals in Punjabi cosmology. People the world over employ a variety of simple and complex symbols to communicate their world-view. This is particularly true when core cultural ideas need to be expressed. In nineteenth-century Punjab the cow signified notions of ritual purity and impurity and helped map out the sacred terrain as distinct from the profane. In an essay demonstrating the homology between social structure and animal classification, Mary Douglas comments 'taxonomy organizes nature so that the categories of animals mirror and reinforce social rules...'.[31]

It is commonly acknowledged that animal taxonomies are influenced by social structures, reflect social concerns and help human beings think about the world around them. Through the animal world and the folklore concerning it, people in diverse cultures have constructed symbolic oppositions between pure and impure, good and bad, industrious and lazy, lucky and unlucky, culture and nature.[32] In classifying animals Punjabis much as in other cultural traditions distinguish between wild and domesticated varieties. Those labelled wild belong to the realm of Nature while those classed within the domesticated taxonomy belong to human culture. The wild pig, a dreaded scourge for the crops, was viewed with great hostility by the peasants and placed beyond the frontiers of human society. The cow, as we will shortly see, belongs to the realm of human culture with an exceptionally high ritual standing among domesticated animals. Its special position in the hierarchy of domesticated animals may be epitomized in contrast to its nearest relative the buffalo.[33] To begin with, Punjabi language categorically distinguishes between the two through a variety of linguistic terms. Second, the cow as an anthropomorphic figure occupies the position of a deity while the buffalo is considered both malevolent and inauspicious and commonly called a 'black ghost'. Third, the cow is a stall animal and the ox harnessed for farm labour. The buffalo is tethered in the open and its male classed as intractable and considered not amenable to ploughing. A proverb current in nineteenth-century Punjab stated 'threshing for a male buffalo, grinding for a man and travelling for a woman, these are all unsuitable'.[34] Fourth, a barren she-buffalo is easily pressed into ploughing fields. The same task is inconceivable for a barren cow and interestingly there is no Punjabi word for it. Finally, these cultural antinomies posit cow's milk as highly desirable for a superior intellect while the buffalo's product is deemed suitable only for physical strength.

Punjabis address cow as *gau mata* or 'mother of man', exhibiting a close association between human life and the sacred animal. By speaking of the cow in the same language as one's kin group they easily substitute human beings for the cow. Paul Hershman, an anthropologist, while carrying out his fieldwork in the Punjab often heard the expression, 'A man is the calf of the cow'.[35] Therefore just as a human mother feeds her child milk, the cow provides milk to the humans. The cow as a mother figure in Punjabi thought represents the indigenous ideal of womanhood: virtuous, domesticated, amenable and productive. Constitutive of this maternal image is the identification of the mother who produces children with the cow that produces calves. On certain occasions the cow is identified with a virgin, *Gau dan* or gift of a cow is undertaken at the same time as *kanya dan* or gift of virgin in marriage. Both are garlanded, anointed in red upon the forehead and clothed in red garments on ritual occasions.

For the purpose at hand, the most crucial aspect of the cow is its capacity to act as a channel of purification. While the organic eruptions of human beings: faeces, urine, saliva, the milk of a woman, are highly impure and polluting, the exudations of a cow are not only pure in themselves but also have a power to purify impurer elements. It undoubtedly possesses the power to overcome the most impure and polluting processes in life and death.[36] The cow performs a role akin to that of Louis Dumont's 'specialists in impurity'—the low caste individuals who by obliterating the unclean and defiled keep the high castes in their state of ritual purity.[37] The fundamental difference between the cow and human carriers of impurity is that while humans remain permanently impure, the cow is intrinsically pure. In being empowered to invert impurity, the cow mediates the division between the pure and impure. For the Kuka Sikhs, who are much more preoccupied than their fellow Punjabis with the boundaries of the ritually clean and unclean, the importance of the cow can hardly be exaggerated. An anthropomorphic deity, firmly established in the framework of indigenous culture, the cow signalled the most fundamental ideas in the Kuka universe: ideas concerning the sacred and the profane and separation of the holy from the unholy.

To the British imperial mind imbued with an ethnocentric logic, the cow had very different connotations from those of the Sikhs. For an English administrator brought up in an alternative cosmogony the cow was simply a profane animal to be slaughtered and its meat devoured. Once British authority felt secure in the Punjab it made cow slaughter legal. Even in Amritsar, the sacred city of the Sikhs, where once the ever sensitive Henry Lawrence had extended a concession by forbidding cow slaughter, butcher shops were given the go ahead in 1849.

Administrative restrictions on the sale of beef within cities were hard to maintain and more often breached than adhered to. Cases where butchers were apprehended for selling beef within city limits were not unknown.[38] A district official in Amritsar candidly admitted 'though there does not appear to have been any systematic violation of rules, it is certain that beef has been brought openly and carelessly into the city to the disgust of the Hindoo community'.[39] In the eyes of the civic population, butchers violating rules were too often let off without severe penalties by the colonial authorities. A Sikh zealot, Deva Singh, a disciple of the famous Bhai Bir Singh, shocked everyone when in April 1871 he produced a beef bone before the holy book within the Golden Temple. He claimed he had found the bone within the precincts of the temple. This well planned publicity stunt visibly angered large sections of the Hindu–Sikh population in the city who now started a vociferous campaign against the sale of beef in the city and demanded a complete ban on cow slaughter in Amritsar. The circulation of a rumour that the administration was thinking of allowing a butcher shop in front of the Golden Temple further angered the protestors. During the months of April and May several minor riots involving Sikh–Hindu groups and Muslims took place in Amritsar. Barely a month later, when the administration appeared to be completely insensitive to public feelings, the Kukas struck against the butchers at Amritsar, killing four of them in the attack. The subsequent violence against the butchers at Raikot and the march on Malerkotla noted at the outset, were part of the same cycle of events.

British incomprehension, together with rigid policies, bred a moral repulsion among Kuka Sikhs. For them British Raj was mleccha Raj. The frequent use of the highly loaded word mleccha among the Kukas for the English rulers, pointedly illuminates Kuka mentalities and the deep seated contempt they harboured towards the alien rulers. Linguistic categories encode collectively-held cultural principles and beliefs. Labelling is a universal mode to carry on a dialogue with social reality and to order diffuse human experiences into comprehensible categories. By naming the English as mleccha the Kukas were following an ancient Indian convention that helped them make the crucial cultural distinction between 'us' and 'them'. It was an index of their distance from the British ethos. Over the last two millenia sections of Indian society have employed the term mleccha for those barbarians, like the Greeks, Scythians and Huns, who were of foreign origin, spoke an alien language, did not perform the prescribed sacred rites, were impure in their food and drinking habits, breached rules of ritual purity and were thus beyond the pale of civilization.[40] Coming into contact with such barbarians carried the danger of being polluted. Theoretically, the Hindu legal treatises prohibited such contacts and there were dire punishments for those who violated prescribed rules. But at the same time there were special rites to overcome one's loss of purity. In the early medieval period the high caste orthodox Hindus used the concept of mleccha to designate the beef-eating and casteless Muslims who swept across north India. Now the Kukas applied it to their British adversaries who, in less than a generation, had turned the familiar world upside down. Kahn Singh Nabha, a model of contemporary Sikh learning, noted in his well-known encyclopaedia of Sikh thought that the word mleccha is used for individuals who consume beef, inveigh against the Vedas and are devoid of a noble character.[41] From the Kuka viewpoint the impure British exactly fitted this classic description of a barbarian. Much like earlier hordes of barbarians one needed to avoid them and hope that the gods would help in their destruction.

A universe created and ordered by God needed to be defended and decontaminated by men of God before the unholy mlecchas completely smashed its coherence, classifications and what appeared to be eternal visions. Unwilling to share the normative values of the British Raj, the Kukas created their own symbolic universe. They refused to travel by trains (a British innovation) and had no use for the newly introduced postal facilities. Devout Kukas exhibited their abhorrence for English textiles by wearing garments made out of Indian fabrics. In addition, they stayed aloof from the British judicial system, the English schools and sometimes even government jobs. As members of a millenarian community headed by a prophetic figure, the Kuka Sikhs promptly acted against adversaries who violated their symbolic order. The centrality of the cow in this symbolic universe made butchers a prime target; murdering them was perceived by the Kuka Sikhs as bestowing great religious merit. Ram Singh personally instructed his followers to destroy those who killed cows. He is reported to have stated: 'if my followers were true to their religion, instead of fighting among themselves they would purify the land from the slaughter of cows, and make some arrangement to stop the work of butchers'.[42] His adherents, true to the words of their master, made such arrangements when they murdered the butchers at Amritsar and Raikot, and undertook the march to Malerkotla to dispatch the butchers in the Muslim principality. By doing so they were translating the articles of their faith into action and defending those ultimate values which they believed were ordained by the Absolute.

Interpretations of the Kuka movement tend to swing between two extremes: one side dismisses them as an incoherent band, virtually mad, what T. Gordon Walker, the British Settlement Officer in Ludhiana district described as the 'insane proceedings of a small body of fanatics', [43] the other extreme eulogizes them for their anti-imperialist fervour. In this paper I have tried to steer clear of these volatile judgements and sought to show that there was coherence in both the thinking and actions of the Kuka Sikhs. If their logic was different from ours, it does not mean they were illogical. Within the prevailing belief system their strategies and millenarian visions were plausible. In a society where the sacred was always intervening in human affairs their use of miracles, symbols, prophecies and rituals was perfectly reasonable and by the standards of their culture capable of yielding results. There was nothing psychopathological in their behaviour, as many colonial officers insisted. Their symbolic and ideological universe was closely related to Sikh cosmology and Indic cultural assumptions. Without the indigenous conceptions of holiness, the binary opposition between the pure and impure, the widespread practice among the Sikhs of circulating prophecies, it is hard to imagine the emergence and consolidation of the Kuka movement. The Kuka Sikhs did not invent a novel world-view *de novo;* they had a long history behind them which made them oppose the imposition of a new cultural code imported by the 'unholy English'. This may make them heroes for some and frenzied obscurantists for others; collectively they represented one paradigm of a counter-colonial discourse in nineteenth-century north India.

Our study of Kuka insurgents and their symbolic universe also suggests some larger conclusions on the nature of empowerment and resistance in colonial India. In the last decade historians interested in mapping out the tropes of indigenous resistance have had recourse to two distinct strategies. The initial push was towards probing modes of resistance by looking at tribal uprisings, grain riots, peasant rebellions and other confrontational popular movements. [44]More recently, influenced by the writings of Michel Foucault, some scholars have begun to argue that if our goal is to recover the history of resistance it is imperative to look at everyday forms of struggle and humbler forms of defiance, rather than studying spectacular riots and short-lived violent upheavals which are anyway rare in the course of South Asian history. [45] Contrary to these highly polarized positions we would like to argue that if our objective is the history of dissent and counterhegemonic ideologies it is futile to pose the problem by simply dichotomizing lived experience into dramatic episodes of confrontation and quotidian modes of defiance. Our reappraisal of Kuka experience in the second half of the nineteenth century points towards the simultaneous existence of insurrection and everyday forms of struggle. In the spring of 1872 when the Kuka crowd undertook a collective march from the village of Bhaini to the Muslim principality of Malerkotla and en route began to turn things upside down, we see in their actions evidence of what would be classified as dramatic assertion and resistance. However, when Kukas in their day-to-day life carved out their own administrative apparatus, refused to travel by British trains, did not enrol their children in Western schools, rejected European clothing and constructed their own semiotic universe, we can read in their collective behaviour and rituals what James Scott would call everyday forms of resistance.[46] Any project that seeks to write a holistic social history of resistance in South Asia will thus have to incorporate both the dramatic and the quotidian, without idealizing either.

NOTES

1 This perspective is clearly reflected in Memorandum on Ram Singh and the Kukas by J.W. Macnabb, Officiating Commissioner, Ambala Division, 4 November 1871, reproduced in Nahar Singh, *Goroo Ram Singh and the Kuka Sikhs,*vol. I, New Delhi: Amrit Books, 1965, pp. 143–52. Nahar Singh in a very useful three-volume collection has compiled British official documents on the Kukas available at the National Archives of India, New Delhi. Vols I and II are published from New Delhi, 1965 and 1966. The final volume is from Sri Jiwan Nagar, 1967 (hereafter these vols are cited as *KS*).

2 For this interpretation see Macnabb's memorandum cited above.

3 This line of thought is clearly seen in Fauja Singh Bajwa, *Kuka Movement: An Important Phase in Punjab's Role in India's Struggle for Freedom*, Delhi: Motilal Banarsidass, 1965; M.M. Ahluwalia, *Kukas: The Freedom Fighters of the Panjab*, Bombay, Allied Publishers, 1965; and Joginder Singh, *Kuka Movement: Freedom Struggle in Punjab*, New Delhi: Atlantic Publishers, 1985.

4 W.H. McLeod, 'The Kukas: A Millenarian Sect of the Punjab', in G.A. Wood and P.S. O'Connor (eds), *W. P. Morrell: A Tribute*, Dunedin: University of Otago Press, 1973, pp. 85–103.

5 Reproduced in Ganda Singh, *Kukian di Vithia,* Amritsar: Khalsa College, 1944, letter number 4, p. 25, my translation (hereafter *Vithia*).

6 Examination of the accused number 3, Kaisra Singh in 'Copy of the Correspondence, or Extracts from Correspondence, relating to Kooka Outbreak', *Parliamentary Papers*, vol. 45, 1872, p. 43.

7 On the importance of a moral order for peasant societies particularly in the 'economic' domain see the well-known work of James C. Scott, *The Moral Economy of the Peasant: Rebellion and Subsistence in Southeast Asia*, New Haven: Yale University Press, 1976). For its ramifications in the Indian sphere see Barbara Daly Metcalf (ed.), *Moral Conduct and Authority*, California: University of California Press,

1984, pp. 1–22. Although she surveys the importance of the moral order in Islam, her study can illuminate similar concepts among other Indian traditions.

8 I have often used the term Kuka Sikhs here because the differences between the Kukas and the Sikhs had not fully crystallized in the nineteenth century and the two categories often overlapped. This is one reason why the British authorities found it so hard to judge the exact number of Kukas in the Punjab. But at the same time it must be acknowledged there were certain differences between sectors of the Sikh tradition and the Kukas, particularly doctrinal ones, which came to a head when Ram Singh visited the Anandpur shrine.

9 This brief biographical note is based on Ganda Singh, *Vithia* and Nahar Singh, *Namdhari Itihias*, Delhi: published by author, 1955 (hereafter *Itihias*). Both these works have made extensive use of primary sources in Urdu and Panjabi, particularly the literature produced by the Kukas themselves. For instance Santokh Singh, 'satgur Bilds' (unpublished manuscript), Dhian Singh, *Sri Salguru Bilas*, Bhaini Sahib: Namdhari Publications, 1942, and Nidhan Singh Alam, *Jug Paltau Satgurii,* (Delhi: Satguru Publications, 1947).

10 F.A. Steel, 'Folklore in the Punjab', *The Indian Antiquary,* vol. II, 1882, p. 42.

11 Ganda Singh, *Vithia*, letter number 44, p. 302.

12 On how the pure impure antinomy has influenced different cultures see Mary Douglas, *Purity and Danger*, London: Routledge & Kegan Paul, 1966.

13 Sikh concerns with purity and pollution are clearly reflected in the *Sau Sakhian* anthology circulated within the community in the nineteenth century. In a list of sixty-four injunctions in the anthology, several are concerned with the maintenance of purity. For an English translation of the original text see Attar Singh, *Sakhe Book or the Description of Gooroo Gobind Singh's Religion and Doctrines*, Benares: Medical Hall Press, 1873, pp. 18–24.

14 M. Eliade, *Patterns in Comparative Religion*, London: Sheed & Ward, 1958, p. 194, cited in Douglas, *Purity and Danger*, p. 161.

15 For an early attempt at conceptualizing purity and impurity in India see an unsigned essay by Louis Dumont and David F. Pocock, 'Pure and Impure', *Contributions to Indian Sociology,* vol. 3, 1959, pp. 9–39.

16 Nahar Singh, *Itihas*, p. 51.

17 Reproduced in Ganda Singh, *Vithia*, pp. 313–14. Above passage translated by W.H. McLeod, *Textual Sources for the Study of Sikhism*, Manchester: Manchester University Press, 1984, p. 129.

18 Swaran Singh Sanehi, 'Kukas they Live', in John C.B. Webster (ed.), *Popular Religion in the Punjab Today*, Delhi: Institute for Sikh Studies, 1974, pp. 30–1.

19 Ganda Singh, *Vithia*, p. 288.

20 Inspector General of Police, Punjab, to Secretary to Government, Punjab, 20 January 1868, Nahar Singh, *KS* 1, p. 64.

21 Dumont and Pocock, 'Pure and Impure', p. 31.

22 Andrew J. Major, 'Return to Empire: The Sikhs and the British in the Punjab 1839–1872', unpubished PhD thesis, the Australian National University, Canberra, 1981, p. 320.

23 Edmund Leach, *Culture and Communication*, Cambridge: Cambridge University Press, 1976, p. 39.

24 On how the British administration repeatedly tried to disassociate its political authority from the local religious culture in the Punjab, although often without any success, see Ian J. Kerr, 'British relationships with the Golden Temple, 1849–1900', *The Indian Economic and Social History Review*, 21 (2), 1984, pp. 139–45; and David Gilmartin, 'Tribe, Land and Religion in the Punjab: Muslim Politics and the Making of Pakistan', unpublished PhD thesis, University of California, Berkeley, 1979, pp. 53–105.

25 Marvin Harris, an anthropologist, in numerous writings has argued that Indian attitudes towards cattle have to do with ecological adaptation, nutritional efficiency and bioenergetic productivity. For instance, see his 'The Cultural Ecology of India's Sacred Cattle', *Current Anthropology*, 7 (1), 1966, pp. 51–66 and 'India's Sacred Cow', *Human Nature*, 1 (2), 1978, pp. 28–36. This perspective has been bitterly opposed by Paul Diener, Donald Nonini, and Eugene E. Robkin, 'The Dialectics of the Sacred Cow: Ecological Adaptation Versus Political Appropriation in the Origin of India's Cattle Complex', *Dialectical Anthropology*, vol. 3, 1978, pp. 221–41. These authors argue the position of the cow can be understood through an analysis of class conflict, power equations, appropriation of surplus and the rise of Indian empires. Both these approaches remain locked within the polemics of materialism and are uninterested in cow symbolism or its sacredness.

26 W.N. Brown, 'The Sanctity of Cow in Hinduism', *Economic Weekly*, vol. 16, 1964, pp. 245–55.

27 Quoted in Edward Rice, *Eastern Definitions*, New York: Doubleday Publishing, 1978, p. 111.

28 Benjamin Walker, *The Hindu World: An Encyclopedic Survey of Hinduism*, vol. 1, New York: Praeger, 1968, p. 256.

29 William Crooke, *Religion and Folklore of Northern India*, Oxford: Oxford University Press, 1926), p. 364.

30 John R. McLane, *Indian Nationalism and the Early Congress*, Oxford: Princeton University Press, 1926, p. 279

31 Mary Douglas, *Implicit Meanings*, London: Routledge & Kegan Paul Ltd, 1975, p. 285.

32 The literature on this subject is vast, see especially Claude Levi Strauss, *The Savage Mind*, Chicago: Chicago University Press 1966; Edmund Leach, 'Anthropological Aspects of Language: Animal Categories and Verbal Abuse', in Erik H. Lenneberg (ed.), *New Directions in the Study of Language*, Cambridge, Mass.: MIT Press, 1964, pp. 23–63; Ralph Bulmer, 'Why is the Cassowary not a Bird? A Problem of Zoological Taxonomy Among the Karam of the New Guinea Highlands', *Man* (n.s.), vol. 2, 1967, pp. 5–25.

33 For the following observations on the ritual importance of the cow I am indebted to an essay by Paul Hershman, 'Virgin and Mother', in I.M. Lewis (ed.), *Symbols and Sentiments*, London: Academic Press, 1977, pp. 269–92. Although this work is based on a study carried out in the 1970s there is no evidence to show the situation was any different in the nineteenth century. Occasionally, I have supplemented Hershman's findings with other contemporary sources.

34 W.E. Purser, *Revised Settlement of the Jullundur District*,Lahore: Civil and Military Gazette Press, 1892, p. 33.

35 Hershman, 'Virgin and Mother', p. 281.

36 For an explicit Sikh statement on this see Giani Gian Singh, *Pustak Khalsa Dharam Patit Pavan Bhag*, Amritsar: Wazir Hind Press, 1930, p. 20.

37 Louis Dumont, *Homo Hierarchicus*, London: Grafton, 1972, pp. 85–7.

38 For several instances see Nahar Singh, *Itihas*, pp. 119–20.

39 Home Judicial Proceedings, 29 July 1871, (A) 45–61, National Archives of India, New Delhi.

40 Romila Thapar, 'The Image of the Barbarian in Early India', *Comparative Studies in Society and History*, vol. 13, 1971, pp. 408–36, a comprehensive paper, on the evolution of the ideology of mleccha, the nuances and subtle distinctions in its usage and its cultural implications for Indian history, particularly when the term was used for indigenous populations.

41 Kahan Singh Nabha, *Gurshabad Ratankaar Mahan Kosh*, Patiala: Punjab Language Department, 1960, first published 1930, p. 957.

42 Memorandum by Lieutenant Colonel G. McAndrew, Deputy Inspector General of Police, Ambalah Circle, 20 November 1871, Nahar Singh, *KS*, 1, p. 152. Ram Singh expressed similar views in a letter reproduced in Ganda Singh, *Vithia*, letter number, p. 245.

43 T. Gordon Walker, *Final Report on the Revision of Settlement 1878–83 of the Ludhiana District*, Calcutta: Central Press Company, 1884, p. 36.

44 For numerous examples of this genre see Ranajit Guha (ed.), *Subaltern Studies, Writings on South Asian History and Society*, New Delhi: Oxford University Press, vol. II, 1983.

45 Rosalind O' Hanlon, 'Recovering the Subject: Subaltern Studies and Histories of Resistance in Colonial South Asia', *Modern Asian Studies*, 22 (1), 1988, pp. 213–15.

46 See James C. Scott, *Weapons of the Weak: Everyday Forms of Peasant Resistance*, New Haven: Yale University Press, 1985.

7

Anshu Malhotra†

Panths and Piety in the Nineteenth Century

THE GULABDASIS OF PUNJAB

Bakhsiye sabhī gunāh mere lokan vāṅg maiṅ satguru jāndī saṅ
Musalmān maiṅ jānke āp taiṅ Hindu tusaṅ nuṅ paī pachhāndī saṅ (Piro,
Siharfī, 2)
Forgive my sins (for) I perceived you satguru as others did
I knew myself a Musalman, and saw you as Hindu.

Jitrī bājī na hār kuṛe aes janam na phir āvṇaī...
Turak Hinduaṅ da rāh chhoṛ Pīro gur mursadaṅ de rāh jāvṇaī (Piro, Siharfī, 8)[1]
Don't lose a won game girl, this birth will come but once...
Leave the path of Turks and Hindus, Piro follow the path of the guru
murshid.

These lines from Piro's poetry point to the limited vision of ordinary folk who are quick to slot people into recognizable categories of
Hindus and Muslims. Piro confesses to having precisely such a narrow

†I wish to thank Farina Mir and Upinder Singh for their close reading of
the essay and their helpful comments. I also wish to acknowledge the help
of Vijendra Das, Farrukh Khan, Iqbal Qaiser, and Mahima Manchanda in
the collection of some materials for this essay. William Glover managed to
'clean' the images used here and I thank him for his generous help.

perspective before her initiation into the Gulabdasi sect. Following the path of the guru, the above lines suggest, sets her free from conforming to the identities of Turks or Hindus. In other words, adherence to the guru's path made the exteriority of religious practice, whether bodily markers or rituals, irrelevant to the novice on the soteriological path. A world of such devotional practice is explored in this essay.

This essay will look at the Gulabdasi/Gulabdasia sect set up by Guru Gulabdas (d. 1873), with its main establishment (*ḍerā*) in Chathianwala, near Lahore, in the Kasur district of colonial Punjab. The dera was set up sometime during the reign of Ranjit Singh (1799–1839). A brief survey of the different sources available on the Gulabdasis, including the significant 'Nirmala' Sikh ones, will show the various accretive traditions that contributed to the efflorescence of this sect. They will reveal the manner in which the *sant* tradition was assimilated and appropriated by different groups in the nineteenth century, and also depict its resonance in our times. Daniel Gold has studied the multiple sects that developed around the persona of the guru in the late bhakti period in north India with their variable manner of tracing guru lineages. The guru in this imaginary was the exponent of *sant mat*, the teachings of the sants, he was the human guide on the spiritual path, and was also the accessible and immanent manifestation of the divine.[2] The Gulabdasi sect can be placed within this wider north Indian phenomenon of varied *panth*s that grew around the charismatic and benevolent personality of the holy man.

The idea of the guru in Punjab is also associated with Sikh religion that has an established lineage of ten gurus (there were sub-lineages which contested this). Though the tradition of the living guru ended with the demise of the tenth guru Gobind Singh (d.1708), who invested authority in the sacred scripture (*granth*) and the Sikh community (panth) for future guidance, the notion of guru lineage remained significant. The Gulabdasis, with their antecedents within certain Sikh sects, as will be demonstrated below, were also inheritors of this Sikh tradition in some ways. One of the sources of sat mat in Punjab was the Sikh Granth that included the *bāni* of significant *bhagat*s including Kabir, though it is evident from Piro's writings that the Gulabdasis were deeply immersed in the bhakti tradition that came to them from a variety of sources.

This essay will also examine the writings of an important woman follower of Gulabdas, Piro (d.1872), quoted above, who in all her works emphasized the accessibility of the Gulabdasi sect to all irrespective of caste or creed. This was important for Piro to assert, as she was a low-caste Muslim prostitute of Lahore who made a place for herself within the dera. Speaking of Hindu–Muslim difference emerges as something of an obsession in her verses. She refers to it to condemn those tied to fetishistic outward religiosity as the various upholders of faith were in her assessment; and to stress the irrelevance of Hindu–Muslim distinction on the path to inner spiritual growth. To an extent this was an attitude that was closely associated with some bhakti sants, for example the acerbic *padas* of Kabir that were a defining influence in Piro's writings.[3] The path opened by the guru, in other words, showed in relief the hollow claims of traditional religious authorities. Gold summarized the alterity of the sant tradition when he noted, 'To those who recognized the received traditions of neither Hinduism nor Islam as unquestionably true, the sants could present the mystery of the guru as an alternative basis of faith'.[4] It was this faith in the guru and his ability to bless and guide the disciple and the devotee that Piro repeatedly affirmed.

However for Piro, Hindu–Muslim distinctness was also imbricated in the story of her life, as her autobiographical *Ik Sau Saṭh Kāfiaṅ* (*160 Kāfis*) testify. These will be discussed in some detail and used along with her *30 Kāfis*.[5] How Piro tied her personal story to the perceived religious identities of her time will be elaborated. More salient, however, was Piro's manner of telling, the relating of her tale. Her narrative, with its language, imagery and emotional content, emphatically linked her with diverse aspects of Punjabi literary, devotional and popular culture. The *kāfis* (rhyming verses) of the Sufis and the *qissās* of Punjab, the *nirguṇa* (without attributes) poetry of the *bhakta*s and the *saguṇa* (with attributes) imagery of Vaishnavas, all found a place in her writings. Some of these linkages, especially the broad bhakti and Sufi aspects of her writings, were fundamental to the religious expression of the Gulabdasi sect.

Thus multifarious and eclectic traditions went into the making of the Gulabdasi sect and in giving voice to the piety of its members. Despite Piro's frequent references to Hindu–Muslim dissimilarities, indeed animosities, we are not in the world of concretized religious identities that apparently came to define the Hindus, Muslims and Sikhs of late colonial Punjab. Even though the Gulabdasi sect straddled the pre-colonial and colonial periods, and the decade of Gulabdas' and Piro's demise coincided with the establishment of movements that worked towards sharpening religious identities, Gulabdasi religiosity had little to do with such polemics. How do we then best understand the complex ways in which different traditions were assimilated within the Gulabdasi theology, cultural expression and social practice? How do we comprehend Piro's poetry that spoke simultaneously of distinction and sameness of different religious traditions?

In this context I wish to re-examine the concept of syncretism whose utility of late has come to be critically probed by scholars. Over the last two decades scholars have questioned the usefulness of the term—critiques coming from historians with expertise in textual sources[6] to anthropologists looking at religions in practice, especially those studying active and contested religious sites.[7] They see syncretism as an inadequate concept because it assumes an amalgamation of separate religious traditions, allowing the viewing of religions as self-contained entities that can be mixed and harmonized into a synthesis. That is to say, the processual and open-ended character of religions is overlaid with the idea of their inherent completeness. Conversely, scholars have pointed to the interrelatedness of all human actions, including exchange in the religious sphere.[8] If such is the case, then the value of a term like syncretism amounts to little as no tradition can historically be shown to be exclusive—borrowing and appropriating from varied cultures being the norm. Syncretism, in this understanding, adds little analytical value towards deciphering religious phenomena. The commonsensical way in which the term was used in earlier scholarship is therefore no longer adequate.

In South Asia the term has carried a positive connotation, as historians used examples of 'syncretism' to show religions in practice. The term syncretism was invested with the load of demonstrating composite cultures, shared religious sites and religiously mixed following of tombs and saints that acted as antidote to the pathology of communalism that scarred colonial and post-colonial histories. Negating the burden of colonialist accusations that saw the colonized as intrinsically divided, the concept of syncretism was deployed to show the nascent nation's 'composite' culture. As mentioned by Shahid Amin, syncretism in this understanding came fully formed, 'bleaching' histories of conquest and conflict.[9] Peter van der Veer has shown mixed following of a saint may not exclude hierarchies of access and worship in these sites.[10] Wary of such usage today, historians are carefully examining their own conscious or unconscious implication in the agendas of writing 'secular' histories.[11]

Two further interventions in this debate are of interest here. An argument based on interaction and relatedness of cultures has been put forward by Tony Stewart in the context of the seemingly syncretic language used to establish Islamic theological ideas in medieval Bengal. Stewart does not see the language that deployed 'Hindu' equivalents to convey the ideas of Islam as a case of syncretic amalgamation. Rather he prefers to see in this borrowing a desire to locate 'theological equivalences' on the part of religious figures disseminating Islamic ideals in this peripheral region of India.[12] The theology of the interlocutors was rooted in Islamic traditions, but the project of its diffusion required a language that was easily comprehensible to the people. In an argument that too underlined the need for greater care in assuming syncretism from outward appearances of convergence, Carl Ernst studied the extensive texts that showed a relationship between the Sufis and Yogis of India. Acknowledging the many points of equivalence and cultural conversation between them, Ernst stressed that exchange often took place from being grounded in one's tradition, and included an inclination towards contestation and appropriation.[13] While both arguments explicitly reject syncretism as an analytic, they show constant and innovative interaction between cultures, to evolve as traditions and face challenges of different historical situations. I will use aspects of both these arguments to show the manner in which the Gulabdasis absorbed and intersected with the religious environment of mid-nineteenth century Punjab.

However, I do not wish to altogether abandon the conceptual advantages that 'syncretism' as a term offers. Though cultures may not amalgamate in equal parts, we still need to show open-endedness, borrowing, absorption and appropriation, as the stuff of cultural exchange, when groups worked towards such fluid intercourse. As Charles

Stewart points out, when the complexities and ambiguities inherent in a phenomenon like religious traditions and their interaction are multi-dimensional and subjective, it is not possible for objective terms to carry the whole range of interpretive meanings.[14] Thus syncretism may help us understand how, when and why cultures interact and inter-animate each other, though it may not rule out hierarchical or other ways of cataloguing them. The cultural pores that allow exchange may be, to use a biological term, osmotic, that is sieving some influences through while blocking others. Syncretism as a concept will help us grasp this mien of fluidity and highlight the attitude of curiosity that leads to exchange and cultural flows. Discarding it may deprive us of a concept that stresses interactive development as a given aspect of some traditions as against others' investment in exclusivity. As Dominique-Sila Khan writes—'Syncretic and liminal traditions or communities can be perceived as cohesive forces in the social fabric, powerful links in the uninterrupted chain of religious traditions'. Fuzzy thinking in her understanding points to a world comfortable with multitudinous values as against one embedded in bivalent either/or logic.[15] Sects like the Gulabdasis appealed to peoples of different religious traditions, and also wished to appropriate and claim parallel theological concepts. In such an environment syncretism facilitates the underscoring of shared moral and emotional structures for which the language of religion remained salient. This includes the sharing of moral principles—which can be variously referred to as '*dharma*' or '*shara*'[16]—that cut across community lines and were a part of a 'moral economy' that had an emotional charge in Punjab. Recourse to such multivalent values and revelling in their heuristic possibilities will be shown in the last section of the paper. In this case the theological equivalences noted will not develop out of a novel situation as for example shown by Stewart. Here the gradual layering of thought and the sedimentation of ideas (geological terms that highlight accretion/acculturation) occurred over time and came to fashion modes of being.

THE GULABDASIS: SOURCES AND CONTROVERSIES

Two distinct traditions on the life of the founder of the sect, Gulabdas, are available. One emanates from the scholarly and ascetic sects within

Sikhism, the Udasis and the Nirmalas and links Gulabdasis to them.[17] Colonial ethnography mostly follows this account,[18] though sometimes gives additional information.[19] This is the more historical narration, and some of the figures linked with it, for example Giani Gian Singh, were beginning to be associated with Sikh reformism of the Singh Sabhas.[20] Gian Singh's *Panth Prakāsh* was a detailed history of the eighteenth century, along with narratives on the Sikh gurus, especially the first and the tenth. Towards the end of this massive history in Braj verse, Singh gives accounts of Sikh sects, including the Nirmalas, Udasis, Nihangs, Kukas, and smaller ones like the Gulabdasis. The Gulabdasis in this tradition were seen to be a part of this varied Sikh heritage.

A more mythologized reading of Gulabdas' life comes from a Sindhi younger disciple of Gulabdas, Vishandas, who stayed with Gulabdas for six and a half months in his youth, and whose father, Nehalchand was also a Gulabdasi follower. Vishandas later became a successful businessman and a landlord in Sindh, who also dabbled in Congress-led politics.[21] A sub-lineage of the Gulabdasis, in our present times, based in Hansi, Haryana, in India, also endorses this mythic reading of the guru's life.[22]

According to the scholarly Sikh accounts, Gulabdas was born in village Ratol, Tarn Taran district, near Amritsar, Punjab in 1809. The young Gulabdas spent a period serving a Sikh chief militarily, after which he was attracted to ascetic life under the aegis of the Udasis. Udasis are the oldest sect within Sikhism, inaugurated by Siri Chand, the elder son of the founder of Sikhism, Guru Nanak. Resembling the ascetic orders that flourished in north India in more ways than the householder movement established by Nanak, the Udasis are a part of the Sikh community, with their history connected to the lives of Sikh gurus and their progeny.[23] They had a strong presence in Punjab historically, but were also found in cities and pilgrimage centres of the north Indian plains. A preceptor from among the Sangatsahibs, one of the sub-divisions within the Udasis, may have initiated Gulabdas. Under their influence he smeared ashes on his body, and joined the ranks of the *nangās*, or celibate Udasis. His tutor within the Udasi fold is variously referred to as Brahmdas or Hiradas.

Interestingly, while the eighteenth and the early nineteenth centuries are usually associated in Sikh and Punjabi history as a period that established the political and religious power of the Khalsa, the sect within Sikhism whose genesis is traced to the tenth and the last Sikh guru Gobind, the Udasi order too flourished in this period. It seems political consolidation under Ranjit Singh played a positive role in providing sustained patronage. Apparently sixty new Udasi centres came to be established,[24] and by mid nineteenth century Udasi establishments exceeded 250.[25] The multiple references to Udasi *samādh*s (commemoratives shrines over the ashes of deceased holy men), *akhāra*s and deras (establishments) in Ganesh Das' *Chār Bāgh-i-Panjāb*, an 1849 history, confirm the importance of this sect.[26]

Nirmalas too, in these accounts, played an important role in grooming Gulabdas. Under various teachers—Dhyandas of Dhanaula, Haridas Giridhar, and Deva Singh 'Nirmala', he learnt the art of composing poetry and became acquainted with the philosophy of Vedanta— both aspects vital in Gulabdasi theology and literary culture. The story of the origin of Nirmalas also links them to Guru Gobind, who is said to have sent three disciples to Benaras to learn Sanskrit and blessed them when they came back calling them 'Nirmala' (stainless). Known for keeping hair unshorn in the fashion of the Khalsa, the Nirmalas were celibate and immersed in Vedic and Sanskrit teaching.[27]

Gulabdas, in these Nirmala Sikh accounts then, spent his early years in the eclectic world of Sikh asceticism and scholarship, aspects of which link up with the multivalent cosmos of Indic ascetic and philosophical traditions. There was yet another influence on Gulabdas, presented as deleterious by the contemporary/near-contemporary Sikh historians Gian Singh and Ganesha Singh. This was time spent with the *faqīr*s of a Sufi order mentioned as Bulleh Shahi.[28] While both these historians were appreciative of Gulabdas' intellectual acuity, they condemned what they saw as his follies. They accused him of slack and hedonistic habits due to this faqir influence, outside the fold of Sikh sects that had apparently nurtured him.

From the above accounts it becomes clear that when Gulabdas set up his own dera, he diverged from both the Udasis and the Nirmalas. However, Vedanta, important to the two orders, continued to be a defining influence, as seen in Gulabdas' and Piro's writings. These show his inclination towards Vedantic monism, denying a duality between God and the world, and solipsism, the self as the knowable truth. This may have led him to call himself *Brahm*, an aspect of the divine, underlining the influence of *Advaitā*, and the basis of a defining mantra of the Gulabdasis, *soham* (I am He). However, his contemporaries accused him of atheism,[29] his ideas too esoteric and wayward for their comfort. He was also disapproved of for his general disregard for maintaining any symbols that would distinguish his sect from others, allowing his followers to keep their hair short or unshorn, dressing well himself and allowing the same for his followers. He invited all castes into his fold, removing restrictions on food consumed or the manner of its consumption. He also admitted Muslims into his sect.[30] It was this openness of Gulabdas's sect that a Muslim prostitute like Piro entered its ranks. However, his own intimate relations with her, as our two historians suggest, along with admittance of other prostitutes as followers, led his sect to be seen as opprobrious—*beshar* (literally in contravention to the practice of *shari'ah*) for the Nirmala historians. Gian Singh discountenanced by saying that Gulabdas gave up following accepted moral principles (*taji sharā sab keri*), and Ganesha Singh accused him of insulting (*nindiyā*) the law and moral rules (*sharā*) of Hindus and Musalmans.[31]

In a major divergence from the Sikh sources, the succinct description of Gulabdas' life in Vishandas' account gives him a long life of 151 years. According to Vishandas he was born in 1723 and died in 1874, though the name of his village and district remain identical to Sikh narratives.[32] The guru is said to have left his home at the age of eleven to wander, as many a holy man, to pilgrimage sites and conversing with men of wisdom. He set up his dera in Chathianwala in 1814. The salience of a long life in these alternate accounts can be read as establishing the miraculous and mythical powers of the guru, his stature above that of mere mortals. More significantly, the long span allows the guru interlocution with a variety of mystics of the past, including the eminent Sindhi Sufi, Shah Abdul Latif Bhitai (1689–1752), whose spiritual verses inscribed in the *Risālo* still echo in Sindh.[33] Not only does the guru glow in association with the charisma of one such as Abdul Latif, but Vishandas also establishes a special relationship of Gulabdas with the land of Sindh from which he hailed. Accordingly, guru's interaction with other Sindhi personalities is mentioned—Sri Bankhandi, Rohal Faqir—along with a number of disciples from this region that are not mentioned in other sources (see Figure 7.1).

Figure 7.1 Title page of Gulabdas's *Gulab Chaman.* The title in Gurmukhi reads *Pothi Gulab Chaman Di.* Text below:
Printed at the request of Abdul Haq, Taj Kutub, Lahore, Bazaar Kashmiri, for the benefit of all. The picture depicts Gulabdas seated on his *gaddi*, his sword and shield lying next to him, an aigrette in his turban, and his head framed by a halo. Behind him holding the fly whisk is most likely his appointed successor Hargobind. To his right is his disciple and poet Kishan Singh Arif. The picture underscores the majestic aura of the guru

Vijendra Das of Hansi's account too gives Gulabdas a life of 150 years (1723–1873).[34] Shri Vijendra's introduction to Piro's oeuvre is partially driven by establishing the fantastical power of the guru. Thus like Vishandas, he too speaks of guru's meetings with Shah Abdul Latif, and moreover, Bulleh Shah (1680–1752), the famous Qadiri-Shattari Sufi from Kasur, the district where Chathianwala is, and whose faqirs even the Sikh sources disapprovingly noted as having influenced Gulabdas. In this account Gulabdas is said to have travelled to religious places in India and Europe, besides Islam's sacred sites of Mecca and Medina. The respect for different religious traditions in this narration is underlined by highlighting Gulabdasi followers from different communities. But Vijendra also anachronistically places the concerns evolving from India's present communal tensions to the reading of his Gulabdasi inheritance, even though religious difference was, as noted, acknowledged in that time. Shri Vijendra refers to the Chathianwala tomb where Gulabdas and Piro are buried as '*sadbhāvna sthal*', a place marked by (communal) harmony and cordiality.

Additionally Das wishes to clear '*mātā*' (mother) Piro's name of any infamy attached to it as a consequence of her previous career in prostitution or her relations with her guru. Piro in his portrayal appears as a helpless woman—*abalā*—exploited (a far cry from what her poetry reveals) and looking for a way out of her condition. Guru's long life also fulfils the agenda of proving the purity of Piro's relations with him, for he is said to have met her when he was a 100 years old and she a waif of fourteen or fifteen. Shri Vijendra's introduction to Piro's life and writings also imitates academic scholarship in so far as he gives footnotes and references where possible. However, he succeeds in lending modern historicity to his work only marginally, narration of anecdote and miracle an important aspect in his writing that seeks a balance between academic scholarship and worshipful devoutness.

The Gulabdasis in Sikh histories, then, originated from within a broad Sikh universe, linked to a larger world of Indic philosophical and spiritual rigours. While the Gulabdasis rejected abstemiousness and austerity later, they are presented as retaining principles of monastic life, of a special place of the preceptor (guru, *murshid*), and the scholarly pursuits associated with the Udasis. The Nirmalas, with their antecedents in Vedic learning and interest in Vedanta also fuelled the Gulabdasi imagination, as they did their scholarly bent. From within this capacious world, they created a niche for themselves, their separate identity based on certain theological emphasis, but also the minutiae of daily conduct (in their case that they maintained no restrictions). In Vishandas and Shri Vijendra's narratives these aspects of Gulabdasi sect are overtaken by a desire to link them with wider religious networks of Punjab (and Sindh), an ecumenism that enhanced Gulabdas' spiritual aura and popular allure. This appeal extended to all communities, they emphasize. The Nirmala sources display some discomfort with Gulabdas' relations with faqirs and specifically with his following among prostitutes, even referring to attempts to suppress the sect in the 1850s because of their notoriety on these grounds.[35] The latter accounts are not only sanguine about the sect's ostensible misdemeanours, but also celebratory about the Gulabdasi appeal to all peoples.

In this context of fluid boundaries, whether between Sikh and Hindu sects, or between bhakti sects in dialogue with Sufis, Piro's writings are an important opening to decipher notions of belonging and identity or their superfluous comforts. She both tells us what it meant to belong to a community and also how relations between communities were perceived in the mid-nineteenth century. Piro also displays deep knowledge of Gulabdasi theology and its piety that linked it to different expressions of Punjabi culture.

DISTINCTION AND SAMENESS IN PIRO'S WRITINGS

Though not prolific, Piro was an author in her own right.[36] As noted, here I use her autobiographical *160 Kafis* and her mystical *30 Kafis* to elucidate her religiosity. Appositely placed to write on religious contentiousness, Piro elaborated on the difference between Hindus and Muslims, and between her own and the many sects present in Punjab. She borrowed from wide cultural attitudes in her writing; indeed these constitute a strong emotional element in her works. Acceptance of, even overt assertion of distinction, in other words, did not halt the process of cultural exchange.

The personal details of Piro's life, and the choices she exercised, place her at the cusp of religious friction, or at least she portrayed it as such in *160 Kafis*. A Muslim prostitute of Lahore, she decided to leave her known life and go to the dera of guru Gulabdas at Chathianwala, near Lahore. However cutting off links from her past was easier imagined than accomplished. Piro writes of the anger of her clan members (*kuṭumb*), who eventually abduct her and take her to Wazirabad, north of Lahore on the eastern bank of the Chenab, where she was held in captivity. This becomes an occasion for Piro to rant both against the self-appointed upholders of faith, the *mullāhs*/*mulāṇās*, for she is accused of apostasy; and the *musalmāns* more generally, as the perpetrators of her mistreatment. Fact and fiction mix seamlessly in Piro's narrative—as she assumes the mantle of Sita, the heroine of the epic Ramayana, in her moment of incarceration, and her guru that of Rama, organizing her rescue. This, in turn, makes suspect her version of the events as 'authentic' facts, as Piro employs rich mythology to state her case, unencumbered by the need to sieve the factual and the probable from the make-believe. For wouldn't such a portrayal of victimization help her garner the sympathy that may ease her entry into the dera, where she faced some opposition to her presence? However, a later account of the events specifically mentions strife over her person, locating its genesis in the desire of a powerful suitor (Ilahi Bakhsh, a general of Ranjit Singh) for Piro's attentions. At the behest of this client, an apparent clash took place between her guardians and Gulabdas' men. In this version though, the scene of the skirmish shifts near the tomb of Mian Mir in Lahore, rather than the theatre of Wazirabad as depicted by Piro.[37] Despite some disparity between the two accounts, we are pushed back into a world of real possibilities, where political and religious discord could ensnare a person in a vortex of conflict. In the context of Piro's writings, the exaggerated animus between Hindus and Muslims is as much of narrative trope, as it is her understanding of her circumstances, or any reflection of her times.

It is also important to note that the primary religious distinction that Piro underscores is between Hindus and Muslims. Sikh identity remains amorphous. Specific Sikh sects are mentioned—Udasis,

Nirmalas, Akalis, Khalsas—but as just that—sects (panth), even though she has a notion of *sikhī*, the Sikh way. This is much the same way that Ganesh Das could refer to the Udasi dervishes of Nanak Shah at one juncture and Akali faqirs at another, without necessarily qualifying them as Sikh.

Acrimonious relations between Hindus and Muslims is a strong leitmotif in Piro's writings, though more powerful is the idea that religious authorities are self-seeking, corrupt and out to ensnare people with their shenanigans. The differences between their religious beliefs and rituals is brought out in statements like—*Hindu path haiṅ bed ko yeh Turak Qurāne* (*160*-18)[38]—Hindus study the Veda, the Turks, the Quran; or *Turak japde aur ko yeh Hindu aure* (*160*-18)—Turks worship something else and Hindus quite another. In a similar vein she states that while one prays (facing) the west, the other to the south (*160*-131); or that one set discuss the Quran and are cow-slayers while the other preach sitting in cow-shelters (*160*-154). Speaking against ritualism and exteriority of religious practice Piro notes that circumcision and a style of facial hair define Turk men, the sacred thread and the topknot the Hindus (*160*-44). Thus Piro implies implacable religious differences between the two.

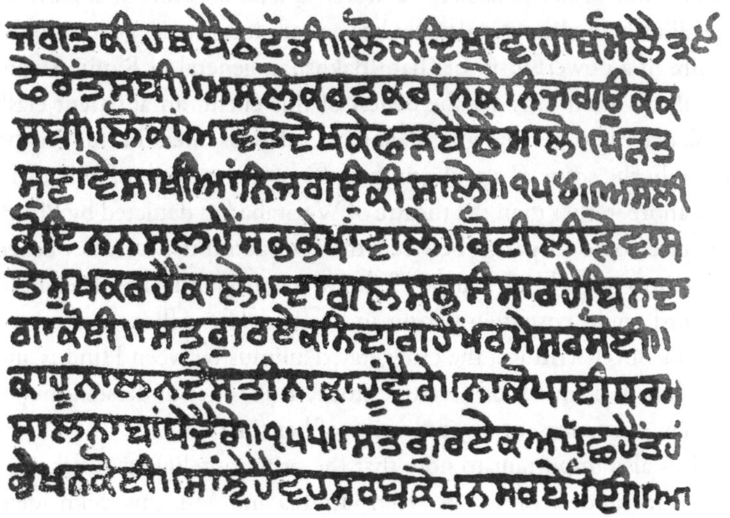

Figure 7.2 A page from Piro's *Ik Sau Sath Kafian* (*160 Kafis*) showing *Kafis* 154 and 155

The investment that the upholders of fetishistic outward religiosity make in maintaining the symbols of religion and power over people is exemplified in Piro's own bitter confrontation with the mullahs as depicted in her *160 Kafis*. In Piro's rendition of events she is persuaded by her clan to leave the dera and accompany them which she does hoping to come back after perhaps convincing them of her decision. Once back with her clan she has a showdown with the mullahs/*qāzis* (*mulānel kājī*), who are brought in because she is accused of apostasy, even conversion (*is majbar lāhī*). Mullahs are depicted coming bearing down with books and religious knowledge—*mār katebañ bagal mo mulvāne āye* (*160*-25)—(tucking their books under their arms the mullahs came); and though all present bow before them, Piro refuses to do so. The mullahs call her a *kāfir* (unbeliever), of having taken pork (forbidden for Muslims), and urge her to say the Muslim prayers including the *kalmā* (*kalīmā*, the Islamic creedal formula) to purify her. Piro in turn accuses them of being 'dogs of religion' (*majbañ ke tum kūkre*), kafir for their inability to discern a true gnostic (*ārif*), of practicing *harām* (unlawful) rather than *halāl* (lawful), and that she herself has become purified on meeting her guru. Along with this vituperative tête-à-tête with the mullahs, Piro also explicates the true message of her sect in appropriate monist, pantheistic language—of God who is limitless (*behad*) and omnipresent, the truth that pervades all. In this context she also asserts that she is neither a Hindu nor a Muslim—*nā maiñ Musalmānī nā Hiñdu hosañ* (*160*-150)—pointing to her Gulabdasi identity that could transcend given identities.

Piro thus draws out the manner in which the Hindu and Islamic creeds diverge, and then creates one of the many dramatic moments in her narrative—her contretemps with the Islamic religious and judicial authorities to firstly emphasize their narrow minded religiosity; and secondly to delineate the theology of her sect in contradistinction to Muslim and Hindu ritualism. However, equally important in Piro's verbal sparring with the mullahs, her mullah baiting, is that such sentiment has deep roots in Punjabi culture. This anti-mullah rhetoric that underscores the exteriority of religious practice is visible in the kafis of the popular Sufi poets of Punjab. They make fun of the mullah's learning whose end is self-aggrandizement, and make a virtue of the Sufis' purported indifference to bookish knowledge.

The Sufis often emphasize how reading the first letter of the Arabic alphabet, *alif*, is enough, written as an upright line, signifying the unity of God, and his name, Allah. The only other letter they care for is *mīm*, standing for Prophet Mohammad.[39] Expressing revulsion for the self-motivated scholarship of the mullah, the seventeenth century Sufi poet Sultan Bahu writes:

> Quran scholars read and aggrandize themselves, priests act sanctimonious.
> Like rain clouds in the monsoon, they wander heavy with books.
> They recite more wherever they see greater gain and plenty.
> Bahu, those who sell and eat up their earnings lose both worlds.[40]

The same sensibility runs through many of Bulleh Shah's *kafis,* whose followers are said to have influenced Gulabdas—for instance when he writes against the knowledge of Quran scholars—

> Becoming a Quran scholar you memorize it.
> Constant reading makes you glib.
> Then your attention is drawn towards favours and gifts.
> Your heart goes wandering like a messenger.[41]

Thus when Piro writes similarly of Islamic scholars she is expressing a common sentiment.

> *Ghāfal sain nām bin tum kāfar kājī*
> *Sarghī ghar ghar khāvso kar jagat muthājī* (160-28)

> Oblivious of the name of the master, infidel qazis
> You go begging from door to door for meals like the indigent.

While a Sultan Bahu or a Bulleh Shah generalized the condition of the sanctimonious and selfish mullahs, in Piro's writing the confrontation with them acquires a personal tone, a portrayal by Piro of what supposedly occurred to her. It is this sliding between different registers, of the factual and the imagined, that bestows her text with a peculiar quality of blending cultural moods with her apparently lived history. Her contest with the mullahs is reminiscent of the episode in the most popular Punjabi qissa—of Hir and Ranjha—where Hir tears to shreds the legalistic/moralistic stance of the qazi who urges her to obey her parents and maintain sexual propriety. Hir demonstrates the empty legalism of the qazi, underscoring her superior morality towards her love to his bookish harangue.[42] Piro repeatedly uses given literary topoi and their emotional structures to string together what is purportedly her story. What makes her tale more compelling, however, is the manner in which she weaves in strife between Hindus and Muslims at the very heart of her story, rather than mere dismissal of such differentiation one may find in the writing of a Bulleh. Did this insistence on Hindu–Muslim dissension, enumerating the manner in which their creeds differ, or placing them at the nub of her own tale make Piro singular? Let us look at another nineteenth century variant of a saga of Hindu–Muslim fracas to see the larger point being made.

Ganesh Das Badhera's *Chārs Bāgh-i-Panjāb* has been introduced earlier. J.S. Grewal and Indu Banga's translation of 150 pages of a work completed in 1849 shows the author's expertise in the administrative history of Punjab, even as he makes his case for the continuing patronage of the state before the newly established colonial power. The text is focused on the role of the Khatris, the service gentry, as historically important cogs in the functioning of the state, and as men of knowledge and piety. Ganesh Das gives an elaborate description of parts of Punjab, especially the Rachna and Chaj *doābs*,[43] creating in the process a sacred topography of Punjab. Along with men (and occasionally women) of learning and skill the holy personages belonging to each sub-region are enumerated. Numerous *sādh*s, faqirs, dervishes (mendicants) *sanyāsī*s, *bairāgī*s, (renunciants) *jogī*s (renunciant Naths) *pīr*s (Sufi masters) and a rare *agāmī* (a follower of *tantrā*) fill his account, as do a number of samadhs (memorial shrines) *thākurdwārā*s (temples) *khānqāh*s (Sufi habitations) *masīt*s (mosques) and *dharamsālā*s (Sikh temples). His native Gujrat, for instance, is associated with the deeds and miracles of its most renowned saint Hazrat Shah Daula, including a fascinating account of the saint saving Gujrat from the wrath of the sixth Sikh guru Hargobind annoyed at the irrepressible banter of Gujrati men.[44] Equally remarkably the famous qissas of Punjab, mostly romantic stories of tragic loves with their polyvalent significations including spiritual interpretations, are interwoven in his regional histories, occupying almost one-third of the text.[45] It is here, while describing the Rachna doab between rivers Ravi and Chenab, and his ancestral roots in Gujrat–Dakhan, that Das relates the piteous tale of the righteous Hindu martyr, the fourteen-year old Haqiqat Rai, son of the rich Khatri Bhag Mal Puri.[46]

In brief, the story relates the cruel fate of Haqiqat Rai, who as a pupil of a *maktāb* (the mosque school) in Sialkot once enters a discussion about the composition of verses with a *mullāzādā* (son of a mullah). Unable to dispute Haqiqat Rai's point the mullazada accuses him of displaying disrespect to the Prophet of Islam, an accusation supported by the musalmans of the city. The young lad is given the choice of conversion to Islam or death as punishment for his blasphemy. His desperate father is able to have the case transferred to Lahore where the governor is Zakariya Khan. Though convinced of Haqiqat Rai's innocence, the Khan leaves the matter to the *maulvīs* (scholars of Islam), who once again place before him the (non) choice of conversion or death. Though Bhag Mal tries to convince his son of the benefits of conversion and the value of Islam, the son refuses to convert. He underlines the narrowness of the orthodox creed of Islamic scholars as against the catholicity of the Persian poets, exposition of whose literary labours began his troubles. The next day Haqiqat Rai is almost stoned to death, but for a soldier who beheads him out of compassion. Haqiqat Rai the martyr is cremated, with a samadh built for him in Lahore, and a *maṛhi* (memorial built at the site of cremation) in Sialkot, both of which subsequently became places of pilgrimage.

At one level this story is about the inexorable distance between the Hindus and the Muslims—Haqiqat Rai is evidently a martyr to the Hindu cause (refusal to convert), when Muslims exercise political power. Located in a particular historical context, the period of the governorship of Zakariya Khan in Punjab in the first half of the eighteenth century, unlike the mythic time of most qissas, the story is reminiscent of the martyrdom of Guru Tegh Bahadur, who too was ostensibly asked by the Mughal emperor Aurangzeb to choose between conversion to Islam and death.[47] However, unlike the imperial frame of the guru's tale, that of Haqiqat Rai has a local flavour. Also unlike the guru's martyrdom, that became an important anecdote in the enduring hostility between the subsequently created Khalsa and the Mughal state, Haqiqat Rai's saga merely reiterates what the Sufis of Punjab had been singing all along—the arbitrary, unbending, and wrongly applied power of the legalistic religious authorities. Though Haqiqat Rai dies for being a Hindu who refuses conversion, the conflict that his story invokes is between Islamic authority and the catholicity of Persian poets, the dispute after all on composition of verses that initiates the tragedy. That the common people are not implicated in the murder is reinforced by the compassionate act of mercy of beheading performed by a common soldier, though who the persecuting musalmans are (men with conspicuous religiosity?) remains ambiguous. A story apparently embedded in implacable Hindu–Muslim antagonism, on closer scrutiny reveals a deeper timbre of hostility towards dogmatic and capricious power.

How do we then view Piro's tale of her own clearly voluntary conversion, her turning a Muslim renegade? There is no doubt that Piro wishes to evoke the anti-authority mood that the many qissas, and Punjabi Sufi poetry were imbricated in. This dialogic relationship with Punjabi culture makes her saga a rendering of her own story, as it is a recapitulation of the congealed emotions of Punjabi literary imagination. Though hers is not a story of martyrdom, she nevertheless tries to dress it as one of wrongly applied power and assumes the moral high ground of a woman hounded by the upholders of religious power. I have suggested elsewhere that Piro is caught in a dilemma of choosing between pursuing the life opened for her in the Gulabdasi dera, and the obligations she owes to those in her profession as a daughter and a prostitute.[48] The difficulty in exercising her will, but playing with given anti-authority attitudes, helps her lend a moral weight to her cause. The freedom to fashion her life-story, once shielded in the dera, gives it the gravitas of a person wronged.

Some observations may be made at this stage to link up with the larger issue of syncretism. The recognition of creedal distinction, indeed of emphasizing it, as Piro does, or as is evident in the qissa of Haqiqat Rai, did not mean nothing was shared between people following different faiths. The underscoring of religious, especially ritualistic or external differences itself was a formula meant to enhance the validity of a Sufi path, or that of different panths. The evocation of bigotry of Hindus and Muslims emphasized the all-embracing nature of panths. Even when the antipathy between religious practitioners could lead to tragic ends, as with Haqiqat Rai, at least one of the possible lessons to be drawn from the story was about the irrelevance of dogmatism. It would be difficult to gauge what the emotions of those who flocked to the samadh of Haqiqat Rai were, or those who read the vituperations of Piro against her co-religionists. Yet there is no denying that there were ways in which the emotional and cultural moods evoked by each could also reinforce what people shared across religious gulfs. What this points to is that the acknowledgement of distinction did not obstruct the reworking of these stories with the potential of recasting communities that could accommodate difference, and where conciliation could be knit into the fabric of everyday life. Did this cultural mood of lampooning high authority, available among various communities amount to syncretism? Whether one agrees with that or not, what it did mean was that any development that may be regarded as syncretic had to work on a cultural and emotional plane that was shared across peoples from separate traditions.

THEOLOGICAL EQUIVALENCES AND SYNCRETISTIC POSSIBILITIES

Though at one time scholars assumed that Sufism was derived from Hinduism—Vedanta and the Hatha Yoga of medieval Jogis as the sources of this borrowing[49]—such an assertion is now seen to be completely unfounded. Schimmel showed the deep roots of Sufism in the region that is the crucible of Islam.[50] Recently, Ernst has drawn attention to the polythetic analysis of religion, noting how one might read the shared characteristics of religions without succumbing to an essentialist thesis.[51] There were many points of correspondence between Sufi and Yogic practices, for instance the *dhikr* of the Sufis and the exercise of breath control of the Jogis. For Ernst the preferred way of understanding these commonalities is to show how these allowed Sufis and Jogis to assimilate and appropriate from each other, while installed within their traditions. Even the contests between them to establish superiority, that Simon Digby draws our attention to, emanated from location within their own systems.[52] It is only later that such assimilations, even as they continued, contributed to the emergence of 'communal' identities.[53]

To understand Gulabdasi appropriations from aspects of Sufi thought while at home with their specific understanding of Vedanta, let us look at Piro's sophisticated engagement with the theology of her sect.

The cornerstone of this was the Vedanta belief in the identity between the Self/*Atman* and *Brāhmaṇ* (Supreme Being), the notion that the deepest part of our being is one with the essence of the world.[54] This idea found expression in the mystical mantra of soham (I am S/He)[55] of the Gulabdasis, as with Gulabdas calling himself Brahm. The continuum between the body, the empirical reality, the undifferentiated consciousness and the universe is seen in Piro's words—*ek sarīr anātma, ātam brhamāṇḍe* (*160*-148), and again *batak tukham kā rūp jyoṅ houṅ sarab akhaṅḍe* (*160*-144)—like a tree is a form of seed so I am one with the universe. God as the essence of the world pervades it—*sarab rūp moṅ jāniyoṅ jyoṅ nīr taraṅge* (*30*-16)—and is found in every form, like waves in water. The same thought can be seen in Gulabdas' words: *ek bīj jiveṅ baṭ phail rahā har tarā hai yagat bilās terā*—like a seed spreads as a tree you play expansively in the universe.[56] The Supreme Reality was both immanent and transcendent for the Gulabdasis, and their path involved the solipsistic belief of locating within the self the essence of creation.

This philosophy of the Gulabdasis came overlaid with the ideas of bhakti. In Piro's writings, the ultimate Reality is imagined in nirguna terms, though she takes recourse to Vaishnava imagery when required. However, the ability to follow the path to seek Reality rested on the guru—illuminating the significance of the preceptor both in the ascetic tradition and within the bhakti imaginary, as within Sufi praxis. Piro deliberately and often blurs the line between guru and god, a phenomenon Gold notes as ubiquitous in the later bhakti movement.[57] Piro captures these esoteric ideas in her kafi that refers to this formless Supreme Being, arrived at through working out different negations, but underlines the positive role of the guru:

> *saiṅ hameṅ ajāt hai na hiṅdu turkā*
> *janam maraṇ to bāhrā na nārī purkhā*
> *hadaṅ pare behad hai na hadaṅ māhī*
> *Pīro guru dikhāvsī aiuṅ dekhe nāhī.* (*30*-4)

The master is without attributes neither Hindu nor Turk.
Outside (the cycle) of birth and death, neither woman nor man.
Beyond bounds, is limitless, not confined within limits.
Piro (says) guru will reveal, unfathomable otherwise.

The immanence of death, and therefore the plea to make the most of this birth was an important notion within the bhakti devotional world:

Pīro baṅdiye jāg le huṇ jāgaṇ velā
aise janam malāvṛa phir hoe na melā. (30-3)

Piro woman, awake, it is time to rise
You will get but one birth.

The idea of death staring at all and so waking up to its reality can be traced back to the *sakhi*s of the fifteenth century bhakti saint Kabir, the most popular of bhakti saints of medieval north India.[58] The stamp of Kabir on the mystical writing of Piro is enormous, as noted earlier. Piro's baiting of mullahs and pandits, as discussed above, is akin to Kabir's. Moreover, her critique of circumcision as practiced by Muslims—*use sampūraṇ bhejīyo tum dāg lagāiyo* (160-40)—you were sent complete but have put a stain—resembles Kabir's taunting of this Islamic ritual.[59] It is in Piro's use of cryptic and paradoxical language that one especially senses Kabir's presence in her mystical writing. The manner in which Kabir alluded to the inexpressible experience of the mystical *sahaj* state—'the sugar of the mute'—the adage according to Charlotte Vaudeville that was borrowed from Nath and Tantric traditions, is imitated by Piro. Focusing on the soham mantra, Piro shows the significance of its repetition (like the repetition on *Nām*/Name) by unravelling its mystical dimensions, and exposing its inexpressible joys.

Soham nām pukārdā kyoṅ maiṅ te nasaṅ
Gūngā guṛ ko khai jo maiṅ man vich hasaṅ (30-7)

Soham the word is calling out, why do I run?
Like jaggery to the mute, I smile to myself.

Similarly, Piro mimics the 'eastern' (*pūrbī*) language of Kabir associated with mystical depths to demonstrate her ineffable experience. Her words:

Pīro bolī pūrbī samjhe nahiṅ koī,
jo pūrab kā hovsī samjhegā soī (30-15)

Piro speaks the Eastern language, no one understands
The one from the East, only he will understand.

—are verbatim of Kabir's

My language is of the East—none understands me:
He alone understands me who is from the farthest East.[60]

References to Mira's popular poetry are also seen—*Piro pī pyālṛā matvārī hoī* (*30*-18); on drinking from the cup Piro became intoxicated[61]—showing the sedimentation of bhakti poetry and hagiography in the many sects of North India, and among the Gulabdasis as seen in Piro's poetry.

Indubitably Piro was deeply entrenched in the Vedantic nuances and the bhakti spirituality of her sect. The finer details of the monist cast of the Gulabdasis are worked out in her writing along with the bhakti heritage that was a patrimony of north Indian devotional sects. The guru as the initiator of a lineage, a figure of reverence, and the link to the path of liberation is crucial in her world, and her works reflect all these essentials of her religious life. The broad Indic dimensions of her spiritual life are plain to see. In terms of philosophical roots the Gulabdasis stayed within a broad Hindu–Sikh cosmos. However, some of their central philosophical tenets had striking parallels within popular Sufi thought in Punjab, and the Gulabdasis were quick to absorb and exploit this analogous theology. This appropriation lent them a universalism that the Gulabdasis relished.

While expounding on the ideals of non-duality between the Self and the Supreme —soham—an expression of Piro's immediately opens up the universe of Islamicate Sufi heritage —*anal haq* or 'I am the Absolute Truth.' This expression is attributed to the mystic martyr of Baghdad Mansur al-Hallaj, who inspired in the Islamic world deep enraptured love among some Sufis who looked at him as a model of suffering. He also however invoked venomous hatred from the orthodox, who tortured and hung him in 922 CE.[62] Schimmel, writing the history of Sufism through its classical period, notes that scholars have compared this mystical expression to the Upanishad's *aham brahmāsmi* (I am Brahman). She also shows the strong controversies, interpretations and reactions anal haq garnered in the Muslim world, particularly, whether it should be seen in pantheistic or strictly monotheistic terms.

Here the important point is the manner in which the expression anal haq was used in Punjab to elucidate the idea of Unity of Being, and how theological equivalence was made with Advaita philosophy, though one need not conclude that one was derived from the other. In Punjab, the resonance of anal haq was twofold—its association with Mansur, the Sufi who ostensibly visited Punjab in his peregrinations, and the theological interpretative possibilities opened up by the expression itself. The popularity of Mansur in Punjab is easy to demonstrate and links up with the idea explored earlier—of dogmatic and bookish knowledge, and wrongly applied power by those in authority to perpetuate it. The self-image of the Sufi in this context is of his being the impecunious man of god—a faqir—tortured for his truth, and willingly accepting suffering. Thus any allusion to Mansur is almost always in reference to his torture and unjust hanging.[63] To quote Bulleh Shah for an example:

> Beloved, be careful when you fall in love, or you'll regret it later.
> There, one had his skin flayed,
> One was cut open with axes,
> One was hung on the gallows,
> There, you too will be beheaded.[64]

Similar allusions are found in the poems of Sultan Bahu.

> Like Mansur, those privy to all secrets were hung from the gallows.
>
> Do not raise your head from prostration, Bahu, even if thousands call you an infidel.[65]

The Gulabdasis equally spoke of the tortures of Mansur and others in the same emotional frame as the Sufis of Punjab. Gulabdas writes:

> *has has ke khal lahiyan ne chaṛe sūliyan haq pukārde nī*
>
> Smiling while being flayed, they have climbed gallows calling out *haq* (truth).[66]

And Piro echoes:

> *Pīro kehsi satgurū in sarā piyārī*
> *gote diye Kabīr ko in binā vichārī*
> *sulī diyo Mansūr ko khal samas lāhī*
> *aur dukhāye keṛe ham ket sunāhī. (160-22)*
>
> Piro says *satguru* they love the *shara*.
> Without giving it a thought they tried to drown Kabir.
> They hung Mansur flaying him.
> What more tortures shall I relate?

Mansur was hence easily assimilated into the cultural world of Punjab. The tortures that al-Hallaj suffered with stoicism in Baghdad were appropriated by the Punjabi Sufis, and others like the Gulabdasis, to the self-image and vocabulary of righteous suffering, their unbending adherence to the Truth. Piro's indignation in her face-off with the mullahs exhibits this sense of injustice, the ill treatment that was inevitably meted out to the righteous by those seemingly upholding the tenets of Islamic law.

How was anal haq, the signature words of Mansur that opened a long history of scholarly discourses, interpreted by the Gulabdasis? In Piro's writing anal haq at one level extends the usage of 'Mansur'—to highlight the continuous history of persecution.

jeko ne sat kehat haiṅ taṅh khal lahese
jeko kehsī anal haq bardār kareṅse (160-140)

those who speak the Truth, they strip their flesh
those who say anal haq, they disinherit them.

In this sense Bulleh Shah too uses the term, tongue-in-cheek he cautions

Bullya g̱hair sharā na ho...
Muṅho na anal haq bago
Char̤ sulī ḍhale gāveṅgā.

Bullya don't step out of shari'ah...
Don't say anal haq
Or you will be singing (swinging) on the gallows.[67]

Piro, however, also employs the term as a mantra, a chant specifically of her sect. In her interlocution with the mullahs who urge her to recite the Quranic formula—kalima—to reincorporate her into Islam, Piro proffers anal haq as the right formula—*kaho sabūtī anal haq yeh kalmā sācho* (160-30)—affirm anal haq the true kalma.

However, most often, the term is deployed to highlight the permeation of one Truth in the universe. It is in this sense that it is used as a theological equivalent of the monist ideas of the Gulabdasis. It refers to the one Reality that infuses the universe, the Truth that the guru opens one's heart to:

khol kuvāṛe jikar ke tum dayo hamāre
haq majūd dikhlāyo kul ālam yāre. (*160*-144)

you have opened the doors of my heart
showing the Truth that pervades the universe.

Thus as a mantra, similar in its import to soham, as a universal Reality, and as the Truth that penetrates the world as the self, anal haq resonates with multiple valences with the Gulabdasis.

What do we make of this appropriation and assimilation of anal haq by the Gulabdasis to the Vedanta theology particular to their sect? In one perspective—Piro's—it can be read as a deliberate attempt at synthesis of theologies derived from Indic and Islamicate traditions to underline the openness of sects like hers, especially to recruit adherents from all communities and castes. Just as she had stakes in reifying Hindu–Muslim identities at one end of the social scale, showing authority to be recalcitrant and unbending in order to galvanize an anti-authority mood to her own tale, she had much to gain by expanding the intrinsic porosity of her sect. If the Gulabdasis could be presented as genuine obliterators of sectarian difference, then her own position in her sect was cemented, besides creating a utopia of harmony that her own lamentations against her guardians belied. Thus for Piro it was important to state that her sect and guru were open to Hindus and Muslims—*mālak turkāṅ hinduaṅ ham uskī chāho* (*160*-16)—I seek the master of Hindus and Turks. It was also necessary to show that they were beyond the confines of Hinduism and Islam—*turkāṅ guṅ na dekhyā na hindu koī* (*160*-151)—there are no virtues in the Turks or Hindus—opening a path beyond narrow confines. Or even that the qualities of both the Hindus and Muslims were present in her guru, though he himself was above and beyond them—*sāṇjhe turkāṅ hinduaṅ guṇ taṅh athohe* (*160*-151)—the virtues of Turks and Hindus are jointly present in him (guru).

SHARĀ: SHARED ETHICS

For individuals like Piro, the need to look beyond religious differentiation and to focus on social spaces and spiritual forms that emphasized irrelevance of distinction was important because their contested identities created dissension in society. It was because individuals like her had stakes in envisioning alternative pluralistic spaces that the scope of these traditions expanded, inflating innate and inchoate proclivities that existed in sects like the Gulabdasis. The Manichean Hindu–Muslim antagonism was as much a literary device, a cultural trope, as it was the ingredient that gave a particular twist to her lived tale. Her story banked on a range of emotional repertoire that had traction in the everyday fabric of life in Punjab. The constellation of congealed nuances that packed into the term shara, for instance, exemplified the complex of legal, social and cultural moralities that defined 'Punjabiyat' beyond narrow identities. While the mullahs and the qazis came to be ribbed by the Sufis and the Gulabdasis for being too legalistic in their interpretations of the shari'ah, the Sikh historians, Gian Singh and Ganesha Singh in turn accused the Gulabdasis of living outside shara in their purportedly epicurean habits. It is the availability of a spectrum of sentiments ranged over a shared moral world that was tapped by those seeking to expand horizons of religious, spiritual and social life.

The Gulabdasi penchant for looking for theological equivalences in Vedanta non-dualism and the Sufi doctrine of anal haq exploited this vision. Was their appropriation of al-Hallaj tradition a case of syncretism? Did it make them 'crypto-Sufis' as a historian has posed in another but similar context?[68] This essay has shown the gradual sedimentation of varied influences and traditions layering the making of the Gulabdasi sect. They were comfortable in the manner in which advaita philosophy and bhakti esotericism embossed itself on them via Sikh sects and other routes of transmission in north India. They were open to parallel theological concepts that permeated the Punjabi landscape, because they were willing to absorb and play with the widest cultural possibilities around them. This stake in openness didn't dilute what they inherited from their bhakti heritage as much as render it intelligible and accessible to those who wished to participate in it.

Syncretism is then not an amalgamated alloy that carries proportionate parts of different religious traditions. It may be understood in terms of attitudes that allow a range of interpretive plausibility, create spaces where cultural conversations happen, disseminating multifarious messages. Syncretistic dispositions don't rule out religious conflict, and syncretism is not a given in the pre-colonial or any other period. As a term it must simply be seen to inform peoples and structures that revel in variegated borrowings, absorbing them through a process of osmosis, appropriation and incorporation, or as a deliberate play with multitudinous cultural possibilities.

NOTES

1 This *Siharfi* is available in a manuscript of Piro's writings being compiled and readied for publication by Jigyasu Sant Vijendra Das titled '*Guru Mā Pīro kā Safar: Mahā Punjāb kī Pratham Kavyitrī*'. Shri Vijendra heads a sub-lineage of the Gulabdasis based in Hansi, Haryana.

2 Daniel Gold, *The Lord as Guru: Hindi Sants in North Indian Tradition*, New York: Oxford University Press, 1989.

3 Linda Hess, 'Kabir's Rough Rhetoric', in Karine Schomer and W.H. McLeod (eds), *The Sants: Studies in a Devotional Tradition of India*, Delhi: Motilal Banarsidas, 1987, pp. 143–65.

4 Gold, *The Lord as Guru*, p. 4.

5 Here I have used the *160 Kāfis* available in Ms. 888, (Bhai Gurdas Library, Guru Nanak Dev University, hereafter GNDU). This ms. also has her *30 Kāfis*. These latter will be referred to as such, as they were titled simply 'Kafis written by Mata Piro'. Kafis are free flowing rhyming verses, the favourite genre of the Punjabi Sufis. Thirty verses in effect make this poem a *siharfi*, a genre Piro was familiar with. However, unlike a siharfi, every new stanza of this poem did not commence with a specific alphabet of the Indo-Persian script—hence Piro refers to this hybrid genre as kafis. For a detailed reading of the *160 Kafis* see Anshu Malhotra, 'Telling her Tale? Unravelling a Life in Conflict in Peero's *Ik Sau Sath Kāfian* (*160 Kāfis*)', *Indian Economic and Social History Review*, 46 (4), 2009, pp. 541–78.

6 Carl W. Ernst, 'Situating Sufism and Yoga', *Journal of the Royal Asiatic Society*, 15 (1), 2005, pp. 15–43.

7 Peter van der Veer, 'Syncretism, Multiculturalism and the Discourse of Tolerance', in Charles Stewart and Rosalind Shaw (eds), *Syncretism/Anti-Syncretism: The Politics of Religious Synthesis,* London: Routledge, 1994, pp. 196–211; Robert M. Hayden, 'Antagonistic Tolerance: Competitive Sharing of Religious Sites in South Asia and the Balkans', *Current Anthropology*, 43 (1), February 2002, pp. 205–19.

8 Ernst, 'Situating Sufism and Yoga'.

9 Shahid Amin, 'Un Saint Guerrier: Sur la Conquete del' Inde du Nord par les Tures au xi Siecle', *Annales—Histoire, Sciences Sociales*, 6 (2),

March–April 2005, pp. 262–92. I thank the author for sharing the English version of the paper with me.

10 van der Veer, 'Syncretism, Multiculturalism and the Discourse of Tolerance'.

11 Neeladri Bhattacharya, 'Predicaments of Secular Histories', *Public Culture*, 20 (1), 2008, pp. 57–73.

12 Tony K. Stewart, 'In Search of Equivalence: Conceiving Muslim–Hindu Encounter Through Translation Theory', *History of Religions*, 40 (3), 2001, pp. 260–87.

13 Ernst, 'Situating Sufism and Yoga'.

14 Charles Stewart, 'Syncretism and its Synonyms: Reflections on Cultural Mixture', *Diacritics*, 29 (3), 1999, pp. 40–62.

15 Dominique-Sila Khan, *Crossing the Threshold: Understanding Religious Identities in South Asia*, London: I.B. Tauris Publishers, 2004, pp. 6–7.

16 *Sharā* is the colloquial Punjabi form of shari'ah or shari'at, the Islamic canonical law. The usage of shara here carries a complex of significations that include legal and moral strictures.

17 Giani Gian Singh, *Sri Guru Panth Prakāsh* (hereafter *PP*), Patiala: Bhasha Vibhag, 1970[1880], pp. 1292–5. Gian Singh was the pupil of the famous Nirmala scholar Pandit Tara Singh Narottam. Another Nirmala account is of Ganesha Singh, *Bhārat Mat Darpaṇ* (hereafter *BMD*), Amritsar: Vaidak Bhandar, 1926, pp. 127–30.

18 H.A. Rose, *A Glossary of the Tribes and Castes of the Punjab and the North-West Frontier Province* (hereafter *Glossary*), Patiala: Languages Department Punjab, 1970 [1911], pp. 319–20. A.H. Bingley, *Sikhs*, Patiala: Languages Department, 1970, p. 91.

19 Leslie S. Saunders, *Report on the Revised Land Revenue Settlement of the Lahore District 1865–69*, Lahore: Central Jail Press, 1873, pp. 53–4.

20 On Giani Gian Singh, see Harbans Singh (ed.), *The Encylopaedia of Sikhism*, Vol. II, Patiala: Punjabi University, 1996, pp. 82–3. Another scholarly Singh Sabha account is of Kahn Singh 'Nabha', *Mahān Kosh: Encyclopaedia of Sikh Literature*, Patiala: Bhasha Vibhag, 1981 [1930], p. 423.

21 Zafar Iqbal Mirza (tr.), *Seṭh Vishandās: A Great Philanthropist*, Sehwan Sharif: Sain Publishers, 1997 (This is a translation of a biography of Seth Vishandas in Urdu titled *Ratanjot* and has been compiled by Khadim Hussain Soomro).

22 Vijendra Das, *Guru Ma Pīro*.

23 On the Udasis see *PP*, pp. 1269–2. *Glossary*, pp. 479–81; Also H.A. Rose, 'Udasis,' in James Hastings (ed.), *Encylopaedia of Religion and Ethics*, vol. XII, Edinburgh: T. & T. Clark, 1958 [1921], pp. 504–5.

24 Sulakhan Singh, 'Patronage of the Udasis', in Indu Banga and J.S. Grewal (eds), *Maharaja Ranjit Singh: The State and Society*, Amritsar: GNDU 2001, p. 140.

25 Sulakhan Singh, 'The Udasis in the Early Nineteenth Century', *The Journal of Regional History*, vol. 2, 1981, pp. 35–42.

26 References to the Udasis are ubiquitous in this history of the geographical and administrative regions of Punjab. J.S. Grewal and Indu Banga (tr. and ed.), *Early Nineteenth Century Panjab From Ganesh Dās's Chār Bāgh-i-Panjāb*, Amritsar: GNDU, 1975.

27 *PP*, pp. 1244–63; *Glossary*, p. 172. For a discussion of the Nirmalas also see Harjot Oberoi, *The Construction of Religious Boundaries: Culture, Identity and Diversity in the Sikh Tradition*, New Delhi: Oxford University Press, 1994, pp. 124–30.

28 *BMD*.

29 *PP*.

30 Ghulam Sarvar Qureshi, a contemporary, notes a Shia Sayyid Mohammad Shah as a follower of Gulabdas. See his *Tarīkh Makhzāne Punjāb*, Lahore: Dost Associates, 1996 [1877], pp. 567–8.

31 *PP*, p. 1293; *BMD*, p. 127.

32 Mirza, *Seth Vishandās*, pp. 31–9.

33 Annemarie Schimmel, *Mystical Dimensions of Islam*, Delhi: Yoda Press, 2007 [1975], pp. 390–3.

34 Vijendra Das, *Guru Mā Pīro*, pp. 30–4.

35 Nirmala historians point to the efforts of the ruler of Patiala, and the British in suppressing the sect around the mid-1850s.

36 Besides her autobiographical *160 Kafis*, she wrote a set of kafis, a siharfi, a joint siharfi with her guru, and poems set to *rāgas* in the *Rāg Sāgar*.

37 *BMD*.

38 The kafi number from the *160 Kafis* will be shown as (*160-*), and from *30 Kafis* as (*30-*).

39 See Jamal J. Elias, *Death Before Dying: The Sufi Poems of Sultan Bahu*, Berkeley: University of California Press, 1998, p. 4.

40 This is Elias' translation of Bahu's *Hāfaz Padh Padh Karan Taqbīr*, see Elias, *Death Before Dying*, p. 59.

41 '*Ik Alaf Padho Chhutkārā Hai*'. See Namwar Singh (ed.), *Bulleh Shāh kī Kāfian*, Delhi: National Institute of Punjab Studies, 2003, p. 43. All translations of Bulleh's verses are mine.

42 The romance of Hir and Ranjha was circulating in the oral tradition of Punjab for over 400 years. Among the literary renditions of it, the most famous was the eighteenth century one of Varis Shah. See Farina Mir, *The Social Space of Language: Vernacular Culture in British Colonial Punjab*, Ranikhet: Permanent Black, 2010, pp. 1–2. On this episode see

ibid., pp. 140–9, and Jeevan Deol, 'Sex, Social Critique and the Female Figure in Pre-Modern Punjabi Poetry: Varis Shah's Hir', *Modern Asian Studies*, 36 (1), 2002, pp. 141–71.

43 Grewal and Banga, *Early Nineteenth Century Panjab*, p. 10.

44 Ibid., p. 63.

45 Ibid., p. 10.

46 Ibid., pp. 87, 152–4.

47 On this episode and its discussion in *Gurbilās* literature and the development of the trope of conversion see Anne Murphy's paper in this volume.

48 Malhotra, 'Telling her Tale'.

49 Lajwanti Rama Krishna, *Punjabi Sufi Poets 1460–1900*, Karachi: Indus Publications, 1977.

50 Schimmel, *The Mystical Dimensions of Islam*.

51 Ernst, 'Situating Sufism and Yoga'.

52 Simon Digby (tr.), *Wonder-Tales of South Asia*, Jersey: Orient Monographs, 2000.

53 Nile Green, 'Breathing in India, c. 1890', *Modern Asian Studies*, 42 (2/3), 2008, pp. 283–315.

54 On Advaita, see S. Radhakrishnan and Charles A. Moore (eds), *A Source Book in Indian Philosophy*, Princeton: University of Princeton Press, 1957, pp. 506–7.

55 On the self-understanding of female spiritual leaders and their 'theological identification' with a feminine deity see Rita Das Gupta Sherma, '"Sa Ham: I am She": Woman as Goddess', in Alf Hiltebeitel and Kathleen M. Erndl (eds), *Is the Goddess a Feminist: The Politics of South Asian Goddesses*, Sheffield: Academic Press, 2000, pp. 24–51.

56 This line is from an incomplete siharfi (20) of Gulabdas in Ms. 888.

57 Gold, *The Lord as Guru*.

58 On Kabir see Charlotte Vaudeville, *A Weaver Named Kabir*, New Delhi: Oxford University Press, 2005 [1993]. For a discussion on death see pp. 106–7.

59 Ibid., p.47. Also John S. Hawley and Mark Juergensmeyer, *Songs of the Saints of India*, New Delhi: Oxford University Press, 2004 [1988], pp. 35–6.

60 Vaudeville, *A Weaver Named Kabir*, p. 118.

61 On Mirabai, and how her poetry reflected her biography see Hawley and Juergensmeyer, *Songs of the Saints*, pp. 119–40.

62 Schimmel, *Mystical Dimensions of Islam*, pp. 62–77.

63 Mansur was often referred to in conjunction with other tortured souls like Shams Tabriz, said to be the preceptor of the great Jalaluddin Rumi. In Punjabi folk parlance he was skinned alive.

64 Singh (ed.), *Bulleh Shah*, p. 142 (*Pyāriaṅ Sambhal ke Nehu Lagā*)
65 Elias, *Death Before Dying*, p. 86.
66 Ms. 888.
67 Singh, *Bulleh Shah*, p. 143.
68 H. Van Skyhawk, 'Sufi Influence in the Eknathi Bhagvat: Some Observations on the Text and its Historical Context', in R.S. McGregor (ed.), *Devotional Literature in South Asia: Current Research*, Cambridge: Cambridge University Press, 1992, pp. 67–79.

8

Farina Mir

Genre and Devotion in Punjabi Popular Narratives

RETHINKING CULTURAL AND RELIGIOUS SYNCRETISM[*]

In 1849, administrator-turned-historian Ganesh Das Vadhera completed *Char Bagh-i-Panjab*, a history of his native region in India, the Punjab. The *Char Bagh* was a Persian manuscript written as the Sikh Kingdom of Lahore was being dismantled and the Punjab incorporated into British India, and documented the establishment, decline, and fall of Sikh rule in the area. Vadhera's account was more than a political history of the Punjab, however; it also gave detailed descriptions of many of the towns, cities, and villages of the region leading some contemporary scholars to refer to it as a geography.[1] Guru Nanak Dev University recognized Vadhera's Persian text as being not only a historical account but a source of valuable 'information on social, religious, and cultural life of the Panjab', and published it in 1965.[2] Two scholars of the region published a partial English translation a decade later.[3]

* Originally published as Farina Mir, 'Genre and Devotion in Punjabi Popular Narratives: Rethinking Cultural and Religious Syncretism', *Comparative Studies in Society and History*, 48 (3), 2006, pp. 727–58. © Society for the Comparative Study of Society and History, published by Cambridge University Press.

The English translation of the *Char Bagh* excludes Vadhera's review and analysis of the Punjab's political history (which the translators' synopsize in their introduction) and presents instead a 150-page section of the original text devoted to a description of the region. This section, the translators tell us, 'furnishes most of the [text's] topographical, sociological and cultural data on the Panjab'.[4] The English translation makes a curious change to the text, however, one that raises important questions about literature's place in the writing of history. Nestled within Vadhera's description of the Punjab—but absent from the main text of its English translation—is an extensive narration of fictional romances. Indeed, one-third of Vadhera's description of the Punjab is devoted to recounting *qisse* (epic-romances; sing. *qissa*), Punjabi-language romances that historically circulated in both oral and textual form.[5] Their centrality to the original text suggests that Vadhera thought qisse were crucial to an understanding of the Punjab and its history.

Ganesh Das Vadhera, unfortunately, never elaborated on why he thought a series of qisse, all drawn from the Punjabi oral tradition, were fundamental to writing the region's history. The answer to that question—why, or how, do qisse inform an understanding of the Punjab's history?—is not self-evident. As historical texts or sources, qisse are certainly enigmatic. They are clearly fictional narratives, sometimes even fantastical. We know little about those who composed them, even less about those who performed the tales orally, and almost nothing about audience reception. Perhaps these considerations, which make qisse elusive historical texts or sources, explain their marginal role in the *Char Bagh*'s English translation, a text produced by two of Punjab's eminent historians for its value as a primary source.

Taking a cue from Ganesh Das Vadhera's unexpurgated *Char Bagh-i-Panjab*, this essay argues that Punjabi qisse are integral to understanding Punjab's history, particularly its colonial history (1849–1947). I will illustrate their usefulness as historical sources by concentrating my analysis on two aspects of Punjabi qisse: first, I will examine invocations as a literary convention that helps constitute the qissa as a genre; and, second, I will analyse representations of piety, a central motif of qissa narratives. This focus will elucidate how qisse contribute, in particular, to an understanding of aesthetic and religious culture in colonial Punjab.

I open my analysis by examining the qissa genre as it emerges in South Asia generally, and the Punjab specifically, during the medieval and early modern periods. Punjabi language qisse, I will show, lie at the nexus of Perso-Islamic and local Punjabi aesthetic forms. I argue that Punjabi qissa writers drew heavily upon the literary conventions of Persian qisse, drawing their compositions into the sphere of Perso-Islamic literary aesthetics. At the same time, Punjabi qisse constitute a regional tradition, one that incorporated local aesthetic principles and responded to the religious plurality and social organization of the Punjab.[6] While a Perso-Islamic aesthetic provides an important foundation for the Punjab's qissa tradition, this does not limit the qissa to being an Islamic or Muslim genre. In the context of the late nineteenth century, however, the Perso-Islamic component of the Punjabi qissa takes on particular historical significance as questions of religious difference became entwined with aesthetic, literary, and linguistic choices in the Punjab, as in other parts of colonial India. That the qissa continued to be one of the most popular literary forms of the time suggests that there were currents in late nineteenth-century society that were not affected by the era's increasingly communal political environment.

The latter portion of this essay shifts attention from the significance of genre to an examination of the content of a range of qisse composed during the colonial period. Although qisse narratives are located in real Punjabi locales or sometimes make reference to real historical persons or events, their contribution to Punjab's history rests not in any kernels of empirical evidence to be drawn from them, but rather in their engagement with issues that were relevant to Punjab's inhabitants. Working within the bounds of the genre as well as within the strictures of centuries-old and well-known narratives, Punjabi poets were nonetheless able to argue and debate issues of contemporary social, cultural, and religious importance through qisse.

While authors took up a range of issues in their qissa compositions, I focus here on one theme that figures prominently in late nineteenth- and early twentieth-century texts: the proper performance of piety.

As a rich body of scholarship has emphasized, many late nineteenth-century socio-religious reform organizations were concerned with defining both proper and pious conduct for their co-religionists.[7] An analysis of qisse makes two important contributions to the history of Punjab's socio-religious culture during this dynamic period. First, qisse add a regional and non-sectarian perspective to our understanding of late nineteenth-century debates about the definition of piety. In providing a point of view that is not grounded in any one religious tradition, qisse are remarkably different from the tracts, treatises, newspapers, and modern genres of literature, most of which were produced by religious reformers, that have been important sources for scholarly studies of the period.[8] Second, Punjabi qisse provide evidence that Punjabis shared notions of pious behaviour irrespective of their affiliations to different religions. Put another way, Punjabi qisse present a vision of late nineteenth-century sociality and religiosity in which religious community—Hindu, Muslim, Sikh, or Christian—was not of paramount importance.

Representations of devotion in Punjabi qisse provide insights into the nature of contemporary Punjabi beliefs and practices, but these representations do not map comfortably onto contemporary notions of discrete religious communities. And yet the practices represented in qisse do not exclude those notions. What qisse underscore is the multiplicity of religious practices in which Punjabis participated. This complexity of religious belief has been difficult to integrate into the history of late nineteenth-century Punjab given the scholarly emphasis on this period as a time of sharpening religious boundaries and increasing political discord between members of different religious communities.[9] Indeed, India's Partition in 1947 along ostensibly religious lines, which resulted in religious violence in which as many as a million people were killed in the Punjab alone, serves to reinforce this perception of Punjab's colonial past. The Partition has remained salient in South Asia and South Asian historiography, whether gauged through the ever-present political tensions between India and Pakistan, the rhetoric that accompanies communal pogroms in India,[10] or scholars' 'Partition industry', a recent spate of works trying to understand the event and particularly the violence it engendered.[11] This has undoubtedly obscured aspects of Punjabi experience that were shared by people of all religions. With Partition always explic-itly or implicitly as the backdrop, scholarship on the region's colonial history has emphasized increasing political tensions between religious groups. However, qisse from the same period indicate that an ethos of piety continued to be both salient to and shared by Punjabis, despite this political context.

Syncretism Reconsidered

As my introductory comments indicate, the Punjabi qissa tradition, in form and content, lies at the interstices of different cultural and religious formations. In terms of genre, it blends Perso-Islamic and local aesthetics into a coherent and recognizable regional genre. In their representations of devotional practice, Punjabi qisse emphasize a kind of piety that was shared across religious traditions as opposed to one affiliated to a single religion. In both the realms of genre and devotional practice, Punjabi qisse represent ideas that do not fit comfortably within existing categories or taxonomies, whether liter-ary/aesthetic or religious. Because qisse draw on multiple cultural and religious traditions, this essay seeks to assess the usefulness of the theoretical apparatus most often used to describe and analyse cul-tural and religious exchange, interaction, and mixture: syncretism.

Syncretism has a long and checkered history in academic discourse. As a concept, its roots lie in religious studies, where it continues to be used to describe theologies that draw on two or more individual—and independent—theological systems. Its use as an analytic concept has moved well beyond matters of religion, however. Today, syncre-tism is a critical term in cultural studies that, along with concepts such as hybridity and creolization, is used to describe cultural mix-ture. In recent years, scholars from a number of disciplines, working in a variety of historical and geographical contexts, have reflected on the merits of syncretism as an analytical category.[12] Charles Stewart, for example, argues in his 'Syncretism and Its Synonyms' that the pejorative connotations syncretism assumed in the European context due to the seventeenth-century 'syncretistic controversies' need not circumscribe the use of the concept today.[13] Similarly, he suggests that the negative connotations of syncretism in the African context, where the religious practices of local African churches were interpreted by some as impure forms of Christianity, should not prevent contemporary anthropologists or other social scientists from using the concept as an analytical tool.[14] Indeed, Stewart argues that the term syncretism can be re-appropriated to describe 'the cultural borrowing and interpenetration through which cultures constitute themselves'.[15] He argues for this re-appropriation with self-conscious attention to two widely held criticisms of the term. First, that 'syncretism is a pejorative term, one that derides mixture', and second, that 'syncretism presupposes "purity" in the traditions that combine'.[16] I will return to the latter criticism presently, particularly as it relates to South Asian scholarship. But first, let me address whether syncretism necessarily holds pejorative connotations.

If one moves beyond the history of Christianity in Europe and its missionary activities in parts of Africa and Asia, syncretism has not, by-and-large, been seen as pejorative.[17] South Asian scholars, in particular, have relied heavily on syncretism as a descriptive and analytic term, particularly in their studies of religious practice.[18] They have invariably used syncretism to suggest a simple mixture of two or more otherwise distinct religious traditions. In contrast to the negative connotations associated with syncretism in the context of Christianity and Europe, when used by scholars of South Asia syncretism often has positive connotations since it implies reconciliation between religious traditions and communities otherwise taken to be at odds. Brian Hatcher, for example, underscores this aspect of syncretism in the South Asian context: 'It is not sufficient when speaking of syncretism, to refer only to the process of encounter and appropriation; one must also speak of merging, accommodation, and amalgamation. Syncretism involves blending, synthesizing, or *harmonizing*'.[19] That harmonizing (suggesting reconciliation) is an aspect of syncretism as the concept is used in the South Asian context suggests that the traditions being drawn on are, a priori, in conflict. Thus, the term syncretism takes specific moments or histories of contestation and conflict between religious communities and applies them as the starting point of interactions between religious traditions. In South Asian scholarship, then, syncretism as religious mixture is not so much derided, as in the European or African cases, as celebrated. This celebration, however, is grounded in an assumption that relationships between religious traditions are always conflictual. Such an assumption is not substantiated by historical analysis, as I will show. In addition, given that religious conflicts between Hindus and Muslims, or Muslims and Sikhs are the focus of much of the scholarship on north India's late nineteenth- and early twentieth-century history (due to a telos toward India's Partition), syncretism is deployed as an analytic space standing in opposition to religious orthopraxy on one hand, and religious communalism on the other.

If syncretism in South Asian scholarship is not given a pejorative valence, it nonetheless falls into the second of Taylor's above-mentioned broad criticisms of the term: that it relies on purity (or coherence, one might add) in the traditions that combine. Few scholars who rely on syncretism in their studies of South Asian religious practices address this concern. An exception is Tony Stewart, a scholar of early modern religious practices in India. Stewart argues the limitations of syncretism on the grounds that religious traditions in the early modern period had not yet cohered in the ways that syncretism imagines of or imposes on them: 'the myriad forms of the concept of syncretism (when used as an interpretive, rather than strictly descriptive, category) become highly problematic in nearly all their applications because they nearly uniformly read into the history the very institutional (ritual, theological, social) structures that are not yet present in an enduring way'.[20] Stewart's criticism of syncretism is grounded in his study of early modern, pre-colonial Bengal. But what of the modern, colonial period when the institutional structures of South Asia's religions were perhaps better entrenched?

I argue that for the modern period as well, syncretism continues to be problematic as an analytic for the study of South Asian religious practices. For if institutional structures became better established in the modern period, they did not go unchallenged. Modern South Asian history is marked by reform and revival movements that have in some cases contested the institutional structures of their religions and in others reworked them altogether.[21] While the modern period might point to more and less dominant strands in any of South Asia's major religious traditions, diversity of opinion, thought, and belief continued to be a hallmark *within* the Hindu, Muslim, Sikh, and Christian traditions. The use of syncretism as an analytic elides precisely such diversity.

For those scholars of South Asia who would avoid the term syncretism, the problem of how to represent social and religious practices that incorporate people from multiple religious traditions remains a vexing one. One of the primary difficulties is how to move beyond analysing such practices only as they relate to pre-existing identities and traditions. Or, to put the dilemma somewhat differently, must religious identity—Hindu, Muslim, Sikh, Christian—always be the primary category of analysis? Take, for example, Peter Gottschalk's *Beyond Hindu and Muslim: Multiple Identity in Narratives from Village India*.[22] This monograph is in many ways a sensitive study of contemporary north Indian identity. Its aim is to examine social formations that defy religious homogeneity. Gottschalk, however, writes about shared practices only as they relate to pre-existing identities and traditions. For example, a section of the book devoted specifically to describing 'a common public sphere' in the village of Arampur, one of Gottschalk's ethnographic sites, is titled 'Constructing and Affirming an *Intercommunal* Public Sphere'.[23] By using the term 'intercommunal', Gottschalk limits the possibilities of his analysis in two ways. One, this designation continues to privilege well-defined religious identities (the communal) above all else. And two, by doing so, he leaves little room for exploring precisely what is being constructed and affirmed in this public sphere. For that, we must adduce language that moves beyond 'intercommunal', beyond the centrality of Hindu and Muslim in scholarly discourse, and grapples with locally specific relationships and social and religious values.

My concerns with the use of syncretism in South Asian scholarship are grounded in a desire to discern whether the notion of syncretism helps or hinders an analysis of the historical significance of the Punjabi qissa tradition. Specifically, does syncretism provide an adequate analytic to historically situate a literary genre that draws on both Perso-Islamic and Punjabi local aesthetics? Does the notion of syncretism contribute to a nuanced understanding of devotional practices in which Hindus, Muslims, Christians, and Sikhs all participated? Simply put, the answer to both questions is 'no'. Syncretism, whether applied to literary or religious spheres, is unhelpful. In the literary realm, syncretism leaves us with only a most generic idea of mixture. As an analytic, it does not address the specific implications of mixture. As I will show through an analysis of the form in which the Punjabi qissa tradition coheres, the significance of mixture rests not in the fact that it occurs, but in its specific historical context.

If the main shortcoming of syncretism as an analytic in the literary realm is that it leaves one with nothing but a generic idea of mixture, then in the study of religion the problems with the term are compounded. In the context of scholarship on South Asian religiosity, syncretism suggests an a priori conflictual relationship between religious traditions, implies that these traditions are coherent, if not pure, and privileges pre-existing religious identities as paramount. I contend that the devotional practices described and privileged in Punjabi qisse are better understood as reflecting shared notions of piety, and that participating in the forms of devotion that accompanied this piety was not predicated on one's pre-existing religious identity. It is in this latter sense that the concept of shared piety opens up more conceptual and analytical space than that accorded by the notion of syncretism. Before exploring piety as represented in Punjabi qisse, however, let me first address questions of form, or genre, in the Punjabi qissa tradition.

THE PERSO-ISLAMIC FOUNDATIONS OF THE QISSA TRADITION

The term qissa, used widely in north Indian languages to mean story, is derived from Arabic. In the Arabic context, the cognate verb *qassa*, 'to tell a story, narrate', appears in the Quran often, while qissa itself first appears in hadith literature.[24] In the early Islamic era, the term qissa was used to describe tales told by popular religious storytellers. With time, however, Arab story-tellers (*qussas*) increasingly narrated tales with no religious character and the term qissa came to mean 'story' more generally. Adopted into the Persian lexicon with the spread of Islam, the term follows a somewhat similar trajectory, initially carrying religious overtones, but by the second millennium CE, increasingly used outside a religious context.[25]

The earliest use of qissa in Persian suggests that it meant 'biography', usually the biographies of prophets or other religious figures.

Qissa was also used to designate 'pseudo-biographical' works of a largely fictional nature such as the *Qissa-e-Hamza* or *Hamzanama*, a text about the prophet Muhammad's uncle dating back to at least the ninth century.[26] By the second millennium CE, the term was increasingly associated with stories, particularly romances, with no religious overtones.

In tracing the evolution of the qissa—albeit briefly—and its transmission from the Middle East to South Asia, it is particularly instructive to focus on the romance, one specific type of qissa that evolved in Persia/Persian literature in the first centuries of the second millennium. This romance tradition was refined by the eminent Persian poets Gurgani (d. after 1055) and Ansari (d. 1088), and reached its apogee with the compositions of Nezami (d. 1209). The romances composed by these literary greats, as well as their lesser-known peers, drew on both Arab and Persian tales (*Laila-Majnun* [Arab] and *Khusraw-Shirin* [Persian], for example) and shared a specific poetic form: the *masnavi*, or epic poem in rhymed couplets.[27] Indeed, the masnavi form came to define those Persian qisse that were romances.

Persian romances were incorporated into the literary and oral traditions of South Asia during the medieval period, likely crossing regional boundaries with court poets, merchants, traders, Sufis, and mendicants. The earliest existing evidence for this comes from the compositions of Amir Khusraw (1254–1325). Amir Khusraw is best remembered in literary circles as one of the earliest exponents of Hindvi (an early Indian vernacular language), for his innovations in compositional styles, and for laying the early foundations of north Indian classical music.[28] A gifted poet and musician, Khusraw composed in various languages, among them Persian. His Persian compositions provide insights into the transmission of the qissa, especially the romance, to South Asia. Khusraw composed renditions of the romances *Laila-Majnun* and *Khusraw-Shirin*, in Persian and in the masnavi form, which illustrates that Arab and Persian tales, and Persian literary forms, were incorporated into South Asian literary production as early as the fourteenth century, albeit into the Persianate literary culture of the time. Over the following centuries, however, these romances and their genre would also be incorporated into Indian vernacular oral and textual traditions.

Whether qisse first entered South Asia's vernacular literature through texts or orally is impossible to discern. What is clear, though, is that by the seventeenth century qisse were circulating in India's vernacular languages both orally and in textual form. One example that points to this comes from the Punjabi writings of the Sikh religious figure, Bhai Gurdas Bhalla (d. 1633). In his *Var* 27,1, Bhai Gurdas mentions a series of love stories, including *Laila-Majnun*.[29] However, he gives no explanation of their narratives, but rather assumes his audience's familiarity with these tales. This reference points to the contemporary orality of these tales because Bhai Gurdas' poetry was not limited to Punjab's literate elites; his compositions were meant for oral dissemination among people of all social classes (hence their role in making the message of Sikhism broadly accessible), most of whom were illiterate. Given this context, Bhai Gurdas' reference to *Laila-Majnun* and other romances—a reference that takes their stories as already known by his audience—suggests that qisse were circulating orally in his native area of Punjab, and in its regional vernacular, Punjabi.

In the Punjab, the term qissa has historically referred to any of a series of epic-length verse romances that circulated in the region. Many of these romances, as suggested above, were drawn from Arab and Persian literary traditions, and circulated in the Punjab in Persian (the language of high culture in the region from the eleventh through nineteenth centuries) and in Punjabi (dialects of which were spoken by the region's inhabitants from the twelfth century onwards). The term qissa in the Punjab also refers to a genre, the verse romance epic, whether in Persian or in the vernacular, Punjabi. There is a critical difference, however, between the Persian and Punjabi qisse produced in the Punjab: Persian-language qisse follow the rhyme and metre of Persian masnavi rather carefully; Punjabi-language qisse, though born of the Persian tradition, share only their rhyme scheme with the masnavi. The meters of Punjabi qisse (by this I mean those qisse composed in the Punjabi language) are indigenous, leading critic Denis Matringe to refer to them as 'a confluence of two traditions', the Persian and the Punjabi.[30] This bringing together of the extra-local and the local is also mirrored in the content of Punjabi qisse. While some of the romances popular in the Punjab, north India, and beyond were originally from the Arabian peninsula and Persia, many of the tales in the Punjabi qissa tradition are local in origin, situated in the local landscape and embedded in local social relations.[31] Among these, some of which continue to be popular beyond the geographic locale of the Punjab, are the qisse *Puran-Bhagat*, *Sohni-Mahival*, *Mirza-Sahiban*, and, perhaps most popular of all, *Hir-Ranjha*.

A number of Punjabi poets took to the qissa as their principle genre from the early seventeenth century onward. By the late nineteenth century, qisse accounted for an overwhelming preponderance in the Punjabi publishing industry, suggesting their popularity as a literary form.[32] If both early-modern manuscripts and nineteenth-century printed texts point to the popularity of qisse in literary circles, then colonial ethnographic records indicate their corresponding popularity as oral texts. In their examination and documentation of 'native practices', colonial ethnographers noted the centrality of qisse in Punjabi cultural life, particularly those qisse based on indigenous narratives. The *Gazetteer of the Lahore District 1883–1884*, for example, recorded that: 'music, singing and dancing are all amusements much enjoyed by the natives…Of the songs in vogue … the most popular are the ballads *Mirza Sahiba ki Sur* and *Waris Shah ki Hir*'—both indigenous Punjabi qisse.[33]

THE INVOCATION IN PERSIAN AND PUNJABI QISSE

Whether a tale is local or extra-local in origin, Punjabi qisse as a genre, share certain elements with the Perso-Islamic narrative or storytelling tradition.[34] Due to inadequate documentation and sources, it is difficult to relate the precise history of how literatures, oral and textual, were transmitted in the medieval period from the Middle East to South Asia. Despite the inability to trace the exact chains of transmission, however, similarities of form between the Persian and Punjabi qissa traditions suggest distinct links. While others have pointed to the similarities in formal prosody that link these two traditions,[35] my interest lies in the similarity of content and language that ties these two traditions together. As such, I will concentrate on the use of invocations, referred to in Punjabi as the *hamd* or *mangalacharan*, as one aspect of the Perso-Islamic heritage of the Punjabi qissa tradition. In order to underscore the continuities between Persian and Punjabi qisse, I will first examine the invocation as it was used in the Persian romance tradition.

Let me turn, then, to Fakhr ud-Din Gurgani's eleventh-century composition, *Vis and Ramin*, 'the first great achievement of the romantic epic in Iran'.[36] The poem opens with a section in praise of God in which the poet also describes the creation of the universe. Then comes a section in praise of the prophet Muhammad, followed by sections on the paramount Sultan of the time, Tughrilbeg, his chief minister (*vizier*), and lastly the governor of Isfahan. While the invocation is too long to quote here in its entirety, an excerpt will provide the outlines of Gurgani's form:

To the King who brought into being the world and ourselves, thanks and blessing!..

Now I shall speak praises of the Prophet, our guide to God ...

God created him of blessing and chose him out of all the pure and elect ...

Three kinds of obedience are obligatory to the reasonable man, and those three are connected ...

One is the command of the judge of the world, which liberates the soul forever.

Second, the command of the Prophet Muhammad, which is rejected by a faithless unbeliever.

Third, the command of the Sultan that rules the world, splendor of the religion of God in the realm.[37]

Functioning outside the narrative of the story, Gurgani's invocation frames the tale (which was drawn from a pre-Islamic past) with his obeisance to the spiritual and temporal powers of his own time. It also describes the genesis of the composition itself. The author suggests that he wrote upon God's request, a request to enhance the beauty of a tale that had been composed by 'authorities of the past'.[38] Gurgani's invocation accomplishes two important tasks. First, it invokes and praises spiritual and temporal authority, bringing divine and worldly blessing on his text. Second, the invocation highlights the (purported) circumstances of composition, bringing his reader and/or listener into the tale not at the beginning of the narrative, but at the composition's genesis. Only then does Gurgani begin his epic.

Eminent Persian poets such as Nezami followed Gurgani's narrative strategy, and Amir Khusraw, in turn, incorporated the invocation as a literary convention in his Persian compositions. 'Like Nezami', R.C. Burgel writes in his essay on the Persian romance, 'Amir Khusrow begins [his *Quintet*] with a number of introductory chapters devoted to praise of God, Muhammad, of a patron prince ... and reasons for writing the book'.[39] While the correlation between Khusraw's and Nezami's Persian compositions appears evident, particularly since critics argue that Khusraw was imitating Nezami's *Quintet*, tracing the broader contours of the qissa's transmission from present-day Iran and Afghanistan to the Punjab is difficult. The adoption of the invocation in the Punjabi qissa tradition suggests one literary link between the two traditions.

Of all Punjabi qisse, the tale of *Hir-Ranjha* has perhaps enjoyed the greatest popularity historically. It is the earliest extant Punjabi language qissa, and, gauging from existing manuscripts from the medieval and early modern periods, and publishing information from the colonial period, *Hir-Ranjha* was among the most commonly composed qisse. From the repertoire of texts produced over at least four centuries (sixteenth–twentieth), Waris Shah's rendition of the tale (ca. 1766) is surely the most famous; it is also, without doubt, the most critically-acclaimed text of the genre.[40] Waris Shah's *Hir-Ranjha* was not the first rendition of the narrative, however. In fact, his text drew heavily on the work of his immediate literary predecessor, Hafiz Shah Jahan Muqbal, who composed a rendition of *Hir-Ranjha* some twenty years earlier.[41] Both Muqbal and Waris Shah used invocations at the outset of their *Hir-Ranjha* compositions. Excerpts from the two invocations underscore both their similarity to one another, and the similarity of Punjabi invocations to that of Gurgani's Persian text. Muqbal's text opens:[42]

First let me remember the name of Allah,
let me recite 'I begin with the name of Allah' one lakh [100,000] times...
I would sacrifice my life for His friend,
whose name is the Prophet of God [*nabi rasool Allah*]...
Came together a group of passionate ones and said to Muqbal,
recite for us the tale of Hir's love.
I said to the passionate ones I agree to your command,

I will join together the tale of Hir and Ranjha ...
My poetry will only be accepted, when I wrap it in the name of the Lord.
When with each breath I provide the pure soul of the Prophet with praise.
I bow before all four, Abu Bakr, Umar, Usman, and Ali [the first four caliphs of Islam].
I will lace the entire tale of Hir and Ranjha with weeping and lamentation.[43]

Waris Shah's invocation follows Muqbal's closely in form and content, as seen from this excerpt:

Let us first repeat praise for the Lord ...
The second praise is for the Prophet ...
Also I praise the four friends of the Prophet ...
Abu Bakr and Umar, Usman, Ali ...
they are exalted, they are the Lord's slaves.
Next I must sing praise with love for that pir [Sufi spiritual guide],
who counts holy men among his followers ...[44]
Maudud's beloved, the Chishti pir, Masood Shakar-Ganj [Shaikh Farid] is plenitude itself ...
When one takes up the job of love, first meditate on the name of the lord.
Then, with each breath provide praise to the messenger of God and the prophets.
Friends came to me and asked me a question, will you make a new composition on the love of Hir?...
Bringing together exotic and beautiful poetry, I have written of the union of Hir and Ranjha.[45]

Muqbal's and Waris Shah's eighteenth-century texts present a template for invocations in Punjabi qisse. This template, employed by poets composing in subsequent centuries, suggests that invocations were a literary convention of Punjabi qisse. While invocations of some sort are familiar in a variety of South Asian literary genres, the particular form of invocations employed in Punjabi qisse—related to the model presented by Persian qisse—helps define the Punjabi qissa tradition. Tracing the use of invocations in late nineteenth-century renditions of *Hir-Ranjha* both underscores how invocations in these later texts are related to earlier models in the tradition, and also illustrates the coherence of the Punjabi qissa tradition.

Late nineteenth-century *Hir-Ranjha* texts do not invariably open with invocations. The practice was common enough, however, to suggest that it continued to be a literary convention of the genre into this period. Or, to think about it in a slightly different manner, the use of an invocation so closely styled on the template described above was a method of linking one's composition to the qissa tradition. The following examples of opening passages from late nineteenth-century *Hir-Ranjha* texts highlight their similarity with the invocations composed by Muqbal and Waris Shah.

The first is from Muhammad Shah Sakin's *Qissa Hir wa Ranjha*. The text is comprised of four *si harfian* that narrate the story of Hir and Ranjha. *Si harfi* is a genre of Persian poetry based on couplets that begin with successive letters of the Persian alphabet (pl. *si harfian*). Sakin's first two stanzas are devoted to an invocation:

First is praise for God, and then the prophet, the certain friend of the Lord ...
Then one must praise the companions of the prophet ...
My pir is Muhammad Shah Ghaus al-Aztam,
just taking his name pushes away all pain.[46]

The second example is *Faryad Hir* by Khaksar al-Baksh of Lahore, who wrote under the penname Munir. This text opens:

First praise for the Lord, who is the bestower to all.
... Let me say praise for the beloved friend of the Lord [Muhammad].
[Let me praise] Abu Bakr, Umar, and Usman, the fourth exalted one being Ali.
[Let me praise] Ghaus Azm Shah Gilani, whose benevolence is present in all the world.[47]

These opening passages follow the conventional form of invocations in the Punjabi qissa, opening with praise for God, followed by praise for the prophet Muhammad and the first four caliphs. Each poet also invokes more local spiritual figures, represented by pirs. These invocations are, to some extent, formulaic. They do not belabor their point. Their inclusion—no matter how truncated the form—suggests that these poets saw invocations as a convention of the qissa genre. At the same time, the use of invocations by late nineteenth-century authors suggests that they were literary devices that allowed them to identify their texts with a regional qissa tradition, while also pointing to the coherence of that tradition in the Punjab.

If invocations point to the coherence of the Punjabi qissa tradition, the late nineteenth-century texts presented above show that this tradition was not rigidly defined. While the texts by Sakin and Munir share the literary device of the invocation with Muqbal and Waris Shah, the texts by the former authors are very different from those of their predecessors in a host of ways. Most obvious, perhaps, is that the later texts are not epic-length renditions that give a detailed treatment to the tale of Hir and Ranjha. Rather, they are significantly shorter renditions, eight or sixteen pages in length, that concentrate on a single or a limited number of episodes from the broader narrative. The colonial-era texts also represent an eclectic mix of poetic styles. While some late nineteenth-century Punjabi qissa poets continued to use the rhyme scheme associated with the masnavi, many did not. Sakin's text, for example, was composed in si harfi, a genre in its own right.

Although the poetic forms used by late nineteenth-century poets show little consistency, they should all be read as part of the qissa tradition. Certainly, that is the way they were presented to the public. Sakin's text, for example, was published under the title *Qissa Hir wa Ranjha* despite its use of the si harfi form. This suggests that in the qissa's transition to the Punjabi context, many of the formal features of the Persian genre became more malleable. The inclusion of different poetic forms (and meters, as mentioned above) was not the only way that poets shaped the qissa to local taste and context. The invocation also proved an adaptable literary convention. From the earliest existing Punjabi qisse, poets opened their texts by invoking spiritual authorities other than those associated with Islam.

MOVING BEYOND THE ISLAMIC IDIOM

If stemming from an Islamic milieu, as the nature of traditional invocations that praise Allah, Muhammad, and the first four caliphs suggests, then the use of invocations praising alternate genealogies, or ones that simply praise God without using an idiom associated with a particular religious tradition, points to the ways the Punjabi qissa reflected the religious plurality of the Punjab. Adhering to a literary convention that links the qissa to its Perso-Islamic heritage and, at the same time, adapting that convention to suit its local context underscores how the Punjabi qissa functions as a regional literary tradition.

The Hindu poet Damodar, as far as we know, was the first person to compose an epic-length Punjabi text of *Hir-Ranjha*. Composed in the early seventeenth century, Damodar's text includes the following invocation:[48]

First let us take the name of the Lord [*sahib*], who created this world.
Who made land and sky, the heavens and evil with his divine power.
Who created the moon and the sun, that in every place should be his shadow.
My name is Damodar, my zat [caste, kinship group] Gulati, I have created this qissa.[49]

Damodar draws on a source of spiritual authority in his invocation using the term sahib, described as the creator. Although the word sahib has an Arabic etymology, its use in the Punjabi language is not associated with Islam alone; it serves as a term for God that is not particular to any one religious community or denomination more than another.

Similar examples abound, particularly from the late nineteenth century. Take, for example, Kishan Singh 'Arif's *Qissa Hir te Ranjhe da*. Published in 1889, this text opens with an invocation that self-consciously avoids using any one religious idiom:

In the beginning, the end, and throughout time, there is only one true one [*sucha subhan*] to be praised.
Without that grace [*subhan*], all the world would be false.
He has not one name alone: either Ram, Rabb, or Bhagwan.
Under God's writ, all the world exists,
the sun, the stars, the moon, water, land, and sky,
the life within each thing, each life, and the soul within each body.
Kishan Singh says, there is one God [*Brahm*], the Vedas and Quran speak the truth.[50]

In his reference to a divine power/God, 'Arif self-consciously avoids using the language of a single religious genealogy or tradition. Instead, he praises a supreme deity (*sucha subhan*) in terms equally accessible to people from all of the Punjab's religious faiths, and uses terms associated with each of the Punjab's major religions (Ram, Rabb, Bhagwan). Hindu and Sikh authors need not limit themselves to praise of a generic deity in their invocations, however. Bhai Rann Singh, for example, uses an invocation in his *Navan Qissa Hir* that adopts a Sikh idiom: 'Repeat the name of the Lord. Who has made the whole world…Who has brought us the land and water. He who is in every soul. He is the ruler of all the world. Then let us take the name of the fifth king [Guru Arjun]. He who made the corpus, the Guru Granth Sahib'.[51]

While Damodar's, 'Arif's, and Rann Singh's invocations differ stylistically and in content—Damodar's and 'Arif's drawing on a generic deity and Rann Singh's drawing on a Sikh genealogy—these texts exemplify the adoption of the invocation as a literary convention that ties the Punjabi qissa to the Perso-Islamic tradition while simultaneously showing how the convention was molded to reflect the cultural and religious context in which qisse in the Punjab were composed and circulated.

That poets used invocations to identify specific sources of spiritual authority, underlining their own religious identity in the process, raises the question of whether Punjabi qisse were understood as either Muslim, Hindu, or Sikh texts by their authors or audiences. The answer to this question can only be speculative given the limited sources on authorial intent, performers' perspectives, or audience reception, whether that of readers or of those who heard qisse through oral performances. On the basis of qissa texts themselves, it appears that while authors used invocations to reflect their religious affiliations, religious affiliations had little impact on the way the narrative was recounted; the narrative of *Hir-Ranjha* has remained remarkably consistent in tellings across many centuries. Representations of the love story and the regional motifs at the heart of this narrative tradition—specific villages, towns, landscapes, rivers, and recognizable figures such as the greedy boatman, his licentious wife, or the immoral Muslim cleric (*mullah*)—were not informed by a religiously communitarian perspective. To put it another way, in the framing of the text authors were able to reflect on or include their class, caste, sectarian, religious, and geographic affiliations and predilections. This sort of self-referentiality is barely discernible in the narrative itself, however. In addition, religious identity does not appear to have informed the formation of audiences for Punjabi qisse. Readers of qissa texts and audiences at their public performances were religiously plural up to and into the early twentieth century. Rather than suggesting the division of the Punjabi qissa tradition into Hindu, Muslim, and Sikh segments, invocations that move beyond the Islamic idiom suggest that invocations were an important literary convention in the Punjabi qissa tradition, one that both linked it to a Perso-Islamic heritage and, at the same time, was flexible enough to allow the Punjabi qissa to reflect local beliefs, and aesthetic and cultural practices. By precisely such adaptations, Punjabi poets made the qissa genre a regional literary tradition despite its extra-local roots.

The significance of the Perso-Islamic foundations of the Punjabi qissa tradition is two-fold. First, and perhaps most obviously, establishing the relationship with the Persian (and, latently, the Arabic) literary traditions brings historical depth to our understanding of this Indian literary tradition. Second, recognizing the links—and the divergences—between these literary traditions contributes to an understanding of late nineteenth-century India's cultural history. In particular, an analysis of the Perso-Islamic foundations of Punjabi qisse contributes to a rich and burgeoning body of scholarship on language and religious community.[52] The colonial context of the late nineteenth (and indeed early twentieth) century, this scholarship shows, produced movements that associated languages (and scripts) with particular religious communities: advocates argued that Hindi (in the Devnagri script) was the language of Hindus, Urdu (in the Indo-Persian script) that of Muslims, and Punjabi (in the Gurmukhi script) that of Sikhs. Linguistic activists waged their political battles, in the Punjab as elsewhere in north India, not only with petitions to the colonial state asking for official recognition of their claims,[53] but also through literary journals and societies that advocated (or appropriated) particular genres (and scripts) as emblematic of their aspirations.[54] In this context, the Perso-Islamic foundations and conventions of Punjabi qisse take on particular historical salience. This is not only because qisse were extremely popular as both published (in Indo-Persian and Gurmukhi scripts) (Figures 8.1 and 8.2) and oral texts in the late nineteenth century, but also because invocations—Perso-Islamic links notwithstanding—continued to be a hallmark of the genre.

The significance of the invocation in late nineteenth-century Punjabi qisse, then, is that it underscores that this regional literary tradition did not adhere or conform to the increasingly politicized environment—linguistic and literary—of contemporary colonial north India. That Punjabi qisse were very popular throughout the

Figure 8.1 Title page of *Qissa Hir Jog Singh*, lithograph, Lahore, 1882. The script is Indo-Persian. The image depicts Hir and Ranjha sitting before the *panj pir*

Figure 8.2 Title page of Kishan Singh 'Arif, *Qissa Hir te Ranjhe da*, lithograph, Amritsar, 1889. The script is Gurmukhi. The image depicts Hir and Ranjha

late nineteenth century suggests that traditions that did not adhere to an increasingly communalized and communalizing discourse were central, rather than marginal, to Punjabi cultural life. What accounts for the vitality and popularity of the Punjabi qissa tradition in spite of a changing political and cultural context that worked to categorize languages, scripts, and literary production into communally demar-cated boxes? One answer, I suggest, is that qisse debated issues of importance to the Punjab's inhabitants and articulated ideas and practices that resonated with their audiences. One such issue that appears in a series of late nineteenth-century Punjabi qisse is the con-stitution of pious behaviour.

REPRESENTATIONS OF PIETY IN LATE NINETEENTH-CENTURY PUNJABI QISSE

Punjabi qisse historically circulated through manuscripts (from the seventeenth century), published versions (in the nineteenth and twentieth centuries), and, perhaps more commonly, through public performances that were familiar to both urban and rural people. References to these performances in colonial records rarely go beyond noting their ubiquity, as suggested, for example, in Muhammad Latif's colonial-era history of Lahore. 'Young people in the streets recite epic and other poetry', wrote Latif, 'or sing songs descriptive of love and intrigue'.[55] Unfortunately, there are few detailed sources on late nineteenth-century oral performances of qisse in the Punjab, and those that exist are of limited value.[56] Printed qisse from this period, however, allow one to gauge pub-lishing trends and thus literary history in the region. While these texts are not an imprint of the oral tradition of the time, they do provide insights into the Punjab's oral culture since qisse were com-posed in meters meant for oral dissemination, usually with musical accompaniment.

Of those qisse published in the late nineteenth century, *Hir-Ranjha* was among the most popular. The tale of Hir and Ranjha is a simple love story. The tale's main male protagonist is Dhido, a young man referred to in the narrative by the name of his kinship group, Ranjha. Ranjha is the son of a landowner in the village of Takht Hazara in the Punjab. Upon his father's death, Ranjha's brothers cheat him out of a viable parcel of their father's land and this prompts Ranjha to leave home. His epic journey takes him in search of a renowned beauty named Hir. Through trials and tribulations Ranjha makes his way to Hir's village, Jhang, where the two fall in love. Conspiring to keep Ranjha close-at-hand, Hir arranges for him to become her father's cowherd. While Hir and Ranjha believe this ruse will keep their relationship a secret, they are eventually found out by Hir's parents who immediately force her into a marriage with someone they consider more suitable. Sometimes this tale ends with Hir and Ranjha reunited and living happily ever after. More often, however, the tale ends in tragedy as Hir and Ranjha die for their love.

The *Hir-Ranjha* narrative has been important to Punjab's culture since at least the sixteenth century. While Damodar's early seventeenth-century composition is the earliest existing text of the tale in its entirety, evidence of *Hir-Ranjha* compositions produced during Mughal emperor Akbar's reign (1556–1605) suggests that Damodar gave literary expression to a tale that was already circulating in the region.[57] After Damodar, many others gave poetic expression to the tale. With access to printing presses in the Punjab from the mid-nineteenth century, renditions of this qissa proliferated. In the words of Sirani, an author of *Hir-Ranjha*, the narrative served as a means to 'open the history of the times'.[58] Sirani's comment suggests that poets were engaging with issues germane to their day while composing within the conventions of this narrative tradition. If this was the case, then certainly what constituted pious behaviour was an important issue in late nineteenth-century Punjab, for it surfaces repeatedly as a motif in contemporary *Hir-Ranjha* texts. Piety in *Hir-Ranjha* is inextricably linked to the practice of saint veneration, particularly of Sufi pirs, a practice that Punjabis from an array of religions and classes participated in during the colonial period.

The practices associated with Sufi pirs and their shrines in the Punjab have been the focus of excellent studies that have demarcated their religious, social, and political functions. David Gilmartin has shown that Sufi pirs held considerable political power in their local context, and that they played an instrumental role in connecting local religious practices to broader conceptions of Islam.[59] Richard Eaton's work on Sufism generally, and on the shrine of Shaikh Farid of Pakpattan in particular, argues that Sufi pirs acted as intermediaries between individuals and God and that they made Islam accessible to many of the non-Muslims among whom they lived.[60] While Gilmartin and Eaton emphasize different aspects of the various roles Sufi pirs and their shrines play in Punjab's history, they share a focus on the Sufi pir or his or her shrine as the locus of study.

In contrast, Harjot Oberoi examines the veneration of Sufi saints in colonial Punjab from the perspective of non-Muslim participation in this form of devotion. In *The Construction of Religious Boundaries*, Oberoi argues that in the late nineteenth century Sikh reformers advanced an increasingly rigid definition of Sikhism, one that sought to cleanse the community of devotional practices now deemed unacceptable to proper Sikh conduct. To provide a context for this Sikh reformist activity, Oberoi describes the religious practices of late nineteenth-century Punjab's 'subordinate social sector', one that participated in an 'enchanted universe' of popular religion marked by miracle saints, malevolent goddesses, village sacred sites, evil spirits, and witchcraft.[61] The veneration of saints (Sufi pirs in the Punjabi context) is among the myriad aspects of 'popular religion' that Oberoi analyses. As Gilmartin, Eaton, and Oberoi all point out, the veneration of Sufi pirs was not limited to individuals who considered themselves adherents of the Sufi way, or even of Islam more generally. Hindus, Sikhs, and Christians participated in the veneration of Muslim saints in the Punjab with as much vigour as their Muslim contemporaries.[62] Seeking to understand such non-Muslim participation, Oberoi suggests that it was grounded in a syncretic tradition of shrines that drew on Hindu, Muslim, and Sikh normative traditions, on one hand, and 'cognitive frameworks of illness and healing' on the other.[63]

These interpretations, however, even if taken together, do not adequately explain the widespread Punjabi participation in shrine activities, or in the veneration of saints. At issue is Oberoi's reliance on syncretism as an analytic. Oberoi writes: '[T]he cultural space of the shrine, its architectural fusion, and the icons it enshrined contained elements from the "great" religious traditions of Punjab, enabling it to generate popular devotion'.[64] This argument suggests that participation in shrine activities was a result of the elements of the 'great' religious traditions embedded therein. What remains the foundation of Oberoi's analysis, then, is an individual's 'normative' religious identity, Hindu, Muslim, or Sikh. Perhaps Oberoi's reliance on syncretism and 'illness and healing' to understand widespread participation in saint veneration rests on his assertion that it is difficult to reconstruct 'popular religion' or to pinpoint 'the concepts around which the fabric of popular religion was woven'.[65] At best, he writes, one must use elite sources—newspapers, journals, reformers' tracts, and other things.—to deduce the impetus towards popular devotional practices by the vast majority of Punjab's inhabitants. Other types of sources from the late nineteenth century are available, however, that reflect on popular religious sentiments. In particular, popular literature such as qisse allow one to pursue an understanding of saint veneration that is not based on the religious ideals of Punjabi elites, many of whom were actively involved in religious reform movements that called for curtailing this form of devotional practice.

My reading of late nineteenth-century *Hir-Ranjha* texts reveals that a discourse on piety was central to them; this discourse shapes the discernible contours of a spiritual community symbolized by the practices of saint veneration. Rather than understanding saint veneration in these texts as solely symbolic of adherence to Sufi values (though that meaning, too, is important), the discourse on piety in *Hir-Ranjha* texts portrays saint veneration as a form of piety in which all Punjabis could participate. This shared piety, without conflicting with an individual's nominative religious identity, constituted a sphere of religiosity and devotion that cut across the boundaries that distinguished the Punjab's major religious traditions.

My focus on representations of piety in *Hir-Ranjha* texts is prompted by the centrality of this theme in late nineteenth-century texts themselves. While piety has many definitions and associations, two meanings are central to the *Hir-Ranjha* narrative. The first is the sense of personal devotion to religious observance. The second is that of dutifulness, often articulated as duty to one's parents or elders. While these meanings may appear unrelated, both senses of piety are imbricated in the *Hir-Ranjha* narrative as its characters struggle over the proper forms that piety should take.

Na'at di Hir, published in 1880, exemplifies this. In this short text, the poet Na'at highlights a single episode from the larger *Hir-Ranjha* narrative: a conversation between Hir and a *qazi*, or Muslim judge. Their conversation is really more of a dispute, as Hir and the qazi argue about her conduct. The qazi, whose authority is grounded in his capacity as an arbiter of Islamic law, argues that Hir should marry her parents' choice of suitor.[66] Although the qazi's argument does not explicitly draw on Islamic law, it is clear that he is urging Hir to acquiesce to her parents' wishes on the grounds that this would fulfil both her religious and moral duties. In contrast, Hir argues that her position—to be faithful to Ranjha—is truer to the spirit of Islam. What we find in this text is not a denial of the religious law upon which the qazi's authority is grounded, but a discourse on the proper interpretation of that law—with the question of pious conduct laying at the very core.

In Na'at's text, the qazi's authority is taken for granted; it need not be elaborated upon. By virtue of being a qazi, he has the sanction of Islamic law behind him. Hir, however, does not cower before the qazi's authority and insists on her right to marry a man of her choice. Realizing that his religious authority alone is not bending Hir to his (and her parents') will, the qazi adds a moral tenor to the discussion, arguing that it is Hir's moral duty to abide by her parents' wishes. The weight of religion and familial duty—or one might say the patriarchal structure—come together when the qazi tells Hir: 'Where the parents are willing, and the qazi is also willing, only by accepting that same place will you be happy'.[67] Hir rejects the qazi's argument, responding, 'I will not be separated from my beloved. My body and soul are his'.[68] The qazi chastises Hir for this comment: 'Do not forego your shame', he tells her, 'protect your parents' honor'.[69] Hir's reply suggests the strength of her convictions, as she says, 'I would sacrifice my life as well as my faith [for Ranjha]'.[70] If the qazi is attempting to persuade Hir to marry the correct suitor by invoking an obligation of duty to one's parents, Hir changes the terms of the debate altogether.

Notice how in her rebuttal Hir reinterprets the concept of piety in which filial and religious duty is grounded. Hir's description of her devotion to Ranjha points to her interpretation of proper conduct: 'Everyday like a slave I take Ranjha's name, without him, oh qazi, to eat or drink would be forbidden [*haram*]'.[71] The language Hir uses, especially the use of the term haram, co-opts a language associated with the doctrinal Islam of the qazi in which actions are deemed halal or haram, sanctioned or forbidden. Hir is being subversive when she uses the same language to very different ends. Instead of adhering to an order of behavior as sanctioned or forbidden under Islamic law and social custom, Hir defines a code of behaviour, anchored in her devotion to her lover, which has its own set of principles.

Hir points to these principles in her conversation with the qazi. She first rejects the qazi's moral universe for its corruption and suggests that to abide by her parents wishes would bring her into conflict with her own beliefs, her own sense of pious conduct. 'I asked for Ranjha from the shrine, from true belief and purity itself', she tells the qazi.[72] If one recalls that earlier in the text Hir had conflated her devotion to Ranjha with devotion to God (everyday like a slave I take Ranjha's name), this reference to the shrine as the source for Ranjha suggests that the shrine is also the source for Hir's understanding of pious action (for it represents true belief and purity itself) and that it is the locus of her devotion. While one might interpret the conflict between the qazi and Hir as representing a duality between doctrinal Islam and Sufi Islam, this is not being suggested in this text. Rather, it appears that Hir is anchoring her beliefs in an institutional site with deep foundations in the Punjab, and simultaneously deploying the language and concept of the Sufi shrine to challenge the authority, social norms, and notions of duty argued for by the qazi.

This becomes clearer if one examines a rendition of *Hir-Ranjha* composed by the poet Roshan. Entitled *Hir Roshan* and published repeatedly between 1873 and 1900, Roshan's text, like Na'at's, focuses on a particular episode from the larger *Hir-Ranjha* narrative. In this case, the text is a conversation between Hir and her mother, Malki. At issue, as in Na'at's text, is Hir's resistance to the marriage arranged by her parents. In *Hir Roshan*, Malki attempts to convince Hir to abide by her parents' wishes. Malki frames their debate around religious obligation; she argues that in order to behave in ways that coincide with honour, right conduct, and religious duty, Hir must marry the man her parents have chosen for her.

The conversation between the two opens with Malki admonishing Hir to behave in accordance with Islamic law, or *shari'a*. 'Abide by the shari'a Hir', Malki tells her daughter, 'do not go the way of the devil, oh my daughter'.[73] Hir's response both prevents her mother from pursuing this line of argument further and serves to introduce Hir's notion of right conduct and religious duty. Hir responds, 'If I were to turn my face away from Ranjha, I would die an infidel [*kafir*], oh mother. I hold the dictates of religious law dearly, I would not take one step outside of them, oh mother'.[74] As in Na'at's use of the term haram in the example above, Roshan's use of the word kafir brings with it a wealth of meaning.

In this exchange between Hir and her mother, Roshan sets up a duality with concepts that initially appear opposed to one another. One is shari'a, or Islamic law, the other is the notion of a kafir, or an individual who does not believe in, or does not abide by the tenets of Islam. In their conversation, Malki argues that Islamic law prescribes that Hir obey her parents in order to be a good Muslim. Hir's response follows the same logic, only reverses its terms. Hir's rebuttal argues that to give up Ranjha, precisely what her parents desire, would make her an infidel, one who turns her back on God. Hir's response also suggests that her interpretation of Islamic law results in very different ends than does her mother's. In challenging Malki's interpretation of what behaviour is in accordance with shari'a, what constitutes a kafir, Hir is challenging her mother's interpretation of pious conduct. Hir's actions in the text suggest that the religious law she adheres to defines pious conduct in very different ways from Malki. While Roshan never goes on to describe the parameters of this alternative, parallel realm of belief, other renditions of *Hir-Ranjha* bring some of its associations into clearer focus.

Hir Husain, a text comprised of two si harfian, was extremely popular throughout the late nineteenth century. First published in 1871, *Hir Husain* was republished at least a dozen times through the late 1880s. The first si harfi is a dialogue between Hir and Ranjha and the second is a dialogue between Hir and Malki. In this text the author Husain does not introduce events from the earlier parts of the narrative, or treat the narrative in its entirety. Instead, he explores two points of conflict in detail: the conflict between

Hir and Ranjha over her betrothal to Seido Khera (her parents' choice of suitor) and that between Hir and Malki over the former's relationship with Ranjha. Both exchanges portray Hir as a woman firm in her convictions as she defends herself against Ranjha's accusations of infidelity, and counters her mother's laments about her immorality. *Hir Husain* also reveals, in very subtle shades, Hir's piety and its heavy emphasis on saint veneration.

Husain's first si harfi opens with Ranjha leaving Jhang, accusing Hir of being unfaithful to him. Agitated by Hir's betrothal to Seido Khera, Ranjha exclaims, 'get up and manage your cattle Hir, Ranjha is laying off this yoke... Your thoughts are always with the Kheras, you have no consideration for Ranjha, oh Hir'.[75] Through the rest of the si harfi, Hir defends herself against Ranjha's accusations. Hir's strength of character is depicted in the last lines she utters to Ranjha in which she urges him to remember her faithfulness and that she 'broke the bonds of family and religion' for his sake.[76] What religion has Hir broken away from, and to what form of piety does she turn? The answers to these questions are alluded to in the text's second half.

Husain's second si harfi is a dialogue in which Malki implores Hir to give up what society deems to be her shameful behaviour. Hir's response shows that her mother is using more than the pressure of social norms to sway her daughter's behaviour; Malki is relying on religious concepts as well. Hir's response to her mother's censure is: 'Stop mother, don't tell me any more, I have understood your meaning. You are making me turn my back on the ka'aba, by speaking of the hadith and the Kheras in the same breath'.[77] Hir's comment clearly indicates that Malki is relying on arguments about proper religious conduct to persuade Hir to marry Seido Khera. Hir's rejection of the husband chosen for her marks a rejection not of those religious symbols, but rather the associations upon which her mother's argument rests. In rejecting her mother's dictates, Hir does not wish to, literally, 'turn [her] back on the ka'aba' and the hadith. Instead, Hir challenges the very structures upon which her mother's arguments are based. This is evident from a comment directed at Ranjha. In the following line we see a glimpse of where, and in what, Hir vests her piety. Cognizant of the challenges facing them both, in a poignant closing line to Ranjha, Hir says, 'I, Hir, am your slave. Keep your trust and hope in the *panj pir*, oh Ranjha'.[78] The panj pir, which literally means five saints, is as much a cultural as a religious symbol. An allusion to the Punjab's greatest Sufi saints, the panj pir are icons of the region's Sufi tradition. Because of the piety with which they are associated, the panj pir are revered by Punjabis irrespective of their formal religious identity. In advocating belief in the panj pir, Hir's words are full of hope and belief. By asking Ranjha to keep his faith in them, Hir is signalling her belief in an order symbolized by the archetypal saints of the Punjab.

Thus far, my discussion has focused on texts by Muslim authors. The discourse on religion and piety in these texts is decidedly in a Muslim idiom. That the qissa tradition was a regional literary tradition participated in by poets of all religions necessitates the question: what representations of piety are found in texts by Sikh and Hindu authors? Are the representations of piety in such texts markedly different from those discussed above? Or do they also represent participation and belief in an order symbolized by saint veneration? Examination of a series of texts by Hindu and Sikh authors suggests that, in these texts as well, the privileged form of piety is that associated with saint veneration.

Take, for example, *Navan Qissa Hir* by the poet Kishore Chand (a Hindu). The earlier portions of this text are set in Takht Hazara and follow Ranjha's disappointments after his father's death. Dejected by his (dis)inheritance, Ranjha one day goes to sit with a group of religious mendicants (*faqirs*) who are camped on the outskirts of Takht Hazara. Ranjha tells the mendicants of his sorrows, and they in turn console him by referring to the intervention of the panj pir. Upon hearing his tale they say: 'the *panj pir* will always help you. We have given our solemn pledge'.[79] With these words, Ranjha's fears are assuaged and, under the protection of the panj pir, he leaves Takht Hazara on his epic journey in search of Hir.

The importance of saints also surfaces in the rendition of *Hir-Ranjha* by Kishan Singh 'Arif. Here again one sees saint veneration privileged as a form of devotion. This is initially evidenced in the composition through the intervention of the panj pir. In 'Arif's text, the panj pir come to Ranjha in a dream as he travels from Takht Hazara to Jhang. The reader or listener is told, 'along the way he came in contact with some pirs. The *panj pir* themselves came to him in a dream, a wondrous miracle. Kishan Singh says, to meet the *panj pir* is to know God's way'.[80] Ranjha's respect for and devotion to these individuals is represented through his reaction to the meeting. 'Ranjha put his two hands together as he prostrated in salutation', 'Arif wrote, 'saying to them, I am your ... slave'.[81] Although the panj pir initially chastise Ranjha for leaving home at too young an age, upon hearing of his devotion to Hir they support his endeavour: 'go now and meet Hir, for this we pray. We will meet you again in Jhang. If you encounter any difficulty, remember us in your heart. Kishan Singh says, with each breath focus your soul's attention on the Lord'.[82] The exchange between Ranjha and the panj pir ends with this injunction: 'Kishan Singh says, to live without one's beloved is forbidden [haram] in this world'.[83] That 'Arif, a Sikh, should use haram, a word steeped with Islamic connotations, suggests that the Islamic idiom of *Hir-Ranjha* texts is just that: an idiom, rather than a discourse specifically on Islam. 'Arif's use of haram not only indicates that an Islamic idiom was the literary norm of this narrative tradition, but also that irrespective of its Islamic idiom, the sentiments being depicted in *Hir-Ranjha* texts were relevant beyond a Muslim community. If one were to engage the multivalence of the language used in these texts, then haram connotes forbidden under shari'a in an Islamic context, and, in a broader context, suggests that which is forbidden under the tenets of religion. At a broader level, the Islamic idiom used in *Hir-Ranjha* texts was the language employed for a discourse on piety that was not, at the levels of either production or consumption, limited to Muslims alone.

* * *

In an essay on the Ramayana narrative tradition, A.K. Ramanujan writes that its plot—as is the case with many Indian popular narrative traditions, including *Hir-Ranjha*—is 'always already there'.[84] The audience does not read or listen to this narrative to learn what happens; they read or listen out of an appreciation for the art of poetic composition or artistic performance. The audience, then, of Kishan Singh 'Arif's text knew from the outset that the relationship between

Hir and Ranjha would be in conflict with an interpretation of religious obligation used to buttress the authority of Hir's parents. Thus,
to suggest that Ranjha's living without his beloved is haram suggests
beliefs that are not coterminous with that interpretation of Islam that
will be associated later in the text with Hir's family. In short, what
the brief meeting between Ranjha and the panj pir in 'Arif's text illustrates is both the privileging of saint veneration above other forms of
religiosity and the allusion to a set of beliefs, to forms of piety, that do
not conform to the injunctions of religion as practiced by the dominant forces in society. Instead, the *Hir-Ranjha* narrative privileges
an understanding of religious obligation that challenges authority
structures, and represents a vision of piety that is distinct from the
religiosity of characters such as the qazi and Hir's parents. This piety
is articulated through reference to Sufi saints and shrines, institutions
and institutional sites that were prominent across the Punjab, and
were patronized by people from all walks of life. *Hir-Ranjha* texts,
then, point to an articulation of piety centred on saint veneration, a
form of piety that was shared by Punjab's inhabitants.

That saint veneration is so central to these texts is clear. It is also
clear, however, that the depictions of saint veneration make little
reference to Punjab's major religious traditions. Characters' participation in this world of devotional practice seems to bear no direct
relation to Islam, Hinduism, Sikhism, or any other religion. The way
saint veneration is represented in these texts points to an independent
set of beliefs that are neither in conflict with nor coterminous with
Punjab's major religious traditions. *Hir-Ranjha* texts portray a religious world—with remarkable consistency—that operates as a parallel
arena of belief. Hir, after all, does not want to be in conflict with the
shari'a, she does not want to be a kafir. But she is also not satisfied
with the religious world that her parents and the qazi represent. The
relationship between these spheres of religiosity as represented in *Hir-
Ranjha* texts, however, is ill represented by the notion of syncretism.
Hir's beliefs are neither an amalgam of Hindu and Muslim practice,
nor does her participation in the religious world of the shrine appear
in any way predicated on her religious identity as a Muslim.

Punjabi qisse were remarkably consistent in their representations
of piety, always privileging saint veneration. This was a form of piety

that accommodated all Punjabis, irrespective of differences of religion, class, or caste. Indeed, we know that Punjabis of all backgrounds actively participated in devotional activities at shrines in the late nineteenth century. That this particular form of piety is a core concept in a tradition of Punjabi popular narratives such as *Hir-Ranjha*, however, suggests that it represents more than religious conviction alone. These texts, after all, were not religious tracts, but popular narratives circulating through print and performance. The centrality of representations of piety in these texts points to the importance of saint veneration to the region's cultural imagination. Put another way, the piety represented in the Punjabi qissa is clearly an integral aspect of a regional cultural identity. That this cultural identity—which encompassed people of all religions (much like the qissa tradition itself)—has been muted in scholarly representations of the Punjab's colonial past is not surprising, not only given the lingering effects of India's Partition, but also because it is less pronounced in the colonial archive, where conflict and contestation between religious communities was a prominent aspect of political discourse. By turning to the Punjabi qissa and reading it as a historical source—perhaps in the way that Ganesh Das Vadhera imagined when he recounted qisse in his history of the Punjab—this aspect of Punjab's colonial history comes into clearer focus.

Notes

1 Michael Brand and James Westcoat, Jr., Bibliography for the Mughal Gardens Project. www.mughalgardens.org/PDF/lahore_bibliography. pdf. Retrieved on 1 May 2011.

2 As cited in J.S. Grewal and Indu Banga (trans. and eds), *Early Nineteenth Century Panjab: From Ganesh Das's Char Bagh-i-Panjab*, Amritsar: Guru Nanak Dev University, 1975, p. 9.

3 Grewal and Banga, *Early Nineteenth Century Panjab*.

4 Ibid., p. 10.

5 Rather than including these romances in their entirety, the translators provide abridged translations, and this only in an appendix.

6 Three major religions have long been practiced in the Punjab: Hinduism, Islam, and Sikhism. By the late nineteenth century there was also a growing Christian community. The reference to 'social organization' is

to *zat* (caste, kinship group), a kinship system that continues to mark Hindu, Muslim, Christian, and Sikh social organization in the region.

7 Yohanan Friedmann, *Prophecy Continuous: Aspects of Ahmadi Religious Thought and its Medieval Background*, Berkeley: University of California Press, 1989; Kenneth Jones, *Arya Dharm: Hindu Consciousness in 19th-Century Punjab*, New Delhi: Manohar, 1989 [1976]; Kenneth Jones, *Socio-Religious Reform Movements in British India*, Albany: State University of New York Press, 1992; Ikram Ali Malik, 'Muslim Anjumans in the Punjab', *Journal of Regional History*, vol. 5, 1984, pp. 97–115; Ikram Ali Malik, 'Muslim Anjumans and Communitarian Consciousness', in Indu Banga (ed.), *Five Punjabi Centuries: Polity, Economy, Society and Culture, c. 1500–1990*, New Delhi: Manohar, 1997, pp. 112–25; Barbara Metcalf, *Islamic Revival in British India: Deoband, 1860–1900*, Princeton: Princeton University Press, 1982; Gail Minault, *Secluded Scholars: Women's Education and Muslim Social Reform in Colonial India*, New Delhi: Oxford University Press, 1999, pp. 158–214; Harjot Oberoi, *The Construction of Religious Boundaries: Culture, Identity and Diversity in the Sikh Tradition*, New Delhi: Oxford University Press, 1997 [1994]; Razi Wasti, 'Anjuman Himayat-i-Islam, Lahore—A Brief History', in Razi Wasti (ed.), *The Political Triangle in India*, Lahore: People's Publishing House, 1976, pp. 25–36.

8 It is important to note that qisse were not the only type of popular Punjabi fiction in the late nineteenth and early twentieth centuries. A comparable form of narrative was the novel, introduced into Punjabi literature in 1898. As a genre, however, the novel (as was true of Punjabi-language tracts, treatises, and newspapers) was introduced and promoted by socio-religious reformers (particularly the Sikh Singh Sabha). The Singh Sabha regarded Punjabi as a specifically Sikh language, and one of its leading proponents, Bhai Vir Singh, saw the novel as a good vehicle for its reformist agendas (N.G. Barrier, *The Sikhs and their Literature*, New Delhi: Manohar, 1970; Ganda Singh (ed.), *Bhai Vir Singh*, special issue of *Panjab Past and Present*, 6 (2), 1972). Such new, modern genres differ markedly from qisse not only in their novelty, but in their circulation, being limited principally to a reading public.

9 Oberoi, *The Construction of Religious Boundaries*; Nonica Datta, *Forming an Identity: A Social History of the Jats*, New Delhi: Oxford University Press, 1999; Jones, *Arya Dharm*.

10 Gyanendra Pandey, 'In Defense of the Fragment: Writing about Hindu-Muslim Riots Today', *Representations*, vol. 37, 1992, pp. 27–55.

11 Suvir Kaul, 'Introduction', in Suvir Kaul (ed.), *The Partitions of Memory*, Bloomington: Indiana University Press, 2002 [2001], pp. 1–29.

12 David Frankfurter, 'Syncretism and the Holy Man in Late Antique Egypt', *Journal of Early Christian Studies*, 11 (3), 2003, pp. 339–85; Vassilis Lambropoulos, 'Syncretism as Mixture and as Method', *Journal of Modern Greek Studies*, vol. 19, 2001, pp. 221–35; Andrew Beatty, 'Adam and Eve and Vishnu: Syncretism in the Javanese Slametan', *The Journal of the Royal Anthropological Institute*, 2 (2), 1996, pp. 271–88; Charles Stewart and Rosalind Shaw (eds), *Syncretism/Anti-syncretism: The Politics of Religious Synthesis*, New York: Routledge, 1994.

13 Charles Stewart, 'Syncretism and its Synonyms: Reflections on Cultural Mixture', *Diacritics*, 29 (3), 1999, p. 46.

14 Stewart, 'Syncretism and Its Synonyms'. See also, Stewart and Shaw, *Syncretism/Anti-syncretism*; and Richard Werbner, 'The Suffering Body: Passion and Ritual Allegory in Christian Encounters', *Journal of Southern African Studies*, 23 (2), 1997, pp. 311–24.

15 Stewart, 'Syncretism and its Synonyms', p. 41.

16 Ibid., pp. 40–1.

17 An exception from South Asia is a genre of colonial writing on South Asian religious traditions, specifically on Sikhism. In this scholarship, the description of Sikhism as syncretic was undoubtedly pejorative. Syncretism in this context connoted that Sikhism was not a religious tradition on par with Islam or Hinduism, and that because it was a syncretistic tradition it would not last.

18 Susan Bayly, 'Islam in Southern India: Purist or Syncretic?', in Christopher A. Bayly and D.H.A. Kolff (eds), *Two Colonial Empires*, Boston: Martinus Nijhoff, 1986, pp. 35–73; Derryl MacLean, *Religion and Society in Arab Sind*, Leiden: E. J. Brill, 1989; Asim Roy, *The Islamic Syncretistic Tradition in Bengal*, Princeton: Princeton University Press, 1983; M. Waseem (trans. and ed.), *On Becoming an Indian Muslim: French Essays on Aspects of Syncretism*, New Delhi: Oxford University Press, 2003.

19 Brian Hatcher, *Eclecticism and Modern Hindu Discourse*, New York: Oxford University Press, 1999, p. 8; emphasis added.

20 Tony K. Stewart, 'In Search of Equivalence: Conceiving Muslim-Hindu Encounter Through Translation Theory', *History of Religions*, 40 (3), 2001, p. 262.

21 Friedmann, *Prophesy Continuous*; Jones, *Arya Dharm*; Oberoi, *The Construction of Religious Boundaries*.

22 Peter Gottschalk, *Beyond Hindu and Muslim: Multiple Identity in Narratives from Village India*, New York: Oxford University Press, 2000.

23 Ibid., pp. 151–8; emphasis added.

24 'Kissa', in C.E. Bosworth, Evan Donzel, W.P. Heinrichs, and C. Pellat. (eds), *Encyclopedia of Islam*, new edition, 5 (1), Leiden: E. J. Brill, 1986, pp. 185–207. *Hadith* are the reputed sayings and actions of the Prophet Muhammad. They are a fundamental component of Islamic law.

25 Ibid.

26 Ibid.

27 Masnavi is defined as 'a series of distitchs in rhyming pairs (aa, bb, cc, and others). It contains the whole of [Persian pre-modern] heroic, historic and *romantic* poetry'. Jan Rypka, *History of Iranian Literature*, Dordrecht: Reidel, 1968, p. 91; emphasis added.

28 Mohammed Wahid Mirza, *Life and Works of Amir Khusrau*, Lahore: Punjab University, 1962; Sunil Sharma, *Amir Khusraw: The Poet of Sufis and Sultans*, Oxford: Oneworld, 2005.

29 Mohan Singh Dewana, *A History of Panjabi Literature (1100–1932)*, Jalandhar: Bharat Prakashan, 1971, p. 76.

30 Denis Matringe, '*Hir* Waris Shah', in Waseem, *On Becoming an Indian Muslim*, p. 214.

31 Christopher Shackle suggests that the qissa genre was a particularly powerful medium for expressing regional attachments, writing, 'few genres show a more powerful attachment to the specificities of place than the Panjabi verse romance called qissa'. 'Beyond Turk and Hindu: Crossing the Boundaries in Indo-Muslim Romance', in David Gilmartin and Bruce B. Lawrence (eds), *Beyond Turk and Hindu: Rethinking Religious Identities in Islamicate South Asia*, Gainesville: University Press of Florida, 2000, p. 59.

32 Despite a somewhat slow start, Punjabi books were published in large numbers by the closing decades of the nineteenth century. By 1887, for example, 473 Punjabi titles were published, with print runs of anywhere from 100 to 2,400 copies, and sometimes more. These statistics are drawn from 'Publications Issued and Published in 1887', in *Selections from the Records of the Government of India*, No. 247, Calcutta: Office of the Superintendent of Government Printing, n.d..

33 *Gazetteer of the Lahore District 1883–1884*, Lahore: Sang-e-Meel Publications, 1989 [1884], p. 49.

34 While Persian and Arabic storytelling traditions have a pre-Islamic heritage, their migration to South Asia was intrinsically related to the spread of Islam in the region. Therefore, in the South Asian context, I refer to this storytelling tradition as Perso-Islamic.

35 Matringe, '*Hir* Waris Shah'; Jeevan Deol, 'Sex, Social Critique and the Female Figure in Premodern Punjabi Poetry: Varis Shah's "Hir"', *Modern Asian Studies*, 36 (1), 2002, pp. 141–71.

36 J.C. Burgel, 'The Romance', in Ehsan Yarshater (ed.), *Persian Literature*, [Albany]: Bibliotecha Persica, 1988, p. 164.

37 Fakhr al-Din Gurgani, *Vis and Ramin*, George Morrison (trans.), New York: Columbia University Press, 1972, pp. 1–10.

38 Ibid., p. 18.

39 Burgel, 'The Romance', p. 171.

40 Christopher Shackle, 'Transition and Transformation in Varis Shah's Hir', in Christopher Shackle and Rupert Snell (eds), *The Indian Narrative*, Wiesbaden: Otto Harrassowitz, 1992, pp. 241–63.

41 Maula Baksh Kushta, *Punjabi Shairan da Tazkira* (A Dictionary of Punjabi Poets), Chaudhry Muhammad Afzal Khan (ed.), Lahore: Aziz Publishers, 1988, p. 108.

42 This and all subsequent translations from Punjabi are mine.

43 Shah Jahan Muqbal, *Hir Muqbal*, Faqir Muhammad Faqir (ed.), n.p.: n.p., n.d. [1990], pp. 1–2.

44 According to Sant Singh Sekhon, the reference is to the Sufi saint Sayyid Jalal ud-din Bukhari of Multan. See Waris Shah, *The Love of Hir and Ranjha*, Sant Singh Sekhon (trans.), Ludhiana: Punjab Agricultural University, 1978, p. 264.

45 Waris Shah, *Hir*, Muhammad Baqir (ed.), Lahore: Pakistan Punjabi Adabi Board, 1993 [1988], pp. 1–2.

46 Pir Muhammad Shah Sakin, *Qissa Hir wa Ranjha*, Lahore, Malik Din Muhammad and Sons, n.d., p. 2.

47 Khaksar al-Baksh [Munir], *Faryad Hir* (Hir's Plea), Lahore: Munshi Aziz al-Din Najm al-Din, n.d., p. 2.

48 The exact placement of Damodar's invocation is contested. In Asif Khan's critical edition, Damodar's text begins with seven self-referential stanzas in which the author claims to have witnessed the events he narrates in the qissa. In this edition, it is these seven stanzas that frame the text. They are, however, followed by the invocation cited, that opens the narrative section of the poem. See Damodar, *Hir Damodar*, Muhammad Asif Khan (ed.), Lahore: Pakistan Punjabi Adabi Board, 1986. Other critical editions begin Damodar's text with this invocation. See, for example, Damodar, *Hir Damodar*, Jagtar Singh (ed.), Patiala: Punjabi University, 1987.

49 Damodar, *Hir Damodar*, Muhammad Asif Khan (ed.), p. 37.

50 Kishan Singh 'Arif, *Qissa Hir te Ranjhe da*, Amritsar: Bhai Vasava Singh Juneja Pustak Wale, 1889, p. 2.

51 Bhai Rann Singh, *Navan Qissa Hir*, Amritsar: n.p., 1913, p. 2.

52 Vasudha Dalmia, *The Nationalization of Hindu Traditions: Bharatendu Harischandra and Nineteenth–Century Banaras*, New Delhi: Oxford University Press, 1997; Christopher King, *One Language, Two Scripts: The Hindi Movement in Nineteenth Century North India*, New Delhi: Oxford

University Press, 1994; Veena Naregal, *Language Politics, Elites and the Public Sphere*, London: Anthem Press, 2001; Oberoi, *The Construction of Religious Boundaries*; Francesca Orsini, *The Hindi Public Sphere 1920–1940*, New Delhi: Oxford University Press, 2002; Alok Rai, *Hindi Nationalism*, Hyderabad: Orient Longman, 2001.

53 Ayesha Jalal, *Self and Sovereignty: Individual and Community in South Asian Islam since 1850*, New York: Routledge, 2000, pp. 102–38.

54 Dalmia, *The Nationalization of Hindu Traditions*; King, *One Language, Two Scripts*; Oberoi, *The Construction of Religious Boundaries*.

55 Syed Muhammad Latif, *Lahore: Its History, Architectural Remains and Antiquities*, Lahore: Sang-e-Meel Publications, 1994 [1892], p. 267.

56 Colonial folklorists and ethnographers took some pains to record and translate Punjabi 'folktales', many of which were qisse. See, for example, R.C. Temple, *Legends of the Panjab*, Lahore: Sang-e-Meel Publications, 1981 [1884]; Flora Annie Steel, *Tales of the Punjab Told by the People*, New Delhi: Asian Educational Services, 1989 [1894]; H.A. Rose, 'Hir and Ranjha', *Indian Antiquary*, vol. 52, 1923, pp. 65–78; H.A. Rose, 'A Version of Hir and Ranjha by Asa Singh of Maghiana, Jhang District', *Indian Antiquary*, vol. 54, 1925, pp. 176–9, 210–19; H.A. Rose, 'The Sequel to Hir and Ranjha Told by a Peasant Proprietor of Jhang', *Indian Antiquary*, vol. 55, 1926, pp. 14–19, 36–8; and Charles Swynnerton, *Romantic Tales from the Panjab*, London: Archibald Constable and Co., 1903. These materials, however, are of limited value in reconstructing oral performances because the settings and contexts for colonial performances of 'folk' literature were so contrived that it would be a mistake to construe them as indigenous cultural practices.

57 Jit Singh Sital, 'Authentic Text of the Heer of Waris Shah', PhD dissertation, Panjab University, 1958, pp. 20–1.

58 Malik Ahmad Baksh Toba Sirani, *Qissa Hir wa Ranjha*, Lahore: Matba' Kadimi Lahore, n.d., p. 3.

59 David Gilmartin, *Empire and Islam: Punjab and the Making of Pakistan*, London: I.B. Tauris, 1988; and David Gilmartin, 'Shrines, Succession and Sources of Moral Authority', in Barbara Metcalf (ed.), *Moral Conduct and Authority*, Berkeley: University of California Press, 1984, pp. 221–40.

60 Richard Eaton, 'The Political and Religious Authority of the Shrine of Baba Farid', in Metcalf, *Moral Conduct and Authority*, pp. 333–56; and Richard Eaton, *The Sufis of Bijapur, 1300–1700*, Princeton: Princeton University Press, 1977.

61 Oberoi, *The Construction of Religious Boundaries*, pp. 139–206.

62 To cite just one example, the 1911 colonial census listed approximately 79,000 Sikh adherents of Sakhi Sarwar, a twelfth-century Muslim saint whose shrine is located in Southern Punjab. See ibid., p. 148.

63 Ibid., p. 156.
64 Ibid., p. 151.
65 Ibid., pp. 144–5.
66 While the qazi is often a character of derision in Punjabi popular litera-
    ture for his self-interest and corruptibility, he is simultaneously a figure
    of religious and legal authority. He is learned in Islamic jurisprudence,
    can perform religious services, and in pre-colonial, and often in colonial
    India as well, served in an official (state) role as a local judge.
67 Abd al-Karim Na'at, *Na'at di Hir*, Multan: Hafiz Muhammad al-Din
    Aziz al-Din Bashir al-Din Tajran Kutab, n.d. [c. 1880], p. 3.
68 Ibid.
69 Ibid.
70 Ibid., p. 4.
71 Ibid., p. 5.
72 Ibid., p. 6.
73 Roshan, *Hir Roshan*, Lahore: Mian Chiragh al-Din, n.d. [c. 1873], p. 4.
74 Ibid., p. 5.
75 Husain, *Hir Husain, Si Harfi Ashraf, Si Harfi Arora Rai, Si Harfi
    Ghulam*, Lahore: Matbah Sultani, 1873, p. 2.
76 Ibid., p. 4.
77 Ibid., p. 5.
78 Ibid., p. 4.
79 Kishore Chand, *Navan Qissa Hir Kishore Chand*, Amritsar: Bhai
    Harnam Singh Karam Singh, 1914, p. 4.
80 'Arif, *Qisse Hir te Ranjhe da*, p. 40.
81 Ibid.
82 Ibid., p. 44.
83 Ibid.
84 A.K. Ramanujan, 'Three Hundred Ramayanas: Five Examples and Three
    Thoughts on Translation', in Paula Richman (ed.), *Many Ramayanas:
    The Diversity of a Narrative Tradition in South Asia*, Berkeley: University
    of California Press, 1991, p. 46.

9

C.S. Adcock

Brave Converts in the Arya Samaj

THE CASE OF DHARM PAL

The Arya Samaj was a reaction to the influence of Islam and Christianity, more especially the former... It introduced proselytization into Hinduism and thus tended to come into conflict with other proselytizing religions.

— Jawaharlal Nehru[1]

We, if a Musalmaan was coming along the road, and we shook hands with him, and we had, say, a box of food or something in our hand, that would then become soiled and we would not eat it: if we are holding a dog in one hand and food in the other, there's nothing wrong with that food.

— Recollection of Bir Bahadur Singh[2]

Among the many organizations that pursued reform during the nineteenth century, the Arya Samaj has long been distinguished in historical scholarship as the forerunner of Hindu nationalist politics and exemplar of Hindu religious intolerance.[3] Arya Samaj practices that can be classed as proselytizing lie at the heart of this scholarly assessment: practices of *religious controversy*, which included print polemics and face-to-face debate with contending Hindu, Muslim, Sikh, and Christian organizations; and the *shuddhi* ritual of conversion or 'purification'. It is true that Arya Samaj controversialists were infamous for their unrestrained anti-Muslim polemics; and Arya Samajists worked alongside members of the Hindu nationalist organization, the Hindu Mahasabha, during the expanded Shuddhi Movement of the 1920s. However, scholars' understandings of the so-called 'proselytizing' activities of the Arya Samaj during the preceding decades have been circumscribed by the framing narrative of *Hindu Tolerance*.

Hindu Tolerance characterizes proselytizing religiosity as necessarily intolerant and damaging to religious harmony, by contrast with a putative flexible, accommodating and syncretic style of religiosity that is sometimes described as more characteristic of the subcontinent.[4] Hindu Tolerance has been widely influential in scholarship on religion, where it continues to inform scholars' evaluative judgments of types of religious expression in South Asia despite suggestions that the distinction between 'syncretic' and 'dogmatic', tolerant and intolerant religiosity cannot withstand scrutiny.[5] Hindu Tolerance also colours the historiography of Indian political culture.[6] According to the Hindu Tolerance narrative, proselytizing contributed to Hindu–Muslim tensions during the late nineteenth and early twentieth centuries, ultimately feeding Hindu nationalist politics: Hindus in the Arya Samaj used shuddhi to target non-Hindus for conversion; their proselytizing efforts polarized religious identities and fuelled communal competition and conflict.

One shortcoming of the Hindu Tolerance narrative is that it focuses on the motives or intentions of the proselytizers—in this case, caste Hindu elites in the Arya Samaj—to the point of virtually excluding from consideration the aims of those who chose to accept shuddhi or who actively pursued conversion. That prospective converts often did play an active role is now clear: it was not Christian missionaries, for example, but Dalits or so-called 'untouchables' who initiated the 'mass conversion' movements in Punjab that catalyzed Arya Samaj shuddhi efforts after 1900.[7] Similarly, far from passive recipients of upper-caste reform efforts, in Punjab both ritually low-caste Jats, and Chamars and other 'untouchable' castes selectively appropriated elements of Arya Samaj teachings—or rejected them—as it suited their objectives of social status and equality.[8] Building on this attention to a wider

Arya Samaj membership, this essay considers proselytizing from the point of view of members of the Arya Samaj who were born Muslim. It will focus, in particular, on the Arya Samaj controversialist and former Muslim, Dharm Pal, who pursued shuddhi as a step toward radical caste reform.

Dharm Pal was associated with the Arya Samaj during the first decade of the twentieth century, but scholarly understandings of Arya Samaj proselytizing are inextricable from the surrounding decades: the Hindu Tolerance perspective on conversion became prevalent in the 1920s, and it colours perspectives on religious polemics of the nineteenth century. The essay therefore begins in the 1920s and travels back to the 1880s and 1890s before turning to Dharm Pal's time in the Arya Samaj. When shuddhi is viewed from the perspective of those who pursued conversion, its subversive potential becomes visible. Dharm Pal appropriated the proselytizing mission of the Arya Samaj in service of a radical critique of the caste practices or *chūt* that subordinated the lowest classes of north Indian society.

***

Although the first Arya Samaj was founded in Bombay in 1875, the organization took root in the western districts of the United Provinces (UP) and in Punjab. Scholars have often noted the peculiar religious diversity of Punjab as a factor in the Arya Samaj's popularity in that province: British census figures show a Muslim majority in the province as a whole, but with sizeable Hindu and Sikh minorities, and active Christian missionary activity. A less noted feature of diversity in Punjab is the high proportion of castes deemed 'untouchable'. If in 1901 Arya Samaj membership consisted overwhelmingly of Hindu upper-castes, by 1911 the Punjab membership had quadrupled, and the census estimated that as many as two-thirds of the Arya Samajists of Punjab hailed from the lowest castes.[9] These lowest castes included groups counted as Muslim, Christian, Sikh, or Hindu; the former religious affiliation of Arya Samajists of untouchable caste background was not generally recorded. Additionally, as Dharm Pal observed, caste Hindus in Punjab observed varying degrees of 'untouchability' or *chūt* toward not only the lowest castes, but also Muslims and Christians.

Although Dharm Pal was converted in Punjab and based in Lahore, this essay includes the United Provinces in its scope. Arya Samaj controversialists—professional or volunteer speakers and champions of debate—circulated between Punjab and western UP, as did many of their opponents in debate. This was particularly the case with the Gurukul Party within the Arya Samaj with which Dharm Pal was associated. Several Gurukul Party leaders are important to his story: Pt Lekh Ram, Swami Shraddhanand, Swami Darshananand, and Pt Bhoj Datt. After the death of Arya Samaj founder Swami Dayanand Saraswati in 1883, significant differences of opinion caused a rift in the Punjab Arya Samaj. When the Arya Samaj split into two 'parties' in 1893, Pt Lekh Ram and Swami Shraddhanand headed the Gurukul Party, so named after the school established by Swami Shraddhanand at Kangri, outside Hardwar, UP in 1901.[10] Swami Shraddhanand and Swami Darshananand were responsible for bringing the Gurukul Party's emphasis on the universal dissemination of the Vedas (*ved prachār*) from Punjab to UP, where it was dominant by 1896. Swami Darshananand was born in Punjab, but was an important figure in Arya Samaj circles in UP until his death in 1913.[11] He carried on the tradition of controversial engagement with Islam established in Punjab by Pt Lekh Ram in UP, as did the infamous Pt Bhoj Datt, who was based in Agra. Dharm Pal—formerly Abdul Ghafur—underwent shuddhi in 1903 at Gujranwala, Punjab during the first years of Arya Samaj conversion or uplift of Muslims and untouchables. Dharm Pal reiterated many of the Arya Samaj polemic attacks against Islam and the Quran, drawing Muslims' protest as had infamous Arya Samajists (and upper caste Hindus) like Pt Lekh Ram before him. During his seven years in the Arya Samaj, Dharm Pal extolled shuddhi as a step toward the elimination of caste distinctions and purity rules, even as he challenged Arya Samajists to live up to the ideals of Vedic dharma.

HINDU TOLERANCE AND HISTORIOGRAPHY

Mohandas Gandhi promulgated the Hindu Tolerance ideal during the expanded Shuddhi Movement of the 1920s. The Arya Samaj had initiated this campaign to 'reconvert' the Muslim Malkana Rajputs to the religion of their ancestors, but in the political context of the 1920s the Shuddhi Movement received broad support from the representatives of Hindu orthodoxy and from Hindu nationalists in the Hindu Mahasabha. In response, the Indian National Congress endeavoured to quash what it portrayed as the aggressive proselytizing of the Arya Samaj. Gandhi in particular insisted that Hinduism was an essentially tolerant religion that accommodated a diversity of doctrinal positions. Authentic Hindu religiosity, he argued, recognizes that all religions contain a kernel of truth; true Hindu religiosity teaches that all paths lead to the same goal. Given its flexible stance on doctrinal difference, this vision of authentic Hinduism had no place for proselytizing.[12]

Because the shuddhi practices of the Arya Samaj were evidently fed in part by a political concern with augmenting Hindu numbers, it might appear to be imperative to condemn proselytizing. However, Gandhi's invocation of Hindu Tolerance framed shuddhi as a matter of Hindu proselytizing—Hindus targeting Muslims for conversion—and therefore as an expression of intolerance for religious difference. In doing so, it elided the fact that untouchables also resorted to shuddhi, pursuing substantial caste reform by in effect 'converting' to caste Hindu status. Hindu Tolerance had the effect of obscuring caste politics.

Historians have viewed the Arya Samaj shuddhi ritual as a means by which high caste Hindus sought to preserve their privileges, not least by securing the loyalties of low-caste groups.[13] This view has supported historical narratives that trace a direct continuity between the Hindu nationalism promoted since the 1920s by the Rashtriya Swayamsevak Sangh and its family of affiliated organizations, and Arya Samaj proselytizing of the preceding decades. Hindu nationalism was characterized by a preoccupation with Hindu political strength—including numerical strength—vis-à-vis what Hindu nationalists portrayed as their main political rival: the Muslim community. As long as Arya Samaj shuddhi has been understood primarily as a method of competition with Muslims, therefore, the continuity with Hindu nationalist politics has seemed clear.[14] A closer understanding of Arya Samaj shuddhi in the early period makes it possible to revise this established view.

A significant discontinuity between Hindu nationalism and the politics of the early Arya Samaj is evident in their respective solutions to the problem untouchables posed for Hindu unity.[15] In the first decades of the twentieth century, the relationship of untouchables to Hindus was uncertain: were untouchables part of Hindu society, or, as persons deemed beneath the order of castes, were they outside it? Given untouchables' sizeable numbers, this was no idle question. The Hindu nationalist approach to securing untouchables to Hindu society was 'symbolic' in nature: Hindu nationalists held that untouchables should be considered Hindus, and counted as such for political purposes, regardless of their relations with caste Hindus. The symbolic approach to Hindu unity had become dominant in Arya Samaj circles by the close of the 1920s, owing to the combined effects of the extension of separate electorates for Muslims under the constitutional reforms of 1919, and the highly influential Hindu nationalist ideology of Hindutva or 'Hindu-ness', published in 1923. To be sure, the problem of untouchables had first presented itself during the Gait Circular controversy of 1910, when Hindus learned that the British colonial government might begin to count untouchables separately from Hindus in the decennial census.[16] But prior to 1927, a significant number of more 'radical' Arya Samajists rejected the symbolic solution to Hindu unity in favour of substantial reform. Their pursuit of shuddhi cannot be characterized as simply an effort to shore up high caste Hindu interests. By using shuddhi to initiate untouchables into the Vedic rites hitherto reserved for high caste Hindus, they challenged the very distinctions of purity and impurity that organized caste society. Beginning in 1900 and continuing into the 1920s, untouchables and low castes pursued shuddhi as a provocative form of self-assertion, and often met violent opposition by high caste Hindus. Arya Samaj shuddhi among untouchables was more complex than simply adding to Hindu numbers for political gain; in the field of caste reform, what has been classed as Arya Samaj proselytizing had a radical edge.

When Congress polemicists invoked Hindu Tolerance during the Shuddhi Movement, they portrayed the Indian National Congress as an organization that continued a pre-colonial tradition of religious synthesis and tolerance, serving the interests of all Indians. At the

same time, Hindu Tolerance cast proselytizing as uniquely conducive to Hindu politics. But the Congress' position was not so distant
from Hindu nationalists' 'symbolic' approach to Hindu unity: as
would become evident in the 1930s, Gandhi held the position that
untouchables should be considered Hindus, and staunchly opposed
schemes for enumerating them otherwise for political purposes.[17]
During the 1920s, Hindu Tolerance enabled Gandhi to oppose all
shuddhi activities without qualification by directing attention away
from caste politics to Hindu–Muslim relations, away from the prospective convert to the intentions of the 'proselytizer'. One lasting
legacy of the Hindu tolerance frame on historiography has been to
elide issues of caste.

***

Accounts of the transformation in religion in India during the
colonial period resonate distinctly with the Hindu Tolerance narrative that Congress leaders put forward. Scholars have traced
continuity between nineteenth century reform organizations like the
Arya Samaj and the Hindu nationalist politics that developed in the
1920s by pointing to a transformation in Indian styles of religiosity brought about by religious controversy. The 'Semiticization of
Hinduism' thesis,[18] for example, holds that Hinduism was transformed by nineteenth century reformers—the example cited is
always the Arya Samaj—who imitated Christian and Islamic styles of
religiosity, particularly proselytizing. Historians argue that reformers
popularized a new conception of religion that emphasized doctrinal truth claims; rivalry over truth claims then gave rise to a rigid,
exclusive form of identification with doctrinal community. In these
accounts, practices of religious debate and proselytizing were both
expressions of this new religiosity, and served to disseminate it. But
the assumption that a dogmatic formulation of Hindu religiosity was
linked to Hindu nationalist politics is questionable. Instead it seems
Hindu nationalism was premised on a vague definition of Hinduism
more conducive to the symbolic approach to demarcating a unified
community of Hindus.[19]

The Semiticization of Hinduism thesis has found its way into
seminal works on Hindu nationalism.[20] Variations on this account
also dominate treatments of nineteenth century controversy: the

religious polemics of the nineteenth century are understood to have been an important contributing factor in the polarization of Hindu and Muslim identities.[21] In this view, controversy gave rise to a sense of Hinduism and Islam as distinct and clearly demarcated religious systems, even in the many cases when Hindu and Muslim did not confront each other directly in the debate arena. But in drawing a contrast between proselytizing and forms of religiosity that supposedly came before, the Hindu Tolerance perspective exaggerates the importance of doctrine and the rigidity of identity in the culture of public debate.

The Arya Samaj gained popularity during the last decades of the nineteenth century in the context of a dynamic culture of controversy. Controversialists toured the countryside lecturing and answering rivals, and staked out positions in bazaars, railway stations, and at pilgrimage centres, sometimes kitty-corner from their opponents. In cities such as Lahore and Delhi, performances by controversialists drew large audiences to town halls and other public venues, to temples and to private homes. Gail Minault's observation about Lahore of the 1870s and 1880s—that debate between Christian missionaries and Muslim 'ulama 'was obviously the most exciting game in town'—applies equally to the more diverse debate culture of the ensuing decades.[22] Controversy was an exciting form of entertainment that showcased orators' skills in argument, language play and mocking humour.

In the 1880s and 1890s, controversialists were connected to Christian missions, Sikh, Jain, and Hindu organizations. Muslims of the reformist Madrassah at Deoband specialized in controversy with non-Muslims and with Muslims associated with the Aligarh, Ahl-e-Sunnat (Barelwi), and Ahl-i-Hadith schools of Islam, each of which also debated Arya Samajists and Christians. By 1890, the Ahmadiyyas, a new Islamic sect focused on the person of Mirza Ghulam Ahmad, began to send their own lecturers and debaters into the field to engage with Christian, Muslim, and Arya Samaj opponents. Controversialists professing to defend Hindu orthodoxy, including the Sanatan Dharm Sabha among other non-reformist (Pauranik or Sanatanist) Hindus, took on the Arya Samaj and other Hindu reformers.

Scholars have remarked with good reason upon the repetitive, predictable nature of most controversial arguments, and the doctrinal commitments of participating organizations are now well documented. However, doctrinal commitments did not determine the alignments that would result from individual debates: organizations could be allied as well as divided by their positions on points of doctrine, ritual practice or textual authority. Flexibility in the boundaries between 'communities of doctrine' allowed for alliances and alignments that the Hindu Tolerance narrative omits.

A formal debate (*shāstrārth*) between controversialists of the Sanatan Dharm Sabha and the Arya Samaj held at Kirana, Muzaffarnagar District, UP in 1893 on the subject of image-worship (*mūrtipūjā*) illustrates this possibility.[23] The doctrinal stances of the two organizations were clear: the Sanatan Dharm side supported image-worship, while the Arya Samaj rejected it. Since Arya Samajists did not accept later Sanskrit texts, particularly the Puranas, as authoritative, when setting the terms of the debate the Sanatan Dharm side had been forced to restrict their textual proofs for idol-worship only to the four Vedic *samhita*s. When this caused them difficulties in the course of the debate, the Sanatan Dharm speaker turned to Muslims in the audience for support, saying, 'if some person accepting fifteen *sipār*s of the Holy Quran were to say, prove something or other from this much only, then what remedy is there? In this way these people accept only the samhita, one part of the Vedas, and say from this much only prove mūrtipūjā.' Towards the end of the debate, the Arya Samaj account reported, many in the audience stood up crying out victory for the Sanatan Dharm party; and 'while rising some Pauraniks caused one common Muslim to say, "In my understanding the Arya Pandit is talking like the Naturiyyas, and the Hindus like we members of Islam."' The Naturiyyas, the followers of Sayyid Ahmad Khan, were held by many Muslims of north India to have deviated radically from the path of Islam by subjecting the Quran to an erroneous interpretation, putting human reason before revelation.

Arya Samajists went to great lengths to refute the comparison, as their publication of this pamphlet in the aftermath of the debate testifies. The pamphlet proclaimed that 'in the end many famous *rais*

Muslims put their signatures in connection with the strength of the Aryas' side', and that 'to oppose the one Muslim who compared the Aryas to the Naturis and the Hindus to the Muslims, many Muslim Raises and Maulvis proved the victory of the Aryas' by written testimony. Indeed, the Arya Samaj pamphlet reproduced the testimony of seven Muslims following the text of the debate, to vindicate the Arya Samaj from this damaging comparison to Sayyid Ahmad Khan.

This example illustrates the complex array of alignments, including inter-sectarian concerns with the relative weight of reason and revelation, tradition and innovation, as well as social factors of class and status (common and rais noble) that could be brought into play in controversial encounters. These shaped an array of commitments and did not merely reinforce fixed oppositions between doctrinal communities, or between polarized Hindu and Muslim identities. Instead, they provided a repertoire of positions of contention and agreement from which controversialists could draw to suit their audiences and their strategic aims.

Religious controversy and proselytizing have also been described to have contributed to an exclusive, 'either/or' form of religious identification. Evidence of repeated conversions to and from the Arya Samaj confirms this characterization, since it involved individuals changing their affiliations, and not only their private observances. But at the same time, stress on 'either/or' identities can obscure the degree to which converts accumulated multiple identities, or held commitments that transsected the boundaries of controversial organizations. By its focus on 'proselytizer' more than 'proselytized', it hampers recognition of the fluidity of identities—conversions and reconversions—that the culture of debate engendered. For example, many of the most outspoken Arya Samajists to engage in polemics against Islam were former Muslims. If scholars have been content to treat them simply as (intolerant) Hindus, in the context of controversy their former affiliations remained clearly in view, shading their identities as members of the Arya Samaj.

After leaving the Arya Samaj and returning to Islam, Dharm Pal would take the name Ghazi Mahmud, but would continue to be known as Ghazi Mahmud Dharm Pal.[24] Formerly Muslim Arya Samajists who have attracted the attention of scholars for their harsh polemics include Satya Deo (whose tract *Afshai Raz* was the occasion for protest meetings of Muslims in Delhi in 1911) and Dharm Bir (whose lecture against the Quran became the occasion for an important lawsuit in 1915).[25] Brief details concerning the changing affiliations— conversions and reconversions—of Arya Samajists were recorded by the Criminal Intelligence Department during the 1920s, when the Shuddhi Movement among the Malkana Rajputs was at its height and the governments of UP and Punjab were intent on controlling the movements of controversialists. Ghazi Mahmud–Dharm Pal attracted official attention for his polemics against the Arya Samaj in this decade.[26] The CID for UP took note of a number of converts from Islam lecturing on behalf of the Arya Samaj who apparently did not reconvert: Shanti Sarup, Pt Vidya Dhar, Gyan Indar Deo, Dharm Chand, Dharm Raj Singh, and Dharm Sewak.[27] CID records also document a number of former Muslim converts to the Arya Samaj who were speaking and publishing against the Arya Samaj in this decade: Zulfiqar Haidar *alias* Ved Prakash of Balliah, Ghazi Akhtar ul Islam, a former Arya Samajist of Delhi, and Baba Khalil Das, who converted to Islam in 1925.[28] Pt Bahadur Singh, who took the name Muhammad Ahmad when he converted to Islam in 1925, had been described in 1915 as a strident Arya Samajist closely associated with Pt Bhoj Datt.[29] Chandra Prakash, formerly Abdur Rahman of Hardoi, spoke on behalf of the Arya Samaj in 1924–5, then reverted to Islam, only to quickly return to the Arya Samaj in 1925.[30]

How did Muslim converts perceive shuddhi? We know that the use of shuddhi among untouchables carried a radical potential in the first decades of its use, before the 'symbolic' approach to Hindu unity grew dominant in the 1920s. Evidence of Muslim converts to the Arya Samaj before the 1920s is more scarce. We know that in 1911, three Muslim converts left the Arya Samaj to return to Islam: Dharmvir, Satya Deo, and Dharm Pal.[31] But detailed information about individual Muslim converts is hard to come by. Because he was both a prolific controversialist and the focus of much discussion among Muslims and Arya Samajists, Dharm Pal's case is exceptionally well documented.

Dharm Pal underwent shuddhi in 1903, and renounced the Arya Samaj in 1911 after seven years as an ardent controversialist.

This means that he converted after the Gurukul Party of the Arya Samaj had extended the use of shuddhi to untouchables in 1900, and before two milestone events in the politicization of religious identity: the Government of India Act of 1909 which introduced separate electorates for Muslims, giving new structure to political competition between Hindu and Muslim; and the Gait Circular of 1910, which raised the question of whether untouchables would continue to be counted as Hindus.[32]

DHARM PAL, ARYA SAMAJ CONTROVERSIALIST

Dharm Pal, formerly Abdul Ghafur, was one of the most famous Muslim converts to the Arya Samaj. Arya Samaj sources recall that Dharm Pal was a particularly valued convert, because 'such a highly educated Musalman had never entered into the Arya Samaj'.[33] At the time of his conversion, Arya Samajists described him as a Muslim graduate who had been employed as headmaster of an Islamic school. Dharm Pal quickly emerged as a prominent controversialist, engaging in polemics against Islamic organizations in pamphlets and in the two newspapers he edited. As a result, during his seven years in the Arya Samaj, Dharm Pal was the target of polemic attacks by Muslim controversialists who sought to diminish his influence by disparaging his qualifications to speak knowledgeably about Islam. His return to Islam in 1911 was therefore a dramatic event that required significant damage control on the part of the Arya Samaj leadership; Swami Shraddhanand himself turned his pen to this effort.

Within a year of his conversion, Dharm Pal was immersed in controversy with some of the most outspoken and determined Muslim critics of the Arya Samaj. His first publication, *Tark Islam* (*The Logic of Islam*), which purported to be a record of the speech he gave at the time of his conversion, will be the focus of this discussion. He published a second polemic text in the same year, *Tahzib ul Islam* (*The Refinement of Islam*), by way of reply to two prominent Muslim polemicists against the Arya Samaj:[34] Nur-ud-din, a prominent Ahmadiyya Muslim; and Maulvi Sana-ullah of Amritsar, a member of the Ahl-i-Hadith who had written a damaging critique of Swami Dayanand's criticism of Islam, and who was frequently engaged in controversy with Bhoj Datt's newspaper, the *Musafir*.[35] Dharm Pal would continue this controversial engagement in the pages of his journals, the *Arjun* and the *Indar* of Lahore, until 1911. He and another Arya Samaj convert from Islam, Sham Lal, mocked the passionate character of the Prophet Muhammad, jeered about the spirit of *jihad* in Islam, and described the oppressions of Muslim rule under Aurangzeb in the pages of the *Arjun*.[36]

Dharm Pal's polemics reiterated established Arya Samaj positions on points of doctrinal disagreement with Islam. The bulk of *Tark Islam* was taken up by a list of mocking or humorous criticisms of what Dharm Pal described as the 'teachings of the Quran' that cited Quranic verses and derived absurd, outrageous, and immoral meanings from them. These criticisms were made in service of the basic Arya Samaj position that the Quran was not a divinely revealed text.[37] Arya Samajists did not recognize Muhammad as Prophet; adopting Islamic terminology, they rejected this position as *shirk*, or associating another with God. They often rejected the Quran as a text fabricated by Muhammad for selfish purposes—echoing their rejection of the Hindu Puranas as the fabrications of selfish and greedy Brahman 'popes'. In *Tark Islam*, Dharm Pal reiterated these Arya Samaj polemics. Like other Arya Samajists who engaged in polemics against Islam, Dharm Pal gave extraordinary emphasis to *tauhid*, the unity of God, and to the condemnation of shirk, the association of another with God.[38]

Dharm Pal followed established Arya Samaj polemic style when he employed the Puranas as the measure of religious error.[39] Dharm Pal compared the foolishness of the Quran and of Muslim maulvis to that of the Puranas and '*Pauranik*' pandits. Wrote Dharm Pal, 'the Quran teaches that Lord Christ revived the dead… then if a *maulvi sāhab* says that the teaching of the Quran is in accord with the laws of nature, why shouldn't I reject him. Here is an even greater *lilā* than in the Puranas'; 'how could anything be more full of false stories than the Quran or the Puranas?'[40] And he measured the teachings of the Quran against the central tenets of Arya Samaj moral practice as understood by the Gurukul Party, namely *brahmacharya* (chastity) and a vegetarian diet. Elaborating on the conventional Arya Samaj mockery of the supposed Quranic description of heaven as populated by fair youths and beautiful women, Dharm Pal declared, 'a brahmachari considers it a great a sin even to be in the presence of such obscene things. Shame! Shame!'[41] He expanded at length on the importance of a vegetarian diet for morality: 'the Quran's teachings can't in any way make men compassionate, because where there's meat-eating and animal-sacrifice, how can compassion exist?'[42] Scholars have generally viewed Muslim converts like Dharm Pal as paid spokesmen who parroted the Arya Samaj party line; and it is true that the polemic Dharm Pal unfurled in *Tark Islam* was largely unoriginal. But Dharm Pal did more than replicate well-worn Arya Samaj positions; he also propounded a radical interpretation of the Arya Samaj teaching of universalism.

Dharm Pal's radical universalism may have been inspired by his own caste background, though this is difficult to ascertain.[43] Muslim controversialists derided the low caste status of Dharm Pal and other Muslim converts to the Arya Samaj. Inasmuch as the Muslim *ashraf* viewed birth and Islamic learning as linked, such criticisms were closely tied to the denunciation of the authority of these individuals to speak for Islamic teachings. In addition to accusing Dharm Pal of having joined the Arya Samaj to feed his passions rather than out of religious conviction,[44] they cast doubt on his educational credentials and his character, and challenged him to sit for an examination that would test his claims to Islamic learning.[45] But he was also said to 'bark and indulge in nonsensical yapping like a blind dog', and was described as a 'renegade weaver', implying that he was born to a caste of weavers, generally considered of low birth.[46] Muslim controversialists denounced Satya Deo, another Muslim convert to the Arya Samaj who would become Dharm Pal's companion, in similar terms. Although Satya Deo claimed Sayyid origin,[47] they derided him as an untouchable *Chamar*—a caste associated with leather-working—and mocked his polemic tract, 'The New Quran', saying 'the stench of hides... seems to have fouled his brain' so that 'filthy words' issue from his lips.[48] Another paper commented on Muslim converts to the Arya Samaj collectively, saying, 'poor and hungry [low caste] Dhunias and Jolahas readily accept the Arya faith to eke out their livelihood'.[49] To be sure, such charges of low birth were a common controversialist strategy, used by Sanatan Dharm Hindus against the Arya Samaj, and used by Arya Samajists, too, during the 1920s in a like effort to defame the character of Muslim converts who reverted to Islam.[50] In Dharm Pal's case there may have been more to this charge. Whether or not Dharm Pal came from a low caste background as his critics alleged, he repeatedly advocated that caste distinctions of impurity be eliminated, including untouchability.

This is evidenced in Dharm Pal's response to the Gait Circular controversy. Dharm Pal upheld the ideal of caste reform espoused by radical reformers within the Gurukul Party, and condemned the 'symbolic' approach to Hindu unity. In 1911, some Arya Samaj papers praised what they portrayed as the transformative effect of Arya Samaj teachings on the attitudes of Hindu orthodoxy, citing 'the attitude of the Pundits of Benares and other Sanatan Dharm Sabhas towards the untouchable in the recent Gait Circular controversy'. Giving voice to a symbolic approach to Hindu reform, they celebrated the fact that Hindu society has now 'declared it in bold and unambiguous terms that the Depressed Classes are part and parcel of the Hindu body politic'.[51] Dharm Pal reportedly condemned this merely symbolic approach to Hindu unity in favour of a radical reform that would eliminate the distinctions of caste, commenting 'that it is not fair on the part of Hindus to include the depressed classes in their category for political purposes only when they have no social connection with them'[52] and advocating that 'the leaders of the Hindu community should assemble at some place and dine with the depressed classes with the object of raising their status'.[53]

Dharm Pal praised shuddhi and the universalist ideal of the Gurukul Party as a step towards the elimination of caste distinctions. As recorded in *Tark Islam*, Dharm Pal's first remarks at the time of his conversion praised the universalism the Arya Samaj had shown in disregarding the conventional boundaries of twice-born Hindu society to admit him. These boundaries were marked by purity rules that excluded those born as untouchables or as Muslims from caste Hindu society. Dharm Pal says,

The pure teaching of the Vedas has given rise to such a society, and such men, who truly understand that truth is one! Fifty years before today, the feet of a born-Muslim man would have been thought to pollute this temple and this platform. But the situation today is different. The teachings of the

Vedas have demonstrated that just as a born Brahman of good conduct has the right to publish the Vedic mantras and their truth before all ordinary people, likewise even a born Muslim of good conduct can stand in this temple on this platform, having received the true knowledge of the Vedas, and cause his voice to reach the ears of many seekers after Vedic knowledge. Without doubt just as the light of the pure teaching of the Vedas will be spread, just so will barbarism and darkness be removed.[54]

Dharm Pal thus praised the universalist reform of the Arya Samaj that premised the right to learn and teach Vedic dharma on merit, rather than birth—of which his own shuddhi was an example. He criticized Muslims on the same universalist grounds, decrying Islam for purportedly labeling non-Muslims kafirs and idolaters (*musharik*), considering them impure, and teaching Muslims to stay away from them. This, he said, 'has struck a blow at the root of all Islam's teachings about unity or equality (*mel*)'.[55] The publication of such statements in the pages of *Tark Islam* could be interpreted as no more than a restatement of the Gurukul Party's position of Vedic universalism; but in the coming years, Dharm Pal would go further: he would challenge Arya Samaj leaders to live up to this radically universalist ideal.

It is easy to forget that Arya Samaj use of shuddhi to 'purify' Muslims was, from the point of view of caste Hindu society, as radical as was the use of shuddhi to uplift untouchables. In 1910 and 1911, several Muslim papers of Punjab would protest the contempt Hindus showed Muslims in treating them as polluting. They rejected Hindus' defence that the 'Hindu institution of *chūt*... is based on medical considerations and it is foolish to impart a religious colour to the same', and denounced chūt as 'rude and humiliating, an insult to the entire Muhammadan community'. They protested that an object 'touched by the filthiest thread-wearer, needs only be cleansed with earth' when things touched by a Muslim must be cleansed by fire.[56] Several decades later, one Partition survivor would see fit to ascribe the Partition of India to the practice: 'We don't have such dealings with our lower castes as Hindus and Sikhs did with the Musalmans'.[57] Arya Samaj contravention of these caste practices was no small step, and Sanatanist leaders denounced Arya Samajists' disrespect for caste purity. A prominent Sanatan Dharmist of Punjab, Gopinath, insisted that 'Sanatanists would never tolerate... elevation of Muhammadans to the status of brahmacharyas'.[58] In response to shuddhi initiatives in UP in 1909 several Sanatanist newspapers called on Hindus to out-caste Arya Samajists who sought to inter-dine or inter-marry with Christian and Muslim converts.[59]

Dharm Pal expressed great optimism about the work the Arya Samaj was doing to eliminate the distinctions of caste. In a lecture at Lahore in 1906 he is reported to have boasted that 'he had received letters from hundreds of Musalmans and Christians in which they expressed their willingness to enter the Arya Samaj', provided Arya Samajists showed their readiness to admit them into caste.[60] Speaking of the religious awakening which the Arya Samaj was affecting among Hindus by 'starting to break down the barriers of caste', the *Arjun* declared in 1910 that 'the day Hindus open the gates of their society to Muhammadans, the latter... will rush in in immense numbers' and that the 'future religion of the country will consist of the faith professed by the seven crores of untouchables who are being trampled by the Hindus. Islam is not in the running'; the 'religious salvation of India lies between Christ and Dayanand'.[61] Dharm Pal maintained his optimism about shuddhi even while he was criticizing Arya Samajists.

By the end of 1909, Dharm Pal was already at the centre of a commotion in the Gurukul Party.[62] Dharm Pal was publishing what leading Arya Samajists perceived to be troublesome criticisms of Arya Samaj leadership including Swami Shraddhanand and the Arya Pratinidhi Sabha, of Swami Dayanand and the *Satyarth Prakash*. By April of 1910, Arya Samaj attempts at damage control had begun: Arya Samajist Lachman Das published a book attempting to defame him, *Dharmpal ki khud kushi* (The Suicide of Dharmpal).[63] Nonetheless, in June of 1911, a month before he would leave the Arya Samaj, Dharm Pal was still enjoining Arya Samajists to 'devote themselves, heart and soul, to the dissemination of the Vedas'.[64] Hence Arya Samaj papers' protests: he 'writes against the Arya Samaj, but poses as a member of that body'.[65]

Dharm Pal continued to hold the conduct of Arya Samajists up to the model of Swami Dayanand's teachings until his departure. Dharm Pal's article, 'Fight for Liberty in the Arya Samaj' published in January 1911 was written in the midst of what was apparently a struggle over continued practices of caste inequality within the Arya Samaj. Dharm Pal extolled Swami Dayanand's effort to emancipate untouchable castes from their position of subordination to the upper castes, and he praised Arya Samajists for extending the invitation to non-Hindus to adopt Vedic dharma. But he condemned the continued prevalence of caste practices within the Arya Samaj, adopting the language of Arya Samaj criticism of Pauranik Hindu Brahmans ('popes') to do so. When some Muslims and Christians accepted Arya Samajists' invitation to undergo shuddhi, Dharm Pal wrote, 'they found chains of slavery waiting for them'. Those 'brave Muhammadan and Christian converts' who 'did not consent to put themselves into "priestly" chains' within the Arya Samaj 'stepped boldly forward and there ensued a religious and social struggle between them and the "popes" of the Samaj'.[66]

At the same time, however, Dharm Pal embedded his vision of Vedic universalism within an anti-caste discourse that drew language from several so-called 'doctrinal communities'. Dharm Pal's anti-caste polemics drew upon the languages of low-caste movements and Christianity, and echoed the polemics of Ahmadiyya Muslims. In the course of the controversy within the Arya Samaj just described, Dharm Pal commented that 'when the ancient Aryas were divested of their ruling powers they had established a social kingdom and reduced 10 crores of women and 6 crores of sweepers, chamars, etc. to the position of slaves'. He thereby invoked a historical narrative of caste oppression that is more usually associated with the ideologies of non-Brahman and untouchable movements. Moreover, this narrative inverted Arya Samaj histories, according to which the ancient Aryas were 'noble' people (not a racial group) who adhered to the true Vedic teachings of caste as a merit-based ranking in which untouchability held no place. Ahmadiyya controversialists were ready to appropriate such low caste narratives for the purpose of attacking the Arya Samaj. One Ahmadiyya paper argued that

[s]ince the *Aryas* came here from Central Asia several thousand years back, moral, spiritual and social evils have been rampant in the land, which was previously immune from the same. The *Aryas* destroyed the nationality, religion and traditions of the aborigines of India, set the latter down as

Shudras and deprived them even of their birthrights and their privileges as human beings...[67]

The paper went on to describe the Vedas as the 'fountain-head of tyranny and oppression'.[68] When rejecting the continued oppression of Muslim and Christian converts within the Arya Samaj, Dharm Pal also echoed the Christian Bible: 'these brave converts can never consent to work as hewers of wood and drawers of water, nay, they will breathe a spirit of social liberty even to the "slaves" of Hindus (women and the untouchables)'.[69] The protests of Bhoj Datt some months later suggest that Dharm Pal continued to disregard the boundaries of controversialist organizations: Bhoj Datt painted Dharm Pal as someone 'who not only propagates the doctrines of Christianity but openly accuses and shamelessly criticizes the conduct of Arya saints and their much respected *rishis* simply to defend Christ'.[70] The language of Dharm Pal's anti-caste polemics transsected the boundaries of Arya Samaj, Islam, and Christianity.

There is some evidence that Dharm Pal's anti-caste discourse gained him a following within the Arya Samaj. This is suggested by Bhoj Datt's lament: 'The case of some Aryas who have entirely lost themselves in human worship is certainly much to be regretted, as they have given their money, earned with the sweat of their brow, for this man... Alas ! how regrettable it is indeed that... he is... making disreputable allegations against the Arya saints and the respected *rishis*, with the help of the Aryas themselves'. Several months before Dharm Pal was to leave the Arya Samaj, Bhoj Datt's paper warned: 'selfish persons will get into your society simply to break up at a blow your united power'; 'listen to the advice of the *Musafir*. Remove from your necks the polluted hands of your treacherous friends'.[71]

Dharm Pal maintained his condemnation of caste prejudice in his replies to these attacks by the Arya Samaj leadership. Deriding Pt Bhoj Datt's underhanded tactics in controversy with Muslims, he remarked, 'it was once suggested by the *Musafir* that the non-Hindus "purified" into the Vedic fold should receive lessons... But how can those, who themselves tell lies, practice deception, and commit forgery, act as teachers of others?', posing the ironic question 'why Pt Bhoj Dat, whose habits were not impure and "Muhammadan"' should have shown such behaviour.[72] Dharm Pal condemned Arya Samajists for imputing baseness of character to those born outside high-caste Hindu society—low castes, untouchables, and other non-Hindus—in their efforts to contain the challenge Dharm Pal and his supporters posed. Dharm Pal criticized the efforts of 'those conservative "popes" within the Samaj' who 'stooped to the dodge that the gate to the spring [of Vedic dharma] should be closed upon the *mleccha*s for the following reasons: 1) that Muhammadans and Christians being given to very evil deeds injure the Samaj after entering it; 2) that as non-Hindu converts to the Arya religion are assigned a position which they do not deserve they lose their heads'.[73] It is evident from Dharm Pal's criticisms that caste prejudices were indeed prevalent within the Arya Samaj. But for seven years before leaving the organization, Dharm Pal appropriated the Gurukul Party's Vedic universalism for the purposes of a radical critique of caste, employing the languages of Vedic dharma, of Christianity, and of low-caste movements in his effort to chastise Arya Samajists who clung to caste prejudice—while presumably encouraging his supporters and fellow converts.

Although Dharm Pal's polemics reiterated established Arya Samaj doctrinal positions, to understand them simply as intolerant 'Hindu' attacks on 'Islam' is to miss the struggle in which Dharm Pal was engaged. Above and beyond any identification with Hindus, and without regard to the doctrinal boundaries of the Arya Samaj, Dharm Pal upheld a commitment to the radical reform of caste.

From the perspective of this 'born Muslim' member of the Arya Samaj, shuddhi was one element of a challenge to the distinctions of purity and impurity organizing caste society; for Dharm Pal, shuddhi of Muslim and Christian non-Hindus carried a radical potential comparable to the shuddhi of untouchables. To be sure, even before the 1920s many members of the Arya Samaj supported a politics of Hindu unity, and expressed concerns over Hindus' political strength. Arya Samajists advocated the 'symbolic' approach to securing untouchables for the enumerated community of Hindus, and the reconversion of Muslims and Christians to shore up Hindu numbers. But to class Arya Samaj shuddhi as 'Hindu proselytizing' does not capture the complexities of this story. The framing narrative of

Hindu Tolerance discourages attention to the perspectives of those who pursued shuddhi, and obscures the place of shuddhi in a politics of caste reform.

NOTES

1 Jawaharlal Nehru, *The Discovery of India,* New Delhi: Jawaharlal Nehru Memorial Fund, 1999, pp. 335–6.

2 Recollection of Bir Bahadur Singh, formerly of Thoa Khalsa Village, district Rawalpindi, Punjab about Hindus and Sikhs observing *chūt,* untouchability towards Muslims in Punjab before Partition. Recorded by Urvashi Butalia, *The Other Side of Silence: Voices from the Partition of India,* New Delhi: Penguin Books, 1998, pp. 221–2.

3 See especially the works of Christophe Jaffrelot; find a summary of his argument in the introduction to his *Hindu Nationalism: A Reader,* Princeton: Princeton University Press, 2007. See also Kenneth W. Jones, 'Communalism in the Punjab: The Arya Samaj Contribution', *Journal of Asian Studies,* 28 (1), November 1968, pp. 39–54.

4 See, for example, Romila Thapar, 'Imagined Religious Communities? Ancient History and the Modern Search for a Hindu Identity', *Modern Asian Studies,* 23 (2), 1989, pp. 209–31, and 'Syndicated Hinduism', in Gunther-Dietz Sontheimer and Hermann Kulke (eds), *Hinduism Reconsidered,* New Delhi: Manohar, 1997; and Robert E. Frykenberg, 'The Emergence of Modern "Hinduism" as a Concept and as an Institution: A Reappraisal with Special Reference to South India', in *Hinduism Reconsidered,* pp. 82–107.

5 Scholars are inclined to favour what they represent to be 'syncretic' forms of Hindu religiosity (one favourite is the poet-saint Kabir, who criticized Hindu pandits and Muslim maulvis equally) and to celebrate Sufi forms of Islam as purportedly more tolerant, plural, and indigenous. By contrast, they portray Islamic reformism as almost 'a mirror image of Hindu fundamentalism: polarizing identities and disrupting inclusiveness and religious toleration.' Filippo Osella and Caroline Osella, 'Introduction: Islamic Reformism in South Asia', *Modern South Asia,* 42 (2–3), 2008, p. 249. See also Peter Van der Veer, 'Syncretism, Multiculturalism and the Discourse of Tolerance', in Charles Stewart and Rosalind Shaw (eds), *Syncretism/Anti-Syncretism: The Politics of Religious Synthesis,* London, Routledge, 1994, pp. 196–211.

6 Neeladri Bhattacharya reflects on how historians' search for 'syncretism and tolerance' in the Indian past has limited historical understanding

in his 'Predicaments of Secular History', *Public Culture*, vol. 20, 2008, pp. 57–73.

7 John C. B. Webster, *A History of the Dalit Christians in India* San Francisco: Mellen Research University Press, 1992), chap. 2. The term 'untouchable' most accurately denotes an upper-caste attitude. I use the term to refer to those who suffer from this attitude so as to keep the practices of social prejudice clearly in view.

8 Nonica Datta, *Forming an Identity: A Social History of the Jats*, New Delhi: Oxford University Press, 1999; Mark Juergensmeyer, *Religion as Social Vision: The Movement against Untouchability in 20th Century Punjab*, Berkeley: University of California Press, 1982.

9 It included large numbers of Rahtias, Meghs, Ods, and Chamars: as many as three-fifths of the population of Meghs and half of the Ods in some districts of Punjab identified as Aryas in 1911. *Census of India*, 1911, 1 (1), Calcutta: Superintendent of Government Printing, 1912, pp. 123–4. The trend continued to 1921. *Census of India*, 1921, vol. 15 Punjab and Delhi, part 1, Calcutta: Superintendent Government Printing, 1922, p. 181.

10 The Dayanand Anglo-Vedic College Party of Punjab would remain separate from the Gurukul Party and from the Sarvadeshik Arya Pratinidhi Sabha, the central Arya Samaj representative organization. Satyaketu Vidyālankār, Haridatt Vedālankār, tathā Bhavānīlāl Bhāratiya, *Ārya Samāj kā itihās*, vol. 2 Nayī Dilli: Ārya Svādhyāya Kendra, 1984, p. 219.

11 Bhavānīlāl Bhāratiya, *Ārya Samāj ke bīs balidāni*, Dillī: Vijayakumāra Govindarāma Hāsānanda, 2007, pp. 44, 48.

12 Mohandas Gandhi, 'Hindu-Muslim Tension: Its Cause and Cure', in *Young India, 1924–1927*, New York: Viking Press, 1927, pp. 21–60.

13 Christophe Jaffrelot, 'The Genesis and Development of Hindu Nationalism in the Punjab: from the Arya Samaj to the Hindu Sabha (1875–1910)', *Indo-British Review*, 21 (1) (1995), pp. 3–39; also Harald Fischer-Tiné, '"Kindly Elders of the Hindu Biradri": The Ārya Samāj's Struggle for Influence and its Effect on Hindu-Muslim Relations, 1880–1925', in Antony Copley (ed.), *Gurus and their Followers: New Religious Reform Movements in Colonial India*, New Delhi: Oxford University Press, 2000, pp. 107–27.

14 Jaffrelot, 'Genesis'; Fischer-Tiné, 'Kindly Elders', pp.111–14.

15 John Zavos, *The Emergence of Hindu Nationalism in India*, New Delhi: Oxford University Press, 2000.

16 Kenneth W. Jones, 'Religious Identity and the Indian Census', in N. Gerald Barrier (ed.), *The Census in British India: New Perspectives*, New Delhi: Manohar, 1981, pp. 93–4.

17 On the Poona Pact, see William Gould, 'The UP Congress and "Hindu Unity": Untouchables and the Minority Question in the 1930s', *Modern Asian Studies,* 39 (4), 2005, pp. 849–60. For dalits' perspective, see Ramnarayan S. Rawat, 'Making Claims for Power: A New Agenda in Dalit Politics of Uttar Pradesh, 1946–48', *Modern Asian Studies,* 37 (3), 2003, pp. 585–612.

18 For the 'Semiticization of Hinduism' thesis, see Thapar, 'Imagined Religious Communities'; Frykenberg, 'Modern "Hinduism"'.

19 Brian K. Smith, 'Questioning Authority: Constructions and Deconstructions of Hinduism', in J.E. Llewellyn (ed.), *Defining Hinduism: A Reader,* New York: Routledge, 2005, pp.117–18.

20 Thomas Blom Hansen, *The Saffron Wave: Democracy and Hindu Nationalism in Modern India,* Princeton, NJ: Princeton University Press, 1999, pp. 71–2.

21 Barbara Metcalf has aptly summarized the scholarly consensus: Barbara Daly Metcalf, 'Imagining Community: Polemical Debates in Colonial India', in Kenneth W. Jones (ed.), *Religious Controversy in British India: Dialogues in South Asian Languages,* Albany: State University of New York Press, 1992, p. 230. This edited volume provides a useful survey of the environment of controversy.

22 Gail Minault, 'Sayyid Mumtaz 'Ali and Tahzib un-Niswan: Women's Rights in Islam and Women's Journalism in Urdu', in Jones, *Religious Controversy,* p. 183.

23 *Shāstrārth Kirāṇā (zilā, Muzaffarnagar), jo 15 disambar se 19 disambar san 93 ī. tak āryyoṃ tathā hinduoṃ ke madhya huvā,* 1894, Allahabad: Sarasvatīyantrālay, 1894.

24 Dharm Pal proceeded to write polemics against the Arya Samaj together with another former Arya Samajist, Dharm Vir, who was now known as Abdul Kabir (*Musafir* (Agra) 6 July, 1917, *Selections from the Vernacular Press, United Provinces* (henceforth *SVPUP*) 1917, pp. 418–19). He also published a journal, *Al-Muslim.* National Archives of India, New Delhi (hence forth NAI), Home Political B September 1915 no. 205–7, pp. 3–4.

25 Both discussed by G. R. Thursby, *Hindu-Muslim Relations in British India: A Study of Controversy, Conflict, and Communal Movements in Northern India 1923–1928,* Leiden: Brill, 1975.

26 *Police Abstracts of Intelligence,* UP government (hence forth *PAI*), 16 January 1926, no. 2, p. 32; *PAI,* 1923, p. 3; *PAI* 3 October 1925, no. 38, p. 408; *PAI,* 16 January 1926, no. 2, p. 32; *PAI,* 27 February 1926, no. 8, p. 114; *PAI,* 8 May 1926, no. 17, p. 248; *PAI,* 21 April 1928, no. 15, p. 147.

27 *PAI,* 1922–7.

28 *PAI*, 19 June 1926, para. 23, 332; *PAI*, 1927; *PAI*, 1925, 1927.

29 *PAI*, 1925; UP General Administration Department (hence forth UPGAD), file 321, box 293, 1915, 26–7.

30 *PAI*, 13 December 1924, para. 48, p. 416; *PAI*, 25 January 1925, para. 4, p. 46; *PAI*, 18 April 1925, para. 14, p. 164.

31 '*Pulīs ke dvār par andher Svāmi Dayānand ko musalmānon kī gāliyaṇ "satyārthprakāsh ko jalāyā jāve"'. Saddharm Prachārak* (hereafter *SDP*) *Jesht* 31, 1914, 12.

32 Webster finds that the 'politics of numbers' first began to transform conversion in 1909 (Dalit Christians, 73).

33 Ārya Pratinidhi Sabhā, *Pañjāb kā sachitra itihās* (Lahaura: Bhimsen Vidyālankar, 1935), p. 312.

34 Swami Shraddhanand reviewed the book in *SDP* 2 December 1904, p. 290.

35 *SVPUP* 1907–12; *Musafir* (Agra), 6 January 1911 and 15 September 1911, *SVPUP* 1911, 32, p. 867.

36 *Arjun* (Lahore), 28 January, 4 February, 11 February, 18 February, 1910, *Selections from the Vernacular Press, Punjab* (hence forth *SVPP*) 1910, pp. 148, 149, 151–2, 173–4, 177, 198.

37 Darshanānand Saraswati, *Darshanānand Granthamālā*, Calcutta: Govindārām Hāsānand, 1927.

38 Dharma Pāl, *Tark Islām*, Nayī Dilli: Sārvadeshik Ārya Pratinidhi Sabhā, [1904] 1996, p. 7; hereafter *TI*. Swami Darshananand described the Quran as guilty of shirk because it imputed Prophetic status to Muhammad, arguing that to suggest God had need of Prophet or angels was to imply limits to God's omnipotence and unity (*Darshanānand Granthamālā*).

39 Jones, *Arya Dharm*, p. 145.

40 *TI*, pp. 49, 52.

41 *TI*, p. 31.

42 *TI*, pp. 32–3.

43 Arya Samaj shuddhi among Muslims is generally associated with their 'reconversion' of the higher caste Muslim Rajputs, which began in 1907; Dharm Pal's shuddhi predated this initiative by several years. *Riyaz-i-Faiz* (Pilibhit), 4 September 1907, *SVPUP* 1907, p. 1062; see also *Hindosthan* (Kalakankar), 28 January 1907, *SVPUP* 1907, p. 129. *Zia-ul-Islam* (Moradabad), December, 1907, *SVPUP* 1908, p. 27; *Qulqul* (Bijnor) 16 December 1907, *SVPUP* 1908, p. 27; and *Al-Bashir* (Etawah), 31 March 1907, in *SVPUP* 1907 p. 325.

44 Actioned issue of the *Shahna-i-Hind* (Meerut), 16 August 1910, in NAI, Home Political A, March 1917, no. 374–5 & KW, pp. 203–4.

45 *Mujaddad* (Lahore), March 1910, *SVPP* 1910, pp. 350–1.

46 *The Hunter* (Lahore), 7 April 1910, *SVPP* 1910, pp. 351–2; *Mujaddad* (Lahore), March 1910, *SVPP* 1910, pp. 350–1.

47 *The Hunter* (Lahore), 21 May 1910, *SVPP* 1910, p. 467; *Hidayat* (Delhi), 25 May 1910, *SVPP* 1910, p. 489. On the role of controversial practice in assertions of elevated ashraf status, see Justin Jones, 'The Local Experiences of Reformist Islam in a "Muslim" Town in Colonial India: The Case of Amroha', *Modern Asian Studies,* 43 (4), 2009, pp. 871–908.

48 *The Hunter* (Lahore), 21 May 1910, *SVPP* 1910, p. 467.

49 *Shahna-i-Hind* (Meerut), 16 July 1910, *SVPUP* 1910, p. 691.

50 The Criminal Intelligence Department noted of Abul Karim and Hakim Shifa, '[b]oth were formerly Aryas and local Arya Samajists have issued a manifesto warning Hindus against them, declaring them uneducated' and not to be listened to. *PAI*, 11 September 1926, para 35, p. 484.

51 'The Social Outlook', *Arya Patrika*, 14 January 1911, *SVPP* 1911, p. 83.

52 *Al Bashir* (Etawah), 31 January 1911, *SVPUP* 1911, p. 98.

53 *Indar*, discussed in the *Hindustani* (Lucknow), 3 April 1911, *SVPUP* 1911, p. 289.

54 *TI*, p. 8.

55 *TI*, p. 10.

56 *Afghan* (Peshawar), 28 July 1911, *SVPP* 1911, p. 808; *Jhang Sial* (Jhang), 28 October 1911, *SVPP* 1911, pp. 1121–2. See also *Paisa Akhbar* (Lahore), 2 May 1910, *SVPP* 1910, p. 407, *Paisa Akhbar* (Lahore), 2 May 1910, *SVPP* 1910, p. 408.

57 Recorded in Butalia, *Silence*, pp. 221–2.

58' Pandit Gopi Nath's lecture on the Arya Samaj', *Hindustan* (Lahore), 21 January 1910, *SVPP* 1910, pp. 85–6.

59 *Brahman Saraswa* (Etawah), June 1909, *SVPUP* 1909, p. 560; *Sanatan Dharma Pataka* (Moradabad), June 1909, *SVPUP* 1909, p. 574; *Shri Yadavendra* (Allahabad), September 1909, *SVPUP* 1909, p. 681; *Samrat* (Kalakankar), 16 September 1909, *SVPUP* 1909, p. 681.

60 *Al Bashir* (Etawah), 8 May 1906, *SVPUP* 1905–6, p. 301.

61 *Arjun*, 20 May 1910, *SVPP* 1910, 468. See also *Arjun*, 27 May 1910, *SVPP* 1910, p. 490.

62 *Brihasapati* (Lahore), 15 November 1909, *SVPP* 1910, pp. 25–6.

63 The book is described in *The Hunter* (Lahore), 7 April, 21 May 1910, *SVPP* 1910, pp. 351–2, 467.

64 *Indar* (Lahore), June 1911, *SVPP* 1911, p. 632. By the end of July the *Arjun* was moribund, and Dharm Pal's reversion to Islam was being discussed in the press: *Musafir* (Agra), 21 July 1911, *SVPUP* 1911, p. 688.

65　*Parkash*, 11 July 1911, *SVPP* 1911, p. 746.

66　*Indar* (Lahore), January 1911, *SVPP* 1911, p. 109.

67　The blessings of the Vedas and the existing misfortunes of India', *Haq* (Delhi), 20 May 1910, *SVPP* 1910, pp. 520–1.

68　Ibid.

69　*Indar* (Lahore), January 1911, *SVPP* 1911, p. 109.

70　*Musafir* (Agra), 16 April 1911, *SVPUP* 1911, p. 323.

71　Ibid.

72　*Arjun* (Lahore), 27 May 1910, *SVPP* 1911, p. 186.

73　*Indar* (Lahore), January 1911, *SVPP* 1911, p. 109.

Part IV

Colonialism: Rural and Urban Cultures

10

David Gilmartin

Environmental History, *Biradari*, and the Making of Pakistani Punjab

The creation of Pakistan has often been portrayed as a process peculiarly divorced from the history of the land that is today Pakistan. At the time of its creation, some viewed Pakistan as an 'ideological state', a state somehow disconnected from the particular land on which it was forced to settle.[1] In the decades since that time, historians and others have explored the connections between Pakistan's history and the distinctive cultures of the geographical regions it encompassed.[2] But there has been surprisingly little work linking the history of Pakistan's creation to the massive environmental changes that during the colonial era shaped the Indus Basin, the heartland of today's Pakistan. The Indus Basin region—and particularly the Punjab—witnessed, through the expansion of irrigation and agriculture, one of the world's great environmental transformations in the nineteenth and twentieth centuries. This article attempts to link the narrative of this environmental transformation to the cultural history of modern Punjab—and to the story of the coming of partition and Pakistan's creation in 1947.

The relationship between cultural and ecological change is an extremely important one, though relatively little explored in the history of modern India. The most important work exploring this connection historically has been that of Richard Eaton dealing with Bengal. Eaton has highlighted the importance of the relationship between environmental and cultural change in Mughal Bengal, showing the close connections between the transformation of east Bengal into a predominantly rice-growing agricultural region, and the conversion of the majority of the population of east Bengal to Islam. Ecological changes—particularly the long-term shift of the Ganges delta toward the east—provided the link, in Eaton's argument, between the history of production and the history of religion.

Sedentarization and the intensification of agriculture, as Eaton sees it, brought dramatic cultural changes to east Bengal. But the key to these changes lay in the historical intersection of environmental change with the establishment of new structures of state power. Environmental change—and sedentarization—aligned with the incorporation of the region into a Mughal economic and cultural world. This was a process in which reformulations of local community arising from new forms of settled agriculture led to gradual processes of cultural assimilation to Islam, loosely associated with the Mughal state but locally embodied in new village mosques and shrines. 'From the perspective of Mughal authorities in Dhaka or Murshidabad', Eaton writes,

the hundreds of tiny rural mosques and shrines established in the interior of eastern Bengal served as agents for the transformation of jungle into arable land and the construction of stable microsocieties loyal to the Mughal state. From a religious perspective, however, these same institutions facilitated the diffusion of uniquely Islamic conceptions of divine and human authority among groups under their socioeconomic influence.[3]

Though the processes of cultural interaction between Mughal elites, western Bengali Hindus, and indigenous east Bengali tribal worldviews were complex, Eaton's work suggests the importance of environmental history for understanding the spread of Islam into eastern Bengal, and also for understanding the nature of the Bengali Islam that emerged. New understandings of power associated with the state gained distinctive meaning as new adaptations to a changing natural environment restructured local culture and local communities.

Similar processes shaped Punjab during the medieval period—yet in Punjab the most dramatic transformations of the environment awaited the colonial period. Agriculture in the Indus Basin, of course, dates back millennia. But as Irfan Habib has argued, the introduction and dissemination of the Persian wheel on the Indus plains in the period after the coming of the Muslims had profound effects on the whole region. The harnessing of animal power to irrigation triggered a significant extension of settlement in central Punjab, encouraging as well an acceleration of Jat migrations up the Indus rivers toward the central Punjab. Habib argues that the widespread settlement of formerly pastoral Jats may in fact have been connected with the extensive conversion of Jats in central Punjab to Sikhism, a religion whose rejection of agrarian caste hierarchies may have reflected the region's pastoral history. This thesis has in fact been challenged, both by those who have questioned the role of the Persian wheel in Punjab's settlement and by those who have pointed to the lack of solid evidence linking settlement patterns directly to Jat conversions to Sikhism.[4] Whatever the case, however, Punjab differed significantly from Bengal in that, even by the late Mughal era, it remained a region only very partially transformed by agriculture. Under the Mughals, significant extensions of agriculture had occurred in central Punjab, in the districts bordering on the hills and in narrow strips along the river valleys, and in the post-Mughal period, increasing inundation canal construction led to the expansion of agriculture in the river valleys of southwestern Punjab.[5] But the eighteenth century also witnessed the contraction of agriculture in many areas. Indeed, the great bulk of the western Punjabi areas which today provide the heartlands of Pakistani agriculture, were not settled, even at the height of the Mughal Empire, but occupied by pastoralists, often practicing temporary and shifting agriculture. The development of a close connection between Muslim cultural identity and farming had thus not developed in Punjab—as it had in Bengal—in the period before colonial rule.

Though generalizations about culture as an abstract concept are always dangerous, the dominant patterns of Punjabi religious culture appear to have reflected the ongoing interaction between tribal pastoralism, trade, and settled, river valley agriculture that defined

Punjab's ecology. This shaped, for example, the important networks of Sufi shrines that dominated the region. In her book on the *pirs* of Sind, Sarah Ansari has argued that the broad significance of pirs in the life of Sind at the opening of British rule grew from their social, political and religious roles in the intermediate environment between pastoralism and settled society in the lower Indus Basin, an environment in some ways similar to that of western Punjab. 'Pirs carried out a series of basic functions vital to the process by which tribesmen became peasants', she writes. 'They linked the nomadic and the settled worlds, and bridged the gap between countryside and town in a way that tribal chiefs increasingly could not'.[6] Indeed, they defined an Islamic ethos centred on mediation that was closely tied to the ongoing tensions generated by a long-standing agricultural frontier. Many of the same elements can be seen in the networks of Sufi shrines that dominated much of western Punjab in the post-Mughal period, shrines often located on the margins between interacting settled and pastoral environments in the river valleys, and at key nodes on the trading routes that crisscrossed the region.

These Sufi shrines helped also to define the basic patterns of authority that shaped the character of Punjabi Muslim identity. Many of the most important Punjabi literary works of the era, such as the *Hir Ranjha* story of the eighteenth century poet, Waris Shah, are both infused with Sufism and reveal the tensions of this partly agricultural and partly pastoral society. In the *Hir Ranjha* story, as in many other Punjabi folk stories of the era, images of both pastoralism and settled agriculture are prominent, even though the stories reveal, in the words of Neeladri Bhattacharya, 'a complex of ambivalent and conflicting attitudes' toward them.[7] Indeed, it can be argued that this tension gave particular power to the Sufi imagery that suffused such stories. In *Hir Ranjha*, the metaphorical Sufi language of divine longing, embodied in the doomed love of the uprooted farmer, Ranjha, and the pastoral princess, Hir, drew together symbolically the worlds of settlement and wandering, even as they were transformed into metaphors for irresolvable cosmic and human tensions. The literature of this era also suggested the importance of another feature of the Punjabi cultural world, and one reflective of Punjab's distinctive ecological balance—the power of genealogy.[8] Waris Shah was himself a member of 'that rural Muslim religious elite whose values', in the words of Christopher Shackle, 'so largely determine (d) the overall character of the surviving literature'.[9] And Waris Shah, a Sayyid, claiming descent from the Prophet, gained cultural authority, like the Sufis associated with Punjab's great shrines, largely on the basis of his sacred descent. Though the existence of an important agricultural community in Punjab shaped strongly many of Waris Shah's descriptions of Punjab in *Hir Ranjha*, it was not attachment to the land and the statuses associated with it that provided the primary foundations for Punjabi social order in this world, but the ordering power of genealogy, stretching across the boundaries between wandering and settlement. Sacred genealogy, as much as mysticism, legitimized the power of Sufi religious leaders and storytellers alike to articulate in the eighteenth century the dominant Punjabi Muslim cultural ethos operating on the fluid margin between pastoralism and settled agriculture.

Such an emphasis on Sufism and genealogy oversimplifies the complexities of Punjabi Islam in this period—and the cultural flux created by the various states that ruled parts of Punjab during the era—but it provides a critical backdrop for understanding the connections between environment and culture that occurred during the period of British rule. Central to the effects of British rule on the expression of Punjabi identity were the sweeping agricultural transformations that marked the British period. With the construction of a massive system of state-run canals in the Indus Basin in the nineteenth and twentieth centuries, unprecedented in scope not only in India at that time, but in the world as a whole, the British transformed western Punjab in a period of about seventy-five years into an overwhelmingly settled, agricultural society. But critically, as with the case of Eaton's Mughal Bengal, such changes were associated with far-reaching cultural effects.

In Punjab, such changes were not, of course, primarily those of religious conversion. The British state did not project Christianity as a hegemonic state culture during the time in which these environmental transformations occurred. But they *were* associated with a state-projected moral discourse—in this case a hegemonic discourse linked to property, law, and cultural objectification—that, as in Eaton's story, played out in transformations in the meaning of local community that were no less fundamental than those associated in the late Mughal period with east Bengal's gradual conversion to Islam. On one level, changes brought by the British were intended, as in the case of the Mughals, to facilitate revenue collection through the establishment of stable, loyal communities linked, often through intermediaries, to the imperial regime. But no less than the framing power of Islam under the Mughals, colonial principles of rule operated as a universalizing moral discourse defined not just by the immediate authority of the colonial state but by its claims to be the bearer of a moral universalism that transcended all specific cultures. This by no means meant a complete transformation in local culture, any more than did the conversion to Islam in Bengal. But it did mean key changes in the place and culture of the local community within wider political and natural frameworks, both in its relationship to the state and to the land.

Nothing perhaps illustrates this more clearly than the colonial attack on pastoralism and wandering, both in its relationship to the structuring of community and as a mode of adaptation to the Indus Basin environment. That the encouragement of agricultural settlement should be associated with an attack on pastoralism is no surprise; settled communities were central to the British revenue structure.[10] What is noteworthy is that this attack was explicitly constructed by the British as inextricably linked to a vision of private property as a universal moral good. Though British records are not without romantic statements of sympathy for the Indus Basin's pastoral peoples, the overwhelmingly dominant colonial view, shaped by nineteenth century liberal thinking, was that pastoralism was both an economically and morally backward system. By failing to allow for the accumulation of landed, private property, pastoralism stunted the growth of individual moral responsibility that was, in the eyes of most British administrators, the hallmark of the modern era—and an element in the hegemony of the new colonial state. Canal policy in the Indus Basin was aimed deliberately by the British toward extending fixed agricultural settlement in the Indus Basin to the greatest extent possible. Not only were formerly pastoral peoples thus given lands to encourage them to settle, but, far more important, agricultural colonists were also imported in large numbers onto newly opened canal colony lands in western Punjab, thus closing off the ecological possibilities of continued pastoral liveli-hood even for those who resisted settlement. Those who continued to wander were either forced to the extreme margins of production or stigmatized as socially inferior and morally bankrupt 'criminal tribes', both in the eyes of the British and, increasingly, in the eyes of many settled Punjabi agriculturists themselves. From the beginning the attack on pastoralism was thus not *only* about facilitating settlement, it was also about underscoring the new hegemony of a cultural vision associated with fixed rights in property, as the foundation, in essence, for a new overarching vision of civilization. And ultimately, it was the physical transformation of the environment under colonial auspices that gave this new vision powerful local meaning.

Indeed, the transformative power of the British regime on the Indus Basin in this context was seen nowhere more clearly than in its critical impact on genealogy as an ordering principle of community and life. Genealogy, that is, the emphasis on a language of commu-nity rooted preeminently in the claims of common descent, remained a central organizing social and political principle under the British, but its meanings were radically transformed under the new British cultural and environmental order. The diagnostic marker of these changes was the critical rise of *biradari*, or brotherhood of extended kin, as the preeminent form of social organization in the new, settled agricultural society of the Punjab. This is not to say that biradari was in any way new in the Indus Basin at this time, for its earlier his-tory as a concept of genealogical reckoning is clearly suggested by the Persian origins of the term. But no longer was genealogy primarily a form of social ordering whose power derived from its role in facilitat-ing social relations across the ecological boundaries of settlement and wandering, and in adapting (at least for Muslims) local power to an assimilative Islamic framework. Rather, its new role lay in assimilating local power relations to a hegemonic imperial ideology undergirded by the moral authority attached to property, now justiciable by the courts. Property in some ways defined a new rights-bearing image of the legal individual, but individuals were assimilated to this uni-versalizing moral realm under the British as members of biradaris, their prestige, honour and rights as property holders cast in the now appropriated language of genealogical authority. And in the process, of course, the very meaning of biradari itself was transformed.

The structuring of this system was accomplished in the second half of the nineteenth century through Punjab's massive revenue settlements, which fixed both individual property rights and biradari relationships to the land. Though the most sweeping environmental changes came with the opening of Punjab's canal colonies, beginning in the late 1880s, the association of land 'settlements' in Punjab with an emphasis on physical settlement as well was pronounced in Punjab's bureaucratic traditions from the first decades after the establishment of British rule, as the British built their administration in a region that had faced serious displacements from the land. The opening of the Bari Doab canal in central Punjab in the 1850s, the Sirhind canal in the east, and the significant expansion of inundation canal construction along the Jhelum, Chenab and Indus in the west, were all connected with the reconstruction of communities within the framework of a new environmental and bureaucratic order, even before the great expansions of irrigated land settlement in the canal colonies. Such processes built, of course, on older histories of settlement shaped by lineage organization.[11] But the combination of linked environmental and legal/administrative transformation—though varying in different parts of Punjab—defined a new frame that had, by the end of the nineteenth century, produced far-reaching cultural transformations in the province.

The touchstone of these transformations was the structure of biradari as the defining form of community at the base of the system, which had an important impact on politics and social organization in all of Punjab's religious communities. The clearest marker of this was the structuring of colonial property law. The key was the embedding of the property owner simultaneously in two systems of law, a contract law that governed individual property rights and exchange, and a structure of personal, 'customary law' that controlled inheritance and embedded it in a framework of biradari constraints.[12] Fundamental to the reconstruction of biradari in this era was thus the fact that it was built on the demarcation and recording of individual property rights on a vast scale within the framework of Punjab's nineteenth century land settlements. Though this process was marked by significant regional variations in the Punjab (relating to both social structure and environment), individual property rights were recorded in settlement records in all parts of the province.[13] But even as individual rights were recorded, British land settlement policies embedded these rights in stabilizing local communities defined in terms of recorded genealogies. This was evident, for example, in the village pedigrees carefully recorded by the British in most parts of the province as charters for settled village communities (or sometimes for segments of villages), which dictated the structure of inheritance rights as embodied in Punjab's system of customary law. It was also evident in the protections the law offered to the dominance of the male 'proprietary body' (or village community) over the generally non-landholding subordinate classes in the village: artisans (*kamins*), tenants, and women. British bureaucratic and legal policies thus intersected with older ideas about genealogy to define a distinctive landholding ethos in Punjab, one linked to notions of genealogically-based and gender-based honour (or *izzat*) but one that strongly linked status as well to the existence, and protection through politics and the courts, of state-recorded individual property rights.[14] Grounding in a biradari was, in other words, defined simultaneously in the language of both honour and law.

A full discussion of the local operation of biradari under the British is well beyond the scope of this article.[15] But several critical features marked its transformation in colonial Punjab. Biradaris were generally not corporate groups in this system; they were fluid, transactional entities dominated by individual landholders (often using highly personalized idioms). Nor were they in any way synonymous with 'village communities' as a fixed administrative category, however important the village 'proprietary body' was as a biradari model. In practice, biradari organization was quite elastic, taking different forms in different contexts.[16] But the primary significance of biradari lay in the fact that it grounded the individual in a civilizational moral order defined by property—a moral order that legitimized the colonial state—even as it underscored the primacy of a cultural structure in rural Punjab shaped by the local, particularistic—and semi-autonomous—ordering power of genealogy. It was a system that bound landowners to the state, and yet defined a primary idiom of local cultural calculation that could never be *fully* subsumed within the colonial bureaucratic/legal order. And it gained extraordinary traction in Punjab precisely because it developed at the intersection of a changing structure of state authority and a changing relationship to nature as Punjab came to be a province of settled agricultural communities.

Biradari idioms powerfully influenced developing structures of rural political leadership under the colonial regime. Genealogical calculation played a critical role in structuring the state's cooptation of a landed elite to mediate between the state and the great bulk of the rural population. In many Punjab districts, the British recognized an emerging 'landed gentry', legitimized by genealogical claims to authority sometimes reaching back to a pastoral past, whose pedigrees were carefully recorded in the genealogies attached to accounts such as Lepel Griffin's *Punjab Chiefs*. Large-scale control of land was critical to these intermediaries (and this control was bolstered by the British policy of distributing sizeable land grants in the canal colonies). But the foundations of this system rested on more than landholding alone. For the British, the 'landed gentry' were part of a larger class of landed leaders, reaching down to the village level, whose legitimacy was based on the joint props of property rights and genealogy. The idiom of biradari thus played a critical role in conjuring an image of Punjabi 'society' (and of rural political leadership) as resting on indigenous foundations conceptualized, through genealogy, as prior to the political structure of the colonial regime (even as, in actual fact, the influence of most colonial landed intermediaries was in significant part a product of British land settlements themselves). The political salience of this framing was in fact given statutory dimension in the definition of a protected political class associated with the 'agricultural tribes' as defined in the Punjab Alienation of Land Act of 1901. The Land Alienation Act was intended to protect the lands of these intermediaries from their creditors, but its language translated into usable political terms the linking of property interests (now conceptualized in terms of 'class' interests) and biradari-based (or tribal) honour that defined the new rural order. This linkage took concrete political form in the 1920s with the launching of the Punjab Unionist Party.

Yet, if the Unionist Party defined a provincial political coalition built politically on Punjab's landholding/biradari structure, it defined no province-wide *cultural* mobilization linked to this structure. One of the most noteworthy features of the new cultural order in the Punjab, was the sharply limited character of any attempt to transform the culture of biradari into a framework for an emerging vision of a broader, or distinctly Punjabi, cultural identity—an identity that could make claims to culturally challenge the colonial state. Indeed, this highlights a central feature of the new biradari order that had emerged in the late nineteenth century, namely its deeply parochial character. The very power of biradari lay in its particularism, in its providing a frame for individual adaptation to the new property order even as it underscored the local cultural autonomy of rural life. Though, as Farina Mir has shown, Punjabi literary production linked to the genres of an earlier era continued under the British (and in some ways expanded in the new realm of print), this gained little in the way of state patronage.[17] In an environment in which Punjab's landed elites depended on British land grants as the agricultural transformation of western Punjab proceeded, the British in fact discouraged elite patronage of a literary reformulation of Punjab's old cultural traditions in the new political and ecological environment of the era.[18] Neither the British nor the Unionists made any efforts to link their power to the patronage of Punjabi as a regional language.[19] As Hanif Ramay has argued, the *jagirdar*s of the Punjab, as he calls them, remained parochial in their cultural outlook throughout, even as they served as political mediators within the new colonial system.[20] Though property (and a language of rights) provided a potentially universalizing moral frame linking the state to individual landholders under British rule, the linking of property rights to new forms of localized genealogical community defined, at the same time, a deep cultural separation between society and state. Indeed, the cultural separation of the state from society and the parochialization of indigenous Punjabi culture were the twin foundations on which the new, settled agricultural order of Punjab was established.

Here the comparison of the colonial Punjab with Eaton's account of Bengal may again be instructive. The commonality between the two cases lay in the emergence of new, transformative forms of local community, drawing on the past, but linked simultaneously with a new state system and with a new productive relationship to nature. But the difference between the two cases was also marked. In Punjab's case these new local communities were both framed by, and penetrated by, the state in ways unimaginable in Mughal Bengal. Not only was the state's canal-building role central to the environmental transformations that produced these settled communities, but the reformulations of local biradari (and of the position of the individual within it) were also defined fundamentally by the state's legal property order whose establishment was a key to biradari's new definition. At the same time, however, Punjab's new biradari order was built on a conceptual cultural separation between the state and the local community that was quite different from the moral visions shaping Islam's overarching role in Mughal Bengal. Biradari was, in a sense, 'captured' within the rational and moral/legal order of the colonial state, but it was also a vessel for a form of cultural and moral autonomy, based on genealogy and rights of property, that in its very parochialism claimed a cultural space that stood apart, in critical ways, from the state's authority.

BIRADARI, THE STATE, AND COMMUNALISM IN TWENTIETH-CENTURY PUNJAB

The impact of this biradari structure in shaping relations between state and society is one of twentieth century Punjab's most important stories. It is the argument here that the analysis of this biradari-based order helps us to make sense of many of the paradoxes that have marked Punjab's twentieth century history.

Perhaps the best place to begin such an exploration is with the ongoing story of environmental change itself. If expanding irrigation and settlement were, as has been argued here, at the heart of a new property-based cultural order after 1850, the expansion of irrigation and of settled agriculture continued apace in the first half of the twentieth century. But the principles on which this expansion occurred were not static or fixed, and the interaction between Punjab's biradari-based property order and the subsequent evolution of new visions of state-directed environmental change illustrate as clearly as any other historical development the importance of the deep entrenchment of the cultural changes that were occurring. In fact, new visions of professional engineering and technical efficiency promised new avenues for direct state control over nature as the canal colonies expanded in the twentieth century.[21] The first decades of the twentieth century witnessed a vast expansion of arid 'wastelands' that were brought, through irrigation, under agricultural settlement. But shifts in the state's developmental strategies only highlighted the degree to which cultural patterns of state–society relations associated with biradari had already crystallized by the turn of the twentieth century—and came to act as a constraint even on state policy itself.

This was in fact the context for the eruption of serious popular protests against British canal colony policies in 1907. Protests emerged first in the Chenab colony, and extended to communities along the Bari Doab canal as well, challenging British efforts to impose intrusive rules on colony residents (and other irrigators), and to define a new framework of state control over colony villages. These protests took on special danger in the eyes of many British officials as they linked grievances among rural agriculturalists to urban-based (and to some degree, nationalist) challenges to the British, and the British thus moved swiftly to try to suppress them. But the outcome of the protests also showed how central the cultural dynamics of Punjab's property order had become to state–society relations in the province. A key complaint of many of the protestors was that their settlement on long-term colony leases had made them subject to state intrusions that differentiated them from property-holders elsewhere in the province. Critically, the demand for proprietary rights also reflected a demand for the full recognition of the cultural primacy of customary law (and biradari) as it operated in the proprietary village. The ultimate British capitulation to this demand hardly represented the end of Punjab's ongoing process of irrigation expansion and state-led environmental transformation, or of new ideologies of state-led technical developmentalism. But the protests, and their outcome, suggested the strength of Punjab's nineteenth century property order (and of an elastic, reformulated vision of biradari within that order) as the key prop in defining the state's relations to society.[22]

The history of the 1907 protests can thus be read as the coming of age of a colonial cultural structure linked to biradari and property. Fifty years earlier, in 1857, when Ahmad Khan Kharral, and other semi-pastoral groups attacked the British in the Gugera uprising, theirs was a revolt built on the old roles of genealogical calculation in mobilizing support across the divides of pastoralism and agriculture. This drew on an older genealogical order that was not encapsulated within colonial structures and was mobilized to challenge colonial rule. By 1907 rural protests were built on a different genealogical ideology, one linked to individual property interests and community solidarity. The success of these protests was in fact, as Imran Ali has argued, a 'political watershed'. Yet this was a watershed defined not simply by the capitulation of a nascent developmental state to peasant conservatism (as Ali explains it), but by the strength of a new rural order that simultaneously bound agricultural communities to the colonial system and, at the same time, defined a space of local cultural autonomy within it. [23]

The distinctive impact of this biradari order in the twentieth century can also be measured, if perhaps somewhat more speculatively, through its role in shaping the form of politics for which Punjab is perhaps best known—the politics of communalism. The narrative of Punjab's history of communalism has long been a subject of some controversy because it was shaped by a central paradox: while communal conflict was as virulent in Punjab as in any other province in India (reaching its pinnacle in the horrendous violence of 1947), the province was at the same time the home of some of the most vibrant cross-religious political alliances in India. Indeed, for all the ferocity of the communal riots that marked partition, Punjab was the last of the major provinces in India affected by partition to fall into a structure of communally-based political oppositions. An analysis of the structure of biradari in fact helps us to make sense of both sides of this apparent paradox.

The relationship between biradari and religion in Punjab's modern history is of course a complex one. But it is difficult to track the emergence of religious identity as a foundation for communalism except against the backdrop of biradari identities as they emerged within the context of Punjab's settled agricultural transformation. Though it is certainly true that the British projected an image of Punjabi society (through the census and other mechanisms) that built on religious communities as much as on genealogy, it was biradari, rather than religion, that provided the central idiom of local community in Punjab as the region was physically transformed in the nineteenth century into an overwhelmingly agricultural, propertied society. Biradari, rather than religion, emerged in the second half of the nineteenth century as the central idiom of community shaping local life, binding together concepts of both honour and rights of property. No evocation of religion as a category of community could thus easily gain a foothold in Punjab except in relationship to this frame. For Hindus, Muslims, and Sikhs alike, notions of religious community and of biradari were thus intimately intertwined. At times, biradari provided a model for the imagining of the religious community itself (as in the occasional usage of the terms 'Hindu biradari' or 'Sikh biradari', for example), but more often, the use of biradari idioms and religious idioms were bound together at the local level in complex relationships.[24] Even models of individual religious reform, such as Anshu Malhotra discusses in her book on gender and community among middle-class Punjabi Hindus, were often cast, sometimes in highly ambiguous ways, against the backdrop of a social world in which idioms of biradari were central.[25]

But the very power of this model of biradari, forged at intersection of legal/bureaucratic and physical/environmental transformation, spawned powerful reactions as well. One can see this in part as a product of the fact that certain groups, particularly in the cities, were only partially assimilated into the world of agricultural biradari, and that the British manipulated divisions between countryside and city, between agriculturist and non-agriculturist, in the twentieth century for their own purposes. In such circumstances the appeal by excluded groups to a vision of religious community as a moral alternative to the world that biradari created is perhaps not a surprise. Historians have thus often emphasized the urban roots of communalism in the Punjab, and seen its manifestation in the emerging, largely urban, world of print. But to push this too far would be a mistake, for there is little doubt that the world of biradari extended across the rural-urban divide even into Punjab's cities, which contained increasing numbers of migrants from rural and small-town Punjab.

Rather, it is more plausible to see the emergence of a distinct, highly idealized, form of communal politics in twentieth century Punjab as not so much a product of the limits of the biradari idiom, but rather as a reaction to its ubiquitousness—and, perhaps most importantly, to the utterly parochial character of the political worlds that biradari idioms created. Though biradari idioms shaped forms of politics that, as we have seen, offered room for autonomous manoeuvre, even, at times, for limiting the power of the state, this was a politics significantly divorced from the universalizing promise of moral individualism that the British invested in their own visions of property (even as the concept of 'rights', of course, gestured toward this vision). Property rights were culturally contained for rural Punjabis within a world of genealogy and 'custom' that was largely separated within the colonial legal regime from *any* universalizing moral ideology.[26] Though the growth of communalism in Punjab no doubt owed much to the same pressures of state policy and reform that one can see elsewhere in India, its distinctive Punjabi emphasis was thus a product of the Punjab's distinctive experience. The development of a particular brand of communalism in Punjab that was in significant ways configured in stark opposition to the local, the particular, and the everyday (and was, for this very reason—though this is highly speculative—perhaps particularly prone to violence), was arguably a product of the very hold that biradari had gained in Punjabi life within the context of Punjab's dramatic nineteenth–twentieth century environmental transformations.

To say this is not to deny the varied and complex forms that communalism took in twentieth century Punjab, or the significant differences in its manifestations within the Hindu, Sikh and Muslim communities. It was the Hindu community that was most deeply affected by the distinctions between agriculturalists and non-agriculturalists that had been shaped by the Land Alienation Act. Debates on the meaning of Hindu community in twentieth century Punjabi politics could hardly escape this backdrop. Some non-agriculturist Hindu leaders in the cities responded to the increasing centrality of biradari in Punjabi politics by attempting to project a new vision of Hindu community rooted in the explicit moral rejection of biradari politics. In doing so, some attempted to conflate the category 'agricultural tribes' (and the politicization of biradari that went with it) with Punjab's Muslims, though this, of course, involved a wilful denial of the large numbers of Hindus (particularly Hindu Jats) who, under the leadership of Ch Chhotu Ram, were actively involved in the Unionist Party (and actively engaged in the mobilization of biradari idioms in politics).[27] But of equal importance was the fact that many urban Hindus projected a vision of a self-controlled moral self, transcending the worldly snares of biradari, as a key to a new normative construction of Hindu community.[28] The degree to which this produced a harder-edged vision of Hindu community in the 1920s and 1930s, rooted precisely in a rejection of religion's deep entanglements in local life, is a subject that could use considerably more research. But there is little doubt that tensions surrounding the role of biradari played an important part in shaping the social world in which Hindu communalism developed.

The role of biradari in shaping the distinctive development of Sikh and Muslim communalism is more readily evident. The relationship of biradari (and other diverse local practices) to the development of Sikh communalism has been perhaps most persuasively delineated by Harjot Oberoi.[29] Oberoi's work demonstrates clearly the critical ways that an attempt to homogenize and unify 'Sikh community' through attacks on diverse religious (and local biradari) practices, transformed Sikh tradition in the late nineteenth and the early twentieth centuries. But Oberoi tends to see these local practices and forms of biradari organization as largely remnants of an older order. In fact, the nature of the processes he describes—and the relationship of biradari to religious communalism—is clearer if we see the more homogenizing Tat Khalsa Sikhism he describes as not simply a response to older world-views (a response fomented and facilitated by colonial army recruiting policies and census delineations), but as a counterpoint to the powerful structures of property rights and parochial community that were associated with the *new* nineteenth century agrarian order—an order that had significantly influenced local Sikh life. In this light, newly idealized visions of Sikh moral community, enacted and delineated in the twentieth century public sphere, developed not to suppress an older order, but in ongoing juxtaposition with vibrant—and yet parochial—notions of genealogical honour and individual property rights that were themselves, in significant part, a product of the colonial property order itself.

It was precisely this juxtaposition that was productive of the distinctive forms that twentieth century Sikh communalism took. To get a sense of the vitality of these tensions, one has only to compare the highly idealized visions of Khalsa community that marked the Gurdwara reform movement and the later Khalistan movement (visions of community imagined for many as divorced from local social structure and biradari-based genealogy), with the highly personalized, biradari-based forms of political competition for honour, power and property that maintained, *at the very same time*, their holds on the everyday worlds of twentieth century Sikh politics—as dramatically illustrated, for example, in Joyce Pettigrew's *Robber Noblemen*.[30] Indeed, one can see the ongoing replication of these tensions in the years after the Sikh Gurdwaras and Shrines Act of 1925 in the history of the Central Gurdwara Management Committee, which was simultaneously a symbol of Khalsa unity *and* an arena for the continual and pervasive staging of these personalized, parochial, biradari-based political oppositions. The history of biradari and of strong Sikh communalism can thus be viewed in critical ways as opposite sides of the same coin.

The same pattern—though with significant variations—shaped Muslim politics. As among Sikhs, Punjabi Muslims witnessed strong currents of reformism in the late nineteenth and early twentieth centuries focused on the development of a more homogenous vision of Muslim community—a vision that at times directly challenged local structures of biradari. Tensions between biradari and idealized visions of community were expressed, for example, in the writings of some *ulama*, who contrasted the divisive pull of local kinship-based 'custom' (and customary law) with commitment to Muslim law (*shariat*). Communal definitions of Muslim community in fact developed most strongly among urban elites, including those associated with the British bureaucracy (Hamza Alavi's salariat), who saw a new emphasis on an idealized vision of Muslim community as a moral antidote to the parochial character of biradari-based mobilization.[31]

Still, for most rural Muslim leaders the political impact of this challenge to biradari was initially limited, for biradari dominated the world of property in rural Punjab. In fact, rural leaders in Punjab had, historically, seen little conceptual or moral opposition between religious community and local 'tribal' organization. Nevertheless, in the twentieth century, as the moral foundations of the colonial political order were increasingly debated, these leaders too were hardly immune to the moral pressures of reformist attacks on biradari organization, particularly in the years after separate electorates were extended into rural Punjab in 1919.

As among the Sikhs, however, the appeal of Muslim communal solidarity gained traction among these leaders precisely as it came to be cast in terms of an abstracted individual commitment to religious ideals that, whatever its juxtaposition against biradari, was in reality conceptually divorced from *any* connection to the actual structure of local life and local politics. Muhammad Iqbal, for example, in the 1930s linked a vision of a new Muslim state to an idealized vision of an Islamic self (*khudi*), cast in sharp opposition to the 'earth-rootedness' of biradari.[32] Iqbal's vision of individualized moral community was in fact less a concrete attack on biradari as an actual framework for local life, than an attempt to define a vision of Muslim community set free from all sociological moorings and linked only to idealized individual commitments.[33] Such a vision, which cast the appeal for Pakistan in idealized terms, influenced Jinnah as well, who in the mid-1940s pushed the Pakistan movement toward an abstracted, unitary structure of community imagining of Pakistan, defined as transcending society's parochialized constraints. This was the context in which many of Punjab's landed Muslim classes shifted their support toward the Muslim League and Pakistan in the 1940s, in spite of the rhetorical opposition between Pakistan as an ideal and Punjab's deep-seated biradari structure. In practice, pro-Pakistan rhetoric was directed toward providing moral and symbolic foundations for a state that was imagined as having only limited connections to the parochial structures defining rural society itself. It was precisely as a counterpoint to the ongoing entrenchment of a property order powerfully linked to structures of biradari that the vision of the Pakistan state as a symbol of idealized moral community gained its most powerful meanings.[34]

Some have, in fact, seen this movement of landed leaders into the Pakistan movement in the last years before 1947 as representing a 'capture' of the movement by backward 'feudal' elements who were survivals of an earlier era, a throwback to an earlier world. But, as in the case of the Sikhs, to see Punjab's rural propertied elites in these terms is to significantly distort what had happened. Most of the rural leaders who gained control of the Punjab Muslim League in the mid-1940s were men whose visions had been forged in the interlinked processes of environmental and legal transformation marking the colonial era. Most saw the Pakistan idea as a frame for the moral reformulation of the authority of a state, like the colonial state, standing morally apart from the structures actually organizing rural society. If Pakistan offered a new vision of the state linked to an idealized sense of Muslim selfhood, it was an ideal that was, by its very abstraction from the actual structure of society, calculated to disassociate itself from the parochial local world of biradari organized around the twin interests of genealogical honour and property rights.

LEGACIES FOR PAKISTANI PUNJAB

Pakistan's creation thus embodied in some ways the contradictions that had been built into the cultural structure of Punjab's newly emerging agrarian order of the nineteenth century. These contradictions were subsequently played out in an independent Pakistan. An overarching discussion of the cultural impact of colonial environmental transformation on the history of Pakistan is necessarily highly speculative, but we can trace briefly the cultural legacies of Punjab's colonial environmental transformations in three interconnected realms.

First was the realm of state-led developmentalism, which continued to bear the marks of the state–society accommodations that had emerged from the canal colony protests of 1907. In fact, state-led intensification of Pakistan's environmental transformations continued apace in the 1950s and 1960s, increasingly supported by foreign experts and foreign capital, particularly during the Ayub era. This was the era of vast new projects and of the first great Indus basin dams. In some ways the creation of a new national state, linked to an idealized vision of a Muslim national community, provided a framework for new forms of state intervention in local society, extending well

beyond those of the colonial era. But with the persistence of biradari as a hegemonic form of local Punjabi organization—and one
deeply embedded in the legal property order—the basic structures
of state-society relations that had emerged in the colonial era were
not seriously altered. On one level, local biradaris, in their very
multiplicity, provided a dense social framework of local social order
and leadership in rural Pakistani Punjab that in some ways facilitated local stability even in the face of change. But on another level,
biradari structures have continued to limit state penetration into
society. They have facilitated the persistence of an imagined separation between a state defined in terms of idealized developmental,
national, and religious/moral models (an image that has itself facilitated, and in turn been enhanced by, Pakistan's bouts of military
rule), and a parochial, honour-based (and rights-based) culture,
linked to biradari. This tension has influenced state policies as
diverse as local government reform and ongoing irrigation development. As Douglas Merrey's work has suggested, the tension between
bureaucratized water management and local honour-based biradari
influence has remained a defining feature of Pakistani Punjab's canal
systems.[35] Indeed, Punjabi development politics have been shaped by
an imagined cultural fault line between society and state in Pakistan,
however dense the actual networks of personalized (and kinship)
connections crossing this imaginary line. Whatever the shifts that
Pakistan has experienced since 1947, one can thus trace the outlines
of a number of critical, broad developmental patterns back to the
nature of the cultural order that emerged from Punjab's nineteenth
century agrarian and environmental transformations.

These tensions have also come to be closely related to a second
vital realm, the checkered history since 1947 of Islam in shaping these
state–society relations. Nothing has captured this more clearly than
debates in Pakistan on the implementation of (and, indeed, meaning
of) shariat within Pakistani law. However much rural Punjabi leaders
rhetorically supported the shariat during the Pakistan movement, they
had little practical use for those aspects of shariat-based law, particularly a concern for the inheritance rights of women, that potentially
threatened the links between biradari and settled property interests.
Despite the passage of the West Punjab Shariat Application Act of

1948, and even in the face of Ayub's new family laws in the 1960s and General Zia's Islamizing reforms of the 1980s (with their very different statist approaches to Islam), rural Punjabi elites have generally continued to deploy their local resources, as Matthew Nelson has recently shown, to protect rural Punjab's property-holding structure, and have thus worked systematically to block the implementation of shariat-based inheritance rights for daughters.[36] The gap between shariat as a universalizing sign of individual transformation and moral community, and the actual implementation of rules of shariat that might challenge the structure of inequality underlying rural property holding and biradari organization, has thus been large. To some degree this has led to an emphasis within popular interpretations of the shariat on those aspects of Islamic law seemingly reconcilable to the maintenance of biradari-based authority, particularly those emphasizing not female inheritance, but strong male control over the conduct of women (which has also, as a result, produced a movement among some women to contest such an interpretation). But a widespread vision of shariat as an idealized system has persisted, and has fuelled sectarian competition (occasionally violent) focused on idealized visions of religious law and religious community, usually divorced from the realities of local life. The overall tenor of controversy surrounding the shariat in Punjab's politics—though hardly capturing all the varied aspects of Islam's changing roles in Punjab since 1947—thus suggests also the persistence of tensions rooted in the history of agricultural settlement.[37]

Perhaps most interestingly, the history of these transformations also provides a critical window on a third realm: the story of the abortive efforts since 1947 to develop a distinctive Punjabi regional identity within Pakistan. The legacies of Punjab's environmental transformations are perhaps clearest in this arena. One of the noteworthy features marking Punjab's history since 1947 has, in fact, been the lack of a popular movement of Punjabi identity drawing on the projection of a folk identity of Punjabis as 'sons of the soil'—and this in an overwhelming agrarian province. This is in contrast with many parts of India, and, indeed, with Bengal, and has sometimes been cited as a reason for the weakness of democracy in west Punjab.[38] The reasons for this are, of course, complex. But the context for the historical emergence of a predominantly agricultural society in Punjab, amidst the environmental changes of the nineteenth and early twentieth centuries, undoubtedly played a significant role.

Unlike in Bengal under the Mughals, Punjab's agricultural settlement did not produce a strong cultural association between Islam and farming. This was not because Islamic identity was unimportant to Punjabi agriculturalists, as there was, as we have seen, an old and deeply embedded tradition of indigenous rural Islam in the Punjab, preeminently associated with Sufism and with the popular Punjabi *qisse*, dating back to a mixed pastoral/agricultural era. But it was the emergence of biradari as the dominant, yet parochial, form of local community that shaped most profoundly Punjab's cultural adaptation to a new, propertied agricultural order. Though a culture of Punjabi identity associated with Sufism and with the great qisse survived (and in some ways even thrived) under colonial rule, as Farina Mir has shown, it provided no unifying cultural frame for a political movement during the British period based on the popular mobilization of reified Punjabi identity (as was evident even in the history of the Unionist Party).

This did not prevent some urban intellectuals attempting in the years after 1947 to mobilize Punjab's cultural traditions as a frame for resistance to the statism of the new Pakistani order. Yet, strikingly, it was pastoralism, and the values of freedom associated with it, that were now mobilized to try to free Punjabi culture from the parochial space that an emphasis on local biradari had defined for it within the great agricultural/property transformation that occurred under the British. As Fateh Mohammad Malik has described it, intellectuals 'rediscovered in the folk-lore, heroes of resistance and revolt against an oppressive system and symbols of egalitarian change in an exploitative economic order and wove poems, stories and plays around them'.[39] Indeed, pastoralism was associated precisely with a universalizing spirit of individual freedom that was now projected as having been lost in the great process of environmental change and agricultural settlement. As one Punjabi poet, Rashid Hassan Rana, put it, lamenting the loss of this pastoral spirit: 'We used to be called Kharrals and Raaths; now we have become thieves... Mother earth, find yourself other sons'.[40] A pre-colonial (and pre-settlement) past, often associated with Sufism, became the foundation for a new folk vision of Punjabi culture that could be juxtaposed against the bureaucratic authority of the state. As one author put it, the sixteenth century Sufi poet, Shah Husain, could serve as 'a kind of Murshid who is calling everyone to go with him to the Jhok [pastoral camp] of Ranjhan', the pastoral locus of both universal, intrinsically human values—and Punjabi identity—that had been lost in the new environmental/legal framework for Punjab's agricultural transformation.[41]

But this literary appeal to old pastoral and Sufi traditions, as foundations for a new, folk identity defining the culture of Punjab, gained significance precisely because the agricultural transformation of Punjab was now virtually complete, and a semi-pastoral economy only a memory.[42] However much the appeal to pastoralism as the key to the authentic spirit of the folk resonated with some intellectuals, it had limited appeal to contemporary rural biradari leaders who remained enmeshed in a bureaucratized structure of state-controlled irrigation and agricultural production that also protected rural property rights. Though Sufism and Punjabi qisse were indeed at times popularly mobilized in literature and popular culture as a counterpoint to the power of the Pakistani state, such appeals were in practice meaningful less as a mode of resistance to state power, than as a reflection of the complicit structures of power associated with biradari organization, and with the rights of property, that had long allowed rural leaders both to engage with, and yet, at the same time, define a realm of cultural distance from, the state.[43]

Such contradictions were in some ways tellingly encapsulated by the small controversy that erupted in the mid-1970s regarding the renaming of the city of Lyallpur, the major commercial and agricultural mart of western Punjab—and the central city of Punjab's old canal colonies. Lyallpur in some ways epitomized Punjab's agricultural revolution under colonial rule. Named for Punjab Lt-Gov. James B. Lyall, one of the administrative and intellectual architects of what we might call Punjab's nineteenth century 'cultural settlement', Lyallpur came into existence at the end of the nineteenth century as the commercial hub for the colonies, and grew by the 1980s to be a city of over a million people. It lay at the heart of modern agricultural Punjab, and yet, as the colonial name Lyallpur suggested, its symbolic role as a cultural centre after Pakistan's creation was ambiguous. Among the suggestions for a new name in the 1970s, none seemed more calculated to link the city to its indigenous regional roots than a name in honour of Ahmad Khan Kharral, the pastoral leader of the tribes who revolted against the British in 1857. But before a decision could be reached on this by Zulfiqar Ali Bhutto and the Pakistan People's Party, the elections of 1977, and the coup of General Zia intervened. In asserting his own statist power, Zia wasted little time in officially renaming the city, in September 1977, as Faisalabad in honor of King Faisal of Saudi Arabia. Whatever Zia's concern in playing for Saudi support, the cultural implications of his actions were unmistakable. As a symbolic statement of the power of the state to define the culture of Pakistan, independently of any direct connection to the indigenous, rural traditions of the Punjab—or to Punjabi society—the significance of Zia's act could hardly have been clearer.

Though the renaming of Lyallpur was in itself an act with little direct political significance for the country, it suggested the ongoing tension in Pakistan between the conceptual separation of the biradari-based structure of Pakistani society from an essentially statist Islamic culture (here drawing sustenance from its international Islamic and developmental links). Central to the history of this tension is an understanding of the cultural framework for the modern ecological transformation of the Punjab. Western Punjab was transformed into an overwhelmingly settled agricultural region only in the nineteenth and early twentieth centuries, and within a colonial bureaucratic framework in which indigenous culture was self-consciously neither replaced nor destroyed, but parochialized and deliberately separated from the idealized vision of a unifying culture defining the state. Settled property rights bound individuals to the state system, even as the linking of such rights to biradari grounded the individual culturally in parochialized local communities. This defined a particular form of cultural separation between state and society that has had a profound effect on Punjab's politics. But perhaps most importantly, this story also suggests the importance for historians of grounding the history of the Punjab, in all its intersecting social, religious and developmental aspects, in a larger history of changing relationships to the environment and the land. This is an ongoing agenda, that in its vast local variation and detail—and in its overarching long-term historical significance—historians are just beginning to pursue.

NOTES

1 See, for example, F.K. Khan Durrani, *The Meaning of Pakistan*, Lahore: Islamic Book Service, 1983.

2 Perhaps the most noteworthy book that attempted this was the study by the prominent Pakistani lawyer, Aitzaz Ahsan, *The Indus Saga and the Making of Pakistan*, New York: Oxford, 1996.

3 Richard M. Eaton, *The Rise of Islam and the Bengal Frontier*, Berkeley: University of California Press, 1993, p. 268.

4 Habib argues, admittedly somewhat speculatively, that the Persian wheel shaped Jat migration and settlement in the Punjab and the subsequent development of Jat culture, including the development of Sikhism. See Irfan Habib, 'Presidential Address', in *Proceedings of the Indian History Congress*, 31st Session, Varanasi, 1969, Patna: Indian History Congress, 1970, pp. 149–55, and 'Jatts in Medieval Punjab', in Reeta Grewal and Sheena Pall (eds), *Precolonial and Colonial Punjab: Society, Economy, Politics and Culture*, Delhi: Manohar, 1992, pp. 63–75. For a critique of Habib's views, see Chetan Singh, 'Well-irrigation Methods in Medieval Punjab: The Persian Wheel Reconsidered', *Indian Economic and Social History Review*, XXII (1), January–March 1985, pp. 73–87.

5 This was particularly marked in the region around Multan and Bahawalpur. See Richard B. Barnett, 'The Greening of Bahawalpur: Ecological Pragmatism and State Formation in Pre-British Western India, 1730–1870', *Indo-British Review: A Journal of History*, 15 (2), December 1988.

6 Sarah F.D. Ansari, *Sufi Saints and State Power: The Pirs of Sind, 1843–1947*, Cambridge: Cambridge University Press, 1992, p. 35.

7 Neeladri Bhattacharya, 'Pastoralists in a Colonial World', in David Arnold and Ramachandra Guha (eds), *Nature, Culture, Imperialism: Essays on the Environmental History of South Asia*, New Delhi: Oxford University Press, 1995, p. 80.

8 The importance of 'clans' (at least partly pastoral) in many Punjabi *qissa*s has been noted by Harjot Oberoi: 'The popular folk-songs of Hir-Ranjha, Mirza-Sahiban and Sassi-Punnu, recited by minstrels all over the province, illustrate both the existence of clan rules and how conflict, retribution and bloodshed followed when these rules were violated'. Harjot Oberoi, *The Construction of Religious Boundaries: Culture,*

Identity, and Diversity in the Sikh Tradition, Chicago: University of Chicago Press, 1994, p. 419.

9 Christopher Shackle, 'Transition and Transformation in Varis Shah's Hir', in Christopher Shackle and R. Snell (eds), *The Indian Narrative: Perspectives and Patterns*, Wiesbaden: Harrassowitz, 1992, pp. 241–63.

10 The British did, in fact, attempt to collect revenue from pastoralists through the *tirni* tax, but many viewed this as an encouragement to settle. See Brian Caton, 'Settling the State: Pastoralists and Colonial Rule in Southwestern Panjab, 1840–1900', PhD dissertation, University of Pennsylvania, 2003. Caton's work is pioneering in linking the story of settlement in western Punjab to a narrative of the structural transformation of the state.

11 A good history of the intersection of lineage and settlement is found in Tom G. Kessinger, *Vilyatpur, 1848–1968: Social and Economic Change in a North Indian Village*, Berkeley: University of California Press, 1974, who also discusses how lineage was transformed to produce new patterns under the legal framing of property by the British (though Kessinger does not much use the term 'biradari' in his analysis).

12 These constraints initially affected primarily inheritance, but they also restricted land sales, both under the laws of preemption and under the statutory framing of the Punjab Alienation of Land Act. The general tensions in colonial law between free individual land control and indigenous cultural constraints on individual land control is discussed in David Washbrook, 'Law, State, and Agrarian Society in Colonial India', *Modern Asian Studies*, 15 (3), 1981, though he does not discuss the distinctive relationship of the law to forms of genealogy-based local organization.

13 For a good, short introduction to this process, not only from an administrative, but also from an intellectual point of view, see the Introduction in Clive Dewey, *The Settlement Literature of the Greater Punjab: A Handbook*, Delhi: Manohar, 1991. The most detailed examination of the implications of these records in shaping emerging ideas of community is in Richard Saumarez Smith, *Rule by Records: Land Registration and Village Custom in Early British Panjab*, New Delhi: Oxford University Press, 1996.

14 For a discussion of the imaginative power of the *kaghazi raj* (empire of paper) created by British bureaucracy and property law, see Matthew S. Hull, 'The File: Agency, Authority, and Autography in an Islamabad Bureaucracy', *Language & Communication*, vol. 23, 2003, p. 293. See also David Gilmartin, 'The Strange Career of the Rule of Law in Colonial Punjab', *Pakistan Vision*, 10 (2), December 2009, pp. 1–21.

15 There is a somewhat fuller discussion in David Gilmartin, '*Biraderi* and Bureaucracy: The Politics of Muslim Kinship Solidarity in 20th

Century Punjab', *International Journal of Punjab Studies*, 1 (1), January–June 1994, pp. 1–29. The term biradari is of course one that overlapped with, and was in varying circumstances ambiguously related to, a variety of other similar terms (in English, Urdu, and Punjabi), including tribe, *qaum, got*, and *zat*. But I have conflated these under the term biradari here to suggest the distinctive ways these all came to be loosely connected within the new moral/cultural framework of the colonial system in the late nineteenth century, even if, in specific circumstances, they had varied and sometimes distinctive meanings.

16 This elasticity is captured in Prakash Tandon, *Punjabi Century*, Berkeley: University of California Press, 1961, p. 82; Biradari referents shifted in the local setting, he noted, depending on the context: 'There was an Overall Hindu biradari', he writes, 'There was a Khatri biradari, an Aurora biradari, and biradaris of sub-castes and each service caste, Hindu or Muslim. These biradaris were loose and undefined, but in time of need they formed themselves into close-knit groups. They gave you certain rights and expected some duties'. As geographical contexts expanded in the twentieth century, biradaris too took on larger referents sometimes encompassing very large numbers in the context of provincial politics (as, for example, in references to the Jat or Arain biradaris in provincial politics). Biradaris also existed, though in perhaps somewhat different form, among non-property owning groups.

17 See Farina Mir, *The Social Space of Language: Vernacular Culture in British Colonial Punjab*, Berkeley: University of California Press, 2010.

18 At Aitchison Chiefs College, for example, the British encouraged the maintenance by this elite of pride in genealogy, respect for their religious heritage, and respect for the cultural trappings of their parochial, tribal identities, including their folk culture and Sufi associations. But at the same time, they sought to divorce this from any high cultural tradition, providing instead an intellectual education for this elite that was overwhelmingly English in its emphases.

19 See Mir, *The Social Space of Language*.

20 Hanif Ramay, *Panjab ka Muqaddimah*, Lahore: Jang Pablisharz, 1985, pp. 51–67.

21 The ideology of state control in the canal colonies bears comparison with many of those projects discussed in James C. Scott, *Seeing Like a State: How Certain Schemes to Improve the Human Condition have Failed*, New Haven: Yale University Press, 1998.

22 The British in fact emphasized in the Punjab Colonies Committee Report following the protests the central importance of property to the whole structure of popular consent which they saw underlying their rule: 'No considerable body of persons have in northern India ever held

directly under the British Government otherwise than as proprietors', the Committee declared, 'and it has become an ingrained and cherished belief that this status implies security of tenure and moderation and justice in regard to the revenue demand'. Punjab Government, *Report of the Colonies Committee, 1907–08*, Lahore: Civil and Military Gazette Press, 1908, p. 18.

23 See Imran Ali, *The Punjab Under Imperialism, 1885–1947*, Princeton: Princeton University Press, 1988, p. 70, and Imran Ali, 'Malign Growth? Agricultural Colonization and the Roots of Backwardness in the Punjab', *Past and Present*, vol. 114, February 1987, pp. 110–32.

24 An excellent example of this is provided in Prem Chowdhry's discussion of the relationship of mobilization along religious lines to local conflicts based on 'caste' in Haryana: Prem Chowdhry, 'Contours of Communalism: Religion, Caste and Identity in South-East Punjab', *Social Scientist*, 24 (4/6), 1996, pp. 130–63.

25 Malhotra says that the authority of the 'caste-based *biradari* or patrilineage' was declining among urban Hindus, but in some ways, as she also implies, the referents for biradari were expanding. What is most striking is the way that the biradari idiom itself shifted from its original moorings to encompass multiple visions of community solidarity in local (and provincial) life. It is thus significant that one can find the term used even to refer to 'the biradari of the Arya Samajis'. Anshu Malhotra, *Gender, Caste, and Religious Identities: Restructuring Class in Colonial Punjab*, New Delhi: Oxford University Press, 2002, pp. 36–41.

26 There were, of course, some ongoing efforts under the British to link biradari identities to the larger structures of sacred genealogy that had long shaped some 'tribal' histories in the Punjab. For some discussion of this, see David Gilmartin, '*Biraderi* and Bureaucracy', p. 17.

27 For a good study of this, see Prem Chowdhry, *Punjab Politics: The Role of Chhotu Ram*, New Delhi: Vikas, 1984.

28 The relationship of the development of communalism to different visions of the self (and relations to society) deserves considerably more work, but some discussion of this with respect to the Arya Samaj is in C. S. Adcock, 'Religious Freedom and Political Culture: The Arya Samaj in Colonial North India', Unpublished PhD Thesis, University of Chicago, 2007. See also Neeti Nair, *Changing Homelands: Hindu Politics and the Partition of India*, Cambridge: Harvard University Press, 2011.

29 Harjot Oberoi, *The Construction of Religious Boundaries: Culture, Identity, and Diversity in the Sikh Tradition*, Chicago: University of Chicago Press, 1994.

30 Joyce Pettigrew, *Robber Noblemen: A Study of the Political System of the Sikh Jats*, London: Routledge & Kegan Paul, 1975.

31 Alavi does not specifically make this argument with respect to biradari, but for the idea of the salariat, see Hamza Alavi, 'Formation of the Social Structure of South Asia under the Impact of Colonialism', in Hamza Alavi and John Harriss (eds), *Sociology of Developing Societies: South Asia*, London: Macmillan, 1989, pp. 5–19.

32 'Blood relationship is earth-rootedness', Iqbal had written in *The Reconstruction of Religious Thought in Islam*, Lahore: Sh. Muhammad Ashraf, 1971, p. 146. See also Iqbal's poem, 'To a Panjab Peasant', D.J. Matthews (ed. and trans.), *Iqbal: A Selection of the Urdu Verse*, London: SOAS, 1993, pp. 122–3. Such developments in Islamic thinking were not, of course, a product only of the history of Punjab, and there is a large context for studying their roots in a history of Islamic reform that is well beyond the scope of this article.

33 Such a vision of Pakistan paralleled the urban politics of abstracted, individual community identification, a 'politics against society' that Markus Daechsel associates with the growth of urban consumer society in Punjab during this era. Markus Daechsel, *The Politics of Self-expression: the Urdu Middle-class Milieu in Mid-twentieth century India and Pakistan*, London: Routledge, 2006.

34 Visions of radical structural change were present among some Pakistan supporters, and found concrete expression in documents such as the Punjab Muslim League Manifesto of 1944. But more typical, as the end of British rule approached, was the framing found in the Muslim League's electoral appeals of 1946, in which the demand for Pakistan was juxtaposed against a social world dominated by everyday structures of power, kinship, and biradari, even as the League itself made continuing use of these social structures for political purposes. See David Gilmartin (trans.), 'Muslim League Appeals to the Voters of Punjab for Support of Pakistan' in Barbara Metcalf (ed.), *Islam in South Asia in Practice*, Princeton: Princeton University Press, 2009, pp. 409–23.

35 Douglas J. Merrey, 'Irrigation and Honor: Cultural Impediments to the Improvement of Local Level Water Management in Pakistan', in Michael R. Dove and Carol Carpenter (eds), *Sociology of Natural Resources in Pakistan and Adjoining Countries*, Lahore: Vanguard Books, 1992, pp. 126–60.

36 Matthew Nelson, *In the Shadow of Shari'ah: Islam, Islamic Law, and Democracy in Pakistan*, New York: Columbia University Press, 2011. See also Veena Talwar Oldenburg, *Dowry Murder: The Imperial Origins of a Cultural Crime*, New York: Oxford University Press, 2002. This is not to suggest, of course, that these issues have not been the subject of conflict and variation both geographically and over time.

37 One can see some of these tensions reflected also in contestations about the role of pirs in Punjabi society—and in Pakistani Islam—after 1947. For some discussion of this see David Gilmartin, 'Sufism, Exemplary Lives, and Social Science in Pakistan', in Carl W. Ernst and Richard C. Martin (eds), *Rethinking Islamic Studies: From Orientalism to Cosmopolitanism*, Columbia: University of South Carolina Press, 2010, pp. 159–78.

38 For one comparative analysis of this (which emphasizes also the weaknesses of land reform in Pakistani Punjab in the postcolonial era), see Robert W. Stern, *Democracy and Dictatorship in South Asia: Dominant Classes and Political Outcomes in India, Pakistan, and Bangladesh*, Westport, CT: Praeger, 2001, pp. 49–74.

39 Fateh Mohammad Malik, *Punjabi Identity*, Lahore: Sang-e-Meel Publications, 1989, p. 14.

40 Ibid., pp. 22–35. Hanif Ramay, for example, held up the biographies of pastoral leaders such as Dullah Bhatti, who led a revolt against the Mughals from the Sandal Bar, and Ahmad Khan Kharral as models of Punjabi men embodying the inner spirit of Punjabi Muslim identity. Hanif Ramay, *Panjab ka Muqaddimah*, pp. 114–24.

41 The quotation about Ranjha is from a defense by Aitzaz Ahsan of a Punjabi novel by the PPP activist, Fakhar Zaman, quoted in Fateh Mohammad Malik, *Punjabi Identity*, p. 35. The use of Ranjha by Najam Hussain Sayad as a symbol of the search for the Punjabi self is discussed more fully in Fahmida Riaz, *Pakistan Literature and Society*, New Delhi: Patriot Publishers, 1986, pp. 93–5.

42 Some, however, continued to associate this ideology of freedom with pastoralism where it still survived in Pakistan. See, for example, Akbar S. Ahmed, 'Nomadism as Ideological Expression: The Case of Gomal Nomads', *Economic and Political Weekly*, 17 (27), 3 July 1982, pp. 1101–06.

43 This in part explains the paradoxical character, as Alyssa Ayres has noted, of the appeal by some intellectual elites to Punjabi language and culture as a sign of resistance to oppression, even as Punjabi elites have enjoyed a privileged place in the overall structure of power in Pakistan. Alyssa Ayres, 'Language, the Nation, and Symbolic Capital: The Case of Punjab', *Journal of Asian Studies*, 67 (3), August 2008, pp. 917–46.

11

Markus Daechsel

Being Middle Class in Late Colonial Punjab

There is nothing strange about locating a 'middle class' in contemporary Punjab. On the Indian side of the 1947 border such an association is in fact intuitive: one thinks immediately of one of the richest farming strata in post-colonial India, be they predominantly Sikh as in east Punjab proper, or Hindu Jat in Haryana. Less geographically contiguous, but equally clear is the association between Punjabis and an urban middle class: when one speaks of Delhi as a 'Punjabi' city by virtue of its numerous Partition refugees from Lahore, Rawalpindi or the canal colony towns which are now in Pakistan, one also thinks of their proverbially middle-class lifestyle; industriousness and self-help, entrepreneurship and mercantile skill, and above all, their taste for consumerism and the fruits of liberalization. A similar association also exists in Pakistan, although it is often couched more in political than economic terms. Here, being middle class and Punjabi means being an aspiring member of the Pakistani elite. More specifically it denotes urban constituencies that espouse the values of education and political responsibility, which are often seen in contrast to the 'religious fundamentalism' of the poor and the 'feudal' cynicism of the land-owning rich.

To associate *colonial* Punjab with middle-class development is far less intuitive, however. At least at first glance, it is almost a contradiction in terms. The dominant focus of politics and social development in the pre-1947 province revolves around the relationship of landed elites and their dependents. We know of canal colonies and colonial agricultural developments, of Sufi pirs and their peasant followers, and of the politics of the Punjab Unionist party, which in so many ways epitomized the successful installation of a regime of landed grandees in the face of social mobility and political pressures from below.[1] For most historians, middle-class development in colonial India may be an appropriate topic of study in Bombay and Calcutta, even perhaps in Delhi or the cities of United Province (UP)[2] but it seems out of place in the 'granary of India'.

At least in part, this contrast between colonial and post-colonial Punjab is simply down to changing political hegemons. The British had claimed the very possibility of being 'middle class' almost entirely for themselves. Throughout the nineteenth century, such a label had meant being progressive and reasonable, a force for the future pitted against 'Old Corruption'.[3] The colonial enterprise was in many ways a global expression of this historic role at home. Ruling India for the sake of a civilizing mission was for large sections of the British public a self-avowedly 'middle class' mission.[4] It follows that even to grant the possibility of middle-class development amongst the ruled would have amounted to an intellectual self-dissolution of the colonial project. But the denial of a middle class also threw down the gauntlet for the political ambitions of aspirant Indians. In order to become truly free they too had to become middle class in some form or other; in order to claim their rights they had to claim their rights as a middle class.

Such aspirations received a powerful boost after decolonization, when US modernization theory became the most powerful paradigm of development sociology. Having a 'new middle class' became a key criterion for obtaining support and development aid. Both the US and the Soviet Union eager to seek 'progressive' allies amongst the newly decolonized nations around the globe no longer denied the existence of a middle class in the poor South, but actively demanded it.[5] It is no coincidence that Pakistanis enthusiastically adopted a language of the middle class when their relationship with the US grew ever closer under Ayub Khan's military dictatorship, even though this language was used by so many and with such empirical imprecision that it became almost meaningless as an actual social category on the ground.[6] Something similar happened in India more recently, after the demise of the Nehruvian state. When India became the model of successful globalization in the wake of economic liberalization and ever-closer strategic ties with the US, there was again talk about the 'great Indian middle class', which was meant to add a social foundation to political ambition.[7]

Even if it was only in the post-independence period that a language of being 'middle class' became fully available as a powerful self-description to the people of South Asia, it is still worth questioning whether there really was no place for a middle class in colonial Punjab. By its own logic, colonial rule itself both posited the possibility of a middle class (what else should a successful civilizing mission produce?) and made its articulation impossible in an artificial straightjacket of paternalism and tradition. Although it existed to some extent everywhere in India, this contradiction was nowhere more drastic than in Punjab. The very process of creating a prosperous, stable and landlord dominated political economy was impossible without far-reaching modernization measures which immediately called into being a service stratum that was amongst the most modernized anywhere in the subcontinent. There were no canal colonies without revenue officials, surveyors, railway and irrigation engineers; no peace amongst the 'sturdy' landowning zamindars without an overgrown legal establishment, no agricultural production without insurance houses, banks and moneylenders, no cotton or wheat for world market sale without transport infrastructure, brokers, wholesalers and auxiliary light industry; in turn, there were no lawyers, bankers or administrators without teachers and professors, print workers, publishers and journalists; not to mention the purveyors of soda waters and office suits, hunter beef and family photographs, potency pills and kerosene fans.

This essay is about how these people experienced, fashioned and made sense of their lives as a 'class'. Unlike their post-colonial descendants they did not have at their disposal an overt and officially sanctioned discourse of a middle class that could provide them with a central axis of identification. Their colonial middle-class identities were highly contested and 'fractured', to use Sanjay Joshi's phrase,[8] dispersed, as it were, across a whole range of discursive arenas and experiences, in pedagogy, lifestyle, and social reform, in consumerism and politics. As this essay will show, they never quite made it to become 'a', let alone, 'the' middle class. Their only—still fleeting and self-destructive—sense of identity emerged in political struggle, which not only destroyed the colonial straightjacket that had produced them, but also pitted different sections of the Punjabi middle class mercilessly against each other.

WHAT MAKES THE 'MIDDLE CLASS' A 'CLASS'?

Before investigating the possibilities and limits of middle-class articulation in different arenas of colonial life and culture, it is necessary to clarify some conceptual issues. This essay is based on an un-ashamedly holistic reading of 'class'; one that maintains at least as a question—as it was posed by the colonial gauntlet of development itself—that class bundles different aspects of social existence and unites them in one meta-historical subjectivity. This means 'Class' with a capital 'C', something that still has an aftertaste of the kind of class Marx talked about when he sought to identify a social agent that could make and break capitalism; or indeed, of the kind of class that underlies much past and present talk about 'the' middle class as the harbinger of progress, democracy and general prosperity.

Much scholarly analysis of class in general, and of the middle class in South Asia in particular, has rejected such a holistic view. On the one hand, there have been attempts to pin down 'the middle class' as an empirical reality with the help of objective social science indicators, such as educational status, income, modes of employment etc. Such precision has tended to splinter 'class' into a plethora of substrata that have lost any connection with a special mission or meta-historical drive.[9] From a force for change, class has—beyond the narrow confines of social mobility—become a descriptive of order. In the case of South Asia this approach has been adopted in much sociological and anthropological work, presenting case studies of how various variants of middle class in different localities appear in their social and cultural practices.[10] In the field of history, a similar strategy of micro-analysis has led to the rejection of class as a meaningful category altogether. In analysing actual political relationships in localities, the adherents of the so-called Cambridge School, have concluded that political favouritism, loyalties of caste, *biradari* or religious community tended to connect people vertically from top to bottom, rather than horizontally across class loyalties.[11]

On the other hand, class has been re-conceptualized as a 'language' or discourse. In the first instance, this was a reaction to fundamental critiques of the meta-historical master narratives that gave Class with a capital 'C', its foundation. At its most radical, post-linguistic-turn scholars have conceded the possibility of 'class' only insofar as it appeared in overt usages of the term in political and social discourse;[12] an option that is a priori meaningless in a context like colonial Punjab where local people precisely did not describe themselves as 'middle class', in fact, barely possessed the linguistic possibilities to do so.[13] Other interpretations would cast the net wider and occasionally ascribe a class character to a whole range of not always entirely explicit social discourses about status and aspiration. The latter has been the preferred strategy of most recent historians of 'a' middle class in colonial India who sought to locate the existence of such a formation in the growing output of vernacular print publishing from the late nineteenth century onwards.[14] Middle class appears in their account wherever educated Indians wrote about history, language reform, the betterment of women, a reformulation of religious practice, or in new ideas about how to make everyday life more orderly, punctual and hygienic. The most recent scholarship has discovered another important additional register of discourse analysis that goes well with this focus on social reformism: the messages contained in consumer goods and advertising, where, once again, a middle-class ethos could be detected, particularly as far as the very last decades of the colonial period was concerned.[15]

While there is much to learn from all these revisionist approaches, there are several reasons to hark back to 'Class' in the older and stronger sense. In the first instance, it has to do with the need to interpret social and cultural discourses within their appropriate contexts, which can only be conceived as social totalities. It is all well and good to describe Indian social reformism or consumerism as 'middle class-ness' because they easily map on to similar 'middle class' ideas in nineteenth century Europe. But we can only be sure what these discourses really meant in their local context by relating them to the struggles and experiences of Indians who adopted them. A second reason for maintaining at least some sense of class in the strong sense lies in the need to acknowledge the extraordinary power that such an idea continues to exercise over people's lives. Sociological or linguistic analyses that deconstruct the middle class and its underlying master narrative of modernization into non-existence can only ring hollow in a context where the prestige and real-life purchase of these ideas has never been higher. At least for the sake of having a fruitful argument, it is worth not looking quite so closely and carefully at 'class' as a precise category, but to accept the challenge of working with a grandly flawed but 'live' concept.

What makes a class a class—and not simply a 'stratum' or a 'discourse'—is the fact that it has some 'beef'. It arouses love and hate, knows who its enemies and friends are. It is not—or at least not merely—a descriptive category but a concept born of struggle. To say this is not necessarily a fallback to crude Marxism predicated on the assumption that social ideology and identity formation, 'in the last instance', relate to hard economic facts, to objective relationships with the means of production. Rather, I wish to adopt a view inspired by Nietzschean genealogy; one that does not seek to reduce class conflict to any particular cause, but rather focuses on the conflict itself, the heat it generates, the pain as well as the exhilaration that the experience of power entails. It is still the social context as a whole that generates this conflict, because conflict itself is only imaginable as a relational category; it can never be explained by looking at one partner in the conflict alone. The 'beef'—the sense of resentment, fear, hatred and aspiration—that characterized the middle class in colonial Punjab was, as we shall see, never reducible to a simple anxiety over jobs and wealth. There was much more involved: sexual identity, relationship with one's body, political self-fulfilment and so on. But the functioning of the colonial political economy remains an important starting point, not the least because it provided the necessary context to discussions of culture that will follow later on in this essay.

COLONIAL AGRICULTURAL CAPITALISM

Punjab was set apart from the rest of India by a number of unique features which have been explored in more detail throughout this volume: conquered and annexed as late as 1848, Punjab was a spectacular case for rapid 'development' in the colonial era. While the Raj was entirely content not to follow up its rhetoric of a civilizing mission and to run a government 'on the cheap' in almost all other parts of India, it was much more seriously committed to social and economic interventionism in Punjab. The main reasons were military and strategic: Punjab lay on what was then considered the traditional 'invasion route' of India from the North West and had to be especially protected. More importantly, Punjab had acquired a reputation for providing loyal soldiers to the Imperial Army who were to fight for the crown from the trenches of Flanders to Singapore, from Eritrea to Hong Kong. [16]

The measures adopted to create Punjab as the proverbial land of stability and loyalty drew heavily on the lessons learnt from experiences of anti-colonial rebellion, particularly the Great Uprising of 1857: a prosperous and stable class of agricultural owners–cultivators had to be created and protected, and the landed elites that exercised some control over them had to be accommodated politically. What one wanted to avoid was the combination of radicalized landless peasants, disgruntled post-Mughal lords and nationalist city professionals that undermined stability in neighbouring UP. In Punjab, soldiers and farmers had to be kept as far apart as possible from city populations and from uncontrolled processes of social change. This was achieved through two trademark Punjabi policies: first, the state got heavily involved in land development and irrigation, particularly in the canal colonies, where land could be directly allocated to those deemed especially loyal to crown. Second, and an intricate system of land-ownership legislation based on the anthropological distinction between 'agricultural' and 'non-agricultural' tribes and castes was used to keep the right to hold farming properties across the province firmly in the hands of the kind of loyalist constituencies identified above. The special favourites of the crown included Hindu Jat, Muslim Rajputs, Arains and a host of other 'tribal' groupings, and in addition, most 'orthodox' Khalsa Sikhs, while also leaving many 'non-agriculturalists' from all three religious communities beyond the purview of favouritism.[17]

Even at its most 'developmentalist', the colonial state remained extractive, however. Monetized tax-collection depended on an intricate system of loans and insurance schemes, which were provided to cultivators by village moneylenders, who were in their majority Hindu (and Sikh) Khatris. The contradiction between ensuring a level of agricultural prosperity to keep the zamindar class loyal, and the need to raise revenue in the interest of the colonial enterprise could only be bridged with ever-increasing levels of rural indebtedness. In consequence, the power of moneylending and commercial constituencies increased dramatically over the course of the late nineteenth century. They transformed from proverbial itinerant '*sahukar*s' who were always at risk of violent peasant reprisals into a highly urbanized stratum with connections into the colonial bureaucracy and an ambition to elite status. Although by no means uniformly anti-colonial, this constituency proved on several occasions over the late nineteenth century that it could be a powerful and occasionally radical political force.[18]

It is before this background that the contours of middle-class development in Punjab emerged. To exemplify what happened let us turn to the life of one man that demonstrates both the opportunities and constraints of the colonial political economy. Lala Harkishan Lal— according to an obituary 'the man who put Punjab on the industrial map'[19]—was born in 1864 in a remote country town on the border to the Pakhtun frontier, as son of Lala Chhela Ram, a rich Hindu grain trader and agricultural moneylender. Between 1881 and 1887, the young Harkishan Lal was educated at Government College, Lahore, which had at that very point become part of the recently created Punjab University, the nucleus of one of the largest and best-regarded educational institutions in all of India. This was a time when many advanced clerical and professional positions still had to be filled by recruits from the much older and more anglicized province of Bengal, and an

Anglophone Punjabi service elite was still in its infancy. Harkishan Lal's performance at university earned him a scholarship to study law at Trinity College, Cambridge. In 1893, he stopped practising law in his hometown, Dera Ismail Khan, with its sharp communal conflicts and limited economic opportunities. Like so many others from a similar background, he shifted to Lahore, the capital of a province where the agricultural economy was rapidly expanding and integrated into a global capitalist market.[20]

As a designated 'non-agriculturalist', Harkishan Lal was legally barred from investing his growing capital in agricultural land. In search for alternative investment opportunities Harkishan Lal founded a number of more or less unstable 'modern' financial institutions that went well beyond the scope of the 'traditional' moneylending business that had characterized his father's generation: the Punjab National Bank, the Bharat Insurance Company and the People's Bank, all employing a growing number of white collar workers. In anticipation of technological change, he also initiated and chaired the Lahore Electrical Supply Company, and owned or founded the Punjab Cotton Press, the Bhatinda Flour Mills, the Century Flour Mills, the Lucknow Flour Mills, the Lahore Sugar Mills, the Mahalakhshmi Sugar Works and the Bharat Ice Factory.[21] This list demonstrates once again where a nouveau riche non-agriculturalist could and could not make money: there was some scope for the manufacture of consumer perishables, and for the first stage processing of agricultural commodities, but in accordance with government policy not for large scale industrial production, which would have undercut the very primacy of agriculture on which the governability of the province depended so crucially.[22]

Harkishan Lal's rise to a finance bourgeois of sorts was forever endangered, and in the end fatally undermined, by his inability to cultivate lasting government support and to survive in the world of factional intrigue. Although the Raj gave certain recognition to the man—by making him a minister under the new system of 'dyarchy' after the First World War, no less—it ultimately remained suspicious of an Indian tycoon who became too big for his boots. Despite his efforts to stay close to power, Harkishan Lal had lost control over the Punjab National Bank early on and went bankrupt with the People's

Bank twice, once in 1913, and again in 1931, when he even received a six-months prison sentence. This second bankruptcy received considerable attention around India as Lahore Chief Justice Douglas Young, a man at the top of the British colonial establishment, was alleged to have colluded with Harkishan Lal's local business rivals to enable them to ruin him.[23] Harkishan Lal's children defended a certain position of wealth, however, but not without displaying an almost chameleon-like ability to subvert colonial social identities. Khalid Latif Gauba, his son, took the extraordinary step of converting to Islam in the early 1930s to get married to the daughter of a high-ranking Muslim Civil Servant. Later he stood in the 1937 elections and became a Member of Legislative Assembly (MLA) for the Unionist Party, voice-piece of loyalist and agriculturalist interest led by Sir Sikandar Hayat Khan. Instrumental in his ability to cross the sacrosanct land-owning–non-landowning divide was a wave of religious sympathy which he carefully cultivated by publishing, amongst other things, a reformist hagiography of the Prophet Muhammad in English.[24]

URBANIZATION AND SERVICE PATRONAGE

Key to the kind of social advancement that Harkishan Lal enjoyed on his path from mufassilite moneylender to urban banker was rapid urban development. The spaces where a new Punjabi middle class could emerge were the cities, particularly the capital Lahore. Despite the inescapable and omnipresent links between most economic activity and the colonial land-economy, Punjab's capital grew an exponential rate over the late colonial period, in the case of the provincial capital from 228,687 to 671,649 between 1911 and 1941, an increase of 193 per cent (compared to a 44 per cent overall population growth over the same period). It was not only urbanization amongst large sections of agricultural financiers that drove this development. Similarly, many members of the agriculturalist classes, particularly their non-inheriting sons, also moved to the city to invest in higher education and become lawyers, teachers or journalists. The most important employer for white-collar workers was government itself, which expanded unabatedly from its humble beginnings in the 1850s until the first major wave of retrenchment after the First World War. Of particular importance within the government sector were the North-Western Railways that employed not only a large number of clerks and engineers, but also ran Lahore's only large industrial establishment, the Mughalpura Railway workshops.[25]

The government service sector was particularly attractive for urban and often 'non-agricultural' Muslims who lacked the family expertise and capital to establish themselves in the Hindu and Khatri Sikh-dominated commercial sector. The numbers of these aspiring 'middle class' Muslims included government and military contractors,[26] and in growing numbers also urban professionals. The family of one Sufi Pir Bakhsh, born around 1870 into a family of suitcase-makers inside Shehranwala Gate, within the old city walls of Lahore, can serve as a good example.[27] Pir Bakhsh's *zat* or 'caste' was 'Shaikh', denoting a Muslim business family of medium social ranking with a relatively recent conversion history to Islam. In contrast to the more notable, highly politicized and 'agriculturalist' Arains of Lahore, his was a weak 'caste' identity that did not mean much in terms of professional or political advancement. Unlike his brothers, Sufi Pir Bakhsh did not take up the box-making trade, but began working in a printing press, which was then one of the most important bazaar industries in Lahore, satisfying the needs of law, education, commerce and other aspects of the colonial administration. He never got a chance to attend school, but started to become an autodidact and avid reader from the age of 16 —according to family lore mastering several languages including Sanskrit. After marrying a not family-related woman of similar background from Mocchi Gate, another Old City locality, Sufi Pir Bakhsh joined official service in the Punjab Government Printing Press, from where he was to eventually retire in the position of a Superintendent. As for so many other Muslims in the city, it was government service, not commerce, which secured an income large enough for upward social mobility. Pir Bakhsh's success was sealed, when some years before his death in 1936, he moved with his family from the overcrowded inner city area of Shehranwala Gate to Momenpura, Ravi Road, a Muslim-dominated new housing colony north-west of the walled city.

Although the family as a whole never lost touch with the world of bazaar artisanship and small-scale commercial enterprise, Sufi Pir

Bakhsh's lineage won and defended their upwardly mobile status over the course of the twentieth century on the basis of the same factors that had helped Sufi Pir Bakhsh himself: education and government service. His son Muhammad Yusuf (1896–1967) eventually became a headmaster in a colonial high school, his grandchildren rose to important position in the Pakistani military and academia. It is an excellent indication of the family ethos that one of Muhammad Yusuf's sons was told by his father to celebrate the day he joined primary school as his 'official' birthday—even though both were perfectly aware when the 'real' birthday was.

Despite their undeniable individual achievements in education, people like Harkishan Lal and Sufi Pir Bakhsh and his family had to pursue their social aspirations in an environment that was far from meritocratic. It was not only the colonial state itself whose patronage had to be constantly sought for success. The social space, in which middle-class development could take place, was structured around new 'civil society' institutions through which members of the Punjabi elite sought to exercise their influence. Education and religious reform were the most important concerns, and they were often closely linked on the ground. Reformist institutions like the *Anjuman-e Himayat-e Islam* or the *Arya Samaj* organized lecture cycles and women's groups, maintained mosques and temples and, most importantly, ran the most important schools and colleges that were not directly part of the government sector. Funding came in large measure from those on top of the provincial hierarchy, large landowners and members of the most important financier families. Participation in these bodies and access to their resources was largely determined by religious affiliation, which leant an immediate communal flavour to much of middle-class life itself.

Once again, Harkishan Lal's fortunes are a good example. As one of the most prosperous businessman in the province, he sought to establish himself in the provincial elite by patronizing society institutions directly: he was a trustee of Dyal Singh College and *The Tribune* and made contributions to the Benares Hindu University. But his religious affiliations let him down. Harkishan Lal was closely associated with the Brahmo Samaj, the oldest branch of reformist neo-Hinduism. The movement enjoyed a strong following in

Bengal, but in Punjab had only a smattering of support amongst intellectuals, journalists, and bureaucrats. The most powerful Hindu organization in Lahore was the Arya Samaj, which with its vast network of Dayananda Anglo-Vedic Colleges and schools was by far the largest provider of middle-class Hindu education in the city and elsewhere in the province. Harkishan Lal's strong dislike for the Arya Samaj was never only of a religious nature; when he was ruined in trumped up bankruptcy proceedings, he pointed the finger directly at the machinations of powerful Arya Samajis who had plotted against him all his life.[28] Similarly, when Muhammad Yusuf, Sufi Pir Bakhsh's son, failed to obtain a physics lectureship at Government College Lahore, he blamed it on the machinations of 'Hindu' corruption networks; and in order to advance his career he would naturally seek the communal safety of Muslim-financed Islamia College.[29]

THE LIMITS OF THE PATRONAGE SYSTEM

A space for 'middle-class' development in Punjab existed only in the shadows of the agricultural economy, in its subsidiary industries and financial activities, and in a growing service sector directly linked to the state itself. For the most part, this space was ordered by the kind of network politics that the Raj had successfully institutionalized for its own governmental convenience. Direct government patronage mattered the most, and for much of what stood outside direct government control, it was elite patronage—both from landowning grandees and loyalist commercial men—that bound most aspirant city dwellers into the colonial system. The extent to which it even included figures outwardly strongly opposed to colonial system is nicely illustrated in Bhim Sen Sacchar's Sunlight Insurance Company, set up in 1931. Sacchar was a prominent Lahore Congresswalla (and after 1947 Chief Minister of east Punjab), who acted as the spokesman of secular nationalism and social revolution in the Nehruvian mould. But in his private life, he was both a patron himself, and subject to elite patronage from above. The Sunlight Insurance Company hardly employed any Muslims in its clerical staff, but had an illustrative cross-section of the provincial elite on its board of directors: Bhai Parmanand of the Hindu Mahasabha, doyen of loyalist Hindu interests, Mian Daultana of the Unionist Party and later the Muslim League, one of the quintessential 'feudal' lords of Punjab; and finally Raja Raghbir Singh, a Sikh loyalist from Amritsar.[30]

This system of control was never watertight, however, particularly in moments of economic crisis, and in the urban spaces that rapid agricultural modernization had created as an unwanted by-product. In the period between the end of the First World War and Partition, changes in the global political economy had severely limited a further expansion of the agricultural economy and its managerial sector. The state bureaucracy had grown to such an extent that it could no longer be maintained according to the extractive prerogatives of the colonial regime. Large-scale retrenchment followed, and from the 1920s onwards there would be a shortage of government employment opportunities, leading to the widespread emergence of 'educated unemployment' as a much talked about social problem.[31] The World Economic Crisis of the early 1930s drastically reduced returns from the agricultural sector and limited the ability of landowners and agricultural financiers to 'water' the patronage channels with which they sought to control the rest of society. Big business ventures like Harkishan Lal's, collapsed in a climate of tough intra-elite competition, while the sons of impoverished landowners and village artisans flocked to the cities in search for a foothold in a shrinking service economy. They ended up competing with unemployed university graduates for often very precarious jobs. Fears of social decline became widespread. Sons of even relatively well-off families attempted to stay afloat by producing homemade soap, hair oils and medicines; for which they would find do-it-yourself recipes in a burgeoning market of self-help literature for the unemployed city dweller.[32]

When agricultural prices rose again as a consequence of the Second World War, this did not lead to a reintegration of the patronage system, but to hard economic antagonisms that had the potential to turn into open class conflict. While salaried families in the cities were struggling to cope with their dearness allowances to afford even daily necessities, the landowning and financial elite experienced a profit bonanza and a 'golden age' of affluence.[33] Motorcars and

European luxury goods became more visible than ever in Lahore thoroughfares; woollen cloths, kerosene, cement and sugar had to be rationed to support the war effort. As the colonial bureaucracy got more deeply involved into the actual distribution of goods in a system of rationing than ever before, patronage lost its benevolent character and emerged in popular view as a 'connections economy' in which 'corruption' was rife.[34]

The potential class character of widespread dissatisfaction was often immediately blunted by the gravitational pull of All-India nationalist politics, however. Middle-class discontent played a crucial role in the falling out between the Punjab Unionist Party and the All India Muslim League, for instance, which owed its political breakthrough in the cities to middle-class hatred for their erstwhile 'feudal' patrons;[35] but as is well known, the League never became a middle-class party. Most of the feudal patrons quickly jumped on the bandwagon of Muslim nationalism themselves, which took them out of the ideological firing line and allowed them to shore up their preeminence for many decades to come.[36] The Punjab Congress came closer to representing interests that could be described as 'middle class'. Loyalist Hindu financial families would refer to it behind closed doors as the congregation of those who had not really made it in the colonial system. But as the national leadership was only too aware, its support base in Punjab remained highly factionalized and unable to reach out across communal boundaries. Its main selling point was that it was a government in waiting at an all-India level. For most Muslim middle-class circles this simply stoked fears of an impending 'Hindu Raj', while a large number of erstwhile Hindu loyalists from a similar background joined the ranks of the Rashtriya Swayamsevak Sangh (RSS) to prevent the establishment of a 'Muslim Raj' associated with the Pakistan movement.

Middle-class politics in late colonial Punjab does not map on easily to official electoral and nationalist politics, although it is possible to detect elements of class antagonism in the complicated but well-known story of the coming of independence in the province. As we shall see, if there was indeed something like a distinctive middle-class politics during the period, it emerged in a particular *style* of doing politics that cut across established political camps. To perceive this style most distinctly we have to move away from the great stories of South Asian nation creation and listen to more marginal political voices, which have subsequently often been forgotten. Moreover, the Punjabi middle class did not find its political identity in a clear-cut language of economic self-interests, which would be immediately intelligible to old-fashioned Marxists or adherents of the Cambridge School. It is important to keep the broad outlines of the colonial political economy and its contradictions at the back of our mind, but to truly understand how the Punjabi middle class experienced and understood its class position we will now have to turn to an analysis of culture.

REFORMISM AND ITS LIMITS

A link between colonial middle-class development in South Asia and reformist discourse has often been suggested in South Asia scholarship. Many of the ideals espoused by a burgeoning market in vernacular print publishing have a strong middle-class flavour, or at least a resonance with what passes as middle-class values in other parts of the world. Religion was made commensurate with 'science' and tailored more strongly than before around ideas of an individualized, unmediated, and action-oriented relationship with the divine.[37] Gender norms were reformulated around ideals of thrift, hygiene, respectability and a clear demarcation from subaltern and folk practices.[38] Education and self-discipline became the new bywords of success.[39] It is tempting to read these discourses as an Indian response to the colonial presence that right from the start included a project of social and political self-determination, exactly of the kind that the global myth of modernization ascribes to the middle-class tout court. But seen in the light of ground realities in a place like Punjab, a more limited and conservative reading of this discourse suggests itself. Social reformism was not—at least not initially and not primarily—a vehicle for Indian middle-class ambition, but rather the ideological glue required by the colonial political economy of patronage outlined above. It was through the patronage of hospitals, schools, colleges, and women reformers, that the colonial elite of Punjab demonstrated its allegiance to the colonial presence, and simultaneously laid down the ideological ground rules for aspiring others. Only by developing the kind of reformist subjectivity that this master discourse demanded, could Indians earn their ability to serve at the nerve centre of a modernized agricultural system. Moreover, their journey of self-fashioning led them almost invariably into dependency on the colonial state, in educational institutions and in their quest for jobs. If there was indeed a relationship between reformist discourse and middle-class development, it was exactly not one of ideological congruence, but rather it's opposite. As we will demonstrate in more detail in the last section of this essay, it was only through a rejection or subversion of social reformism that a middle class could find something like its own voice.

The system-conformist character of much reformist publishing can be read directly from some of the contradictions that are inherent in this discourse itself. There is always something 'misplaced' or 'out of kilter' about the kind of exhortations to cultivate personal responsibility and thrift, to earn a place on the sunny side of modernity, as they were presented to literate Punjabis of all religious background. As a starting point let us consider two Urdu pamphlets about women's improvement by loyalist Muslim authors. They are in many ways typical for the Punjabi middle-class milieu regardless of religious affiliation as very similar messages were also churned out by Hindu and Sikh writers of the period.[40]

The first is an Urdu booklet entitled *Arsi: the mirror of good housekeeping*, authored by one Maulvi Muhammad Amin who had received the colonially-sanctioned honorific 'Shams ul-ʿUlama', and published by the Dar ul-Ishaʿat-e Panjab, a typical elite-financed publishing house with a strong loyalist and reformist agenda. The booklet appeared first in 1913—alongside many other similar publications by different authors and publishers, including the famous *Bihishti Zewar* of Maulana Ashraf Ali Thanawi of Deoband, which is until today regarded as the authoritative statement of a 'traditionalist' reformist sense of womanhood. Aside from restating some established wisdom on correct religious observance, on home economics and childcare, the pamphlet also targeted some basics of everyday life that would demarcate the *sharif* housewife both from the old elites and from the urban poor: the importance of cross-ventilation and sewerage in dwellings and the need for regular exercise in the open air, for instance, demanded new forms of living that were incommensurate with the old neighbourhoods in old cities like Lahore and suggested the more spacious facilities of new suburbs.[41] New cooking recipes stressed light and non-spicy foods and directly rejected the more sumptuous ideas of the good life espoused by the rajas or zamindars of old.[42] The espousal of a new material culture based on Western imports was recommended in the replacement of earthen pots with metalware, the purchase of hygienically sealed storage jars and meat boxes, and most importantly of all, in the wide-scale use of detergents and disinfectants. Idleness and spending a long time in bed were singled out as sources of evil, and the daily wash under running water and with a lot of soap admonished.[43]

Although it is tempting to see a new 'middle class' woman behind the reader of such a publication this would not amount to a full interpretation of *Arsi*. Seen from the perspective of the strongly loyalist and elite publisher, the pamphlet demonstrates above all a quest for ideological hegemony. Aspiring women could not become 'modern' out of their own devices. As the frequently condemnatory and strongly pedagogic tone suggests, they required tuition from above in almost all aspects of their daily and corporeal existence. Not even the correct use of soap, it appears could be left to their own agency. Self-improvement along the lines suggested here were in no way meant to lead to a new ambitious class consciousness, but rather to an ever-closer incorporation into the colonial system.

This interpretation is strengthened when we consider the second example, a morality tale by the same publisher, again addressed at women and eager to make a reformed domesticity the centre of a new social identity. The title is *Sharif Biwi—the story of poor Sayyida—who advanced from poverty to the highest echelons of wealth by virtue of her education and accomplishment.*[44] Sayyida is a poor but well-brought up woman married to the idle and ill-disciplined Muhammad Ja'far, who does not advance in his meagre government job and spends most of his time playing chess or chatting to friends. Sayyida is unwilling to maintain a standard of 'middle class' respectability by getting into debt; instead she convinces both her husband and her mother-in-law that she should set up her own sewing business to keep the

family afloat. She starts an advertising campaign and then assidu-
ously works her way up from a few orders to obtaining an agency of a
textile firm. As her income reaches mind-boggling amounts she earns
the respect of her husband, family, and biradari. But then the story
offers a very revealing twist: Sayyida's crowning achievement is not
her business wealth, but her ability to inspire her husband to work a
little harder and to network with high colonial officials. In the end it
is *his* becoming Deputy Collector, the birth of a son and happy phil-
anthropic retirement that stand at the end of Sayyida's spectacular
'advance'. The concern for women's employment advocated here is in
part a real recognition of the economic crisis of the post-First World
War era. Many aspiring families had discovered that their further
advance into the colonial elite had become blocked, or that previous
gains could no longer be maintained by the new generation. The
point about all this, however, is that the kind of middle-class work
ethic advocated in the pamphlet was not meant to lead to demands
that could explode the established political economy of favouritism. Aspiring middle-class Punjabis are told to alleviate its position
through its own efforts, but also reminded that the sole source of real
achievement was still patronage.

Another relevant body of literature where such contradictions can
be observed is children's literature. Ever since the first commercial
children's newspaper *Bacchon ka Akhbar* appeared in Lahore in the
early twentieth century, young readers were inundated with a heavily
pedagogic celebration of thrift and upward social mobility. They learnt
how the likes of Benjamin Franklin and James Watt overcame their
bitterly poor childhoods through hard work;[45] even more revealingly,
perhaps, they were meant to sing in an Urdu rendition of *Twinkle
Twinkle Little Star* that their greatest wish should be to become first
of their class and then to join the colonial civil service in a high position.[46] As children's literature matured some of the crude pedagogy
in such publications was softened. The relentless demand for self-
improvement, in contrast, remained as strong as ever. Imtiaz Ali Taj,
perhaps the most important author of children's books in Urdu, of his
generation and editor of magazines and pocket books that influenced
a whole generation of the future 'middle class' Punjabis of all backgrounds, is no exception. A relevant example may be a short-story

entitled 'Purani Haveli'.[47] The story is included in an edition of his
so-called *Paisa Library*, which encouraged the saving of one paisa per
day, so pocket money would be spent on uplifting books rather than
on sweets and other money wasters. Once again the story tells the
changing fortunes of an old sharif family that had fallen upon hard
times after the great depression. An erstwhile successful industrialist
of the late nineteenth century boom, who had wasted his wealth on
a lavish lifestyle and who had been idle and complacent in his business dealings, has to sell the last remaining family asset—an ancient
townhouse inherited from the Mughal past—to meet his creditor's
demands. The children heroes of the stories play one last time in
the old building and discover an ancient treasure that subsequently
saves the family from ruin. The moral of the story is spelt out in the
concluding dialogue between father and children: in modern times
success can only be secured by hard and diligent work, and by the
clever investment of surplus capital. Although the treasure has saved
them for now, the practice of burying money for the benefit of future
generations is in itself reprehensible. True to reformist ideology, the
belief in a meritocratic system based on transparent economic laws
is affirmed—but this morale does not quite follow from the story
itself. A more accurate and alternative conclusion that would have
tallied with the life experience of the readers much better would hold
that economic success in the environment of late colonial Punjab
was highly precarious and dependent on strikes of luck as well as on
inherited status and political connections.

What we find in reformist discourse is exactly the simultaneous
imposition and denial of a middle-class identity that we have identified at the very heart of the colonial project at the beginning of this
article; reformism and through it, some sense of becoming middle
class-*like* was necessary, because the colonial rulers had claimed
such values for themselves in order to justify their own hegemonic
project. But precisely because they had to remain the subordinates of
colonialism, reformist Indians could never be more than especially
hygiene-obsessed, education-driven and self-motivated minions
working along the vertical fault-lines of the colonial political economy. Being more than that, being middle class in a full sense, could
never be primarily a cultural project, it had to be a political one.

MIDDLE-CLASS CONSUMERISM

There was an order of cultural discourses that could function as a bridge between reformist habitus and politics, and more importantly that could at least in some form shake reformist values out of the patronage straight jacket—the world of everyday goods and their encoding as consumer products, as they became ever more prevalent from the 1920s onward.

A quick conceptual clarification is in order here.[48] In the first instance, consumerism is different from the simple and more or less fixed relationship between social identities and material goods as status symbols that has existed throughout history. Consumerism's radical promise is that the free choice of material goods on the capitalist market place can directly translate into free choice in the construction of social identities; I can be what I buy. It is immediately obvious that the consumerist promise is deeply flawed. Not only is access to material goods determined by wealth, but the very identity value that is ascribed to certain consumer goods is also always open to struggle that tends to favour those already in positions of prominence. Once something that has been a marker of luxury and good taste becomes available to the many, it is discarded as valueless by the few who will seek new markers of difference elsewhere. But despite this inherent hierarchy-affirming tendency, consumerism does inject a new sense of dynamism into social relationships, as it subjects all participants in consumer culture to be constantly on their watch, to constantly assess the identity value of consumer goods, and to play games to catch-up with each other. Consumerism gives rise to status anxiety, and more importantly, it turns real social relationships between people into sometimes strongly fetishistic relationships with material objects. Consumerism thus internalizes and individualizes collective social relationships, which is precisely why it has had so much appeal for self-avowedly individualistic and self-oriented middle-class projects the world over.

In the late nineteenth and early twentieth century when branded consumer goods were only beginning to be available in Indian markets on a limited scale, many Indians were perfectly able to see through the false promise of consumerism. A good indication is the genre of social satire literature, which flourished over this period. Its preferred target were people, often called the 'young men of fashion' or 'sons of the times', who were seen as ridiculous precisely because they were unable to see that their demonstrative use of Western fashions, eating habits and general lifestyles would never turn them into people of substance.[49]

A Punjabi (written in Persian script) tract from 1922—*Ajkal fashion da phuka gentleman*[50] ('the puffed-up [or hollow] gentleman of today's fashion')—may serve as a good example of the main argument made in this literature. The topic is a young man who comically fails to keep up appearances to claim some form of middle-class status. He rents a large flat despite having no money, brandishes his European clothes and his bicycle, eats and drinks expensively, and smokes cigarettes. Whenever he is about to be found out by his creditors he tries to conceal his poverty—his pocket according to one verse only contains dried chickpeas but no money—with the help of a brash anglicized demeanour. What the object of fun here is not so much the attempt of Westernization itself, which would be highlighted in the older literature in Urdu, but the *false* assumption of a Westernized identity by somebody who did not have the requisite status to claim such an identity. The use of the westernizing sign objects mentioned in the poem was presumably reserved for *real* members of the elite who could actually afford them. Similar ridicule about the discrepancy between being and appearance was heaped by British officials on some of their less fortunate clerical subordinates, who lived in hovels but still insisted on wearing expensive Western clothes in public.[51]

Within the context of the colonial connections economy the assumption of new social identities through the appropriation of sign objects could only ever work to a limited extent. The social knowledge of its participants was too accurate and comprehensive to allow much room for deception. But as urbanization and social dislocation proceeded in the interwar ear and beyond, this clear-sighted unmasking of the miracle of consumerism began to fade out of print discourse. Social satire was first displaced into cheap and local language publishing like the Punjabi tract quoted above, and subsequently crowded out by the expansion of a new Urdu publishing culture where such genres no longer had an important place. The erstwhile hollow gentleman of fashion, it seems, had now become the main producers of literature. They were still sometimes made fun off, particularly in the new genre of film and film criticism, but strikingly, they had become social stereotypes that could be caricatured, rather than social imposters to be un-masked.[52]

The expansion and changed nature of advertising discourse in the 1930s offered new opportunities for middle-class people to fashion themselves in increasingly variegated ways. The presence of often very sophisticated marketing techniques of global brands such as Gillette, Lipton Tea or Horlicks lent international standards of credibility and a sense of mystique to even cheap products of everyday use. The range of consumer identities that could be constructed around material sign-objects expanded far beyond the stereotype of the 'Westernized' gentleman of yesteryears. Urdu advertising appealed to anti-Westernized positions and a sense of religious traditionalism as much as it created the 'man of the world'.[53] There were products advertised specifically with a Muslim twist, others with a Sikh or Hindu twist, allowing for an easy transposition of communal conflict into lifestyle choices. [54] Despite this differentiation, however, advertising discourse was remarkably consistent on one point that betrayed its continuing entanglement with reformist discourse: there was no room for an open espousal of conspicuous consumption, even of more oblique ways of communicating privilege; furthermore, there were very few adverts that directly appealed to pleasure and enjoyment as what a product had to offer. Almost unanimously, advertising would portray products as 'useful', as educational tools or aids in the struggle for social betterment more generally. Soap was not about beauty but about cleansing the mind for better office performance;[55] tonics and patent medicines would produce first-class BA students;[56] lamps were desirable because they extended the study time of the inhabitants of a room,[57] even detective novels were not read for enjoyment, but because they could offer useful advice when joining the colonial police service.[58] Once again, this cult of use-value betrays the fact that the middle-class milieu was unable to move out of the hegemonic field of reformist discourse. But the encapsulation of such discourses in consumer products also changed and inverted the original meaning of reformism. A somewhat surrogate reformist stance could now be self-assembled—involving only the expenditure of relatively small amounts for goods of everyday necessity; it was no longer dependent on participation in the political economy of favour.

New internalized and individualistic relationships with commodities promised to secure middle-class identity in an easy and miraculous way. Take a particularly elaborate and sophisticated comic-strip advertisement for Horlicks energy drink, which appeared first in the 1930s but was reprinted in both English and Urdu until well into the 1950s.[59] Atiya, a sickly middle-class housewife, fails to conform to established norms of domesticity: her house is untidy, her children are unpunctual at school; she cannot even make herself presentable when a senior colonial official visits her subaltern husband. In the end, things get so bad that the husband is scolded by his mother about the dismal performance of his wife; the help of a doctor is sought who recommends the intake of a glass of Horlicks every day; as a result all domestic duties are from now on performed meticulously. This advertisement perhaps not only reflects the all too real burdens that the self-confessed reformist housewife had to face in the 1930s, it also represents metaphorically the general malaise of a frustrated middle class in the form of Atiya's illness. The whole point about Horlicks energy drink is that it instantaneously and effortlessly relieves the pressures associated with middle-class life while at the same time reaffirming that a true middle-class identity can only be born of sweat and toil. The fictional Atiya is meant to suffer so that the real female recipient of the advert can enjoy a middle-class identity without suffering.

The miraculous nature of consumer goods could never dispense with a certain sense of unease, which was increasingly expressed in popular medical culture and social commentary. Unlike the provincial elite who used sign-objects in a much more clearly referential way and whose status and position in society could be objectively measured, middle-class consumerism could never vouchsafe the identities it produced. This applied to social identities in general, but was particularly acute where political or religious commitment was expressed in terms of consumer choice. How could one be sure to be a true *Congresswala*, for instance, if the *swadeshi* cloth one bought in accordance with nationalist prescriptions was really Japanese and falsely re-labelled as swadeshi by unscrupulous shopkeepers?; or what

if one's preferred brand of swadeshi soap was, according to the advertising slogan of a competitor and alarmist reports in the vernacular
newspapers, not truly swadeshi at all, but contaminated with foreign
oils?[60] This sense of insecurity about the exact meaning of sign-objects
was transformed into a very middle-class anxiety about consumption
that revolved around the search for an unreachable sense of authenticity. Increasingly, the very products that promised the miraculous
construction of middleclass-ness—particularly novelty foods such as
toast, chocolate, vegetable ghee, biscuits and the like—were seen as
a mortal danger to the middle-class self. With the help of humoural
traditions of medicine the intake of such 'inauthentic' items was
linked to a whole range of typically middle-class diseases: a feeling
of weariness and listlessness, constipation and impurity of the blood,
sexual dysfunction and loss of strength.[61] At the same time, the old
enemies of reformist discourse—the sumptuous, 'hot' and sexually
active body of the old-fashioned 'feudal', or of the muscular strength
of *pahlwan* and body-builder fed on more natural foods—emerged as
an object of middle-class fascination in which envy was ill-concealed
behind professed revulsion. The project of middle class self-fashioning through consumption had left to self-emasculation, as Ghulam
Jilani Barque, a *mufasselite* publicist and social critic writing in the
1940s and 1950s pointed out. The young men of today had become
listless and idle, and were no longer able to succeed in the fight for
life, which he perceived as 'a perpendicular rock to climb'.[62]

Consumerism did not offer an emerging Punjabi middle class
a stable and self-secure identity; but it did facilitate an encoding
of the fundamental contradiction between the reformist demand
for self-improvements and the constraints of the colonial political
economy that could now be experienced in recognizable middle-class ways. Middle-class consciousness emerged as a medical
syndrome, as a corporeal anxiety that cut across distinctions of
religion, caste or biradari background. This unhappy state of being
could not be resolved through a closer adherence to reformist
ideas, nor through the use of middle-class products that dominated the landscape of consumer choice. Both had offered false
promises before and were only going to make the middle-class
malaise worse.

THE POLITICS OF MIDDLE CLASS SELF-EXPRESSION

A sense of liberation from this unhappy state of being emerged in a style of radical politics—'a politics of self-expression'—that existed both within and outside of the established nationalist movements of the time. As I have pointed out at length elsewhere,[63] this politics stood out by promising individual salvation to its adherents, rather than the redress of socio-economic grievances or alternative societal visions. It spoke to frustrated government servants, urban artisans and above all, to the young of middle-class backgrounds, who felt that the reformist respectability of their parents' generation had become a dead-end. Impossible to locate with any precision on a conventional left–right political spectrum, this politics borrowed freely and sometimes explicitly from revolutionary ideologies of socialist and fascist provenance.

A good example for this new politics was Inayatullah Khan Al-Mashriqi's Khaksar movement set up with direct reference to German National Socialism. The members of the movement were recruited both from the artisan class of the cities as well from disaffected educated members of the middling strata. Inayatullah Khan in many ways embodied a thwarted middle-class experience in his own person. As a strikingly successful example of upward social mobility through education in the late nineteenth century he had progressed to become a civil servant and later college headmaster of some importance. But after the First World War his reformist certainties mutated into the very opposite.[64] Under his new *nome de guerre* 'Al-Mashriqi', he became a strong advocate of war as the most rewarding and natural state of human existence and turned political 'action' and, at least at the rhetorical level, advocated violence and action as experiential values in their own right.[65] In line with these larger aims, he launched savage attacks on the pillars of the reformist consensus: in his view, the family strangulated the development of true man- and woman-hood, economic advancement made people listless and idle, the question of female education was as futile as education in general because it did not prepare the young of the nation for war; cultural regeneration and religious reform as conventionally understood were acts of appeasement and out of sync with the Social Darwinist lessons of history.[66] But this schoolmaster turned anti-educationist could not really escape his roots. Within the Khaksar movement itself, many of the established norms of reformism were turned into fetishes: people who came late to weekly paramilitary drill sessions, who smoked without permission or appeared in filthy attire were publicly flogged. The experience of pain and hardship were meant to liberate all members of the movement from their reformist sensibilities, but they did so in a strikingly reformist way.

This desire to experience a new way of life, which had broken free from conventional reformist respectability while at the same time reaffirming many of the staples of this respectability in the garb of a revolutionary methodology, was not unique to the Khaksars. It was also found in other movements that attracted disaffected middle-class support. Punjabi activists of the Communist Party of India celebrated cold baths as pathways to national liberation;[67] the 'terrorist' left experimented with self-mutilation and physical endurance tests.[68] The Muslim League of Jinnah—who once famously said that national liberation started with all Muslims cleaning up after themselves—existed side by side with the Muslim League of the Punjab Muslim Student federation who believed that the experience of killing Hindus could liberate them from the constraints of a society ruled by elders.[69]

Affective states were central to this politics. Just like the magical consumer goods described earlier, they translated socio-economic aspirations into individual experiences of pain and elation. The weak and listless body—contaminated as it was by unwholesome lifestyles and too much learning—became the microcosm of the middle-class struggle. It was only at the corporeal level—in a deliberately de-intellectualized and de-societalized state—that the problem of thwarted middle-class development could be properly worked through. Exercises deliberately designed to inflict pain heightened the more generalized malaise of middle-class existence in each individual body into an intense physical experience that could now be mastered. As the pain ebbed away, as the endurance test was passed, the middle-class body could enjoy a feeling of finally having overcome its own inadequacies. Beyond pain stood intoxication and elation, as was often enough pointed out by figures as politically diverse as Subhas Chandra Bose and Maulana Zafar Ali Khan when addressing Punjabi middle-class audiences.[70] When attempting to answer what Pakistan stood for, a Muslim League propaganda poem simply stated that it was *'chain'*—a state of comfort and ease.[71]

While this corporeal politics could leave conventional political programmatics and societal analysis aside, it was nevertheless very precise in expressing a clearly identifiable middle class sense of resentment. The middle-class body—most often but not exclusively the middle-class *male* body—as it was awakened and steeled by pain, had acquired the ability to ward off corporeal challenges from both above and below. The middle class's social and political enemies were never only that; they were directly and individually felt as physical threats to one's own body. In the first instance, there was colonial rule itself, which was couched in its own peculiar body politics of superior masculine strength, designing Indian subjects into effeminacy and submission.[72] But there were also striking differences in the predominant image of the corporeal 'other' between Hindu and Muslim middle-class elements. For Muslims, middle-class bodies had to become stronger and more self-controlled than the sexually profligate and luxury-bloated bodies of the provincial elites—their erstwhile masters in patronage; and at the same time more disciplined and more hygienic than those of the labouring poor. For middle-class Hindu Punjabis their 'other' was typically couched in terms of the 'wild' body of a Muslim underclass, the proverbial 'rapists' and conquerors of India prone to inexplicable outbursts of violence. Communal antagonism, which the fault-lines of the colonial patronage system had institutionalized, was embodied alongside a shared middle-class identity.[73]

In its preoccupation with affective states and corporeal experiences and its emphasis on personal authenticity, this new style of politics overlapped considerably with the world of middle-class consumerism described above. The false and inauthentic middle-class strength acquired from a cup of Horlicks was in a way only the mirror image of the successful middle-class body toned in paramilitary training. This link to consumer culture was hardly surprising. The political climate of nationalist mass mobilizations both demanded and validated the widespread use of material sign objects—or branded goods—for the purpose of identity construction. The precedent established by earlier Indian nationalist campaigns around the boycott of foreign goods prompted other political groups to develop 'life-style' packages that expressed political preference. Leading nationalist politicians of all camps lent their names to a whole range of marketing campaigns from swadeshi soaps, to books and insurance bonds.[74] The self-styled Gandhian would wear *khaddar*, refrain from chocolate and biscuits and, if he deemed such a beverage suitable at all, prefer a type of tea that according to its advertising copy represented the sweat of the toiling masses of India;[75] the Muslim Leaguer would purchase a Jinnah cap, an *acchkan* and try to boycott products produced or sold by Hindus and Sikhs. In the astute and cutting observations of Ismat Chughtai, a feminist novelist and contemporary, the self-styled 'revolutionary' was somebody who deliberately wore shabby clothes, kept his hair unkempt and carried a collection of vintage photographs around with him to impress the girls with his romantic sensitivity.[76]

Middle-class politics in Punjab became identifiable as such not through the clear-headed pursuit of 'middle-class' interests, as they have been so glowingly depicted in the myth of a reasonable, democratizing force bound to destroy the hegemony of old elites and to usher in a new age of meritocracy, rationality and general prosperity. Although 'objective' class divisions certainly existed in the Punjabi colonial economy and were even directly perceived in moments of crisis, they were internalized rather than analysed. In place of a marching plan towards a better social order, the politics of middle class self-expression was in love with individual emotional states; in place of rationalism and social reformism stood an often self-conscious espousal of irrationalism and an open disdain for the achievements of bourgeois society. The Punjabi middle class was a class that could not make sense of itself as a class, only as the shared malaise of its individualized bodies and their yearning for redress.

As suggested right at the outset of this discussion, middle-class development in colonial Punjab was indeed fatally flawed, thwarted by the straightjacket of a hegemonic land economy and divided along communal and caste lines imposed by colonial governmentality. But—and this is the most important conclusion to be drawn from this essay—a middle class did nevertheless exist; it existed not so much in any particular sociological formation on the ground, as it were, but in the immense emotional energy that the politics of self-expression itself generated. There is no question at all that the Punjab middle class had plenty of 'beef'; that there was a very significant amount of middle class resentment in evidence during the time period under review. It is very important to note that the kind of radical politics that otherwise flourished only in the recognized centres of colonial modernity—urban Bengal and urban western India— would also find such a significant home in Punjab. The land of the five rivers was never only the land of zamindars, moneylenders and Unionists, but also that of 'terrorists', romantic communists and a wide array of fascist sympathizers. In this sense, Punjab had been a quintessentially middle-class province for much longer than contemporary celebrations of middle-class development suggest; what is more, it epitomized a strikingly 'dark' version of middle-class development that should caution against all too simplistic and optimistic expectations of our new middle class age in India and elsewhere.

NOTES

1 Classic 'Punjab' histories in this vein include Imran Ali, *The Punjab under Imperialism 1885–1947*, Princeton: Princeton University Press, 1988; Ian Talbot, *Punjab and the Raj, 1849–1947*, New Delhi: Manohar, 1988; N. Gerald Barrier, *The Punjab Alienation of Land Bill of 1900*, Durham: Duke University Program in Comparative Studies on Southern Asia, 1966; Richard Gabriel Fox, *Lions of the Punjab: Culture in the Making*, Berkeley, London: University of California Press, 1985. The need for an analysis of urban Punjabi politics is formulated powerfully in David Gilmartin, *Empire and Islam: Punjab and the Making of Pakistan*, Comparative Studies on Muslim Societies; 7 Berkeley: University of California Press, 1988.

2 See, for instance, Sanjay Joshi, *Fractured Modernity: Making of a Middle Class in Colonial North India*, New Delhi: Oxford University Press, 2001; Prashant Kidambi, 'Consumption, Domestic Economy and the Idea of the "Middle Class" in Late Colonial Bombay', in Doughlas E. Haynes, Abigail McGowan, Tirthankar Roy, and Haruka Yanagisawa (eds), *Towards a History of Consumption in South Asia*, New Delhi: Oxford University Press, 2009, pp. 108–35; Tithi Bhattacharya, *The Sentinels of Culture: Class, Education, and the Colonial Intellectual in Bengal (1848–85)*, New Delhi: Oxford University Press, 2005.

3   Dror Wahrman, *Imagining the Middle Class: The Political Representation of Class in Britain, c. 1780–1840*, Cambridge: New York: Cambridge University Press, 1995.

4   'India has from first to last been a middleclass possession, won by middleclass ambition and sagacity', 'governed at home by middleclass agency' and 'administered by middleclass instrumentality'. *The Daily News,* London, 3 October 1857.

5   With special reference to a new middle class in military dictatorships in the Muslim world (including Pakistan) see Manfred Halpern, *The Politics of Social Change in the Middle East and North Africa*, Princeton: Princeton University Press, 1963. For a wider take in a similar vein see John J. Johnson (ed.), *The Role of the Military in Underdeveloped Countries*, Princeton: Princeton University Press, 1962.

6   Good examples were the public pronouncements of Ayub Khan's finance minister, Muhammad Shoaib; and subsequent depositions by self-acclaimed middle-class constituencies; reported in *Dawn*, 20 January 1959, 10 February,1 April, 1959 and other similar occasions.

7   See for example Pavan K. Varma, *Great Indian Middle Class*, New Delhi: Penguin, 1998.

8   Regarding the middle class in colonial Lucknow, see Joshi, *Fractured Modernity* .

9   See for example Pamela M. Pilbeam, *The Middle Classes in Europe, 1789–1914: France, Germany, Italy, and Russia*, Themes in Comparative History, Houndmills, Basingstoke, Hampshire: Macmillan, 1990. More generally this is the approach preferred by scholarship in the wake of Max Weber. For a discussion of this literature see Mark Liechty, *Suitably Modern: Making Middle-Class Culture in a New Consumer Society*, Princeton, NJ: Princeton University Press, 2003, pp. 11–16.

10 Henrike Donner (ed.), *A Way of Life: Changing Middle-class Identities in Postliberalisation India*, London: Routledge, 2010.

11 As set out in John Gallagher, Gordon Johnson, and Anil Seal, *Locality, Province and Nation: Essays on Indian Politics 1870 to 1940: Reprinted from Modern Asian Studies 1973*, Cambridge: Cambridge University Press, 1973.

12 The classic formulation in labour history is Gareth Stedman Jones, *Languages of Class: Studies in English Working Class History, 1832–1982*, Cambridge: Cambridge University Press, 1983.For an application of a similar methodology to the field of middle class studies see Wahrman, *Imagining the Middle Class.*

13 The Arabic etymology and late nineteenth century usage of terms like *tabqa* does not suggest a great awareness of class as a powerful agent of transformation, which is so fundamental to the middle class myth.

Rather, it suggest a classification of order—a horizontal 'layer' as part of a stable social edifice, similar to the German 'schicht', which is often read as linguistic testimony to a suppression of class struggle in twentieth century German history. Platt, who records late nineteenth century usage does not yet list 'class' in the sociological sense amongst the meanings of *tabqa* (although it does mention class in the early nineteenth century sense of 'degree, rank, order').

14 Amongst many others Anshu Malhotra, *Gender, Caste, and Religious Identities: Restructuring Class in Colonial Punjab*, New Delhi: Oxford: Oxford University Press, 2004; Anindita Ghosh, *Power in Print: Popular Publishing and the Politics of Language and Culture in a Colonial Society, 1778–1905*, New Delhi: Oxford University Press, 2006; Bhattacharya, *The Sentinels of Culture*; Francesca Orsini, *The Hindi Public Sphere 1920–1940: Language and Literature in the Age of Nationalism*, New Delhi; New York: Oxford University Press, 2002; Ulrike Stark, *An Empire of Books: The Naval Kishore Press and the Diffusion of the Printed Word in Colonial India*, Ranikhet: Permanent Black, 2007; Margrit Pernau, *Bürger Mit Turban: Muslime in Delhi Im 19. Jahrhundert*, Bürgertum N.F., Bd. 5, Göttingen: Vandenhoeck & Ruprecht, 2008.

15 For a recent collection see Haynes (ed.), *Towards a History of Consumption in South Asia*.

16 Ali, *The Punjab under Imperialism*, Mustapha Kamal Pasha, *Colonial Political Economy: Recruitment and Underdevelopment in the Punjab*, Karachi, New York: Oxford University Press, 1998; Rajit K. Mazumder, *The Indian Army and the Making of Punjab*, Ranikhet: Permanent Black, 2003.

17 Barrier, *The Punjab Alienation of Land Bill of 1900*; P.H.M. van den Dungen, *The Punjab Tradition: Influence and Authority in Nineteenth-Century India*, London: Allen & Unwin, 1972; Gilmartin, *Empire and Islam: Punjab and the Making of Pakistan*, chap. 1; Fox, *Lions of the Punjab*.

18 Richard G. Fox, 'Urban Class and Communal Consciousness in Colonial Punjab: The Genesis of India's Intermediate Regime', *Modern Asian Studies*, 18 (3), 1984, pp. 459–89; Norman G. Barrier, 'The Arya Samaj and Congress Politics in the Punjab 1894–1908', *Journal of Asian Studies*, XXVI (3), 1967, pp. 363–80.

19 *The Tribune*, 14 February 1937.

20 Ibid.; also *Oral History Transcript Khalid Latif Gauba*, Nehru Memorial Museum and Library, New Delhi; Khalid Latif Gauba, *The Rebel Minister*, Lahore: Premier Publishing House, 1938.

21 *The Tribune*, 14 February 1937.

22 This was the conclusion reached by the Indian industrial commission as cited in B.R. Tomlinson, *The Political Economy of the Raj, 1914–1947: The Economics of Decolonization in India*, Cambridge Commonwealth Series, London: Macmillan Press, 1979, p. 12. See also Statement H. Calvert, Registrar of Cooperative Societies in Punjab. *Minutes of Evidence taken by the Indian Industrial Commission, 1916–18*, Calcutta 1918; vol. VI—Confidential Evidence, p.196.

23 For his first bankruptcy see Ravinder Kumar, 'The Rowlatt Satyagraha in Lahore', in Ravinder Kumar (ed.), *Essays on Gandhian Politics: The Rowlatt Satyagraha of 1919* (Oxford: Clarendon Press, 1971), pp. 253–8; for his second Gauba, *The Rebel Minister*, p. xxx, Gauba's version was confirmed to me by Daniyal Latifi, Interview, New Delhi, February 1999.

24 Khalid Latif Gauba, *The Prophet of the Desert*, Lahore: Muhammad Ashraf, 1934.

25 Ian Kerr, *The Railway Workshops of Lahore and Their Employees, 1863–1930*, Surjit Dulai and Arthur Helweg (eds), Punjab in Perspective, South Asia Series, Occasional Paper No. 39, East Lansing: Michigan State University, 1991; Ian Kerr, 'Urbanization and Colonial Rule in 19th Century India: Lahore and Amritsar 1849–1881', *The Punjab Past and Present*, 14 (1), 1980.

26 Ian Kerr, 'Social Change in Lahore 1849–1875', *Journal of Indian History*, 57 (2–3), 1979, .

27 All information about him and his family is derived from extensive interviews with his son, Usman Khalid, London, 2000–06, and his daughter Fatima Kaniz Yusuf, Islamabad, 1999.

28 *Oral History Transcript Khalid Latif Gauba*.

29 Interview Usman Khalid, London, 2000.

30 Interview Daniyal Latifi, New Delhi, 1999; G.S. Bhargava, *Bhim Sen Sachar: An Intimate Biography*, New Delhi: Har-Anand Publications, 1997, p. 87.

31 As discussed for instance in Brij Narain, *India in the Crisis*, Allahabad: Indian Press Ltd, 1934, pp. 365–71.

32 Pren Nevile, *Lahore: A Sentimental Journey*, New Delhi: Allied Publishers, 1993, p. 55. For a wider discussion of this literature see Markus Daechsel, *The Politics of Self-Expression: The Urdu Middle-Class Milieu in Mid-Twentieth Century India and Pakistan*,London: Routledge, 2006, pp. 190–2.

33 Nevile, *Lahore*, pp. 164–70.

34 Oriental and India Office Collection (OIOC): File L/P&J/5/248, Fortnightly Report for Punjab, First Half of June. TM: All India

Congress Committee (AICC) File P-16, 1942–46, Letter Duni Chand to AICC, 5 March 1946, Teen Murti. AFM: File 345, Representation to Baldev Singh, Punjab Muslim League, 5 March 1946, p. 68.

35 *Manifesto of the Punjab Provincial Muslim League*, 1944, pp. 6, 9–10.

36 Talbot, *Punjab and the Raj*.

37 See for example, Francis Robinson, 'Religious Change and the Self in Muslim South Asia since 1800', *South Asia*, 20 (1), pp. 1–15; Kenneth W. Jones, *Socio-Religious Reform Movements in British India*, New Cambridge History of India. 3, the Indian Empire and the Beginnings of Modern Society; 1, Cambridge: Cambridge University Press, 1989.

38 For example, Charu Gupta, *Sexuality, Obscenity, Community: Women, Muslims, and the Hindu Public in Colonial India* Palgrave, 2002; Malhotra, *Gender, Caste, and Religious Identities*.

39 For example, Harald Fischer-Tiné, 'Character Building and Manly Games—Viktorianische Männlichkeitsideale Und Ihre Aneignung Im Frühen Hindu-Nationalismus', *Historische Anthropologie*, 9 (3), 2001, pp. 432–55; Carey Watt, 'Education for National Effiency: Constructive Nationalism in North India 1909–1916', *Modern Asian Studies*, 31 (2), 1997, pp. 339–74.

40 Malhotra, *Gender, Caste, and Religious Identities*, pp. 116–64.

41 Maulawī Muhammad Amīn, *Ārsī - Ghardārī Kā Āʾinah*, Lahore: Dār ul-Ishāʿat-e-Panjāb, 1929, pp. 138–41.

42 Ibid., p. 136. For the wider context of corporeal models see Daechsel, *The Politics of Self-Expression*, pp. 94–9.

43 Amīn, *Ārsī*, p. 143.

44 Anonymous, *Sharīf Bīwī: Gharīb Sayyidah Kā Qissā*, Lahore: Dār ul-Ishāʿat-e-Panjāb, 1935.

45 *Bacchon ka akhbar*, June 1903, p. 2.

46 *Bacchon ka akhbar*, November 1903, p. 33.

47 *Khazānūn Kī Kahāniyān*, ed. Imtiyāz Alī Tāj, *Paysah Lāʾibrērī*, Lahore: Dār ul-Ishāʿat-e-Panjāb, 1946.

48 Based largely on Jean Baudrillard's early work, Jean Baudrillard, *The Consumer Society*, London, Thousand Oaks: Sage, 1998. And Jean Baudrillard, *The System of Objects*, London: New York: Verso, 1996.

49 For a widely read classic of this genre see 'Deputy' Nazir Ahmed, *Ibn ul-Waqt*.

50 Munshi Muhammad Bakhsh Amritsari, *Ājkal Dā Phūkā Gentleman*, Lahore: Munshi Azizuddin, 1922.

51 *District Gazetteer for Lahore*, Lahore: Government of Punjab, 1916, p.149.

52 Daechsel, *The Politics of Self-Expression*, p.196.

53 Ibid., pp. 176–83.

54 Shops were frequently advertised with reference to communal loyalties, for instance *Inqilab*, 15 October 1936; *Zamindar*, 15 February 1938, 10 July 1940.

55 *Inqilab*, 18 March 1944.

56 *Zamindar*, 5 January 1941; *The Tribune*, 23 December 1937.

57 *Wikli Tej*, Krishna Number, 21 August 1935.

58 Publisher's preface to A. Conan Doyle, *Yadgar-e Sharlak Homz,* Lahore: Indian Publishing Company, 1927.

59 *Zamindar*, 22 June 1940.

60 *Paisa Akhbar*, 4 January 1934; *Wikli Tej*, 22 July 1936, p.11.

61 Daechsel, *The Politics of Self-Expression*, pp. 101–4.

62 Ghulam Jilani Barq, *Islam: The Religion of Humanity*, trans. Fazl-i-Ahmad Kuraishi, Lahore: 1956, p. 358.

63 Daechsel, *The Politics of Self-Expression*, pp. 35–92.

64 Muhammad Aslam Malik, *Allama Inayatullah Khan Mashriqi: A Political Biography*, Karachi: Oxford University Press, 2000, pp. 1–42.

65 Markus Daechsel, 'Scientism and its Discontents: The Indo-Muslim "Fascism" of Inayatullah Khan al-Mashriqi', *Modern Intellectual History*, 3 (3), 2006, p. 443.

66 Inyatullah Khan Mashriqi, 'Islam Ki Askari Zindigi', *Al-Islah*, 29 May 1936.

67 Rajbans Kishen, 'Fragments from a guerilla diary', *People's War*, 2 August 1942.

68 A self-acclaimed cell of leftwing terrorists tested their preparedness for torture in colonial prisons by timing how long they could hold their elbows over a candle flame. Interview Mian Nizam Din, Lahore, September 1999.

69 Jinnah: Speech on All India Radio, Id, 13 November 1939, reprinted in Khurshid Ahmad Khan Yusufi (ed.), *Speeches, Statements & Messages of the Qaid-E-Azam*, Lahore: Bazm-e-Iqbal, 1996, p. 1062. Punjab Muslim Student Federation: *Khilāfat-e Pākistān Iskīm*, Lahore: Punjab Muslim Student Federation, 1939.

70 Daechsel, *The Politics of Self-Expression*, pp. 64–8.

71 Qaid-e Azam Paper Project: Poems about Qaid-e Azam, Punjabi, pp. 3, 4, 7; Institute of Historical and Cultural Research, Islamabad: 'Muslim', *Namghah-e Pakistan*, n.d. p.11.

72 For a classic exposition with special reference to Bengal see Mrinalini Sinha, *Colonial Masculinity: The 'Manly Englishman' and the 'Effeminate Bengali' in the Late Nineteenth Century*, Studies in Imperialism, Manchester, England, Manchester, New York: Manchester University Press. For the wider colonial context see Anne McClintock, *Imperial*

Leather: Race, Gender, and Sexuality in the Colonial Contest, New York: Routledge, 1995.

73 Daechsel, *The Politics of Self-Expression*, pp. 118–26.

74 For instance *Wikli Tej*, 18 March 1935, p. 29. Dasarathi Mishra, *Advertising in Indian Newspapers, 1780–1947*, Berhanpur: Ishani Publications, 1987, pp. 63,72.

75 Ismat Chughtāi, *The Crooked Line = (Terhi Lakir)*, trans. Tahira Naqvi, Karachi: Oxford University Press, 1995, p. 261. See 'Hindustan Chai' advertising in the nationalist papers *Hindustan*, 29 March 1940; and *Wikli Tej*, 29 April 1935.

76 Ibid., pp. 261–2.

William J. Glover

Translating the Public in Colonial Punjab*

Use of the term 'public space' to describe municipally-owned or controlled urban land is commonplace in many parts of the world today.
Use of the term to describe more metaphysical things—for example,
'public space' as an incorporeal realm of political engagement—is
also commonplace. While this essay is more concerned with the
former use, both illustrate how context-dependent the term is, and
how alternate meanings may remain submerged in ordinary usage.
In particular, even though the term is context-sensitive, the 'public'
part of public space endows the term with a particular historicity: as
political theorist Seyla Benhabib reminds us, 'whatever other applications and resonances they might have, the terms "public", "public
space", [and] "*res publica*" will never lose their intimate rootedness in
the domain of [Western] political life'.[1] Keeping Benhabib's point
in mind, this chapter presents a small number of legal cases from
colonial Punjab in which the English term and concept 'public' was
applied to a building or spatial practice in an urban area. These cases

* Originally published as William J. Glover, 'Construing Urban Space as
"Public" in Colonial India: Some Notes from the Punjab', *Journal of Punjab
Studies*, 14 (2), 2007, pp. 211–24.

illustrate a number of different ways the concept of public space refracted through more long-standing indigenous concepts and spatial practices in Punjab. They also reveal how the institutionalization of public space as a prerogative of colonial municipal authority gradually changed the configurations and meanings of those shared spaces that were a traditional feature of every Indian city. These colonial-era cases thus point to the newness of public space, as both a concept and a corporeal substance, and its associated urban phenomena in late-nineteenth century Punjab.

The concept of 'public' accrued its particular meanings throughout a long history, one that stretches back to Western classical antiquity and forward to the present. It is important to remember, however, that the modern concept developed within a relatively narrow geographical and cultural context. Widespread use of the term 'public' to describe a type of urban space, one accessible to all of a town's residents and owned by none in particular, probably began in medieval northern Europe. A legal distinction between 'individual' and 'public' forms of urban property was codified as early as the thirteenth century in England, and appears elsewhere around the same time.[2] Scholars have shown that defining and codifying types of urban property acquired importance during the medieval period, the first sustained period of urbanization in Europe. By the late medieval period, the term 'public space' had acquired a set of distinctive connotations that linked it with municipal authority.

It was during this period that municipal authorities extended their scope of interest to the management of public life. By setting fixed locations for markets, regulating exchange, and imposing controls over social activity in towns, municipal authorities helped constitute the physical attributes of public space in towns, and imbued it with particular qualities:

For example, municipal regulations about streetwalking, begging, or gambling, all of which multiplied in the late medieval period, served both to define the legitimate market and to constitute public space in specific ways . . . public space was closed for certain kinds of exchange and opened for others. The 'public' became associated with spaces that were, by definition, risk-averse, propertied, and sexually restricted.[3]

The association of urban public space with municipal order and the protection of propertied interests has been durable in Anglo-European cities. It has also become meaningful beyond its original context, particularly in areas colonized by European powers. Despite what are relatively narrow geographical and historical origins, therefore, the category 'public space' has become common currency in cities across the globe. Nevertheless, to recite an earlier point, the many 'resonances and applications' the term has acquired in its extension across the globe all necessarily point back to a particular 'domain of political life'.

This becomes apparent if we consider how public space entered into discourse in Indian cities during the late nineteenth century, while India was under British colonial rule.[4] Prior to this period, Indian cities had physical spaces that were shared in common, accessible to all or most of the city's residents, and in many ways physically identical to what the colonial government would later call 'public' urban space. Newness, in other words, did not derive from novel physical arrangements of space or entirely unprecedented protocols of use. Rather, by naming certain urban properties and spaces 'public', drafting rules governing what activities could take place there, and enforcing these rules through new urban institutions the colonial government created both a concept and a substance—public space—that had no prior history in the Indian city. Put somewhat differently, while pre-colonial and colonial urban spaces may have sometimes looked the same, invisible differences between the two were significant.

The colonial Indian metropolis contained many of the same phenomena that prompted municipal reform of public space in nineteenth-century European cities, including over crowding, filth, and illegal transactions in property. British observers saw the indigenous districts of Indian cities—with what they deemed to be filthy bazaars and inscrutably tangled streets—as indicative of a faulty mode of life. Urban dwellers were considered to be indifferent to their surroundings, lacking in civic spirit, and prone by both race and environmental circumstance to harbour transmittable diseases. At the same time, both British and Indian intellectuals interested in the social artifact of the city (along with the concomitant social

worlds that term implied), assumed that social life in the Indian city
was more malleable, less tied to custom and superstition, than social
life in Indian villages.[5] If social life was malleable, moreover, then
reshaping the everyday environment of the city held out the promise
of reshaping the very core of society.

Colonial officials were reluctant to intervene physically in the
indigenous quarters of cities; however, they showed little hesitation
in reshaping the legal traditions that governed urban space and property. In colonial India, the central institution governing the legal
affairs of a city was the Municipal Committee, a body comprised of
elected members drawn from the city's Indian and European communities.[6] Municipal Committees were formed beginning in 1862,
and they initiated a new regime of municipal record-keeping and
control over building activity in towns and cities. From that point
onward, municipalities passed by-laws governing the placement of,
and uses allowed in, new or remodelled buildings and streets. These
by-laws derived from standards established in Britain, for the most
part, and they replaced a range of pre-existing spatial practices in
the Punjab urban context whose origins go back most directly to
Mughal—and later, Sikh—custom. While there is not space here
to discuss the important question of what those previous practices
were, and research has barely begun on this question, suffice it to say
that the colonial city in India was produced over time through separate, sometimes overlapping notions about the proper relationship
between society and its material containers. Urban reform in colonial
India thus entailed radical changes in the way the city was conceived,
if not always in the way it looked.

In what follows, I explore changes in the conception of one
dimension of city life by analysing a small number of legal cases in
which a modern Anglo-European notion of the 'public'—and the
spatial qualities associated with this notion—was put in place in the
colonial city as a series of propositions about who could do what
where, and under what authority. While my examples are all drawn
from cities in Punjab province, the general processes they elucidate
were repeated elsewhere in British India, at least in every city large
enough to have a Municipal Committee. In the cases that follow, I
focus on both different interpretations of the term 'public' that were

at stake in each case, and on the process of translation from one domain of urban practice to another that each case entailed. These interpretations and translations came about in Punjab, as in the rest of colonial India, as a result of the colonial government requiring different traditions of owning, inhabiting, and conceptualizing space in north India to be reduced to a common legal frame, one enshrined in English common law and the corresponding notion of 'good government' it upheld.

In British legal tradition, good government implied the protection of the public good—or public interest—from the depredations of sectarian or purely private self-interest. Other traditions of governance co-existed with this legal tradition in India, but during the colonial period the prerogative to protect rights based on a liberal notion of the 'public'—and to identify certain physical spaces and objects as themselves possessing qualities of public-ness—was dominant and enforced by law. This fact produced fundamental constraints on the way people could conceptualize the relationship between society and space in the colonial city, and forcefully altered older traditions of spatial practice.

My first example illustrates the nature of those constraints by showing how the notion of 'public' was used over time, in increasingly sophisticated ways, to authorize practices that derived from more longstanding urban practices in India for which the notion of 'public' was previously irrelevant. Consider the case of Nabi Baksh, a shopkeeper from Sialkot who initiated construction of a mosque without permission on land owned by the government in Sialkot's Sadar Bazaar.[7] Before the mosque was fully complete, in March 1874, Baksh was asked by the colonial authorities to stop construction, which he appears to have done. Some days later, however, Baksh and several Muslim shopkeepers from his neighbourhood petitioned the government to allow them to finish the mosque and begin using it. Baksh promised that the mosque would 'not be used as a place of public prayer'; rather, according to a report filed on the case, the mosque would be used 'purely for the private accommodation and convenience of [himself and his friends]' (142). The officer in charge reluctantly agreed to this restricted use of the building until it became apparent several weeks later that the *azan* [call to prayer] was regularly being heard from the mosque, and 'the public generally in the bazaar' was using the mosque.

Baksh was called back in by the municipal authority; this time he was ordered to post a 500 rupee bond guaranteeing that he would not have the azan called at the mosque again. He responded by writing a petition that reversed his earlier claim in important ways: 'This *masjid* [mosque] is not my private property, but property devoted to pious uses. For this reason I object to give security. . . No Muslim law prohibits [worship because of] fear or other scruples. No masjid is the private property of any person...nor do I invite anyone to pray in this masjid—and from this date, I will not go there myself'. He continued: 'I have no manner of authority to prevent people from resorting to it, but you have authority to make such arrangements as you please, [but remember that] there are five masjids in the cantonment, and 184 in the city; the azan is heard in all of them' (144).

I do not have access to Baksh's original petition; an English translation is all that is recorded in the government file on the case. Nevertheless, the translation reveals that Baksh had a sophisticated sense of key elements of the new municipal regime he was forced to frame his argument within. This skill, I would argue, is crucial to understanding the history of colonial urbanism in India. In the first place, notice that Baksh was careful to disavow any purely private claims on the appropriated land in his petition. Instead, he argued that the mosque was a pious endowment for the benefit of the community and, by tradition, the building thereby acquired qualities that placed the regulation of its use outside his private authority— just as a range of other spaces in the city were, according to colonial law, beyond the reach of merely private control. Secondly, if authority was to be exercised to keep people from using the mosque, then Baksh implied that such authority would have to derive from caprice or superior might, rather than from any benevolent conception of public good: as Baksh put it—and not without irony—the government had the authority to 'make arrangements as [it] please[d]' (144). Finally, in the concluding passage of his petition, Baksh appealed to yet another central tenet of the tradition he found himself subject to, where he wrote: 'In 1858 there was a large assembly, and the Queen's proclamation was read. I recollect it was therein written that

Government would not interfere with anyone's religion. However, You are ruler and judge. And I am your subject. Act as you please' (144). What pleased the authorities, in this case, was a 500 rupee bond, which Baksh was required to pay.

This first example dates from the 1870s, and the word 'public' appears only in an English translation of Baksh's original petition; we don't know what term he actually used. The case illustrates, I believe, how certain features of a liberal notion of public-ness—its antithetical relationship to private interest, its putative openness to all members of the urban community—could be selectively translated and re-deployed to support claims that derived from outside that tradition, even when the concept of 'community' Baksh upheld was not coincident with British notions of the 'public'. By the 1880s, and possibly earlier, the term 'public', along with its new connotations, was commonplace in disputes over the use of urban land in Punjab. To illustrate the point, I want to consider a case that arose in Hoshiarpur, beginning in 1885.

According to colonial records, a resident of that city named Hamir Chand, in a 'very flagrant fashion, invaded the rights of the public by erecting a wall, so as to take possession of a well, [which he admits is] public property'.[8] The well Hamir Chand enclosed with his wall was located on part of a public lane, and that wall was built in such a way as to make it appear that part of the public lane was his private property. This event seemed, on the surface, to be a simple case of illegal encroachment. The details of the case reveal that Hamir Chand's actions were far more complicated than that, however. They provide a different example of the way colonial cities in India acquired their particular form through negotiation with the concepts and institutions that authorized colonial rule.

In the first place, and much to the surprise of higher authorities, the municipal committee of Hoshiarpur was divided over what action to take on the matter. The European and Muslim members of the committee were in favour of removing the newly constructed wall, while the majority Hindu members 'joined sides with the offender, and voted that no interference should be attempted'.[9] After two unsuccessful attempts to get the municipal committee to reconsider their vote, the deputy commissioner of the district formally intervened in the case. His first action was to ask Ram Nath, a trusted judge in the district court, to ascertain the facts of the case since, he reasoned, 'it is…desirable that an officer of Hamir Chand's own religion should inquire into the case'—an idea that called for no further justification.[10] The judge discovered that Hamir Chand knowingly built the wall on a public thoroughfare, but that he nevertheless had no intention of prohibiting Muslims or anyone else from using the well. It also emerged that Chand had been advised by his lawyer friends that since the municipal committee had decided in his favour, he could not be legally compelled to remove his wall. Finally, the judge concluded his investigation by observing that 'there appears to be no religious disputes in this matter, [indeed] Hamir Chand's Hindu enemies are at the bottom [of this]'.[11]

The Deputy Commissioner, an Irishman named Reginald Clarke, was uncertain about how to proceed: '[Hamir Chand] acted deliberately throughout in defiance of the law…I should insist on the [removal of the wall]. But how to compel him? He has taken legal advice and thinks that with a majority of the Committee in his favour he can snap his fingers at the Deputy Commissioner and the minority'. To complicate matters further, Hamir Chand's legal advice was indeed accurate, and there was very little the deputy commissioner could do to legally compel Chand to remove the obstruction. A new municipal Act that would have allowed Clarke to dismiss the municipal committee outright under extraordinary circumstances was not yet in effect in Hoshiarpur. In addition, it was doubtful that Hamir Chand could be convicted on criminal charges unless 'the District Magistrate will condescend to pack the jury', Clarke wrote, adding that 'as an Irishman, I reprobate [such a] process, having seen what it leads to'. The only remedy appeared to be to let 'any one who feels himself injured by the well being enclosed [seek redress in Civil Court]'.[12]

The latter remedy was rejected out of hand by Punjab's Lieutenant-Governor, Charles Aitchison, the province's highest official. Aitcheson's secretary wrote the following: 'The case appears to the Lieutenant-Governor to be a very gross one, in which it is not right that private persons shall be left to obtain their [public rights] by resource to the Civil Courts. The Municipality are the guardians of the public interests committed to their care. On the supposition, which seems to be clearly established, that the well is a public well, and the street a public street, the proceedings of the [Municipal] Committee are manifestly illegal, and it is the duty of the...Government to require them to amend their proceedings'.[13] After this rebuke from the lieutenant-governor, the municipal committee in Hoshiarpur met once again to vote on the matter—and once again decided not to proceed against Hamir Chand's obstruction.

By virtue of their failure to guard 'the public interests committed to their care', the municipal committee was next put on notice that unless steps were taken to have the obstructions removed within fifteen days, they would be dissolved as a body and a newly constituted committee put in their place. This authoritarian action was sanctioned under a new municipal Act, which was simultaneously extended by Government decree to cover the municipality of Hoshiarpur. As a first step in the process, the governor annulled all former resolutions passed by the committee allowing Hamir Chand's wall to remain standing. 'His Honor considers that two things are essential', wrote the Lieutenant-Governor's secretary in a final memo on the case; 'First, the Municipal Committee must do its duty, and secondly, the public rights should be substantially vindicated and secured'.[14] Under pressure of prosecution, and nine months after the case first received notice, the municipal committee of Hoshiarpur finally forced Hamir Chand to remove his wall. In a poetic gesture of disapproval, Chand removed all but three inches of the offending wall, something the committee agreed to ignore.

The case of Hamir Chand is interesting for several reasons. His actions were sanctioned by a majority of elected members of the Hoshiarpur Municipal Committee. While the committee was split between a Hindu majority, and a Muslim and European minority, a district court judge sent to inquire about the case concluded there were 'no religious disputes in this matter'. That conclusion, importantly, was accepted by the superior authorities. Instead, the issue revolved around two separate points. First was the issue of Hamir Chand's private 'absorption' of 'public rights' by obstructing a 'public' lane. Second was the question of whether or not the municipal committee had acted legally by sanctioning Chand's actions.

Note that until the Lieutenant-Governor extended by decree a new Act to include the municipality of Hoshiarpur, the city's municipal committee did indeed act within the law. Accordingly, the committee's majority decision to sanction Hamir Chand's wall has to be seen as a particular interpretation of the proper use of public space, though one which challenged the notion of 'public interests' the committee was expected to uphold. This is why the only challenge available to the Deputy Commissioner, Reginald Clarke, was to try Hamir Chand in criminal court. In Clarke's opinion, however, the only way to secure a conviction would be to 'pack the jury'—something Clarke, 'as an Irishman', and thus himself a subject of British colonial rule—could not support on moral grounds. In the end, the 'public interests' recognized by the state could only be secured by superseding the elected committee's authority, annulling their resolutions, and threatening the committee with dissolution. This was a high-handed—indeed illiberal—resort to superior force, in other words, and it indicates how far the colonial government was willing to go in an effort to secure its own definition of what constituted the public interest.

The Hamir Chand case also illustrates an increasingly sophisticated use by Indian subjects of the legal apparatus of the colonial state as a mechanism for positing the legitimacy of values, attachments, and customary practices that were incommensurate with British traditions. There were a number of ambiguities built into concepts like the 'public', and people were quick to exploit these. The particular ambiguity Hamir Chand seems to have targeted is the notion that 'public interest' was something that could be decided upon by taking a vote, since elected authority, by definition, upheld the public interest. While on the surface of things this assumption does not appear to be particularly ambiguous, the final disposition of the case illustrates that the legal tradition that defined 'public' space in the city, like all philosophical and practical traditions, had to secure its ends through a continual struggle to define terms. One wonders, for instance, what course deputy commissioner Clarke would have taken had he not been self-consciously 'Irish', something he drew attention to in an official government document. It seems clear that Clarke's personal history was equally decisive in the history of this case as any static definition of a fixed legal tradition. The result of the Hoshiarpur municipal committee's negotiation with that tradition has to be seen, therefore, as part of the historical process by which Anglo-European traditions of community organization and policing extended their claims in the colonial setting rather than an example of the corruption of public interest, as observers at the time chose to see it.

A final example illustrates some of the points I've already raised. At the same time, the case illustrates how the difficulty of translating between new and old practices, foreign and local concepts in the city can lead to the perception of wrongdoing. As I will argue in my conclusion, charges of municipal wrongdoing—often generically glossed as 'corruption'—may be an important effect of the historical process I have been tracing. The collection of records on this final case was prompted by an article published in an Urdu-language daily, the *Paisa Akhbar*, on 22 June 1927. The article was entitled, 'Baldia Lahore ko Dhoka' (Municipality of Lahore Deceived).[15] The author of the article claimed that the widow of Ram Mal, the owner of a *janj ghar* (wedding hall) in the city, was renting out rooms in the hall for personal profit rather than providing the hall to the public for its use. The latter was a condition of the owner's original agreement when he purchased the property from the municipality some years earlier, and the author of the article insisted that if this accusation was true, then the president of the municipal committee should take measures to protect the public interest.

The accusatory article prompted research into the matter, which revealed that this particular case had begun more than twenty years earlier. At that time, in 1906, a resident named Ram Rakha Mal requested permission to purchase a small property owned by the municipality which fronted onto a house he owned. 'I propose converting the property owned by me into a public reception room for the accommodation of strangers visiting the city', Mal wrote, 'and if the Municipality will kindly allow me to purchase the property owned by them, it will enable me to improve the place and afford greater accommodation'.[16] Ram Mal was fulfilling a charitable request by his father, who left money at the time of his death to endow a 'public' facility for the use of visitors to the city, 'as there is no inn or any other place especially set apart in the centre of the city for such [purposes]', Mal wrote. 'As the object for which I am making this request is charitable', he continued, 'I am sure the Municipal Committee will oblige me by acceding to my request'.[17]

The property Mal wanted to buy was occupied by a small three-room shed, a building the municipal committee used to house its fire engine and a few employees connected with it. Suitable space could be found to relocate the engine nearby, Mal argued, and eventually the municipal committee agreed. Under the initial draft agreement worked out between Mal and the city, the former was to pay for the property and the building materials on the property. In all, the amount came to around 1650 rupees, an amount that Mal found 'excessive', but which he nevertheless agreed to pay.[18] By the time a second, more formal agreement had been drafted, several months later, the price had risen by 600 rupees. The case languished for a period of a few years at this point, and a debate took place over whether Mal had to pay for the construction of a new fire shed. In the final agreement, Mal was required to pay for the new construction in addition to the land and buildings on the old site. The amount had almost doubled from the original estimate, to about Rs 3200. Mal reluctantly agreed to this final figure as well, and he deposited the money in the municipality's account in September 1915, nine years after his initial request was written.[19]

More time passed, during which the agreement with Mal was refined, altered, and made more detrimental to him, which he did not object to. Instead, Mal began to complain about the time the whole process had taken. 'I have waited all through these years to build this useful, charitable rest-house for the public visiting the capital of the Punjab', Mal complained in a letter written around the time he made his deposit; 'but [I] have not been able to do so up to this time'.[20] Throughout the lengthy negotiations over the price of the land, and the elaboration of conditions under which Mal could acquire it (including a provision that would require him to give the land back if the city ever needed it again), the underlying benevolence of the project was never questioned. 'The land must be sold to the applicant because it is for charitable purposes and it is not particularly used by the committee', wrote Mool Chand, a member of the committee, in 1913.[21] The same year, Mohammad Shafi, a distinguished jurist and municipal committee member wrote that 'the object which Lala Ram Rakha Mal has in view being a laudable one and the public spirit which he is showing in spending a large sum for the benefit of travelers and others being one worthy of encouragement, I am of the opinion that the land should be given to him on easy terms'.[22] Once the money was in hand, the municipal committee began building a new engine shed on a nearby plot, and Mal was asked to wait until that was completed before taking over possession of the old shed.

A few months into the construction project, however, another city resident, Sukh Dyal, sued the city for blocking his right of access to his property given the placement of the new building. His suit stuck, and the case was appealed several times.[23] This suit extended the janj ghar case two more years, during which time Ram Mal was unable to possess the building he had more than adequately paid for. In addition, during the wait, another survey was carried out on the property Mal had purchased that showed it to be slightly larger than was originally described. This meant that the agreement with Mal had to be drafted over again. Shortly thereafter, the new agreement went missing in the city engineer's office, having been misplaced at the back of an open almirah, leaving Ram Mal without any record in the case.

Two years further on, in August 1919, Ram Mal wrote the following note to the municipality: 'Sir, I beg to state that I paid your price of a city fire station building purchased from you long ago. You have neither given me possession of it nor the house is registered up to now. Please note that I shall hold you responsible for rent from the date I paid you the price'.[24] This letter seems to have prompted action, and in august of 1919, the paperwork was rediscovered. [25] This discovery allowed Ram to take possession of his property for the first time. His possession was not legally registered, however, until 1923. The entire process, from Mal's original request to the registration of his deed to the land, had taken seventeen years.

Ram Mal died in 1925, two years after the process was complete. In his will, Mal attached the income from other properties he owned in the city to ensure that the janj ghar could be run as a charitable institution. When this was revealed to the president of the municipal committee, who inquired into the case in 1927 in response to the newspaper article I referred to earlier, Ram Mal's widow was acquitted of any suspicion of private gain.[26] Ram Mal's janj ghar quietly disappears from the historical record at this point, after accumulating a file that stretched over twenty-one years.

My purpose in describing this final case is two-fold. First, notice how the term 'public' is appropriated and given new meanings by Ram Mal's effort to carry out his father's pious wish. A public rest-house, sometimes called a janj ghar and sometimes called by another term, is a stable fixture in towns and villages of the Punjab. These are usually endowed by private persons, but provided for the use of whoever is in need. Ram Mal and the municipal committee members continually referred to the 'public' nature of his project, a reference that served in each case to underscore its suitability to the interests of the municipal government. In 1927, when a complaint was lodged in a Lahore newspaper over the suspected violation of the terms of the building's deed, it was once again the 'public' who was said to be aggrieved. Each of these statements thus helps assimilate a traditional piece of urban furniture into the orbit of 'public' spaces authorized in British municipal law.

Secondly, I have underlined the extraordinary length of time it took to transact the sale of a small property and construct a simple 30' x 60' shed on a new site—twenty-one years—in order to call into question what is sometimes presumed to be the efficiency of the colonial municipal government. The process was slowed down in several ways: first by discussion over whether the uses proposed by Mal were appropriate justifications for selling municipal land; next, by the filing of a suit by a third party over the infringement of his 'public rights of way' caused by the placement of the new city fire shed; and finally by prolonged efforts to restrict Ram Mal's rights over access to surrounding space, the terms of possession he could enjoy, and the final cost he should be made to pay. We shall set aside the addition of two years to the process caused by Ram Mal's agreement getting lost in the city engineer's office.

These delays reveal a growing sophistication in the use of civil courts to adjudicate questions of public right by the city's residents.

Certainly that is how we should understand Sukh Dyal's suit over the placement of the new fire station. But I think the delays also reveal the difficulty of translating an object like the janj ghar—by placing limits on the rights of possession, by calculating the costs it should entail, and by developing a range of enforceable legal instruments to describe it—into a setting endowed with the status of 'public' space.

In the colonial city, these kinds of translations were ubiquitous; they also helped produce the urban space of the contemporary Indian city in important ways. Understanding the difficulty entailed in this process of translation opens up a possibility for seeing something more than official 'corruption' laying behind many of the contentious spatial practices that characterize urban life in South Asia, particularly those which entail struggles over the illegal, improper, or unwarranted use of urban space. Indeed, in every large South Asian city public rights-of-way are regularly taken over by vendors, vacant lots are illegally built upon, and public streets are obstructed to provide space for private occupations. The term most-often used to describe these violations, 'encroachment', derives from the French *croc*, cognate to the English word 'crook', and has come to mean the advance—gradual or otherwise—beyond 'due limits'. What these limits are, as this article has argued, depends on the particular traditions of property ownership and use, as well as on mechanisms for marking and enforcing spatial boundaries that separate private from public uses in any given setting.

Encroachment is necessarily denounced by every political candidate for municipal office. In every large city in South Asia, a week does not go by without a letter being published in a local newspaper calling for action to be taken against encroachers. At irregular intervals, sudden—and often violent—anti-encroachment campaigns are carried out to remove illegal occupations from city streets.[27] Conversely, encroachment is sometimes denounced in thinly veiled tones of admiration; there is a certain pleasure involved in subverting authority, after all, and the more brazen the violation, the more likely complaints about it may be saturated with irony. There is an almost constant discourse in the popular press, however, around local authority's attempts and failures to order, administer, and control space in the Indian city. This kind of discourse is framed most often in an idiom that mixes cynicism with nostalgia: cynicism about the city's willingness to enforce regulations, and nostalgia for a previous era when urban life was imagined to be more decorous, less congested, and more civil than it is today.

The latter claim, I hope to have shown, is at the very least an oversimplification. While both present-day and historical cases of encroachment are regularly described as examples of corruption and the narrow-minded self interest of private citizens, the colonial history of how public space became a familiar category in South Asia suggests a different approach to what encroachment may entail. The sorts of translations that made public space an essential component of South Asian cities—along with the many physical places and practices in cities where that concept simply has no relevance— suggest that alternative ways of conceptualizing benevolent forms of urban living may have a long history in the Indian city. The tentative resolutions those translations establish with municipal law and the 'public interests' the latter upholds, are almost always more complex than they appear.

NOTES

1 Seyla Benhabib, 'Models of Public Space: Hannah Arendt, the Liberal Tradition, and Jurgen Habermas', in Craig Calhoun (ed.), *Habermas and the Public Sphere*, Cambridge, MA: The MIT Press, 1992, pp. 22–78, esp. 74.

2 In the medieval record of English common law, *De Legibus Et Consuetudinibus Angliae* (The Laws and Customs of England), written ca. 1220 and credited to Henry of Bracton, a clear distinction is made between 'public', 'common', 'universal', 'individual', and 'sacred' property, and rights are ascribed for both corporeal (immovable) and incorporeal 'things'.

3 Peter Arnade, Martha C. Howell, and Walter Simons, 'Fertile Spaces: The Productivity of Urban Space in Northern Europe', *Journal of Interdisciplinary History*, 32 (4), Spring 2002, pp. 515–58, esp. 547.

4 Works that foreground differences between European and Indian concepts and uses of public and private space include several articles collected in Sandria Frietag (ed.), *The Public and its Meanings in Colonial South Asia, Special Issue of South Asia*, 14 (1), 1991. In particular, see

the works in this volume by Jim Masselos, 'Appropriating Urban Space: Social Constructs of Bombay in the Time of the Raj', pp. 33–63; Faisal Devji, 'Gender and the Politics of Space: The Movement for Women's Reform in Muslim India, 1857–1900', pp. 141–53; and Sandria Freitag, 'Introduction', pp. 1–13; and Freitag, 'Enactments of Ram's Story and the Changing Nature of "The Public" in British India', pp. 65–90.

5 See Jyoti Hosagrahar, *Indigenous Modernities: Negotiating Architecture and Urbanism*, London: Routledge, 2005; Swati Chattopadhyay, *Representing Calcutta: Modernity, Nationalism, and the Colonial Uncanny*, London: Routledge, 2005; William J. Glover, *Making Lahore Modern: Constructing and Imagining a Colonial City*, Minneapolis: University of Minnesota Press, 2008.

6 The Punjab Municipal Act of 1867 provided for the appointment of both official and non-official members from the European and Indian communities to municipal committees, with the district commissioner serving as the committee's president. A revised Act in 1870 provided for the election of some committee members and the appointment others, but it was not until 1882, following Lord Ripon's Resolution on Self-Government, that municipal elections were undertaken regularly in Punjab's cities. In 1884, the Municipal Act was amended to provide for the election of the president as well. In 1891, a further revision set fixed proportions for electing Muslim, Hindu, and Christian members to the committee. See British Library, Oriental and India Office Collections, V/24/2839 'Report on the Working of Municipalities in the Punjab During the Year 1893–94'.

7 Government of Punjab, Home Department Proceedings (General), Proceeding no. 15, March 1874, p. 141. Page numbers in parentheses in this section of the paper all derive from this file.

8 Government of Punjab, Home Department Proceedings (Municipal), Proceeding no. 18, 7 August 1885, 'Letter from Lieutenant Colonel G. Gordon Young, Commissioner and Superintendent, Jullundur Division, to the Secretary to Government, Punjab', n.p.

9 Government of Punjab, Home Department Proceedings (Municipal), Proceeding no. 18, 7 August, 1885, 'Letter from Lieutenant Colonel G. Gordon Young, Commissioner and Superintendent, Jullundur Division, to the Secretary to Government, Punjab', n.p.

10 Government of Punjab, Home Department Proceedings (Municipal), Proceeding no. 18, 4 July, 1885, 'Memorandum by R. Clarke, Esquire, Deputy Commissioner, Hoshiarpur', n.p.

11 Government of Punjab, Home Department Proceedings (Municipal), Proceeding no. 18, 13 July 1885, 'Memorandum by Diwan Ram Nath, District Judge, Hoshiarpur', n.p.

12 Government of Punjab, Home Department Proceedings (Municipal), Proceeding no. 18, 20 July, 'Memorandum by R. Clarke, Esquire, Deputy Commissioner, Hoshiarpur', n.p.

13 Government of Punjab, Home Department Proceedings (Municipal), Proceeding no. 19, 1 September 1885, 'Letter from C.L. Tupper, Esquire, Officiating Secretary to Government, Punjab, to The Government Advocate, Punjab', n.p.

14 Government of Punjab, Home Department Proceedings (Boards and Committees), Proceeding no. 18, May 1886, 'Letter from Secretary to the Government (Lahore) to the Commissioner of Jullundur Division', n.p.

15 The archival material on this case is collected in the Lahore Municipal Corporation (LMC) Old Record Room in a paper-bound file of correspondence. The cover of the file is labelled 'Case LH-3/3-1906'. Subsequent references to materials in this file will be identified by their title or type, date, and page number(s) in the file of correspondence.

16 Lahore Municipal Corporation, LH-3/3-1906, 'Letter of Petition from Ram Rakha Mal, banker, Suabazaar, Lahore', 26 June 1906, p. 1.

17 Lahore Municipal Corporation, LH-3/3-1906, 'Letter from Ram Rakha Mal', 3 September 1906, p. 5.

18 Lahore Municipal Corporation, LH-3/3-1906, 'Letter from the Chairman, Public Works Subcommittee', 20 November 1906, pp. 16–19.

19 Lahore Municipal Corporation, LH-3/3-1906, File Note, 15 September 1915, p. 59.

20 Lahore Municipal Corporation, LH-3/3-1906, 'Letter from Ram Rakha Mal to Secretary, Lahore Municipal Committee', 6 January 1914, p. 23.

21 Lahore Municipal Corporation, LH-3/3-1906, 'Letters of Support from Ram Sarin Dass, Sunder Dass, Seraj Ud Din, Mool Chand, etc.', 25 December 1913, p. 25.

22 Lahore Municipal Corporation, LH-3/3-1906, 'Letters of Support from Ram Sarin Dass, Sunder Dass, Seraj Ud Din, Mool Chand, etc.', 25 December 1913, p. 25.

23 Lahore Municipal Corporation, LH-3/3-1906, 'Suit Filed by Sukh Dyal, Son of L. Shib Dyal, of Langemandi Bazaar, Lahore', 28 August 1914, pp. 33a–c.

24 Lahore Municipal Corporation, LH-3/3-1906, 'Letter from Ram Mal', 25 June 1919,p. 135.

25 In August 1919, Ram Mal was informed that his papers on the case, including his purchase receipt for the property, were 'lost in the engineering department for a long time but were finally found in the open

almirah of the city overseer'. See Lahore Municipal Corporation, LH-3/3-1906, 'File Note', 15 August 1919, p. 143.

26 The final entry in the case is written in response to claims in the 1927 *Paisa Akhbar* article that accused Ram Mal's widow of defrauding the city. The author of the note, S. Das, concluded the following: 'I have gone through these papers of the widow of L. Ram Rakhamal [sic] has sent me a copy of the will left by the deceased. A perusal of the will, will show that this property has been left for charitable purposes and a trust has been created to look after it. Other property yielding an income of Rs.130 p.m. has been attached to it for this purpose of the chart papers to be filed'. See Lahore Municipal Corporation, LH-3/3-1906, 12 April 1930, p. 159.

27 For a recent study on urban displacement of this sort in Delhi see Amita Baviskar, 'Between Violence and Desire: Space, Power, and Identity in the Making of Metropolitan Delhi', *International Social Science Journal*, (175), 2003, pp. 89–98.

Part V

Cosmopolitanisms: Historical and Contemporary

13

Simona Sawhney†

Bhagat Singh

A POLITICS OF DEATH AND HOPE

The only city where the great sacrifice of Bhagat Singh and his comrades created a
political movement among the left was Lahore.

—Bipan Chandra[1]

Asān tān joban rute marnā
We will die in the season of youth.

—Shiv Kumar Batalvi[2]

LAHORE NOW AND THEN

Over ninety worshippers were killed and many others injured as
seven assailants including three suicide bombers attacked Ahmadiyya
mosques in the Model Town and Garhi Shahu areas of Lahore on
28 May 2010. At least one of the attackers is described by the press
as a young Pashto-speaking teenager from the tribal areas. In past

† Earlier drafts of this essay were presented in October 2010 at the Political
Theory Colloquium, University of Minnesota and at a conference on 'Love
and Revolution', Centre for Humanities Research, University of the Western
Cape, South Africa. I am grateful to the organizers and members of the
audience at both venues for their comments and questions. Special thanks

attacks in Lahore attributed to the Taliban, commentators have likewise alluded to the youth of some of the assailants.

I have not been able to find any more information about the Pashto youth who was arrested on 28 May. What was he willing to kill—and to die—for? Why did the supposed 'heresy' of the Ahmadi sect become the focus of his rage? The common narrative, as we know, links these attacks to the orthodox believers' intolerance of Ahmadi heterodoxy. The Ahmadis constitute a very small minority in Pakistan, yet have been the object of much scrutiny. Though Ahmadis consider themselves Muslim, their belief in the prophethood of the sect's founder Mirza Ghulam Ahmad (1835–1908) is considered heretical by many other Muslims. Indeed, Ahmadis were declared non-Muslims by the Pakistani state in 1974 and their beliefs are considered blasphemous under Pakistan's 'blasphemy law' (Section 295-C of the Penal Code). Human Rights Watch reports that in 2009 alone, at least fifty Ahmadis were charged under various provisions of the blasphemy law—a law that has been often used to target members of minority communities.[3]

The news tells us that responsibility for this attack was claimed by the 'Punjabi wing' of Al-Qaeda. A text message from the group sent to various media outlets issued a final warning to the Ahmadis, asking them to 'leave Pakistan or prepare for death at the hands of Muhammad's devotees'.[4] Witnesses contend that the first people killed at the Darul Zikr mosque in the Garhi Shahu neighborhood of Lahore were also young boys—unarmed boys standing outside and 'guarding' the mosque. The events provoked the Interior Minister Rahman Malik to admit to the existence of a Punjabi Taliban in south Punjab and to admit that militant groups in south Punjab were now part of Al-Qaeda.[5]

No doubt what induces some of 'Muhammad's devotees' to kill and die is a complex and powerful force—indeed, a complex of

to Naheed Aaftaab, G. Arunima, Abir Bazaz, Patricia Hayes, Premesh Lalu, Ajay Skaria, and Antonio Vasquez-Arroyo for their questions—some of which still remain to be addressed. I am also grateful to the editors of this volume, Anshu Malhotra and Farina Mir, for their thoughtful suggestions, encouragement, and patience.

such forces. These are forces that belong to our world; they are not only a part of it but in fact they constitute it; this world of whose globalization, or, to use a different idiom, of whose world-ness, comprehensiveness, and interconnectedness, we have barely a glimpse. To what extent is the intensity of such attacks related to internal questions of orthodoxy and heterodoxy in Islam, to the strangely besieged figure of Muhammad himself, whose status as the last Prophet is so decisive for some of his followers? To what extent has that status become a charged but shifting signifier in the internal dynamics of a Pakistani state unable to articulate a meaningful or defensible relation to its minorities? To what extent is the very sign of Muhammad today inextricably linked to US imperialism in South Asia and the Middle East, to drone attacks over Afghanistan and Pakistan, scores and scores of remote-killings—now of suspected warriors, now of their families, of wedding parties and market places?[6] All this, and much more, intersects in the horrific slaughter of Ahmadis in Lahore. Indeed, one feels, uneasily, that even such attempts to gesture toward the political and historical contours of the phenomenon remain at a superficial level. How would one begin to articulate the relation between the explosive forces of political economy on the one hand, and on the other the intense psychic drama that such an economy energizes? How would one begin to take account of unemployment and despair, of rage and passion, of the secret paths of identification, of jealousy, desire, testosterone, and youth's smoldering, inarticulate fascination with death?

It might seem that I am primarily interested in weaving a narrative that would implicitly excuse or justify the actions of the young men who recently turned themselves into weapons of mass destruction in Punjab. That is not my intention. If at all possible, I would like to move away from the language of blame and praise. Instead, I would like to juxtapose these contemporary images of calculated public violence in Lahore with the contested legacy of another time. In the early decades of the twentieth century, several men were hanged in Central Jail, Lahore, on charges of sedition, criminality, or conspiracy. Like many young men in Lahore today, these men were accused of terrorism. They too were willing to kill and die for their beliefs. And they too used violent methods to protest a government perceived as tyrannical and unjust. Among the early twentieth century 'terrorists' of Lahore, perhaps the one most often recalled is Bhagat Singh who was hanged in 1931 along with his comrades Sukhdev and Rajguru for the murder of J.P. Saunders, Deputy Superintendent of Police. Saunders was killed in retaliation for the death of veteran nationalist leader Lala Lajpat Rai, who died of injuries suffered in the brutal police repression of a march to protest the Simon Commission in 1928.

Bhagat Singh (1907–1931) came from a politically active family in Lyallpur district in Punjab. He was the nephew of Ajit Singh, a leader of the Kisan (peasant) movement. Inspired by the Young Italy movement established by Giuseppe Mazzini in 1831, Bhagat Singh played a central role in organizing the Naujawan Bharat Sabha (The Young India Society) in Lahore in 1926. He was deeply impressed by the heroes of the Ghadar movement that had started in San Francisco, and especially by Kartar Singh Sarabha, who had been executed in Lahore in 1915 at the young age of nineteen. Bhagat Singh became a member of the Hindustan Republican Association and seems to have been largely responsible for changing its name to the Hindustan Socialist Republican Association in 1928. After the murder of Saunders, he initially escaped from Lahore, but then courted arrest in April 1929. Inspired by the actions of the French anarchist Edouard Vaillant, Bhagat Singh and his comrade Batukeshwar Dutt threw bombs in the Central Assembly in Delhi to protest against the Public Safety Bill and the Trade Dispute Bill. Along with the bombs, copies of a leaflet titled 'To Make the Deaf Hear' were scattered. Bhagat Singh's real fame on the national stage, however, may have come later, when, as a prisoner, he, along with his comrades, went on a sixty-three day hunger strike to protest against the differential treatment of British and Indian prisoners, and to insist that the category of 'political prisoner' be recognized and applied to the revolutionaries. The strike created immense solidarity for the prisoners in public consciousness of the time. Bhagat Singh, Rajguru, and Sukhdev were sentenced to death by a special tribunal created under an emergency ordinance, and hanged in Lahore on 23 March 1931, at an unscheduled time in order to prevent public rioting.

There may be many reasons for Bhagat Singh's current prominence and popularity—and doubtless reasons too to be suspicious of what he represents today, especially in divided Punjab, where, on the Indian side, he is frequently associated with Sikh militant separatists of the 1980s, even as the mainstream media constantly attempts to rehabilitate him as a consummate nationalist. In this essay, I want to explore how we might rethink the significance of Bhagat Singh's work and thought. Is it possible to distinguish between the violent political acts of Bhagat Singh and his friends on the one hand, and those of young 'terrorists' in Lahore today—and if so, on what grounds? From a nationalist position, of course the former are heroes and the latter misguided fundamentalists. If we didn't succumb to such labels, and instead compared the role of the religious community and the significance of religious identity in the thought–work of each group, I suspect the answer might be more complicated. Bhagat Singh himself is often remembered, at least in secular–left circles, as an 'atheist', based on his own late essay, 'Why I am an Atheist'. But regardless of religious belief, his political thinking, especially in the early years of his youth, had been formed by debates surrounding religio-political institutions. In his formative years he had been affected by Sikh political activism of the time as well as Arya Samaj ideals. Conversely, contemporary radical Islamic groups often evoke a strong anti-imperial sentiment and focus on Muslims in terms of the *political* oppression they suffer—in other words, their focus is usually on Muslims as the political victims of imperialism, whether in Palestine, Kashmir, or Afghanistan. In this regard, they are not unlike earlier third world nationalists.

One may notice other similarities as well: for example, the contention that the exercise of violence by the oppressed is a means of 'equalizing' political space by re-distributing, as it were, aggression and vulnerability; and most importantly, the belief that the ability to sacrifice oneself is the true measure of commitment. And yet we cannot disregard the differences either. Perhaps the most salient difference has to do with our current access to the thinking that leads to political violence. Whereas we are able to read the writings of many of the young people who were involved in anti-colonial struggles in the early twentieth century, we have less access to the ideas of the contemporary foot-soldiers of the Punjabi Taliban. They are spoken for by other, more prominent leaders, which perhaps attests to the scale of the current movement. What is most easily available, at least in the Western and other English-language media, are the writings and speeches of Osama bin Laden and Ayman al-Zawahiri; consequently it is difficult to know whether, and to what extent, young recruits see themselves not just as actors, but also as intellectual and political thinkers, as analysts. At times I have wondered what young recruits of the Punjabi Taliban today would make of Bhagat Singh's work: whether it would appear to them as a startling and perhaps unnerving mirror. I do not know.

However, it seems to me that Bhagat Singh's work (as well as the work of some of his comrades) also reveals some crucial and fundamental differences between that earlier world and the world of contemporary Lahore. In this essay I would like to think about this different 'world' that Bhagat Singh inhabited and that enabled him not only to take seriously his own reading of international politics, but also—indeed, as a sign of this seriousness—to continually question and revise his political stances. How did Bhagat Singh and his friends—mostly middle class youth with limited access to resources—perceive their actions? What did they want? How may we read today their willingness to suffer and die for an abstract cause? Where may we discern the shape and force of a commitment, and if we call this a *political* commitment, on what grounds would we do so?

To this end, I would like to look more closely at the terms, the phrases, the repetitions that appear in Bhagat Singh's work.[7] Of course, these writings do not give us any immediate access to desire, intention, or sensibility. But perhaps we may be able to decipher in these texts a kind of symbolic economy: the discursive ground, if you will, that enabled and validated decisions to kill and die. It seems to me that immense energy gathers in these writings around two fundamental elements: hope and death. They provide the essential and elemental shape of ethico-political action—which in this case may be defined as action undertaken in pursuit of a morally valourized vision of a necessarily 'imagined' community. I am interested in asking what enabled Bhagat Singh's and his comrades' belief that ordinary men have agency, that their words and actions can affect and shape hierarchies and distributions of power—what, in short, may have accounted for their astonishing hope. The second characteristic that marks this discourse is the central place it accords to the willingness to die. This is of course a trait it shares with all kinds of other discourses—and especially those we call 'revolutionary'. Here, I am less interested in the idea of 'dying to give life'—a phrase that Talal Asad evokes in his work on suicide bombing, and that he relates to liberalism's own disavowed genealogy.[8] Rather, I am interested in the way the ability to die becomes a testament to the strength and indeed, the veracity, of commitment. Surely this is by no means a 'natural' or transhistorical phenomenon. In early Indian texts, when warriors proclaim their willingness to die, they do not mention their beliefs—they might die for their own or their kinsmen's honour, or to prove their courage, or to fulfil their caste duties—and though of course we might discern a politics in all this, it seems quite clear that they do not die because they want to change the world. Dying in order to change the world (rather than redeeming or saving it in a theological sense) may be a characteristically modern phenomenon, one that testifies to the emergence of a global political subject. Keeping these tentative and preliminary remarks in mind, let me attempt to articulate in this essay the historical specificity of the work of these early twentieth century revolutionaries by thinking about their conception of community, action, hope, and death.

Bhagat Singh was executed before he had turned twenty-four. His many articles, essays, speeches, pamphlets and letters reveal a persistently restless and astonishingly cosmopolitan mind, searching for new and convincing analyses of the poverty, oppression, and misery he saw around him. Most striking perhaps is the confidence and conviction with which he and his friends wrote about the future. Despite moments of doubt and despair, they were more or less convinced that a better and brighter world could be built, and all that was needed to build it was the dedication and courage of young people. The strength of this conviction seems inextricably connected to Bhagat Singh's sense of himself as a citizen of the world. Though his immediate concern was with Indian independence from British rule, the shape of such independence increasingly became a question for him. Convinced that capitalist democracy would only substitute the Indian elite for the British rulers, he read and wrote extensively about anarchism and communism. Events in France, Italy, Russia, the US, Ireland, and Japan are of urgent and absorbing significance for him, as are the thoughts and writings of a diverse group of Russian, European, and American intellectuals.

One of the most obvious but nonetheless noteworthy effects of colonial occupation was its construction of the 'West' as an interlocutor for many Indians. This West was not, however, perceived as monolithic. This is crucial for understanding how Bhagat Singh's optimism—the astonishing faith and conviction with which he and his comrades approached the political field—cannot be accounted for only in terms of a modern belief in historical progress. Such a belief is doubtless discernible in their work, but it is propped up and supported by the perception that the West is not one: that the West is, indeed, at war with itself, on many fronts, and that consequently it is not only possible, but at times inevitable, exhilarating, and necessary, for third world nationalists to understand and establish their own critique of the warring ideologies of the West. The figure of a fissured Europe, divided not only by intra-state wars, but more crucially, by radically different visions of a European and world future—enabled Bhagat Singh and his comrades to conceive of their own cosmopolitan and historical significance in terms that may no longer be available to youth in the third world. Neither a narrative that focuses exclusively on the resurgence of religion in the wake of cold war politics in the postcolonial world, nor one that emphasizes socio-economic discontent and resistance to modernity, nor indeed any other narrative that remains focused on the internal dynamics of the Middle East or South Asia can adequately explain the difference between contemporary Islamic militancy and third world militancy of the early twentieth century. In thinking this difference, we must also think of the West's own consolidation in our times—its internal defeat of some of the most powerful evocations of egalitarian communal life to have appeared in modernity. I focus on Bhagat Singh's work partly because it puts this defeat most strongly in relief.

What would it mean to read this work as a text—not so much as an argument, but as a web, a discourse? How may we take into account its variegated strands: its undeniable romance with violence and young death, its fundamental absorption in a cult of male friendship and love, its reliance on figures of male *honour*, no less than its astonishing confidence—the confidence and hope of an anti-colonial thought-and-work that sees itself participating in an international challenge to authoritarianism and a global quest for more egalitarian political communities.[9]

Much has been written about Bhagat Singh's life and work.[10] A strand that emerges often in discussions concerning this work is its (mis)appropriation by various forces: those of the Left and the Right; those that speak in the name of religion and those that don't; those aligned with a nationalism, and those aligned with a Marxism.[11] Such appropriations are sometimes contested by highlighting certain elements in Bhagat Singh's work and challenging or marginalizing others.[12] However, in reading his writings, I am indeed struck by the diversity of tropes, elements, and indeed, discourses, which intersect in this work and render it, in effect, appropriable by several forces that we might consider formally opposed. In an early and astute essay, the Marxist historian Bipan Chandra puts this very perceptively: 'The new generation of terrorist revolutionaries were men of ideas and ideologies. Their ideas were, of course, rapidly developing and *cannot be studied except in motion,* so to speak'.[13] As soon as one thinks about this phrase, one realizes that any idea worth the name is always in motion—the idea that is studied no less than the idea that studies. The question then is: how to make such motion visible or legible, without attempting to circumscribe or limit it, without immediately reading it in terms of a contradiction—as Chandra proceeds to do. Indeed, it seems to me that by resorting too quickly to the category of contradiction, Chandra perhaps gives up on the task of pursuing a more complex analysis. His argument is as follows. He is struck by the 'historical paradox' that though most of the revolutionary terrorists were committed to a version of Marxism, their own deeds and words were appropriated by the nationalist leadership:

Basically their failure can be expressed in a series of contradictions *between their ideology and their work.* While in theory they were committed to socialism, in practice they could not go beyond nationalism. While in theory they desired mass action and armed struggle, in practice they could not rise above terrorist or individual action… While in theory they wanted to create and lead a mass movement, in practice they remained a small band of heroic youth.[14]

The failure of the revolutionaries, according to him, 'was not merely that of not linking their practice with their theory', but also 'that of not integrating nationalism and socialism at the theoretical and programmatic plane'. Their political aspiration was to 'accomplish at one stroke the nationalist as well as the socialist revolutions', but since historical conditions could not allow them to do that, they were forced to keep the two ideals distinct.

Let us consider for a moment the terms of this analysis. Two pairs are central: nationalism/socialism on the one hand, theory/practice on the other. Chandra first asserts that nationalism appropriates (and hence negates) socialism, then proposes that perhaps the revolutionaries themselves could not integrate the two, either at the level of theory or at the level of practice. This is a suggestive analysis—and all the more powerful because it is evidently written from a perspective that reads this moment in light of its political significance for the future. At the same time, however, I wonder whether by taking *as given* the limits of each of his central terms, Chandra also does not thereby limit his analysis. For what emerges most powerfully in his discussion and in the movement of his text is indeed the confusion, the slippage and the mutual instability of the terms of each pair. Should one not then re-think the work performed by these in the colonial context? If it was not possible for the revolutionaries to either integrate or segregate what is called 'nationalism' and 'socialism', maybe these concepts do not provide a strong enough frame to articulate the forces that were most insistent in the thought/praxis of the revolutionaries. If, finally, the revolutionaries found themselves unable—in theory or practice—to renounce a certain attachment to the figure of the nation, we should likewise ask whether the shape of this attachment should be necessarily subsumed under available concepts of nationalism. In what follows, I will make a few steps in this direction. I am aware that a more substantial analysis of this kind would require that instead of focusing on Bhagat Singh, we read as well the work of several writers of this 'generation of terrorist-revolutionaries' as Chandra calls them. Though I will occasionally mention some of these other figures, my remarks here will mostly be limited to the corpus of writings that are recognized as Bhagat Singh's—even though he wrote under several pseudonyms.

APNE-PARĀYE (ONE'S OWN/THE OTHER)

An early essay, '*Punjabi kī bhāshā aur lipī kī samasyā*' (The Problem of the Punjabi Language and Script),[15] which won an award from the Punjab Hindi Sahitya Sammelan, was written in 1924 but published posthumously in 1933. It is an interesting study in the tensions between several kinds of solidarity: to the region, the nation, and the world. Ultimately, the young Bhagat Singh writes, Indians should be guided by the ideal of unifying the entire world, but before that, they must create one language, one script, one ideal and one nation (*rāshtra*) in India. Language is of primary significance in this regard because it will enable mutual understanding. In the essay, Punjab emerges as an especially appropriate example of the national problem, since, unlike other states, it has no unifying language. Moreover, Bhagat Singh connects this lack of a common language to religious division, and in particular to the Muslim community which insists on the importance of its own language, Urdu. Here the essay takes a turn that we sometimes see in Bhagat Singh's early writings, though it is almost entirely absent in his later work:

Like other states, the language of Punjab should be Punjabi, then why didn't it happen, this question naturally arises, but the local Muslims adopted Urdu.[16] Muslims entirely lack Indianness (*musalmānon men bhārtīyatā kā sarvathā abhāv hai*), that is why, not perceiving the importance of Indianness for India, they want to propagate the Arabic script and Persian language. They do not understand that it is important for all of India to have one language and that too Hindi. That is why they kept up their chant of Urdu and sat aside.[17]

Though the essay goes on to indict all religious communities—Sikhs, Hindus, and Muslims—for their attachment to their own language and script, and for their role in the communalization of language and culture in Punjab, Muslims are obviously singled out, and a familiar trope that reiterates the 'outsider' status of Muslims and the Urdu script is repeated.[18] Indeed, despite all its evocations of regional, national, and international unity, in effect the essay dramatizes precisely the difficulty of conceiving such unity. More importantly, it dramatizes the difficulty of reconciling the force of local attachment and singular history with abstract ideals of community. This difficulty is at the crux of the young Bhagat Singh's deliberations on language, and his advocacy of a shared language. On the one hand, he is attracted to the idea of a single national language, and advocates that this language be Hindi. On the other, he is also convinced that the Punjabi language *speaks to* Punjabis in a way that Hindi cannot. A hesitation regarding the status of Hindi is thus hard to miss, in spite of his general argument in favor of adopting the Hindi script in Punjab.

Arguing that the language of Punjab should be Punjabi, but a Punjabi written in the Hindi script, the essay at first seeks to demolish Urdu's claim. It discusses how Punjabi Urdu poets exhibit a pervasive lack of 'Indianness' (*Bhārtīyatā*), and how the Urdu script cannot be called full-limbed (*sarvāngsampūrṇa*) on account of its inability to accurately represent the vowels and consonants of Hindi and Punjabi. Towards the end, however, as Bhagat Singh evokes several popular Punjabi verses, he also suggests that the Punjabi language, the one whose rhythm and vocabulary is most familiar and beloved in Punjab, might actually be further from Hindi than from Farsi: 'It [Hindi] as yet seems rather outsiderly (*parāyī-sī*). The reason is that Hindi is based on Sanskrit. Punjab is now leagues apart from it. Farsi has kept a strong influence on Punjabi...I mean to say that in spite of being close to Punjabi [perhaps from the perspective of historical linguistics], Hindi is yet quite far from the Punjabi heart' (45). Writing Punjabi in the Hindi script is therefore presented as the solution to this problem: 'Yes, when the Punjabi language is written in the Hindi script and when an attempt is made to [thus] produce a [Punjabi] literature, then it will certainly come closer to Hindi' (45). Where is Farsi in this map? It is at the same time near and far; it is closer to Punjabi than Hindi, but propagating its use is anti-Indian.

We cannot disregard this ambivalence about the status of Urdu, Farsi, and Muslims that surfaces at several moments in Bhagat Singh's early writing, in spite of its ostensible commitment to an 'anti-communal' stance. What does this ambivalence signal? To what other tropes, patterns, and discourses is it related? Is it possible to follow the Marxist historian Irfan Habib in believing that the Naujawan Bharat Sabha (Young India Society), formed by Bhagat Singh and his friends in 1926, was 'above all petty religious politics of the times and stood for secularism'?[19] While the Sabha might indeed have 'stood for' secularism, *how* did it think the secular—what were the elements it drew upon to conceive of the political community, or even community itself in its most fundamental sense? Could community be thought outside the distinction between *apnā/parāyā* (one's own and the other, the outsider) evoked by Bhagat Singh? And if not, then in what sense is it possible to idealize a world community? These seem to be the very complex and thorny questions that lie beneath ostensible confusions regarding nationalism, socialism, and internationalism. Indeed, this early essay on language is only one text among several others that signal a persistent engagement with the tropes of the near and the far, one's own and the other, the intimate and the foreign. In one way or another, this engagement circulates through many of Bhagat Singh's writings. In reading this work, we are struck by the *difficulties* it encounters in articulating a vision of cosmopolitanism. At the same time, we become aware of the moving coordinates of the world that Bhagat Singh inhabited—a world in which Mazzini,[20] Garibaldi, and Lenin at times appear to be closer to Bhagat Singh than contemporary Indian thinkers.

In the essay titled 'Vishva Prem' (Love of the World), published in November 1924 under the pseudonym 'Balvant Singh' in the Calcutta weekly 'Matvala', Bhagat Singh glosses the concept of the other (*parāyā*) in terms of hierarchy. To wish for an end to otherness, he indicates, is not to wish for the end of difference, but rather to wish for the end of hierarchical relations. The 'other' thus emerges here as not a racial or national other, but instead as the one who is differentiated by a structural and unjust hierarchy.

'World-Friendship'—I, for one, understand this as nothing else but equality in the world (*Sāmyavād*, world wide equality in the true sense).

How lofty is that thought! That everyone be one's own. No one be an other. How joyous [*sukhmaya*] that time will be, when otherness will be entirely destroyed in the world...

Trade will be at the epitome of progress that day, but there will not be terrible wars between Germany and France in the name of trade. Both America and Japan will exist, but there won't be westerness and easterness [*pūrvīya aur paścimīyapan*] in them. Black and White will exist, but the residents of America will not be able to burn alive the black residents (Red Indians). There will be peace but not the necessity of a penal code. The British and the Indians will both exist, but they will not understand themselves as slaves and rulers.[21]

Here, his consciousness of hierarchy and inequality gives rise to an amalgam of hatred and compassion towards the weak: a symptom perhaps all the more clearly visible in the writing of a seventeen-year-old boy who does not mask his words. Castigating those who fear the bloodshed and anarchy of revolt, he writes:

Let unrest [*ashānti*] spread if it will, it will also mean the end of dependence. Let anarchy spread if it will, it will also mean the destruction of subjection. Ah! The weak will be ground down in that struggle. [*Us kashmakash men kamzor pis jāyenge*]. This daily weeping will end. [*Roz roz kā ronā band ho jāyegā*]. The weak will no longer exist, *there will be friendship among the strong*. Those who have strength will be close to one another. There will be love among them, and it will be possible to propagate universal love in the world.

Yes, yes, the weak will have to be ground down, once and for all. They are the culprits of the entire world. They are responsible for terrible unrest [*ghor ashānti*]. Let everyone become strong, otherwise they will become grist in this mill.[22]

The ensuing argument appears to be at least partially a response to Gandhi. Bhagat Singh, like many of his comrades, had participated in the non-cooperation movement that was called off by Gandhi after the violence of Chauri-Chaura in 1922, much to the dismay of many of the young men who saw the incident as part of the unavoidable violence of political conflict. Universal friendship and brotherhood, Bhagat Singh writes, only has value as a principle when it is articulated and practiced by the strong; if a weak human being claims that he does not resist oppression because he is a follower of universal brotherhood, his statement has no significance since it is likely to be read as indicative of his powerlessness rather than as a principled stance. In essence, he makes an argument that was often made by the revolutionaries: non-violence truly makes an impact only when it is practiced by those who have the ability to be violent. It must be chosen, not adopted expediently by those who have no other means to resist.

At the same time, the weak are also *necessary* for the way in which political and ethical struggle is envisioned, here as well as in other writings. In this political imagination, the world is divided into oppressors, victims, and heroes. Ultimately, the hero is the one who is unable to witness suffering, and instead, is himself willing to suffer. This image appears at several moments in Bhagat Singh's work. In this essay, for instance, he writes that the aim of the revolutionaries is to spread anarchy on the sites of those imperial states that, blinded by power, have caused the agony of millions. It is the duty of revolutionaries to save the suffering, the exploited. The true proponent of universal love is one who takes on suffering in order to save others.[23] This seems to unite figures as diverse as Lenin (who suffered unspeakable hardships), Brutus (who, for his birthland, murdered his beloved Caesar with his own hands, and then committed suicide) and Savarkar (carried away by universal love, he would stop while walking on the grass so that tender leaves may not be crushed beneath his feet).[24] These are the fundamental ingredients of heroism: first, an inability to witness the suffering of the weak, and second, a capacity to both inflict and suffer violence. The former—a capacity for boundless compassion—justifies the violence of the hero and differentiates it from the violence of the oppressor.[25] The hero's violence is born out of intense compassion and sensitivity, and it is, moreover, employed not for one's own benefit but for the benefit of others. Indeed, its primary task is to expose the oppressor's own vulnerability and strip him of his apparent immunity. In so far as it is directed toward exposing the weakness of the strong—toward exposing the strong as weak, as mortal, as living in the midst of the same battlefield as those who are more regularly attacked and crushed—it may be guided by a powerful impulse to render public space more 'egalitarian'.

In this context, we might also recall Osama bin Laden's words after the 2004 Madrid bombings: 'It is well known that security is a vital necessity for every human being. We will not let you monopolize it for yourselves [...]'.[26] As Faisal Devji notes in his analysis, for Al-Qaeda, terror becomes 'the only form in which global freedom and equality are now available'.[27] Devji reads this as a sign of Al-Qaeda's profound implication in a vision of globality eviscerated of ideology and politics.

In this sense, he reads Al-Qaeda as participating, albeit perversely, in the same logic that governs humanitarianisms that privilege the interrelatedness of the global community at the cost of historical and political analyses. Though I am not at present persuaded by all aspects of Devji's argument,[28] I share his sense that, despite rhetorical and other similarities, there are also important differences between contemporary Islamic militancy and earlier insurgent or revolutionary movements. Contemporary militancy, he writes, 'unlike all previous forms of terrorist or insurgent action, refuses to set up an alternative utopia for itself, something that even anarchists are not immune to'.[29] My question may be similar to, but simpler than the one Devji confronts: I wish to explore what *enabled* Bhagat Singh and his comrades to imagine such a utopia—to imagine its nearness, and, moreover, to believe that they themselves could be instrumental in realizing it. To this end, I attempt to re-read the significance of the terms that are privileged in their writings. For example: death. Is it only sacrifice that beckons when death beckons?

MIT JĀNE KĪ HASRAT (THE DESIRE TO BE ERASED)

One of Bhagat Singh's most famous articles, '*Holi ke Din Rakt ki Chinte*' (Splashes of Blood on Holi), published under the name '*Ek Punjabi Yuvak*' (A Punjabi Youth) in *Pratap* in March 1926, commemorates six members of the Babbar Akalis who were hanged in Lahore Central Jail a few weeks earlier, on 27 February.[30] The Babbar Akalis were a radical splinter group of the Akali movement for the reform of Sikh temples. Excusing any mistakes or follies these men might have committed, Bhagat Singh insists that we view their actions in terms of their devotion to 'this unfortunate land': 'They could not bear injustice, could not bear to watch the fallen state of the country, the cruelties inflicted on the weak became unbearable for them, they could not stand the exploitation of the common people…'.[31] Such phrases are repeated countless times in Bhagat Singh's hagiographic accounts of the Babbar Akalis, the Kakori heroes, and other revolutionaries. These phrases are evidently not merely descriptive, but rather prescriptive in their intent. Indeed, if these two qualities are repeatedly valourized—an inability to witness the suffering of the weak, and the corresponding ability to challenge or attack wrong-doers, even in the face of death—it is perhaps because in the analytic perspective of the revolutionaries these were the qualities most vividly lacking in the Indian public. Fear of death, in this analysis, inoculates in advance, as it were, against compassion. Correspondingly, the true measure of compassion is the overcoming of such fear. It has become a truism that colonial discourse and practice produced and sustained an image of the weak and effete Indian male and so one could read the revolutionary position as a response—indeed a challenge to such an image. Evocations of male honour and the importance of fighting humiliation are scattered through Bhagat Singh's writings. Idealized manhood is figured, first, as that which does not publicly submit to domination, and second, as capable of great, immense love—not, of course, for women—but either for the motherland or for other heroes. Such love, the love of heroes for one another, is predicated on overcoming fear and is the most cherished and precious of all human bonds.[32] The idea of overcoming fear is crucial to the political, moral, and aesthetic sensibility of the revolutionaries. At the risk of stating the obvious, let me attempt to parse this.

In a site of extreme and visible hierarchy, the political domain cannot but appear as the arena of a moral war in which those who exercise power are in some immediate sense wrong, immoral, unjust, and only able to hold on to their position because of force. Correlatively, those who submit to an obviously unjust force would only do so—in this view—out of fear. For the revolutionaries, what sustained the power of the British in India was not the consent of the ruled, but neither was it just the coercive power of the ruler. Moral responsibility for colonial rule was assigned—in fact, *appropriated*—through this focus on, and indictment of, fear and in the final analysis fear was understood essentially as fear of death. In a long exchange with Gandhi, Sachindranath Sanyal, one of the founding members of the Hindustan Republican Army, writes at length about this:

If you mean that these reforms [the annulment of the Bengal partition; the Minto-Morley reforms; the Montford reform] are no index to true progress, then I would venture to say that this revolutionary movement has achieved no mean progress in the moral advancement of India. Indians were miserably afraid of death and this revolutionary party once more made the Indians realize the grandeur and the beauty that lay in dying for a noble cause. The revolutionaries have once again demonstrated that death has a certain charm and is not always a dreadful thing. To die for one's own beliefs and convictions, to die in the consciousness that by so dying one is serving god and the nation, to accept death or to risk one's life when there is every probability of death, for a cause which one honestly believes to be just and legitimate—is this no moral progress?[33]

In a similar vein, in 1928 Bhagat Singh writes an essay extolling Madan Lal Dhingra, who was hanged in 1909 for killing Sir Curzon Wyllie, political aide-de-camp to the Secretary of State for India. The essay was published in the journal *Kirti* as part of a series 'Martyrs for Freedom' (*Āzādī kī bhent shahādaten*), under the name '*Vidrohi*' (Rebel). The aim of the series was to explain to readers 'how Punjab awakened, how work was carried out, and for what actions, what ideas, these martyrs dedicated (even) their lives'.[34] The essay cites Madan Lal's final testimony in English: '...I believe that a nation held down by foreign bayonets is in a perpetual state of war...The only lesson required in India at present is to learn how to die, and the only way to teach it is by dying ourselves'.[35]

The colonial situation powerfully corroborated this vision of the world, which perceived suffering and inequality as a consequence of the greed and arrogance of those in power, and thus legitimated actions that would diminish and undermine the colonizer's sense of immunity: 'The British government exists, because the Britishers have been successful in terrorizing the whole of India. How are we to meet this official terrorism? Only counter-terrorism on the part of revolutionaries can checkmate effectively this bureaucratic bullying'.[36]

But it is clear that the existential dimension of courting death also presented to the revolutionaries a vision of political work that was very far from what they saw as the drab work of compromise and negotiation followed by professional politicians. In place of the professional politician, they wanted the professional revolutionary. 'We require—to use the term so dear to Lenin—the "professional revolutionaries". The whole-time workers who have no other ambitions or life-work except the revolution'.[37] Several distinct but related images mesh in the valourization of a life entirely saturated by revolutionary activity and thought, and risked in honorable battle. Images of a glorious death, no doubt—a 'beautiful death' (*kalos thanatos*) not unlike the one valorized in epic narratives of war.[38] Such a death is beautiful because it erases the inexplicable futility of human life and death. Revolution 'uses up' both life and death and in this use, gives both the value that otherwise eludes them. In a fascinating letter to Sukhdev written during their hunger strike, Bhagat Singh relates an incident when he was advised by secret service agents to aid the British and save his life. In the presence of his father, these agents said that since he was not prepared to do so, he must be deeply unhappy and desirous of death. In effect they argued, Bhagat Singh writes, that his death in these circumstances would be akin to suicide. In response, he told them that a person of his beliefs could not bear to die in vain. 'We wish to obtain the utmost value for our lives [*Hum to apne jīvan kā adhik se adhik mūlya prāpt karnā chāhte hain*]. We wish to render as much service as possible to humanity. Particularly a person like me, whose life is not unhappy or anxious in any way—far from committing suicide, such a person doesn't consider it appropriate to even let such a thought enter his heart'.[39]

Suicide carries connotations of cowardice or despair, and hence seems to be the inverse of the heroic death desired by revolutionaries.[40] Indeed Bhagat Singh's letter to Sukhdev makes several arguments against the legitimacy of suicide as a personal or political act. But though suicide is distinguished from what Bipan Chandra calls 'propaganda by death'[41] in terms of its motives, occasionally a different note may be heard in passages of revolutionary writing: a note which suggests that death itself may, indeed, have become sweet or desirable. One of Bhagat Singh's most famous comrades, Ram Prasad 'Bismil', was hanged in 1928 in the Kakori conspiracy case. In his adulatory essay about the Kakori prisoners, Bhagat Singh describes in detail his last moments. Just as he is about to be hanged, Bismil recites several passages of poetry. Among them, the following:

Ab na ahle valvale hain, aur na armānon kī bhīrh
Ek mit jāne kī hasrat, ab dil-e-bismil men hai.[42]

No more now fruitless passion, nor throngs of hope
Now, in this wounded heart (the heart of 'Bismil'), one desire: to be
erased.

How should we understand this desire to be erased? The desire to
extinguish all desires? To be sure, we may read it in a spiritual register,
for Bismil was by all accounts a devout believer. Another verse he is
reported to have recited in the moments before ascending the gallows
starts thus:

Mālik terī razā rahe aur tū hi tū rahe
Bāqī na main rahūn, na merī ārzū rahe.[43]

Lord, may your will remain and may you alone remain
Apart from that, let neither me nor my desire remain.

Yet I would suggest that the spiritual register may not entirely exhaust
Bismil's '*mit jāne kī hasrat*', just as the heroic may not entirely account
for Bhagat Singh's own movement toward death. Let us take note of
two cryptic entries in the *Jail Notebook*:

Tujhe zabāh karne kī khushī, mujhe marne kā shauq,
Merī bhī marzī vohī hai, jo mere sayyād kī hai.[44]

You delight in slaughter, I am drawn to death
My wish is the same, as that of my executioner.

And many pages later, a short citation from Rousseau's *Émile*: 'If we
were immortal we should all be miserable; no doubt it is hard to die,
but is sweet to think that we shall not live for ever'.[45]

I am treading on thin ground here. If I draw attention to a fascination with death that surfaces at moments in the writings of the
revolutionaries, and that appears to exceed what we usually understand
as spiritual or political motives, I do so neither to circumscribe and thus
dam the spiritual and the political, nor to drain them in some swamp of
the psyche. I am aware that both can become colonial moves. Instead,
I do so in order to indicate the deep and complex relation between the
political, the spiritual, and the psychic, and to underline the centrality of death in this understanding of politics. I would not deny that
the recurrence of the trope of sacrifice in Bhagat Singh's writings—
especially his earlier writings commemorating other heroes—should

be read as part of the repertoire of religious nationalism; nor would I deny that nineteenth and early twentieth revolutionary thought was nourished in part by the energies of romanticism and in particular by romantic images of heroic death. In his famous essay 'Why I am an Atheist' Bhagat Singh himself suggests that up till about 1926 he was 'only a romantic idealist revolutionary'. Nevertheless, moving at a tangent from those readings, I want to underline that an existential approach to the political remained in a crucial sense foundational for revolutionary thought. By an existential approach I do not mean an approach influenced by Western existentialist thinkers, but rather an approach for which the essential mortality of human life and the question of political community were mutually implicated and gave meaning to one another. In a context where political community was difficult to imagine and describe (as the tensions arising from regional, religious and linguistic, not to speak of ideological difference demonstrate), death was recruited, as it were, in the task of creating community. But this is not a politics of despair. On the contrary, I want to draw attention to the essentially hopeful and confident strain in this approach, as made evident in the writings and acts of the revolutionaries of the early twentieth century.

HOPE IN A WORLD AT WAR

This hopeful strain arose from a certain reading of Marxism, as well as a certain understanding of world politics. But even more importantly, it arose from a certain condition of the world. That is to say, it was not just a matter of what and how the young Indian revolutionaries were reading. It was also a matter of what was happening in a world, which, as I have suggested before, presented itself as fundamentally fissured and on the brink of momentous change. Most crucially, this fissure did not appear as a fissure between the west and the rest, but rather as a growing divide between authoritarian regimes of various kinds and challenges to them—a divide that ran through the West as much as it did through the East. It is important to remember in this context that the Public Safety and Trade Dispute Bills that provided the occasion for Bhagat Singh's and B.K. Dutt's spectacular agitation at the Central Assembly were introduced after the South Indian Railway and the Bombay Textile workers strikes in 1928. Both bills were aimed at the growing labour movement and an immediate objective of the Public Safety Bill was the deportation of British communists helping to organize workers in Bengal and Bombay.[46] Commenting on this moment, Sumit Sarkar convincingly argues that Bhagat Singh's interest in Marxism 'must be placed in the context of what was in some ways the most striking feature of 1928–29—a massive labour upsurge (particularly in railways, cotton textiles, and jute), accompanied by considerable Communist penetration into trade unions'.[47] Where the pamphlet 'To Make the Deaf Hear' opposes the 'indiscriminate arrests of labour leaders working in the open field' it clearly refers to the thirty-one communist and labour leaders who were arrested on 20 March 1929. Three of these men were British. The arrests led to the famous Meerut Conspiracy Case; those arrested were charged with being aligned with the Communist International, with inciting antagonism between Capital and Labour, creating workers' and peasants' parties, youth leagues, and other such organizations, and ultimately, with conspiring to overthrow the government. Among the organizations listed by the prosecution as 'co-conspirators' were the League Against Imperialism as well as The League for National Independence, of whose executive committee Jawaharlal Nehru was a member.[48]

It is clear from Bhagat Singh's Jail Notebook as well as other writings that he had read at least some texts by Marx, Engels, and Lenin. From these he had distilled an understanding of history that, on the one hand, set him apart, and on the other, oddly converged with the more spiritual leanings of some of his friends in emphasizing the relative insignificance of the individual. A striking passage in his letter to Sukhdev (written in 1929), cited earlier, offers a glimpse of this understanding. It is unfortunate that Sukhdev's letter, to which Bhagat Singh systematically responds, has been lost. But the response indicates that Sukhdev had expressed despair over the hardships of prison life, wondered about the futility of political work, suggested that suicide might be appropriate in certain circumstances, and expressed a new conviction about the significance of (erotic) love in human life. Bhagat Singh's letter is long and thoughtful, addressing several of Sukhdev's concerns, and in the process discussing some of the changes that have occurred over the years in their respective perspectives. I will cite an extended passage here, translated from the original Hindi:

Do you mean to imply that if we had not stepped into this field, no revolutionary work would have been done at all? If so, you are mistaken. While it is correct that we too have proved helpful in changing the environment to a considerable extent, we have merely been produced by the necessities of our time [*hum to keval apne samaye kī āvashyaktā kī upaj hain*].

I would in fact also say that the father of communism,[49] Marx, was not in reality the one who gave birth to this idea. Actually the industrial revolution in Europe had produced people of a particular way of thinking. Marx was one among them. Yes, doubtless Marx was to some extent helpful in giving the wheel of time a particular kind of speed.

I (and you) have not given birth to socialist and communist ideas in this country; they are the result of the impress of our time and circumstances upon us.[50]

Let us note two moves here. An analytic move: historical conditions produce certain necessities, needs. The Hindi word *āvashyaktā*, from *āvashya*—that which cannot be brought under control or conquered, that which must be—brings together the idea of necessity with the idea of need. But the necessary—that which cannot be subdued, that to which one *must* submit—no longer signifies what it once did. Fate has been recast and reshaped, as it were, by historical determinism. Now it is history that determines the necessary. Thus the relative insignificance of the individual: the individual is not the original author of his ideas, but should instead be seen as the proponent of ideas that are produced by the necessities, the needs of time and circumstance.

This theoretical humility, if we may thus name it, does not, however, translate into personal humility. The letter presents Bhagat Singh and Sukhdev as political actors in the world, their situation analogous to Marx's. This is the other move, and it seems to be as significant as the first one. By using a term such as 'humility' I certainly do not mean to suggest that its lack signals an ethical flaw in the revolutionaries. Rather I want to draw attention to the way in which these young activists saw themselves as part of a global historical process and found models and comrades in various far away spaces. Later in the same letter, Bhagat Singh writes,

Do we not have in front of us examples of such revolutionary workers who returned after enduring prison sentences and are still working? If Bakunin had thought like you, he would have committed suicide at the very beginning. Today you may see countless such revolutionaries who occupy responsible posts in the Russian state and who have spent most of their lives under sentence in prison. Man should attempt to stand firmly and unwaveringly by his beliefs. No one can predict the future.[51]

That Russia was a powerful inspiration is evident from several different essays. The anarchist writers Bakunin and Prince Kropotkin are approvingly cited in various places, and especially in the series of essays on anarchism (*arājaktāvād*) published in 1928. Bakunin's life is here described with reference to a chain of political events: labour and peasant revolts in Poland, France, Spain, and Italy. Four of his followers are then singled out: the Italians Carlo Cafiero and Malatesta, the French Paul Brousse, and the Russian Peter Kropotkin. Bhagat Singh briefly paints a picture of a Europe in revolt: peasant revolts in Italy and France in the late nineteenth century; two unsuccessful attempts to assassinate the Italian king Umberto followed by his (successful) assassination in 1900; two assassination attempts on Kaiser Wilhelm I within three weeks of one another; the killing of police officers by radical anarchists in Vienna in 1883–4; the revolts of silk workers in Lyons; the 'haymarket' riots in Chicago in 1886; the throwing of a bomb in the Chamber of Deputies in France by Auguste Vaillant in 1893. His aim is both to provide a 'plot history' of anarchist actions, and to demonstrate to his readers the motives behind the violent actions undertaken by anarchists all over the world. Anarchists, he writes, are not blood thirsty and cruel people who delight in destruction, but rather those who are willing to sacrifice their lives in fighting for the rights of the poor against capitalists and authoritarian rulers.[52]

The essay seems to foreshadow a passage in Benedict Anderson's book *Under Three Flags*, where Anderson succinctly describes an 'imagined community' that has not gained quite the same recognition as the one described in his book on nationalism. This is not the community imagined by any particular nationalism, but rather the community of the revolutionary-assassins who operated in various parts of the world, yet shared a common stage:

But beginning in the early 1880s the preliminary tremors were being felt of the earthquake that we remember variously as the Great War or the First World War. Tsar Alexander II's assassination in 1881 by bomb-throwing radicals calling themselves The People's Will was followed over the next twenty-five years by the killing of a French president, an Italian monarch, an Austrian empress and an heir-apparent, a Portuguese king and his heir, a Spanish prime minister, two American presidents, a king of Greece, a king of Serbia, and powerful conservative politicians in Russia, Ireland, and Japan. Of course, a much larger number of attentats failed. The earliest and most spectacular of these assassinations were carried out by anarchists, but nationalists soon followed in their wake. In most cases the immediate aftermath was a mass of draconian 'anti-terrorist' legislation, summary executions, and sharp rise in torture by police forces, public and secret, as well as militaries. But the assassins, some of whom could well be described as early suicide-bombers, understood themselves as acting for a world-audience of news agencies, newspapers, religious progressives, working-class and peasant organizations, and so on.[53]

As I have attempted to demonstrate, such assassins had a powerful impact on Bhagat Singh; at various moments in his writings, he attempts to yoke the Indian nationalist movement to an international movement for the liberation of the oppressed. Because in describing these events, he focuses in a very general way on the fact of oppression, and the moral and physical courage of those who challenge the powerful and the wealthy, he is spared the labour of distinguishing too carefully between nationalists and anarchists, republicans and Marxists. What is of significance for him is the very possibility of international uprising on the grounds of an ethico-political critique of inequality and imperialism—however hazy or amorphous such a critique may be.

In this brief series of comments I have by no means been able to do any justice either to Bhagat Singh's own work and thought, or to the complex forces that structured his word. In conclusion, let me attempt to pull together some of the strands that I have highlighted and summarize my argument in two general remarks. First, the focus on death and sacrifice in the thought of Bhagat Singh and his comrades, a focus partially enabled by the vocabulary of a religio-nationalism, and partially by a masculinist discourse of honour and action, must also be read in terms of an existential approach to the political. This may be a stronger force than has hitherto been recognized—a force more primary than the nationalist, Marxist, or anarchist ideas that Bhagat Singh was, at different moments, attracted to and invested in. Though such an approach becomes most evident at certain times and among certain groups, and though it can quickly become associated with a fascism, we must also ask ourselves whether any commitment to an ideal of community can be articulated at a distance or a remove from it. This existential approach was linked to a new figure of the 'world' that had become available as an object of concern, care and love. To love the world meant risking one's life in order to affect its possible futures.

And second, the actions of nationalists and anarchists at the end of the nineteenth century, the First World War, and above all perhaps, the Russian revolution had a profound impact on Bhagat Singh and his comrades. Perhaps, taking a cue from Bhagat Singh's own understanding of history, we may say that what separates today's young Punjabi terrorists from the Punjabi revolutionaries of the last century is less a difference of individual capacity or perspective, and more a worldly difference—a difference in the world they inhabit. What Bhagat Singh saw was a deeply divided West: a West perhaps on the brink of transforming itself by making a stupendous commitment to a politics of equality. That is why nowhere in his work do we see the kind of sweeping suspicion of the West that we see in the writings and speeches of contemporary terrorists, for whom America and her satellites present a stark monolith, barren of any meaningful internal dissent. Could we say that Bhagat Singh lived in a world where war—that is to say, the confrontation of sovereign powers—was still possible and that hope, in that world, arose precisely from the dark fertility of that possibility?

NOTES

1 Bipan Chandra, *Nationalism and Colonialism in Modern India*, Hyderabad: Orient Longman, 1996 [1979], pp. 251–2.
2 Shiv Kumar, *Sampuran Kāv Sangreh*, Ludhiana: Lahore Book Shop, 1997, p. 259.

3 http://www.hrw.org/en/news_/2010/05/31/pakistan-massacre-minori-ty-ahmadis. Accessed on 30 April 2011.

4 http://www.independent.co.uk_/news/world/asia/worshippers-slaugh-tered-in-deadly-final-warning-1986188.html. Accessed on 30 April 2011.

5 http://www.nytimes.com/2010/06/03/world/asia/03pstan.html. Accessed on 30 April 2011.

6 This essay was written before the US Special Forces operation that killed Osama bin Laden on 1 May 2011.

7 Bhagat Singh wrote in Hindi, Punjabi, Urdu, and English. His writings include letters; articles published in journals such as *Pratāp* (Kanpur), *Kīrti* (Amritsar), *Mahārathi* (Delhi), *Chānd* (Allahabad), and *Arjun* (Delhi); statements at court; a Hindi adaptation/translation of Dan Breen's *My Fight for Irish Freedom* (Breen's book was published in 1924); and a Jail notebook mostly consisting of citations from, and notes about, the books he was reading in prison. Hindi readers will find extremely useful the collection of his writings edited by Chaman Lal, *Bhagat Singh ke Sampūrṇa Dastāvez*, Panchkula: Adhar Prakashan, 2004. The collection includes a comprehensive and very informative Introduction by the editor. I am not able to treat Bhagat Singh's work in its entirety in this essay, but will refer only to selected texts.

8 'I want to suggest', writes Asad, 'that the cult of sacrifice, blood, and death that secular liberals find so repellent in pre-liberal Christianity is a part of the genealogy of modern liberalism itself, in which violence and tenderness go together'. See Talal Asad, *On Suicide Bombing*, New York: Columbia University Press, 2007, p. 88.

9 Mazzini's influence is a telling example in this regard. Discussing this influence, C.A. Bayly writes, 'The hermeneutic that interpreted him to Indians was the mid-nineteenth-century conjuncture in Eurasia. This finally destroyed the papacy's secular power, and announced the "springtime of peoples in Europe". It also shook the sultanate, destroyed the vestiges of Mughal legitimacy, and called into question the efficacy of Brahminical ritual'. See C.A. Bayly, 'Liberalism at Large: Mazzini and Nineteenth-Century Indian Thought', in C.A. Bayly and Eugenio F. Biagini (eds), *Giuseppe Mazzini and the Globalization of Democratic Nationalism 1830–1920*, Oxford: Oxford University Press, 2008, p. 365.

10 Some recent books include: Irfan Habib, *To Make the Deaf Hear: Ideology and Programme of Bhagat Singh and his Comrades*, Gurgaon: Three Essays Collective, 2007; P.M.S. Grewal, *Bhagat Singh: Liberation's Blazing Star*, Delhi: LeftWord Books, 2007; Ishwar Dayal Gaur, *Martyr*

as Bridegroom: A Folk Representation of Bhagat Singh, New Delhi: Anthem Press, 2008; and Jose George, Manoj Kumar, and Avinash Khandare (eds), *Rethinking Radicalism in Indian Society: Bhagat Singh and Beyond*, Jaipur: Rawat Publications, 2009.

11 A fascinating study of such appropriations is a 1990 documentary by Anand Patwardhan titled *Unā Mitrān di Yād Piyārī* (In Memory of Friends).

12 Bhagat Singh's appropriation by nationalist discourse is sometimes challenged by focusing on his Marxism. See for example Jose George and Manoj Kumar, 'Bhagat Singh: Transformation from a Patriotic Nationalist to a Revolutionary Communist' and Datta Desai, 'Revisiting Bhagat Singh: Ideology and Politics', in George, Kumar, and Khandare (eds), *Rethinking Radicalism in Indian Society: Bhagat Singh and Beyond*, Jaipur: Rawat Publications, 2009.

13 Chandra, *Nationalism and Colonialism*, p. 232.

14 Ibid., p. 249 (emphasis added).

15 Chaman Lal, *Bhagatsingh ke Sampūrṇa dastāvez*, pp. 39–46. This and all other translations from Hindi texts are mine.

16 I have attempted, as far as possible, to preserve the syntax of the Hindi essay.

17 Ibid., p. 42.

18 For example, following a standard Hindu–Sikh narrative, Muslims are presented as needlessly cruel and provocative in an article about the Kuka rebellion. See Chaman Lal, *Bhagatsingh*, pp. 73–84.

19 Irfan Habib, *To Make the Deaf Hear: Ideology and Programme of Bhagat Singh and his Comrades*, Gurgaon: Three Essays Collective, 2007, p. 43.

20 Mazzini's influence requires greater exploration. S.N. Bannerjee wrote and spoke extensively about him, and Lajpat Rai translated Mazzini's *Duties of Man* in Urdu. In 1895 he wrote a biography of Mazzini as well. Savarkar also translated his biography in Marathi—a book that became immensely popular, and was widely read and discussed. It was the first book to be banned by the Indian Press Act. See Gita Srivastava, *Mazzini and His Impact on the Indian National Movement*, Allahabad: Chugh Publications, 1982. Though one finds references to Mazzini in many texts of the period, of particular interest in this regard is a short story about Mazzini's life by Premchand, *Ishke Duniyā va hubbe vatan*, Love of the World and Attachment to the Homeland. Published in Urdu in *Zamana* in 1908, it is considered to be Premchand's first Urdu story. It was included in the collection *Soz-e-Vatan* (Dirge of the Nation)—most copies of the book were confiscated and burnt by the colonial government. See Premchand, *Soze vatan tathā anya zabtshudā*

kahāniyān, ed. Balram Agrawal, Delhi: Manu Prakashan, 2008, pp. 26–34.

21 Chaman Lal, *Bhagatsingh*, p. 47. Parenthetical phrases are from the original text. Words in square brackets are added to indicate the words of the original.

22 Ibid., p. 49. Emphasis added.

23 Writing about his 'revolutionary friend' in *Young India* in May 1925, Gandhi says, 'I have a soft corner for him in my heart for there is one thing in common between him and me—the ability to suffer'. Manmathnath Gupta, *They Lived Dangerously: Reminiscences of a Revolutionary*, New Delhi: People's Publishing House, 1969, p. 85.

24 Chaman Lal, *Bhagatsingh*, p. 51.

25 In her analysis of the French Revolution, Hannah Arendt has written about the moment when 'compassion became the driving force of the revolutionaries' (Hannah Arendt, *On Revolution*, London: Penguin Books, 1990, p. 75). Arendt is suspicious of compassion as a political virtue because she reads it as a passion, and hence as constitutively incapable of entering the mediated realm of human discourse. Intensely focused on the particular suffering being it encounters, compassion has, she writes, no capacity for generalization. In her taxonomy, compassion is opposed to pity on the one hand, and solidarity on the other—the latter obviously being the most suited for political action. While I am not able at present to engage with this argument in any detail, it seems to me that perhaps we could question this strict division posited by Arendt between compassion and solidarity. This division evidently draws its meaning from the division between the private and the public that structures Arendt's thinking, and hence perhaps remains tied to a limited concept of the political.

26 Lawrence (ed.), *Messages to the World: The Statements of Osama Bin Laden*, London: Verso, 2005, p. 234. Cited in Faisal Devji, *The Terrorist in Search of Humanity: Militant Islam and Global Politics*, New York: Columbia University Press, 2008, p. 43.

27 Ibid.

28 In brief, I would articulate my discomfort in the following way: Devji's critique of humanitarianism draws on Hannah Arendt's work and reads humanitarianism as an imperialist discourse that replaces the category of the citizen with that of the human being, whose rights cannot be guaranteed by any political entity. Thus Devji writes, 'It is possible even in our own times to see imperialism at work as a global project in the steady replacement of the citizen by the human being, whose biological security now routinely trumps his rights of citizenship in anti-terror measures at home and humanitarian interventions abroad' (*The Terrorist*

in Search of Humanity, p. 7). On this view, humanitarianism functions as a dehistoricized and depoliticized discourse; it hides its imperialist moorings. However, if contemporary Jihadi discourse mimics or shares the tropes of humanitarianism, does it also share its imperialist aspirations? On this point, Devji is not very clear. Further, I am not persuaded that humanitarianism as such can be entirely exhausted or accounted for by this critique. I am not sure if the anti-statist move that humanitarianisms and ecological discourses make can always be subsumed within imperialist politics, even though they often appear to function in the interests of imperial powers. These are preliminary thoughts; at some point I would like to engage Devji's intriguing work in a more systematic way.

29 Ibid., p. 45.
30 On the historical context of the Babbar Akalis, as well as the Kuka movement and the Ghadar movement, see, for example, Mridula Mukherjee, *Peasants in India's Non-Violent Revolution: Practice and Theory*, New Delhi: Sage Publications, 2004, pp. 25–45. See also Susana Devalle and Harjot S. Oberoi, 'Sacred Shrines, Secular Protest and Peasant-Participation: The Babbar Akalis Reconsidered', *Punjab Journal of Politics*, 7 (2), July–December 1983, pp. 27–62.
31 Chaman Lal, *Bhagatsingh*, p. 56.
32 Of particular interest in this regard is Bhagat Singh's description of a meeting between Madan Lal Dhingra and V.D. Savarkar in England. After a rite of exhibiting and demonstrating commitment, the heroes embrace. 'Ah, how beautiful was that moment. How invaluable and rare those tears. How beautiful, how exalted, was that meeting. How would we worldly people—we who are cowards and fearful even of the thought of death—how would we know how lofty, how pure, and how worship-worthy are those who give their lives for their nation and community' (Chaman Lal, *Bhagatsingh*, p. 90).
33 Gupta, *They Lived Dangerously*, pp. 74–5. Gandhi's response to the revolutionaries is complex and expresses his fundamental belief in non-violent politics. For instance, he writes, 'Armed conspiracies against something satanic is like matching satans against satan. But since one satan is one too many for me, I would not multiply him...I do not regard killing or assassination or terrorism as good in any circumstances whatsoever'. Gupta, *They Lived Dangerously*, p. 82. This seems to be a categorical denunciation of violence as such. At other moments, however, his arguments are less powerful and his words almost appear to validate some of the grounds of revolutionary activity. Let me cite an extended passage from the same letter: 'The revolutionaries are at liberty to reject the whole of my philosophy. To them I merely present my own experience as a co-worker in the same cause even as I have successfully

presented them to the Ali Brothers and many other friends. They can and do applaud whole-heartedly the action of Mustafa Kamal Pasha and possibly De Valera and Lenin. But they realize with me that India is not like Turkey or Ireland or Russia and that revolutionary activity is suicidal at this stage of the country's life at any rate, if not for all time in a country so vast, so hopelessly divided and with the masses so deeply sunk in pauperism and so fearfully terror-struck'. Gupta, *They Lived Dangerously*, p. 84. It is one thing to categorically oppose violent methods in political life and quite another to argue that the particular conditions of India—the pitiable conditions of its 'masses'—render it unsuitable for revolutionary activity. It seems this confusion between a pragmatic and an ethical opposition to violence continually aggravated the revolutionaries. An interesting comparison of Bhagat Singh and Gandhi's thought is offered by Neeti Nair in her article, 'Bhagat Singh as "Satyagrahi": The Limits to Non-Violence in Late Colonial India', *Modern Asian Studies*, 43 (3), 2009, pp. 649–81.

34 Chaman Lal, *Bhagatsingh*, p. 87.

35 Ibid., p. 91.

36 *Manifesto of the Hindustan Socialist Republican Association*, prepared by B.C. Vohra, and widely distributed in 1929, at the time of the Lahore session of the Congress. Shiv Verma (ed.), *Selected Writings of Shaheed Bhagat Singh*, New Delhi: National Book Center, 1986, p. 186.

37 Bhagat Singh, *Message to Young Political Workers* (1931) in Gupta, *They Lived Dangerously*, p. 46.

38 Certainly there is a link between the idea of the beautiful (young) death, and the injunction to remember that constantly appears in Bhagat Singh's writings about heroes.

39 Chaman Lal, *Bhagatsingh*, p. 226.

40 In his last letter to his comrades, Bhagat Singh writes, 'My name has become a symbol of the Indian revolution, and the ideals and sacrifices of the revolutionary group have carried me very high—so high that in the event of living on, I could never be higher than this. Today my weaknesses are not in the public eye. If I escape hanging, they will become manifest, and the symbol of the revolution will fade or possibly be erased. But if I boldly accept the noose with laughter, Indian mothers will wish for their children to become like Bhagat Singh, and the number of those who sacrifice for freedom will so increase that it will no longer be possible for imperialism or any evil power to stop the revolution' (Chaman Lal, *Bhagatsingh*, p. 232).

41 Chandra, *Nationalism and Colonialism*, p. 251.

42 Chaman Lal, *Bhagatsingh*, p. 71.

43 Ibid., p. 71

44 Bhagat Singh, *The Jail Notebook and Other Writings*, compiled by Chaman Lal and annotated by Bhupendar Hooja, New Delhi: LeftWord Books, 2007, p. 48.

45 Ibid., p. 115.

46 See Sumit Sarkar, *Modern India: 1885–1947*, Delhi: Macmillan India, 1983, pp. 269–274.

47 Ibid., p. 269.

48 See *History of the Communist Movement in India, I: The Formative Years 1920–1933,* New Delhi: LeftWord Books, 2005, p. 176.

49 The Hindi word for 'communism' is *sāmyavād*, literally 'the discourse of equality'.

50 Chaman Lal, *Bhagatsingh*, p. 224.

51 Ibid., p. 225.

52 Ibid., pp. 138–41.

53 Benedict Anderson, *Under Three Flags: Anarchism and the Anti-Colonial Imagination*, London: Verso, 2005, pp. 3–4 (emphasis added).

14

Anna Bigelow[†]

Post-Partition Pluralism

PLACING ISLAM IN INDIAN PUNJAB

Punjab is often treated in both media and scholarship as a primordially and perennially conflicted region. From Alexander's invasion to Mahmud of Ghazna's raids to Bhindranwale's campaigns, Punjab can seem like the gateway to and battleground of the subcontinent. To emphasize these aspects of Punjab's history, however, is to focus on only a fraction of a more complex story of coexistence between multiple religious groups, coexistence forged and practiced over centuries. Within this Punjabi epic, among the most revealing stages upon which interreligious interaction takes place are the myriad shared sacred sites that proliferate from Multan to Malerkotla. In Punjab, as elsewhere in India, shared sacred sites are often depicted as flashpoints for conflict, ticking time bombs, and places

[†] I would like to thank the editors of this volume, Anshu Malhotra and Farina Mir, for their helpful comments. In addition the essay benefited from feedback from Glenn Bowman, David Gilmartin, the members of the North Carolina Consortium for South Asian Studies, and the participants in a series of conferences on shared sacred sites sponsored by Columbia University's Center for Democracy, Toleration, and Religion. Any errors are, of course, mine.

of antagonistic contestation between religions. Although such cases certainly exist and have a profound effect on interreligious relations, it is important to recognize that many, many shared sites not only allow but actually promote pro-social encounters. The conflicts that occur at places like the Babri Masjid/ Ramjanmabhumi in Ayodhya or Shahid Ganj Mosque/Gurdwara in Amritsar serve to remind us of the symbolic power of shared sites and that controlling them is an important strategy for the demonstration of authority.[1] But the reality of conflict is not the whole story. At sacred sites people communicate most directly with their sense of ultimate reality, and at these sites the transcendent power of the ultimate becomes manifest and accessible. Controlling these sites demonstrates and validates both worldly and spiritual authority. As Roger Friedland and Richard Hecht have argued, disputes over sacred space are also necessarily struggles over the choreography of daily life.[2] In this essay an examination of effective interactive choreography at three shared sites will illuminate modes, systems, and strategies of exchange that substantively contribute to, or detract from, the production and perpetuation of peace. In particular, attention will be paid to the ritual, narrative, and administrative arenas of exchange that are produced and grounded in shared sacred sites. The quality of these interactions is a key indicator of the degree of conflict or cooperation at such places, and the ways in which these places affect the communities in which each is situated. All of the sites in this study are located in Punjab and each is identified to some extent as Muslim, though the clientele and custodians are from various religious backgrounds: one is a *dargah* (tomb shrine of a Sufi saint), another is a shrine memorializing a Sufi saint's presence in the region, and the last is a *maseet* (mosque).

The dynamics of Punjab's shared sacred spaces are particularly interesting given the region's history of inter-religious conflict, especially during the Partition of the subcontinent in 1947. As many as a million died and millions were displaced during the migration that accompanied the independence of these two countries from the British Empire. In Indian Punjab, the turmoil of Partition resulted in the outmigration of huge numbers of Punjabi Muslims, leaving just a few places with substantial populations of indigenous Muslims.

Whereas pre-Partition united Punjab had a slight Muslim majority of 53.2 per cent according to the 1941 census, in 1951 the Muslim population in Indian Punjab was below one per cent, and remains below two per cent to this day.[3] In spite of the relative absence of Muslims, Islamic shrines continue to animate the religious landscape. Indeed, in Punjab today, these sites sometimes serve as the repositories of nostalgia for the more diverse pre-Partition demographics and an idealized shared Punjabi culture. At these sites Sikh, Hindu, and Muslim pilgrims engage together in a variety of encounters that demonstrate how shared sacred places in many instances express and facilitate the convergence of complex and contradictory beliefs and actions, rather than provide points for disputation and the articulation of oppositional identities.[4] After discussing the challenges of sharing such places, I will examine three shared sites, highlighting points of manifest variation between religions, such as disparate modes and methods of worship, and pointing out the potential for ritual conflicts around the timing of events or the acceptability of particular practices. Then I will elucidate how the constituent communities of caretakers, ritual specialists, and devotees choreograph their interactions and express their variant conceptions and claims in order to mitigate possible tension. In each case, the physical spaces, narrative traditions, and administrative regimes are differently configured, but all the sites are engaged by plural communities in such a way as to facilitate the simultaneous presence of multiple and even conflicting beliefs and behaviours.

Although this essay focuses on inter-religious engagements that are largely peaceful or even amicable, relations between religions in South Asia can be conflicted and violent. One of the most devastating recent examples took place in the western state of Gujarat in 2002 when a conflagration on a train loaded with Hindu pilgrims ignited a systematic anti-Muslim pogrom resulting in hundreds of deaths and over 125,000 refugees. Indeed, in 2003 and 2004 the United States Commission on International Religious Freedom (USCIRF), an agency of the US State Department, listed India as a 'Country of Particular Concern',[5] In 2004 the USCIRF wrote, 'despite India's democratic traditions, religious minorities in India have periodically been subject to severe violence, including mass killings', and further noted that 'those responsible for the violence are rarely ever held to account'.[6] The report implicates the Hindu nationalist BJP (Bharatiya Janata Party) government that has ruled in Gujarat from 1999 to the present. The BJP also ruled at the national level from 1999–2004, but lost power after promised economic development did not reach most people. However, in Gujarat, in spite of the riots in 2002, the BJP has been reelected twice, most recently in December of 2007. The USCIRF report noted that in India, 'an increase in such violence has coincided with the rise in political influence of groups associated with the Sangh Parivar'. The empowerment of the Hindu nationalist BJP and its affiliated organizations (the Sangh Parivar) has resulted in a growing 'climate of immunity for the perpetrators of attacks on minorities'.[7] In this climate of fear, amid clear evidence that pogroms against Muslims will not only go unpunished but also provide substantial electoral gains, the nature of daily interactions between Hindus, Muslims, Sikhs, and others throughout India becomes a matter of urgent concern. The foot soldiers of Hindu nationalism frequently target sacred sites of Muslims and Christians, regarding these communities as fundamentally alien to Indian culture.[8] The Hindu nationalist ideology of *Hindutva* (Hinduness), to which the BJP and its allies adhere, equates being Indian with being Hindu. As put by V.D. Savarkar, one of the chief ideologues of Hindutva,

These are the essentials of Hindutva—a common nation (*rashtra*), a common race (*jati*), and a common civilization (*sanskriti*). All these essentials could best be summed up by stating in brief that he is a Hindu to whom Sindhusthan [India] is not only a [Fatherland] but also a [Holy Land]. For the first two essentials of Hindutva—nation and *jati*—are clearly denoted and connoted by the word *pitrabhumi* [Fatherland] while the third essential of civilization is pre-eminently implied by the word *punyabhumi* [Holy Land].[9]

In this sense, Hindutva indicates a profoundly Indian cultural and territorial identity that excludes from national membership those whose holy lands are outside the borders of India. Since Muslims and Christians identify with religions that are not only associated with former imperial powers but also have roots and their holiest places in the Middle East, they are seen as suspect and only partially loyal to the fatherland of India.

However, there are countless Muslim holy places in India that sacralize the landscape and integrate Islam into the fabric of Indian social life. Mosques, tomb shrines, and other places associated with Sufi saints are all evidence that India is also a Muslim holy land. Indeed certain shrines are so significant that some Muslims declare that a pilgrimage to places like the tomb of Khwaja Muinuddin Chishti in Ajmer, for example, can substitute for the hajj to Mecca if one cannot afford the longer journey. Significantly, these profoundly Islamic sites are often revered by non-Muslim Indians as well. The uneventful daily reality of coexistence and interaction at shared sites belies the religious chauvinism extant within all the traditions whose adherents collectively acknowledge the sacred power of these places. Given India and Punjab's experiences of religious tension and conflict, it is all the more important to understand how such sites function within communities to establish positive community relations and stable civil societies.

In addition to the transactions between the mundane and the divine occurring at shared sacred sites, such places also mediate transactions between multiple actors and divine agencies through a diverse repertoire of rituals, narratives and authoritative schemes. In some cases this multiplicity and simultaneity occurs uneventfully. Other situations require highly elaborate systems—such as the time-share arrangement at the Holy Sepulcher and the Church of the Nativity in Jerusalem—or even regulatory personnel—such as police or military.[10] However, as the phenomenologist of space, Edward Casey, asserts, one of the unique qualities of place is its ability to incorporate without conflict the most diverse elements constituting its being. He writes: 'there is a peculiar power to place and its ability to contain multiple meanings, diverse intentions, contradictory interactions. Surpassing the capacity of humans to sustain such a *gathering*, place permits a simultaneity and a filtering of experience, history, imagination, action'.[11] The multiplicity itself, the suspended tensions of contradictory beliefs and practices, and the gathering power of spatial and narrative symbols constitute, in part, the significance of shared sacred sites. In other words, by physically and discursively connecting people and their practices at a single site, by gathering and then maintaining that gathering, place is animated, enlivened and made meaningful.

This view is not without its critics. In a provocative article entitled 'Antagonistic Tolerance', anthropologist Robert Hayden disavows the possibility of non-contentious sharing of sacred space. In his view, sites that scholars portray as uncontested are in fact exemplary of a 'negative definition of tolerance as passive noninterference'.[12] For Hayden, depictions of 'un-contested' or peaceful shrines require a false erasure of time from the theoretical analysis that obscures a socially enforced political stasis. Synthesis of traditions, he writes, is a 'temporal manifestation of relations between social groups, which continue to differentiate themselves from each other'.[13] It is, indeed, irresponsible and inaccurate to claim that shared sites are perpetually devoid of competition or the possibility of antagonism. However, given the situation on the ground at many shared sites, Hayden over-states his case by asserting that the competitive sharing of sacred space is inherently antagonistic.[14] Competition at shared sites may be episodic and contextual. For example, the ownership of a site may be clear, but ritual authority less so as in the case of the tomb of Haider Shaykh in Punjab that will be discussed below. There the hereditary caretakers, *khalifah*s, are descended from the saint and oversee an entirely different complex of rituals than those mediated by the *chelas*—literally meaning disciple, but in this context refer-ring to those individuals who are possessed by the saint's spirit. This example is one of many in which even a site with multiple owners and ritual authorities is neither inevitably antagonistic nor perpetually harmonious. Clearly, we must examine specific situations of sharing to determine patterns of conflict and cooperation. Conditions facili-tating non-conflictual sharing may be unusual, as political scientist Ron Hassner argues, but such sharing is not impossible and depends in no small part upon the active roles of religious leaders, constituent communities, and political authorities in facilitating the process.[15]

In addition to the issue of leadership in determining usage and access to sacred places shared sacred sites may also thwart categoriza-tion in terms of architecture or iconography. At shrines dedicated to Gugga Pir, for example, across northwest India, images of Guru Nanak or Ganesha are juxtaposed with the Ka'ba and the Buraq. In some cases, attendees of these shrines indicate how misguided notions of fixed religious identity may be by not identifying themselves with an institutional religion, that is, 'Hinduism' or 'Islam'. While Joyce Flueckiger, in her study of a Muslim healer in Hyderabad (India), points out that 'differences between Hindus and Muslims matter very much' in relation to some issues or concerns (marriage, employment, admissions, elections), in certain situations, such as in the healing room she describes, 'these differences are overridden by what is shared'.[16] Flueckiger's study further demonstrates that it is not merely the need for healing that is shared, but also the 'ritual grammar' that bespeaks efficacy.

The rejection of sectarian religious identity within the confines or environs of a shared sanctuary does not mean that religious identity has no significance. Religious identities *do* matter to people in understanding how, when, and why it is essential to our perception of the broader phenomenon of inter-religious relations. This is particularly important in relation to minority religious groups who must situate themselves amid sometimes competing national and local level identity discourses. The national level requires minority populations to project a defensive image emphasizing their non-threatening, pacific identity while the local demands that inter-religious friction be suppressed and denied to maintain the dominant ethic of harmony. The shared space of dargahs and other Muslim shrines provides an ideal stage upon which to perform this ethic of harmony and promote a collective identity rejecting communalism. This enables minority Muslims to demonstrate their integration into the secular Indian polity and proactively counter the criticism that they are somehow less Indian than others. Shared sites provide loci for actors to publicly reject sectarianism, communalism, and the religious orthodoxies that criticize shared practices. India was founded as a secular country, and its constitution guarantees significant rights of religious autonomy and self-determination without establishing any one faith as the religion of the state. Hindu politicians from secular national or regionally based parties court the minority vote, whether Muslim, Sikh, Christian, or other, and are often dependent upon these constituencies to secure election against communally-based parties like the BJP. Politically speaking, therefore, secularism is an ideology of enlightened self-interest in some circumstances. Socially speaking, in mixed communities there is social capital to be gained by being known as a secular person who can be trusted to fairly arbitrate disputes, give equal treatment to customers, clients, or employees, and associate openly and universally with people of all religions. Shared sacred sites are ideal stages upon which to demonstrate one's secular credentials.

The public performance of secular sentiment and shared pietistic practice is observable at the three shared sacred sites under examination. First, located in Malerkotla, is the dargah, or tomb shrine, of Haider Shaykh, a fifteenth century Sufi saint.[17] The cult of Haider Shaykh draws devotees from all over Punjab and its diaspora. Since Partition in 1947 and the exodus of most Muslims from the region these pilgrims are mostly Sikhs and Hindus, but the popularity of the site has only grown in recent years. The second site is a complex of shrines sacred to Baba Farid Shakarganj in and around the town of Faridkot near the Pakistani border. Baba Farid is one of the most famous South Asian Sufi saints and is said to have passed through this area carrying out a *chilla* or forty-day retreat and performing several miracles. There are very few Punjabi Muslims in Faridkot, but local Sikhs and Hindus maintain their connection to the saint through several narrative strategies, as does the growing population of non-Punjabi Muslims. The third shrine is a mosque in Sri Hargobindpur widely believed to have been built by the sixth Sikh Guru, Hargobind for his Muslim followers.[18] In the post-Partition absence of any Muslim population the mosque has been cared for by a group of Nihang Sikhs. As we shall see, some Muslim activists from outside recently challenged their custodial role, but those efforts to establish an exclusive identity for the site have thus far failed to take root. These are three different types of sacred spaces located in different regions of Indian Punjab, making a comparison of their dynamics of sharing particularly illuminating for the purposes of this volume.

MALERKOTLA: RITUAL INTEGRATION

Despite the low percentage of Muslims in postcolonial Indian Punjab, in Malerkotla the Muslim population actually increased as Muslims in the region fled during the crisis to this former princely state for protection, as it was ruled by Muslims.[19] In 1948 the princely state was dissolved and became a town, developing into an industrial centre in district Sangrur. Today the Muslim population is approximately 70 per cent of Malerkotla's 106,000 people, with the remainder mostly Sikhs and Hindus. Malerkotla is famous throughout Punjab, not only for its Muslim population, but also because no one there was killed in inter-religious violence during the traumas of Partition.[20] Many locals and visitors believe that it was through the blessings of Haider Shaykh, who is credited with founding the town and for the fact that the town remained unscathed. Furthermore, Sikhs and Hindus in far greater numbers than Muslims attend the festivals for Haider Shaykh, though the Muslim descendants of the saint continue to own and manage the site and local Muslims attend the shrine, although mostly on non-festival occasions. However, the non-Muslim clientele is not a new phenomenon at all. For example, the Maler Kotla State Gazetteer of 1904 puzzles over the saint's festivals, saying, 'it is strange that these fairs are mostly attended by Hindus, though Sadr-ud-Din was a Muhammadan Saint'.[21] The multi-religious appeal of this shrine—as in all such places—draws from perceived efficacy, an ecumenical identity, and a non-sectarian ethos.

Haider Shaykh's tomb is a primary marker of local identity and is an important site for religiously-based strategies of community building. Local and regional politicians visit the dargah as a crucial gesture of respect for the state's only Muslim constituency. Both the descendents of the town's former princes and the caretakers of the tomb shrine are descended from the saint and they remain influential even after the dissolution of the princely state of Malerkotla in 1948, often serving as elected representatives to local and state office. Pilgrims from all over the world come to the tomb to make and fulfil vows, pay homage, honour family traditions, and experience the multicultural *communitas* that characterizes saints' shrines throughout the subcontinent. In this way, the shrine sustains and is sustained by other local centres of power—the government, the home, the neighbourhood. Temporal authorities must attend the saint and devotees must enter a public sphere of exchange where inter-religious interaction is likely, if not inevitable. Though the possibility of inter-religious encounters could be minimized through careful timing, the shrine is universally celebrated for its plural appeal. The saint *is* the past of the town and one's presence there acknowledges that debt and entails encounter between self and other through the mediating presence of the saint, the space, and the multivocal interlocutors of the saint's spirit and traditions. Exchanges occur at the dargah not only between visitors and the dead saint, but also between pilgrims and the caretakers, who may belong to other religious traditions.

In order to sustain multiple practices and perceptions, the ritual life of the shrine exceeds a single religious idiom. Indeed, many rituals enacted at the shrine—such as prostration, circumambulation, distribution of items or food blessed by contact with the tomb (called *tabarruk* or *prasad*), occasional devotional music performances, possession, and offerings—are not exclusive to one religion or another.[22] Rather, these ritual performances defy communal limitations and involve a range of localizing practices that situate Haider Shaykh and his devotees within a self-identifying community of faith and practice.[23]

These site-based ritual performances give rise to potential conflict over the appropriate form of ritual action at the shrine. One of several possible points of contestation is the fact that the status of the saintly dead is understood quite differently within each religion. Many Hindu and Sikh devotees express their understandings by asserting that the saint is, in fact, God. Time and again Sikhs and Hindus at the tomb of Haider Shaykh informed me '*voh hamare bhagwan hai*'—he is our god. Such declarations are antithetical to the Muslim perspective in which the unity and singularity of Allah is unassailable. Muslim constituents are aware of these different beliefs and the Muslim khalifahs, who are the caretakers of the dargah and descendents of the saint, facilitate the ritual devotions of Hindus and Sikhs in full consciousness of these conflicting ideas about the nature of the saint. For example, the ritual life of the tomb includes many *chelas*, people who profess to be possessed by the spirit of Haider Shaykh who come with large retinues of followers who believe the chelas will transmit to them the blessings and the advice of the saint. Rather than monopolizing the devotional energies of their entourages, the chelas often refer their disciples to the tomb itself and direct them to seek the mediating power of the khalifahs to secure their blessings, an encounter that may also include financial offerings. In a less materialistic example of making space for the other, I was present when a khalifah and chela discussed their theological differences and concluded that their contrasting beliefs were in fact part of God's plan. Agreeing upon the divine origin of humanity, they both perceived the variety of humans as God's will and therefore the variant perspectives and practices must also be sanctioned.

Another potential source of conflict is the presence of two categories of ritual specialists mentioned above. First there are the khalifahs, descendants of Haider Shaykh who sit at the tomb, collect offerings, return tabarruk, and provide blessings to the faithful. Occasionally they provide spiritual guidance, but largely their role is to facilitate temporally limited devotions at the shrine. Though some pilgrims have long standing relations with the khalifahs, the overwhelming majority only encounter them long enough to touch their feet or knees or simply to bow in their direction. However, as descendants of the saint they bear his blood, and therefore also his *baraka*. Thus physical contact with a khalifah is regarded as an essential element of ritual efficacy by many of those in attendance, especially non-Muslims. In addition to the saint's descendants, the saint's baraka is made present through the bodies of certain devotees who are possessed by his spirit. These individuals, often called chelas, are overwhelmingly Sikh and Hindu.[24] The Sikh and Hindu chelas come to the shrine for festivals and, occasionally, on Thursday nights along with groups of followers, ranging from a few to a few hundred. In addition to paying respects at the dargah and receiving blessings from the khalifahs, the chelas and their entourages set up satellite ritual spaces, called *chaunki*, in which the spirit of Haider Shaykh is invoked into the body of the chela through whom his spiritual, personal, medical, and psychological healing powers are made available to the gathering. Although these supplementary spaces could potentially provoke clashes between the Muslim owner/caretaker khalifahs and the Sikh and Hindu itinerant chelas, this does not occur. One might expect the khalifahs to ban or exile the chelas from the dargah's environs in that they are the undisputed owners of the site. That they do not do this is significant, particularly in light of Ron Hassner's claims that it is the *lack* of an absolute monopoly on hierocratic religious authority that is a key factor in producing conflict over sacred space by opening space for competition. In this instance, however, the lack does not give rise to competition and antagonistic contestation. Rather, the two ritual systems exist side by side, with many devotees transacting without inhibitions between them. Indeed, the fact that khalifahs and chelas perceive an economic symbiosis in their cooperation is an important factor in their continued coexistence. But these relations go beyond mutual self-interest as both parties often seek ways to validate each other, even though they may not participate in, support, or agree with one another's perspectives or ritual practices.

This validation is vividly illustrated by a conversation between a khalifah (who does not sit at the tomb) and a Hindu chela during which the subject of apparent contradictions between Hindu and Muslim rituals and beliefs arose. The khalifah described a spiritual encounter in which Haider Shaykh manifested himself to him and his teacher, summoning them to a conversation in an empty building. During this vision of Haider Shaykh the khalifah took the opportunity to pose the question of difference and how it should be managed and understood. He asked the saint,

'Hazrat, people come here, they come for a wish. They come for a boy child, some say our business is not going well. But it is written in our book that whatever you ask, ask it from God. But thousands of people come and ask from you. So what is the order for us, and what are the orders for them?' And so he [i.e. Haider Shaykh] responded, 'This is the secret of God,' he said. 'Let them do their work and you do yours.' He didn't say you are right or they are right, he said 'these are the secrets of God. I asked what are those secrets and he said that only God knows.' [25]

By leaving judgement over these contradictory practices and conceptions up to God, the khalifah was able to establish his own authority and simultaneously legitimate the beliefs and practices of the Hindu devotee. Furthermore, the khalifah asserted his credentials as an orthodox Muslim by prefacing his account saying that the interview occurred when he had just returned from the Hajj. Finally, he concluded his narrative with Haider Shaykh's declamation 'Let them do their work and you do yours'. This assertion evokes the 109th *Surat al-Kafirun* of the Qur'an, which ends 'to you be your

religion, and to me, mine'. Thus, by directly addressing the difference between Muslim, Hindu and Sikh ritual practices, the khalifah
received a carefully worded reply reminding the audience that Allah
alone knows best why he created people to believe and act in a variety
of ways.

For his part, the Hindu chela acknowledged that the khalifah,
as a descendant of the saint, was able to meet the saint personally,
while he and those with him had to negotiate a different sort of
relationship with Haider Shaykh. This relationship includes rules
for behaviour that do not apply to Muslims. For example, Hindu
and Sikh devotees are often instructed by Haider Shaykh during
chaunkis to abjure the consumption of meat. Yet Muslim descendants do eat meat, which is regarded by the non-Muslim followers as
a special dispensation for them. Such encounters demonstrate that
interactions at the dargah are capable of actually facilitating ritual
and theological variance rather than contesting or prohibiting it.
This demonstrates also that given conditions of support from both
groups of religious authorities, the potentially divisive factor of a
multivocal religious tradition is neutralized by the leaders and validated by the constituency.

BABA FARID GANJ-E SHAKAR: NARRATIVE EXCHANGE

Shared sacred sites are engaged narratively as well as ritually.
Owners, patrons, caretakers, and pilgrims imagine and articulate
a site's identity through the body of oral and written lore about a
shrine. Multi-confessional sites require a degree of multivocality,
enabling fluid interactions and thwarting the aggressive articulation of oppositional identities. In Faridkot, near the Pakistan
border, there are two shrines sacred to the thirteenth century Sufi
saint Baba Farid Shakarganj (d. 1265). He is not only one of the
most influential saints of the powerful South Asian Chishti lineage, but is also beloved by Sikhs who include poetic compositions
attributed to him in the holy book of the Sikhs, the Guru Granth
Sahib. In Faridkot, Baba Farid is narratively appropriated and
incorporated into the landscape, personal lives, and oral traditions
of the largely Sikh population through stories of the origins of the

shrines, accounts of miracles past and present, and the strategic performance of poetic works attributed to the saint.

Every resident and devotee I encountered at the shrines dedicated to Baba Farid knew the story of the saint's connection with the area. After performing a solitary chilla there, Baba Farid was pressed into labour by soldiers of the local Hindu ruler to help build a new fort. But rather than struggling under the burden of bearing bricks, Farid made his basket float in the air above his head, apparently weightless. The ruler, recognizing him as a holy man, begged forgiveness for showing the saint disrespect and renamed his domain Faridkot. Today there are two shrines in the area. One is called Tilla Baba Farid and consists of three structures—a relic shrine, a *gurdwara* (lit. house of the guru; Sikh place of worship), and a mosque— providing ritual spaces for all Baba Farid's devotees. These sites memorialize the saint's encounter with a Hindu king who became his devotee but *did not convert*. This encounter sets a local precedent for non-Muslims who can participate in the worship of a Muslim holy man without abandoning their own religious identities.[26] The other site is called Godhri Sahib Gurdwara and is just outside of town at a site believed to be the place where Baba Farid performed his meditational chilla.

The small Muslim community in Faridkot is mostly non-Punjabi, but they also take great pride in their connection to the famous saint. The current imam of the Baba Farid mosque next door to Tilla Baba Farid is from Uttar Pradesh and does not frequent the neighbouring shrine, nor does he encourage Muslims to do so. In fact, he actively discourages Muslims from making offerings at the shrine, pointing out that it is not a tomb and therefore not, in his view, appropriate to worship Baba Farid in that place. Still, the imam does revere Baba Farid and invokes blessings upon him, '*rehmat Allah alayhi* ' (mercy of God be upon him), whenever he mentions his name. He does not oppose Sikh and Hindu patronage of Tilla Baba Farid and has congenial relations with the Tilla management. The brother of the mosque's imam expresses the special bond between the Muslim community and Baba Farid saying:

We also fully love Baba Farid's place [the Tilla], we respect it, but in our religion, to prostrate before any photo or idol is banned. This is because you can prostrate only before God who made this world. That is why we believe in Baba Farid completely with a full heart. He was our *wali* [saint], a *buzurg* [pious elder], he has shown us good ways.[27]

Here Baba Farid's *Muslim* identity is emphasized—he is 'our wali'—and the distinctions between Muslim and non-Muslim worship are clearly drawn. The imam himself also highlights the reality of difference between these communities, and asserts the importance of holding fast to one's own faith, no matter what that faith might be. He says 'any religion, Hindu, Muslim, Sikh, Christian, in whichever religion one is, one should hold it properly. Hold the rope of one religion tightly; do not try to hold the ropes of other religions. You should sail in one boat, if you sail in two boats you will sink'. However, although the Imam advocates singular religious affiliation, he also frequently provides counsel and produces healing amulets called *tawiz* for a largely non-Muslim clientele. So even if difference is articulated, potential conflict is obviated, at least in part, through ritual exchange. Thus his symbolic authority as the local Muslim leader, with perhaps a natural affinity for or even a privileged relationship with Baba Farid, is established and the site is validated as a Muslim space with a multi-confessional clientele.

However, the tacit, though peaceful competition over the significance of Baba Farid is evident in the non-Punjabi Muslim population's efforts to celebrate the Punjabi saint's legacy in spite of their small number and status as outsiders to the region. For example, the local Muslims contributed their energies to the annual festival marking Baba Farid's arrival in the area, which is mostly organized and sponsored by the non-Muslim majority in Faridkot. In addition, a local group called the Muslim Welfare Society, composed of Muslims, Sikhs, and Hindus, sponsored a *Vishal Dharmik Samaroh* (Religious Gathering) at which several well-known Muslim preachers gave speeches on the importance of true religion as something internally realized and universal rather than dependent on a particular faith. This gathering was comparatively small, with perhaps one hundred in attendance, while thousands swarmed the Tilla and attended the *kirtan darbar* (gathering for devotional music). Nonetheless the activities geared towards the Muslim population not only gave the Muslim minority an opportunity to take centre stage, but gave the whole proceedings additional legitimacy as an event celebrated by Baba Farid's co-religionists as well as non-Muslim devotees. For similar reasons the main organizers of the festival take care to invite a group of Muslim *qawwals* (singers of Sufi devotional music) from Delhi to perform Baba Farid's *kalam* (spiritual compositions) at the kirtan darbar.

The baraka of Baba Farid's presence is also associated with the Godri Sahib Gurdwara, about five kilometres from Tilla Baba Farid. At this site, almost exclusively visited by Sikhs, Baba Farid's retreat is rendered into a Sikh religious idiom narratively, ritually, and practically. This is evidenced by the words of an elderly male Sikh devotee who explained the power of the site thus:

This is a place where Baba did *bhagati* [worship] and this place gathered powers. This place has special importance, so whenever somebody comes here and bows and touches their forehead here, some power comes in us, if we are ill we get well, if we are unhappy we will get happiness, that is one becomes healthy. When for the first time someone comes here with *sharda* (faith) he gets blessed.[28]

Hindus and Sikhs employ non-Islamic terms of reference for the Muslim saint's activities (that is, *bhagati* (devotion) instead of chilla, *khalwa* (seclusion), or *murakaba* (meditation) and *sharda* (faith) instead of *iman* (Arabic for faith). Some people described Baba Farid's *murshid*, (spiritual guide), Khwaja Qutb ud-Din Bakhtiyar Kaki, as his *guru* (teacher or master). Next to Godri Sahib Gurdwara is a shrine with a tree to which devotees attach *godris*, or small cushions for sitting such as the one on which the saint would have meditated. Here there is an interesting ritual acknowledgement of Baba Farid's piety in that rather than performing meditative retreats, the Sikh and Hindu devotees offer forty days of *seva*, or service, at the gurdwara. This is an example of non-Muslims reworking a Muslim practice in their own religious terms, replacing murakaba with seva, but still making a ritual link with the 700-year-old saint. The Sikh religion advocates discipline, but not asceticism, and fasting—a practice for which Baba Farid was famous—is generally rejected as disrespectful of the body. These features demonstrate a narrative as well as ritual appropriation of Baba Farid, effectively incorporating him into a non-Muslim idiom.

Baba Farid's continuing presence in Indian Punjab is most deeply and pervasively manifest through the frequent deployment of verses attributed to him from the Guru Granth Sahib. Although debates among scholars rage on concerning the authorship of these Punjabi verses, they are popularly seen as unquestionably Farid's.[29] Furthermore, many people believe them to be the very first compositions in the Punjabi language. Most Sikhs know portions of the Guru Granth Sahib by heart and many of those in attendance were able to recite upon request. The verses of Baba Farid most often volunteered by Sikh devotees are several that emphasize the importance of forgiving those who strike you, resisting anger, and avoiding provocative and insulting speech. Among these, two of the most commonly cited compositions are:

> Farid, if you are wise, then do not write evil against others
> Look into your own heart instead
> Farid, do not turn and strike those who strike you
> Kiss their feet, and return to your own home[30]

Many times these two passages, and others, were recited to me unsolicited, merely as conversational examples of the essence of Baba Farid's teachings and his philosophy of life. The popularity of such verses is generally ascribed to their sentiment as they express a conciliatory, forbearing, and magnanimous ideal of behaviour. The recitation and repetition of poetic compositions attributed to Baba Farid ground the saint's sentiments of forbearance, tolerance, and forgiveness in the earth at his shrines in Faridkot. By narratively establishing a privileged relationship with the holy man, the Sikh and Muslim community in Faridkot creates space for specificity of belief while maintaining the multivocality of the traditions associated with the saint and his shrines.

Historical studies of shared narrative traditions, such as Tony Stewart's examination of the rich body of literature on the Hindu–Muslim traditions of Satya Pir in Bengal, indicate that these stories may provide indices of the quality and depth of interreligious exchange.[31] Furthermore, studying change in such traditions over time may provide crucial early warning signals of heightened communal tension in the gradual or abrupt erasure of Muslim, Sikh and/or Hindu elements from an active repertoire. These ritual and narrative arenas of exchange are almost entirely neglected by social scientists and policy analysts seeking to understand religious conflict. However, it is clear that these cases demonstrate the possibility of deep conceptual links between religious groups, observable in integrated spiritual and ritual vocabularies. The interactive choreography facilitating the simultaneous presence of difference may also enable the trust building conducive to peaceful communities.

SRI HARGOBINDPUR: ADMINISTRATIVE COOPERATION

In the final case, the administration of a mosque is shared by multiple religions.[32] In Sri Hargobindpur, District Gurdaspur, Punjab there is a seventeenth-century mosque known as the *Guru ki Maseet*, or Guru's mosque, which is cared for by a group of Sikhs. According to popular tradition, the sixth Sikh Guru, Hargobind, after defeating a Mughal army in battle, insisted on building not only a gurdwara but also temples and a mosque so that all the residents of the region would have places to worship.[33] This firmly established the Sikh leader as a patron and benefactor of the Muslim minority community. Sikh proprietary claims remain in force even today as, since Partition, there has been no Muslim population in this small town of just under 4000; no Muslim worship has taken place in the mosque for over fifty years. Although Muslim religious sites and endowments abandoned in 1947 nominally became property of the Waqf Board, in reality many Muslim properties became temples, houses, shops and even barns. In Sri Hargobindpur the Guru ki Maseet was not wholly neglected even though it was inactive as a mosque and declining in condition. A local band of Nihang Sikhs, a sect who style themselves the Guru's army, took over the site in the 1980s.[34] A Nihang caretaker erected a small building at the side of the mosque and resided there, doing his seva, or service to the Guru, caring for the mosque, placing the Guru Granth Sahib in the mosque, and erecting a Sikh flag outside. As these are standard markers of Sikh sacred space, the building's identity as a maseet (mosque) became questionable.

In 1997, a survey team with an architectural restoration group called Cultural Resource Conservation Initiative (CRCI) came to Sri

Hargobindpur, saw the maseet, heard the story of its construction, and undertook itsrestoration. In conjunction with the conservation of the mosque, the CRCI worked to re-establish links between the site, the idealized event it represents, and the citizens of the town by hiring and training locals in the work, running programmes in the schools, and initiating other development projects. Through this process the ostensibly Muslim space, in a majority Sikh and Hindu town, appropriated by Nihang Sikhs, began to embody meanings both old and new for the residents of Sri Hargobindpur. Local residents organized a seva with a *langar* (communal kitchen) that brought people from the entire region to work on the maseet. These activities served to incorporate the site into local religious life, as seva and langar are two of the principal expressions of devotion and affirmation of community in the Sikh tradition.

However the process was not wholly smooth. Publicity about the site brought a challenge to the process of restoration and to the Nihangs' role as caretakers. A leading Muslim activist and former Member of Parliament, Syed Shihabuddin, who has been instrumental in the Babri Masjid Action Committee and legal efforts to restore the mosque at Ayodhya heard about the Guru ki Maseet from newspaper accounts and raised objections. Dismayed by what appeared to be yet another case of non-Muslims usurping Muslim property in a place where few Muslims lived and could defend their legal ownership, Shihabuddin lodged a complaint with the United Nations Commission on Human Rights (UNCHR) and alerted the Waqf Council. Waqf representatives visited the site and the police were called to take statements from CRCI and locals about the mosque's history and status. The situation became tense, and the site that had begun to be heralded in the press as evidence of India's rich, plural culture was in danger of becoming another example of politicized religion and contestation not unlike Ayodhya. Yet this did not happen.

Instead, measures were taken to preserve the identity of the site and maintain its cohesive nature over and against efforts to manipulate, appropriate, or politicize its public meaning. A new space was built and the Guru Granth Sahib was moved out of the maseet. Various officials visited the maseet to observe the status of the site. In February

2001 the Secretary of the Central Waqf Council and the head of the Nihang group met in order to determine the future management of the Guru ki Maseet. At one point during the meeting the octogenarian Nihang leader declared, 'Nobody can damage this maseet. We will protect it like it was a gurdwara. This maseet was established by our Guru. If anyone tries to damage it, we will kill him'. These efforts to find common ground resulted in a Memorandum of Understanding establishing terms of joint management of the mosque. Under the agreement, the Nihangs continue the daily upkeep of the shrine and the Waqf reserves all proprietary rights. The multiple identities and plural appeal of the site are acknowledged in the Memorandum itself, which opens by declaring that Guru Hargobind 'conceptualized this Maseet as a symbol of peace and unity between the Sikhs, Muslims and the Hindus'. Finally, on 23 April 2002 *namaz* (Muslim daily ritual prayer) was performed in the mosque for the first time since 1947. This event was widely reported in India's Muslim press as a much-needed gesture of goodwill and harmony during the dark days following anti-Muslim pogroms that took place in Gujarat two months earlier. In the *Islamic Voice* Andalib Akhtar wrote 'at a time when the nation is at the crossroads of communal hatred and disbelief, the Sikhs of this small village...have set a unique example of love, brotherhood and communal harmony. They quietly handed over "Guru ki Maseet", a historical Masjid built by the sixth Sikh Guru Hargovind in the early 17th century, to the Muslims'.[35]

Due to the history of the site and the process of its restoration, the Guru ki Maseet is sacred to multiple religions. Interestingly, in this case, it was possible for the mosque to be integrated into the community and to take on multiple meanings for the various constituents only after all parties acknowledged the single identity of the site as a *mosque*. Successful negotiation was possible in part because, although the interests and intentions of the parties involved were divergent in some areas, the overall will of the decision makers and the community was to promote understanding and effect a resolution. This challenges Hayden's assertion that representations of shared religious sites as non-conflictual is a function of the analyst's failure to historicize the shrine. Here we see a historical process in which competition is managed and conflict averted. Through the struggles over the Guru ki Maseet's admin-istration, the place was *made* a kind of secular monument, the very existence of which contests religious divisions and represents an ideal of peaceful exchange both in the past and the present. Significantly this did not occur through an uncontested, spontane-ous, or unconscious acknowledgement of the site's identity. Rather this came about through dialogue and a series of compromises and strategic efforts by the interested parties giving everyone a stake in the success of the restoration, maintenance, and ongoing signifi-cance of the Guru ki Maseet.[36]

PLURALISM, SECULARISM, AND THE SACRED

Having surveyed three different dimensions of inter-religious rela-tions at three different shared sacred sites in Punjab, India, it is important to recall that situations of peaceful exchange are not exclu-sive to Punjab or to India. In his study of sites shared by Muslims and Christians in Palestine, Glenn Bowman described those shrines as *semantically multivocal*.[37] Semantic multivocality allows mul-tiple users to maintain relations with a site that is central to their local and/or religious identity without over-determining the site and rendering it fixed and unavailable to contradictory uses and interpretations. In Bowman's study in Palestine, as in my study in Punjab, the openness of a shrine is deliberately maintained through actions and interactions among the constituents that are intended to allow for a lack of uniformity of belief and practice. Indeed, the communities in which such places are situated often value shared sites precisely for their quality of openness. As Bowman found in his research in the Palestinian Territories, 'while the miraculous power seen to be resident there [that is, at Mar Elyas, a site dedicated to the prophet Elijah] served as a general pretext for the gathering of local persons of Muslim and various Christian persuasions, the specific reasons people gave for attending ranged from the need for cures through the demands of religion, to the pleasures of conviviality'.[38] Thus a common primary motivator for allegiance to Mar Elyas, its miraculous power, facilitates and perhaps even draws from another powerful factor in the site's appeal: its multi-religious constituency.

Furthermore, part of the appeal for the Muslim and Christian groups under Israeli rule was the opportunity to experience and demonstrate solidarity against the Israeli regime.[39] At least within the confines of a shrine, normally disempowered minorities exercise a degree of autonomy. United in their resistance to Israeli authority, the symbolic value of public exchange at a sacred site demonstrates an unforeseen power of the usually divisive religious politics in Israel–Palestine to intensify the bonds between the disempowered.

Ritual, narrative, and administrative dimensions of these three sacred sites in Punjab demonstrate how shared shrines are able to promote, and even generate, a dynamic of inter-religious engagement deliberately designed to support cooperation and discourage discord. In particular, these shared shrines illuminate the ways in which the highly fraught relations between Hindus, Sikhs, and Muslims are negotiated on a daily basis through symbolic zones of exchange. At these sites non-Muslims and Muslims alike engage Islamic space ritually and discursively, deriving spiritual and political benefit from the inter-religious experience. In the case of Haider Shaykh's shrine cult, ritual conflicts are circumvented through dialogue and mutual validation. At Faridkot, stories and poetic performances ground the Muslim saint in a Sikh community. And finally, at the Guru ki Maseet, proprietary competition is managed and the claims of each party ultimately affirmed. In each case there is a twofold dynamic, one which particularizes, specifies, and personalizes the saint and the site, and the other which simultaneously generalizes, incorporates, and includes. Contrary to the assumption that shared shrines are inherently conflictual, these places show that, although distinctions between religions are often made, discrepancies are rarely seen as antagonistic or threatening. On the contrary, the multivocality of the shared ritual, narrative, and administrative life of the shrines is not only part of the appeal but is also a source of their effective power. Thus, these shared sacred places serve as powerful resources for community building and the promotion of harmonious civil society. As interactive nodes between individuals, religions, genders, classes, age groups, and so on, the bodily and discursive practices and experiences at these sites are opportunities for the public performance of community and individual identities characterized by openness and inclusiveness rather than exclusivity and hostility.

Notes

1 For more on the Babri Masjid, see Ashis Nandy, Shikha Trivedy, Shail Mayaram, and Achyut Yagnik, *Creating a Nationality: The Ramjanmabhumi Movement and Fear of the Self*, New Delhi: Oxford University Press, 1995. For a discussion of the Shahid Ganj Mosque/Gurdwara, see David Gilmartin, 'The Shahidganj Mosque Incident: A Prelude to Pakistan', in Ira M. Lapidus and Edmund Burke III (eds), *Islam, Politics, and Social Movements*, Berkeley: University of California Press, 1988, pp. 146–68.

2 Roger Friedland and Richard Hecht, 'The Bodies of Nations: A Comparative Study of Religious Violence in Jerusalem and Ayodhya', *History of Religions*, 38 (2), 1998, p. 101.

3 Gopal Krishan, 'Demography of Punjab, 18-1947', *Journal of Punjab Studies*, 11 (1), 2004, p. 89. Current census data is available for registered users at: http://www.censusindia.gov.in/Census_Data_2001/Census_Data_Online/Social_and_cultural/Religion.aspx?cki=feCEiLeZOMU, accessed on 24 October 2009.

4 There are Christians, Jains, and Buddhists in Punjab, but the majority of shrine attendees are Muslim, Hindu, and Sikh.

5 *Annual Report 2003*, United States Commission on International Religious Freedom (USCIRF), US Dept. of State. Retrieved 20 December 2007 from http://www.uscirf.gov/countries/region/south_asia/india/india.html

6 *Countries of Particular Concern: India*, United States Commission on International Religious Freedom, US Dept. of State, 2004. Retrieved 20 December 2007 from http://www.uscirf.gov/countries/countries-concerns/Countries/India.html

7 USCIRF 2004.

8 As recently as Christmas 2007, a number of Christian villages in Orissa were attacked, their churches burned, and their residents terrorized into fleeing.

9 V.D. Savarkar, *Hindutva, or Who is a Hindu?*, Bombay: Veer Savarkar Prakashan, 1969 [1923], p. 116. N.B. Savarkar used the term 'Sindhusthan' to designate what is more commonly called Hindustan, geographically the same, that is, the land east and south of the Indus River.

10 Richard Hecht, 'The Construction and Management of Sacred Time and Space: The *Sabta Nur* at the Church of the Holy Sepulchre', in Roger Friedland and D. Bowen (eds), *Nowhere: Space, Time and Modernity*, Berkeley: University of California Press, 1994, pp. 181-235.

11 Edward S. Casey, 'How to Get from Space to Place in a Fairly Short Stretch of Time: Phenomenological Prolegomena', in Steven Feld and

Keith Basso (eds), *Senses of Place*, Santa Fe, NM: School of American Research Press, 1996, p. 26.

12 Robert Hayden, 'Antagonistic Tolerance: Competitive Sharing of Religious Sites in South Asia and the Balkans', *Current Anthropology*, 43 (2), 2002, p. 206.

13 Ibid., p. 207.

14 This view is typical of conflict studies scholars such as Sissela Bok who view the activation of conflicts as the strategic action of rationally motivated actors taking advantage of perceived opportunities to advance their interests. Sissela Bok, *Strategies for Peace: Human Values and the Threat of War*, NY: Vintage,1990.

15 Ron E. Hassner, 'Understanding and Resolving Disputes over Sacred Space', Stanford Center on Conflict and Negotiation Working Paper, 62, 2002, p. 11.

16 Joyce Burkhalter Flueckiger, *In Amma's Healing Room: Gender and Vernacular Islam in India*, Bloomington; Indiana University Press, 2006, pp.168–9.

17 Shaykh Sadruddin Sadri Jahan is the saint's full name, but he is popularly known as Haider Shaykh.

18 In the period of Guru Hargobind (1595–1644) the Sikh community was still taking shape as a religious entity, and many of the Guru's followers were Muslims and Hindus who did not abandon their religious identities even as they were loyal to the Guru.

19 Ian Copland, 'The Master and the Maharajas: The Sikh Princes and the East Punjab Massacres of 1947', *Modern Asian Studies,* 36 (2), 2002, p. 682.

20 Malerkotla's history and religious culture are the subjects of my book, *Sharing the Sacred: Practicing Pluralism in Muslim North India*, New York: Oxford University Press, 2010.

21 *Malerkotla State Gazetteer*, Lahore: The Civil and Military Gazette Press, 1904, p. 44.

22 *Tabarruk* and *prasad* are respectively the Islamic and Hindu terms for the items returned to devotees after being offered at a shrine. Having come into contact with the shrine's sacred precincts the items are regarded as possessing residual power. In the case of Islam, this is *baraka* (spiritual power) that clings to the place of interment of a holy person in the case of saint's tombs, or a point of access to the divine such as the Ka'ba. In Hindu traditions, prasad is understood as the leftovers of the divine being who has gathered the pure and rarefied essence of whatever has been offered. The portion returned to the devotee is seen as *jutha*, or polluted by prior consumption, but is still far more pure than something consumed by a human, and thus by receiving prasad, the devotee

is purified. In both cases, a portion of the items offered is retained at the shrine and a portion returned to the offerer.

23 A term often adopted by devotees is the *pirpanth*, or party of the saint, a designation that draws on the Muslim honorific *pir* and *panth*, meaning group or sect. Thus those in the pirpanth do not see their primary religious identity as Hindu, Muslim or Sikh but as particular to the traditions of the saint's worship.

24 In fact in a year and a half I never witnessed or heard of a Muslim who was 'played' by the spirit of the saint at this shrine. A common term for being possessed by the saint is *khelna*, or playing.

25 Interview, 5 June 2001.

26 In addition, the town and shrine have gained a heightened status in post-Partition Punjab as the actual dargah of Baba Farid is in Pakpattan in Pakistan and is therefore inaccessible to most Indian devotees.

27 Interview, 23 September 2000.

28 Interview, 22 September 2001.

29 Some scholars have argued that the verses are likely the work of Baba Farid's descendant, Shaykh Ibrahim. However, Christopher Shackle points out in his essay in this volume that a number of contemporary researchers claim that Shaykh Farid Ganj-e Shakar was in fact the true author, even if some alterations occurred during the various stages of recording and compiling the Granth. See his, 'Punjabi Sufi Poetry from Farid to Farid'.

30 Interviews, 22–24 September 2000 and 21–23 September 2000. These verses were also written on the walls and ceiling beams of the community hall adjacent to the Godhri Sahib Gurdwara.

31 Tony Stewart, 'In Search of Equivalence: Conceiving the Muslim–Hindu Encounter through Translation Theory', *History of Religions,* 40 (3), 2001, pp. 260–87.

32 A more complete account of this process can be found in Anna Bigelow, 'Unifying Structures, Structuring Unity: Negotiating the Sharing of the Guru's Mosque', *Radical History Review*, Issue 99, Fall 2007, pp. 158–72.

33 This is described in Macauliffe's section on Guru Hargobind in *History of the Sikhs*, 'He projected the construction of a Sikh temple, but it occurred to him that his Muhammadan troops and laborers would also require a temple for their worship. He therefore constructed with thoughtful impartiality both a temple and a mosque'. M.A. Macauliffe, *The Sikh Religion*, Delhi: Low Price Publications, 2000 [1909], p. 119.

34 'Nihangs or Nihang Singhs, originally known as Akalis or Akali Nihangs, are endearingly designated the Guru's knights or the Guru's beloved for

the military air they bear and the heroic style they continue to cultivate. They constitute a distinct order among the Sikhs and are readily recognised by their dark blue loose apparel and their ample, peaked turbans festooned with quoits, insignia of the Khalsa and rosaries, all made of steel. They are always armed, and are usually seen mounted heavily laden with weapons such as swords, daggers, spears, rifles, shot-guns and pistols.' 'The Encyclopaedia of Sikhism', Harbans Singh, editor. Retrieved 27 August 2003 from http://thesikhencyclopedia.com/

35 Andalib Akhter, 'Creating History at Hargovindpur', *Islamic Voice*, May 2002. Retrieved 21 September 2002 from www.islamicvoice.com/may.2002/secular.htm.

36 The joint oversight of the Guru ki Maseet by the Waqf Board, the Nihangs, and CRCI displays associational links. These links, according to political scientist Ashutosh Varshney, are instrumental in preserving inter-religious peace. Such links were forged between the Nihangs, the Waqf, and the community throughout the negotiations. Ashutosh Varshney, *Ethnic Conflict and Civic Life: Hindus and Muslims in India*, New Haven: Yale University Press, 2002.

37 Glenn Bowman, 'Nationalising the Sacred: Shrines and Shifting Identities in the Israeli-Occupied Territories', *Man*, 28, 1993, p. 431.

38 Glenn Bowman, 'Response to Robert Hayden', *Current Anthropology*, 43 (2), 2002, p. 220.

39 Bowman, 'Nationalising the Sacred', pp. 442–8.

15

Tony Ballantyne

Migration, Cultural Legibility, and the Politics of Identity in the Making of British Sikh Communities

This essay explores the development of Sikh communities in Britain during the second half of the twentieth century. It is particularly concerned with the ways in which Sikhs have positioned themselves in the public sphere and attempted to win recognition as a distinct community from the British state. What I offer here is essentially an interactionist reading of the development of Sikhs in Britain, arguing that their legal and political successes reflect the ability of Sikhs to offer clear and legible definitions of their tradition to the British state. In delineating Sikh 'identity', community leaders and the state have inscribed clear boundaries that mark Sikhs from other religious groups and migrant communities, including Punjabi Hindus and Muslims. In embracing the politics of religious identity, Sikhs have largely rejected the possibility of inter-racial and inter-faith alliances and marginalized members of the *panth* (community) who have been reluctant to embrace this clear vision of what a Sikh should be.

In arguing that Sikh culture was simultaneously shaped by debates within the community in Britain and engagements with other migrant communities, white Britons, and the British state, this essay navigates a path between what I have elsewhere identified as the 'internalist' and 'externalist' readings of Sikh history.[1] Internalist readings see Sikhism as essentially the product of the Gurus' teachings and the outlook of the Gurus' followers, discounting the importance of state regimes, imperial powers, and mobility as factors in shaping the panth.[2] Conversely, historians of British colonialism have offered externalist readings that reject the importance of pre-colonial teachings and practices as they see modern Sikh identity as essentially the product of the exigencies of colonial rule as the East India Company and then the Crown Raj worked hard to reconfigure the Sikh community into a bulwark of colonial authority.[3] In the exchanges over the nature of Sikhism and Sikh identity surveyed here, Sikhs mobilized the words of the Gurus, the injunctions of the *rahit* (code of belief and discipline), and popular understandings of regional and religious identity to define their faith and make claims for Sikhism in the British public sphere. In other words, they attempted to deploy key elements of the textual tradition produced by the Gurus and historical leaders of the panth to define the boundaries of contemporary community. Of course, the logic of the British state and the contingencies of recent politics have invested the construction of these boundaries with particular urgency. In particular, the politics of Sikhism in Britain has been given a particular inflection by the nature of liberal multiculturalism as well as the frequently heated debates over Britishness and its limits.

This essay begins by exploring the profound disjuncture between the protection afforded to Sikhism as a distinctive 'religious community' under colonial law in India and the lack of legal recognition that framed the status and experience of the Punjabi migrants who settled in Britain in large numbers after World War II. It then explores the efforts of British Sikhs to gain concessions through the courts and the passage of legislation to ensure that the community was able to maintain many of its key religious symbols and cultural practices. Here I note that this legal and political struggle co-existed with Punjabi youths growing engagement with British culture and, in particular, the culture and politics of the Afro-Caribbean migrants. I then examine how these fledgling connections were severed during the 1990s as Sikhs increasingly stressed the self-contained nature of the panth, rejecting the politics of affiliation that might have connected them to other migrant communities. The essay concludes by examining recent Sikh efforts to reposition themselves within Britain's cultural landscape, particularly their insistence that Sikhs are an integral part of British culture, contrasting themselves in particular with British Muslims who are frequently identified as threats to both British identity and national security after the September 11 attacks and the bombings in London on 7 July 2005.

***

James Scott has suggested that over the last two centuries 'legibility' has been 'a central problem in statecraft' as modern states have been committed to rendering their domains and populations legible. Bureaucrats and government officials have consistently displayed a desire to delimit the bounds of their territorial sovereignty, to measure the landscape, and count the population. Gathering and organizing this kind of data has been fundamental to the operation of governance as states seek to render these complex forms of knowledge into 'legible and administratively more convenient forms' that can be used to shape policies and measure their outcomes.[4] The consolidation of maps and atlases, censuses and ethnographic reports as state instruments during the long nineteenth century were an important marker of the epistemic commonalities that underpin state regimes of various types. By 1900, it was common for governments to think about their citizens through a set of categories—religion, language, race and ethnicity—that had achieved a level of global authority, even as they were inflected in particular ways in specific locales.

A substantial body of work has recovered the centrality of these ways of organizing information and thinking about populations in British India. The colonial state's concern with social classification and its commitment to the value of statistics as instruments for making sense of India has led several scholars to suggest that an 'enumerative state' developed in British India.[5] Sikh leaders in nineteenth century Punjab quickly grasped both the colonial state's deep concern with categorization and the weight it attached to statistics. This understanding was an important spur to the efforts of urban leaders and religious reformers to formulate clear visions of their communities,

emphasize their distinctive characteristics, delineate newly systema-
tized visions of 'identity', and inscribe religious boundaries onto a
very complex cultural landscape with an assertive confidence. By the
1870s, a range of Punjabi leaders and intellectuals were attempting
to have their visions of the Punjabi cultural order legitimated by the
colonial state. While Arya Samajis were suggesting that Sikhism was
not an independent tradition and Sikhs were really just Hindus, the
Tat Khalsa faction of the Singh Sabha, the influential Sikh reform
movement, worked hard to mark off Sikhs from their Hindu neighbours, constructing a large literature on Sikh identity and a new cycle
of life rituals to establish the distinctiveness of Sikhism. Although it
drew on the long standing prescriptive tradition of the *rahit-namas*,
the Tat Khalsa programme was innovative in that it accepted the
notion of 'religion' as a coherent, self-contained system and deployed
print culture to produce a distinctive bodily order that made Sikh
identity legible to both the colonial state and the Punjabi population
as a whole.[6] But the clear vision of Sikh identity espoused by these
reformers was constantly in tension with complexity and diversity of
Sikh life and practice. Singh Sabha reformers worked very hard to
inscribe boundaries that clearly marked Sikhs off from other Punjabi
communities, but such acts of cultural definition always marginalized
some groups whose life-ways were as odds with dominant visions of
orthodoxy and orthopraxy.

Sikh reformers identified military service as a domain that could
produce, reproduce and police their vision of a coherent Sikh identity. The British were also invested in maintaining the distinctiveness
of the panth as Sikhs were increasingly prominent in the Indian army
from the 1860s. As more Sikhs were recruited by the British state,
some colonial authorities worried that the allures of colonial towns
and the influence of Hindu reformers were undercutting the martial
culture of Sikhism. This was an alarming idea given the prominence
of Sikhs in colonial military service both within India and a host of
other Biriths colonies. These anxieties over the 'decay of Sikhism'
were at the heart of British recruiting efforts in the final third of
the nineteenth century.[7] R.W. Falcon's 1896 officer's handbook suggested that recruitment should be aimed only at 'real Sikhs'. The
ultimate test of 'Sikh-ness' was whether an individual maintained

the external symbols of the Khalsa: 'Singhs, the members of the Khalsa; these are the only Sikhs who are reckoned as true Sikhs. … The best practical test of a true Sikh is to ascertain whether calling himself a Sikh he wears uncut hair [*kes-dhari*] and abstains from smoking tobacco.'[8] The various non-kes-dhari groups (*sahaj-dhari*s, shaven *mona*s and *patit* Sikhs, for example) who might have identified themselves with the Sikh tradition were to be avoided. Only Khalsa Sikhs were 'true' Sikhs and it was they who would exhibit the true values of a warrior. Falcon mapped these martial qualities across the different regions of Punjab, warning officers away from eastern and southern regions where the 'Hindustani type' was prevalent and against those regions where Sikh identity was 'very diluted by Hinduism'.[9] Once recruited Sikh troops were placed in Sikh regiments, kes-dhari Sikhs who were not *amrit-dhari* were required to undergo the Khalsa's *khande di pahul* initiation rite, all Sikh troops were to maintain the external symbols of their religious identity and were expected to accept the authority of the *granthi*s (reader of the Granth) appointed by the Army.[10] To help maintain these regimens, Falcon provided translated excerpts from various rahit-namas to guide British military men: recruiters and commanding officers were not only to inculcate military discipline in their troops but they were to police religious discipline as well.[11]

The state's preoccupation with the nature and limits of Sikh identity was made most clear in its willingness to enshrine legal definitions of Sikhism in law. As a consequence of its long-running dialogues with Sikh community leaders and through the heated public exchanges over religious boundaries within Punjab more generally, the colonial state felt it should define who was a Sikh. In 1925 the Punjab Government passed the Sikh Gurdwaras Act to regularize the management of Harmandir Sahib (the Golden Temple in Amritsar) and the panth's gurdwaras. This legislation included a definition of Sikh identity that was grounded in an orthodox set of beliefs: 'I solemnly affirm that I am a Sikh, that I believe in the Guru Granth Sahib, that I believe in the Ten Gurus, and that I have no other religion.'[12] Later colonial legislation elaborated on this definition and in so doing it codified hierarchies within community. Act XI of 1944, which amended the 1925 Act, defined a 'patit' (Fallen) Sikh as 'a person who being a Keshdhari Sikh, trims or shaves his beard or keshas or who after taking AMRIT commits any one or more of the four kurahits'.[13] In turn, authoritative Sikh texts reinforced these hierarchies that marked off Sikhs who adopted the Khalsa discipline from other members of the panth. Where the 1925 Act did not include any mention of the Khalsa, the formal definition of a Sikh promulgated in the Sikh Rahit Marayada of 1950 noted that Sikhs not only believed in Akal Purakh, the teachings of the Gurus and the Guru Granth Sahib, but also accepted the authority of the Khalsa initiation ceremony.[14] This new rahit also spelled out the penalties for rejecting the disciplines at the heart of the Khalsa order. Members of the panth were enjoined to avoid all contact with patit individuals: in fact, eating with a patit Sikh meant being defined as a *tankhahia* (offender liable to religious penalty).[15]

***

One of the chief lessons of the colonial order was that 'cultural visibility' was central to the definition of community and, in turn, dictated the socio-economic and political possibilities open to a community within a larger social order.[16] But the Sikhs who began to settle in Britain in the wake of India and Pakistan's independence made their new homes in a society that did not afford any formal recognition or protection to their religious identity. While travelogues, adventure stories and imperial romances, advertising images, photographs and films meant a steady stream of images of Sikhs—at least of the bearded and turbaned kes-dhari male—were accessible to the British public through the media, these images did not translate into legal recognition for Sikhs settled in Britain. The Sikh Gurdwaras Act, with its specific definitions of Sikh identity, had no legal purchase in Britain and like other recent migrants from the Commonwealth, Punjabis found themselves operating in a British society where the legal system operated quite differently from the 'British' law they had encountered in the colonies.

The cultural dislocation produced by this legal disjuncture between colony and metropole was heightened by the very different religious landscape the migrants were entering. Sikhs who settled in Britain in the 1950s and 1960s encountered a society where Christianity implicitly framed many social conventions, cultural attitudes and the provisions of the law. Even though the long and very uneven proc-esses of secularisation had removed most of the legal disabilities that had traditionally restricted Catholic, Non-Conformists, and Jews and weakened the authority of the Church of England in the public domain, Christianity's cultural power remained potent. Most impor-tantly, in the middle of the twentieth century, the law still reinforced and defended certain elements of Christianity—such as the status of the Sabbath (through Sunday trading laws) and the authority of Christian teaching (blasphemy laws)—while affording no positive protection to non-Christian groups.[17] The Punjabi migrants of the 1950s and early 1960s settled in a Britain where non-Christian faiths remained unusual, where chapels, church, and church halls remained important sites of community, and were powerful Protestant teach-ings had a broad cultural sway and moulded ideas about respectability and the social order.[18]

So although imperial transportation and communication net-works enabled the extension and acceleration of migration from Punjab to the United Kingdom, these 'webs of empire' did not pro-duce a homogenous imperial order. Ocean liners and aeroplanes underwrote important demographic and economic interdependences between Punjab and Britain, but the cultural and legal terrain of the empire was never seamless and smooth. Many Punjabi Sikhs who migrated to Britain drew strong contrasts between the alienation of living in '*Vilayat*' (Britain as the foreign land) and the comforts of their Punjabi '*desh mulk*'—homeland. Sikh migrants who arrived in Britain in the early 1970s after being expelled from east Africa had to adjust to a cultural order that was very different from Kenya and Uganda where they had been settled for the previous six decades.[19]

***

By the late 1950s, Sikhs were responding effectively to the diffi-culties they had in translating their practices into British life. In most places where significant numbers of Sikhs clustered, Indian Workers' Associations (IWAs) were either reactivated or established.[20] Before 1947, IWAs were primarily concerned with supporting the struggle for freedom at 'home', but in the 1950s they increasingly functioned as associational movements that connected migrants and helped improve their living conditions.[21] The IWAs effectively functioned as political umbrella organizations, bringing together a range of South Asian political affiliations into local chapters and the national body. While connections back to Indian political parties fed the schismatic tendencies of the IWAs, they did not prevent these institutions from functioning as important sites for community discussion in the 1950s and 1960s. Given the strength of both the Communist party and Indian National Congress affiliations in shaping the agenda of the IWAs, it is not surprising that these latter organizations were deeply concerned with questions relating to class and labour. They also slowly developed the ability to offer some basic social services. But their class-based ideology meant that they were not in a strong position to forward claims about the particular needs and rights of Sikhs as a distinct community.

Ultimately British Sikhs won state recognition through the courts rather than class-based worker's associations. Of central importance was the recognition of the turban, an issue that became more pressing with the arrival of growing numbers of east African Sikhs, who were reluctant to trim their *kesh* and who routinely wore turbans. The example of these new arrivals were partly responsible for the increasing willingness of other Sikh men to keep their hair untrimmed and to wear turbans as public markers of their identity. But this shift was also produced by the growing number of female migrants and the formation of more traditional family structures.[22] For many Britons, however, turbans and beards were potent signs of otherness and these symbols were read as indicating the unwillingness of migrants to 'fit into' British life. Nevertheless, the growing willingness of Sikh men to maintain turbans and beards came at a moment when state policy aims were shifting. Until 1962, the British state had relatively few immigration controls, but this was sharply reversed as it quickly implemented a regime that greatly restricted migration from the Commonwealth. This new policing of the border was accompanied by a new concern with anti-discrimination legislation as the state attempted to manage increasingly prominent and organized migrant communities. A key initiative was the 1965 Race Relations Act, which marked an important legislative shift towards multiculturalism. This law created a new institutional framework, supported by both the Labour and Conservative parties, for the protection of minority communities by outlawing discrimination in public places on the 'grounds of colour, race, or ethnic or national origins'.[23]

The first significant debate over the legal status of markers of Sikh identity predated this 1965 legislation, occurring instead when the question of Commonwealth migration was subject to sustained debate in the late 1950s, spurred in part by the anti-black violence of the Notting Hill riots of 1958. The campaign was launched by G. S. S. Sagar, who had applied for a position as a bus conductor in Manchester's department of transportation in 1959. His application had been turned down as his turban was considered to be a violation of the company's dress code and his subsequent offer to wear a blue turban with the company's badge was also rejected. With the support of his gurdwara, Sagar launched an extensive letter-writing campaign and a legal challenge to these rulings, but it took seven years for the transport committee of Manchester City Council to reverse the decision, by which point Sagar was too old to take up the position he had initially applied for. In 1967 another dispute over the status of turbans played out in a very different manner in Wolverhampton, where 150 Sikh drivers, none of whom routinely kept their kesh or wore a turban, were employed by the city's transportation service. But one driver, Tarsem Singh Sandhu, returned to work after an illness and resolved to maintain his kesh and a turban. He was sent home for violating dress regulations and after two weeks he lost his job. West Indian as well as Punjabi drivers supported the campaign against his dismissal and it drew considerable national attention after a large public demonstration was staged in Wolverhampton in support of Sandhu. More sensationally, one Sikh leader—Sohan Singh Jolly of Hounslow—caused a national uproar after promising to burn himself alive if no resolution was found in the dispute; an action that angered Wolverhampton's Sikh community as well as most Britons. Ultimately the Wolverhampton transport Committee ceded to Sandhu's request. While this dispute certainly underlined the turban's status as a marker of Sikh identity, it reinforced many white Britons scepticism about the place of religion in the public sphere and caused them to question Sikhs' investment in British life.[24]

This scepticism resurfaced in the public debate over what proved to be the pivotal public struggle over the turban: whether Sikhs could be forced to comply with the requirement to wear helmets on motorcycles as stipulated by of the Road Traffic Act of 1972. Some commentators opposed any exemption to the safety legislation and others questioned the religious status of the turban. But Sikhs won significant support from outside of their community, not only on the basis of the argument that the turban was an essential religious symbol, but by also stressing the strong shared history they saw as knitting together Sikhs and the British. It was the close connections that the Sikh community had established with the Labour Member of Parliament for Ealing–Southall, Sidney Bidwell, that enabled the passage of the Motorcycle Crash Helmets (Religious Exemption Act (1976)). Labour Parliamentarians supported this controversial legislation—which exempted Sikhs from wearing the helmets required for all other motorcyclists—because it supported the principle of religious tolerance, an ideal that was seen as ultimately outweighing safety concerns.[25] In the House of Lords, Lord Avebury insisted that turban was 'an essential article of faith', one endorsed by Guru Nanak and enjoined by the 'rehat namas'.[26] This legislation established an important principle that was later extended by the Employment Act of 1989. It exempted turban wearing Sikhs from the necessity of donning hard hats on construction sites, an important concession given that over 4000 Sikhs were employed in the construction industry, primarily turban-wearing Ramgarhia Sikhs of east African origin.[27]

Sikh leaders also sort legal protection for wearing *kirpan*, the ceremonial dagger that was one of the five *ks* that marked the identity of Khalsa Sikhs. Initially it seemed that it would be relatively easy to win concessions around the kirpan in light of the recognition extended to the turban as a religious symbol. However the hijacking of an Indian Airlines flight in 1982 by Sikhs wielding kirpans and the suspected role of Sikh separatists in the bombing of Air India flight 182 in 1985 hardened government attitudes and public opinion towards any special dispensation for kirpans. These crises dissipated with time: the ability of Sikh leaders to sustain their arguments and navigate the multicultural state, meant that arguments for the recognition of the kirpan ultimately gained purchase. Sikh rights to carry the kirpan gained some formal protection through the provisions of section 139 of the Criminal Justice Act 1988 and sections 3 and 4 of the

Offensive Weapons Act 1996, which allow Sikhs to carry a kirpan as it is deemed a necessary part of their religion. Residual anxieties over the kirpan mean that it remains subject to intermittent debate given fears around hijacking, terrorism, and the growing prevalence of inter-personal knife violence in British cities.[28]

The British state's slow and hesitant move towards multiculturalism between the 1960s and the 1990s effectively encouraged 'minority' communities to define the markers of identity and social practices that they saw as requiring legal protection. The logic of this state regime was reactive rather than actively interventionist: essentially the law provided an instrument that individuals and communities could mobilize to protect their interests. Sikhs have also succeeded in winning these concessions because a commitment to religious pluralism has threaded this vision of multiculturalism. The particular legal supports that traditionally favoured Christianity have largely been removed since the 1950s, the state's religious studies curriculum introduces students to a range of 'world religions' (including Sikhism and Christianity), and Christian churches have been quite willing to engage in inter-faith dialogues with the aim of increasing cross-cultural understanding within Britain as well as cementing the legitimacy of religion in the public sphere. Just as the movement of migrants into Britain has forced these legal and cultural shifts, the British state's move towards multiculturalism has in turn encouraged leaders of 'minority' communities to produce increasingly regularized and coherent visions of their identity.

***

Sikh appeals for formal recognition of their community's distinctiveness echoed the Sikh tradition of engagement with the state that was firmly established in Punjab during the final third of the nineteenth century. Indeed, in the final third of the twentieth century these leaders were faced with some of the same issues that Singh Sabha leaders had earlier grappled with: how were Sikh identities to be reproduced and policed? How could they ensure that their ordered and prescriptive vision of identity be reconciled with the innovations and messiness that seemed so characteristic of everyday life?[29]

Many of these questions played out within families where questions over practice and the politics of identity were subject to considerable contestation. This was particularly the case because the framework of Punjabi migrant families was quite different than the organization of work and the family in Punjab itself. Even when increasing numbers of women joined their husbands and the community began consolidating and reproducing itself in the 1960s, traditional family structures, especially the joint-family, were not prevalent amongst diasporic Punjabis in Britain. Moreover, because the early community was born out of migration rather reproduction within Britain, migrant Punjabi families developed stronger horizontal social networks (brothers, sisters and cousins) rather than the complex inter-generational structures that shape life within Punjab itself.[30] The resulting simplification of kin-structures created greater space for some teenagers, as many households lacked the grandparents and the uncles and aunts who might supervise children while parents were working. Punjabi women, frequently identified as the upholders of tradition, were in fact extremely active in the formal workforce (especially in the case of Punjabis who migrated to Britain from east Africa) and their participation rates eclipsed those of other South Asian women and British women as a whole. This strong engagement with the labour market inevitably devolved some domestic responsibilities onto daughters and it also meant that many Punjabi children were not under the direct motherly supervision that remained common in Punjab. This allowed some Sikh and Punjabi youths to associate with non-Punjabi friends, to engage widely with their urban environments, and to explore other cultures. These inquisitive needs were deeply felt by many second and third generation Punjabi Britons. Reflecting in 1988, Harwant Singh Bains, a prominent Southall youth worker and anti-racist campaigner, observed '[a]mongst many of my friends, both boys and girls, there is often a yearning to escape from the confines of Southall...and to embrace the fugitive freedoms of the "outside world".' [31]

That outside world placed particular pressures on migrants. Most importantly, many Sikh men were compelled to downplay their identity in order to enhance their economic prospects and to 'fit in' socially. We have already seen, for example, 150 Sikh bus-drivers in Wolverhampton had abandoned maintaining their kesh in order to keep their jobs. This was not an isolated incident: in fact, various court cases, especially over the status of the kesh in light of the laws governing food hygiene and workplace safety, highlighted the pressures that have forced many Sikh men to at least temporally set aside the turban and trim their kesh.[32] The deep commitment of east African Sikh men to maintaining these symbols and the embrace of the turban and beard as political markers by early advocates of the creation of a Khalistan—a Sikh homeland in India—exacerbated tensions within the community. For some, the maintenance of the kesh and the turban became indexes of the spiritual commitment or political orientation of individuals and families. This remains the case as prominent Sikh businessmen, community leaders, and sportsmen are scrutinized in print culture editorials, internet bulletin boards, and informal conversation.[33]

These kind of debates in Britain not only reflect anxieties within British Sikh communities about maintaining the faith, but they are also energized by the deepening preoccupation with identity which has reshaped British politics and culture since the 1960s. As multiculturalism developed as the primary mechanism for managing the consequences of non-white immigration and the failure of assimilation, the state has been increasingly concerned with defining and reproducing 'minority' identities. Eleanor Nesbitt's work on Sikhism's place in British multicultural education has shown the ways in which school textbooks have produced hierarchies within the panth by drawing hard boundaries between 'Sikhs' and 'real Sikhs', 'true Sikhs' and 'proper Sikhs'. The latter group is only seen to include amritdhari or Khalsa Sikhs, excluding other members of the panth who have not taken amrit and, especially, those that do not maintain the five ks and wear the turban.[34] Nesbitt's study has made it clear that British Sikhs' devotional beliefs and practices exhibit a considerable range, as well as a depth and complexity that are not conveyed in the textbooks used for multicultural education. Moreover, these understandings manifest themselves in a vibrant popular religiosity that is not controlled by supposedly authoritative texts and normative prescriptions. But, as Nesbitt's ethnographic work has shown, textbooks and school teachers' questions help reinforce supposedly 'orthodox' identities within the community, while querying the authenticity or validity of beliefs, practices or identities that seem at odds with how a community 'should be'.[35] This is particularly the case with Ravidasi Dalit Punjabis who have had strong historical connections to the panth and whose distinctive practices are heavily inflected by Sikhism. Within the British cultural landscape, however, Ravidasis are not seen as 'real Sikhs'.[36] In part because of the distinctive teachings that shape Ravidasi beliefs and in part because of the cohesive Dalit identity that underwrites the Ravidasi community, many British Sikhs believe that Ravidasas have no connection to the panth or else constitute a challenge to it. These arguments are part of wider set of exchanges within the global panth over the boundaries of Sikhism. In rural Punjab these debates frequently focus on the practices of Dalit Sikhs which Jat and Khatri Sikhs frequently see as heterodox. Chamar and Mazhabi Sikhs within the Punjab have been inclined towards a more open-ended interpretation of the Sikh tradition, have increasingly pursued the construction of their own gurdwaras, and frequently images of the fifteenth century Chamar Sant Ravidas sit alongside the ten Gurus within these gurdwaras.[37]

Thus the kinds of oppositions that some British Sikhs draw between 'real Sikhs' and other Punjabis are an attempt to impose order on a cultural field that is actually complex, dynamic and contradictory. Sikh migrants in Britain had to adjust to an economic system, sets of cultural expectations, and a political culture that was very different from that of independent India. They have also been preoccupied with broader markers of their regional identity as Punjabis as well as the narrower signs of their Sikhi. For Punjabi Sikh families in Britain, the dislocations that they have experienced have invested some cultural elements with particular salience as markers of a distinctive 'Punjabiyat'—Punjabi culture and identity—in Britain. *Saag* (mustard leaves), for example, have been invoked as an everyday symbol of Punjabiness, a marker invested with particular significance in a diasporic context. Lyricists and writers have invoked saag as a symbol of a distant homeland, while Marie Gillespie's work has shown that Southall mothers and aunties in the 1980s understood saag as a signifier of 'tradition' and that it was set against the 'unhealthy' physical and cultural influence of 'western food'.[38] In a similar vein, the salwar kameez, the 'Punjabi suit', was an important sign of the growing visibility of north Indian migrants in Britain in the 1960s. As migrant families were consolidated and the community grew in demographic significance it was increasingly adopted as a routine garment for Punjabi women. But even as some migrant women reworked key design elements in new ways in Britain, white Britons often read the salwar kameez as an exotic oddity—a 'night suit'. For many Britons the salwar kameez was a potent signifier of the priorities of 'Asians', they were read as a sign that migrants were not willing to assimilate into 'mainstream' culture or were seen as proof of the 'backwardness' of gender relations within India.[39] Most significantly, perhaps, the importance attached to the salwar kameez within the community as a sign of cultural continuity reminds us that for migrant families female dress was invested with considerable symbolic freight while male youths and men were free to wear western clothing. It is important to note here, however, that the salwar kameez was primarily a marker of a regional Punjabi identity: it was not primarily a marker of religious affiliation in the way that the distinctive Sikh turban was for men.

The filmmaker Gurinder Chadha has observed that during the early 1980s fashion, music and language were interconnected as Punjabi youths re-evaluated their own cultural inheritance and questioned assumptions about identity promulgated by their parents, grandparents and aunties and uncles.[40] Parminder Bhachu has noted the growing significance of bhangra in the British cultural landscape and the growing prominence of the salwar kameez were interconnected.[41] Both clothing and music enabled youths to experiment with Punjabi aesthetics with a degree of autonomy from their families and within a larger cultural landscape that was increasingly attuned to the performance of identity. It is particularly important to recognize that the transformation of *bhangra* in Britain in the 1980s was dependent on a set of new social contacts and cultural exchanges between Punjabi youths and their Black counterparts. Young Punjabi men particularly engaged with Black culture, which as Gillespie observed, enjoyed a 'very high status' among Southall youth who admired Afro-Caribbeans for their personal style, musical taste, and greater personal freedoms. As a result, Black culture became a powerful object of desire for young Punjabis and some were quick to adopt Afro-Caribbean idioms and vocal mannerisms, fashion and music. But, as Gillespie reminds us, South Asian girls could not engage as openly with Black culture. When Punjabi girls attended bhangra gigs at the Hammersmith Palais or the Empire in Leicester Square, they typically wore 'traditional' salwar kameez while their male kin were able to adopt 'hipper' street wear influenced by African-American culture and the style of their Black classmates in Southall.[42]

These engagements developed in a milieu shot through with widespread anxieties about contacts across racial lines. Concerns about community boundaries particularly focused on the 'dangers' of inter-racial sex, an issue that was brought into the wider public sphere by Gurinder Chadha's 1993 film *Bhaji on the Beach*. While Chadha's work illuminated the particular fears that British Punjabis expressed about the consequences of social and especially sexual contact between their daughters and Black Britons, ethnographic work by Kathleen Hall on Leeds and Marie Gillespie on Southall clearly demonstrated the complex mechanisms of social control that controlled the behaviour of young British Sikh women. The strict policing of their movement, the careful monitoring of their dress and use of makeup, a generalized culture of surveillance where uncles, aunties, cousins and family acquaintances observed and reported on the behaviour of young females, and the power of gossip and rumour were all designed to protect the *izzat* (face, prestige) of families and the reputation of the community as a whole.[43]

Despite the worries that many parents articulated about the consequences of cross-cultural contact, the assertion of a reworked Punjabi identity through new forms of bhangra was an important proclamation of distinctiveness. Bhangra also garnered considerable media interest and it was an important instrument that allowed Punjabis to emphasize both their distinctive heritage *and* their engagement with British culture. Highlighting their multiple positions in relation to Britain gave these diasporic subjects the ability to critique the British state from within (or, at least, from the margins). Within this context, the rapid embrace of new forms of bhangra by Punjabi youths was part of this rejection of assimilation and must be viewed as part of a broader contest over the nature of British South Asian identity and the limits of Britishness itself.[44] These kinds of cultural and political affiliations that enabled the lacing of some elements of Afro-Caribbean culture in bhangra in the 1980s were not durable. Most Punjabis Sikhs were reluctant to identify as being 'black'. In the face of the new forms of bhangra being produced by younger members of the community who were engaging with black musical traditions, many Punjabis responded by reasserting the primacy of 'tradition', upholding the unquestioned authority of the cultural forms that they had transplanted to Britain, and nurturing a powerful nostalgia for 'their Punjab'. A strong desire for 'traditional' bhangra over the new styles of bhangra fashioned in Southall or Handsworth was often an important element of this stress on cultural continuity, especially among older Punjabis or in towns with smaller South Asian populations.

This emphasis on cultural continuity reflected deeper debates within the British Sikh community in the 1980s as divisions flared over political and religious priorities. Neither the Southall IWA, which had a strong Congress inflection and articulated a commitment to serving all Indians in Britain, or the more narrowly Marxist politics of the national body IWA (GB) were strongly positioned to serve growing desire amongst some British Sikhs to stress their religious identity.[45] While a small minority of British Sikhs were supporters of the struggle to establish Khalistan as a Sikh homeland, not all sympathizers were solely energized by the idea that Sikhs were in danger of becoming a permanently persecuted minority in Hindustan.[46] For a significant number of British Sikhs the idea of Khalistan was not so much about the creation of a territorial homeland to which they could return, but rather the construction of a spiritual homeland that could be used to distinguish themselves as a distinctive group within Britain, marking them off from other communities of South Asian origin, peoples who might have simply been understood as 'Asians' by white Britons, or worse still as 'Pakis'.

A majority of British Sikhs, however, adopted a different strategy as they strove to highlight the particular and unique interconnections between Britain and the Sikh community. This strategy focused on stressing shared values and especially the military contribution of Sikhs to the defence of Britain and its empire. As I have shown elsewhere, this strategy required an energetic reworking of the past. Some British Sikhs, for example, have celebrated Maharaja Dalip Singh as the embodiment of this shared history, a position that requires them to downplay the deep rift that developed between the Maharaja and Queen Victoria and his clumsy attempts to construct a global alliance that would rise up against British interests and influence. Groups like the Maharajah Duleep Singh Centenary Trust have, in fact, consistently stressed the loyalty of Sikhs to Britain, distancing themselves from the radical claims of Khalistanis.[47] By stressing their place as a special community *within* the British nation, Sikh leaders were deeply concerned about how the community is seen by British politicians and the public. Eager to distance themselves from the arguments and demands made by some British Muslims from the time of the Rushdie affair, British Sikhs have worked hard to win recognition and support from the British state, rather than articulating positions that could be read as challenging the authority of the law or the state more generally.

In fact, positioning Sikhism against Islam has been a key strategy over the past decade when international conflicts and 'domestic terrorism' has sharpened attention on the relationships between religion and the state in Britain. Sikh community leaders mobilized quickly in response to the media coverage of September 11 that featured the widespread circulation of images of a bearded and turbaned Osama bin Laden. They worked hard to not only protect members of their own community but to also remind the British media and broader public of the distinctiveness of Sikh identity.[48] The suspicion, abuse and violence directed toward the community in the wake of the attacks revealed the limits of multiculturalism and the provisional nature of the acceptance of 'Asians', including Sikhs, as 'Britons'. Sukhpreet Grewal, from Hillingdon, explained to a reporter that 'I don't think we're feeling part of mainstream Britain any more...But because of the experiences I've had, if I've not been accepted as being British, it's very difficult for me to feel British...We see ourselves as the truly dispossessed. I don't see India as my home, but I don't think we'll ever be accepted in Britain.'[49]

Even before September 11 the Sikh Federation, like the Hindu Forum, were actively arguing that social workers, journalists, academics and politicians should abandon the term 'Asian' as a catchall for Britons of South Asian origins and instead argued that people should be identified by their religious affiliation, a move that they hoped would allow violence to be equated narrowly with British Muslims.[50] The journalist and broadcaster Safraz Manzoor have vigorously made this argument for the primacy of religious identities from a very different political vantage point. Manzoor has claimed that 'Asian' was essentially a colonial and colonizing category and that more recent emphasis on religious identities marks the greater autonomy and confidence of migrant communities, without necessarily implying any desire to repudiate Britishness.[51] This kind of argument has won support from many Sikh groups. In particular, the Sikh Federation has led a long running struggle to ensure that the state sees Sikhs as distinct from other migrant and minority communities. It has argued that the government needs to disaggregate census statistics, abandon the use of collective terms like 'Asian', and insists that Sikhs should be identified as a distinct 'ethnic' or 'racial group'.[52]

After the London bombings of July 2005 British Sikhs felt that these questions of cultural legibility were especially urgent. Against a backdrop of violence targeted towards Sikh men and the firebombing of gurdwaras, some Sikh men began to wear t-shirts, stickers and badges with the slogan 'Don't Freak, I'm a Sikh'.[53] Both September 11 and the London bombings convinced many Sikhs that cultural legibility was not only an important way of winning resources and protection from the state, but it was also crucial if they were to ensure the safety of the community.

In the heated debates over the nature of British Muslim communities, some Sikhs have assumed prominent roles in anti-Muslim politics. The recently established English Defence League (EDL), for example, has garnered some support from Sikhs. Amit Singh, a British-born Sikh, has been a prominent spokesman for the group's campaign against 'Muslim extremism', an agenda that has seen the EDL oppose mosque construction, attack supporters of Palestinian sovereignty, and oppose migration to Britain from Muslim nations.[54] Rajinder Singh, a retired schoolteacher and British Sikh who migrated from India in 1967, has been prominent for much longer, arguing since 2001 that Sikhs should support the British National Party (BNP) because of its criticisms of Islam. He has suggested that Britain is in danger of being 'overrun' by Muslims, a community that he sees as being innately opposed to democratic principles.[55] He has suggested the 'violence [of jihadists] sprung from the Koran' and the 'Muslim answer to reasoned argument is knife, dagger and bomb.' In March 2010 he became the

BNP's first non-white member. Rajinder Singh's family was displaced from its Lahore home and father was killed during Partition in 1947 and he continues to hold Muslims responsible for the upheaval and violence that engulfed Punjab in the second half of the 1940s.[56] The long shadows of Partition stretch not just over the history of India, Pakistan, and Bangladesh, but also provide a potent set of narratives that can be mobilized in contemporary debates over religion and politics in Britain.

Sikh leaders have been critical of Rajinder Singh and more generally have consistently repudiated the racist politics that underpin British far right politics, but they have been less willing to challenge the anti-Islamic sentiment that has underpinned the rise of the British right in the first decade of the twenty-first. Just as the class-based connections of the IWAs were set aside and potential links with Afro-Caribbean communities were neglected, so now are the possible connections with British Muslims, the majority of whom are of South Asian origin and many of whom are themselves Punjabis. In engaging with the growing power of multiculturalism, British Sikhs have exhibited resourcefulness, tenacity, and considerable skill in winning state recognition and protection. This strategic quest for recognition has been preoccupied with the legibility of Sikh identity to ensure that Sikhs enjoy rights to freely practice their religion and enjoy full social citizenship in Britain. At the same time, however, this political priority has consolidated oppositions between 'real' Khalsa Sikhs and other members of the panth. It has fed anxieties over the consequences of the cultural innovations and real social change that has been the consequence of migration and community building so far from Punjab. How these tensions will be resolved will be crucial in determining the contours of the community and its political orientation in the future.

NOTES

1 Tony Ballantyne, *Between Colonialism and Diaspora: Sikh Cultural Formations in an Imperial World*, Durham, NC: Duke University Press, 2006, pp. 4–19, 35–6, 119, 160–1.

2 Probably the most important articulation of the 'internalist' interpretative tradition is W.H. McLeod, *The Sikhs of the Khalsa: A History of the*

Khalsa Rahit, New Delhi: Oxford University Press, 2003. The works of Gurinder Singh Mann and Pashaura Singh offer sophisticated internalist interpretations of the panth grounded in the close reading of the textual tradition. See, for example, Pashaura Singh, *The Guru Granth Sahib: Canon, Meaning and Authority*, New Delhi: Oxford University Press, 2000 and Gurinder Singh Mann, *The Making of Sikh Scripture*, New York: Oxford University Press, 2001.

3 Richard G. Fox, *Lions of the Punjab: Culture in the Making*, Berkeley: University of California Press, 1985; Bernard S. Cohn, *Colonialism and its Forms of Knowledge: The British in India*, Princeton: Princeton University Press, 1996, especially p.107.

4 James C. Scott, *Seeing like a State: How Certain Schemes to Improve the Human Condition have Failed*, New Haven: Yale University Press, 1998, pp.2–3.

5 Arjun Appadurai, 'Number in the Colonial Imagination', in Carol A. Breckenridge and Peter van der Veer (eds), *Orientalism and the Postcolonial Predicament: Perspectives on South Asia*, Philadelphia: University of Pennsylvania Press, 1993, pp. 314–39; Bernard S. Cohn, 'The Census, Social Structure and Objectification in South Asia', *An Anthropologist among the Historians and Other Essays*, New Delhi: Oxford University Press, 1990, pp. 224–54 and *Colonialism and its Forms of Knowledge*, p. 8; Nicholas B. Dirks, *Castes of Mind: Colonialism and the Making of Modern India*, Princeton: Princeton University Press, 2001, pp. 43–60.

6 Harjot Oberoi, *The Construction of Religious Boundaries: Culture, Identity, and Diversity in the Sikh Tradition*, Chicago: University of Chicago Press, 1994; McLeod, *Sikhs of the Khalsa*, pp. 206–7; Ballantyne, *Between Colonialism and Diaspora*, especially pp. 35–6.

7 R.W. Falcon, *Handbook on Sikhs for Regimental Officers*, Allahabad: The Pioneer Press, 1896, p. 21.

8 Ibid., p. 15. Also see pp. 61–2.

9 Ibid., pp. 71–3, 98–102.

10 For a first-hand account of this see Vincent Eyre, *The Sikh and European Soldiers of Our Indian Forces*, London: Harrison and Sons, 1867, pp. 7–8. On the kes-dhari–amrit-dhari distinction see W.H. McLeod, *Who is a Sikh?*, Oxford: Clarendon, 1989, pp. 110–15.

11 See, Falcon, *Handbook on Sikhs* especially pp. 6–10 and McLeod, *Sikhs of the Khalsa*, pp. 19, 164, 244.

12 The Sikh Gurdwaras Act, 1925, 2 (9).

13 The four kurahits are: (1) the trimming or shaving of hair (2) eating halal meat (3) sexual contact with anyone other than one's own wife or husband (4) the use of tobacco.

14 McLeod, *Sikhs of the Khalsa*, pp. 162, 178.

15 On the growing identification of the panth with the Khasla see McLeod, *Sikhs of the Khalsa*, p. 179. McLeod notes that 'patit' was a 'Singh Sabha introduction', p. 134 n. 20.

16 Tasha G. Oren, 'Secret Asian Man: Angry Asians and the Politics of Cultural Visibility', in Shilpa Davé, LeiLani Nishime, Tasha G. Oren (eds), *East Main Street: Asian American Popular Culture*, New York: New York University Press, 2005, p. 351.

17 St. John Anthony Robilliard, *Religion and the Law: Religious Liberty in Modern English Law*, Manchester: Manchester University Press, 1984, pp. 25–58.

18 This argument is shaped by Callum G. Brown, *The Death of Christian Britain: Understanding Secularisation, 1800–2000*, London: Routledge, 2000.

19 These east African Sikhs had a very different cultural sensibility from Sikh migrants from Punjab. Sikhs who settled in east Africa had weak connections back to Punjab and did not aspire to return to Punjab at some point.

20 The first IWA had been established in Coventry in 1938.

21 Pnina Werbner and Muhammad Anwar (eds), *Black and Ethnic Leaderships in Britain: The Cultural Dimensions of Political Action*, London: Routledge, 1991, p. 174.

22 Many settlers in Britain in the middle of the twentieth century had dispensed with the turban and cut their kesh to assist their economic prospects and assist the process of making a home in the United Kingdom. Gurharpal Singh and Darshan Singh Tatla, *Sikhs in Britain: The Making of a Community*, London: Zed Books, 2006, p. 127; Michael Banton, *Promoting Racial Harmony*, Cambridge: Cambridge University Press, 1985. pp. 54–5.

23 This argument broadly draws from Hansen, *Citizenship and Immigration in Post-War Britain.*

24 Banton, *Racial Harmony*, pp. 55–6.

25 Singh and Tatla, *Sikhs in Britain*, pp. 129–30. Also see Sidney Bidwell's own discussion of this issue: *Red, White & Black: Race Relations in Britain*, London: Gordon and Cremonesi, 1976, p. 60.

26 *Hansard*, House of Lords, 4 October 1976, vol. 374, cc1055–7.

27 Ramesh Chandra, *Minority: Social and Political Conflict*, Delhi: Isha Books, 2004, p. 26.

28 An important intervention has come from the self-described 'secular Sikh' Hardeep Singh Kohli who has questioned the consequences of seeking protection for religious symbols, particularly the kirpan. The

Guardian, 9 February 2010, http://www.guardian.co.uk/commentis-free/belief/2010/feb/09/dagger-dilemma-sikhism-kirpan-schools

29 Gurinder Singh Mann, 'The Sikh Educational Heritage', in John Stratton Hawley and Gurinder Singh Mann (eds), *Studying the Sikhs: Issues for North America*, Albany, NY: State University of New York Press, 1993, p. 103.

30 These structures are explored in Gerd Baumann, 'Managing in a Polyethnic Milieu: Kinship and Interaction in a London Suburb', *Journal of the Royal Anthropological Institute*, 1 (4), 1995, pp. 725–41.

31 Harwant S. Bains, 'Southall Youth: An Old-Fashioned Story', in Philip Cohen and Harwant S. Bains (eds), *Multi-racist Britain*, Basingstoke: Macmillan, 1988, p. 235.

32 Robilliard, *Religion and the Law*, pp. 124, 170; Avtar Brah, 'The "Asian" in Britain', in Nasreen Ali, Virinder S. Kalra, and Salman Sayyid (eds), *A Postcolonial People: South Asians in Britain*, London: Hurst & Co., 1996, pp. 38–9.

33 *The Tribune*, 12 August 2006; *Outlook India*, 23 October 2006, http://www.outlookindia.com/article.aspx?232931

34 Eleanor Nesbitt, 'Sikhs and Proper Sikhs: Young British Sikhs' Perceptions of their Identity', in Pashaura Singh and N.G. Barrier (eds), *Sikh Identity: Continuity and Change*, Delhi; Manohar, 1999, pp. 315–33.

35 This argument draws upon and reworks Eleanor Nesbitt, '"Splashed with Goodness": The Many Meanings of Amrit for Young British Sikhs', *Journal of Contemporary Religion*, 12 (1), 1997, pp. 17–33 and '"I'm a Gujarati Lohana and a Vaishnav as Well": Religious Identity Formation among Young Coventrian Punjabis and Gujaratis', in S. Coleman and P. Collins (eds), *Religion, Identity and Change: Perspectives on Global Transformations*, London: Ashgate, 2004, pp. 174–90.

36 Eleanor Nesbitt, 'Pitfalls in Religious Taxonomy: Hindus and Sikhs, Valmikis and Ravidasis', *Religion Today*, 6(1), 1990, pp. 9–12; also see Opinderjit Kaur Takhar, *Sikh Identity: An Exploration of Groups among Sikhs*, Burlington: Ashgate, 2005, chapter 4.

37 Indera P. Singh, 'Religion in Daleke: A Sikh Village', in L.P. Vidyarthi (ed.), *Aspects of Religion in Indian Society*, Meerut: Kedar Nath Ram Nath, 1961, pp. 192–3; Surinder S. Jodkha, 'Caste and Untouchability in Rural Punjab', *Economic and Political Weekly*, 11 May 2002, p. 1818.

38 Marie Gillespie, *Television, Ethnicity and Cultural Change*, p. 201; Ballantyne, *Between Colonialism and Diaspora*, pp. 142–3, 170.

39 Parminder Bhachu, *Dangerous Designs: Asian Women, Fashion, and the Diaspora Economies*, London: Routledge, 2004, pp. 11–12.

40 See extended quote from Gurinder Chadha in Bhachu, *Dangerous Designs*, pp. 18–19.

41 Ibid., pp. 16, 18–19.

42 Ibid., pp. 46, 181–2.

43 Kathleen Hall, *Lives in Translation: Sikh Youth as British Citizens*, Philadelphia: University of Pennsylvania Press, 2002, pp. 178–82; Gillespie, *Television, Ethnicity, and Cultural Change*, pp. 142–74, 181–2.

44 Cited in Sanjay Sharma, 'Noisy Asians or 'Asian Noise', p. 32.

45 Werbner and Anwar (eds), *Black and Ethnic Leaderships in Britain*, p. 178.

46 Giorgio Shani, *Sikh Nationalism and Identity in a Global Age*, p. 52.

47 Ballantyne, *Between Colonialism and Diaspora*, chapter 3.

48 For example, 'Sikhs Fear Prejudice Based on Turban', *The Times*, 21 September 2001.

49 'A Bad Time to be Asian in Britain', *The Times*, 27 September 2001.

50 For an excellent overview of this broad issue listen to the BBC Asian Network Special Report, 'Don't Call Me Asian', October 2006, http://www.bbc.co.uk/asiannetwork/documentaries/dontcallmeasian.shtml

51 *The Guardian*, 11 January 2005, http://www.guardian.co.uk/world/2005/jan/11/race.religion

52 http://www.british-sikh-federation.org/EthnicGroup.html; http://www.sikhfederation.com/pdf/SikhsCensusJan2010.pdf;

53 *The Guardian*, 5 September 2005, http://www.guardian.co.uk/world/2005/sep/05/religion.july7

54 *The Times*, 10 August 2009, http://www.timesonline.co.uk/tol/news/uk/article6790067.ece.; *Harrow Times*, 19 August 2009, http://www.harrowtimes.co.uk/news/4553713.Mosque_protest_called_off_after_Sharia_court_denial/; *The Samosa*, 19 January 2010, http://www.thesamosa.co.uk/index.php/news-and-features/society/210-exclusive-f-the-pakis-meet-the-edls-anti-racist-poster-boy.html

55 *The Observer*, 23 December 2001, http://www.guardian.co.uk/uk/2001/dec/23/race.politics

56 *The Guardian*, 11 February 2010, http://www.guardian.co.uk/politics/2010/feb/11/bnp-nonwhites-members-sikh-join; *Sikhs Online*, 3 December 2009, http://www.sikhsonline.co.uk/sikh-news/bnp-anger-raf-hero-but-find-sikh-allies/

Contributors

C.S. Adcock is Assistant Professor of South Asian Studies and Religious Studies in the Department of History at Washington University in St Louis. She is currently working on a monograph, 'The Limits of Tolerance: Indian Secularism and the Politics of Religious Freedom'.

Alyssa Ayres was appointed Deputy Assistant Secretary for South and Central Asia at the United States Department of State in August 2010. (The essay included in this volume much predated her State Department appointment.) She is the author of *Speaking Like a State: Language and Nationalism in Pakistan* (2009).

Tony Ballantyne is Professor of History at University of Otago, New Zealand. He is the author of *Between Colonialism and Diaspora: Sikh Cultural Formations in an Imperial World* (2006) and *Orientalism and Race: Aryanism in the British Empire* (2002).

Anna Bigelow is Associate Professor in the Department of Philosophy and Religious Studies at North Carolina State University. She is the author of *Sharing the Sacred: Practicing Pluralism in Muslim North India* (2010).

MARKUS DAECHSEL is Lecturer in Modern Islamic Societies at Royal Holloway College, University of London. He is the author of *The Politics of Self-Expression: The Urdu Middle-Class Milieu in Mid-20th Century India and Pakistan* (2006).

LOUIS E. FENECH is Professor of History at the University of Northern Iowa. His publications include *The Darbar of the Sikh Gurus: The Court of God in the World of Men* (2008) and *Martyrdom in the Sikh Tradition: Playing the 'Game of Love'* (2000).

DAVID GILMARTIN is Professor of History at North Carolina State University. His publications include *Civilization and Modernity: Narrating the Creation of Pakistan* (forthcoming, 2012) and *Empire and Islam: Punjab and the Making of Pakistan* (1988).

WILLIAM J. GLOVER is Associate Professor of Urban and Architectural History and Theory at the University of Michigan's Taubman College of Architecture and Urban Planning. He is the author of *Making Lahore Modern: Constructing and Imagining a Colonial City* (2008).

ANSHU MALHOTRA is Associate Professor in the Department of History at the University of Delhi. She is the author of *Gender, Caste, and Religious Identities: Restructuring Class in Colonial Punjab* (2002).

GURINDER SINGH MANN is Kapany Professor of Sikh Studies at the University of California, Santa Barbara. His publications include *Sikhism* (2004), *The Making of Sikh Scripture* (2001), and *The Goindval Pothis* (1996).

FARINA MIR is Associate Professor of History at the University of Michigan, Ann Arbor. She is the author of *The Social Space of Language: Vernacular Culture in British Colonial Punjab* (2010).

ANNE MURPHY is Assistant Professor of Asian Studies and holder of the Chair in Punjabi Language, Literature, and Sikh Studies at the University of British Columbia, Vancouver. She is the author of *The Materiality of the Past: History and Representation in Sikh Tradition* (forthcoming).

HARJOT OBEROI is Professor in the Department of Asian Studies at the University of British Columbia, Vancouver. He is the author of

Constructing Religious Boundaries: Culture, Identity, and Diversity in Sikh Tradition (1994).

SIMONA SAWHNEY is Associate Professor in the Department Asian Languages and Literatures at the University of Minnesota. She is the author of *The Modernity of Sanskrit* (2008).

CHRISTOPHER SHACKLE is Emeritus Professor of the modern languages of South Asia at the School of Oriental and African Studies. His most recent publications are *Attar and the Persian Sufi Tradition: The Art of Spiritual Flight*, ed. with Leonard Lewisohn (2006) and *Teachings of the Sikh Gurus: Selections from the Sikh Scriptures*, ed. and trans. with Arvind Pal Mandair (2005).